LYNDON BAINES JOHNSON AND THE USES OF POWER

LYNDON BAINES JOHNSON AND THE USES OF POWER

WITHDRAWN

Edited by Bernard J. Firestone and Robert C. Vogt

Prepared under the auspices of Hofstra University

Contributions in Political Science, Number 221

Greenwood Press
New York • Westport, Connecticut • London

Library of Congress Cataloging-in-Publication Data

Lyndon Baines Johnson and the uses of power / edited by Bernard J.
  Firestone and Robert C. Vogt.
      p.   cm. — (Contributions in political science, ISSN 0147–1066 ;
  no. 221)
      "Prepared under the auspices of Hofstra University."
      Includes index.
      ISBN 0–313–26395–7 (lib. bdg. : alk. paper)
      1. Johnson, Lyndon B. (Lyndon Baines), 1908–1973.   2. United
States—Politics and government—1963–1969.   I. Firestone, Bernard
J.   II. Vogt, Robert C.   III. Series.
E847.L97   1988
973.923′092′4—dc19   88–10250

British Library Cataloguing in Publication Data is available.

Library of Congress Catalog Card Number: 88–10250
ISBN: 0–313–26395–7
ISSN: 0147–1066

First published in 1988

Greenwood Press, Inc.
88 Post Road West, Westport, Connecticut   06881

Printed in the United States of America

The paper used in this book complies with the
Permanent Paper Standard issued by the National
Information Standards Organization (Z39.48–1984).

10 9 8 7 6 5 4 3 2 1

Contents

Tables

Preface

It is difficult to identify a post–World War II American presidency of more
enduring historical importance than the presidency of Lyndon Baines Johnson.
The Johnson legacy can be found today in government programs that feed the
poor, educate the middle class, and provide medical care for the elderly. It
resonates in the voting power and civil equality of black Americans. It achieves
contemporary relevance in the political debate over the wisdom and value of the
Great Society.

The images of the Johnson era—with their sharply contrasting evocations—
live equally in our memories. Etched in our minds are the tragedy at Dallas and
the triumph of the 1964 campaign; the legislative whirlwind and the anguish of
Vietnam; the remarkable eloquence of the president's "We Shall Overcome"
speech and the bitter turbulence of the riots in the streets; the great popularity
of the early presidential years and the stunning fall from public grace; the generous vision of the Great Society and the personal indignities frequently inflicted
on those who worked with Johnson most closely.

Lyndon Johnson, a man of enormous energy and political skill, was, above
all, a product of his times. Nurtured on the ideals of New Deal liberalism,
Johnson came to believe, as did an entire generation of Americans, that government could offer its citizens the promise and reality of a better life. If he was
exceptional, it was not for the boldness of his ideals or the eloquence of his
rhetoric. Instead, Lyndon Johnson managed to seize a strategic moment in the
nation's history—one ignited by the tragic death of his predecessor and sustained
by social revolution—and to translate a vision, partly his own, partly an elab-
oration of New Deal liberalism, into a domestic program of immense and far-
reaching proportions.

Lyndon Johnson was a man of his times in other ways as well. In his view of the world, Johnson embraced the traditional Cold War faith in the superiority of American values and the dangers of appeasement. In Vietnam, Johnson inherited a commitment made by others but confronted a situation far more complex and far more demanding of hard decisions. The broad strokes of his Vietnam policy were fully predictable given the rigidity of his generation's anti-communism. Ironically, Johnson's steadfast support of traditional Cold War assumptions in Vietnam, such as the "domino" theory, contributed not only to the unraveling of his presidency but also to the collapse of the consensus about those very assumptions as guideposts for future policy.

The essays and panel discussions contained in this volume attempt to interpret the Johnson presidency and its legacy. They are drawn from the proceedings of Hofstra University's conference on the Johnson presidency held in April 1986. This conference was the fifth in a continuing series of presidential conferences hosted by the university since 1982.

The bulk of this volume is made up of scholarly essays submitted in response to a nation-wide call for papers. From among approximately fifty papers submitted, some twenty-five were chosen for delivery at the conference. Seventeen are contained herein. Also included are two papers, one by Bruce Murphy and the other by Marlan Blissett, commissioned specifically for this volume.

In making its selections the conference committee was guided by the quality of each submission and a desire to produce coherent and intellectually balanced panels. As it happens, most of the papers submitted were largely favorable in their assessments of the Johnson record in domestic policy and most were unfavorable in their evaluations of the president's handling of the Vietnam War. If there are regrettable lacunae in this volume, they are the absence of a strong, conservative critique of the Great Society and an essay on Vietnam critical of Johnson for not having pursued the war more vigorously.

Besides scholarly essays we are fortunate to be able to include the observations of Johnson adviser Bill D. Moyers and political columnist Tom Wicker. Both Moyers and Wicker delivered addresses at the conference, and both were gracious enough to edit transcripts of their remarks for inclusion here. Moyers provides an eloquent and wide-ranging insider's view of the Johnson White House that leaves very few stones unturned, and Wicker offers a concise and powerful analysis of the gap between expectations generated by Johnson's extraordinary first year in office and the realities of presidential power.

A distinctive feature of Hofstra's presidential conferences is the effort to blend scholarly analysis with retrospective discussions involving people who were once either at the heart of the policy-making system or well known for their political activism. In this volume we include edited transcripts of panel discussions covering the Great Society, civil rights, and the Vietnam War. The Great Society panel brings together former officials of the Johnson administration, who assess the president's legislative skills and largely defend the administration's programs against the conservative challenge of the 1980s. The civil rights panel, including two former attorneys-general and a group of civil rights activists, offers a stirring and at times passionate discussion of the president's leadership in this area. The Vietnam panel, joining administration officials such as W. W. Rostow and William Bundy with anti-war activists such as Tom Hayden, sparks naturally the most controversy. It also provides interesting insights into the president's motivation and moments of fascinating personal introspection.

In preparing each panel transcript for publication, the editors attempted as much as possible to remain faithful to the exact words of the participants. The spoken word, however, is different from the written word, and in some cases words are inserted in brackets to make the proceedings more coherent.

Apart from the introductory essay by Tom Wicker and the concluding essay by Bill Moyers, the book is organized into five sections. Part I examines the establishment of the Great Society and assesses its programs against the test of time. Michael Reopel and Lance Bardsley study two Johnson programs, the Elementary and Secondary Education Act of 1965 and the Demonstration Cities Act of 1966. Sheri David provides a well-documented narrative of the evolution of the Medicare Act, and Marlan Blissett offers a provocative evaluation of the implementation of selected Great Society programs, a subject that normally receives scant attention compared to the debate over their social effectiveness. Responding to the current spate of scholarly criticisms of the Great Society, Attiat Ott and Paul Hughes-Cromwick question the assumptions and methods underlying economists' analyses of the success or failure of the Great Society, and Michael Riccards criticizes the role of the liberal community in the revisionist view of Johnson's domestic program. We conclude with the Great Society panel discussion.

Part II offers a look into Johnson's civil rights program and Supreme Court appointments. Robert Loevy provides an analysis of the legislative fight over the 1964 Civil Rights Act and focuses on the president's leadership. Julie Leininger Pycior covers another facet of Johnson's concern for minorities by examining the president's attitudes toward Mexican Americans, and in the process she paints a vivid sociological portrait of the Mexican American in Johnson's native Texas. David O'Brien assesses the argument that Johnson's court appointments reflected "cronyism," and Bruce Murphy delves into the Johnson–Abe Fortas relationship, particularly as it applied to the justice's advice to the president regarding Vietnam. We conclude with a panel discussion on civil rights.

Part III evaluates the impact of the Vietnam War on the Great Society and the nation's economic health. Donald Pickens employs the role of the Council of Economic Advisers as a useful tool for tracing the effects of the war on economic policy, and Phillip Simpson looks at the legislative battle over tax policy to make some observations about changing political and economic circumstances and their impact on the revenue-raising process. Thomas Riddell provides statistical data which indicate, despite the revisionist view, that the war did in fact fuel inflation. Finally, John Ullmann examines the president's strivings against the backdrop of limited resources.

Part IV offers a useful counterpoint to the contentions that Lyndon Johnson came to the presidency with no previous background in foreign policy and that once in office Vietnam was his sole foreign policy preoccupation. Thomas Gaskin reviews Johnson's foreign policy experience as Senate majority leader, and Elmer Plischke details Johnson's efforts, both as vice president and president, in the area of high level summitry.

Part V deals with the Vietnam War. Kenneth Thompson views the president's war policy in terms of commitments made by previous presidents toward collective security. William Levantrosser examines, on the basis of extensive interviewing and review of archival material, the Gulf of Tonkin incident. Kathleen Turner assesses Johnson's effort to turn public opinion toward the war in April 1965, and Philip Avillo, Jr., takes note of congressional reluctance to support the war as early as 1965. A panel discussion on the war concludes this section.

If the papers submitted and published in this volume suggest anything about history's assessment of Lyndon Baines Johnson two decades after he left the White House, it is that no dramatic revisionism has yet taken place with regard to his presidential reputation. Johnson was recognized during his presidency for the brilliance of his political skills and the sweep, for better or worse, of his social vision. He was attacked, on the other hand, for the quality of his decisions on Vietnam. While contemporary conservative and military revisionists lament the nation's failure to pursue the war to a decisive end, there is no strong body of opinion, even among the revisionists, to suggest that Johnson did the right thing by prosecuting a limited war. The verdict of scholars twenty years later is remarkably close to the verdict of the American people as Johnson left the presidency—that a president who approached greatness in his quest for a more just and equitable society was ultimately brought down by a war he could neither win nor conclude.

We have chosen to title this book *Lyndon Johnson and the Uses of Power* because few presidencies so clearly demonstrate the various ends toward which the immense power of the president can be applied. Nor can other presidencies offer us so dramatic a testimony to the transitory nature of power. The presidency can be a source of social amelioration or a source of war. Its authority can be used skillfully or clumsily. A president may stand high one day and fall low the next. Lyndon Johnson was a master in the uses of political power, but like others who have held his office he discovered that power used problematically can exact a heavy toll on its practitioner.

We would like to thank some of the people involved in helping us produce this volume. Many thanks to all the contributors, and a special word of appreciation to Bill Moyers and Harry Middleton, director of the LBJ Library, who helped us enlist participants in the conference. Thank you to Paul Demery, Joy Woda, and Tomio Narita for their outstanding editorial assistance. Thank you to Marilyn Shepherd, Shari Qwatny, and Hofstra's Special Secretarial Services for their typing assistance. And finally, thank you to the Hofstra University

Cultural Center, its staff, and acting co-directors Natalie Datlof and Alexej Ugrinsky for helping to make the conference a success.

Bernard J. Firestone

Robert C. Vogt

LYNDON BAINES JOHNSON AND THE USES OF POWER

Introduction.
LBJ: The Strength of a Giant

Tom Wicker

I appreciate that introduction very much, those glowing words. After an even more glowing introduction, I once heard President Johnson say that he really liked it, his father would have loved it, and his mother would have believed it.

It's a pleasure to see so many old friends and acquaintances here this morning and to regain with them, for this moment, something of the spirit of a more confident and optimistic time—those remarkable first months and years of Lyndon Johnson's presidency. To many of us who were then concerned with public policy, as officials or observers, all things at last seemed possible, obstacles suddenly puny.

As LBJ led Congress to the completion of the Civil Rights Act of 1964, to a major tax bill, the first significant federal aid to education, and the program of medical care for the aged that had been pending since Harry Truman's day, surely confidence and optimism were not unwarranted.

Then in 1964 the American people seemed to give overwhelming endorsement to these great achievements and to the man who had made them a reality; his reelection was followed by the notable series of legislative victories establishing the Great Society—the most visionary domestic program in American history, and one that, above all, was grounded in a generosity of spirit that I believe is more genuinely characteristic of our people than the complacency and self-seeking that are often pandered to today.

I want particularly to recall that relatively brief period of accomplishment for the Johnson administration—of great accomplishment—and let others dwell, if they will, on the disappointment and decline that came later. My reason for that is not just that the American political system, under the leadership of a man who knew what made it tick, was able to work efficiently and productively to an extent not seen since and not often before. It's also that this moment of great presidential success may hold for us a useful lesson, and I take it that we have come here, as [Hofstra] President [James] Shuart has indicated, not so much to bury Lyndon Johnson or to praise him as to try to learn something from our experience of him and his time.

Despite the relative obscurity of his years in the vice presidency—incidentally, the careers of all who have occupied that office since his time suggest that in the enhancement of the vice presidency so much talked about, there's less than meets the eye. The present incumbent may so find. But despite the relative obscurity of his years in the vice presidency, Lyndon Johnson was known to Washington in 1963 as perhaps the most effective floor leader the Senate had seen. And after he magnificently—there's no other word—rallied the nation following President Kennedy's murder and moved ahead to the remarkable record I've cited, it was easy enough to fall victim to the idea that we had something of a miracle man in the White House. I don't think I was alone in the expectation that Lyndon Johnson might earn a place equal to Franklin Roosevelt's—or greater—in the transformation of modern American life.

We know now that it didn't happen, despite his early successes. This conference probably will be told that the war in Vietnam thwarted further achievement, and no doubt that's true. But I suggest that after 1965 the road might have been downhill anyway, and probably would have been, because no president could have satisfied the expectations that many of us—probably including LBJ himself—had for him, with all his knowledge and skill and strength and desire to be great by doing good. No president can be a miracle man; and if in those fruitful early years Lyndon Johnson came about as close to it as could be expected of mortal man, his fate powerfully symbolizes that truth: No president can be a miracle man.

That's an unpalatable truth to Americans, congenital optimists that they are, and believers in the efficacy of power. Americans like to think—and a history insufficiently studied or understood persuades them—that for everything that's wrong there's bound to be a solution, only needing to be found; and the quicker the fix the better.

If we can't travel in the Mediterranean this summer for fear of terrorism, surely we can next year. We like to think there's nothing we can't achieve if we set our minds to it. We went to the moon, didn't we? And we tend to believe that the worst of problems is just a wreck on the highway; we Americans can clear it off and go on, the way we did when we answered all our race questions with civil rights bills.

"You can't just throw money at problems," goes the popular saying; but Americans don't really believe it, or if they do, they often don't act on it: witness their support for President Reagan's first-term military buildup. Or maybe, Americans keep thinking, things can be fixed up by technology, as in nuclear power too cheap to meter, or a space-based, x-ray lasered missile defense.

Today's most popular cure-all is free enterprise, the magic of the marketplace. Oh yes, the market can make things right from South Africa to the bread lines in the world's richest nation, despite the fact that many of the social programs being starved or dismantled today were made necessary by the cruelties and indifferences of that same market.

Of course if all else fails—sometimes *before* all else fails—there's always military power. Three aircraft carriers in the Gulf of Sidra will clean Khaddafi's clock and show the terrorists who's boss.

So it tends to be with our presidents. If we just elect the right man—maybe some day the right woman—if we just elect the right person, we can get this country moving again. Throw the rascals out, vote in the miracle man, and we can all stand tall; it'll be morning again in America.

Whose finger do you want on the button? Not just the nuclear button but all those magic buttons that when pushed (or mashed, as LBJ used to say) will rev up the economy, face down the Russians, overtake the Japanese, conquer poverty, abolish the deficit, bring back the family farm, eliminate crime, Aids, and herpes, lower insurance premiums, scourge waste, fraud, and inefficiency at the Pentagon—and so on and on.

But an important lesson to be learned even from the glory years of Lyndon Johnson, I believe, is that no president can fix or do it all; no president can change all that needs changing, meet every new circumstance, remove everything outmoded, and persuade the American people, in Harry Truman's phrase, "to do what they ought to do without persuasion."

Some problems are insurmountable, or will yield only to time and the generations, as may well be the case despite all demonstrable gains, many of them owing to LBJ—with the persisting economic and social gaps between white and black Americans.

Some resistance is immovable, like that of most American businessmen to anything, however reasonable, that can be called planning. Some impulses are irresistible—for example, the American instinct that all other societies should be remodeled in our image. And some ills are incurable—as, apparently, is the conviction of so many Americans that they are a chosen people, living in a nation favored of God.

The idea of the miracle man in the White House seems to me to be of a parcel with such delusory notions. It's fostered by the excesses of political campaigning—which itself has been hyped toward fantasy by the deceptive potentialities of television—including, in my judgment, those high-noon shootouts of posturing and misinformation, the so-called presidential debates.

The miracle man myth is propagated also, I fear, by the more gullible and ideological practitioners, of which there are many, among my brethren of the press. And to the extent, which is quite an extent, that scholars and professionals of government climb eagerly aboard the political power train, they too spread the illusion that all we need is the right man, the right party—victory on election day!—and all will be well.

I think the American people feed on quite enough illusions. Now, with another presidential campaign already under way, I wonder if we who knew Lyndon

Johnson and shared in his times, we who marvelled at his works and perhaps
inflated the expectations of a nation—I wonder if in our years and experience
we aren't particularly suited to cast a cold eye on the miracle man myth.

Shouldn't we, more than most, give fair warning that *much is intractable*—
problems persist, programs miss the mark, persuasion fails, even the headiest
vision may be clouded? We aren't going to be friends with the Soviet Union in
the next administration and don't we have good reason to know that even successful efforts, domestic or foreign, sometimes have consequences no one expected or wanted? That as Adlai Stevenson put it, "There are no gains without
pains."

And if we know how excellent a thing it is for a president to have the strength
of a giant, surely we've seen, too, how fatal it can be to use it like a giant—
and that the temptation to do so is the dark lining of the love of power.

Above all, it seems to me, those who in the urge to win and lead perpetuate
the idea of a miracle man in the White House—which is really a cult of personality
of the president—only compound the real problem. They not only mislead the
people about the president; more grievously, they mislead the people about
themselves. For if we are even marginally to improve our society, strengthen
our freedom, and ease the dangers of the world, the burden lies more heavily
on the American people than upon any president.

A president can lead, a president can persuade, a president can act—but the
truth that the miracle man illusion denies is that *it's the people who must understand and follow.* In the long run, it's the people who have to do all those
things that, in an ideal world, they ought to do without leadership or persuasion.

Friends, Americans, countrymen: I've offered these reflections not to tarnish
that long-ago moment that I've characterized as one of optimism and confidence,
but because that moment still represents to me, all these years later, a high-water
mark of my own expectations. Therefore, it means also to me the inevitability
of disillusion and decline—a hard truth that can only ennoble the human effort
that remains necessary.

And if I said in the beginning that I came here neither to bury nor to praise
Lyndon Johnson, still the occasion does cause me further to observe with Mark
Anthony: "The evil that men do lives after them; the good is oft interred with
their bones." But, like Anthony, "I speak not to disprove" what much of the
nation appears to think today about the man we've gathered here to reexamine,
perhaps to reevaluate. Rather, it seems fair to me, on such an occasion, merely
to ask of the American people, as Anthony asked of the Romans: "You all did
love him once, not without cause. What cause withholds you then to mourn for
him?'

Thank you.

I

THE GREAT SOCIETY AND WAR ON POVERTY

1

Strategies for Governance: Domestic Policy Making in the Johnson Administration

Michael R. Reopel and Lance W. Bardsley

Conventional wisdom suggests that President Lyndon Baines Johnson pushed each Congress to the limit to obtain a maximum number of controversial legislative victories. Consequently, slim margins were often expected and indeed planned for. A key Johnson legislative aide, Henry Hall Wilson, made this point explicitly, "When we have a fat Congress as we did in the Eighty-ninth, then we can hike up our demands to fit the situation. When votes are not razor thin in either case, then we are not doing a good job."[1]

The linchpin of the whole system was "the treatment," Johnson's personal techniques of political persuasion and political skill. Johnson used just about everything in his extensive repertoire to get Congress moving and excelled whenever he had the opportunity for direct, one-on-one contact. According to Hugh Sidey, "During 1965 in particular I think Johnson would zero in on a congressman or a senator and get what he wanted, a good deal. I would be amazed at some of the devices he would use. He would lie, beg, cheat, steal a little, threaten, intimidate. But he never lost sight of that ultimate goal, his idea of the Great Society."[2] Substantial preparation was required to identify that congressman or senator who could serve as a swing vote, resulting in a close victory. Corroborations of Hugh Sidey's observations are numerous.[3] For example, Evans and Novak described "the treatment" as an endeavor that could last ten minutes or four hours and "its tone could be supplication, accusation, cajolery, exuberance, scorn, tears, complaint, the hint of threat." With a dominating personality and physical presence, Johnson would move in close, "his face a scant millimeter from his target, his eyes widening and narrowing, his eyebrows rising and falling. From his pockets poured clippings, memos, statistics. Mimicry, humor, and the genius of analogy made 'the treatment' an almost hypnotic experience and rendered the target stunned and helpless."[4]

"Great innovations should not be forced on slender majorities." Kennedy often quoted Jefferson to argue that there was no virtue in fighting legislative battles and losing.[5] Thus, the 1964 Goldwater backlash is frequently and correctly credited with giving President Johnson the added legislative leeway to push his domestic agenda. In 1964 the American voter gave the Democratic ticket the most extensive plurality in history and sent to Congress the largest Democratic majority since 1936 (295 in the House and 67 in the Senate). Goldwater beat Johnson in only one non-Southern state—Arizona, where his margin was embarrassingly close—and carried no congressional districts in thirty-two states outside the South.[6] The 1964 election created a political climate between the president and members of Congress that made "the treatment" an all but irresistible force.[7]

Lobbying for critical votes, the Johnson treatment and the Goldwater backlash are significant explanations for Johnson's domestic policy successes in the eighty-ninth Congress. However, they are neither sufficient nor supported empirically. According to George Edwards, if Johnson's legislative skills did gain him a few critical votes necessary to win top priority legislation, then one should expect he should have won at least a good number of votes by narrow margins. Examining presidential roll call votes in both 1965 and 1967, Edwards found that Johnson did not win many votes by close margins even when a generous definition of marginal victory was employed.[8] In fact, Johnson's key victories in 1965— aid to education, Medicare, voting rights—all had significant majorities.

Although recent scholars have found it difficult to measure presidential effectiveness in influencing Congress and legislative liaison has seemed less significant than conventional wisdom has previously indicated, Johnson nevertheless maintained, "There is only one way for a president to deal with the Congress and that is continuously, incessantly, and without interruption."[9] In his memoirs Johnson explained, "Merely, placing a program before Congress is not enough. Without constant attention from the administration, most legislation moves through the congressional process at the speed of a glacier."[10] For an activist president with a large agenda such attention appears critical. But such attention also costs.[11] Contrary to the opening remarks by Henry Hall Wilson, razor thin victories and multiple demands expend scarce political resources and often require key compromises and face substantial congressional modification and, occasionally, defeat. Larry O'Brien, head of the Office of Congressional Relations under Kennedy and Johnson, related one instance where Johnson telephoned twenty-two members of the House and asked them to sign a discharge petition on a home rule bill for the District of Columbia: "He persuaded and cajoled and pleaded. He spoke movingly of the inequality of denying democratic government. He got the signatures, personally and single-handedly."[12] It was a remarkable performance, but O'Brien should have also noted that the petition failed.[13]

Fortunately for Lyndon Johnson winning big in 1964 gave the president a large number of liberal Democrats in Congress and a mandate to follow his inclinations. However, even in late 1964 Johnson did not really know the details of what he would seek to do. The mandate for domestic policy seemed to have something to do with a Great Society, the war on poverty, civil rights, and maybe, expanding educational opportunity.[14] Even if the Goldwater backlash assured Johnson of stable, not slender, majorities, then the president and his staff still had to develop the legislative program, make public pronouncements, forge needed coalitions, perfect timing sequences, design alternatives, and superintend the legislative process when necessary.[15] This would require early planning and strategic choices of priorities and timing.

This chapter will attempt to move somewhat beyond the conventional analysis and anecdotes of the Johnson presidency. It will also have very little to say concerning the tactics of White House lobbying and congressional liaison. Fortunately, others have commented superbly in this area.[16] Our concern here is a more strategic look at a president's influence on governmental action. Paraphrasing Richard Neustadt, the question is not how a president masters Congress in any particular instance, but what choices he makes early on to boost his chances for mastery in any future instance.[17] The ability to join policy and politics systematically in a realistic time frame has been called the "strategic presidency."[18] Strategic governance means to choose a limited number of "first order" priorities, to force timely action, to integrate the political considerations with the policy process. If successful early, administrations hope that subsequent legislation can be spun out from these initial victories until the administration can no longer control the agenda.[19]

This chapter will focus on the process of policy formulation in the Johnson presidency by examining two domestic initiatives, the Elementary and Secondary Education Act of 1965 and the Demonstration Cities and Metropolitan Development Act of 1966. These initiatives were selected for two reasons. First, both issues were primarily redistributive policies whose impetus came from the executive office. Second, these issues represented both the beginning and end of the eighty-ninth Congress. The Elementary and Secondary Educational Act was the product of an electoral mandate and careful planning prior to the State of the Union message in order to take full opportunity of the presidential honeymoon. Demonstration Cities, on the other hand, was timed just prior to the midterm elections, when presidents are expected to be less assertive and Congress less acquiescent.

One final note is necessary. In examining these two domestic initiatives there are at least three analytical cuts or perspectives: functional, legislative history, and institutional. Although the Domestic Council and Office of Congressional Relations will be discussed implicitly, a complete legislative history will not be found here.[20] The focus will remain functional, the strategic activities outlined below.

STRATEGIC GOVERNANCE

A president must be his own strategic center in order to provide coherence to the rest of the government. The Executive Office of the President (EOP) cannot.

The EOP is overcrowded with staff units charged with overseeing large areas of domestic policy, budgeting, and politics but has no coordinating mechanism for bringing all these perspectives into a strategic focus. Only the president sits where he sits; no one else can feel the weight of his obligations; only he can pull all the relevant aspects of policy and politics together into a genuine strategy for governance. Consequently, he must develop a political battle plan to bring the often competing functions of policy planning, congressional lobbying, press management, public relations, party politics, and budget allocations into a single disciplined and coherent framework called the "president's program."[21] Four strategic actions are available for a president to provide coherence to the rest of government: setting priorities with a proper sense of timing, framing the issue, planning early, and preempting congressional modification. These four actions will be discussed in turn.

Priorities and Political Timing

Ten days after President Johnson was inaugurated in 1965 he called together all of his legislative liaison people in the White House and gave a sermon on political timing:

I want you to get all my legislative proposals during this session, now!... Every day that I am in office, I lose part of my power. Every day that I use power, I have less power left. You must get this legislation through immediately. I want you to talk to those congressmen. I want you to sleep with those congressmen if you have to. I want you to get this legislation through now—while I still have the power.[22]

Upon retirement President Johnson reminisced:

You've got to give it all you can that first year. Doesn't matter what kind of majority you come in with. You've got just one year when they treat you right, and before they start worrying about themselves. The third year, you lose votes.... The fourth year's all politics. You can't put anything through when half of the Congress is thinking how to beat you. So you've got one year. That's why I tried. Well, we gave it a hell of a lick, didn't we?[23]

Paul Light offers evidence to support Johnson's propositions. He has identified two policy cycles—the cycle of decreasing influence and the cycle of increasing effectiveness—that characterize the presidential-congressional relationship. The former is a window of opportunity that incorporates factors such as a president's honeymoon, coattails, electoral mandate, and public prestige. Since most presidents have experienced a decline in public approval ratings over the term of office and since all presidents since Roosevelt in 1934 have suffered midterm losses of party seats in Congress, presidents have been advised to act in the first years of their term and as early as possible within each year. If a president fails to move early, Congress will fill the domestic agenda with its own initiatives.

In short, since a president's opportunities for congressional support are at a maximum early in the first year, he must push his domestic proposals as soon as he enters office. Consequently, this puts tremendous pressures on the president-elect prior to his inaugural to make decisions on the substance, timing, publicity, and priority of legislative proposals to Congress.[24]

The latter cycle, which rests on the premise that presidents and staff learn over time, was less applicable to Johnson.[25] Johnson's experiences as Senate majority leader and his unelected year in office (1964) provided him and his staff with a job training program that simply did not exist for other presidents. Thus, Johnson was able to avoid the hazards of inexperience and miscalculation and concentrate on moving legislation early.

If political timing is a key ingredient to success, to be a successful president one must develop and enforce decision- and action-forcing processes to move contemporary government. The phrasing of congressional messages, the clearance of initiatives, the drafts of the inaugural, economic, and State of the Union messages are all examples of action-forcing mechanisms that require presidential decisions by certain deadlines.[26] Note that wanting early action is not the same thing as enforcing it; only deadlines can compel action. In describing the emergence of President Nixon's domestic program, Richard Nathan has illustrated this relationship between legislative opportunity and deadlines:

During the period from Nixon's inauguration until August 8, 1969, the business of domestic policymaking had dragged out longer than the president wanted. Many protracted meetings had been held on program details and techniques. This was especially true of welfare reform, which at every turn became more difficult and complex than had been originally anticipated. The president was impatient. Early in July he instructed press secretary Ronald Ziegler to state publicly that his domestic program would be announced in the first week of August right after the president returned from an overseas trip. The die was cast, and in this case the deadline was met.[27]

Thus, a president is faced with several strategic choices. He must set enforceable deadlines to prompt early action on his priority initiatives.

According to Johnson, "One of the president's most important jobs is to help Congress concentrate on the five and six dozen bills that make up his legislative program."[28] But such massive, annual presentations have a tendency to blur the impact of any particular bill, scatter attention, and often make deadlines numerous and unmanageable. By sending bills individually, rather than in a complete package, to committees with clear agendas so that they could be considered immediately without time for opposition to coalesce, Johnson was able to avoid this predicament. Johnson's technique of maximum attention in minimum time was his way to avoid congressional policy congestion.[29] Keeping the cycle of decreasing influence in mind, this sequential timing of initiatives is, in actuality, the setting of presidential priorities. Johnson felt that the first impression of his presidency would be crucial. A loss or stalemate at the beginning of his first elected year would be a serious blow. Thus, Johnson's decision to push health and education legislation ahead of home rule for the District of Columbia, for example, resulted from his carefully considered judgment as to the amount of time each of the bills would consume and which measures were most likely to provoke controversy that would drain valuable energy.[30] Their eventual passage gave momentum to the whole Johnson program. Momentum is not mysterious; it is a controllable fact of political life that depends on nothing more exotic than preparation.[31]

Framing the Issue

One of the most powerful and simplifying tools available for a president is "to frame the issue." When any issue arises, the relevant publics both in and outside government typically come to see quite different faces or aspects of the same issue. Where you sit influences what you see as well as where you stand.[32] Rarely will two sets of eyes see the same issue the same way. Consequently, this gives a president a certain amount of flexibility. By educating the relevant publics through the "bully pulpit" a president can sometimes repackage an issue in an attempt to reduce conflict, thus gaining leeway or benefit of the doubt. A most recent illustration occurred in 1985 with the MX missile. If the Reagan administration advocated the MX solely in terms of its capability, cost, basing mode and doctrine, there would have been a strong case for congressional rejection. Instead, President Reagan framed the issue by labelling the MX as a critical "bargaining chip" for the upcoming Geneva summit. Thus, the burden of proof was shifted from the executive to the Congress. The question became not one of force ratios and cost effectiveness but, rather, will the rejection of the MX undercut the feet of the president in Geneva?

Normally a president cannot depend on external events to rescue his position. But he may be able to do one of the following:

• Evoke memories of past performances and commitments.

• Conjure up a prospect for future benefits (or dire consequences).[33]

• Sell conflictual, redistributive policies by emphasizing their distributive features.[34]

• Explain the election returns and interpret the new political climate.

• Argue that opposition would permanently weaken the office of the presidency (e.g., Reagan and AWACS).

• Package the issue in terms of budget necessity and fiscal responsibility rather than its social underpinnings.

• Link national security demands and perceived crises to what otherwise would be domestic policies (e.g., National Defense Education Act).

In a more colorful, less academic way Jack Valenti recalled a Johnson lesson on how to give a congressman a handle to justify his decision to his constituency:

Now, the first thing you have to remember is these men have to go back home and get reelected every two years. They're not going to be impressed if you ask them to vote for something that will give them political leprosy. They have to have a fall-back, something they can talk about in positive terms as to why they voted with us. It has to be something that Cousin Oriole can understand, not some fancy theory about life in the hereafter.[35]

Positively framing an issue early on allows a president to color the mood of its initial congressional reception. This is different from lobbying one on one using several faces of the issue. Although creating a political mood or atmosphere may be impossible to measure, nonetheless it conditions feelings and thoughts, facilitates action, and occasionally determines outcomes.[36]

Strategic Planning

With the developing of a highly specialized liaison staff in the Office of Congressional Relations (OCR) there has come a separation of the policy-planning functions from the overt lobbying functions.[37] Although a clear-cut dichotomy does not exist, certainly more strategic thinking is done during policy planning than legislative liaison. The consequence of this separate lobbying function is that the tactical considerations for each initiative are usually wrestled with quite late in the policy formulation process by the OCR. This early planning function consists of three activities: innovation, insulation, and initiation.

In examining sources of new ideas in government, one observes that the theory of simultaneous—and seemingly spontaneous—invention applies to governments.[38] The successful innovation seems to crop up all at once from multiple sources; in fact, people have almost come to blows in Washington about who should receive the credit. One thing seems certain, routine processes do not warrant the recognition. Expressing his reservations, Johnson wrote:

I had watched this [programming] process for years, and I was convinced that it did not encourage enough fresh or creative ideas. The bureaucracy of the government is too preoccupied with day to day operations, and there is strong bureaucratic inertia dedicated to preserving the status quo. As a result, only the most powerful ideas can survive. . . .

The general theme was not to rock the boat, not to step on anyone's toes, not to interfere with anyone's jurisdiction, but to make some improvements, often remedial, at times incremental, but seldom innovative. The end product was a compromise. Then these same ideas would be pressed forward by the particular agency or department year after year, hoping for ultimate adoption by the administration.[39]

Johnson found his solution for overcoming bureaucratic inertia and repetitiveness:

Hoping for an across-the-board Democratic victory in November 1964, I wanted, if elected, to be able early in 1965 to recommend programs that would deal with the critical problems facing the country,. But those programs depended on a tremendous infusion of objective thinking and new and original ideas. For this reason, we established fourteen task forces in 1964 to study critical areas of our national life, including education.[40]

What significance can we draw from these task forces? First, they were umbilical cords of fresh ideas from the academic community to Washington. Second, they may have short-circuited the bureaucracy, thus prompting action. Third, the debate and negotiation remained inside the EOP ensuring some policy control. Finally, instead of waiting until 1965 to generate new ideas, Johnson was saying the time to act was now to take advantage of the projected landslide.[41] Besides task forces, today sources of ideas for an agenda can come from policy analysts in institutes, commissions, campaign consultants, transition teams, and even congressional committees and agency staffs.

When a president presents the product of his policy formulation process, he presents not suggestions but decisions that are to be defended stubbornly against criticism and change.[42] To ensure against premature release, some degree of political insulation is required. As Bill Moyers, who was responsible for the initial Johnson task forces, explained, "When an idea has surfaced too soon, before it has been examined from every vantage point, it can invite its assassination."[43]

Maintaining secrecy was one of the most important operational characteristics of the Johnson task forces. It allowed the president and his staff to ignore politically unfeasible recommendations, to learn about the policy and political implications of an initiative without having to expend political capital defending preliminary choices, and it allowed selective interest group and congressional litmus checks to test the political waters. On the last point Johnson explained, "My father always impressed me with the importance of trying to know when you walked into a room where your friends and enemies were standing. These initial checks gave us that knowledge."[44]

The initiation phase must be controlled by the president and his principal assistants. It is the phase where policy and politics come together in a realistic time frame. Strategic choices concerning—How to frame the issue? Timing? Public relations? What committee or sponsor?—are made with an eye toward establishing presidential priorities. Stemming from these choices, the government becomes energized by deadlines to prepare presidential messages, legislative drafts, action memos, executive orders, and price out proposals.

It is important to note that the planning activities—innovation, insulation, and initiation—have hidden conflicts and tradeoffs. For example, insulation may prevent the percolation of new ideas from other sources. Also, heavy reliance on outside organizations to short-circuit the bureaucracy may find a cool reception later on during implementation.

Preempting Congressional Modification

What the constitutional convention created, writes Richard Neustadt, was "a government of separated institutions sharing powers" and "what the Constitution separates our political parties do not combine.''[45] Since the president is the primary initiating force in the country, he must break this wall of separation if his legislative program is to be adopted.

According to Steven Shull, domestic policy formation has four substages: agenda setting, initiation, modification, and adoption. In this sequential approach the two most crucial participants are Congress and the president, where the role of the former is greater in modification and adoption and the latter in agenda setting and initiation.[46] In essence this is a refinement of the conventional theory, the president proposes, the Congress disposes. However, this limited partnership was not Lyndon Johnson's theory in the early days of the Great Society. The challenge, remarked Johnson, was ''to crack the wall of separation enough to give the Congress a feeling of participation in creating my bills without exposing my plans at the same time to advance congressional opposition before they even saw the light of day.''[47]

Johnson utilized several techniques based on congressional desires for recognition and avoidance of uncertainty to precook his legislation with those who were essential for its adoption. But from a strategic perspective, by implicating members of Congress in the traditionally executive function of initiating legislation, he received key intelligence on the program's chances of passage, thus confirming his order of priorities. It also gave the president an opportunity to make adjustments, often proposing amendments himself, to improve those chances of adoption. Doris Kearns mentions that these early checks gave the White House an opportunity to redraft its bills and, if necessary, they would be assigned to different and more favorable committees.[48] Others have called it an attempt to superintend the legislative process and still others maintain that functions of the congressional committee were being conducted under the auspices of the executive branch.[49]

In summary, by allowing congressional participation in the initiation substage, Johnson was preempting modification, thus allowing for quicker passage and perhaps a bill more to his liking. Ideally, with early planning and packaging a president could time the modification and adoption substages of a major proposal early during the cycle of decreasing influence, the honeymoon period, where his chances of policy control are at its highest.

ELEMENTARY AND SECONDARY EDUCATION ACT: MOVING BEYOND THE LEGACY

From a presidential perspective, the Elementary and Secondary Education Act of 1965 (ESEA) differs significantly from Demonstration Cities. ESEA was the policy vehicle from which President Johnson moved beyond the ''Kennedy legacy,'' where he transformed his legislative genius into effective executive power. According to biographer Doris Kearns, Johnson in 1964 assumed the responsibility for transforming Kennedy's proposals into legislative victories with the utmost display of humility.[50] But one issue, general aid to education, remained on the back burner since the chastening ordeal over separation of church and state in 1961.[51] There it remained while the first series of Johnson task forces secretly forged a consensus on aiding both public and parochial schools, which formed the base of a distinctively Johnsonian legislative program.[52] The speed and success of this initiative in Congress detached Johnson from any responsibility for another's legacy. In the eyes of the Washington community, he turned the JFK presidency into the LBJ presidency.

The ideas for the education bill had been percolating in Congress since the Eisenhower era and were contained in a report by a presidentially appointed task force led by John W. Gardner, president of the Carnegie Corporation. Before the bill was introduced to Congress, the White House held numerous meetings to iron out a consensus with congressmen, the National Education Association (NEA), the National Catholic Welfare Conference (NCWC), and other interested groups. As a result, ESEA moved through the House with only minor amendments and through the Senate without changes from the House version. The House voted 263 to 153 and the Senate 73 to 18 in favor of the legislation. On 11 April 1965 President Johnson signed the bill into law outside the former one-room schoolhouse at Stonewall, Texas, where he first attended classes.[53]

In hindsight, ESEA seemed like an initiative whose time had come. The issue of aid to segregated schools had been largely settled by the Civil Rights Act of 1964. The ecumenical movement somewhat diffused the church-state issue. The twenty-one day rule gave the speaker a certain amount of leverage over Rules Committee Chairman, "no rules for school," Judge Howard Smith (D-Va.). Finally, the congressional elections since 1961 brought sweeping Democratic victories that replaced Republican opposition.[54] These changes in the political climate may help explain the lopsided vote but certainly not the biggest surprise: ESEA became law in fewer than three months in almost the exact form in which the administration wanted it. To say that ESEA was simply a bill whose time had come belies both the yeoman effort and strategic thinking in the White House as well as the perceptions of the period. Commenting on the 1961 debacle, Hugh D. Price wrote:

The bitterness of the 1961 legislative struggle and the difficulties of reaching a consensus on the status of nonpublic schools will not soon be forgotten. In private, many school-aid supporters admitted that federal aid of the sort proposed by President Kennedy was dead, not just for the 87th Congress, but probably for the decade of the 1960s.[55]

With an eye toward the likely landslide in November, Johnson made education a national priority in his campaign: "I made a personal decision during the 1964 presidential campaign to make education a fundamental issue and to put it high on the nation's agenda."[56] In order to take advantage of this opportunity, the White House would have to get an early start on the 1965 legislative program, wrest the policy initiative from Congress, and force the issue by following a strict time schedule.

In preparation for a Cabinet meeting on 17 January 1964, Horace Busby asked HEW Secretary Anthony Celebrezze and Commissioner Francis Keppel to present recommendations and objectives for a Johnson education program. In attendance was the future head of the task force on education, John W. Gardner.[57] After a few trial speeches, Lyndon Johnson delivered on 22 May 1964 his design for the Great Society in a commencement address at the University of Michigan. In order to build the Great Society in the classrooms, Johnson promised:

We are going to assemble the best thought and broadest knowledge from all over the world to find those answers. I intend to establish working groups to prepare a series of conferences and meetings—on the cities, on natural beauty, on the quality of education, and on other emerging challenges.[58]

To many Americans the Great Society speech established Johnson as his own president.[59] For his principal staff, it was a call to action.

On 30 May Budget Director Kermit Gordon and Chairman of the Council of Economic Advisers Walter Heller sent Bill Moyers a memo proposing fourteen task forces that included education.[60] In June, William Cannon, chief of Education, Manpower and Sciences at BOB (Bureau of the Budget), prepared an education policy issue paper that subsequently served as the agenda for the Gardner task force.[61] On 2 July during a formal cabinet meeting Johnson announced the creation of a number of secret task forces declaring, "The time to begin planning the administration's program for next year—and the years after—is *now*. But you and I are going to be exceedingly busy during the next four months. Therefore, as the first step in drawing up a 1965 program now, I am establishing a number of program task forces made up of outstanding people, from within and without government."[62] Following through, Moyers sent out task force instructions and launched them toward a 10 November deadline.

While the task forces received their marching orders, Chairman Wayne Morse (D-Oreg.) of the Senate education subcommittee introduced a bill prepared by his staff in February 1964 asking for $218 million to be distributed among school districts on the basis of unemployment and welfare statistics. The administration's response was lukewarm, preferring to keep the issue on the back burner. To force the issue, Senator Morse called for a July hearing and subsequently castigated Commissioner Keppel for stalling. Later, in an attempt to tactfully grab policy control, Keppel and HEW Assistant Secretary Wilbur Cohen advised the senator. "The president wants to tell you that we are for your bill. We are even going to expand it."[63]

After monitoring the task force's November deadline, Keppel, Cohen, and White House advisers Douglass Cater and Richard Goodwin put together a number of recommendations for the president's review in December at the LBJ ranch, where he would be working on his State of the Union message. Simultaneously, Moyers chaired several White House strategy sessions and forwarded these proposals to BOB and the Office of Education (OE) for initial drafting.[64]

Although education was somewhat shortchanged in the State of the Union message, the priority was reemphasized in a Cabinet meeting the day prior to the president's message on education to Congress, 12 January 1965:

Tommorow I am sending to the Congress the Message on Education to outline our education program for this year. That is why I have called you here today.

I want—and I intend—education to be the cornerstone on which we build this administration's program and record. Whatever the province of your department or agency, I consider your first priority of responsibility to support education—not merely the legislation, but the cause itself.[65]

In closing he remarked to his Cabinet and confidants:

Today this meeting of the Cabinet is likely to be the last before the Inaugural. Four years ago, most of you began your service here with John Kennedy.

You have served me more faithfully than any man in my situation could ask or expect ...thank you....

And I would like to ask you to join with me in bowing your head for a moment of silent tribute together to the memory of a man beloved to us all—President Kennedy.[66]

By knowing his priorities, and forcing action through deadlines and presidential messages, Johnson in one stroke laid the Kennedy legacy to rest and produced an innovative education proposal before his own inaugural.

President Johnson sent his education bill to Congress with one overriding concern: He was determined to keep the lid on the church-state issue by repackaging the issue.[67] By framing general aid to education in terms of the war on poverty and child benefits, the White House was able to emphasize the distributive aspects of ESEA and shift away from the redistributive focus of race and religion. Consequently, Johnson was determined to put through ESEA with force—draft speed just short of provoking a congressional revolt, without a comma changed, and before the Catholic and Protestant group consensus dissolved over equal aid to parochial schools.[68] As if Keppel controlled the committee system, Johnson instructed:

Look, we've got to do this in a hurry. We've got in with this majority [of sixteen million votes] in the Congress. It doesn't make any difference what we do. We're going to lose them at a rate about a million a month, and under those circumstances, get your subcommittee hearings going. Keppel, when are you starting yours?—I want to see a whole bunch of coonskins on the wall.[69]

Perhaps Congressman Charles Goodell's (R-N.Y.) accusation during the subcommittee hearings can now be put in a different light:

The chairman [Rep. Carl Perkins, D-Ky.] has been very, very kind. . . . Up to this point there has been a very notable lack of balance in the presentations. The thing that bothers me is that the first time we get criticism there apparently is resentment and an attempt to muzzle the witness.[70]

The rediscovery of poverty provided the new rationale for arguing for federal aid to education. As early as mid-February 1964, Commissioner Keppel called poverty the primary target for education before the American Association of School Administrators.[71] Under the supervision of Wilbur Cohen, the HEW staff examined the earlier Morse bill and Gardner recommendations for aiding poor children. With *Everson* v. *Ewing Township* as a precendent, HEW lawyers concluded that new educational programs could be classified as "child benefits" not "school benefits." Hence, the primary purpose of ESEA was to lift the educational level of poor children, whether in public or parochial schools.[72] Framing the issue in these terms had immediate appeal. First, it linked ESEA to Johnson's War on Poverty, which contributed to his landslide election. Second, it was a logical extension of previous assistance to school districts affected by federal activities. Finally, it was a novel approach, as one official suggested: "If we had brought a [school] construction or [teacher] salary bill to the Hill I doubt if it would have had much of an impact—they [the congressmen] would have said: 'So, what else is new?' As it was, they at least had something new to bat around."[73]

It is also important to note that most members of Congress had a personal stake in the outcome of ESEA. The poverty formula meant that federal aid would be distributed in proportion to the numbers of children in families with annual incomes under $2,000. Thus, every congressional district would qualify for some aid. In sum, President Johnson was able to frame the issue sucessfully in terms of prior commitments (War on Poverty), the new political climate (1964 landslide), and by emphasizing the distributive nature of the issue (poverty formula for payments).

Early planning allowed President Johnson to break with tradition by sending his special message on education to Congress before his own inaugural. It also appears that the Gardner Task Force was an important procedural innovation that prompted this early planning.

In trying to ascertain the original parentage of the "child benefit" innovation, certainly Adam Yarmolinsky's theory of simultaneous and spontaneous invention applies to ESEA. For instance, seven people including Senator Abraham Ribicoff, Wilbur Cohen, Francis Keppel, Senator Wayne Morse and his staff aide Charles Lee, Representatives John Dent and Roman Pucinski have all claimed credit for Title I, which tied elementary and secondary aid for education to poverty.[74] Keppel and Congressman Hugh Carey (D-N.Y.) received primary credit for Title II's $300 million program of textbook and library grants to both public and parochial schools. This was the crucial "sweetener" to the Catholics.[75] Did the task force fail as a policy innovator? Apparently the task force did more than pull together existing knowledge and recommendations. Gardner and his task force were the prime initiators of Title III's supplementary education centers, Title IV's research laboratories, and Title V's aid to strengthen state departments of education. Additionally, the Gardner Report began with a plea for concentrating on educational opportunity for the disadvantaged, which subsequently became the prime rationale for Title I.[76]

The history of ESEA is probably the best example of the success of the task force technique and served as a model for subsequent task forces.[77] Richard Goodwin provided the White House liaison and William Cannon of BOB prodded the task force to be venturesome in his role as executive secretary.[78] The membership was not representative; it included pragmatists and professionals committed to federal support of education. Note, clientele groups such as NEA were not represented. All decisions were collegial, allowing a consensus to develop without formal voting.[79]

In 1964 these task forces were "happenings" and their proposals almost immediately became part of Johnson's legislative program.[80] Their novelty gave energy to the executive and their recommendations helped in consensus building. According to Helmer and Maisel, all staffs like to be where the action is, even if only at the margins. If the action is focused on one policy area such as education, health, or housing, then attention tends to be fixed almost exclusively and for long periods in a single area of policy.[81] As long as the Gardner task force and education remained Johnson priorities, the executive branch would dedicate energy to their success. Once the procedural novelty wears off, however, complacency may set in and the desire to circumvent the standard process of legislative agenda formulation will dissipate.[82]

In addition, the use of task forces as a procedural device was consistent with Johnson's triangular mode of decision making. A consensus could be orchestrated by utilizing task force recommendations as a third opinion when confronted with controversial choices. On the other hand, although Commissioner Keppel was a task force member, one would expect the Office of Education to be somewhat resistant to the encroachment on their turf. Cognizant of the possible loss of morale, Johnson demonstrated excellent leadership by personally inspecting the Office of Education on 25 February 1965. Writing to Jack Valenti, Keppel showed his delight: "Nothing in the world could have done our cause more good, or raised morale higher, than the president's visit to this office yesterday."[83]

Frustrated by the secrecy surrounding education task forces, Representative Robert Michel (R-Ill.) told Califano that since "the field of education is no way to be considered a matter of national security, why has it been necessary to cloak the White House efforts in education in secrecy? Isn't the principal purpose of education to open the doors to knowledge rather than to close them?"[84] Secrecy allowed the executive the time to learn about education policy and its political implications and it allowed the staff to send trial balloons to selective interest groups to test and later cement a consensus. Because clientele groups were not represented in the task force and the Office of Education's role in initiating policy declined as a consequence of task force operations, the access of these groups was markedly reduced. Thus, the primary source of information became White House–orchestrated checks. Francis Keppel met with the monsignors of the Catholic church and Jack Valenti served as a liaison with the Vatican's apostolic delegate. Similarly, Lee White dealt with the Jewish organizations; Henry Hall Wilson talked with southern leaders; Douglass Cater, Wilbur Cohen, and Keppel consulted with the education lobbies.[85]

By selective intervention without publicity, the executive branch was able to foster a climate of learning and accommodation between the proponents and opponents of general aid to education. As Sundquist observed:

The sudden turnabout reflects, perhaps most of all, a simple fact: people do learn from experience. First, both sides of the religious controversy had learned. The NEA and its public school allies now knew that an all-or-nothing attitude would mean, for the public schools, nothing. Likewise, Catholic leaders now understood that an equal-treatment-or-nothing position would mean, for the Catholic schools, nothing. For each side the question was whether it preferred to maintain the purity of its ideological position or receive some tangible benefits for its schools.[86]

Policy insulation allowed the White House brokers the ability to manage this climate of "reasoning together," preventing the normal public hardening of viewpoints. Policy insulation also allowed the White House to spring the education proposals ten days prior to the scheduled House hearings, preventing the opposition from planning their own strategy in any detail.

The initial public reaction to ESEA sounded like an ecumenical choir.[87] On the same day as the president's Education Message to Congress, Monsignor Frederick Hockwalt of the NCWC and Robert McKay, chairman of the NEA's Legislative Commission, issued simultaneous statements of support.[88] The timing and the substance of the statements were not coincidental but the culmination of early planning and effort by Keppel and Cater. By the time ESEA became public, the Catholic-Protestant-NEA coalition was forged and the real battle was already over.

At an early stage in the initiation process Bill Moyers coordinated the policy planners with the political operators. In a series of sessions with Larry O'Brien and the principal policy advisers in education, Moyers mapped out a public and legislative strategy that emphasized quick hearings and House adoption followed by Senate ratification. It was decided that Doug Cater should ride herd on the assembling of committee witnesses and the preparation of testimony.[89] Substantive matters were to be referred to Francis Keppel and Wilbur Cohen, but Cater was to make these HEW officials report through him. Questions of parliamentary tactics, favors, audiences with the president, as well as news stories likely to have bearing on congressional action were to be cleared by O'Brien.[90] Additionally, Cater was to provide Moyers advice, free of departmental prejudices, as to which amendments were innocuous or helpful and suggestions for pulling the teeth of harmful proposals that would be impossible to defeat by head-on assault.[91]

The manipulation of congressional hearings was masterful, although Chairman Adam Clayton Powell did provide some anxious moments.[92] For example, Gardner task force members Sidney Marland and James E. Allen, Jr. were co-opted to testify. Following an earlier address to school superintendents by President Johnson, these same superintendents split their resources in half; one group testified before the House, the other before the Senate subcommittee.

John Gardner, Francis Keppel, and Doug Cater all initiated proposals for mustering public support. They organized a citizens' committee for education for the purpose of developing support among school and church organizations and to direct particular efforts toward those congressional constituencies that were being represented in an uncommitted or lukewarm fashion.[93] Other measures included an Education Writers' Association visit to the White House before their annual convention and a luncheon meeting with the heads of various education associations at the White House Mess. Additionally, Mayor Raymond R. Tucker of St. Louis, member of the Gardner task force, offered a resolution at the U.S. Conference of Mayors supporting the education programs, which was reinforced by a special presidential message.[94]

President Johnson involved key members of Congress in the initiation process. Senator Morse and Congressman Perkins became virtual partners in the process at an early stage.[95] Frequent checks were made with Representative Roman Pucinski (D-Ill.), Representative John Brademas (D-Ind.), Senator Abe Ribicoff (D-Conn.), and Senator Lister Hill (D-Ala.). Jack Valenti was given the special charge of consulting with Chairman Adam Clayton Powell (D-N.Y.).[96] As a double check, President Johnson ordered Secretary Celebrezze and Commissioner Keppel to go over the ESEA draft and legislative strategy with the key leaders the night before he sent his message to Congress.[97]

Did this partnership preempt congressional modification? Certainly evidence exists that cooperation between the White House and Congress was fruitful. For example, Congressman Brademas warned the White House that Congressman Alphonzo Bell (R-Calif.) was trying to stir up the religious issue with the National Council of the Church of Christ,[98] and Carl Albert (D-Okla.) circulated the draft materials for the floor debate to Cater and Sam Halperin of HEW.[99] But the White House–congressional partnership can be best demonstrated through three occurrences—the strategic relationship with Senator Morse, the fencing in of Representative Edith Green, and the development of a southern strategy.

In February 1965, Jack Forsythe and Bob Lee, staff members on the education bill for Senators Hill and Morse, respectively, called Mike Manatos to confirm the White House intentions of moving ESEA through the House in such a manner as to permit the Senate to accept the House bill and thus avoid a conference. Recognizing Johnson's limited patience, they also expressed their concern that the White House should not persuade Senator Morse to move early into full committee session on ESEA before House passage, even though its agenda was cleared. They promised that Senator Morse would move with dispatch through committee after House adoption and that he could hold off all amendments.[100]

However, in order to prevent charges of White House steamrolling on the Senate floor, the president later offered Wayne Morse a letter informing the Senate that he did not authorize "anyone in the Administration to try to make suggestions to anyone" and that he "favors the bill passed by the House and hopes that since the Senate Committee reported it unanimously, it will be sympathetically considered by the Senate."[101] With Senator Wayne Morse as the floor manager, the bill was saved from eleven amendments, making it unnecessary to hold a conference committee.

Since ESEA was an old issue, it was easy to identify the potential opposition. With this in mind, Bill Moyers and Doug Cater had a lunch with Congresswoman Edith Green simply to massage her ego and to feel out her position on any specifics of the Education Message. In a "surprise" visit the president dropped by and urged that she help Larry O'Brien and the leaders to move on his bill. After receiving a large colored autographed picture, Green departed after promising him her full support (whatever that meant).[102] When Green finally came out in a biting attack against the bill, Senator Morse expressed the hope that the White House was now convinced that she was a dangerous individual who would "avail herself of every opportunity to throw roadblocks in our way in the Education Bill."[103] In response, Doug Cater, with prior approval of the president and the House leadership, conveyed to her "deep concern at having to report to the president that she is now leading the attack on [his] education program."[104]

The White House and congressional leadership had reasons to fear that the church-state consensus and the "racial thing" would cause substantial trouble for southern congressmen. In order to preempt problems the White House moved on three fronts. First, the initial distribution of funds was heavily slanted toward the southern states.[105] Second, Cater, Keppel, and O'Brien talked at length with Phil Landrum (D-Ga.) of the Rules Committee and provided him with back-up material to influence Judge Smith in making a rule[106] and to prepare Landrum for taking a leading part on the floor fight.[107] Third, Keppel generated a list of southern counties that had made any kind of a creditable showing on integration. The purpose was to have something positive to discuss with southern members on the racial question along the following lines—"X, Y and Z counties in your district have filed reports which possibly can be accepted, though we can give you no assurance now."[108] The truth was that HEW had not yet developed a yardstick about whether to accept or reject the required county reports for federal funds.

By making education a cornerstone of the Great Society, by enforcing timely action, by establishing a secret task force as a procedural innovation to force early and innovative planning, and by forming a partnership with Congress, the religious and philosophical antagonisms engendered by general aid to education were removed from the nation's agenda. From a strategic standpoint, Lyndon Johnson established his political identity and earned the title "Education President."

DEMONSTRATION CITIES: THE STRUGGLE FOR AUTHORIZATION

After the spectacular first session of the eighty-ninth Congress, President Johnson contemplated a minimal program for the second session. He spoke of an early adjournment so that Democratic legislators could have the whole summer to campaign for the 1966 congressional election. But the elaborate machinery geared up by Johnson in 1964 could not be stopped. The flow of new proposals and unfinished business from task forces and departments soon overwhelmed the White House. Consequently, Johnson made an uncharacteristic overestimation of what Congress could handle and for fifty minutes in the 1966 State of the Union message he catalogued an ambitious list of legislative wants. Sooner or later, out of the desire not to be made rubber stamps and from the inevitable pressures of interest groups, the mood of Congress will change and more and more members will vote against the administration.[109] Having misread the mood of Congress by asking too much, Johnson also found himself unable to make the careful advance preparations that characterized his earlier legislative programs.

Demonstration Cities was originally conceived as an idea to teach urban leaders how they could successfully rehabilitate the depressed areas of their cities. The 1964 Wood Task Force on Metropolitan and Urban Problems suggested that Demonstration Cities could be created by a joint effort of local, state, and federal agencies.[110] An expanded version of this concept was formally introduced to the White House in May 1965 when United Auto Workers President Walter Reuther submitted a letter to Dick Goodwin, who had assisted the 1964 Wood Task Force as a White House liaison, outlining a method to rebuild urban slums in six major midwest and east coast cities.[111] Goodwin sent a copy of Reuther's letter to Charles Haar, a Harvard law professor and an administration "idea man," for a feasibility study. Haar approved of Reuther's concept but recommended that further analysis was necessary in order to produce concrete and practical proposals.[112]

Because of Haar's positive response, Califano, Johnson's new special assistant for domestic affairs, arranged for Reuther to present his proposal to the president at the LBJ ranch in early June 1965.[113] Urging a rebuilding program to eliminate urban blight, Reuther's presentation emphasized the integration of modern technology, private industry, local investment, and federal assistance coordinated by local, state, and federal agencies. Johnson assured Reuther that he would establish a group to consider the program.[114]

To Califano, Demonstration Cities represented one potential instrument that might help cure metropolitan decay and produce immediate visible results. With the urging of President Johnson, Califano analyzed the program, and expanded it into a "Marshall Plan" for the cities.[115] He also linked a crime control concept to the program as a coordinated effort to help reduce urban unrest. Califano subsequently created the Task Force on Urban Affairs co-chaired by Charles

Haar and Robert Wood in late October 1965.[116] The cities proposals that emerged from the task force became the basic legislative package submitted to Congress in late January 1966.[117]

Congress was officially notified of a cities program by Special Presidential Message on 26 January 1966. The proposals envisioned one year of planning followed by five years of implementation with an estimated total cost of $2.3 billion, which would cover approximately sixty to seventy participating cities. The Demonstration Cities Act (H.R.12341, S.2842) was introduced in the House on 27 January by the Banking and Currency Committee Chairman Wright Patman (D-Tex.) and in the Senate by Paul Douglas (D-Ill.), a member of the Senate Banking and Currency Committee. Concurrently, six other administration proposals concerning aspects of urban renewal were submitted to the Congress.

Initial reaction to the Demonstration Cities Act was less than enthusiastic. James Kilpatrick's editorial in the *Evening Star* declared the president's proposal "largely a dream . . . and forced neighborhood integration."[118] Also, a *Post* editorial by Russ Wiggins gave a very poor account of the cities bill.[119] This lack of enthusiasm stemmed from the large amount of housing legislation passed in 1964 and 1965. Most members simply felt that further housing legislation was unnecessary.[120]

Once committee time was made available, both bills reached an impasse. In the House, Subcommittee Chairman William Barrett (D-Pa.) faced strong opposition from subcommittee members Thomas Ashley (D-Ohio), William Moorhead (D-Pa.), Henry Reuss (D-Wis.), and the Republican minority under William B. Widnall (R-N.J.). The disagreement centered on eligibility and desegregation requirements.[121] Additionally, the Senate subcommittee did not possess a sponsor for the bill. Chairman John Sparkman (D-Ala.) declined sponsorship because the bill was tainted with racial integration, especially in light of the fair housing fight, which already represented a political liability in his race for reelection of that year.[122] Also, second-ranked subcommittee member Paul Douglas, who introduced the bill, declined sponsorship because his available time was needed for his reelection effort in Illinois.[123] Consequently, Chairman Sparkman, stating that he wanted to get House reaction first, delayed the Senate hearings and indicated that his subcommittee was already overwhelmed by a mass transit bill and a controversial rent supplements bill.

One year after the initial conception of the cities program, the legislation was stalled in the House and Senate subcommittees because of fiscal concerns and its political liabilities. The administration seemed on the verge of suffering a major political setback in Congress. Within the White House even the staff was questioning the desirability of a cities program. Milt Semer, special counsel, and Henry Wilson saw the proposal as a loser.[124] In fact, Wilson stated, "the president has been sold a dog . . . and . . . recognizes this proposal as an outrageous mistake rather than a good bill which a recalcitrant Congress is too stupid to understand."[125]

This lack of congressional enthusiasm for Demonstration Cities provides a stark contrast with the strategic timing and preparation surrounding the Education Act of 1965. The White House expended only a minimal amount of resources early on for Demonstration Cities. In fact, the only documented White House initiative had been Califano's call to Walter Reuther to intercede in order to obtain an official AFL-CIO endorsement for the bill.[126] Unknowingly, the White House would soon be forced to expend critical political resources in order to salvage the Demonstration Cities Act of 1966.

The administration's lack of commitment was rooted in the growing distractions caused by Vietnam and the controversial fight to pass a rent supplements bill, defeated the year before. By conscious choice reflecting the president's priorities, the timing of Demonstration Cities was not fortuitous. Just prior to the midterm elections, when the cycle of decreasing influence marks the eroding of presidential opportunity, Congress was willing and able to give close scrutiny. With the priority given to rent supplements and with the administration handicapped from the rigors of a crowded and complex agenda, the White House was unable to expand the initiation process. Additionally, Johnson violated his technique of maximum attention in minimum time by overwhelming the house subcommittees with several housing and urban proposals at once, thus blurring the impact of any particular bill.

In addition, little attention was devoted to how to frame the issue politically. The administration envisioned a small model cities program with the priority of assistance going to the larger eastern and midwestern cities afflicted with extreme economic and social pressures. Such testimony implied that cities would be required to compete against one another for the program. Therefore, the feeling in the House chamber was that a few big cities of the east coast would win and the medium and small cities would lose. Framed as a redistributive issue, the administration faced stiff opposition from congressmen who did not want their constituents to lose. In order to be adopted, eligibility requirements would have to be expanded.[127]

An amusing but relevant incident to the concept of framing the issue involved the official name change to "model cities." Recent racial demonstrations and riots made the original name for the program quite distasteful to many southern congressmen and Johnson himself.[128]

Inadequate consultation during initiation allowed the administration to misjudge the mood of Congress. Congressmen did not expect any more controversial housing proposals during an election year and displayed their displeasure immediately in the committee rooms. The lack of a sponsor in the Senate was just another indicator of limited partnership. Deprived of key intelligence on Demonstration Cities' chances of passage, the president could not make adjustments prior to its public presentation to Congress.

Improper precooking of the proposal inside the presidency meant there would be no preempting of congressional modification. The fear of an unacceptable committee modification appeared in the form of the Barrett-Barrier proposal in mid-May. The proposal limited the cities bill to a $12 million authorization for planning purposes only. Republicans would support this measure only in return for Democratic support of a mass transit bill. According to *Congressional Quarterly*, the vice president phoned Barrett and implied that the administration would not accept the diluted planning bill.[129]

The lack of attention concerning timing, framing the issue, and consultation resulted from poor strategic planning. Demonstration Cities was presented to Congress before a general consensus was cemented and a constituency for the bill formed. Yet the 1965 Task Force on Urban Affairs incorporated most of the characteristics of the earlier 1964 Task Force on Education: secrecy, a link to the outside world of academics and business, a mandate for innovation. The difference? In 1964 the Gardner task force device was useful as a catalyst in assisting the planners and architects of the Great Society in the White House. In 1965 the Wood task force was created after newly created Housing and Urban Development doubted its ability to handle any more federal projects. Whereas Francis Keppel, commissioner of the Office of Education, became a key contributor in the new task force process, it was only after the appointment of task force members Charles Haar and Bob Wood as deputy secretary and assistant secretary, respectively, that HUD became actively involved in the legislative strategy.[130] Essentially, HUD preferred to concentrate on implementing the previous year's housing legislation.

The most important aspect of the task force device was secrecy, which gave the EOP flexibility in controlling information that enhanced its ability to maintain the initiative. Policy insulation reduced the self-serving interests of the bureaucracy and Congress in order to achieve innovative, not incremental policy. But strategic governance requires the consideration of both policy and politics. Since the principal White House assistants were preoccupied with other priorities, the task of instituting a legislative strategy for Demonstration Cities—obtaining sponsors, designing compromises and fall-back positions, and public support—was downplayed in the planning process. Consequently, policy insulation exacerbated the risk of noninvolvement. Key congressional intelligence on the likelihood of public acceptance was denied and the entire policy formulation process was not backstopped by a resentful HUD. Explaining the impact of task forces, Norman Thomas provided this useful insight:

The flexibility and adaptability of the task force had begun to decline as their operations became increasingly systematized toward the end of the Johnson administration. They were tending to become elaborate instruments of incremental adjustment rather than catalytic agents of change. A leadership technique designed to produce policy innovation worked so well initially that overuse was rendering it counterproductive.[131]

Facing the possibility of a major defeat in Congress, the president urged Califano to organize a meeting to develop a strategy for the administration. A strategy session was held on 6 June 1966 in Califano's office; participating were Wilson, O'Brien, Wood, Harold Barefoot Sanders, Haar, McPherson, Milton Semer, and Manatos.[132] First, Wilson recommended that leadership for Demonstration Cities should be established in the Senate in order to establish a positive cue for House action. It was reasoned that since most states would get one or two cities involved in the program, senatorial constituencies would directly benefit.[133] Second, the group instituted a strong legislation lobbying effort and made preparations for extensive compromises. Finally, it was decided that the administration would begin an immediate public relations campaign to pressure members of Congress.

Why did the administration decide to expend limited political resources for a bill that some White House staffers viewed as useless? Part of the answer appears to come from Wilson's desire to prevent a presidential defeat in Congress, which would decrease White House prestige. Furthermore, Califano expressed to the president that failing to give a determined effort from the White House would destroy presidential credibility with city mayors, civil rights groups, and urban planners.[134]

Because sponsorship in the Senate was the first step to success, the administration had to secure a senator from the housing subcommittee who would lend credibility to the bill as a piece of good policy and also provide a sounding board to test its acceptability. This simple prerequisite limited the choice to six Democratic senators. The final choice was Ed Muskie (D-Maine), who was recommended by Larry O'Brien and Joe Califano.[135] The choice of Muskie was decided probably for two reasons. First, Muskie represented a rural state, therefore his sponsorship would suggest to other senators from rural states, especially southerners and westerners, that the cities bill would provide assistance beyond the industrial north. Second, the administration's first and second choices for sponsorship simply refused to participate for electoral reasons.[136]

The goal of obtaining Muskie's sponsorship was placed in the hands of Larry O'Brien. O'Brien courted Muskie for three weeks before obtaining his cooperation on the bill. The bargain concluded for Muskie's sponsorship required the appointment of a Muskie protege to a federal post. Second, the bill would have to be amended in order to meet Muskie's approval.[137]

The redrafting of the bill was conducted during the first two weeks in July by Larry Levinson and Ashby Foard, representing the White House, and Phil Harris and Dan Nichols, aides to Muskie.[138] The following compromises were made: two years funding, not five; authorization funds for $900 million, not $2 billion; planning funds of $12 million for two years, not one; eligibility requirements changed to allow small and medium-sized cities to participate. The last provision was primarily inserted to ensure Muskie's state of Maine, with its small cities, would receive some benefit.

Significant political capital was expended on White House lobbying. Both the vice president and OCR pressured Chairman Barrett to report a clean bill. In order to attract support for demonstration cities the White House attempted to get an omnibus Urban Development Act that would include a mass transit bill, historic preservation, and rural planning. With amendments, the full House Banking and Currency Committee did report an omnibus version of four administration bills—only to face an impasse in the Rules Committee. The Rules

Committee was split seven to seven, with James Trimble (D-Ark.) as the swing vote. However, Trimble ignored administration pressure because he perceived the bill as a reelection liability. The House version still contained racial stipulations that could allow the federal government to use busing of children to integrated schools as a criterion for eligibility. Because of the deadlock, the White House even considered asking the speaker to invoke the twenty-one–day rule.[139] However, Wilson recommended to O'Brien that the House's Housing Subcommittee reconvene and accept Muskie's Senate bill, S.3708, with S.3711, an omnibus bill that included such diverse provisions as Federal Housing Administration insurance, Alaska housing aid, college housing, historic structures, and cultural center grants.[140] An intensive administrative lobbying effort salvaged the program, but the administration was forced to compromise when considerable opposition arose on the House floor.

Anticipating a rough going, the administration began in mid-June 1966 a large public relations campaign to pressure members of Congress. HUD enlisted support of the U.S. Conference of Mayors, church organizations, NAHRD (National Association of Housing and Rural Development), and the National Association of Home Builders. The president of the National League of Cities sent 600 letters to mayors urging them to contact members of Congress. Finally, the birth of the Urban Alliance, a coalition of labor, cities, and PTA organizations, was organized by the administration in order to orchestrate a new national concern on the problem of cities.[141]

In the White House, President Johnson highlighted the problems of the cities and emphasized his cities program as one cure in ten major addresses, news conferences, and press releases from 24 August to mid-October. In another administration move Senator Ribicoff (D-Conn.) held public hearings on the problems of the cities from mid-August until December. Also, former cities task force members Edgar Kaiser and Bob Heineman were used successfully to secure business's support. Edgar Kaiser sent letters to eighty-three different representatives with Kaiser plants located in their districts asking their support for Demonstration Cities.[142] Additionally, Bob Heineman and Kaiser organized a public statement from twenty major business executives that requested congressional support for the cities bill. Signatories of the statement included Henry Ford II and David Rockefeller, president of the Chase Manhattan Bank.[143]

With significant absenteeism, the Senate, by a 38–22 roll-call vote, and the House, by a 142–126 roll-call vote, adopted Demonstration Cities and sent the omnibus bill to President Johnson, who signed it on 3 November 1966.[144] After nearly a year and a half, an idea finally came to fruition in a piece of public policy that few people were satisfied with, at the high expense of scarce White House political resources.

CONCLUSIONS AND IMPLICATIONS FOR THE FUTURE

Domestic policy success demands that presidents move quickly in their first few months of elected office. To give it all you can in the first year requires careful strategic planning and preparation. As a comparative case study, the Elementary and Secondary Education Act of 1965 and the Demonstration Cities Act of 1966 provide clear contrasts in strategic governance.

The explanation for the prompt passage of the largely intact education bill remains nothing more exotic than preparation and proper setting of priorities. Using a number of devices—campaign speeches, task force deadlines, presidential memos and messages—Lyndon Johnson reminded the Washington community that education was a top priority and action would be forthcoming. Through simultaneous inventions by a number of sources, the issue of general aid to education was reframed away from the previous antagonisms of race and religion to the more recent commitments to the war on poverty. By planning in an insulated environment, the White House was able to cement a consensus among the relevant interest groups and design a legislative strategy with congressional partners. Note that the process of planning, learning, and selective litmus checks to Congress and the public could not have happened overnight. An early start allowed the White House to initiate the suggestion-feedback process that came to a fruition in an unlikely coalition of Catholic, Protestant, and education lobbies and in the co-optation of able floor managers in the Congress.

To be sure, there were compromises in the formulation of education policy. But they occurred under the supervision and policy control of the executive branch during the initiation process, not in the committee rooms of Congress. In terms of presidential power and public perceptions, this is a significant difference. After the quick, largely unmodified passage of the Elementary and Secondary Education Act of 1965, striking comparisons between Roosevelt's seventy-third Congress and Johnson's eighty-ninth were being made around Washington.[145]

By choice, the Demonstration Cities and Metropolitan Development Act of 1966 was not a top priority in the Johnson administration. With minimal preparation and planning this redistributive program was submitted to congressional subcommittees already congested with other controversial housing and urban development proposals. That a sponsor for Demonstration Cities in the Senate was nonexistent is only the most obvious indicator of poor consultation between the branches of government. Adding to the troubles, 1966 was a congressional election year where members would give close scrutiny to any proposal that might upset their constituency. It is of little wonder why Demonstration Cities stalled in Congress.

In order to stave off a presidential defeat before the midterm elections, the White House decided to push Demonstration Cities despite its policy and political deficiencies. The cost in terms of political resources was substantial—bargains and trades, political muscle, presidential involvement, and outside pressure. Political debts were created, but for what benefit? In terms of presidential prestige the administration risked large stakes for a proposal no one particularly cared for.

The major proposition put forth in this chapter is quite simple, but hard for presidents to achieve. Given the party numbers in Congress, knowledge of political timing, priorities, and framing the issue combined with early planning and congressional partnership may result in spectacular legislative victories for a president. However, with the absence of strategic governing, the White House is forced to use expensive lobbying tactics, creating political debts and tough bargains. Consequently, in terms of prestige a president may risk large stakes for uncertain benefits. From this perspective, the Reagan budget and tax cut victories in 1981 may have been seen as a result of strategic governing, whereas the AWACs controversy could be attributed to lack of foresight, resulting in a damage limitation strategy emphasizing expensive White House lobbying and arm twisting.

Several implications for future presidents can be drawn from this chapter, as well as additional questions for research. The questions will be asked first.

The ideal time for implementing the concepts of strategic governance seems to be in the first year of a second term. There the intersection of the two policy cycles of decreasing influence and increasing effectiveness are at an apogee due to a full term's experience. However, why do the histories of second-term presidents, starting with Franklin Roosevelt's, remain so unsupportive of this assessment?

Do early victories set the stage for subsequent victories? Presidents have been encouraged to act early in order to create the impression of effectiveness. But does this impression of effectiveness extend the presidential honeymoon and allow success to pile upon success? It may have happened in both the seventy-third and eighty-ninth Congress but an empirical study would be welcomed.

When and how can a president operationalize the four variables of strategic governance? It appears that the honeymoon period provides the best opportunity for exploiting electoral success for domestic policy achievement. However, with the exception of Johnson's unique circumstances in 1965 and Reagan's success in 1981, few modern administrations have had an opportunity to win a decisive mandate and also to *shape* that mandate. The travails of new administrations, with the Carter transition being most obvious but certainly not unique, often involve a history of missed opportunities. Additionally, most executives have overloaded Congress with so many requests that a widespread feeling of confusion and policy congestion has dominated a presidential term. Thus, with the exception of some first years and perhaps during a few crisis situations, the agenda has seemed so complex and out of presidential control that opportunities for strategic governance have often appeared limited. It would certainly be most useful to devise methods that would allow a president to unfold his domestic program strategically over the entire four-year term rather than just riding herd on his first year.

In this comparative case study Johnson's domestic policy making offers several implications for future presidents in terms of strategy.

1. The task force device and other leadership techniques seem dependent on the strategic setting. If it becomes a catalyst for action it becomes useful for a president. If it

becomes routine it may be counterproductive. Thus, a president should be aware of becoming a hostage to his own procedural innovation.

2. Limiting priorities has the strategic advantage of allocating more time for planning and framing issues. A crowded agenda blurs particular proposals and allocates less time for preparation. Thus, controlling the agenda must become a presidential preoccupation.

3. To govern strategically in the first year will put tremendous pressures on the transition team prior to the inaugural to make decisions on the substance, timing, publicity, and priority of legislative proposals. Thus, great benefits will be given to that candidate who secures his party's nomination early and has time to think strategically not only about the general election but also about governing.

4. More time must be spent in establishing a presidential-congressional partnership. Routines such as precooking legislation must be nurtured to involve key members of Congress in the initiation process. To overlook or antagonize this relationship means a president's program will be subject to significant modification and glacierlike speed. Old issues like ESEA do have advantages in presidential-congressional relations. Sponsors, headcounts, and impediments to enactment are all well known. Thus, partnership in achieving common policy goals rather than advance consultation becomes more descriptive of the presidential-congressional relationship.

5. When does a president drop a loser? If a low priority proposal, such as Demonstration Cities, becomes mired in committee, a president has two alternatives—accept defeat quickly and perhaps quietly or continue the battle publicly by tying his prestige to its outcome. Thus, a president must understand the limits of his political capital and must not be afraid to accept an occasional setback.

One can never be sure that when a citizen becomes the president of the United States his strategic sense will show him how to secure influence in the future. Strategic thinking does not come easy, but opportunities exist, especially during the first year of an administration. Additionally, if strategic planning becomes a trademark of an administration, perhaps a president can exploit other situations to his advantage later in his term. However, many policy controversies defy political resolution and the trademark left by most administrations seems to be one of missed opportunities. Richard Neustadt's warning remains relevant—the presidency is no place for amateurs.

NOTES

1. Doris Kearns, *Lyndon Johnson and the American Dream* (New York: New American Library, 1976), 246.

2. Merle Miller, *Lyndon* (New York: G. P. Putnam's Sons, 1980), 408.

3. For example, see Jack Bell, *The Johnson Treatment: How Lyndon B. Johnson Took Over the Presidency and Made It His Own* (New York: Harper & Row, 1965), 176–181, for a discussion on the treatment applied to Representative Otto Passman; Alfred Steinberg, *Sam Johnson's Boy: A Close-up of the President from Texas* (New York: Macmillan, 1968), 425, on incidents with local Texan politicians; Jack Valenti, *A Very Human President* (New York: Norton, 1975), 182–184, for anecdotes concerning Senator

Dirksen; Charles Roberts, *LBJ's Inner Circle* (New York: Delacorte Press, 1965), for the treatment applied to his staff; and Lyndon Johnson's own *The Vantage Point: Perspectives of the Presidency, 1963–1969* (New York: Popular Library, 1971), 216–217, on Senator Byrd during the Medicare policy process. See Robert Divine's "The Johnson Literature," in Divine, ed., *Exploring the Johnson Years* (Austin: University of Texas Press, 1981), 3–23, and Vaughn Davis Bornet, *The Presidency of Lyndon B. Johnson* (Lawrence: University of Kansas Press, 1983), 385–396, for bibliographical essays on the Johnson presidency.

4. Rowland Evans and Robert Novak, *Lyndon B. Johnson: The Exercise of Power* (New York: Signet, 1966), 104–105.

5. Theodore S. Sorenson, *Kennedy* (New York: Bantam, 1966), 709. See also Arthur M. Schlesinger, Jr., *A Thousand Days: John F. Kennedy in the White House* (Boston: Houghton Mifflin, 1965), 712.

6. Evans and Novak, *Lyndon B. Johnson*, 481.

7. For a better discussion on political moods and climates see Fred I. Greenstein, *Personality and Politics: Problems of Evidence, Inference and Conceptualization* (Chicago: Markham, 1969). For an application to the Reagan administration see Anthony King's "A Mile and a Half Is a Long Way," in King, ed., *Both Ends of the Avenue* (Washington, D.C.: American Enterprise Institute, 1983), 251–265.

8. George C. Edwards III, *Presidential Influence in Congress* (San Francisco: W. H. Freeman and Company, 1980), 197–199. Of the 104 victories in the House, 5 percent were marginal; of the 150 in the Senate, 13 percent were marginal.

9. See Stephen J. Wayne, *The Legislative Presidency* (New York: Harper & Row, 1978), 168–172, and Edwards, *Presidential Influence in Congress*, 198–199.

10. Johnson, *The Vantage Point*, 448; Kearns, *Johnson and the American Dream*, 236.

11. For a discussion on presidential involvement in lobbying see John F. Manley, "White House Lobbying," *Political Science Quarterly*, 93, no. 2 (Summer 1978): 269–271. For a somewhat different perspective see Barbara Kellerman, *The Political Presidency* (New York: Oxford University Press, 1984), 37–43. In her work Kellerman discusses the concept of "ingratiation," a relatively costless behavior designed to influence a particular other person concerning the attractiveness of one's personal qualities.

12. Lawrence F. O'Brien, *No Final Victories* (New York: Ballantine, 1975), 173.

13. Wayne, *The Legislative Presidency*, 150–155, 175.

14. Bornet, *The Presidency of Lyndon B. Johnson*, 117. Bornet points out that Johnson received two mandates. The first was the mandate to carry on the Kennedy legacy. The second was endorsed with the votes in November 1964.

15. Thomas E. Cronin, "The Presidency and Education," in Cronin and Greenberg, eds., *The Presidential Advisory System* (New York: Harper & Row, 1969), 225.

16. These include Wayne, *The Legislative Presidency*; Edwards, *Presidential Influence in Congress*; John F. Manley, "Presidential Power and White House Lobbying," paper presented at the Annual Meeting of the American Political Science Association, September 1977, 255–275; Abraham Holtzman, *Legislative Liaison* (Chicago: Rand McNally, 1970); and Eric L. Davis, "Congressional Liaison: The People and the Institutions," in King, ed., *Both Ends of the Avenue*, 59–95.

17. Richard E. Neustadt, *Presidential Power: The Politics of Leadership from FDR to Carter* (New York: John Wiley, 1980), 4.

18. B. Heinemann, Jr., and C. Hessler, *Memorandum for the President* (New York:

Random House, 1980), Preface and Chapter 1. Heinemann and Hessler argue that the president's plan of governing must be the central organizing concern of his administration.

19. See Wallace E. Walker and Michael R. Reopel, "Startegies for Governance: Transition and Domestic Policymaking in the Reagan Administration," *Presidential Studies Quarterly* (Fall 1986), 734–760.

20. For an institutional focus see John Kessel, *The Domestic Presidency: Decision-Making in the White House* (North Scituate, Mass.: Duxberg Press, 1975), and Steven Hess, *Organizing the Presidency* (Washington, D.C.: Brookings Institution, 1976). For a good legislative history of the Elementary and Secondary Education Act of 1965 see Philip Meranto, *The Politics of Federal Aid to Education in 1965* (Syracuse, N.Y.: Syracuse University Press, 1967), and Stephen Bailey and Edith K. Mosher, *ESEA: The Office of Education Administers a Law* (Syracuse, N.Y.: Syracuse University Press, 1968). For a review of demonstration cities the best source remains the *Congressional Almanac*, 1966.

21. Neustadt, *Presidential Power*, Chapter 1 and "Presidency and Legislation: Planning the President's Program," *American Political Science Review* 49, no. 4 (December 1955): 558–601.

22. Wilbur Cohen in Livingston, Lawrence Dodd, and Richard Schott, eds., *The Presidency and the Congress* (Austin: University of Texas, 1979), 300–301.

23. Quoted from Hess, *Organizing the Presidency*, 22. For an excellent discussion on the rhythmic cycles of presidential leadership and policy making see John Kessel, *Presidential Parties* (Homewood, Ill.: Dorsey Press, 1984), 47–72.

24. Paul Light, *The President's Agenda: Domestic Policy Choice from Kennedy to Carter* (Baltimore: Johns Hopkins University Press, 1983), Chapter 2, 35–61.

25. Charles O. Jones, "Presidential Negotiations with Congress," in King, ed., *Both Ends of the Avenue*, 109.

26. Neustadt, "Planning the President's Program," 600–601.

27. Richard Nathan, *The Administrative Presidency* (New York: John Wiley & Sons, 1983), 18–19. Note that welfare reform never passed Congress.

28. Johnson, *Vantage Point*, 448.

29. Kearns, *Johnson and the American Dream*, 237; Edwards, *Presidential Influence in Congress*, 119.

30. Kearns, *Johnson and the American Dream*, 237.

31. Eric Goldman, *The Tragedy of Lyndon Johnson* (New York: Alfred A. Knopf, 1969), 284.

32,. Graham T. Allison, *Essence of Decision* (Boston: Little, Brown and Company, 1971), 168, 178.

33. The best example was FDR's, "We have nothing to fear but fear itself." But as Neustadt elaborates, those eight words may have conjured up a prospect but without action his phrase would be remembered now with mockery. Neustadt, *Presidential Power*, 76.

34. For further explanation see T. J. Lowi, "Four Systems of Policy, Politics, and Choice," *Public Administration Review* 32 (July/August 1972): 314–325; Randall Ripley and Grace Franklin, *Congress, the Bureaucracy and Public Policy: The Four Arenas of Presidential Power* (Alabama: University of Alabama Press, 1983).

35. Valenti, *A Very Human President*, 190–191.

36. King, "A Mile and a Half," 251–258.

37. Cronin, "The Presidency and Education," 225.

38. Adam Yarmolinsky, "Ideas into Programs," in Cronin and Greenberg, eds., *The Presidential Advisory System*, 95.

39. Wayne, *The Legislative Presidency*, 110. See also Johnson, *Vantage Point*, 326 and "Policy Formation During the Johnson Administration" drafted by James Gaither, LBJ Library.

40. Johnson, *Vantage Point*, 327.

41. See Hugh Davis Graham, "Short-Circuiting the Bureaucracy in the Great Society: Policy Origins in Education," *Presidential Studies Quarterly* 12, no. 3 (Summer 1982): 407–420; William E. Leuchtenburg, "The Genesis of the Great Society," *The Reporter*, 21 April 1966, 36–39; Norman Thomas, ed., *The Presidency in Contemporary Context* (New York: Dodd, Mead & Company, 1975), 318–330; Norman Thomas and Harold L. Wolman, "Policy Formulation in the Institutionalized Presidency: The Johnson Task Forces," in Cronin and Greenberg, eds., *The Presidential Advisory System*, 124–143, and also Wayne, *The Legislative Presidency*, 107–114.

42. James L. Sundquist, *Politics and Policy: The Eisenhower, Kennedy and Johnson Years* (Washington, D.C.: Brookings Institution, 1968), 491–492.

43. Leuchtenburg, "Genesis of the Great Society," 37.

44. Kearns, *Johnson and the American Dream*, 233. See also Thomas, "Policy Formulation for Education: The Johnson Administration," in Thomas, ed., *The Presidency in Contemporary Context*, 322–325.

45. Neustadt, *Presidential Power*, 26.

46. Steven Shull, *Domestic Policy Formation Presidential-Congressional Partnership?* (Westport, Conn.: Greenwood Press, 1983), esp. pp. 5–10 for a quick overview.

47. Kearns, *Johnson and the American Dream*, 231–232.

48. Ibid., 233, and Wayne, *The Legislative Presidency*, 111–112.

49. See Manley, "White House Lobbying," 264–266, for superintending the legislative process.

50. Kearns, *Johnson and the American Dream*, 185.

51. See Sundquist, *Politics and Policy*, Chapter 5, and Hugh Douglas Price, "Race, Religion, and the Rules Committee: The Kennedy Aid-to Education Bills," in Alan F. Westin, ed., *The Uses of Power* (New York: Harcourt Brace and World, 1962), 1–71.

52. Graham, "Short-Circuiting the Bureaucracy in the Great Society," 409.

53. *Congressional Quarterly Almanac*, 1965, 275–276, 282–283, 293.

54. Meranto, *The Politics of Federal Aid to Education in 1965*, 1–6, 13–41. Between 1961 and 1965, the gain in yea votes was +93. Thirty-nine Congressmen who voted nay in 1961 switched their vote to yea in 1965. In the eighty-ninth Congress the Catholic-Methodist breakdown was: Catholics 107, Methodists 88.

55. Ibid., 2.

56. Memo, Douglass Cater to President, 2 Nov. 1964, "Campaign Commitments," Office Files of Douglass Cater, Box 13, LBJ Library. See also Johnson, *Vantage Point*, 207, and Transcript, Dr. Sam Halperin Oral History Interview, 20 Feb. 1975, 26, LBJ Library.

57. Memo, Busby to Celebrezze, 9 Jan. 1964, *Minutes and Documents of the Cabinet Meetings of President Johnson* (Frederick, Md.: University Publications, 1982).

58. Remarks of President Johnson, 22 May 1964, at the University of Michigan in Ann Arbor.

59. Phillip Reed Rulon, *The Compassionate Samaritan* (Chicago: Nelson-Hall, 1981), 208. To see how President Johnson shaped his mandate using the Michigan speech see

Memo, Douglass Cater to President, 3 June 1964, Office Files of Douglass Cater, Box 13, LBJ Library.

60. Memo, Kermit Gordon and Walter Heller to Bill Moyers, 30 May 1964, EX LE2, WHCF, LBJ Library. See also Memo, Moyer to Ackley et al., 6 July 1964, Office Files of Bill Moyers, Box 4, LBJ Library.

61. Graham, "Short-Circuiting the Bureaucracy in the Great Society," 412. Graham notes that Cannon, hence BOB, enjoyed a substantial measure of initiative and control over the education agenda. For reference see: "The Task Force Issue Paper: Education," 17 July 1964, Office Files of Bill Moyers, Box 94, LBJ Library.

62. Roulon, *The Compassionate Samaritan*, 212. See also Leuchtenburg, "Genesis of the Great Society," 37, and Graham, "Short-Circuiting the Bureaucracy in the Great Society," 409.

63. Sundquist, *Politics and Policy*, 210–211.

64. Memo, Anthony Celebrezze to Bill Moyers, 1 Dec. 1964, "Brief on Education," Office Files of Bill Moyers, Box 99, LBJ Library. For a critique of the HEW brief see Memo, Cater to Moyers, 5 Jan. 1965, Folder 4, Office Files of Douglass Cater, Box 22, LBJ Library. Cater complained that the HEW draft did not lay groundwork for education as the heart of the Great Society and really did not explain the poverty theme. Additionally, while Moyers and his staff were at the LBJ ranch, Cater served as the backstop at the White House by providing statistics and other information. See Folder 1, Office Files of Douglass Cater, Box 23, LBJ Library.

65. Memo, Busby to Johnson, 11 Jan. 1965, "Cabinet Meeting Minutes," *Minutes and Documents of the Cabinet Meetings of President Johnson*. See also Memo, Goodwin to Cater, 31 Dec. 1964, Office Files of Douglass Cater, Box 22, LBJ Library.

66. Ibid.

67. Memo, Douglass Cater to President, 7 Jan. 1965, Office Files of Douglass Cater, Box 13, LBJ Library. This memo provided the president with talking points in case he was queried about the church-state conflict. See also Goldman, *The Tragedy of Lyndon Johnson*, 301.

68. Memo, Larry O'Brien to President, 8 March 65, LE FA 2, WHCF, LBJ Library.

69. Graham, "Short-Circuiting the Bureaucracy in the Great Society," 412. Also see Transcript, Keppel Oral History, 21 April 69, page 7, LBJ Library.

70. U.S., House Committee on Education and Labor, Aid to Elementary and Secondary Education, Eighty-ninth Congress, 1st Sess., 1965, 1148–1149.

71. Keppel Transcript, "Poverty: Target for Education," address before the American Association of School Administrators, 15 Feb. 1964 in Atlantic City, N.J.

72. See Douglass Cater, "The Political Struggle for Equal Educational Opportunity," in David C. Warner, ed., *Toward New Human Rights: The Social Policies of Kennedy and Johnson Administrations* (Austin: LBJ School, University of Texas, 1977). See also Transcript, Cater Oral History Interview, 25 Jan. 1972, 12–13, LBJ Library.

73. Meranto, *The Politics of Federal Aid to Education in 1965*, 39.

74. Thomas, "Policy Formulation for Education," 319.

75. Memo Cater to President, 3 Feb. 1965, Office Files of Douglass Cater, Box 13, LBJ Library and Graham, "Short-Circuiting the Bureaucracy in the Great Society," 410.

76. See Robert E. Hawkinson, "Presidential Program Formulation in Education: Lyndon Johnson and the Eighty-ninth Congress" (Ph.D. diss., University of Chicago, 1977), and 1964 Gardner Task Force on Education, 14 Nov. 1964, 19–22, Task Force Collection, LBJ Library.

77. Leuchtenburg, "Genesis of the Great Society," 38.

78. Graham, "Short-Circuiting the Bureaucracy in the Great Society," 412–413. See also "The Task Force Issue Paper: Education," 17 July 1964, Office Files of Bill Moyers, Box 94, LBJ Library.

79. Thomas, "Policy Formulation for Education," 323–325.

80. Thomas and Wolman, "Policy Formulation in the Institutionalized Presidency: The Johnson Task Forces," 129. Note that there was no reluctance to serve on these task forces; see "Policy Formulation During the Johnson Administration," Gaither Papers, Box 300, LBJ Library.

One can follow the program development in education with the sequential array of the following documents:

a. Memo, Moyers to Ackley, Bator, Cater et al., 6 July 1964, Office Files of Bill Moyers, Box 4, LBJ Library.

b. "Task Force Issue Paper: Education," 17 June 1964, Office Files of Bill Moyers, Box 94, LBJ Library.

c. Memo, Gordon to President, 1 Oct. 1964, "Proposed Executive Order to Coordinated Federal Education Program," Education, Box 1, LBJ Library.

d. "Report of the Task Force," Gardner Task Force on Education, 14 Nov. 1964, Task Force Collection, LBJ Library.

e. "1965 Legislative Program Book #3—Task Force Briefs #1," Report to Moyers from Celebrezze, 1 Dec. 1964, Office Files of Bill Moyers, Box 99, LBJ Library.

f. Memo, Boyers to President, Nov. 1964, "Legislative Program Book #6," Office Files of Bill Moyers, Box 100, LBJ Library.

g. Memo, Cohen to Kermit Gordon, 6 Jan. 1965, "Legislative Vehicle for ESEA," Executive LE FA2, WHCF, LBJ Library.

h. Memo to Valenti, Hughes et al., 9 Jan. 1965, "Draft of Education Message," Office Files of Douglass Cater, Folder #1, Box 23, LBJ Library.

i. Telegram, Perkins to Moyers, 1 Feb. 1965, Office Files of Douglass Cater, Folder #1, Box 23, LBJ Library.

81. John Helmer and Louis Maisel, "Analytical Problems in the Study of Presidential Advice: The Domestic Council Staff in Flux," *Presidential Studies Quarterly* (Winter 1978): 46–47. This point was also confirmed by Francis Keppel, Transcript, Oral History Interview, 25 Jan. 1972, 12, LBJ Library.

82. See Richard Neustadt, "Presidency and Legislation: The Growth of Central Clearance," *American Political Science Review* 48, no. 3 (September 1954): 641–671 for the institutionalization of routine legislative clearance.

83. Rulon, *The Compassionate Samaritan*, 229. Letter, Keppel to Valenti, 26 Feb. 1965, GEN FG 165/A-Z, Box 245, WHCF, LBJ Library.

84. Ibid., 214.

85. Johnson, *Vantage Point*, 209. Sam Halperin confirmed that Cohen and Keppel had been lobbying education groups since 1963 (Transcript, Halperin Oral History Interview, 20 Feb. 1965, 12, LBJ Library). HEW Secretary Celebrezze pointed out that interest groups were contacted individually, posed situations, and offered trial balloons (Transcript, Celebrezze Oral History Interview, 24 Sept,. 1971, 16, LBJ Library). For other supporting evidence see Memo, Henry Hall Wilson to Lee C. White, 12 March 1965, Office Files of Henry Hall Wilson, Box 7; Memo, Cater to President, 9 Dec. 1964,

Office Files of Douglass Cater, Box 13, and Transcript, Cater Oral History Interview, 27 Aug. 1971, LBJ Library.

86. Sundquist, *Politics and Policy*, 206.

87. Goldman, *The Tragedy of Lyndon Johnson*, 301; Memo, Cohen to Moyers, 14 Jan. 1965, "Reaction to President Johnson's Message on Education," Office Files of Douglass Cater, Box 25, LBJ Library. Note that advance copies of the education message were distributed to several church groups and education lobbies. See Folder: Material on the Education Bill and Message, Office Files of Douglass Cater, Box 25, LBJ Library.

88. See *New York Times*, 13 Jan. 1965, 21.

89. For example, see Letter, Cater to Theodore Powell, 29 Jan. 1965, Office Files of Douglass Cater, Box 25, LBJ Library.

90. Memo, O'Brien to Moyers, 14 Jan. 1965, Office Files of Bill Moyers, Box 1, LBJ Library.

91. The best example of this occurred during the conflict over the judicial review amendment, which would essentially open the door to endless litigation and virtually paralyze the implementation of ESEA. See Memo, Keppel to Cater, 23 Feb. 1965, Executive LE FA2, WHCF, Box 38, LBJ Library.

92. See the following references on Chairman Powell: Memo, Chuck Daly to Mike Feldman, Office Files of Larry O'Brien, Box 19; Memo, O'Brien to President, 8 April 1965, EX LE FA2, WHCF, Box 38; and Memo, Valenti to President, 24 Feb. 1965, EX LE FA2, WHCF, Box 38, LBJ Library.

93. Memo, Keppel to Cater, 18 Jan. 1965, Office Files of Douglass Cater, Box 13, LBJ Library.

94. Memo, Cater to President, 14 Jan. 1965, Office Files of Douglass Cater, Box 13, LBJ Library.

95. See Sundquist, *Politics and Policy*, 210–216, and Johnson, *Vantage Point*, 208.

96. Valenti, *A Very Human President*, 186–188.

97. Memo, Busby to Johnson, 11 Jan. 1965, "Cabinet Meeting Minutes," *Minutes and Documents of the Cabinet Meetings of President Johnson*.

98. Letter, Brademas to Cater, Folder #1, Office Files of Douglass Cater, Box 23, LBJ Library.

99. Memo, Cater to Halperin, 24 March 1965, Office Files of Douglass Cater, Folder #4, Box 22, LBJ Library.

100. Memo, Manatos to O'Brien, 20 Feb. 1965, Office Files of Mike Manatos, Box 2, LBJ Library.

101. Memo, Cater to Senator Morse, 7 April 1965, Office Files of Douglass Cater, Box 25, LBJ Library.

102. Memo, Moyers to O'Brien, 13 Jan. 1 1965, Office Files of Bill Boyers, Box 1, LBJ Library.

103. Memo, Manatos to O'Brien, 1 March 1965, Office Files of Larry O'Brien, Box 28, LBJ Library.

104. Memo, Cater to President, 24 March 1965, Office Files of Douglass Cater, Box 13, LBJ Library.

105. Memo, O'Brien to President, 8 March 1965, EX LE FA2, WHCF, Box 38, LBJ Library.

106. Memo, O'Brien to President, 6 March 1965, EX LE FA2, WHCF, Box 38, LBJ Library.

107. Memo, Cater to President, 8 March 1965, Office Files of Douglass Cater, Box 13, LBJ Library.

108. Memo, Wilson to O'Brien, 16 March 1965, Office Files of Henry Hall Wilson, Box 7, LBJ Library.

109. See Harry McPherson, *A Political Education* (Boston: Little, Brown, 1972), 267–268.

110. 1964 Metropolitan and Urban Development Task Force, 39, Task Force Collection, Box 1, LBJ Library.

111. Letter, Reuther to President, 13 May 1965, Legislative Background, WHCF, Box 1, LBJ Library.

112. Letter, Haar to Goodwin, 9 June 1965, Legislative Background, WHCF, Box 1, LBJ Library.

113. Letter, Goodwin to Reuther, 4 June 1965, Legislative Background, WHCF, Box 1, LBJ Library.

114. Memo, Califano to President, 10 Sept. 1965, Legislative Background, WHCF, Box 1, LBJ Library.

115. Memo, Califano to Weaver, 4 Aug. 1965, Legislative Background, WHCF, Box 1, LBJ Library.

116. Memo, Califano to President, 9 Oct. 1965, Legislative Background, WHCF, Box 1, LBJ Library.

117. 1965 Task Force on Cities, attached Memo, 9 Dec. 1965, "Cities Folder," Files of McPherson, Box 35, LBJ Library.

118. *Washington Evening Star*, editorial, 10 Feb. 1966.

119. *Washington Post*, editorial, morning ed., 27 Jan. 1966.

120. *Congressional Quarterly Almanac*, 1966, 216.

121. Memo, Wilson to President, 30 May 1966, Legislative Background, WHCF, Box 1, LBJ Library.

122. Ibid.

123. Ibid.

124. Memo, Wilson to O'Brien, 6 June 1966, Legislative Background, WHCF, Box 1, LBJ Library.

125. Memo, Wilson to O'Brien, 6 April 1966, "Model Cities," Office File of Henry Wilson, Box 17, LBJ Library.

126. Memo, McPherson to Haar, 11 Feb. 1966, Legislative Background, WHCF, Box 1, LBJ Library.

127. See Spitzer, *The Presidency and Public Policy*, 150–154, for a good discussion on how Congress tries to take redistributive policies and turn them into distributive ones.

128. *Congressional Quarterly Almanac*, 1966, 217.

129. Ibid., 218.

130. Memo, Wilson to O'Brien, 6 April 1966, "Model Cities," Office File of Henry Wilson, Box 17, LBJ Library.

131. Thomas, "Policy Formulation for Education," 325.

132. Memo, Califano to President, 6 June 1966, Legislative Background, WHCF, Box 2, LBJ Library.

133. Ibid.

134. Ibid.

135. Ibid.

136. Memo, Ashley Foard to Wilson, 3 June 1966, Reports on Pending Legislation File, WHCF, Box 19, LBJ Library.

137. Memo, Califano to President, 6 June 1966, Legislative Background, WHCF, Box 2, LBJ Library.

138. Memo, Califano to President, 13 July 1966, Legislative Background, WHCF, Box 2, LBJ Library.

139. Memo, Foard to Wilson, 7 July 1966, Reports on Pending Legislation, WHCF, Box 22, LBJ Library.

140. Memo, Wilson to O'Brien, 15 July 1966, Legislative Background, WHCF, Box 2, LBJ Library.

141. Memos, Foard to Wilson, June-July, 1966, Reports on Pending Legislation, WHCF, Boxes 18–22, LBJ Library.

142. Letter, Kaiser to Wood, 26 Sept. 1966, Confidential Files, WHCF, Box 31, LBJ Library.

143. Public Statement, Kaiser to White House, 11 Oct. 1966, Legislative Background, WHCF, Box 2, LBJ Library.

144. *Congressional Quarterly Almanac*, 1966, 220.

145. See *Congressional Quarterly*, 14 May 1965, ''CQ Fact Sheet: Eighty-ninth Congress First 100 Days and FDR's First 99 Days,'' 919–925.

2

Medicare: Hallmark of the Great Society

Sheri I. David

The Medicare program was one of the hallmarks of the Great Society. Having recently celebrated its twentieth anniversary, the program has emerged as one of the proudest achievements of Lyndon Johnson's administration. Moreover, while Medicare is not invulnerable to criticism, and even budgetary sniping, the health insurance program for the elderly has withstood the test of time. This chapter will focus on the role that Lyndon Johnson played in getting Medicare passed as law.

Medicare was not originally a Johnson proposal. A bill offering hospital care to those over sixty-five years old was first proposed during the Eisenhower administration. Known as the Forand bill after its congressional sponsor, Aime Forand (D-R.I.), the legislation used the same contributory social insurance approach as the Social Security system. With Eisenhower's insistent opposition, the Forand bill only stirred controversy. Under John Kennedy, the Forand bill became part of the New Frontier but never made it into law. It was Lyndon Johnson who made Medicare a priority and part of the war on poverty.

Medicare was as important to Johnson as fair housing and equal employment and second in priority only to civil rights. Health care for the elderly linked Johnson to his beloved Franklin Roosevelt. In Johnson's mind, getting Medicare passed was a completion of the New Deal's Social Security program. Indeed, a health insurance program was originally intended as part of the 1935 Social Security Act, but was dropped due to expected opposition from the medical and business community.

Health insurance for the elderly fulfilled an obligation that Johnson felt not only for his parents but also all parents.[1] A Medicare program was legislation that could answer a significant filial obligation. "It does not seem fair," the president said, "to ask older people to stoop and bend and plead for funds and be shut out of the state and federal treasury by means of a means test."[2]

Prior to 1965, the bottleneck for Medicare was the two legislative committees responsible for providing the finances for a Medicare-type program: the Senate Finance Committee and the House Ways and Means Committee. Johnson spent hours "talking, cajoling, persuading" members of those two committees to vote favorably on Medicare.[3] The two committee chairmen, Harry F. Byrd (D-Va.) for finance, and Wilbur Mills (D-Ark.) for the ways and means, opposed Medicare—each for his own reasons. Byrd was simply ideologically opposed to a government health program. Mills, on the other hand, worried about financial estimates. He was also not willing to report a bill out of his committee until he was certain that it would pass through the whole House by a respectable majority.

However, by the time Lyndon Johnson took office, Mills was in the process of altering his role as a leading antagonist. In January 1964, the Ways and Means Committee held hearings on a Medicare program—their fourth set since 1957. With a great deal of publicity, Dr. Benjamin Spock arrived in Washington saying, "Babies and children are deprived of things when parents' savings are wiped out by paying for illnesses for grandparents."[4] New York's Mayor Robert Wagner arrived to testify on behalf of Medicare after first holding a rally in New York for older people. Labor leader George Meany also came to Washington. He quipped, "Labor has revised the slogan of the airline industry. They (the elderly) want to pay now and fly later."[5]

The Medicare proposal under discussion specified 60 days of hospital coverage, 180 of skilled nursing home coverage, and 240 days of home health care visits. There was a $10 first day deductible. The bill was sponsored by Clinton Anderson (D-N.M.), an old Senate friend of the president, and Cecil King (D-Calif.). The two had sponsored Medicare legislation since 1960.

A competing bill was offered by several liberal Republicans. Led by Jacob Javits (R-N.Y.), the bill called for forty-five days of hospital coverage and no deductible. According to Javits, he and his colleagues wanted to offer minimum coverage so that private insurance companies could play a role in expanding that coverage.[6]

Even with the publicity, public expectations, a similar Republican bill, and the president's lobbying efforts, no votes were changed on the Ways and Means Committee. Medicare was defeated by eleven to fourteen. In frustration, Eugene Keogh (D-N.Y.) observed, "Patients have been known to die while specialists are conferring."[7]

For Mills, obstacles remained. Mills worried about the role of commercial insurance companies as fiscal intermediaries. He also worried that hospital costs were rising faster than wages. This fact could put the whole program into insolvency before it ever had a chance to prove its worth.[8] Both issues proved to be realistic concerns.

Metaphorically, Medicare was becoming a hardy perennial with no progress beyond the requisite hearings. Yet Johnson was not discouraged. He told the press, "We have just begun to fight."[9] To assist the president in this uphill battle Johnson had a capable staff. Like other parts of the Great Society, Johnson preferred not to get involved with the details of the legislative process. He only wanted results. For Medicare, Johnson's Senate liaison was Mike Manatos. Henry Hall Wilson served as House liaison. It was the responsibility of both to keep tabs on individual lawmakers as well as on the status of Medicare in its respective committees. Wilson and Manatos reported regularly to White House assistant Larry O'Brien. O'Brien in turn reported directly back to the president. Within HEW, Assistant Secretary Wilbur Cohen had the special responsibility of overseeing the progress of Medicare.

In February 1964, Lyndon Johnson delivered a major speech to Congress outlining his ideas on the "Health Needs of Our Nation."[10] The president had budgeted $11 billion for health benefits and programs—many of which related to the elderly. Medicare was included in the list. However, while the Medicare advocates were working through congressional committees, HEW, the White House, and the AFL-CIO, many detractors wanted to change the very structure of the program. Led by Leverett Saltonstall (R-Mass.), several Republicans hoped to create a voluntary medical program for senior citizens. An income test would determine eligibility. Anyone over sixty-five years of age whose income was under $3,000 per year could participate. The $3,000 figure roughly corresponded to the poverty line. After paying a fee that ranged from $10 to $120 a year, the federal government would reimburse the individual for the premium of a private health policy. Approximately 15 percent of the elderly would be eligible to participate in this program.

Aside from changing the structure of Medicare from compulsory to voluntary and from everyone over sixty-five inclusive to income-tested only, there remained another way to sabotage Medicare. This was to raise the tax withholding base for Social Security so high as to preclude adding a wage contributory health program. A 10 percent tax withholding limit was considered the maximum by policymakers. All that remained was for someone like Russell Long (D-La.) to suggest raising Social Security benefits as well as tax withholding to that 10 percent limit.

Against the onslaught of Long's strategy, as well as the Republicans' plea for a voluntary program, and the American Medical Association spending thousands of dollars every month to prevent "socialized medicine," the Medicare program was almost destroyed. Advocates needed to be organized and have a carefully planned strategy. Unfortunately, this did not happen. Hampered by longstanding jealousies over jurisdiction, and by the president's inability to change any except perhaps one vote on the Ways and Means Committee, Medicare floundered. The House Ways and Means Committee reported out a Social Security bill without a health insurance program.[11] If anything was going to save Medicare in 1964, it was going to have to be a new strategy in the Senate. House Majority Whip

Hale Boggs begged White House assistants Bill Moyers and Doug Cater to ask the president to intervene in the Senate so that the nation could have Medicare in 1964.[12]

Abraham Ribicoff (D-Conn.) had a compromise in mind. Ribicoff told the president that someone—presumably Johnson—was going to have to make a decision whether to force Medicare in the Senate, come up with a more acceptable compromise, or give up. Ribicoff wanted to give Social Security beneficiaries a choice: either a case increase or hospital insurance. That choice would leave financing at the 10 percent limit and the wage base stable at $5,400. Nobody would be forced to accept health insurance. The elderly could choose cash instead.[13]

Johnson never responded directly to Ribicoff. Instead, Larry O'Brien, Mike Manatos, Mike Mansfield, Hubert Humphrey, Clinton Anderson, and Abraham Ribicoff held a strategy session in August 1964. Convinced that Medicare would not survive a House and Senate conference committee, even though Ribicoff's plan might, the president decided to let all of the Social Security amendments die.

Events in the Senate did not happen according to plan. Russell Long, George Smathers, and Vance Hartke proposed a Social Security increase that was so high that it would indefinitely preclude Medicare. Albert Gore then hastily added Medicare as a substitute amendment. Gore's amendment was defeated forty-nine to forty-six. So dramatic was the roll call that Barry Goldwater flew to Washington from Arizona solely to vote against Medicare. However close the vote, the telling fact was that two out of the seven Senate conferees and only two out of the House conferees ever supported Medicare. The bill would have died in conference anyway.[14]

Lyndon Johnson informed the press that the chief reason that the country did not have health insurance for the elderly was the one-man blockade exercised by Wilbur Mills. Yet Mills' opposition was only a smokescreen. With the vote for Medicare so close to the 1964 election, many congressmen had privately beseeched Mills not to call the Medicare issue to a vote. They did not want to get caught between the medical profession and its allied business groups, such as the tobacco industry and chambers of commerce, on the one hand and old folks and labor on the other. Mills saved many congressmen from their consciences and took the blame upon himself.[15]

Medicare became a major campaign issue in 1964. Asked by the press if Medicare was going to be on the list of "must" legislation for 1965, Johnson responded, "Just top of the list." In a nine-page summary of goals for the Great Society put together by Johnson's staff, legislation for education was number one, conservation was number two, and health goals, including Medicare, were number three.[16]

The eighty-ninth Congress, elected to office in November 1964, was an overwhelming affirmation of Johnson's liberal goals. In the House there were 67 new Democrats, giving the Democrats a majority of 295 to 140.[17] Three Republicans were replaced by Democrats on the Ways and Means Committee, making it possible for the Johnson administration to report out Medicare even without Mills' support. So sure was Johnson of Medicare's enactment that Clinton Anderson and Cecil King asked for status designation S.1 and H.R.1, respectively, for Medicare legislation. This time in the Senate, Medicare had forty-one co-sponsors, including three Republicans (Jacob Javits, Thomas Kuchel, and Clifford Case).

In his State of the Union Message, 5 January 1965, the president received the loudest applause every time he mentioned Medicare.[18] Wanting to exploit the historical moment, Johnson returned to Capitol Hill two days later to deliver a Special Message on Health. The administration outlined a $6 billion package put together by an Advisory Council on Social Security, a team from HEW headed by Wilbur Cohen, and a group from the AFL-CIO led by Nelson Cruikshank and Leonard Lesser. This package included a health insurance program that offered sixty days of hospital coverage, and 240 home health visits. There would be a $40 deductible roughly equivalent to one day's hospital stay.[19]

The real issue in 1965 was not whether there would be a Medicare bill, but rather in what shape the final bill would evolve. That was precisely the problem that would have such enormous import for the future. Ironically, it was the Republican opposition and the American Medical Association that shaped the final bill. Those who opposed a compulsory health insurance program for the elderly decided to change their strategy. Instead of claiming that Medicare would ruin American medicine, the opposition decided to protest how little the Johnson program would actually achieve! The intent was to frighten the public into preferring a welfare program that on paper looked more comprehensive but in reality was less so.

The AMA created their alternative program, which they called "Eldercare." It proposed to cover 100 percent of all health care, including surgical fees and prescriptions, but used the existing Kerr-Mills program as its vehicle. Kerr-Mills was a medical welfare program, created in 1960, and run by state agencies. The states that wanted to be included received federal reimbursement between 50 percent and 80 percent depending on per capita income. By 1965, twenty states had no program, and those that had varied enormously in services provided.

Republican Congressman John Byrnes offered yet another alternative. Called "Bettercare," Byrnes' bill had the federal government reimburse the purchase of private health insurance premiums for any older persons who qualified by virtue of a means test. The Byrnes program was strictly voluntary and financed out of general tax revenue.

As Wilbur Mills contemplated the King-Anderson bill (Medicare) as well as Eldercare and Bettercare, he had a surprising and creative idea. Instead of viewing the bills as alternatives why not combine all three? The bill that Mills finally approved and reported out of the Ways and Means Committee was a combination of "Elder-Better-Medi-Care" or a "three-layered cake" as it was sometimes called. Mills took the basic hospitalization and nursing home coverage, financed by wage deductions, added the AMA's revamping of Kerr-Mills so that it became Medicaid, and added Byrnes' voluntary program for paying physicians' fees, which then became Part B of the Medicare program.[20]

Lyndon Johnson was delighted by the new legislative proposal. It appeared to be far more than he had anticipated and at the same time would presumably silence the opposition—a brilliant political coup! The three-layered program passed the House 8 April 1965, by a vote of 263 to 153. It went on to the Senate where Russell Long did everything in his power to prevent it from coming to a vote.

On a day when few Democrats were attending Finance Committee hearings, Long presented his own alternative bill. This was a catastrophic health insurance proposal that would be so costly that it would forever preclude Medicare. Long misrepresented his own bill (nobody had had a chance to read it), misused a proxy, and called for a committee vote. Sensing nothing wrong, Long's bill was approved. The president was furious. Johnson personally called each Democrat on the Finance Committee and rebuked him for supporting Long.[21]

Aside from Long's negative evaluation of Medicare, it seemed that Long was using this as an opportunity to express his independence from the Great Society. After Long had supported Johnson's Civil Rights Voting Act, the Louisiana senator needed to distance himself from the administration. It occurred to White House strategists Mike Manatos and Doug Cater that they might compromise with Long, but Clinton Anderson refused.[22] Instead, many Medicare advocates such as Wilbur Cohen, Andrew Biemiller, Nelson Cruikshank, and Elizabeth Wickenden went to work lobbying against Long's catastrophic bill.[23]

The advocates were successful. The three-layered Medicare program passed the Senate 9 July, 1965, albeit with 513 amendments. Clinton Anderson sent a copy of the Senate version to every doctor, hospital, dentist, nursing home, and county welfare director in the nation. After only three days of deliberation the Senate and House conferees reported out the final Medicare program with its three parts intact. Anderson reported to the president that the bill was generally in good shape.

Medicare had gone through so many hurdles from the time that it was first proposed in 1957 and had changed to accommodate so many points of view and vested interests, that the final program, while generally good, carried with it its own future problems. To begin with, Republicans and conservative Democrats, as well as physicians and hospitals, were horrified at the idea of the federal government directly reimbursing health care deliverers for their services. That would have been "state" medicine at its worst. Unfortunately, it also would have been the only way to control future health costs. To counter such fears, private insurance companies, especially Blue Cross, were brought in to serve as fiscal intermediaries. For administration purposes the country was divided into regions. Either one insurance company or a group of companies acted as middlemen between the government and the health care deliverer. The task of fiscal intermediary carried with it the implicit responsibility of cost control. Until recently, that responsibility was not met. For years irresponsible medical and surgical bills, unwarranted services, and too long hospital stays went unquestioned. The insurance industry abdicated a major part of its role.

The second major problem involved the unwillingness on the part of Congress to "offend" physicians and hospitals. Rather than predetermine fair reimbursement fees (such as we are experimenting with currently) the Medicare bill allowed doctors to set their own "customary" fees and hospitals their own "reasonable" rates. Not surprisingly, between the time of the Medicare signing and the date that the program took effect, fees skyrocketed around the nation.

The nursing home industry, infused with sixty days of Medicare money, to say nothing of Medicaid funds, was an opened Pandora's box. Senator Carl Curtis (R-Neb.), one of Medicare's chief detractors, continually harassed the Finance Committee with his worries about government interference in nursing homes. In an effort to placate Curtis and others like him, as well as a general reluctance on the government's part to get involved in an already complicated situation, very few demands were made of nursing homes. The Medicare law required only that minimum health and safety standards be met, that adequate records be kept, that a nurse be on staff twenty-four hours, and that some sort of affiliation be maintained with a hospital. All of the above requirements were handled by state agencies. Too frequently the states avoided their responsibility. It became commonplace for doctors to have an "arrangement" with a nursing home, wander down the corridors, and then submit bills for examining residents who were never examined. Sadly, the elderly were the victims of complacency and compromise.[24]

Even more ambiguous were the home health visits. For practical purposes in 1965, home health care was a fantasy. It existed in Denmark but not in the United States. Where were the elderly to go after being discharged from the hospital or nursing home? Ideally, home health programs would have made a significant difference in the emphasis placed on institutional care. Neither the federal government nor the states desired to create home health facilities.

Finally, and no less seriously, the AMA preferred the Eldercare program, based on a hastily created 1960 Kerr-Mills program, which became the basis for Medicaid. All of the problems that arose from state management of this program in 1960 were no less apparent in 1965. Presumably, Medicaid would dispense medical care to those among the elderly who did not qualify for Medicare or who had run out of benefits and funds. The plan also aided welfare recipients of all ages. Both the enormous potential of Medicaid as well as the fraud and abuse that Medicaid has suffered are the subject of another book.

The fears of socialized medicine, so pronounced during Johnson's administration, seem to have been in vain. Medical students did not stop applying to medical schools. Quite the opposite occurred. Doctors did not flee the country. Older people did not flock to hospitals in order to use them as vacation spots. Families did not "dump" their elder members in hospitals or nursing homes hoping to evade responsibility. There was nothing about the Medicare program that could cause the nation to lose faith in government-sponsored health care or in the Great Society. Even the newest critic of the Great Society, Charles Murray, has chosen to avoid mention of Medicare in his widely publicized book *Losing Ground*.

On the other hand, liberals have every right to lose faith with those who have taken advantage of Medicare. Many physicians, hospitals, x-ray laboratories, pharmacies, "Medicaid mills," and nursing home operators have made unwarranted fortunes from the Medicare program. Private insurance companies have not suffered greatly either. Having offered almost nothing to the elderly in the way of health care policies before 1965, they lost nothing with the government's program. Since Medicare, some private companies have found ways to build "medigap" policies on the basic federal insurance.

Historian Allen Matusow has recently criticized Medicare because it "not only increased the cost of medicine for society as a whole" but also it did not provide enough financial benefits for the elderly. Medicare, according to Matusow, was "the most ambitious effort ever made by the government to furnish in-kind income to some of its citizens." It was, nevertheless, in his judgment a failure of liberalism. It merely transferred money from middle-class taxpayers to middle-class professionals.[25]

Charles Murray does not even include social policy for the elderly in his analysis of poverty in America. He is wrong, however, to separate Medicare from the president's poverty program. The benefits provided by Medicare, economic as well as psychological, have a direct impact on the income and well-being of the families of the aged. If Medicare did not exist, a working-class family, living just above the poverty line, might be forced below that line after paying medical bills of a grandparent. The real import of Medicare is that, for all of its problems, it has worked—and worked well. Very few of today's elderly population live in fear of destitution from illness. At least concerning their medical care they can live, in President Johnson's words, "with dignity."[26]

NOTES

1. Doris Kearns, *Lyndon Johnson and the American Dream* (New York: Harper & Row, 1976), 219.

2. *New York Times*, 2 February 1965, 1.

3. Wilbur Cohen in a recorded interview with Charles Morrissey, 11 November 1966, LBJ Library.

4. *Redbook* 34 (May 1964): 23.

5. *New York Times*, 16 February 1964, IV, 6.

6. House Ways and Means Committee, *Hearings on HR 11865*, 88th Cong., 2d Sess., 1734.

7. *New York Times*, 16 February 1964, IV, 6.

8. "Health Care for the Aged: How the Democrat and Republican Plans Compare," *U.S. News & World Report* 58 (22 February 1965): 46–48.

9. *Vital Speeches* 30 (2 February 1964): 194.

10. *New York Times*, 26 January 1964, 42.

11. Congressional Record, 88th Cong., 2d Sess., 1 April 1964, 7716.

12. O'Brien to Johnson, February 1964, Executive Files LE/ISI, LBJ Library.

13. Bray to Anderson, 27 July 1964, Anderson Papers, Library of Congress, Washington, D.C.

14. O'Brien to Johnson, 14 August 1965, Executive Files, Box 75, LBJ Library.

15. Richard Harrris, *A Sacred Trust* (New York: New American Library, 1966), 166.

16. *New York Times*, 1 November 1965, 63.

17. *New York Times*, 11 November 1964, 24.

18. Wilbur Cohen in a recorded interview with David McComb, 10 May 1969, Tape 3, in LBJ Oral History, LBJ Library.

19. *New York Times*, 8 November 1965, 1.

20. Theodore Marmor, *The Politics of Medicare* (Chicago: Aldine Publishing Co., 1970), 64.

21. "Russell Long's Capers," *The New Republic* 153 (3 July 1965): 6.

22. Harris, *A Sacred Trust*, 199.

23. Cohen, interview with David McComb.

24. Bruce Vladeck, *Unloving Care: The Nursing Home Tragedy* (New York: Basic Books, 1980), 54–56.

25. Allen J. Matusow, *The Unraveling of America: A History of Liberalism in the 1960's* (New York: Harper & Row, 1984), 228–229.

26. Charles Murray, *Losing Ground: American Social Policy, 1950–1980* (New York: Basic Books, 1984), 59–61.

3

The War on Poverty: Two Decades Later

Attiat F. Ott and Paul Hughes-Cromwick

In his last address to Congress on 16 January 1969, President Johnson declared: "No achievement gives me greater pride than the advances in the war on poverty. No social challenge gives me greater concern than the elimination of poverty."[1] Sixteen years later, with an annual level of spending by all units of government on "mean-tested transfers" in the order of 2 to 3 percent of GNP, one would be hard pressed to argue that the war on poverty has been won or that the greatest social concern of the time is the elimination of poverty.

The state of the union today is in sharp contrast to that of the Johnson era. In the 1960s the gain in our gross national product, adjusted for inflation, averaged 3 to 5 percent per annum; the 4 percent unemployment rate, once considered to be the full employment rate, was around 3 percent of the labor force; and the budget and the foreign trade accounts were in balance, if not in surplus. (In 1965 the budget showed a surplus of $2.2 billion; the trade surplus was $6.9 billion.) In the 1960s the American economy was steadily on the march and, as the economy rose to new heights, so did the nation's aspiration for a better future, especially for those who were less fortunate.

The war on poverty was a natural. In the midst of plenty, it was difficult not to do something for those living in poverty. And when, in his 1964 State of the Union message to Congress, President Johnson committed the nation to the fight, Congress confirmed his commitment, and the public applauded his intentions. This pledge, though defensible on moral grounds, its not feasible in today's economy. The U.S. economy has been beset by a series of problems in the 1970s and the first half of the 1980s. In the last decade the overwhelming majority of working American families has seen virtually no gain in their standard of living. The recessions of 1973, 1975, and 1981–1982 and the massive trade and budget deficits, together with the productivity slowdown, left little room for increased support for income transfer programs, let alone the continued fight on behalf of the nation's poor.

To be sure, Johnson's war on poverty has not been won, but we have learned from fighting it that "wars" of this nature, however noble, are seldom winnable. We have also learned that a prerequisite for success is an honest accounting of costs and benefits.

In this chapter, we shall begin with a brief review of Johnson's program and assess its contribution toward shrinking the size of the poverty pool. Next, an evaluation of the program in terms of cost-benefit calculations is made. In the final section, we shall focus on the few lessons we have learned in the course of the war in the hope that they may serve as a guide for future social experimentations.

THE JOHNSON PROGRAM: A REVIEW

The strategy for winning the war on poverty as outlined by President Johnson contained four major elements: sustained economic growth, education and job training, community development, and cash and/or in-kind income transfers. This later aspect—income maintenance—played only a minor role in the initial strategy for reducing poverty. The thinking at that time and hence the design of the war on poverty program were dominated by the view that "poverty" is for the most part an economic phenomenon. The "poor" are poor because of deprivation of economic opportunity. Access to jobs, quality education, and training were deemed necessary to lift the poor out of poverty.[2]

The Johnson advisers were, however, aware that economic growth by itself was not sufficient. For those who lack skills or education, new programs had to be designed and existing ones expanded. Hence came the birth of Head Start, Upward Bound, Follow Through, Teacher Corps, Title I of the Elementary and Secondary Education Act, and the Economic Opportunity Act. Programs that were strengthened included social security, food stamps, public housing, Aid to Families with Dependent Children (AFDC), and Supplemental Security Income (SSI), among others. Along with new and expanded programs, a new institution was created—the Office of Economic Opportunity (OEO)—to lead the assault and direct the nation's efforts on behalf of the poor. The budgetary cost of the war on poverty program during the Johnson years (1965–1969) amounted to $239,259 million (see Table 3.1).

To put the Johnson administration's war efforts in perspective, it is perhaps useful to begin with a brief definition of the terms *poor* and *near poor* and look at the demographic characteristics of these groups.

THE "POOR" AND "NEAR POOR": AN OVERVIEW

In the early 1960s, the Social Security Administration defined a family to be poor or near poor if its consumption fell below a certain minimal standard of

Table 3.1

Great Society Expenditures: Fiscal Years 1965–1969 ($ millions)

	1965	1966	1967	1968	1969	Row Total
I. CASH ASSISTANCE						
A. Social Insurance						
Gen. Ret. & Dis. Ins.	18,128	21,430	22,758	24,552	28,289	115,157
Fed. Employ. Retire.	1,352	1,726	2,076	2,660	1,732	9,546
Unemployment Comp.	2,570	2,206	2,371	2,405	2,577	12,129
B. Public Assistance						
(AFDC, SSI, etc.)	2,828	2,799	2,776	3,243	3,712	15,358
C. Veterans Benefits	5,723	5,923	6,901	6,884	7,642	33,073
Total Cash Assistance	30,601	34,084	36,882	39,744	43,952	185,263
II. IN-KIND ASSISTANCE						
A. Food and Nutrition	299	363	418	505	587	2,172
B. Education						
Element. Sec. & Voca.	720	1,628	2,311	2,517	2,472	9,648
Higher Education	412	705	1,160	1,393	1,232	4,902
C. Housing	231	238	271	312	383	1,435
D. Health						
Health Care Services	881	1,486	2,004	2,694	3,360	10,425
Medicare	0	64	2,763	4,634	5,695	13,156
E. Training & Employment	534	992	1,239	1,590	1,560	5,915
F. Social Services	291	823	1,486	1,791	1,952	6,343
Total In-Kind Assist.	3,368	6,299	11,652	15,436	17,241	53,996
TOTAL EXPENDITURES	33,969	40,383	48,534	55,180	61,193	239,259
TOTAL BUDGET OUTLAYS	118,228	134,532	157,464	178,134	183,640	
GROSS NATIONAL PRODUCT ($ billions)	659.5	724.1	777.3	831.3	910.6	
In-Kind/Total Expenditures	9.9%	15.6%	24.0%	28.0%	28.2%	
Total Expenditures/ Total Budget Outlays	28.7%	30.0%	30.8%	31.0%	33.3%	
Total Expenditures/GNP	5.15%	5.58%	6.24%	6.64%	6.72%	

Source: The Budget of the U.S. Government, Several Issues

living. This standard was defined for a family of three or more to be equal to an amount three times the per capita food requirement established in 1961 by the U.S. Department of Agriculture, the "economy food plan." According to these calculations, the average poverty threshold in 1964 was $3,169 for a family of four. For the near poor, or the "needy," a category of poor whose poverty threshold was 25 percent higher than the poverty line, the income requirement

Table 3.2
Incidence of Poverty, Selected Years, and Groups of Poor (Poverty Rates All Persons)

	1964 (1)	1965 (2)	1967 (3)	1969 (4)	1984 (5)	% Difference Between Columns (4)&(1) (6)	(5)&(4) (7)
All persons	19.0	17.3	14.2	12.1	14.4	-36.3	19.0
White	14.9	13.3	11.0	9.5	11.5	-36.2	21.1
Black	49.6	N.A.	39.3	32.2	33.8	-35.1	5.0
Elderly (65 years and over)	N.A.	N.A.	29.5[a]	25.3	12.4	N.A.	-51.0
Persons in female-headed household	45.9	46.0	40.6	38.4	34.0	-16.3	-11.5

[a]No data were available for elderly poverty prior to 1966 where the poverty rate was 28.5 percent.

Source: U.S. Bureau of the Census, Money Income and Poverty Status of Families and Persons in the U.S.: 1984, Current Population Report, Series P-60, No. 149, August 1985, 20-21.

for the same size family was set at $3,961. Based on these definitions, 36.1 million persons were in poverty in 1964, 19 percent of the population. The poverty rate for the needy stood at 26.3 percent. Twenty years later, in 1984, there were 33.7 million persons (14.4 percent of the population) classified as living in poverty at a cutoff of $10,609 for a family of four. The poverty rate for the needy in 1984 was 19.4 percent.[4]

Although the overall poverty rate has risen rather than fallen since the war on poverty came to a close, the advances made during the Johnson years were not totally dissipated. In effect, those structures that were successful in removing people from poverty were strengthened; others that were not judged to be efficient were dismantled or had their funding reduced. From the data reported in Tables 3.2, 3.3 and 3.4, there has been a dramatic change in the status of the elderly, nonwhites, and female-headed households (see Tables 3.2, 3.3, and 3.4).

Between 1964 and 1969, the poverty rate for all persons was cut by more than one-third for both white and black households. For persons living in households headed by females, the gain was about one-half of that realized by all households. Those 65 years of age and older experienced a major improvement in their poverty status between 1967 and 1968, from 29.5 percent to 25.0 percent, but no further significant gain was accomplished until 1971 when the rate dropped to 21.6 percent.

The incidence of poverty between 1969 and 1984 is in contrast with that of the Johnson era. Whereas the poverty rate rose for all households, poverty among the elderly was cut by more than one-half. Persons living in female-headed households also gained, although the reduction in their poverty rate amounted to only 11.5 percent. For the near poor, though, the poverty rates are uniformly higher, the changes in relative terms follow much the same pattern as those for the poor.

Table 3.3
Incidence of Poverty: The Near Poor—Those Below 125% of the Poverty Level
(Selected Years and Groups)

	1965 (1)	1967 (2)	1969 (3)	1984 (4)	% Difference Between Columns (3)&(1) (5)	(4)&(3) (6)
All persons	24.1	20.0	17.4	19.4	-27.8	11.5
White	19.6	16.3	14.0	16.1	-28.6	15.0
Black	N.A.	49.5	43.2	45.6	N.A.	5.6
Elderly (65 years and over)	N.A.	N.A.	35.2	21.2	N.A.	-39.8
Persons in female- headed households	54.0	48.7	47.8	41.9	-11.5	-12.3

Source: U.S. Bureau of the Census, Money Income and Poverty Status of Families
and Persons in the U.S.: 1984, Current Population Report, Series P-60,
No. 149, August 1985, 20-21.

Table 3.4
Changing Poverty Pool Shares betwen 1966 and 1984 Using 1978 as the
Benchmark (Percent of Total Persons in Families; of Total Persons for Elderly)

Groups of Poor Persons	1984	1978	1969	1966	1984/ 1978	Ratios 1969/ 1978	1966/ 1978
White families	65.4	63.2	66.2	64.8	1.03	1.05	1.03
Black families	30.6	34.1	32.6	34.0	0.90	0.96	1.00
Female headed households	44.7	48.6	35.9	28.8	0.92	0.74	0.59
White families with female heads	22.2	22.9	22.8	15.6	0.97	1.00	0.68
Black families with female heads	21.4	24.7	16.8	13.3	0.87	0.68	0.54
Familes, non- female heads	55.3	51.4	64.1	71.2	1.08	1.25	1.38
White familes, nonfemale heads	43.2	40.3	47.2	49.5	1.07	1.17	1.22
Black families, nonfemale heads	9.2	9.3	15.7	20.7	0.99	1.68	2.23
Elderly	9.9	13.2	19.8	17.9	0.75	1.50	1.36

Source: U.S. Bureau of the Census, Money Income and Poverty Status of Families
and Persons in the U.S., 1984, Current Population Report, Series P-60,
No. 149, August 1985, 20-21.

The differences are all a matter of degree: The rates for the near poor do not decline as much during the Johnson period nor do they increase as much in the period
ending with 1984, as the traditional poverty rates. This reflects a greater resistance
to changes in either specific programs or the state of the economy.

Changes in the poverty rates tell only part of the story, however. Demographic, social, and economic factors alter the poverty pool, which could not be captured by the aggregate index of poverty. As Table 3.4 shows, the pool of poor, although enlarged overall, exhibited a large variation in percentage distribution of poor subgroups across time. Decomposing the period 1964–1984 into two subperiods—from 1964 to 1969 and from 1969 to 1984—the following trends can be observed.

During the Johnson years substantial gains were made by black poor families. Their overall percentage in the poverty pool fell from 34 percent in 1966 to 32.6 percent in 1969. This reduction is attributable to the dramatic drop in the percentage of poor black families other than those headed by females (from 20.7 percent to 15.7 percent). White families other than female-headed families also experienced some gains, but the gain was much smaller than that realized by black families. The percentage of white nonfemale-headed families in the poverty pool fell from 49.5 percent in 1966 to 47.2 percent in 1969.

In contrast to these trends, the percentage of female-headed households in the poverty pool rose rather than fell from 28.8 percent in 1966 to 35.9 percent in 1969. For white female-headed families, the percentage increase was 60 percent, for blacks it was 26 percent. The period 1969 to 1984 shows a reversal of some of these trends. White families with female heads experienced a slight drop in their percentage in the poverty pool—from 22.8 percent in 1969 to 22.2 percent in 1984. The percentage of poor elderly persons also fell from 19.8 percent in 1969 to 9.9 percent in 1984.

To gain a better perspective on the effectiveness of policy instituted during and since the Johnson years, the incidence of poverty, measured in terms of group shares in the pool, in the two subperiods is contrasted with that of a base period. Taking 1978 as the benchmark—the year with the lowest overall poverty rate for all families—the story the comparisons tell is mixed. If one looks at the overall incidence of poverty among black or white families, one is inclined to argue that nothing much has happened between 1966 and 1984—a one-half percentage point rise in the share of poor whites in the poverty pool and a three percentage point fall in the share of blacks in the span of seventeen years. This verdict is a harsh one in view of the substantial improvement in the status of nonfemale-headed poor households. These households show a steady decline in their percentage in the poverty pool from 71.2 percent of the total pool in 1966 to 55.3 percent in 1984. Black, nonfemale-headed families also show a decline in their percentage by more than 50 percent.

The Johnson years, if nothing else, heightened our awareness of the poverty problem. Whereas before Johnson's war on poverty few were aware of how many families lived in or near poverty, today such numbers not only are known for aggregate poverty but for the subgroups of poor as well. Close inspection has been paid to two of these groups—blacks and females. In the former case, it has long been a social, political, and economic concern that this segment of the population be helped via special measures to move them out of poverty. The argument here is that their poverty is largely the result of discrimination. It is certainly a great triumph for the Johnson administration to have set in motion policies designed to attack black poverty on all fronts. Perhaps because of Johnson's efforts, our society has become accustomed to measuring progress against poverty by using the progress of blacks as a yardstick. A look at the figures, especially the disaggregated ones, does reveal a great deal of progress for those blacks living in the traditional family structure: from 33 percent poor in 1966, early in the war on poverty, to a low of 13.4 percent in 1978, before deteriorating economic performance precluded further advances. Poverty for elderly blacks has followed this same pattern, falling from 55.1 percent in 1966 to a low of 33.9 percent in 1978, clearly a great success, although of course the current level of 36.3 percent is still cause for concern. But for changes in family composition—the tremendous rise in female-headed families—progress on this front can be judged quite successful.

Poverty among female-headed households is another matter. While in 1966 female-headed families classified as poor were less than 30 percent of total poor families, their share in the poverty pool increased year after year. As of 1984, nearly 45 percent of all poor families were those headed by females. This trend has given rise to charges and countercharges about the effectiveness of the war on poverty. In effect, some have argued that the poverty programs themselves have contributed to the breakup of the family unit, hence to the rise in the number of female poor. This "feminization" of poverty, more than any other phenomenon, is at the root of the recent charge that Lyndon Johnson's own war on poverty "created" the new poverty problem.[5]

The changing composition of the poverty pool can be explained by three factors: transfer policies, economic progress, and demographic and/or social trends. Researchers working in the poverty area are in agreement that the official census poverty estimates exaggerate the extent of poverty because they exclude about 70 percent of welfare-type or in-kind transfers such as food stamps, public housing, and Medicaid. Other income transfers such as supplemental Social Security income, unemployment insurance, and cash welfare payments are demonstrated to be underreported.[6] Had a comprehensive measure of income been used, the census poverty measure, according to this view, would have been cut drastically.[7]

Without getting bogged down in the details about how to calculate a comprehensive income measure for the poor and whether actual poverty is the same as measured poverty, it is worth noting that the ratio of posttransfer (after adjusting for transfers) to pretransfer poverty must be less than one (or 100 percent) for all positive value of transfers. Changes in this ratio indicate that either pretransfer poverty has changed, transfer policy has changed, or both.

Danziger et al. provide estimates of post- and pretransfer poverty for selected years between 1965 and 1983.[8] According to Danziger, the ratio of post- and pretransfer poverty (official measure adjusted for in-kind transfers and underreporting of income) fell from 77 percent in 1965 to 73 percent in 1970 and to 52 percent in 1979. For 1984, the Census Bureau calculated the posttransfer rate (adjusted for in-kind transfers at market value) to be equal to 9.7 percent compared to the official measure of poverty for 1984 which was equal to 14.4 percent. This puts the post- and pretransfer poverty rate at 67 percent.[9] These statistical findings clearly suggest that income transfers were effective in reducing poverty throughout the 1964 to 1984 period.

Another useful way in assessing the role of transfers in reducing poverty is to investigate the size of the poverty gap. The poverty gap refers to the amount of monies needed to bring the income of all poor households up to the poverty thresholds. Based on pretransfer income, the dollar amount needed was equal to 3.4 percent of personal income in 1968. When pretransfer income of the poor was adjusted by adding to it the market value of in-kind transfers, the poverty gap was found to be equal to only 1 percent of personal income in 1968. Again in 1982, the pretransfer gap, although equal to 4.4 percent, was equal to 1 percent after adjustments to pretransfer income were made.

Since transfer payments are conditioned by age, sex, and status of the head, not all poor persons would be expected to benefit equally from transfer policies of the past two decades. As was expected, the elderly fared best.

Whereas in 1965 cash transfers under Social Security removed 57 percent of aged white and 26 percent of aged black who were classified as poor on the basis of their pretransfer incomes, these transfers removed 78 percent of aged whites and 50 percent of aged blacks out of poverty in 1983. For the nonaged poor, male or female, however, these cash transfers played but a minor role in combating poverty throughout the period. As to nonaged female-headed households, white or black, cash transfers did not contribute to the fall in their poverty. Moreover, the actual percentage of households aided by cash transfers out of poverty fell rather than rose. For white female-headed households with children, the percentage aided declined from 30 percent in 1965 to 14 percent in 1983. For nonwhites, it fell from 10.5 percent to 8 percent.

It is perhaps useful to pause at this moment to speculate about the "feminization" of poverty phenomenon. The increased share of female-headed households in the poverty pool may be explained by factors other than the disincentive effects of transfer policies. Census data underscore the fact that the composition of the population over the past two decades has shifted toward female-headed or single-person households. While the proportion of married-couple families has declined, the share of single-mother families and single persons has more than doubled. Likewise, the proportion of blacks living in female-headed households increased by 94 percent. The extent to which changes in family structure added to poverty was explored by Mary Jo Bane.[10] Using longitudinal data from the Michigan Panel Study of Income Dynamics, her research led her to conclude that the breakup of the family unit was responsible for the majority of white and half of black persons' poverty in the first year after the breakup. Three-quarters of the whites became poor. As for blacks, two-thirds were already poor before the transition into a single-family household.

Economic progress also is a major factor to the observed trends of poverty over the 1964–1984 period. A growing economy is likely to improve the economic opportunity of most, if not all, individuals. Hence, the expectation is that poverty rates rise and fall countercyclically, falling during economic expansions and rising in recessions. This supposition has been supported by empirical evidence reported in numerous studies. The behavior of the poverty rates has been explained by changes in median income, the unemployment rate, as well as policy variables such as transfer policies of a given administration. Using disaggregated data on the poverty pool for the period spanning 1960 to 1983, correlated to levels of real median family income and unemployment, Ott and Hughes-Cromwick show that white families and nonfemale-headed households (black or white) have been the primary beneficiaries of economic growth.[11] Poverty among nonaged black families and female-headed households, black and white, was only weakly correlated with economic variables such as the unemployment rate or the inflation rate.

One finding almost all studies seem to agree on is that poverty rates for persons in white, nonaged, male-headed families with children show great sensitivity to cyclical movement of the economy. While the rate of increase in pretransfer poverty for nonaged white female-headed households was only 9 percent between 1978 and 1983, for nonaged white males the rise amounted to 65 percent between 1978 and 1983. For all persons, the rate of increase between 1978 and 1983 was about 20 percent. Whereas pretransfer poverty for nonwhite male-headed households rose by 33 percent, it has fallen for nonwhite female-headed households.

Two variations to the basic model were also tested. In the first, the "needy" groups replaced the poor in the estimation. This exercise was carried out to determine whether the basic relationships would be altered. This did not turn out to be the case. Those variables that were significant in explaining poverty among subgroups of poor were also significant for the needy subgroups. The only differences we found were for two subgroups of the population—all black needy families and families headed by nonfemale heads. For those two groups the state of the economy turned out to be a significant explanatory variable; that is, poverty among these groups was closely correlated with real median family income and the unemployment rate.

In the second variant, the regression analysis was confined to the subperiod 1960 to 1975 to capture the effects of the stronger than average performance of the economy during the mid-sixties on poverty rates. Although preliminary, the findings do suggest a stronger relation between poverty and the health of the economy in this period compared to the entire 1960–1983 period. This result gives credence to the popular theme, "the rising tide lifts all boats," a theme that was at the center of the Johnson strategy for the war on poverty. As we have yet to experience a resurgence of economic progress at the rate experienced in earlier times, it remains to be seen whether poverty today will respond to that growth as it has earlier or that a fundamental shift in policy or strategy is called for.

It is worth emphasizing at this point what perhaps has been obvious all along— the lack of response of market-determined income to improvement in economic conditions for some groups of poor. This finding means that "some" poverty will continue to persist even under the most optimistic outlook for the economy. Another less obvious finding is that income transfers for certain groups of poor seem not to have been the answer either. Except for the aged, cash and in-kind transfers have done little to alter the fate of some of the nation's poor. The poverty dilemma is summed best by Danziger et al.: "If solving the poverty problem means eliminating reliance on any income support program to obtain nonpoverty incomes, no progress toward a solution is evident," and, "if solving the poverty problem means eliminating the need for public assistance to achieve above poverty incomes, a solution still eludes us."[12]

WAS JOHNSON'S WAR ON POVERTY A FAILURE?

Economists have been engaged in making calculations purporting to show whether a dollar spent on one project yields benefits in excess, equal to, or below the value of that dollar in alternative usage. Given that society's resources are scarce, benefit-cost calculus is at the heart of an efficient allocation of these scarce resources. Cost-benefit calculations take on an added dimension when the public rather than the private sector makes use of these resources. Production efficiency aside, the public sector rarely if ever, "possesses" the resources it uses or allocates. The choices the public sector makes reflect for the most part the choice of the collectivity and not any one individual. In taking and/or allocating the resources it acquires, "excess" burden (cost to society over and above the revenue cost) is likely to accompany both activities. This makes accounting all the more pressing.

Many researchers did that sort of accounting to evaluate the success or failure of the antipoverty programs. Some, like Danziger et al., believe the loss to nonpoor (estimated by them to be equal to 2 to 3 percent of personal income in 1980) was worth the gain to the poor no matter how slim such a gain was. At the other extreme there are those like Charles Murray whose contention is that the observed rise in pretransfer poverty is the result of efforts to eliminate poverty. According to this view a one dollar increase in income transfers to the poor reduces their pretransfer income by more than one dollar. The logical conclusion—"Cut the knot, for there is no way to untie it."[13]

Ellwood and Summers, although they do not share Murray's conclusion, do nevertheless make a strong case against transfer programs.[14] In their view almost all of the variations in the poverty rate can be explained by variations in median family income. Income transfers to the poor, according to their calculations, have had little or no effect on median income.

As economists, we are "creatures" of our discipline; hence, we must abide by the verdict of its tools. However, in assessing Johnson's war on poverty, we argue that the cost-benefit calculus some of us have been engaged in is wanting, for Johnson's war was a social rather than an economic experiment. We believe that another calculus needs to be performed before handing down the final verdict. In this regard two questions ought to be raised: What lessons have we learned? And, did the experiment enhance our ability to address, if not solve, social problems?

Johnson's war posed a challenge to several notions dearly held by the economic profession. Some of these are enumerated below:

1. Poverty is an economic phenomenon.

2. Cash grants are preferable to in-kind transfers.

3. Disincentive effects arising from income transfer schemes are minimal.

4. Policies that aim at redistributing private means are efficient as long as they do not give rise to excess burden.

None of the above notions seems to have survived the challenge unscarred. Today there is no longer a consensus about the validity of any or all of the above-stated propositions. The negative income tax experiment, along with recent studies regarding the supply of labor and savings, shows sizable disincentive effects of tax and transfer schemes that have been instituted for the purpose of distributing income. The choice of a policy instrument is as important as the dollar value attached to that instrument. These lessons, we believe, are the successes or the high marks we ought to attribute to the war on poverty. Without the Johnson social experiment our economic notions would have remained untested.

The challenge to our concepts, essential for the development of economic thoughts and the lessons we have learned, has significantly contributed to our understanding of how economic policy works. Few among us would argue today that all social ills can be eliminated by mere redistribution of economic powers between individuals or between the private and the public sectors. For those who still do, we feel that their advocacy has been somewhat tempered by the "rediscovery" that economics is not an exact science—that what one assumes does not always prevail.

In conclusion, we believe that President Johnson was right in stating that "no social challenge is greater than the elimination of poverty." A world free of poverty may not be tenable today or tomorrow, yet such knowledge should not preclude a leader from aspiring to achieve it.

NOTES

1. The Council of Economic Advisers, *Economic Report of the President* (Washington, D.C.: U.S. Government Printing Office, 1969), 21.

2. See the Council of Economic Advisers, *Economic Report of the President* (Washington, D.C.: U.S. Government Printing Office, 1964), esp. 166–172, "Statement of

Walter W. Heller, Chairman, before the Subcommittee on Employment and Manpower of the Senate Committee on Labor and Public Welfare, October 28, 1963.''

3. This figure represents all federal expenditures on social welfare. Those expenditures soley devoted to poverty relief comprise a much smaller total.

4. For details on selection of poverty thresholds, see Daniel Weinberg, ''Measuring Poverty,'' *Family Economics Review* 2 (April 1985), USDA, Agricultural Research Service; and U.S. Bureau of the Census, *Characteristics of the Population below the Poverty Level: 1983* 147 (February 1985): 175–184, Current Population Report, Series P–60.

5. Charles Murray, *Losing Ground: American Social Policy, 1950–1980* (New York: Basic Books, 1984).

6. Daniel Weinberg cites that on the new census survey of income program participation, only 63 percent of actual AFDC benefits are reported by respondents (Daniel Weinberg, ''Filling the Poverty Gap: Multiple Tranfer Program Participation,'' *Journal of Human Resources* 20 [1985]: 64–89).

7. Morton Paglin, ''How Effective Is Our Multiple Benefit Antipoverty Program?'' in Paul M. Sommers, ed., *Welfare Reform in America* (Boston: Kluwer-Nijhoff, 1982), 78–84.

8. Sheldon H. Danziger, Robert H. Haveman, and Robert D. Plotnick, ''Antipoverty Policy: Effects on the Poor and the Nonpoor,'' in Sheldon H. Danziger and Daniel H. Weinberg, eds., *Fighting Poverty—What Works and What Doesn't?* (Cambridge, Mass.: Harvard University Press, 1986), 54.

9. U.S. Department of Commerce, Bureau of the Census, ''Estimates of Poverty Including the Value of Noncash Benefits: 1984,'' Technical Paper #55 (August 1985).

10. Mary Jo Bane, ''Household Composition and Poverty,'' in Danziger and Weinberg, eds., *Fighting Poverty*, 209–231.

11. Attiat F. Ott, ''Distributional Consequences Arising from Explicit and Implicit Fiscal Actions,'' in Stanley J. Bowers, ed., *Proceedings of the Seventy-Seventh Annual Conference, 1984* (Columbus, Ohio: National Tax Association–Tax Institute of America 1985), 48–59; and Paul F. Hughes-Cromwick, ''Poverty Pools, Transfers, and the Business Cycle'' (Unpublished Manuscript, 1985).

12. Danziger and Weinberg, eds., *Fighting Poverty*, 58.

13. Murray, *Losing Ground*, 228.

14. David T. Ellwood and Lawrence H. Summers, ''Poverty in America: Is Welfare the Answer or the Problem?'' in Danziger and Weinberg, eds., *Fighting Poverty*, 78–105.

4

Untangling the Mess: The Administrative Legacy of President Johnson

Marlan Blissett

In the organization of government we see something of the range and complexity of a presidency. Each president has one or more perspectives on executive organization—what it can do, what it cannot do, how it might be influenced, what its limits are. But through archival materials—oral histories, memos, task force reports, special briefing books, telephone logs, appointment calendars—a larger view begins to emerge. The larger view has at least four reference points or perspectives.[1]

The first can be called the "comprehensive presidential management perspective." From this perspective, administration is viewed as a whole, with responsibility for direction and supervision lodged in the president. Its bedrock principle is integrated organization—one that links related functions from the bottom to the top. The basic rule of organization is to combine functions according to the purposes served, with broader units of purpose enlarging organizational control.

A second perspective is the "tactical presidential perspective." This views organization as it affects the creation and maintenance of executive capacity. Still, many organizational decisions are made in a more limited context, where tactical issues predominate. Seen from this perspective, organizational change is associated with attempts to further certain policy or program objectives and to improve the president's political position. The tactical presidential perspective views organizational ends as limited and specific and organizational decisions as pragmatic and particularistic.

A third perspective of organizational development is the "congressional perspective." Due to the structure of Congress and the nature of its work, its reference points are particularistic. That is, Congress sees the purpose of administration as the implementation of specific statutes. To protect its policies Congress locates them organizationally and protects the locations.

A fourth perspective is the "bureaucratic perspective." Given the diversity of executive departments and agencies, the bureaucratic perspective is particularistic—concerned mainly with the protection of existing functions and resources. The bureaucratic perspective makes presidential guidance and control more difficult.

Taken together, these four perspectives of executive organization suggest that organization is a product of the policy and management needs of government as perceived by the president, the executive branch and Congress. But the president is essential for providing ideas and leadership.

The Johnson presidency was full of new approaches—new ways of thinking and doing. It is not an exaggeration to say that during this period there was an explosion of policy initiatives that forced concern for organization. A war on poverty called for centers of action both within and outside existing structures. New programs in health and education overwhelmed old bureaus with tasks vastly larger than any they had undertaken before. Enforcement of civil rights legislation required new organization within and across departments. New efforts to deal with problems of the cities and with transportation were incorporated into movements for new departments. Many of the new problems of organization were dealt with as they arose, resulting in a new Office of Economic Opportunity, two new departments, reorganizations in education and health and other bureau functions, seventeen reorganization plans, and other initiatives. In most instances these were immediate responses to the program expansions and changes that were occurring.

Leadership was applied to those areas of administrative change that had a chance for success, that is, those that could get the votes in Congress and gain the backing of the executive branch.

Johnson's concern for organization was influenced by many factors, including his own objectives and his desire to project them in public policy, the necessities of program administration, and the initiatives of his own staff in generating proposals for change. Although his responsibility was not transferable, he was assisted by numerous individuals and institutional aides. These included, on occasion, individuals in departments or independent agencies who had separate official responsibilities but whose loyalties to the president led them to look at problems from a presidential perspective. One might call this loosely defined support system the subpresidency.

It is impossible to view the organizational developments under President Johnson—or, for that matter, under any modern president—without considering the impact of the subpresidency. The subpresidency is the institutional component of the presidency. Its institutional core under Johnson was the Bureau of the Budget (BOB) but is also included those who worked for the president either continuously or temporarily, directly or indirectly, in carrying out the functions of the office. This could embrace presidential staff as well as individuals in departments who, although having separate official responsibilities, saw organizational problems from a presidential perspective. The contribution of the subpresidency under Johnson was in monitoring developments, ensuring consistency, protecting the president, and providing information, analysis, and expert guidance.

As an activist president, Johnson was constantly in search of new ideas, demanding of others that they give him new proposals and programs, exacting action from them, and counting achievements in number of things done. Although he always acted to preserve the institutional position of the president, Johnson's main interest in executive organization was tactical, piecemeal, and in reaction to special situations. He showed no comprehensive interest in overall structure or strategies for organizational change.

Johnson's view of the bureaucracy could be compressed in a thimble: it was "dedicated to preserving the status quo" and was "not equipped to solve complex problems that cut across departmental jurisdictions."[2] While such a role is essential for stability and program continuity, Johnson felt it did not bring together the best policy ideas and place them in the broadest possible perspective.

Johnson's approach was to use task forces and other "independent" sources of evaluation and program initiative. The results of these efforts were mixed and messy. Two new departments were created, sixteen reorganization plans were approved, two new programs of national scope and organizational significance (the war on poverty and model cities) were set in motion, and other attempts were made (e.g., a proposal for the creation of a single business and labor department) that failed but that illustrate Johnson's desire for a presidency dominated by policy and not by bureaucratic preference and procedure. The overall impact of the Johnson presidency on executive structure was to create flexibility, uncertainty, and ad hoc solutions at the price of stability and sometimes even predictability. The early signs of what later administrations would inherit from the Great Society began to appear with creation of the first new department under President Johnson—the Department of Housing and Urban Development (HUD).

THE DEPARTMENT OF HOUSING AND URBAN DEVELOPMENT

To help develop a comprehensive urban policy, President Johnson created a Task Force on Metropolitan and Urban Problems under Robert Wood in 1964. The charge to the task force was to come up with fresh, inventive approaches to urban problems. Practical politics were for the moment to be set aside in search of pathways that pointed away from the federal government's traditional emphasis on urban housing.

The task force found that significant imbalances did exist between programs of physical development and human needs within cities, but it also discovered "imbalances between parts of the country, communities of different types, and parts of the population.''[3] Future resources needed to be reallocated to cover social, physical, and economic environments within urban areas. The strategy of the task force was not to divert any existing federal subsidies, but to increase federal funds and provide improved coordination for social service programs within cities, the construction of community facilities, and an increase in federally insured mortgages.

Several new programs and functions were considered—for example, rent supplements, below-market interest subsidies, new communities, block grants, and demonstration cities—but the major organization proposal was for the creation of an urban affairs council in the executive office and a new department of housing and urban development.

Although flexible in its approach, the Task Force on Metropolitan and Urban Problems had confined itself to urban policy and strategy. It dipped occasionally into questions of organization and coordination, but "detailed development" of the proposed new department was left to a sister task force under the leadership of Don K. Price—the Task Force on Government Organization. The organization task force supported a department of housing and community development that incorporated all the functions of the Housing and Home Finance Agency (HHFA) and the Federal Home Loan Bank Board; the home loan functions of the Veterans Administration and the Farmer's Home Administration (Agriculture); and the grant programs for waste treatment facilities (Health, Education, and Welfare), water supply systems in small communities (Agriculture), and urban highway construction (Bureau of Public Roads, Commerce).

The organizational recommendations of the two task forces were under continuous review by BOB—it supplied each with an executive secretary—and, on occasion, a visit by a White House staff member provided linkage to higher levels of policy making. As presidential assistant Bill Moyers expressed it: "We anticipated the reactions of different constituencies that would be served or alienated by the recommendations . . . and made them part of the process in developing the programs. I think that was the most essential, crucial decision that was ever made."[4]

One reaction that was loud and clear was that of Robert Weaver, administrator of HHFA. Weaver argued that the department endorsed by the two task forces should be reduced in scope. It should concentrate mainly on housing and physical assistance functions and not, he wrote Moyers, address "purely social and economic factors involved in the urban programs and the overall urban policy of The Federal Government."[5] Weaver's admonition was timed to coincide with a preliminary evaluation of the Wood and Price recommendations by Moyers, Richard Goodwin of the White House staff, and BOB during December 1964.

The preliminary review favored cabinet status for HHFA, without any additional functions or new legislative mandates. President Johnson seemed to agree with this approach and BOB was instructed to write draft legislation giving the secretary power to change the internal structure of the department. The larger urban role was not addressed.

A second evaluation of the proposed department occurred after agency review of the draft legislation. Nine agencies completely approved, but others raised questions about program jurisdiction, the number of supergrade positions, intergovernmental assistance, and the effect the departmental proposal would have on pending legislation. With the exception of new language that would clarify future legal actions, HHFA and BOB stood firm against additional changes.

The White House wasn't so sure. President Johnson had apparently reverted to an earlier position—a department with the capacity to sustain a broad-based urban policy with new programs and innovative organizational features. HHFA's expectations were more modest. It wanted cabinet status, parity with other departments, protection of its traditional programs, and internal reorganization. What HHFA did not want were jurisdictional conflicts with other agencies, trouble with congressional oversight committees, and an endless dialogue with state and local governments over urban priorities.

The president persisted. In his State of the Union message on 4 January 1965, he again criticized past approaches to the problems of the cities. "The first step," he said, "is to break old patterns—to begin to think, work and plan for the development of entire metropolitan areas. . . . A Department of Housing and Urban Development will be needed to spearhead this effort in our cities."[6] Two months later in his "Special Message to Congress on the Nation's Cities" he once more addressed the question of departmental scope. The proposed department, he insisted, would be primarily responsible for metropolitan area thinking and planning.[7] It would coordinate its activities with those of other federal agencies—particularly in such areas as health, education, employment, and social services—and create a working relationship with mayors, governors, and state legislatures.

When the administration bill was introduced in Congress, many members were still puzzled over what HHFA and BOB were saying—that the new department would deal only with urban physical development—and what President Johnson was advocating—that the department would be "a focal point for thought and innovation and imagination about the problems of our cities."[8] In the end, Congress did not try to clarify or resolve the confusion. It created a department with a secretary, an undersecretary, four assistant secretaries, an assistant secretary for administration, and a director of urban program coordination. Left unaddressed were the nature of the department and specific guidelines for internal integration.

After passage of the act, three centers of activity began to take shape. Two dealt with the comprehensive perspective of the president, although for different reasons. One formed around BOB and the other around a new Presidential Task Force on Urban Problems. A third center with a different organizational perspective clustered around Robert Weaver and HHFA.

WEAVER'S ORGANIZATIONAL RESPONSE

After HUD was created, Weaver would later reflect:

I had assumed that it might be possible that I would become the Secretary. I immediately began to set up machinery for organizing a new department in the event I would be. I got the most experienced people we had here in administration, and I then began to indicate to them the structure and the objectives and so forth that I would want to have— that I would suggest would be done.[9]

Weaver saw organizational structure as an instrument to unify the constituent units of HHFA. "I had a unique problem," he said,

which I suppose any—well, HEW had it and Alan Boyd has had it in Transportation— and that is that we had five little fiefdoms over here, and each one was pretty damned autonomous and had not only its own autonomy, but had something of its own lobby in Congress and its own congressional support. Well, the first thing that was obvious to me was that if we were going to have a department, it didn't mean a tinker's damn if you didn't pull this thing together.[10]

Since Congress had given separate organizational status to programs dealing with the private mortgage market, Weaver's first task was to find some method of integrating the unassigned programs—those that dealt with public housing, metropolitan development, open space, urban renewal, urban beautification, neighborhood facilities, and the urbanizing countryside.

As Weaver put it:

I decided that I would take the other (unassigned) programs and just mix them up, and I had to have a rationale to do this. So I hit on the rationale which was those programs which had to do primarily with the inner city would be put under one assistant secretary; those that had to do with the metropolitan area would be put under another assistant secretary—one assistant secretary primarily for urban renewal and public housing, and the other one for metropolitan development.[11]

With responsibility for existing programs delegated to the assistant secretaries— mortgage credit and commissioner of federal housing, renewal and housing assistance, and metropolitan development—Weaver turned his attention to the remaining positions authorized by the legislation: an undesignated assistant secretary and an assistant secretary for administration. The undesignated slot became the assistant secretary for demonstrations and intergovernmental relations, while the assistant secretary for administration was assigned the task of bringing together and developing department-wide standards for a number of support functions. These included personnel, budgeting, automatic data processing, accounting, auditing, and procurement.

Weaver's organizational design was one that would achieve internal integration and improve program effectiveness. Yet he felt one additional measure was necessary. He planned to give both line and staff responsibilities to his assistant secretaries: "I decided . . . that they were going to be staff insofar as they [were] the top advisory group and they got together on policies and so forth; but line in the sense that they [were] responsible for the administration of particular programs which [fell] under their jurisdiction.''[12]

The final organizational maneuver that Weaver planned for dealt with the relation between headquarters and the field. From Weaver's perspective: ''We wanted to have strong regional offices and we wanted to decentralize up to the point where you could decentralize without losing control.''[13] Even though HHFA had not established a pattern of strong regional administration, Weaver insisted on four major changes:

1. All seven regional administrators would report directly to the secretary.

2. Each would speak for the department on all matters within the region.

3. Under each regional administrator a new position would be created to ensure program and policy consistency within a given community.

4. Finally, regional administrators would assume responsibility for the regional operations of public housing and multifamily FHA programs.

THE ORGANIZATIONAL DESIGNS OF THE PRESIDENT'S TASK FORCE ON URBAN PROBLEMS AND BOB

As Weaver worked over the organizational design of HUD, other efforts were also set in motion, which suggested that President Johnson had not given up on his vision of HUD as the spearhead of urban policy development. In late September 1965 Robert Wood was again summoned to the White House and asked to put together a new urban task force. The new task force—known as the President's Task Force on Urban Problems—was to reconsider the scope of HUD, including its purpose and organizational structure. Within the task force, proposals for reorganization were to be developed by a subcommittee composed of Ben Heineman (president, Chicago and North Western Railway), Charles Haar (law professor, Harvard), and William Rafsky (executive vice president, Old Philadelphia Development Corporation). Each expressed the presidential view that ''the form of organization must be creatively fashioned to be hospitable to inter-governmental cooperation and to local and private action helpful in solving problems of housing, urban development and mass transportation.''[14]

The subcommittee's strategy was two dimensional: (1) change organizational structure to facilitate the integration of the physical and social environments of urban areas and (2) organize the new department so it could coordinate federal programs in both urban and suburban settings. Either dimension of this strategy could have been destroyed had an additional proposal—endorsed by the subcommittee and by a majority of the task force—been used as a basis for action. That proposal was to transfer to HUD all of the community action programs of the Office of Economic Opportunity, then located in the executive office of the president. Although the task force did not devise a rationale for how these programs might be distributed in HUD, the scope and complexity of such an undertaking would have placed severe organizational demands on the new department and made coordination difficult with established agencies administering related programs.

As might be expected, BOB strongly opposed the recommendations of the task force, especially the transfer of community action programs. But it was not in complete agreement with Weaver's design either. Both Weaver and BOB wanted to restrict the scope of HUD to physical development programs, but BOB did not favor Weaver's separation of intercity programs from suburban programs or Weaver's plan to merge line and staff functions in the assistant secretaries. BOB supported strong regional administrators—as did Weaver—but insisted that Weaver's approach would create regional administrators who would serve four masters on functional matters—the four assistant secretaries—and at the same time act "administratively as the Secretary's man in the region."[15]

The choice of organization as well as the appointment of the departmental secretary lay with the White House. President Johnson seemed uncertain which way to go. In the meantime, Weaver's position began to erode. Several key staff in HHFA quit, and rumors began to circulate that Weaver had been passed over. Weaver, too, was uneasy: "You get an image of lack of impetus and the press just preys on this and they decide the President has no confidence in you."[16] Weaver asked for clarification from White House staff but, aside from pleas to hang on, no assurances were given. At that point, Weaver exploded. He let it be known that his "feelings toward President Johnson were less than warm."[17]

Relations between the White House and HUD remained precarious until 19 January 1966 when Johnson announced Weaver's appointment as secretary. At that point Weaver's organization of the department was legitimized, including his line/staff concept and his plans for field operations.

OEO AND MODEL CITIES

President Johnson's decision meant that HUD would continue to focus on housing and the physical aspects of urban development. The new department would not become the center point of an all-out effort to solve urban problems. Still, the question of coordinating federal programs in urban areas remained. Many of these programs derived from the war on poverty and were authorized by Congress in the Economic Opportunity Act of 1964. The legislation created an Office of Economic Opportunity within the executive office of the president, subject to transfer by reorganization plan after one year.

OEO took off quickly, with the result that the number of programs and the organizational problems caused by them seemed to mount by the week. A Job Corps, work training and work study programs, education and information programs, community action programs, rural poverty programs, a domestic peace corps (VISTA), programs for small businesses and many more stretched to the limit the federal government's capacity to guide and control. Despite President Johnson's assurance to Congress that he did "not intend that the war against poverty become a series of uncoordinated and unrelated efforts,"[18] it did. Everywhere one looked some group or organization—whether newly formed or established—was staking out its own turf and daring outsiders to intrude. Cooperation could be forced if enough legal muscle were applied, but always at an extracted price. At the local level, the price was confusion, delay, and an endless battle between established units of local government and community action agencies with their legislative mandate of "maximum feasible participation" for all affected parties. At the federal level—both in the region and in Washington—the price was mismatches between old and new legislation, unattended program overlaps, jurisdictional squabbles, and, in many cases, entrenched opposition from the established departments.

Since the major programs of OEO had urban impacts, the search was on for almost any technique that would serve to pull together physical development activities and social programs within the cities. A number of possibilities had begun to emerge: the interagency agreement, monitoring arrangements, the checkpoint procedure, regional decentralization, and, for some social programs, a common field center with common jurisdictions. The one, however, that caught President Johnson's eye was recommended by the Task Force on Urban Problems. The task force suggested the use of large-scale experiments or demonstrations in selected cities as a method for concentrating and applying federal resources. According to the task force, such experiments could become "models" for the nation, showing "that cities are capable of mobilizing local resources and integrating them with federal assistance to attack urban problems on the huge scale required to create a totally new living environment."[19]

The scope of what the president had in mind became the centerpiece of the Demonstration Cities and Metropolitan Development Act of 1966. The act assigned HUD the responsibility for implementation of the new program in 150 cities and required that the local organization unit—the City Demonstration Agency (CDA)—be a part of city government or have an equivalent legal status as a local public agency. As might be expected, "model cities" severely taxed HUD's decentralized structure and raised doubts that any department—HUD included—could coordinate urban categorical aid programs at the federal level.

Model cities did, however, provide the flexibility to experiment with a variety of methods for representing client interests before city and federal officials, professional and public interest groups, and before state officials who were responsible for administering federal programs. Day-to-day operations were delegated to the field, which left the HUD central office free to concentrate on overall policy guidance and coordination.

Still, results were not encouraging. Neither a "top down" nor a "bottom up" strategy could provide solutions to the complicated problems of urban planning and development. Obstacles to concentrating federal resources were deeply rooted in the practice of American government, including past legislation, a proliferation of special governments, and dispersed administrative responsibilities. But above all, the greatest opposition came from the American people. They did not want it that way.

THE DEPARTMENT OF TRANSPORTATION

The Department of Transportation (DOT) was the second department estab-lished during the Johnson administration. Its pattern of emergence was similar to that of HUD's: numerous task force reviews, presidential intervention (again, Johnson wanted something big), opposition from ongoing programs and agencies, adjustment and accommodation by the subpresidency, and, finally, approval by Congress.

The administrative turf for Transportation was perhaps even more carved up than that of HHFA's before it became HUD. Three commissions were responsible for the economic regulation of transportation: the Civil Aeronautics Board (CAB) (commercial aviation), the Maritime Commission (oceanic transport), and the Interstate Commerce Commission (ICC) (railroads, land-based motor carriers, domestic water carriers, and oil pipelines). Safety regulations were imposed by the CAB, the ICC, the Federal Aviation Administration (FAA) (airplanes), and the Coast Guard (in the Department of Commerce) for the merchant marines.

In addition, certain promotional or nonregulatory functions were performed by the Maritime Administration, the Bureau of Public Roads, the Saint Lawrence Seaway Development Corporation, and the Great Lakes Pilotage Administration (all in the Department of Commerce). Related transportation activities were associated with the U.S. Army Corps of Engineers (inland water traffic), the Alaska Railroad (in the Department of Interior), the Panama Canal Company (under the secretary of the army), and the Housing and Home Finance Agency (mass transit).

The arguments for a Department of Transportation were that it would eliminate the complexity, overlap, and confusion of transportation regulation, provide overall integration for transportation policies, improve federal planning, increase presidential leadership, and give a balanced assessment of federal investments in different modes of transport.

The established transportation interests, both in and out of government, said "no" to the department; the president said "yes," and Congress—unable to find a consensus—resorted to damage control. It did establish a department, but one that ruffled few feathers and that bore almost no resemblance to the arguments advanced for its creation.

The Maritime Commission—due to the work of Paul Hall, president of the Seafarers International Union of North America—was to stay where it was—in the Department of Commerce. Prominent functions such as those dealing with economic and safety regulation were included in the new department, but sorting through the rest of the mess was, for the most part, postponed indefinitely. The legislation contained no new transportation policies or programs, nor did it address changes in the allocation of federal resources. Candidly assessed, the act preserved the status quo, while giving the illusion of progress. At the signing of the bill President Johnson referred to the legislation as "another coonskin on the wall."[20] But in fact it was something else. It was another example of how the president's reorganization efforts—his impulse to do something big—outran his base of support.

REORGANIZATION PLANS

One area of administrative change in which President Johnson did not "think big" was in submitting reorganization plans to Congress. The Reorganization Act of 1949 gave the president the authority, for a specified period, to develop reorganization plans and send them to Congress without going through the existing committee structure. Congress is not permitted to make any amendments and must respond within sixty days. If a majority in either house disapproves, the plan is dead. During the Johnson presidency two extensions were granted.

Altogether President Johnson submitted seventeen reorganization plans; sixteen were approved. Most dealt with minor housekeeping matters and did not lead to controversy. Typical, for example, of such proposals were consideration of locomotive inspection functions in the ICC, elimination of some interdepartmental committees and other committees within departments or other units of government, transfer of certain construction and recreation functions in the District of Columbia, and others of similar scope.

Since reorganization plans were reserved for fine tuning government operations, Johnson usually did not take an active interest. They were given to the president for nighttime reading, but outside a word of caution here or there to his staff, little attention was devoted to them. Johnson's main concern was that they pass Congress.

PRESIDENT JOHNSON'S LEGACY

President Johnson's success with reorganization plans was not matched by his attempts to get home rule for the District of Columbia or a combined department of business and labor. He passed over other possibilities for a variety of reasons: a department of natural resources, a department of education, reorganization of the Small Business Administration, and the Bureau of Indian Affairs. Even in those areas where new organizations were created, President Johnson's visions outpaced his achievements. Looked at sympathetically, the Johnson administration used, explored, or analyzed almost every institutional mechanism available for improving executive branch guidance and control. The Great Society required great administration.

Yet the cumulative effect of Great Society legislation was to produce far greater problems of executive structure and coordination than had existed at any other time, except perhaps during the Civil War, the Great Depression, and World War II. By the twilight of the Johnson presidency it became apparent that the administration apparatus of the Great Society needed attention. Numerous proposals were made, many of which would resurface under subsequent presidents. These included:

- a domestic council
- restructuring of departments
- creating superdepartments
- expanding the executive office
- field integration
- primacy of a particular department for a designated policy area
- bloc grants
- grant consolidation
- revenue sharing

Although no solutions were offered for future executive guidance and control problems, a range of possibilities was identified.

Efforts to untangle the organizational mess of the Johnson presidency have led subsequent presidents to employ several strategies.

First, expansion of the strongest institutional component of the subpresidency—the Bureau of the Budget—into an Office of Management and Budget, with emphasis placed on managerial efficiency and control over agency and departmental budgets

Second, decentralization of administration to the states through block grants and revenue sharing

Third, attempts to eliminate some departments, independent commissions, and other organizational units

Fourth, program cutting, either through reduction in agency budgets by OMB or through automatic reductions

The overall effect of these strategies has been to give a greater role to the states and the private sector in implementing public policy.

At this date, it is difficult to assess the impact on executive structure of these strategies, but when that is done, one cannot ignore the role of the federal budget deficit. Perhaps more than any other development the budget deficit has reduced public commitments and denied departments and agencies the resources they need for experimentation, innovation, and improved operations.

One final point. Executive structure is part of an extremely complex system of presidential guidance and control. It contains unities, disunities, continuities, discontinuities, centralization, decentralization, anomalies, redundancies, and all sorts of institutional relics, accidents, and sports. In short, executive structure contains variety. This is a good thing. It embodies what we know of the past, that is, it serves as our institutional memory, and, finally, in trying to prevent the recurrence of past mistakes, it is a hedge against an unknown future. Periodically, we have to untangle the mess—or part of it. But it is the mess that ensures our survival.

NOTES

1. For an extended discussion of these perspectives see Emmette S. Redford and Marlan Blissett, *Organizing the Executive Branch: The Johnson Presidency* (Chicago: University of Chicago Press, 1981).

2. Lyndon Baines Johnson, *The Vantage Point: Perspectives of the Presidency, 1963–1969* (New York: Holt, Rinehart, and Winston, 1971), 326–327.

3. Staff memo, "Analysis of Programs Which Might Be Transferred to a New Department of Housing and Urban Development," 3 January 1961, Bureau of the Budget, R–4–20, Vol. 1.

4. Hugh Sidey, "The White House Staff vs. the Cabinet," interview with Bill Moyers, *Washington Monthly* (February 1969), 80.

5. Memo, Robert C. Weaver to Bill Moyers, 3 December 1964, "Legislative Proposals, 1965" Folder, Book 4, Box 100, Files of Bill Moyers, LBJ Library.

6. "Annual Message to the Congress on the State of the Union," *Public Papers*, 1965 (4 January 1965), 1: 93.

7. "Special Message to Congress on the Nation's Cities," *Public Papers*, 1965 (2 March 1965), 1: 231.

8. Ibid., 233–234.

9. Transcript, Robert C. Weaver Oral History, 19 November 1965, Tape 1, 33, LBJ Library.

10. Ibid., 41.

11. Ibid., 42.

12. Ibid., 42.

13. Ibid., 3.

14. The President's Task Force on Urban Problems, "Proposed Plan of Organization for the Department of Housing and Urban Development," *Report of the Task Force Subcommittee*, 14 December 1965, 1, Task Force Collection, LBJ Library.

15. Memo, Harold Seidman to Charles Schultze, "Organization of Department of Housing and Urban Development," 18 February 1966, BOB R4–27/66.

16. Weaver Oral History, 35.

17. Ibid.

18. *Public Papers*, 1963–1964, 1: 379.

19. The President's Task Force on Urban Problems, transmitted to the president on 21 December 1965, 5, Task Force Collection, LBJ Library.

20. "Remarks of the President upon Signing a Bill Creating a Department of Transportation," 15 October 1966, press release from Office of the White House Press Secretary, in "Passage and Signature," Legislative Background, Transportation Department, Box 3, LBJ Library.

5

Failure of Nerve: How the Liberals Killed Liberalism

Michael P. Riccards

"In the war on poverty, poverty won."

Ronald Reagan, January 1985

Most conservatives and mainstream liberals may differ about the relative merits of the Reagan administration, but they seem to be in general agreement that the big government public policy experiments symbolized by the Great Society failed. Many reasons are posed for this failure, some quite far reaching in their implications, but taken together the elements of this critique provide much of the intellectual basis for the Reagan assault on the modern American welfare state and for the near paralysis of the national leadership of the Democratic party.

The usual conservative argument against an activist state is well known and has been a part of our political dialogue since at least the advent of the New Deal. The welfare state is seen as sapping individual initiative, thwarting entrepreneurship and political liberty, and distorting the natural equilibrium of the impersonal marketplace. The Reagan attack on the Great Society is not much different from Hoover and Landon's evaluation of the New Deal. Ronald Reagan, of course, is far more able to communicate his discontent and has built up an extensive repertoire of welfare state horror stories—parables on the life and times of the lazy, the promiscuous, and the undeserving. For years, the rubber chicken circuit was regaled by Reagan's tale of the welfare mother from Chicago who spawned eight illegitimate children and rode around the Windy City in a Cadillac purchased from the largesse of the citizenry. The story turned out to be unsubstantiated, but like the parables of the New Testament, it was meant to be a simplified morality tale, signifying a higher set of truths than fact alone will allow.[1]

It is not surprising that traditional Republican circles and conservative economic interests opposed the expansion of the welfare state under Lyndon B. Johnson. Differences in ideology and challenges to the distribution of power and privilege are legitimate controversies in a healthy political system. What is surprising though is that so many liberals, some of them close to the Johnson administration, joined with the conservatives in believing that the Great Society failed, even accepting the overall judgment that national public policy aimed at alleviating poverty in systematic and standardized ways was doomed to over-bureaucracy and unforeseen breakdowns. We are today the heirs to that particular joint legacy, a chapter in the history of American ideas that is both profoundly powerful and yet profoundly incorrect. The basic theme of this chapter is that contrary to this consensus—liberal and conservative—the Great Society actually was rather successful in its hopeful goals of alleviating poverty, closing the income gaps between the races, and fostering a more equitable society.

LOSING OR GAINING GROUND

The most influential critique of American liberal social policy is Charles Murray's study, *Losing Ground*, published in 1984 and celebrated by Reaganites and neoconservatives. Edward Banfield called the book "required reading for every voter," and Nathan Glazer found it remarkable and persuasive in its arguments.[2] Murray maintains that not only did the Great Society fail, but it actually made the lives of the poor, especially the black lower class, substantially worse. The problem is not that we administered good programs improperly, or that sound concepts have been operationalized incorrectly. Instead, the leaders of society changed the rules of the game, thereby making it profitable for "the poor to behave in the short term in ways that were destructive in the long run." The Great Society created more poor, gave them a temporary and misguided incentive to abandon the work ethic, and thereby accelerated the breakdown of the minority family, the further deterioration of urban school systems, and the undoing of individual discipline and productivity. The poor must be given the chance once again to fail, and the reward structures of society should reinforce the behavior of the ambitious, the morally directed, and the upwardly mobile in the lower classes.[3]

Cases of welfare fraud and misrepresentation, of belligerent poverty advocates and incompetent program administrators, of rampant interest group pressures and blatant influence peddling are an extensive part of the 1970s, and surely some of Murray's criticisms are true, especially for programs that span a large and diverse nation. But Murray's critique goes beyond the anecdotes and examples, for he is attacking the very basis of ameliorative legislation and the entire philosophy of the welfare state. His major contentions, which are a social scientist's revision of social Darwinism, rest on statistical data that supposedly show a marked decline in the economic well-being of the poor after the public policy experiments of the 1960s. The Great Society is thus a perverse phenomenon, a set of programs that not only failed, but created (or joined with other phenomena in society to create) the social conditions that led to a further worsening of the very disease the liberals were trying to cure. The curse of liberalism is not that it is bureaucratic and inefficient; the real nemesis of reform is that it produces unexpected consequences that injure the very clients so humanely worried about. Murray's prescription, basically a social "triage" as he calls it, is an end of the national welfare state and, more importantly, a return to social policies that he argues will foster industry, responsibility, and personal direction. Those latter objectives will be accomplished by a restoration of old values and an end to government interventionist public policy.[4]

Murray's volume has been critically reviewed by Christopher Jencks, who has disagreed with some of the book's major theses. First, using the most authoritative data we have—that of the Census Bureau—Jencks finds that the poverty rate fell from 30 percent to 22 percent during the 1950s, and from 22 percent to 13 percent during the 1960s. If noncash benefits are included, the 1980 poverty rate dropped from 13 percent to 10 percent. Jencks further points out that the gap between the infant mortality rates of blacks and whites, which had widened in the 1950s and only narrowed a bit in the early 1960s, closed markedly after 1965. The disparity in life expectancy by race also narrowed after 1965.[5]

Jencks, however, does agree that, apart from health, "the material condition of the poor improved faster from 1950 to 1965 than from 1965 to 1980." He attributes this finding though to the sluggish economy after 1970. In addition, Jencks insists that if total government spending on social welfare programs had been devoted to the poor, poverty would have been abolished. But only a fifth of all social welfare spending went to lower income families, and only a tenth went for providing cash, food, or housing. Most of the expenditures were aimed at the middle class: college loans, Social Security, aid to public schools, military pensions, and similar programs.[6]

Of crucial importance though is that the decline in poverty after 1965 came despite both unfavorable economic conditions and massive demographic changes, which will be addressed later. Jencks does admit that there is empirical evidence that public policy changes in the 1960s that increased AFDC (Aid to Families with Dependent Children) payments helped to accelerate the divorce rate and led to the creation of more single-parent households split off from parents. This finding may mean that higher AFDC benefits allowed single mothers to set up their own households rather than forcing them to live with their parents, to end bad marriages, and to be more selective in remarrying. Jencks adds that while Murray blames the public policy changes of the 1960s for increasing unemployment, especially among blacks, this increase may be due to a rise in the numbers of blacks who were students and also the possibility that the kinds of jobs young blacks have traditionally held may have disappeared structurally in the economy.

Yet Jencks concludes that America in the 1960s did in some ways reward the unworthy, arguing that "we cannot give too many second chances without undermining people's motivation to do well the first time around." He joins Murray in condemning the liberal tendency to blame the "system" for blacks' problems, which consequently led to the "social, cultural, and moral deterioration of black urban communities after 1965." Jencks adds, "That such deterioration occurred in many cities is beyond doubt. Blacks were far more likely to murder, rape and rob one another in 1980 than in 1965. Black males were more likely to father children they did not intend to care for or support. Black teenagers were less likely to be working. More blacks were in school, but despite expanded opportunities for higher education and white-collar employment, black teen-agers were not learning as much." The liberal coalition from 1964 to 1980, then, did help the poor, but it often rewarded folly and vice, and it never insisted that those who violated the rules of social behavior should pay a price for their transgressions. Jencks adds that one of the major problems with Murray's indictment of liberal public policy is that the breakdown of social responsibility, the increase in the crime rate, the decline in sexual fidelity, and the drop in scholastic achievement scores all reflect a much wider change—one that affected vast elements outside of the lower classes.[7] Indeed, it may be speculated that such trends were first set by the middle and upper classes and disseminated through the media.

Both Murray and Jencks accept the popular view that there is a permanent stratum of the poor, a "culture of poverty" with its own deficient life style, world view, and cross-generational value system. However, a longitudinal study of 5,000 families found that nearly one-quarter of the U.S. population experienced at least occasional periods of poverty during the 1969–1978 decade. Only 2.6 percent of the population was persistently poor, that is, poor in eight of the ten years. This group, though, is overwhelmingly black and female and often responsible for dependent children. Thus, more people seem to move in and out of poverty than is usually recognized, and their status is very much linked up with changes in family structure (divorce, widowhood, child-rearing age) as well as with education, sex, and race.[8]

THE GREAT SOCIETY: WAS IT WORKING AFTER ALL?

Despite their points of agreement, the different judgments of Murray and Jencks on the success of the poverty program are critical. The initiatives and cutbacks of the Reagan administration give us additional data by which to compare the effects of the Great Society. If the Great Society were successful, its elimination or pruning back would be felt by a substantial number of people. Conversely, if the Great Society's programs were extraneous or even deleterious to the life of the poor, the Reagan cutbacks would not affect in a negative way that social stratum.

A quite different perspective on the controversy is provided by John E. Schwarz in an insightful book that has received very little notice except among specialists.

Schwarz argues that the Great Society did indeed succeed and that the major cause of our economic woes in the 1970s was the massive number of Americans who came of age. The economy had to expand more rapidly than ever before to provide jobs for an additional 30 million people who entered the work force between 1965 and 1980, a jump of over 40 percent. Remarkably, the economy succeeded and the poverty programs prevented a major increase in deprivation and misery. The really dramatic change, then, was due not to a change in political consciousness nor in the unraveling of our moral code, but to a unique demographic bulge caused by the post World War II baby boom, an event that was almost totally ignored by most leaders in American life in the 1960s and 1970s.[9]

Schwarz argues that economic growth played a small role in the reduction of poverty in that period. Economic growth reduced poverty for one in ten Americans; government intervention reduced poverty for more than one in two over the same period. Using a different method of calculation, Schwarz finds that about 9 percent of the people were below the poverty line by 1972, figures somewhat lower than Jencks' estimate. Nutritional programs reduced flagrant malnutrition in locales of concentrated poverty, and the infant mortality rate dropped by 33 percent from 1965 to 1975; among blacks it fell from 44.5 per 1,000 in 1950 to 40.3 in 1965 to 30.9 in 1970 to 24.2 in 1975.[10]

In terms of manpower retraining programs, a Johns Hopkins study in Baltimore concluded that 40 percent of the enrollees found employment immediately and 56 percent within six months. A later study by the National Academy of Sciences completed in 1978 found, however, a more mixed record for these efforts. Another very visible program of the Great Society, Head Start, reached 300,000 children a year, led to a seven-point immediate increase in IQ (one-half that increase in the long term), and was so successful that graduates of the program were 68 percent less likely to be assigned to special education classes and 45 percent less likely to be held back later. Overall, "in 1980, one in fifteen Americans faced the desperation of poverty," Schwarz declared, "compared with about one in five Americans just a generation earlier. This was accomplished almost entirely by the government." His overall judgments concerning the social programs of the 1960s parallel to large extent a much earlier study by Levitan and Taggart that also found that federal initiatives in welfare, medical care, housing, vocational and job training, remedial education, and civil rights were rather successful. These findings are similar, but not identical to a study done by Plotnick and Skidmore that concluded that in 1965, "as a result of cash transfers, 33% of all pre-transfer poor households were raised out of poverty, by 1972, 44% were raised out of poverty."[11]

Schwarz further argues that, despite the general impression to the contrary, no major growth took place comparatively in the nation's government in the 1960–1980 period. In most respects, the government in relation to the size of the nation's economy grew very slightly. This is the case whether one considers taxation, deficit spending, the size of the bureaucracy, or the amount of regulation. In fact, the size of government grew faster under Eisenhower than it did in the 1960s and 1970s. Combined federal and state income taxes rose modestly from 7.2 percent of American personal income in the 1950s to 10.8 percent in 1960 to 12.9 percent at the end of that decade; about one-half the income tax rise from 1960 to 1979 was due to state, not federal tax increases.[12]

Schwarz's argument runs counter to the conventional wisdom; he finds the poverty program was working, the growth in economic system did not alleviate more than a fraction of the poor's misery, the federal government did not increase in size relative to the economy, government regulatory costs were modest, the 1970s were a period of growth and not stagnation, and productivity in the 1970s exceeded the levels of the 1950s. How, he wonders, did we come to believe we failed, and how did Americans come to adopt the negative consensus about the efficacy of government?[13]

If Schwarz's views are correct, especially about the war on poverty, then the Reagan cutbacks would have major consequences for the poor. The most recent figures indicate that this is what has happened. In May 1985, the Congressional Research Service and the Congressional Budget Office found that poverty among children, for example, had grown deeper and more widespread over the last decade. Children made up 26.8 percent of the nation's total population, but 39.2 percent of the poor. Child poverty in 1983 was "at the highest level since the mid–1960s," the study concluded. Even though the total number of children increased by nine million in the 1968–1983 period, the number of poor children increased by three million. In 1974–1975 the number of poor rose by a million and a half, and by the 1979–1982 period, the increase hit eight million. In 1982, the national poverty rate again reached 15 percent due to the rise in unemployment and cuts in federal social programs. Some 40 percent of the households below the poverty line did not receive Medicaid, housing assistance, or school lunches for children, according to the Census Bureau. By 1984, Robert Greenstein of the Center on Budget and Policy Priorities found that the Reagan administration's budget cuts and rewritten rules led to one million people being denied food stamps, 750,000 children losing free lunches, 500,000 children being eliminated from the summer food service programs, and an overall cut of 30 percent in the child care food programs. By the end of 1984, the poverty rate was reported to be 14.4 percent.[14]

Clearly, then, the Great Society was accomplishing the basic objectives outlined by President Johnson when he created it. The war on poverty, begun in 1964, implemented within a year, and limping along through the late 1960s, had accomplished remarkable progress in less than five years. One can hardly imagine any administration or Congress making a decision to end a weapons system or an agricultural support program based on five years or so experience from idea to implementation. Yet the Great Society has not only been pronounced a failure, but has become a symbol to conservative and large segments of liberal opinion of what government cannot and should not do—that is, use the powers of the federal government to intervene in the social lives of citizens to effect national public policy objectives.

THE FAILURE OF NERVE

The denigration of the reputation of the Great Society came about from a variety of sources. First, as expected, the conservative critics continued their century-long attack on the expansion of the welfare state on familiar grounds. In the 1970s and 1980s, groups of conservative academicians and thinkers, often supported by corporate gifts and organized in research centers, provided systematic critiques of the liberal past and presented an agenda for right-wing reform.

More surprising, though, was the disillusionment of many traditional liberals. Part of their attack on the Great Society was a clear outcome of the personal guerrilla war against Lyndon Johnson. The Kennedy liberals resented his ''style''—a code word for undifferentiated dislike for the successor to the throne. More mainstream liberals split from the president over the war in Vietnam, and by 1967 influential black leaders were expressing reservations about Johnson's foreign policy in Asia. The war on poverty was being elbowed aside by the escalation in Vietnam, proving once again the wisdom of Richard Hofstadter's remark that ''war is the nemesis of reform.'' The liberals never understood or cared to appreciate the extent to which the poverty program especially and the Great Society in general were dependent on Lyndon Johnson. Perhaps even he never realized it either.

One of the architects of the war on poverty, Michael Harrington, has recalled that in 1964 ''the poverty warriors did not know what to do—when asked to come up with a program to end poverty, they were 'intellectually impoverished.' '' Many of the Great Society programs resembled the New Deal because Johnson's advisers resurrected old strategies. It was not just nostalgia and a love of FDR that led them back to the 1930s, it was a dearth of ideas.[15]

Johnson's successes in getting the Great Society through Congress were based in part on an act of faith, on his own considerable skills in persuasion, and by 1965 on the large Democratic majorities in both Houses that arrived after his monumental victory. Only three times in this century has a president ever so mastered Congress, the others being Wilson in 1913 and FDR in his first term. Wilson's triumph came after a generation-long debate over progressive reform; FDR's successes rested on the desperations of the Great Depression. Johnson had neither experience to help lay the groundwork. Kennedy's commitment in 1963 to deal with the poverty problem was apparently known only to Walter Heller and a few others in the government. While some of the reform agendas were influenced by findings being generated and accumulated in the social sciences, there was remarkably little public dialogue on these matters. The only major public event that attracted much attention on the topic was the publication of Michael Harrington's *The Other America*, and, more important the highly favorable long review of the book by critic Dwight MacDonald in the January 1963 issue of *The New Yorker*.[16]

Because of the absence of a period of political gestation, the Great Society programs were highly dependent on the president and his legislative ability—

more dependent than any major policy changes have been on an executive in recent history. Johnson was an incredibly skilled politician: His opponents insisted on calling him in a pejorative way a "political operator," but all agreed he was highly successful in the legislative arts. The war in Vietnam not only cut into his political base and raised the general level of resistance in a once compliant Congress, it also deprived the president of the necessary monies to expand the war on poverty. Johnson's secretary of treasury warned him that he could not increase the level of support for domestic programs if taxes stayed level and military budgets increased.[17]

Yet the growth of the Great Society did not end, as many have charged, because of the war. Through the Republican administrations of the late 1960s and early 1970s, the basic programs of the Johnson administration were funded at still higher levels. Even a staunch critic of the community action programs, such as Daniel Patrick Moynihan, admits that local poverty agencies became entrenched and city halls learned to live with these new advocacy bureaucracies. Medicare and Medicaid became a part of the American support system in the 1970s as expenditures rose from $3.4 billion to $34 billion in the former, and from $770 million to $14 billion in the latter program. Aid to elementary and secondary schools rose from $383 million to $5.4 billion, and aid to higher education went from $538 million to $7.3 billion in the 1968–1977 period. The 1980s also marked a major period of housing and urban development initiatives, becoming in Robert Weaver's words, "the focal point of thought, innovation, and imagination about the problems of our cities."[18]

However, during this era of increased dependency on federal aid, major liberals joined the attack on the legacy of the Great Society—proclaiming it both bankrupt and misguided. The intellectual assault on liberalism by liberals, neoliberals, and former liberals reinforced the assertive right wing critique. One of the major negative perspectives was Moynihan's commentary on community action programs. For Moynihan, at least at this period of his public career, liberal reform seemed to end with the death of Robert Kennedy. The war on poverty, which Moynihan participated in and helped to create, was surely hurt in the early stages by the arrival of community action organizers who challenged the traditional power structures in cities and towns. Moynihan records that Johnson himself was less enamored with CAPs than he was with the basic Great Society benefits programs: Job Corps, aid to education, Medicare, Medicaid, etc.[19]

Moynihan's book is of historical interest because it details some of the bureaucratic infighting over the poverty program, and also because of what it tells us about the turn some liberals took. For all his detailed analysis and balanced perspective, Moynihan never really points to any major Great Society successes. For him, the CAPs are the major story, a great mistake that symbolized the basically bad political strategy that deprived an entire generation of the reform impulse. In a tell-tale way, Moynihan quotes not the liberal patrons of reform: Franklin Roosevelt, Thomas Jefferson, or even reliable John Locke, but instead aligns himself with Edmund Burke, Michael Oakeshott, and Robert Nisbet, articulate figures of the Anglo-American conservative tradition. To Moynihan the lessons of CAPs, the lessons of the Great Society in general, seem to be that "the government did not know what it was doing." Professionals were too willing to "further what was in effect a political agenda of a fairly small group of intellectuals."[20] Since 1969, when Moynihan's volume was published, the disenchanted liberals and reconstructed conservatives have begun a more generalized attack on the national government's public policy programs, using especially the journal pages of *Public Interest* and *The Washington Monthly* to publish their case studies of bureaucratic horror stories and their philosophical tracts against the possibilities of effective nation-wide domestic reform. Ironically by 1986, Moynihan had become the most articulate voice of concern for the increasing ranks of poor people, especially children, in the United States. He argued that overpromising is endemic to political vitality, and that Johnson was fully aware of the complexities the Great Society was addressing. Rather than berating the expensive reform programs, he concluded that if all the "OEO money had gone directly to the poor as income—as most of it did not—each poor person in America would have received about $50–$70 per year."[21]

The new critiques of big government point out some real failings in operations, design, and misplaced sympathies. But the liberal loss of faith runs deeper than historical retrospection. Former House Speaker Thomas O'Neill is correct in exclaiming with some exasperation that the middle class is a creation of the New Deal and subsequent Democratic programs. The difficulty for the Democratic national party was that by the 1960s liberal reform had splintered into a host of agendas, with constituencies often concerned with a single issue: their own. The notion of coalition politics, of compromise, of logrolling became out of date as middle-class politics acquired intensely moralistic, cynical, and antileadership overtones. The attacks on Johnson over the war accelerated these tendencies in the Democratic party. Because the Great Society was so dependent on Johnson and his skills, the assault on the president, for whatever the validity of the reasons, led to an assault on the ability of his party to present a continuous agenda for reform.

The opposition to the war ended up unleashing a party reorganization that destroyed much of the ability of the Democrats to build successful coalitions. The McGovern rules institutionalized these decentralizing tendencies and furthered the dynamics of segmented representation. The disenchantment with the Great Society was a part of the overall view of the 1970s that the federal government was incapable of governing. The Watergate affair became a crisis of legitimacy, and the reforms in campaign financing and in the committee system in Congress led to the rise of political action committees, the breakdown of parties, the extravagance of campaign costs, and the further balkanization of the legislative branch. The handling of the oil crisis in 1973 seemed to confirm that the federal government was incapable of dealing with complex and critical issues.[22]

The lack of nerve, this liberal self-flagellation, achieved its ultimate expression in President Jimmy Carter's speech from the mountain top, which laid out in excruciating detail the alleged narcissistic tendencies of the American people and the reasons for our natural political malaise. Where Johnson was accused of promising too much, Carter told Americans that they had better expect a lot less. The liberal failure of nerve had become national policy.

The Great Society, then, did not fail. It established policies of distribution, amelioration, and reform. Cutbacks in many of these programs in the 1980s have had major impacts on the lives of the poor. Considering that Johnson had a very short time for reform, his policies were rather successful, and the major pillars of the Great Society are mainstays of the American social, educational, and medical establishments. Even the CAPs, so strongly attacked by such an able critic as Moynihan, provided a new generation of leadership in many regions. These organizations were accepted by even wary mayors after a few years.[23] One study of ten California cities found that federal social programs stimulated minority mobilization and incorporation into local government. In the long run though, the CAPs advocates turned out to be correct—the poor need not just benefits but empowerment. The cuts of the Reagan administration have proven that it is power and not feelings of transitory beneficence that is the true protection of the lower classes. The failure of CAPs is not that they encouraged lower-class participation, but that not enough poor people view politics as efficacious activity, for obvious reasons.

Johnson's Great Society is a major contribution to American life. His tragically missed opportunity came from being caught up and finally destroyed by the war in Vietnam—a commitment in which every American president from Truman to Ford concurred. The real enemy of the Great Society was segments of the national liberal leadership with their relentless attack against Johnson for more than his war policies, their assault on the party apparatus, and above all their loss of faith in the future and in the possibilities of collective action. The 1970s and 1980s will be marked as a period in which many Americans seemed overwhelmed by a sense of limits, a nihilism about public institutions, and a depreciation of meaningful citizenship. The great irony of the Reagan administration is that while it has moved to destroy the Great Society, it has restored, in part, confidence in the federal government, in its management of the economy, and in the possibilities of a fairly powerful executive—one different, though, from Franklin Roosevelt and Lyndon Johnson in philosophy and aspirations. Such a restoration in nerve is essential to a renewal of national domestic reform and to an honest reexamination of the Great Society and a more proper evaluation of its patron, Lyndon Johnson.

NOTES

I am grateful to David Colby, Robert Weaver, and Robert Wood for their comments after the first draft of this chapter was presented at the LBJ Conference.

1. Laurence I. Barrett, *Gambling with History: Ronald Reagan in the White House*

(Garden City, N.Y.: Doubleday, 1983); Robert Dallek, *Ronald Reagan: The Politics of Symbolism* (Cambridge, Mass.: Harvard University Press, 1984); Lou Cannon, *Reagan* (New York: G. P. Putnam, 1982); Ronnie Dugger, *On Reagan: The Man and His Personality* (New York: McGraw-Hill, 1983); and Alan Gartner et al., *What Is Reagan Doing To Us* (New York: Harper & Row, 1982).

2. Charles Murray, *Losing Ground: American Social Policy, 1950–1980* (New York: Basic Books, 1984), quotes are on the back cover jacket.

3. Ibid., Chapters 12 and 14.

4. Ibid., Chapters 15 and 16. On the mood of welfare recipients, see Michael Harrington, *The New American Poverty* (New York: Holt, Rinehart and Winston, 1984), 29.

5. Christopher Jencks, "How Poor Are the Poor," *New York Review of Books*, 9 May 1985, 41.

6. Ibid., 42–43. Harrington, *New American Poverty*, 27 points out that from 1961 to 1976 federal spending for the poor increased from $4.6 billion to $34.6 billion, while outlays for the nonpoor went from $29.4 billion to $197.8 billion.

7. Jencks, "How Poor Are the Poor," 45–48.

8. Greg J. Duncan et al., *Years of Poverty, Years of Plenty* (Ann Arbor: Institute of Social Research, 1984), 40–45.

9. John E. Schwarz, *American's Hidden Success: A Reassessment of Twenty Years of Public Policy* (New York: W. W. Norton, 1983), 124, 132.

10. Ibid., 33–35, 38, 45, 47.

11. Ibid., 53, 54, 58; Sar A. Levitan and Robert Taggart, *The Promise of Greatness* (Cambridge, Mass.: Harvard University Press, 1976); Robert D. Plotnick and Felicity Skidmore, *Progress Against Poverty: A Review of the 1964–1974 Decade* (New York: Academic Press, 1975), 173.

12. Ibid., 80–87.

13. Ibid., 100, 132.

14. Robert Pear, "Food Stamp Proposal Would Hurt Poorest Families, a Study Reports," *New York Times*, 14 April 1983; Pear, "US Hunger on Rise Despite Swelling of Food Surpluses," 19 July 1983; Pear, "Halted Growth in NonCash Air Programs," 23 September 1983; Pear, "US Panel Says Hunger Cannot Be Documented," 9 January 1984; Pear, "US Hunger: A New Focus," 12 January 1984; Jean Mayer and Kenneth Schlossberg, "To Insure Nutrition," 28 February 1984; Elin Schoen, "Once Again: Hunger Troubles America," 2 January 1984; Pear, "Study Finds Poverty Among Children Increasing," 23 May 1985; and Pear, "US Poverty Rate Dropped to 14.4 in '84, Bureau Says," 28 August 1985. Increases were further reported by John Herbers, "Hunger in the US is Widening, Study of 'New Poor' Reports," 20 April 1986. This finding is made even more stark by the Associated Press report of 27 July 1986 of a study done by congressional Democrats that the nation's top one-half of one percent of the families in the United States control 35 percent of the total wealth, an increase from 1963 when they held 25 percent of that wealth.

15. Harrington, *New American Poverty*, 13; on gestation, see Daniel Patrick Moynihan, *Maximum Feasible Misunderstanding* (New York: Free Press, 1969), 24. It must be remembered that much of the New Deal was also improvised, but the Great Depression gave Roosevelt considerably more leeway, especially in the first term. David Zarefsky, *President Johnson's War on Poverty: Rhetoric and History* (Alabama: University of Alabama Press, 1986) argues that LBJ's war symbolism hastened the passage of the Economic Opportunity Act.

16. Ongoing research by Robert Wood, former secretary of HUD, leads to the con-

clusion that in education, health, and the environment, new ideas were coming from the stockpile of maturing social science research being done at the time (personal communication to author). Michael Harrington, *The Other America* (New York: Penguin, 1963).

17. Moynihan, *Maximum Feasible Misunderstanding*, 4–5; Harrington, *New American Poverty*, 21.

18. Joseph Califano, *Governing America* (New York: Simon and Schuster, 1981), 24; and Robert C. Weaver, "The First Twenty Years at HUD," *Journal Forum* (Autumn 1985): 463–474.

19. Moynihan, *Maximum Feasible Misunderstanding*, xix, 142–143.

20. Ibid., 170, 190.

21. Peter Steinfels, *The Neo-Conservatives* (New York: Simon and Schuster, 1979); Robert B. Reich, "Toward a New Public Philosophy," *Atlantic Monthly* (May 1985); 68–79. Interestingly, *Public Interest* devoted a whole issue in the Winter 1974 to a series of articles that were generally quite favorable to the social policies of the Great Society. Moynihan's latest concerns are in his Godkin lectures, *Family and Nation* (New York: Harcourt Brace Jovanovich, 1986), 79.

22. Califano, *Governing America*, 140; Harrington, *New American Poverty*, 20–21.

23. Moynihan, *Maximum Feasible Misunderstanding*, 129; Rufus P. Browning, Dale Rogers Marshall, and David H. Tabb, *Protest Is Not Enough* (Berkeley: University of California Press, 1984), 235; David C. Colby, "Black Power, White Resistance, and Public Policy: Political Power and Poverty Program Grants in Mississippi," *Journal of Politics* 47 (1985): 579–595. When the federal government allowed the city halls to take over the community action agencies, only 48 of the 898 agencies suffered that fate; see Moynihan, *Maximum Feasible Misunderstanding*, 159. Interesting reflections on the problems of evaluating public policy in this period are contained in Robert Wood, "The Great Society in 1984: Relic or Reality?" Paper delivered at the University of Colorado, 11–12 June 1984.

6

The Great Society Then and Now: A Panel Discussion

Editors' note: Among the most controversial of President Johnson's legacies is the war against poverty, encompassing a broad range of programs ranging from outright grants to more innovative initiatives designed to involve the poor in their own rehabilitation. But the poor were not the only beneficiaries of Great Society legislation. The president's education policies and successful marshalling of Medicare through Congress substantially widened the scope of government entitlements beyond the poor to the middle class and even the affluent. The following panel discussion includes a number of former government officials who were intimately involved in formulating, winning support for, and implementing the president's Great Society program. The moderator is Sargent Shriver, who served as director of the Peace Corps and Office of Economic Opportunity under Presidents Kennedy and Johnson. Panelists include Johnson's secretary of health, education, and welfare, Wilbur J. Cohen, his commissioner of education, Francis Keppel, and his secretary of HUD (housing and urban development), Robert Weaver. Included also is Adam Yarmolinsky, who occupied a number of important posts under Kennedy and Johnson and who played a large role in fashioning the president's domestic policies.

MODERATOR: SARGENT SHRIVER

In this panel the four people who are the principals are among the most articulate, energetic, feisty, imaginative, hard-hitting executives there have ever been in the federal government in Washington. The first one of whom, after you've heard from him, it will take you a few moments to calm down, because there's never been a cabinet officer or sub-cabinet officer, let alone a Sid Richardson of the University of Texas, comparable to Wilbur Cohen. Wilbur Cohen is the architect and the creator of some of the most imaginative and useful programs the United States government in Washington has ever undertaken in the history of this republic. He is an exemplification, I believe, of the type of social entrepreneur which current government extols when it takes place as entrepreneurship in the private sector, but which they seem to abhor when it takes place in the public sector.

It seems to be perfectly permissible to exert private initiative when it fattens your wallet or your pocketbook, but it's not acceptable to be a social entrepreneur that helps millions of people. Wilbur Cohen will tell you what it's like to be a social entrepreneur and to look back on a career where literally millions of people have benefited from his work.

WILBUR COHEN

My few minutes are going to be devoted to a number of disparate points, since this is one of the few opportunities I have with my other colleagues, some friends here, to make these points.

First then, I spent eight years and two days working for the Kennedy-Johnson administrations. It was the most important episode in my whole life. I don't think any of you can appreciate what it means to work with my colleagues here, and others who had the sparkling dynamism, social idealism, and the practical management to try to make government work for the American people.

I felt that I was engaged in an enterprise far beyond my competence, far beyond my ability, far beyond the capacity really of any human being. And yet, when the president of the United States said, "I am nominating you for this office because I have confidence in you," there is something that envelops you in something that is so much bigger than you are, that you feel everyday should have thirty hours, every week should have eight days, and every year should have 400 days.

To work in an administration under the idealism of President Kennedy and the pragmatism of Lyndon Johnson, were two experiences that I wish everyone could have—men, who whatever their talents, whatever their limitations, were dedicated to the idea that America was a great country, that human beings could be bigger and better than ever before with the help of government. They believed that government was there to help the American people and [that] government was not the problem. Government was there to aid and help, especially the disadvantaged, especially the people who couldn't help themselves. The great willingness of President Kennedy to help the mentally retarded and the mentally ill, the great thrust of Lyndon Johnson to help the Mexican-Americans, and the aged poor, and the boys and girls who needed student financial aid in college. When the president told you that that was his program, he wanted you to go out and work. President Johnson told me many times, "Do whatever you have to do." Twenty-four hours was no limitation on him or any of us.

And you felt you were in a mission so big and so important, that you were willing to do whatever was required. I came in as an appointee for President John F. Kennedy, because I believed that he could make America move again. And the first point I want to make is how fortunate we were in America to have these two men as part of a team as I see it, which most historians don't quite look at that way, because most of the conceptual ideas that were formulated were formulated by the people who worked for Kennedy and most of it was carried out by Lyndon Johnson.

You couldn't think of a combination that brought together two men so different in their backgrounds, and yet being able to build, in a way, a program. I bet I told President Kennedy ten times, "Mr. President, we don't have the votes to do what you want." I never said that to President Johnson, because I didn't have to. But I was constantly telling President Kennedy we ought to put this program down to number ten and move ten to number one so we could probably pick up a couple more votes. One time, President Kennedy said to me, "Wilbur, why don't you get one more Republican to vote for the Education Bill." I got a little annoyed, which I supposed I shouldn't have done, and I said, "Mr. President, why don't you get one more Catholic to vote for it." End of conversation. But I felt I could go to President Kennedy that way. I told my wife everytime I went into the Oval Office for a meeting with the president, "Pack your bags. Tonight we may be leaving at 5:30 because when I go into the president's office, I tell him what I think."

Cap Weinberger, when he got to be secretary of health, education, and welfare, said to me one day, "Wilbur, did you ever appeal to President Johnson over the actions of the Office of Management and Budget?" I said, "Certainly, I did many times." "Oh, I didn't think President Johnson would allow that," he said. I said [the] president would think I was not doing a job if I didn't appeal the decisions of the head of OMB. I said until the president kicked me out of the office, I would keep saying what I had to say because he expected me to.

There was a symbiotic relationship between the Kennedy-Johnson administrations which I find lacking in the academic literature which I read scrupulously. There's always the Kennedy administration [and then] the Johnson administration. It's either the "New Frontier" or the "Great Society." Now you've got people here, who served in both of them and served those two presidents faithfully, and I think, courageously, and see it as a continuum, rather than the way most academic people look at it. Most of the fundamental ideas President Kennedy came in with I helped him plan, as I did others in 1957 and 1958. So when you are enacting legislation in 1965 that's going to be effective in 1980, you are enacting 1957 ideas.

That's part of the penalty we pay in this country because we don't have a parliamentary form of government. We have a different form of government in which you construct ideas in the ethos of one period, then work very hard for about eight or ten years to get them adopted, and then when they are adopted they stay in effect for fifteen or twenty years without much change because we don't have a parliamentary system. That's called incrementalism in the academic environment. That is the nature of the legislative process. And I believe, therefore, that when you come to evaluate the Great Society, you have to keep in mind our form of government. Was the Great Society a failure or a success? Every president has been a failure in some respect, and every president has been a success in some way. It's the nature of our system.

I think that I want to shift to the now and say this. I think we are in the doldrums right now of social reform, and I think the next great period of reform is going to be 1995. I wish I had time to give you my whole thesis, but I'll just summarize it briefly. America goes in great cyclical periods of ups and downs, not merely [in] economics, but in social attitudes. 1905 was one of the great periods of social reforms in the Food and Drug Administration, the later establishment of the Children's Bureau, Mothers' Pensions, Workman's Compensation, and so on. 1935, thirty years later, was the Social Security Act. 1965 was the Medicare Act and all the social legislation.

It's inevitable, but it is only inevitable because of hard work. We are now at the point where the Reagan administration is demonstrating that government cannot work. And they are going to make it a reality by denying money to all the programs Sarge, Keppel, Weaver, Yarmolinsky and I worked so hard for. But the day will come when there will be no Reagan administration. And the day will come when the American people will say, "Gee, we have all these social needs that are not being met." I may not be here then, but there will be someone who will come along and seize the political, intellectual, [and] emotional period, as Kennedy did, and activate the American people.

The things that Sarge did with Headstart and Legal Services for the poor and what we did with maternal and child care, what we did with mental retardation, what we did in library construction and Medicare, someone will come and build upon them. They will not be destroyed, because someone will come along and build on what we have done before. That's in the American tradition and it will come again, and it will come again because in The New Frontier and The Great Society, we built some fundamental institutions.

And those people who tell you that the policy of the federal government is to throw money at problems and that it doesn't work, they don't have any idea how the private economy of the United States works. You can't get anywhere unless you put a lot of money into it. I think that was in the back of the Kennedy and Johnson minds, and certainly what was in the back of my mind and in those of my colleagues: We did not want to establish a welfare state. We didn't want the government to do everything, but we did want to see that there was a social minimum in this country.

We wanted to see that every man and woman, that every boy and girl, every child, had an opportunity. We wanted to see that the system, public and private, federal, state, and local, provided an opportunity for people to have at least a decent minimum upon which they could maximize, through their own efforts, a higher standard of living. I think that was a noble objective now, and it's going to be still an objective of the next administration. It is going to have to remedy what we have been doing for the last six years—not only destroying what we built in the eight years that we were in government, but that has been built since the turn of the century in this country.

MODERATOR: SARGENT SHRIVER

It is particularly appropriate at a university like Hofstra that we hear from the man whose life has been dedicated in large part to education and to higher education. Frank Keppel, as you can see from your program, was United States commissioner of education under President Kennedy and he achieved many significant advances in the field of education similar to the type that Wilbur was talking about in the area of health and human services. He is now not only senior lecturer at Harvard, but associated as senior fellow at the Aspen Institute.

When President Johnson asked me to put together legislation for the so-called war against poverty, in fact I didn't really know what the war against poverty consisted of. So I went scrounging around in the private sector, the public sector, in any sector I could find an idea, to put into this legislation, which didn't even exist, the purpose of which was to minimize, if not eradicate, poverty.

One day, Frank Keppel called up and said, "You know Sarge, I've got this idea, but it wasn't going to be easy to sell it in the Education Committee. Do you think you could put it into the war against poverty?" And he told me and I thought, my God, that's a natural for us, give it to me. And I said fine, and he said to me fine, and I stuck it into the legislation that we sent up to the Hill. It passed. And then to my astonishment, immediately after it passed, Frank Keppel got the president to take it away from us and give it to him. Which should be an object lesson to all of you, how government works.

FRANCIS KEPPEL

I've got three points to make which relate to the then and now, which I understand to be our problem. [In the] early 1960s, the federal government's role in education was really quite small. If you took an estimate, the amount of money the federal government appropriated in relation to the total cost of schools and colleges, [was] 1–2 percent, something like that. Now I guess it's 8–9 percent.

Principally, what the department, then called Office of Education, did was to support vocational education. It had small programs after Sputnik, devised to frighten Khrushchev, by teaching foreign languages and sciences. I'm not sure that it accomplished that, but that's what they did. By the end of Mr. Johnson's time, that figure in dollars, and I don't think that's the proper measure, had probably gone up to 8 or 9 percent or perhaps 10 percent. A relative small percent of the total educational aspect of the United States, but a very great increase in a very short time. What went into that?

[First,] the focus was on the poor and minorities. That was the focus of elementary, secondary, and higher education. There was a clear focus, clearly led by the White House, and as commissioner of education, my job was to wander around and try and get the Congress to pass bills. But it is quite clear what had been there before me and what passed the bills—and here I'll say this for the first time publicly—[was the] antipoverty program. I don't have much doubt about that. There was a focus as to what we were going to do for poor kids in cities and the elementary system, for getting various forms of financial aid, including for higher education. The point [is,] there was a focus. People agreed to that.

The second point I'd like to make is that in those days the legislation would by and large pass through [with] very substantial bipartisan support. And it was quite genuine bipartisan support, and President Johnson was very clear that he wanted bipartisan support when he had plenty of a [partisan] majority in the House in 1965. But my instructions were not to beat the Republicans over the head. My instructions were to build more solidly, and I think we've got a case to make now, and this is my second point. That legislation, although it's been reauthorized a couple of times and voted on God knows how many times in Appropriations, has not fundamentally changed—despite vigorous assaults, partly by the Nixon administration and partly by the present one, but more so by the present one. It simply has been maintained, and by bipartisan support. I think it's a fundamental point again that I'm afraid is often missed.

Now the third point I want to make is one that doesn't have any publicity. I mentioned [that] the Office of Education was collecting statistics, usually late. They were started slowly under Mr. Kennedy and put into effect under Mr. Johnson. We'll give you figures about numbers of buildings, of heat and light and costs and teachers and all that stuff but very little was ever assembled as to what students learned. And starting principally in President Johnson's time, when he put the thing in his budget, we now have samples that can give you data on students' readings in the primary and secondary schools. [We'd] never had it before. I think you can be quite sure that it will continue in the years to come, and I think it may be one of those sleepers. Even the present administration has discovered its virtue. So Mr. Cohen is right. You build on something that was started before.

MODERATOR: SARGENT SHRIVER

I have a particular pleasure in presenting the next member of this panel. My pleasure derives from the very first time I ever met Adam Yarmolinsky right up to the moment now when I find myself sitting next to him in front of you. First time I ever saw Adam was during the period when, at President Kennedy's request, a few of us were trying to put together the cabinet for him. We were in the rented remains of a building that was destined for destruction—it had already been condemned, it was in a very sad state of disrepair—and the door opened. There were about four of us in there, and Adam came walking through, and so far as I know, nobody on the inside really knew who this was. He said, "Is this where you are all working on the campaign putting together the cabinet?" We said, "Yes." He said, "Well, may I help?" Somebody said, "Well, who are you?" and he said what he had been doing. We said, "Take the desk over there." Adam never left. He was the source of more good ideas, he did more research, he created more information about the cabinet than any other single person, and he got paid nothing for it.

I tell that little story because it's almost symbolic of the way many people came to work in what was called the New Frontier and continued on because they believed that they could make the federal government a servant of the people, all the people, especially poor people. But they had a dedication about government which led them to believe that they could enlist in the service of the people of the United States the very best persons in our society.

Looking backward, I hope that there's some erudite professor here who can tell me if I am wrong, but looking backward, I think that the cabinet that was put together, not just the cabinet members themselves, but the subcabinet and then the assistant secretaries in the Kennedy administration, that cabinet stayed in service longer than any cabinet in the twentieth century. And secondly, I believe that the cabinet is the only cabinet in this century no member of which quit under public scrutiny, no member of which was ever convicted of any crime, no member of which ever was accused of fraud, no member of which was ever accused of self-serving or making money at the public's expense. Bob Mc-Namara, and this is just one example, made a quick computation in five minutes, when I saw him for the first time in my life in Detroit, that to join Kennedy's cabinet at a salary of $25,000 a year would cost him and his wife and family between seven and twelve million dollars. That's 1960 now that I'm talking about, 1960–'61. That's as if today a potential cabinet member was being asked to surrender $100 million out of his pocket to go and work for the government.

It took Bob McNamara about thirty seconds to make that decision, and he said to me, "Mr. Shriver, I've got more money already than anybody in the McNamara family ever had. I've got enough money already for my wife and kids. Let's forget the amount of money I will lose if I go to Washington and join the cabinet." That cabinet which Adam did so much to create, as I say, I believe was the best cabinet in this century, but that didn't stop Adam's contribution. Subsequently, when President Johnson proposed the Office of Economic Opportunity, or as he called it the war against poverty, Adam quit the Defense Department, where he was assistant to Secretary McNamara and came over once again as a volunteer, went to work once again in a building which had already been designated for destruction, where it was said it was dangerous to walk up the steps. Adam went to work in the so-called task force to create the war against poverty.

It was he who had the vision to bring the Legal Services Program into creation. It was he who worked out the details of the Job Corps. It was he who was instrumental in working out the detail in every program, in bringing into existence nearly every program, some of the good and bad in the war against poverty, and he continues to be that epitome of a public spirited citizen who has always thought of the general welfare rather than his own.

ADAM YARMOLINSKY

I want to try very briefly to talk to three questions. First, what was the Great Society and what did it amount to, beyond the phrase in the history books? Second, what has it left behind in the somewhat alien climate of the somewhat acquisitive society in which we live today, and third, what lessons, if any, does it teach us for the future, both for the presidency and for American society?

What was it? Well, it was a surge, a tidal wave of social legislation and up-welling of concern in government for those whom the marketplace doesn't always reward, whether they are poor, old, young, or sick. The corner of the Great Society that I worked in was the development of the poverty program, overseeing the drafting of new legislation [and] the creation of a new agency, the Office of Economic Opportunity. I didn't get to work for the program itself, but that is another story.

The poverty program was designed on several fundamental assumptions. I begin if I may with my definition of poverty at the time—and which I have not been able to improve on since—and that is, a person is poor if he or she lacks either the capability or the opportunity to make a contribution to society for which society is willing to reward [him]. I don't tie it to money income. I tie to a kind of reciprocal relationship between the individual and society which poor people just don't have. I think the first fundamental premise of the anti-poverty program really relates to that definition: that it was more important to get people out of poverty than to make them more comfortable, if that were possible, in their condition. Not only did we decide that it was more important to get them out, but it was more important, given the circumstances in the mid–1960s, to prepare people for jobs, because after all, it's useful productive em-ployment that is inconsistent with being in a state of poverty. It's more important to prepare people for jobs than to prepare jobs for people.

One of the reasons for that was that the tax cut, we thought, would be producing the jobs. We also thought that it would take longer to get the hard core poor—the people who not only didn't have skills, but also had not had the opportunity to learn about getting up at the same time in the morning, going to work and doing what the boss said—to learn those basic skills than it was to find the jobs in which they would do them. And we also decided that it was probably more important to concentrate on the rising generation, the younger generation, be-cause those were the people whom if they were not brought out of poverty, would produce the next generation of the under-class, the poverty class. And last but not least important, we understood that we had less than a billion dollars to spend on the first year, and we needed to produce the kind of results that would justify a second year of appropriations, even before the first twelve months of the program were up. That was the primary reason we put so much emphasis on the Job Corps, the residential camps which are still going and still functioning.

Some problems fell by the wayside. We did have an ambitious land reform program, which sounded too much like communist China I guess; it got cut out. We had a program of public service employment, which got cut out because it would cost too much money. The Office of Economic Opportunity itself had two roles; it had the role of operating programs and coordinating the work of other agencies in the war on poverty. That coordinating job, as any student of government will tell you, is a very hard thing for one agency to do to other agencies, and that was not the most successful part of the program.

But look at the legacy, the Job Corps, VISTA [Volunteers in Service to America], which is still going strong, Community Service, Legal Services. There must be a thousand or more Legal Services offices functioning now across the United States. Programs that you may not be aware of, like foster grandparents, which has a certain air perhaps of do-goodism, hung on and works. But I'd like to suggest that perhaps the most important legacy of community action is the idea of mutual reliance, which is at least as old as the country. De Tocqueville notes it, [and] it was certainly reinforced by community action programs. It reinforced solidarity, and it reinforced another great American tradition, and that's "uppityness." It was very good for "uppityness," and I don't think that we are ever going to be able to ever go back to the way [it was] before community action came along.

Of course some of the most troublesome problems that the poverty program was designed to deal with have gotten worse: youth unemployment, family disintegration, teenage pregnancy. We haven't figured out how to deal with them, but one thing I believe is clear—they are not going to solve themselves. Those who have advocated benign neglect don't have the answer.

Last question. What lessons, if any, for the future of the presidency and the future of our society can be derived from that experience? Well, the first lesson, and I think Wilbur was talking about that, is that legislation is very hard to achieve. Dean Acheson had three boxes on his desk, the "in" and "out" boxes and the third box was marked "too hard." Legislative programs mostly belong in that box. Second, I think we've learned that we neglect the unfortunate in our society at our peril. And third, on something of a lighter note, I think one of the lessons for all of us is that government can be fun—an idea I think that would puzzle some of the present incumbents of the offices that we once occupied.

MODERATOR: SARGENT SHRIVER

Our next speaker always got fun out of government, I'm sure of that. He had a second unusual aspect of his record, namely, that he was in the United States government from the very beginning of the Kennedy administration to the very end of the Johnson administration. In other words, he ran the full course, eight years. There were a lot of us who did not have the stamina to stay in there as long as Bob Weaver did.

We all know about the current criticisms of one type or another concerning government housing. We don't hear as much, I think, of what the condition would be for all the people who now live in government housing if there were no housing for them at all. I don't think that it can be said that if there had never been any federal housing or home financing that all these people would be successful entrepreneurs and that they'd all be living out in Scarsdale because they would have made so much money that they could build private housing of their own. I think that it is true that if men like Bob Weaver hadn't created a huge number of housing units for lower income people that today in the U.S. we would have a desolate picture, a desolate reality, with respect to millions and millions of our fellow citizens who would be living without any roof over their heads. So I'm very pleased personally, and happy to be sitting next to him and happy to have a chance to present to you, a man who gave shelter to the homeless here in our own country, at a time when there were millions of Americans who needed it. And that's a wonderful legacy to leave for any public official in any society.

ROBERT WEAVER

I'm going to talk about the Great Society primarily from the point of view of the cities and housing. I do this because Lyndon Johnson brought to the presidency tremendous interest in urban America—an interest that would not be expected from his geographical background, but would be understandable, particularly the housing part, by his legislative background. He had been one of the earlier supporters of the Public Housing Bill and had brought, I believe it was to Austin, certainly to a part of his congressional district, one of the first public housing projects. So he knew about it, he felt about it, and he did about it. I remember too that he was the first president ever to make a message to Congress which was given over exclusively to the problems of the city. On 2 March 1965, he said that the problems of the city represented some of the greatest challenges and the greatest problems of America. He knew what those problems were, and he felt them. He felt that the problems were problems of service, financing for aging infrastructure, and financing for better development and better planning in the urban areas, and also a concern for the aesthetics of the city. [He never forgot] the fact, [however,] that cities are people and people problems are equally as important as the physical problem.

That was the key to his approach to the area in which I operated. I also would like to say that it seems to be, as I look back, that the greatest, although far from the sole contribution of the Great Society, was to move the nation toward a more equitable society, mitigating the problems of the disadvantaged and discriminated. It was to this general background that its chief architect, Lyndon Johnson, brought vision, commitment, and superb political skill. Although there was some hyperbole, particularly in the rhetoric, and sometimes that led to spectacular goals which made the program implausible, most of us survived. As I look back, I am confident that if there had not been some of that hyperbole, if there hadn't been some goals that were accused of being unrealistic at the time, people would not have thought big, and if they didn't think big they couldn't think like Lyndon Johnson thought and they wouldn't have gotten the legislation.

So it wasn't a one-way street, but those of us who had the responsibility of getting the bills enacted in Congress sometimes wished that the speaker hadn't been quite so good. The housing and urban development activities of the Great Society were of such a magnitude as had never been contemplated in this country before. They covered so many areas and they dealt with so many people problems. But they also dealt with economic problems, because the Great Society's approach to housing was not only concerned with housing for low and moderate income families; it was concerned [also] with housing as a source of economic development, economic well-being and employment. And it was also a concern for housing, because housing had so much to do with the family welfare and community well-being.

The list of the Great Society's housing and urban development legislation is lengthy. It not only included such basic laws as rent supplements, model cities, urban mass transit, urban research, urban fellowships, new communities, Title 6 of the Civil Rights Act of 1964, Title 8 of the Civil Rights Act of the following year, and the Housing and Urban Development Act of the same year, but also legislation not specifically focused on urban or housing problems. Included were numerous laws involving taxes, income support, health care, compensatory education, manpower problems, and other statutes which affected the quality of urban life. So this was a broad program, and it was a program which embraced not only what we were doing in HHFA [Housing and Home Finance Agency] and in HUD [Housing and Urban Development] but which many other agencies and departments were doing.

In order to give some notion of what this meant to the country, I have a favorite quotation which I will now share with you. It was written in the fall of 1968 by Ada Louise Huxtable, who was the architectural critic of the *New York Times*. She wrote, and I quote, "The Johnson administration has made a start at providing 26 million houses and apartments in the next ten years, of rebuilding the cities, and of tying physical and social needs and programs together, or visualizing a new urban America. It leaves the three year Department of Housing and Urban Development and the 1968 Housing Bill as the most complicated and sophisticated attack on the nation's ill, to come out of any Congress. For once, political understanding of the urban crisis has gone beyond housing to the total environment. From the advanced planning and financing of new communities, to long overdue governmental programs for innovation in the design and technology of low cost housing." End of quote.

Other major legacies were the forging of an effective broad-based coalition to support HUD and related legislation and new tools for increasing appreciably the volume of low and moderate income housing and for prohibiting racial discrimination itself. At the same time, the initial steps of the Kennedy administration, the humanized urban renewals were greatly expanded and accelerated. Equally significant was the Great Society's achievement of a dramatic rise in the national priority of housing and urban development. It was in that background that the Nixon administration began the process of tearing down what had been built. This was done for philosophical, ideological, and economic reasons. It also was done at a time when neoconservatism had more or less captured academia, and it wasn't fashionable to write about social problems, except to say that they couldn't be solved and you couldn't do anything about them. It was a time when there was a great feeling of animosity toward government, and so it was easy to say none of the programs worked and the Great Society is a failure and nowhere is the failure more apparent than in housing. They said it and they got away with it.

They got away with it in spite of the fact that when the moratorium was placed on all subsidized housing, it took them eight months to get a rationale, and they published that rationale eight months after the fact. It was a very faulted document. Actually, the reason that their attack was made on the subsidized housing wasn't because it was a failure, but because it was too much of a success. So they came up with housing allowances, and one of the reasons they came up with housing allowances was because this demand-oriented type of subsidized housing was equitable, whereas the supply type, such as we had done, the production of housing, was not equitable because some didn't get it. Of course, that was absolute poppycock since determination of whether or not everybody gets shelter isn't in the formula. After they cut off the subsidized housing in the form they had inherited it and had proposed the housing allowances, they did not appropriate the funds for the housing allowances that we are speaking about. So, the equity was lost, and it was a phony issue from the start. The real problem with the programs, particularly the two that were instituted in 1968, one for homeowners and the other for renters, was because of the administration of them. There were tremendous numbers of indictments in the Justice Department. People were hoodwinked, people were sold houses without furnaces, they were sold houses that didn't keep out the rain. And this was done, as we anticipated, because of narrow administration and lax administration. In some instances we even discovered that the low down payment, which was something like 5 percent, would be paid by the person who sold the house, then he'd leave town and would get enough profit and the buyer couldn't find out where he was.

The other problem was of course that the whole idea was *production, production, production*, and with that came great abuses. The General Accounting Office in 1978, long after the thing had sobered down slightly, made an investigation of the rental program. It found that it was a success in the sense that it was the best type of rental program for moderate income housing that had ever been established.

Now after this initial problem, the programs of Housing and Urban Development, particularly the programs of housing, were constantly changed, and before a program could get down to the point where you could sort of resolve its problems, it was supplanted by another program which would have its own problems. And so the usual process of aging and of working out the problems was denied to this part of the Great Society. The Carter administration came in, and for a time brought a breath of fresh air. It reinstituted some of the earlier programs, introduced new ones, and it began to talk about some of the problems that the Great Society had been concerned with. Only at the end [it] fell victim to the conservative fiscal policies that were inaugurated, and its achievements relapsed.

However, the nadir was reached with the present Reagan administration. Here there has been a series of cutbacks, changes of priorities, priorities shifted away from the poor to the affluent. There is a cutback in subsidizing housing, to the point where it was practically wiped out. And the problems that were of major concern to the Great Society have become secondary, if not ignored. The emphasis is upon economic growth, operation of the market, reliance upon the trickle down process to alleviate the deprivation of the needy, and shifting the programs from federal to state and local government.

Now let me say in closing that any program as massive and as complicated as the Great Society is bound to have structural problems. It's bound to present problems of administration, but I think the record will show that the main problem with the Great Society housing and urban development program has not been the nature of the program, but the philosophy, the policies, and the administrative procedures of the four administrations that succeeded it.

Finally, unfortunately we are not as well off in housing as in education. The basic legislation in HUD has been tinkered with and greatly weakened and some of its bases extinguished. I could demonstrate this by simply reading off, which I will not take the time to do; what the budget which was proposed for fiscal year 1986 provided. Cutbacks here, moratoriums there, abolishing programs elsewhere. This not only affected housing, but it also affected those programs within the other agencies which relate to urban development.

There is a sufficient amount of need out there and there is a sufficient amount of basic legislation still in existence to make me not a pessimist, but a guarded optimist. And to say that in all of this, even looking back over these mean years, I consider the eight years that I spent with the Kennedy and Johnson administrations, the association that I had with these and other gentlemen, as the most productive, the most enjoyable and God knows the most exciting years of my life.

MODERATOR: SARGENT SHRIVER

The title of our panel was "The Great Society: Then and Now." It seems to me that really what we have been talking about, from different points of view, is truthfully "The American Society: Then and Now," not just "The Great

Society.'' And I hope that those of you who have been here today will go away with at least one impression. And that is that the people here on this panel and others like them, who could be sitting here, are happy people, they are buoyant people, they are upbeat people. Nobody up here has a sense of defeat or of having suffered a cataclysmic failure, despite what some experts are writing today. A famous governor in New York was described by Franklin Roosevelt way back eons ago as the Happy Warrior. That was Al Smith.

The Happy Warrior phrase or title could be applied to Wilbur Cohen, who certainly has been a happy warrior for the benefit of the poor. To Adam Yarmolinsky, to Bob Weaver, and to Frank Keppel. These people were in the Great Society, but more than that, they were dedicated to the American society as a whole.

II

EQUAL JUSTICE AND THE JUDICIARY

7

"To Write It in the Books of Law": President Lyndon B. Johnson and the Civil Rights Act of 1964

Robert D. Loevy

Enactment of the Civil Rights Act of 1964 has been heralded as one of the great achievements of Lyndon B. Johnson and his presidential administration. The new law banned racial segregation in public facilities throughout the United States, cut off U.S. government funds to public or private programs that practiced discrimination, and outlawed racial and sex bias in employment. More importantly, the new law ended an era of congressional impotence on civil rights legislation and inaugurated a new era of firmness that eventually produced the Voting Rights Act of 1965 and the Housing Rights Act of 1968.

Despite the significance of the Civil Rights Act of 1964, there has been no major study of President Lyndon Johnson's exact role in the enactment of that legislation. Was Lyndon Johnson a key actor in the passage of the bill, or did he merely preside from the White House over legislative efforts carried out mainly by others? There is also the question of whether Lyndon Johnson or his assassinated predecessor, President John F. Kennedy, deserved the most credit for getting such a strong civil rights bill enacted into law.

A review of available congressional and presidential materials indicates that Lyndon Johnson played a more than leading role in the enactment of the Civil Rights Act of 1964. Major conclusions to be drawn are: (1) Lyndon Johnson was a strong supporter of the Civil Rights Bill even before he became president. (2) At the time of the assassination of President Kennedy when Johnson became president, Johnson was viewed by black leaders in the nation as a supporter of civil rights who could be trusted to get a civil rights bill from Congress. (3) President Johnson erred in pressing for a discharge petition to free the Civil Rights Bill from the House Rules Committee, but he quickly saw his error and changed his position. (4) President Johnson did a masterful job of using the publicity powers of the presidency to press for the Civil Rights Bill. (5) Johnson took the lead in opposing Alabama Governor George Wallace's bid for the 1964 Democratic presidential nomination, thereby aiding the Civil Rights Bill, because Wallace based his campaign on opposition to the bill. (6) Johnson took a leading role in getting Senate Republican leader Everett Dirksen to support the bill and thus gained enough Republican votes to end a southern Democratic filibuster in the Senate.

SUPPORT FOR CIVIL RIGHTS AS VICE PRESIDENT

Following major demonstrations opposing racial segregation in Birmingham, Alabama, in May 1963, President John F. Kennedy decided to send a major civil rights bill to Congress. On June 3, 1963, just four days after President Kennedy made that decision, Assistant Attorney General Norbert A. Schlei met with Vice President Lyndon Johnson to discuss the proposed administration bill. After stating his complete loyalty to President Kennedy and his willingness to support whatever decisions the president might make, Johnson then proceeded to outline an extensive plan for getting a major civil rights bill through both the House and the Senate. Item number one on Johnson's list was taking a bipartisan approach.

Johnson told Schlei:

[President Kennedy should] call in the Republican leaders, tell them about the plans and put them on the spot; make them give their promises in blood to support the legislation in an agreed form, indicating that credit would be shared with them for the success achieved and indicating that any failure on their part to agree and to deliver would be laid unmistakably at their doors.[1]

The vice president then proceeded to give Schlei the numerical reasons a bipartisan approach was absolutely essential. Southern Democrats in the Senate would filibuster the proposed Civil Rights Bill, and the only way the Southern tactic could be stopped would be a two-thirds cloture vote. Johnson said:

[The civil rights forces] would need twenty-seven out of the thirty-three Republican votes in the Senate in order to obtain cloture, and as matters now stand we have no prospect at all of getting that many. We would be able to get that many only if we could enlist the full support of Senator Dirksen [the Republican leader in the Senate], among others.[2]

By mid-June 1963, a bipartisan approach similar to the one suggested by Johnson was official Kennedy administration strategy, and it was evident that Senator Everett Dirksen of Illinois would be viewed as the key to getting the bill through the Senate. More importantly, the Schlei meeting with Lyndon Johnson indicated that the vice president was a strong supporter of civil rights legislation before he became president and was more than willing, when asked, to participate in Kennedy administration strategy making to get the bill through Congress.

Vice President Johnson was next involved when President Kennedy called the major civil rights leaders to a conference at the White House to convince them that his Civil Rights Bill was the best that could be achieved under the circumstances. Kennedy gave a brief talk, stressing the need for an all-out effort by everybody in the room to mobilize the public behind his bill.

President Kennedy left the meeting and was replaced by Vice President Johnson. When asked what would happen if civil rights supporters were to lobby Congress hard to strengthen the Kennedy proposed bill, Johnson replied that there must be flexibility in a campaign of this kind, and he saw no problems with the various civil rights groups going beyond the Kennedy administration bill in their demands. Johnson's endorsement of civil rights supporters working to strengthen the Kennedy bill was another indication that the vice president was pro–civil rights prior to his becoming president.[3]

During the fall of 1963 there is no written record of Vice President Johnson being very much involved in the Civil Rights Bill. The Kennedy administration bill advanced through favorable committee hearings in the House of Representatives. At a series of meetings at the White House in late November 1963, President Kennedy and Democratic and Republican leaders hammered out a compromise, bipartisan version of the Civil Rights Bill that all parties agreed to support, both in the House Rules Committee and when the bill came up for a final vote in the House of Representatives.

JOHNSON'S RELATIONSHIP TO BLACK POLITICAL LEADERS

The assassin's bullets that killed President Kennedy in Dallas changed many things, but nothing quite so much as the political situation concerning civil rights. At the time Vice President Johnson became president, there was much comment about the fact that he was a Democrat from the southern state of Texas. At first some national political commentators believed this would doom the Civil Rights Bill, but actually the reverse situation was the case. As a southerner, Lyndon Johnson was mainly concerned with winning political support in the north. He would have to run for reelection in 1964, and he had less than a year to convince skeptical northern and western liberals that a southerner was an acceptable leader for the national Democratic party.

This idea that a southern president such as Lyndon Johnson would work extra hard to prove he was not racist was described by Louis Martin, deputy chairman of the Democratic National Committee under President Johnson. Martin recalled:

Since Johnson was a southerner, he would normally, being a politician, lean over backwards to prove that he was not a racist. Further, there is something in the folklore of Negro life that a reconstructed southerner is really far more liberal than a liberal yankee.[4]

President Johnson seized on the civil rights bill as the perfect instrument for establishing his credentials with northern and western liberals. Five days after

John F. Kennedy's assassination, the new president asked a joint session of the House and Senate to adopt the Civil Rights Bill as a memorial to his slain predecessor. "We have talked long enough in this country about equal rights," Johnson told the Congress. "It is time now to write the next chapter—and to write it in the books of law."[5]

Back on 4 June 1963, when Assistant Attorney General Norbert A. Schlei had interviewed then Vice President Johnson about the strategies for getting a civil rights bill passed, Johnson had outlined to Schlei exactly how he would attempt to get support and loyalty from black political leaders. Schlei reported:

[Johnson] said he would call in all of the Negro leaders of importance in the country and would tell them that the administration was unreservedly on their side in the battle for the objectives they have been seeking. He would tell them that the administration intended to seek civil rights legislation . . . before the end of the session; that the bill would be introduced and considered as soon as the president's tax [cut] program was enacted or defeated, one way or the other and that Congress would stay in Washington until hell freezes over if necessary in order to get the [civil rights] legislation passed. . . . He would tell the Negro leaders that their help would be absolutely essential in getting the Civil Rights Bill enacted. He would tell them that we need . . . Republican votes in the Senate and ask them to get busy on the task of obtaining them. He said he thought what the Negro leaders wanted was an absolute assurance, that we were with them and that we meant business. . . .[6]

Upon becoming president himself, Johnson's first move was to implement the strategy he had outlined to Schlei. He called black leaders and civil rights leaders to well-publicized meetings in the Oval Office at the White House. As Johnson himself told it: "I spoke with black groups and with individual leaders of the black community and told them that John Kennedy's dream of equality had not died with him. I assured them that I was going to press for the Civil Rights Bill with every ounce of energy I possessed."[7]

Apparently the principal black leaders in the nation were ready to believe in Johnson and his commitment to civil rights and the Civil Rights Bill. The oral history statements at the Johnson presidential library indicate that most of the black leaders saw the new president, despite being a southerner from Texas, as pro–civil rights and, in some cases, better able than President Kennedy to get a civil rights bill past the many legislative roadblocks in Congress.

Roy Wilkins, president of the NAACP (National Association for the Advancement of Colored People, a leading civil rights group), saw Johnson's pro–civil rights views as having become visible during the Kennedy administration:

Mr. Johnson began to emerge during the Kennedy administration wholly unexpectedly and to the delight of the civil rights forces in areas that we didn't expect him to be active [in] as vice president. For example, he took a very personal concern on the fair employment business. He . . . called all manner of people—unions and employees[—]all over the country on the matter of increasing their employment of Negroes. Now, for a vice president of the United States to do this, and especially a man who knew his way around . . . Washington, this was very effective.[8]

Clarence Mitchell, Jr., Washington director of the NAACP was receptive to Johnson because Johnson had been friendly to him when other southerners had been unfriendly:

It might be a little difficult for some people who were living in that period to understand this, but the southern contingent in Congress at that time was so hostile that when someone [Lyndon Johnson] came in [from the south] who was not hostile, you immediately felt that here was somebody you could respect and would like to work with, and would like to maintain their friendship.[9]

In addition to reassuring black political leaders of his support for the Civil Rights Bill, President Johnson was urged by White House staff to press these leaders for a reduction in racial protests and demonstrations. One memorandum to the president from White House staff noted: "Although a moratorium on demonstrations is probably not possible, whatever the [black] leadership can do to restrain physical activities or channel energies and interest into such positive programs as education and vocational training should be encouraged."[10]

If there were going to be racial protests and demonstrations, White House staff hoped that President Johnson could get the black political leaders to co-operate with one another and to keep the White House informed about what they were planning to do. A White House memorandum noted that President Johnson was "making a personal plea" to CORE (Congress of Racial Equality, an aggressive pro–civil rights group) to "work with the other [civil rights] groups . . . and try to coordinate . . . activities through the White House. . . ."[11]

JOHNSON AND THE DISCHARGE PETITION

At the time of President Kennedy's assassination, the Civil Rights Bill had cleared the House Judiciary Committee and was waiting to be taken up by the House Rules Committee. Civil rights supporters had good reason to think that the Civil Rights Bill would experience long delay and possibly a slow death before the House Rules Committee. Committee Chairman Howard Smith had a way of vanishing from Washington for days on end when a bill he did not like was before the Rules Committee. In 1957 Smith disappeared to his Virginia farm because, according to him, his dairy barn had burned down. He absented himself again in 1959, claiming that his dairy cattle were sick and required his full attention. On both occasions liberals were awaiting a rule on a bill that Smith strongly opposed.[12]

On 3 December 1963, President Johnson told Democratic congressional leaders he would give full support to a discharge petition to dislodge the Civil Rights Bill from the Rules Committee.[13] If a majority of the members of the House signed the discharge petition, the bill would move directly from the Rules Committee to the House floor.

Apparently, President Johnson believed that, with the successful adoption of a discharge petition, Rules Committee action and House of Representatives action on the Civil Rights Bill could be completed before Christmas of 1963. Immediately following the assassination of President Kennedy, he told an off-the-record gathering of the nation's governors: "We are hoping that we can get a rule on that bill [the Civil Rights Bill] and get it passed [in] the House and as far along in the Senate as we can this session, and then come back in the early part of the next session and finish that."[14]

On 9 December, 1963, House Judiciary Chairman Emanuel Celler officially filed a discharge petition on the Civil Rights Bill. Now that the discharge petition actually existed and could formally be signed by members of the House, President Johnson's support could be more than just verbal. Each day the new president was briefed on who had signed the petition, and "holdouts" would get a personal telephone call directly from the president himself.[15] The White House was so committed to the discharge petition that plans were made to get the assistance of prominent businessmen to lobby representatives who had not signed the petition.[16]

More than 100 representatives signed the discharge petition the first day it was available, but a considerable number resisted signing. The problem was that the discharge petition was opposed by the House Republican leadership. Citing their late-night meetings at the White House with President Kennedy, Republican leaders argued that they had an agreement with the Democratic leadership to furnish Republican votes to clear the bill through the Rules Committee. The only reason the liberal Democrats were circulating the discharge petition, the Republicans charged, was so they could get all the credit for getting the Civil Rights Bill out of the Rules Committee. The Democrats, the Republicans said, wanted to prevent civil rights supporters throughout the nation from seeing that there was strong Republican support for the Civil Rights Bill on the Rules Committee.[17]

President Johnson was aware that the Republicans had agreed to provide the necessary votes to get the Civil Rights Bill out of the Rules Committee. As vice president, he had been present when one of the Republican leaders made his commitment to President Kennedy. In off-the-record remarks to the nation's governors meeting with Johnson at the White House immediately following the assassination, Johnson said, "A Republican leader told President Kennedy in my presence that he would help him get it [the Civil Rights Bill] reported and help get it passed."[18]

Despite the fact that Lyndon Johnson had been present when one of the House Republican leaders had committed himself to the Civil Rights Bill, the strong Republican opposition to the discharge petition came as a surprise to the Johnson White House. In a memorandum to President Johnson dated 29 November 1963, Lawrence F. O'Brien, special assistant to the president for congressional relations, suggested that the White House actively seek Republican signatures for the discharge petition. O'Brien wrote: "[In] order to have the Civil Rights Bill enacted, we must have . . . sixty to seventy House Republicans on the discharge petition. . . . The immediate signal is to push House Republicans generally to sign the discharge petition. . . ."[19]

Five days later, at his first breakfast with the Democratic congressional leadership at the White House, President Johnson proposed that the Republicans be asked to sign the discharge petition "man for man" with the Democrats. The president said, "Does everybody agree that you get as many signatures as you can? Then tell the Republicans they must match us man for man." Later in the breakfast, Johnson stated traditional objections to signing a discharge petition but noted the unusualness of the situation: "I was always reluctant to sign a discharge petition, but you have a great moral issue. People have been denied a right they should have—a discussion in [the House of Representatives].[20]

By 13 December 1963 only 150 of the needed 218 signatures had been obtained, and conspicuously absent from the discharge petition were the names of such key pro–civil rights Democrats as House Speaker John W. McCormack of Massachusetts and House Democratic Leader Carl Albert of Oklahoma. These top Democratic House leaders had negotiated the agreement with the Republican House leaders to vote the bill out of the Rules Committee at the appropriate time, and they were most anxious to in no way disturb that bipartisan agreement. Apparently, President Johnson came to agree with this strategy, because the White House pressure to sign the discharge petition ceased.

On 23 January 1964, House Democratic Leader Carl Albert of Oklahoma announced that the bipartisan Civil Rights Bill would be reported out of the House Rules Committee on 30 January and that floor debate in the House of Representatives would begin the next day. On 30 January by a vote of eleven to four, the bill was sent to the House floor.[21] The Republicans, as they had agreed to do, delivered the needed votes to move the Civil Rights Bill through the Rules Committee.

President Johnson thus appears to have made a mistake in initially supporting the discharge petition without first checking to see how the House Republicans felt about it. He also appears to have backed away quickly from the drive for discharge petition signatures when he learned it would cost him badly needed Republican support in the House.

JOHNSON THE LEGISLATIVE TACTICIAN

At a White House press conference in late January 1964, President Johnson gave what looked like a "go ahead" for some sort of women's rights amendment to be added to the bipartisan Civil Rights Bill when it reached the floor of the House of Representatives. In response to a reporter's question about banning discrimination against women in the Civil Rights Bill, the president said: "I realize there has been discrimination in the employment of women, and I am doing my best to do something about it. I am hopeful that in the next month we will have made substantial advances in that field."[22]

Although the president did not say specifically that he wanted a women's rights amendment added to the Civil Rights Bill, his answer left no doubt that he was a supporter of the principle of equal rights for women, particularly where equal employment opportunity was concerned. He left the option open for the Civil Rights Bill to be amended to ban discrimination on the basis of sex, and such a provision was added to the bill while it was before the House of Representatives.

At the time the Civil Rights Bill was being debated and voted upon in the House of Representatives, Democratic Representative Robert T. Ashmore of South Carolina offered an amendment creating a Community Relations Service to help mediate racial disputes in cities and towns throughout the United States. The idea for a U.S. government agency to mediate between black protesters and local government officials had originated with Lyndon Johnson when he was the Democratic leader in the United States Senate.

The Birmingham demonstrations had given several persons the idea for a Community Relations Service similar to the one that Johnson had been proposing. A memorandum from George E. Reedy to then vice president Lyndon Johnson on 7 June 1963 illustrates this point:

Ramsey Clark has . . . proposals. [One is a] community relations service similar to the one that you have proposed. The amazing part of this to me is that Ramsey, on the basis of one trip to Birmingham, returned thinking precisely along the same lines that you have been thinking for a number of years—that conciliators could perform a world of good in this situation.[23]

Representative Ashmore's amendment creating a Community Relations Service was passed without significant debate. It thus should be noted that Lyndon Johnson made a substantive contribution to the Civil Rights Bill. The Community Relations Service was an idea he had backed both as a senator and vice president. His claim to authorship of that particular provision of the bill is undisputed.

On 10 February 1964, the House of Representatives passed the Civil Rights Bill by a vote of 290 to 130. Exactly as it was designed to do, the bipartisan agreement that President Kennedy had negotiated at the White House back in October 1963 had carried the Civil Rights Bill through both the House Rules Committee and the House of Representatives itself. *Congressional Quarterly* heralded the House bill as "the most sweeping civil rights measure to clear either house of Congress in the 20th Century."[24]

The news media gave much of the credit for getting the Civil Rights Bill through the House to President Lyndon Johnson, although many were careful to point out that "President Kennedy had already laid the groundwork for congressional action."[25]

Apparently, President Johnson was involved in the day-to-day efforts to get the bill through the House. He was so involved, in fact, that several of his close advisers at the White House worried he was overusing his congressional influence. The president's aides, in fact, were warning him that he might be dissipating his considerable influence over Congress with too many phone calls and elbow squeezings. "We don't want him to be one of the boys," said one aide, "we only want to use these calls where they will have maximum impact."[26]

Clearly there was considerable determination on Johnson's part to be intimately involved with congressional passage of the Civil Rights Bill. Two of the lobbyists for civil rights, Clarence Mitchell and Joseph Rauh, had expected to have a moment of rest once the Civil Rights Bill had been passed by the House. There was not rest, however, with Lyndon Johnson running the show. Clarence Mitchell and Joseph Rauh both recalled that the bill had just passed the House when a message came to call the president. "What are you fellows doing about the Senate," the commander-in-chief had said, still very much at his post. "We've got it through the House, and now we've got the big job of getting it through the Senate."[27]

President Lyndon Johnson had very skillfully arranged for the Senate to pass every piece of legislation he considered critical before the civil rights filibuster began. Thus, the Kennedy Tax Cut Bill had been moved out of the Senate before the Civil Rights Bill came over from the House of Representatives. A civil rights lobbyist described the strategy this way:

President Johnson had made it clear . . . that he would not care if the Senate did not do another thing for three months until the Civil Rights Bill was enacted. This removed the filibusterers' greatest weapon—that they could hold out until other needed legislation required the Senate to put aside the Civil Rights Bill.[28]

In an off-the-record conversation with Clarence Mitchell concerning the southerners and their filibuster, President Johnson simply said, "Let them talk until summer."[29]

JOHNSON AND THE PUBLICITY POWERS OF THE PRESIDENCY

President Johnson mobilized the vast publicity powers of the White House in behalf of the Civil Rights Bill. In a memorandum summarizing civil rights activities during President Johnson's first 100 days in office, a White House staff member noted the "urgency and importance that have been given to civil rights." Under the topic of "General Attitude," the memorandum emphasized that "numerous presidential speeches and informal statements have made crystal clear the president's commitment to equal treatment and opportunity for all Americans. . . ."[30]

This presidential publicity campaign began with the president's 1964 State of the Union address to Congress. With its pomp and ceremony and live coverage

by all three major television networks, the State of the Union address offered
Lyndon Johnson an opportunity to restate to the American people his commitment
to the cause of civil rights. Early in the speech the president said:

Let this session of Congress be known as the session that did more for civil rights than
the last hundred sessions combined. . . . As far as the writ of Federal law will run, we
must abolish not some but all racial discrimination. For this is not merely an economic
issue—or a social, political or international issue. It is a moral issue—and it must be met
by the passage this session of the bill now pending in the House.[31]

Johnson's statement was forceful. It was the first time an American president
had ever called for eliminating ''all racial discrimination.'' It was also the first
presidential request that it be done ''as far as the writ of federal law will run.''
Johnson concluded the civil rights portion of this State of the Union address with
a patriotic reference to the increasing role that blacks were playing in the American military: ''Today Americans of all races stand side by side in Berlin and
in Vietnam. They died side by side in Korea. Surely they can work and eat and
travel side by side in their own country.''[32]

President Johnson linked the bipartisan Civil Rights Bill to Abraham Lincoln
and the fact that the nation had recently celebrated (in July of 1963) the one
hundredth anniversary of the Emancipation Proclamation. In response to a reporter's question about the Civil Rights Bill at a White House press conference,
Johnson said:

I hope it is acted upon in the House before the members leave to attend Lincoln Day
birthday meetings throughout the nation, because it would be a great tribute to President
Lincoln to have that bill finally acted upon in the House before we go out to celebrate
his birthday.[33]

By the time the Civil Rights Bill arrived in the Senate, President Johnson was
making virtually a statement a week calling for passage of the bill. One week
the president was quoted by congressional leaders as saying he was ''committed''
to the bill with ''no wheels and no deals.''[34] Another week he stated, ''The
Civil Rights Bill which passed the House is the bill that this administration
recommends. . . . Our position is firm and we stand on the House bill.''[35] A week
after that, the president told a news conference, ''I think we passed a good bill
in the House. I hope the same bill will be passed in the Senate. . . . I hope it
[the Senate] stays on the subject until a bill is passed that is acceptable.''[36]

It was almost as if Lyndon Johnson had a speech writer at the White House
working full time thinking up new ways for the president to express his support
for the bill. In a special press interview marking Johnson's first hundred days
in office, the president said:

I think that when the Senate acts upon the Civil Rights Bill, that we will have the best
civil rights law that has been enacted in 100 years, and I think it will be a substantial

and effective answer to our racial problems. . . . I don't want to predict how long it [the Senate] will be discussing this bill. I am hopeful and I am an optimist and I believe they can pass it and I believe they will pass it and I believe it is their duty to pass it, and I am going to do everything I can to get it passed.[37]

As the filibuster wore on, Johnson began directing his remarks somewhat pointedly at the Senate and its failure to act:

Well, they have been debating [the Civil Rights Bill] for a good many days, and obviously there will be much debate yet in the offing. . . . But I believe, after a reasonable time, the majority of the senators will be ready to vote, and I hope that a vote can be worked out.[38]

A week later the president reiterated the point that the Senate would be a long time passing the bill, but a bill would be passed: "I think it [the filibuster] will go on for some time yet, but I believe at the proper time, after all members have had a chance to present their viewpoints both pro and con, the majority of the Senate will work its will and I believe we will pass the bill."[39]

A week after that Johnson was still hammering away at this now-familiar theme, "We need a good Civil Rights Bill, and the bill now pending in the Senate is a good bill. I hope it can be passed in a reasonable time."[40]

By mid-April, however, even the president appeared to be getting exasperated with the torpor that had gripped the Senate. Giving a prepared address to the American Society of Newspaper Editors, Johnson said: "Our nation will live in tormented ease until the Civil Rights Bill now being considered is written into the book of law. The question is no longer, 'Shall it be passed?' The question is, 'When, when, when will it be passed?' "[41]

Johnson's frequent and unequivocal public statements in support of the Civil Rights Bill were certainly his most visible contributions to its final passage. There could be no question that the president expected the bill to be passed and in essentially unchanged form from the version that was approved in the House of Representatives.

JOHNSON AND THE WALLACE CANDIDACY FOR PRESIDENT

Early in 1964, Alabama Governor George Wallace announced that he was a candidate for the Democratic nomination for president of the United States and that he would run on a platform of all-out opposition to the Civil Rights Bill. Governor Wallace was a formidable candidate running on the anti–civil rights platform. He had gained extensive national publicity when he personally "barred the school house door" at the University of Alabama in his futile attempt to prevent integration of the university by U.S. marshals. Although Wallace had been forced to stand aside and let the university be integrated, he had emerged from the fracas as a southern segregationist hero and as the national symbol of opposition to school integration and black civil rights.

The Wallace candidacy produced quick action on President Lyndon Johnson's part. Unwilling to permit "open season" on his administration by running against Wallace himself, Johnson set to work recruiting stand-in candidates to run against Wallace in three crucial Democratic presidential primaries—Wisconsin, Indiana, and Maryland.

If Wallace could win only one presidential primary outside the old south, it was feared that the chances of beating the filibuster of the Civil Rights Bill would be seriously jeopardized. Johnson himself noted that the Wallace campaign "stiffened the southerners' will to keep on fighting the civil rights measure" in hopes that, following a Wallace primary victory or two, the liberal ranks in the Senate might begin to crumble.[42]

The Wallace campaign began in Wisconsin, where Democratic Governor John W. Reynolds was running as the favorite-son frontman for President Johnson. President Johnson stayed publicly aloof from the Reynolds campaign but did much to help Reynolds from behind the scenes. Johnson sent his postmaster general, John A. Gronouski, a former Wisconsin state official, to campaign for Reynolds in the Polish-American sections of Milwaukee, sections that were close to the black neighborhoods in Milwaukee and regarded as likely to cast a "backlash vote" for Governor Wallace.

On election day, 7 April 1964, Governor Reynolds easily defeated Wallace, collecting 511,000 votes in the process and guaranteeing all of Wisconsin's delegate votes at the Democratic National Convention to President Johnson. Wallace received 264,000 votes, however, many more than many commentators had expected a southern segregationist to receive in a northern state such as Wisconsin.

Following his electoral defeat but publicity triumph in Wisconsin, Governor Wallace turned his attention to the Democratic presidential primary in Indiana scheduled for 5 May 1964. Indiana looked like it might be a rich hunting ground for Wallace. Historically the state had been a northern center of Ku Klux Klan activities, and populous Lake Country, an industrial suburb of Chicago in northwestern Indiana, contained many of the lower-middle-class, second-generation ethnic voters that many commentators feared might vote for Wallace.

President Johnson's favorite-son stand-in in the Indiana primary was Democratic Governor Matthew Welsh. On primary election day Governor Welsh defeated Wallace, and Wallace received a somewhat lower percentage of the vote in Indiana (30 percent) than he had received in Wisconsin (34 percent). *Time's* coverage of the primary election results highlighted the fact that Wallace had not done all that well in the vote count but was continuing to get extensive press coverage for his efforts. *Time* noted: "Governor Matthew Welsh, a favorite-son stand-in for President Johnson, amassed 368,401 votes. But who got the headlines? Why, none other than Alabama's trouble-hunting Governor George Wallace with 170,146."[43]

Wallace's twin defeats in Wisconsin and Indiana did not end the Alabama governor's threat to the Civil Rights Bill. "We are going on to Maryland from here," Wallace said, noting that the Maryland Democratic presidential primary, scheduled for 19 May 1964 would give him one last chance to demonstrate how strong the opposition was to the Civil Rights Bill in the north and the border states.

As the Wallace campaign became organized in Maryland, political analysts began speculating that Wallace might win the Democratic presidential primary contest in Maryland. Although Maryland had not seceded from the Union and joined the Confederacy during the Civil War, it was, after all, a former slave state and south of the Mason-Dixon line. If Wallace could get 30 percent or more of the vote in northern states like Wisconsin and Indiana, he could conceivably get 50 percent or more in a border state like Maryland, and thus win the election.

Fully aware that Wallace had his best chance at a primary victory in Maryland, President Johnson recruited Maryland Senator Daniel B. Brewster, a young (forty years old) freshman senator who had been elected by a wide margin in the 1962 election.

Similar to Governor Reynolds in Wisconsin and Governor Welsh in Indiana, Senator Brewster badly underestimated the depth of racist feeling in his state. He had not anticipated the bitterness that would be generated between himself and committed Wallace supporters as the campaign developed. Brewster explained:

I found that the great popularity I had enjoyed in the 1962 election did not exist in a racial fight. I was called everything from a "cadillac pink" (wealthy Communist sympathizer) to a "race-mixing socialist." I was booed at a political meeting in Baltimore and cursed, jeered, and even spat upon as I campaigned in place of President Johnson. I had never been razzed before in my political career. The Wallace people actually sent "jeering sections" to follow me around and shout me down. Speaking one time at a meeting in College Park, Maryland, with Senator William Proxmire of Wisconsin, who had come over to Maryland to support me, the catcalls and the jeering were so loud that we could not even talk. Another time Assistant Postmaster General Tyler Abel was trying to help me out, but the two of us were just drowned out by the pro-Wallace roar.[44]

President Johnson's political advisers at the White House did everything they could to support Brewster short of an outright presidential endorsement. The Democratic National Committee raised a considerable amount of money and funneled it into Maryland on Brewster's behalf. A key White House aide, Clifton Carter, was dispatched to help Brewster in every way possible. The Johnson forces even arranged for a top campaign publicist to come to Maryland and help Brewster with his campaign speeches and press releases. The White House helped Brewster arrange for leading Democrats in the Senate, including Senators Hubert Humphrey and Edward Kennedy, to come into Maryland and help draw crowds to Brewster's campaign rallies. President Johnson himself scheduled a dramatic helicopter flight to inspect "Appalachian regional problems" in the Catoctin Mountains of western Maryland. The president saw to it that Brewster was at his side every minute he was in Maryland.

According to *Congressional Quarterly*, the Wallace campaign in Maryland had a direct impact on the Senate filibuster of the Civil Rights Bill, particularly where southern Democratic strategy making was concerned. The southerners apparently intentionally waited for the Maryland primary to take place, hoping to pick up votes against cloture after Wallace either won the primary or narrowly missed winning.[45] As the Wallace-Brewster campaign attracted ever more national publicity, the southerners became ever more hopeful that a big Wallace victory in Maryland would convince the uncommitted members of the Senate that sentiment for civil rights was weakening across the nation and it would be in their interest *not* to vote for cloture.

On 19 May 1964, Maryland voters went to the polls to make their choice. Brewster defeated Wallace by a comfortable margin of 57 percent to 42 percent. Since Wallace had done much better than he did in either Wisconsin or Indiana, however, the Alabama governor made his usual claim of winning the election despite coming out on the short end where the votes were concerned.

Brewster's comfortable victory in Maryland, however, ended the southern Democratic senators' hope that Wallace would win or come close in Maryland and thereby start a national groundswell of opposition to the Civil Rights Bill.[46] The Wallace campaign for president was designed to have a direct effect on the fortunes of the Civil Rights Bill in the Senate, and the full responsibility of stopping Wallace fell to President Johnson and his political advisers at the White House. Although the primary elections took place far from the halls of Congress, President Johnson's determined attempts to see that Wallace won no Democratic primaries for president outside the south may have been his most significant contribution to enactment of the Civil Rights Act of 1964.

JOHNSON AND THE "HOOKING" OF SENATOR DIRKSEN

Lyndon Johnson was aware from the moment he became president that the real problem with the Civil Rights Bill would be in the Senate and not in the House of Representatives. On 3 December 1963, he told his first congressional leadership breakfast, "Civil rights has been [in the House of Representatives] since May. . . . We all know the real problem will be in the Senate."[47]

There is much evidence to suggest that, from the very beginning of the Senate debate on the bipartisan Civil Rights Bill, President Johnson and Senate Democratic Whip Hubert Humphrey realized that Senate Republican leader Everett Dirksen of Illinois would hold the key to a successful cloture vote on the bill. Thus, as the drone and drawl of the filibuster dragged on throughout the months of April and May 1964, the most important events taking place were Johnson's and Hubert Humphrey's attempts to find some way of winning Dirksen's support and getting Dirksen to get his Republican allies in the Senate to vote cloture on civil rights.

President Johnson noted in his memoirs that, shortly after President Kennedy's assassination, he telephoned Dirksen and asked him to convey to his Republican colleagues in the Senate that the time had come to forget partisan politics and get the legislative machinery of the United States moving forward. As Johnson recalled the phone conversation:

There was a long pause on the other end of the line and I could hear him [Dirksen] breathing heavily. When he finally spoke, he expressed obvious disappointment that I would even raise the question of marshaling his party behind the president. "Mr. President," he said, "you know I will."[48]

Turning Senator Dirksen's general statement of support for the president into support for a cloture vote on the Civil Rights Bill would be no small task. The strategy designed by Johnson was to give Dirksen the opportunity to be a "hero in history." Johnson noted:

I gave to this fight everything I had in prestige, power, and commitment. At the same time, I deliberately tried to tone down my personal involvement in the daily struggle so that my colleagues on the Hill could take tactical responsibility—and credit so that a hero's niche could be carved out for Senator Dirksen, not me.[49]

The lion's share of the task of winning Everett Dirksen over to the Civil Rights Bill fell to Humphrey, the Democratic whip in the Senate. Humphrey recalled a telephone call from Johnson just as the Civil Rights Bill was arriving in the Senate. The president told Humphrey: "Now you know that this bill can't pass unless you get Ev Dirksen. You and I are going to get him. You make up your mind now that you've got to spend time with Ev Dirksen. You've got to let him have a piece of the action. He's got to look good all the time."[50]

By mid-March 1964, Humphrey was accelerating his efforts at nudging Dirksen into what Johnson had called that "hero's niche." Humphrey recalled that on his first television appearance in connection with the Civil Rights Bill a Sunday morning guest spot on "Meet the Press," he spent most of his time setting up Senator Dirksen, "I praised Dirksen, telling the nation he would help, that he would support a good Civil Rights Bill, that he would put his country above party, that he would look upon this issue as a moral issue and not a partisan issue."[51] Humphrey concluded his television appearance with soaring personal praise for Dirksen: "Senator Dirksen is not only a great senator, he is a great American, and he is going to see the necessity of this legislation. I predict that before this bill is through Senator Dirksen will be its champion."[52]

Apparently, Lyndon Johnson watched Humphrey's performance on "Meet the Press" and believed that Humphrey had done exactly the right thing. In a subsequent telephone call, Johnson continued to urge Humphrey on. The president said:

Boy, that was right. You're doing just right now. You just keep at that. Don't you let those bomb throwers [extremely committed supporters of civil rights] talk you out of seeing Dirksen. You get in there to see Dirksen! You drink with Dirksen! You talk to Dirksen! You listen to Dirksen![53]

Humphrey's legislative assistant described the technique that Johnson and Humphrey were using on Dirksen as "the great man hook!" The legislative assistant, who periodically dictated his thoughts on the progress of the Civil Rights Bill through the Senate, outlined the strategy in considerable detail:

Humphrey has been playing up very strongly the line that this is an opportunity for Dirksen to be the great man of the United States, the man of the hour, the man who saves the Civil Rights Bill. This line has been played up by Humphrey on "Meet the Press," in numerous conversations with journalists. Humphrey instigated Roscoe Drummond's recent article in the Herald Tribune Syndicate pointing up that Dirksen has an opportunity for greatness in the pending civil rights debate. In short, it appears that Dirksen is beginning to swallow the great man hook and, when it is fully digested, we will have ourselves a Civil Rights Bill."[54]

Apparently, Lyndon Johnson was capable of being unpleasant with Dirksen when necessary, as well as being able to maneuver him into a hero's niche. At one point during Senate consideration of the bill Hubert Humphrey became so concerned over the possibility that Dirksen would attempt an early cloture vote on the bill (a vote likely to be lost) that Humphrey endeavored to involve President Johnson in the effort to turn Dirksen off. Humphrey's legislative assistant gave the following account of what happened, based largely on hearsay and rumor:

Finally, one must not leave out President Johnson. The matter [the Civil Rights Bill] was discussed at some length at the Tuesday morning leadership breakfast [with President Johnson at the White House]. At that point, Mansfield raised the possibility of using cloture . . . and the matter was debated at the breakfast but not decided. Subsequently, Humphrey took himself down to the White House to see the president unannounced. He kept [Defense] Secretary [Robert] McNamara and others waiting while he barged into the president's office to lay it on the line. In effect, he told the president that the matter was at the point where victory was in sight but that the law had to be laid down here and now. He set forth the reasons why he opposed cloture. . . . I do not know what Johnson responded. But it has been said that when Dirksen went to the White House at noon today he found Johnson in a tough and noncompromising mood.[55]

There is no record of how much effect President Johnson had on the decision, but the "early vote for cloture" crisis disappeared. Following the Humphrey visit to the White House and the president's "tough and uncompromising mood" with Dirksen, Dirksen stopped talking about an early cloture vote.

JOHNSON AND THE FINAL DRIVE FOR CLOTURE

As the drive for cloture came down to the final days, there appears to have been some, but not very much, influence exerted on wavering senators by President Johnson. Hubert Humphrey recalled: "We did not bother the president very much. The president was not put on the spot. He was not enlisted in the battle particularly. I understand he did contact some of the senators, but not at our insistence."[56]

One theory for President Johnson's uncharacteristic lack of direct involvement was that he did not want to antagonize the southern Democrats unnecessarily and, as always, would need to have their votes on other issues on other days.[57]

President Johnson's low public profile when it came to lobbying Senate votes for cloture produced a critical political comment in a Washington newspaper:

The Civil Rights Bill is not moving according to plan and senators favoring it are beginning to ask each other: "Where's Lyndon?" As majority leader, the president was all muscle and scant conversation. In the present impasse, the criticism is freely heard that the reverse is true. . . . Reporters covering the civil rights story in detail agree that they have seen no traces of the old brooding and impatient Johnson presence that they learned to know so well during the Eisenhower years.[58]

On 9 June 1964, Hubert Humphrey made his final vote calculations in his Capitol office and could count only sixty-six sure votes, one short of the sixty-seven need for cloture. The telephone rang and Humphrey answered it. It was President Johnson, calling to ask about the prospects for the cloture vote. "I think we have enough," Humphrey replied. The president responded to this statement in a harsh tone of voice, "I don't want to know what you think. What's the vote going to be? How many do you have?" Subdued and nervous as a result of the president's impatient manner, Humphrey admitted that he was still one vote short. The search for votes would have to continue into the night.[59]

Despite the instructions from Johnson to continue working, Humphrey was unable that evening to obtain a sixty-seventh senator who would guarantee to vote for cloture. As it turned out, however, five additional senators voted for cloture when the vote was held the next day. The filibuster by the southern Democrats was silenced, and the Civil Rights Bill moved steadily toward final passage in the Senate. Exactly as then Vice President Johnson had predicted in June 1963, it was the votes of Senator Everett Dirksen and his Republican allies in the Senate that made the successful cloture vote possible.

Other than the events described above, there is little written record of the extent to which Lyndon Johnson lobbied senators in order to produce a successful cloture vote on the Civil Rights Bill. One reason for this is that Johnson liked to do most of his lobbying over the telephone, and thus there is no written record of how much pressure he might have applied in the effort to get individual senators to vote for cloture.

Another reason Johnson may not have lobbied too many senators personally was the fact that Johnson had the Justice Department represent his interests to the Senate. Deputy Attorney General Nicholas Katzenbach took the major responsibility for negotiating a version of the bill which Senator Dirksen and his Republican allies could support. Having the Justice Department handle negotiations with Dirksen and other senators concerned about the bill permitted President Johnson's interests to be furthered without Johnson himself having to become publicly involved in the Senate's internal business.[60]

President Johnson does appear to have lobbied one senator directly to vote for cloture, although, ironically, it turned out to be a vote that the president did not need. Senator Carl Hayden, a Democrat from Arizona, did not answer the roll call vote the first time his name was called. Apparently, Hayden had promised his old friend, Lyndon Johnson, that he would stay away if necessary, thereby reducing by one the number of votes needed for cloture. When the roll call was completed and it was clear that the civil rights forces had votes to spare, Senator Hayden walked onto the Senate floor and voted "No." Hayden was anxious to vote against cloture because of the historical fact that a filibuster had been required to win statehood for Arizona back in 1912.

A memorandum to President Johnson from Secretary of the Interior Stewart L. Udall suggests there was something more than friendship involved in Senator Hayden's willingness to not vote if the civil rights forces only had sixty-six votes for cloture. Hayden had long been interested in a major government water project for Arizona known as the Hayden-Brown proposal, and the memorandum suggests that verbal commitments were made to expedite that project in return for Hayden's cooperation on the cloture vote. The memorandum read in part:

The reports I get from Senator Hayden's staff indicate that your gambit on cloture with the senator at our Tuesday meeting was very persuasive. From a tactical standpoint, I think it would be wise for you to defer your final decision on the Hayden-Brown proposal until after the vote on cloture. . . . You are, of course, fully aware of the effect which a Hayden vote for cloture would have: some of the senators tell me that he will carry several other votes with him—such as the two Nevada senators.[61]

A White House staff member provided this summary of President Johnson's negotiations to get the cloture vote of Senator Hayden:

You recall the spade work that has gone into our attempts to work out an arrangement with Senator Hayden and the Central Arizona Project contingent upon the promise of a cloture vote by Hayden on Civil Rights. . . . After last week's Leadership Breakfast the president saw Hayden, and this was a ten-strike because it provided clear evidence of the president's personal interest. . . . I am convinced this can be worked out to Hayden's satisfaction . . . thus gaining one cloture vote. . . .[62]

THE LAW OF THE LAND

Once it was finally passed by the Senate and the House of Representatives, President Lyndon Johnson wasted no time affixing his signature to the Civil Rights Act of 1964. Within hours of House of Representatives approval of the Senate amendments, Johnson had one of the largest bill signing ceremonies in U.S. history arranged at the White House. Ordinarily the president signs bills in the Oval Office, but in order to accommodate as large a crowd of onlookers as possible, President Johnson arranged this particular signing ceremony in the East Room of the White House with more than 100 notables in attendance. The guests included key members of the House and Senate, several Cabinet members, important foreign ambassadors, and the major leaders of the civil rights movement.

The ceremony was carried live on national television at 6:45 P.M., Eastern Daylight Time, on July 2, 1964. The president, who seemingly had spoken more than a million words urging the House and the Senate to pass the Civil Rights Bill, had a few last words to say to the nation:

We believe all men have certain inalienable rights, yet many Americans do not enjoy those rights. We believe all men are entitled to the blessings of liberty. Yet millions are being deprived of those blessings—not because of their own failures, but because of the color of their skin.

The reasons are deeply imbedded in history and tradition and the nature of man. We can understand—without rancor or hatred—how this happened, but it cannot continue. . . . Our Constitution, the foundation of our republic, forbids it. The principles of our freedom forbid it. Morality forbids it. And the law I will sign tonight forbids it.[63]

Following the signing ceremony, President Johnson held a brief meeting with the prominent black political leaders in attendance. The president emphasized the twin themes that there was no longer any need for protest demonstrations and that any court tests on the new civil rights law should be carefully chosen. A White House memorandum summarized the president's remarks to the black political leaders:

The president indicated . . . how essential it was that there be an understanding of the fact that the rights Negroes possessed could now be secured by law, making demonstrations unnecessary and possibly self-defeating. He made clear how important it was that the court tests be carefully selected to guard against any initial decisions ruling the Act unconstitutional [regardless of the fact that ultimately the Supreme Court would find it to be constitutional].[64]

CONCLUSION

Many persons involved with the successful passage of the Civil Rights Act of 1964 commented on the question of whether President Kennedy, had he not been assassinated, could have delivered as strong a civil rights bill as President Johnson did. One of Lyndon Johnson's biographers put the point this way:

The greatest difference between the 1964 Civil Rights Bill as it would probably have been passed in that year under Lyndon was that Lyndon made sure he got everything he asked for. Kennedy, faced with inevitable Senate opposition, would almost surely have compromised somewhere, traded the deletion of one section, say, for the passage of the rest. Lyndon refused to delete, refused to compromise, anywhere.[65]

Robert C. Weaver, a leading black official in the Johnson administration, saw Johnson as both more committed and more skillful than Kennedy in getting a Civil Rights Bill through Congress. Weaver noted:

I think Kennedy had an intellectual commitment for civil rights and a broad view of social legislation. Johnson had a gut commitment for changing the entire social fabric of this country. . . . I don't think we would ever have got the civil rights legislation we did without Johnson. I don't think Kennedy could have done it. He would have gone for it, but he was a lot more cautious than Johnson.[66]

Clarence Mitchell, Jr., of the NAACP, argued that Kennedy could not have won as strong a bill as Johnson did but believed the key difference was in the ability of the two men to lobby Congress. Mitchell explained:

Unhappily it may have been true no bill could have passed without the assassination of President Kennedy. It certainly would have been more difficult if Kennedy had remained as president. Lyndon Johnson just had powers for getting Congress to act that John Kennedy lacked.[67]

A similar view was expressed by Roy Wilkins, national president of the NAACP. He said:

John Fitzgerald Kennedy had a complete comprehension and an identity with the goals of the civil rights movement. Intellectually he was for it. . . . But, I think that precisely the qualities that Lyndon Johnson later exhibited, and which only Lyndon Johnson could have, by reason of his experience and his study and the use of materials of government— precisely that lack in President Kennedy forced him to hesitate and weigh and consider what he should do in the civil rights field. I don't think it was from any inner non-conviction. I think he was convinced that this ought to be done. He just did not know how to manipulate the government to bring it about.[68]

The general consensus seemed to be that President Kennedy probably would have obtained some sort of Civil Rights Bill from Congress in 1964 but that it would not have been anywhere near as strong a bill as Lyndon Johnson obtained. It is sad to have to say it, but virtually all those involved with the Civil Rights Act of 1964 believe that the tragic assassination of President Kennedy helped the final passage of the bill by putting Lyndon Johnson in the White House.

In retrospect, therefore, John F. Kennedy and Lyndon B. Johnson appear to have had something of a symbiotic political relationship (in the sense that each needed something important from the other). With his great speaking ability and his talent for inspiring political followers, John F. Kennedy convinced many Americans of the great need to pass civil rights legislation. Kennedy apparently lacked, however, the ability to get Congress to pass such legislation in a strong enough form to please strong civil rights supporters. Lyndon Johnson, on the other hand, lacked Kennedy's speaking ability and inspirational quality, but he had great talents for getting definite action on Capitol Hill. It might be said of the two men that, in terms of civil rights, President Johnson was able to deliver on the exciting goals and promises so inspirationally presented by President Kennedy.

NOTES

In citing works in the notes, short titles have generally been used. Works frequently cited have been identified by the following abbreviations:

CQWR	*Congressional Quarterly Weekly Report*
HHH Papers	Hubert H. Humphrey Papers, Minnesota Historical Society, St. Paul, Minnesota
JFK Library	John F. Kennedy Library, Boston, Massachusetts
LBJ Library	Lyndon Baines Johnson Library, Austin, Texas

1. Memorandum to the Attorney General from Assistant Attorney General Norbert A. Schlei, Robert F. Kennedy, *General Correspondence*, JFK Library, 4 June 1963, 1.

2. Ibid.

3. Unpublished manuscript on the Civil Rights Act of 1964 by Joseph Rauh, lobbyist for the Leadership Conference on Civil Rights, Washington, D.C., 1964, 5.

4. Interview with Louis Martin, 14 May 1969, Oral History Collection, LBJ Library, 22.

5. *CQWR*, 29 November 1963, 2089.

6. Memorandum to the Attorney General from Assistant Attorney Norbert A. Schlei, Robert F. Kennedy, *General Correspondence*, JFK Library, 4 June 1963, VI.

7. Lyndon Baines Johnson, *The Vantage Point* (New York: Popular Library, 1971), 29.

8. Interview with Roy Wilkins, 1 April 1969, Oral History Collection, LBJ Library, 5.

9. Interview with Clarence Mitchell, Jr., 30 April 1969, Oral History Collection, LBJ Library, 4.

10. Memorandum, Lee White to President Johnson, 29 November 1963, "Suggested Items for Discussion with Roy Wilkins," Appointment File (Diary Back-up), Box 1, LBJ Library, 1. See also Memorandum, Lee C. White to President Johnson, 3 December 1963, "Possible Items for Discussion with Martin Luther King," and Memorandum, Lee C. White to President Johnson, 4 December 1963, "Suggested Items for Discussion with

James Farmer'' (National Director of CORE, the Committee on Racial Equality), EX/HU2, Box 2, LBJ Library.

11. Memorandum, Lee C. White to President Johnson, 4 December 1963, Appointment File (Diary Back-up), Box 2, LBJ Library.

12. *CQWR*, 6 December 1963, 2130.

13. Ibid., 2118.

14. Off-the-Record Remarks to Governors, Appointment File (Diary Back-up), 25 November 1963, LBJ Library, 4.

15. Daniel M. Berman, *A Bill Becomes a Law; Congress Enacts Civil Rights Legislation*, 2d ed. (New York: Macmillan, 1966), 95.

16. Memorandum, Lee C. White to President Johnson, 9 December 1963, ''Assistance of Businessmen on the Discharge Petition,'' EX LE/HU2, Box 65, LBJ Library.

17. *CQWR*, 6 December 1963, 2118.

18. Off-the-Record Remarks to Governors, Appointment File (Diary Back-up), 25 November 1963, LBJ Library, 4.

19. Memorandum, Lawrence F. O'Brien to the President, 29 November 1963, EX LE/HU2, WHCF, Box 65, LBJ Library.

20. Notes on the First Congressional Leadership Breakfast Held by the President on 3 December 1963, Appointment File (Diary Back-up), Box 2, LBJ Library, 1.

21. *CQWR*, 7 February 1964, 250.

22. Ibid., 281.

23. Memorandum, George E. Reedy to the Vice President, 7 June 1963, Office Files of George Reedy, Civil Rights 1963, WDT Box 434(22), Folder #1, LBJ Library. See also Transcript, Ramsey Clark Oral History, 21 March 1969, Tape 1, 14, and 11 February 1969, Tape 1, 11.

24. *CQWR*, 14 February 1964, 293.

25. *Time Magazine*, 14 February 1964, 13.

26. Ibid.

27. Merle Miller, *Lyndon: An Oral Biography* (New York: G. P. Putnam's Sons, 1980), 367. See also Rauh manuscript, 19.

28. Rauh manuscript, 21.

29. Stephen Horn, ''Periodic Log Maintained During the Discussions Concerning the Passage of the Civil Rights Act of 1964,'' unpublished, 24. Horn was legislative assistant to Senator Kuchel.

30. Memorandum, Lee C. White to President Johnson, 15 April 1964, ''Civil Rights Activities During the First 100 Days,'' EX/HU2, LBJ Library, 1.

31. *CQWR*, 10 January 1964, 48.

32. Ibid.

33. *CQWR*, 7 February 1964, 281.

34. *CQWR*, 28 February 1964, 385.

35. *CQWR*, 6 March 1964, 477.

36. *CQWR*, 13 March 1964, 491.

37. *CQWR*, 20 March 1964, 580.

38. *CQWR*, 10 April 1964, 701.

39. *CQWR*, 17 April 1964, 747.

40. *CQWR*, 24 April 1964, 789.

41. Ibid., 797.

42. Johnson, *Vantage Point*, 29.

43. *Time Magazine*, 15 May 1964, 37.

44. Interview with former U.S. Senator Daniel B. Brewster, Baltimore County, Maryland, August 1982.

45. *CQWR*, 15 May 1964, 948.

46. William M. Bates, Press Secretary to Senator Richard B. Russell, 20 April 1966, quoted in Peter Evans Kane, "The Senate Debate on the 1964 Civil Rights Act" (Doctoral dissertation, Purdue University, 1967), 176.

47. "Notes on the First Congressional Leadership Breakfast Held by the President on 3 December 1963," Appointment File (Diary Back-up), Box 2, LBJ Library, 1.

48. Johnson, *Vantage Point*, 30.

49. Ibid., 159.

50. Miller, *Lyndon*, 368.

51. Hubert H. Humphrey, Memorandum on Senate Consideration of the Civil Rights Act of 1964, HHH Papers, Senatorial Legislative Files, Civil Rights, 1964, Box 241, Summer 1964, 13.

52. Miller, *Lyndon*, 368–369.

53. Ibid., 369.

54. Unsigned memorandum titled "Thoughts on the Civil Rights Bill Dictated Wednesday, April 21, 1964," HHH Papers, Senatorial Legislative Files, Civil Rights, 1964, Box 241. The author mailed a copy of the memorandum to Humphrey's legislative assistant, John G. Stewart, who acknowledged authorship. This memorandum and others dictated by Stewart will be referred to as "Stewart notes."

55. Stewart notes, 29 April 1964, 5–6.

56. Humphrey memorandum, 17–18.

57. Winthrop Griffith, *Humphrey: A Candid Biography* (New York: William Morrow, 1965), 283.

58. Doris Fleeson, "They're Asking: 'Where's Lyndon,' Senators Backing Rights Bill Wonder Where Old Johnson Touch Has Gone," *Washington Star*, 22 May 1964. It is an interesting historical note that, when Lyndon Johnson was preparing to leave office in December of 1968, a copy of this newspaper article was found in his middle desk drawer. Marked newspaper article can be found in EX LE/HU2, Box 65, LBJ Library.

59. Griffith, *Humphrey*, 283.

60. John G. Stewart, "Independence and Control, The Challenge of Senatorial Party Leadership" (Doctoral diss., University of Chicago, 1968), 252.

61. Memorandum, Stewart L. Udall to President Johnson, 7 May 1964, EX LE/HU2, LBJ Library.

62. Memorandum, Mike Manatos to Larry O'Brien 11 May 1964, EX/HU2, LBJ Library.

63. *CQWR*, 3 July 1963, 1331.

64. Memorandum, Lee C. White to the Files, 6 July 1964, EX/HU2, Box 65, LBJ Library, 1.

65. Miller, *Lyndon*, 367.

66. Ibid., 345.

67. Interview with Clarence Mitchell, Jr., former Washington director of the NAACP, Baltimore, Maryland, 17 August 1983.

68. Interview with Roy Wilkins, 1 April 1969, Oral History Collection, LBJ Library, 8–9.

8

Lyndon, *La Raza,* and the Paradox of Texas History

Julie Leininger Pycior

Lyndon Baines Johnson had a long, complex relationship with Mexican Americans and many important issues, such as politics, education, civil rights, and labor were reflected in their shared experiences. For example, Johnson's tenure as director of the National Youth Administration offers an opportunity to examine the New Deal policies regarding Hispanics. Mexican American voting patterns can be traced in Johnson's campaigns, from the early, local results to the Parr machine controversies of 1948 and the Viva Kennedy! clubs of 1960.

This is chapter one of the story, the origins of the relationship in Johnson's first job: teaching at a ''Mexican'' school, with all the attendant cultural baggage he and his students brought to the task. The schoolteacher episode is more complex, paradoxical, and important than it seems.

On the evening of 15 March 1965, President Lyndon Johnson spoke before a joint session of Congress and a nation-wide television audience in support of the Voting Rights Bill. This major policy address contained only one personal anecdote:

My first job after college was as a teacher in Cotulla, Texas, in a small Mexican American school. . . . I never thought then, in 1928, that I would be standing here in 1965. It never occurred to me in my fondest dreams that I might have the chance to help the sons and daughters of those students and to help people like them all over this country. But now I do have that chance—and I'll let you in on a secret—I mean to use it.

Johnson considered his Cotulla job one of the most crucial experiences of his life, opening his eyes to true poverty and discrimination. Vice President Hubert Humphrey once remarked:

He was really interested in poor people, truly interested. And he never was able to project that as sincerely as I knew it to be. He never did forget those days when he taught school to those Mexican American kids. He never forgot about it. He romanticized a lot, that I know. And people thought he just used that, but that wasn't true.[1]

Lyndon Johnson the history teacher came by his love of history naturally. His mother, Rebeka Baines Johnson, was an avid genealogist and his father, Sam Johnson, Jr., who always loved history, scored 100 percent in both Texas history and American history. Even more than most Texans both parents conveyed history as interesting, important, and best personified by their illustrious forebears.[2] Johnson's great great uncle, John Wheeler Bunton, immigrated to Texas in 1833 and soon joined the protest against the Mexican government's limits on democracy and its prohibition of slavery. In 1836 he enlisted with a company of volunteers as first sergeant. They camped outside of San Antonio where their captain order a withdrawal. A rump group of several hundred under Ben Milam rebelled and drove a Mexican army four times its size from the city. Four months later the 185 Texans holding the Alamo were killed by Antonio López de Santa Anna. Meanwhile, Bunton signed the Texas declaration of independence at Washington-on-the-Brazos and then fought at the crucial battle of San Jacinto. His captain, Jesse Billington, wrote that Bunton "penetrated so far into the ranks of the defenders . . . that it is miraculous that he was not killed." In gratitude the new republic awarded Bunton 960 acres of land. Johnson's great grandfather, George W. Baines, was a friend of Sam Houston, and Rebeka's cousin, Mary Baines, was a founder of the Daughters of the Republic of Texas, the guardians of Texas history as viewed by the victors. The Daughters lobbied, with the aid of Lyndon's father, to have the state legislature purchase the Alamo and designate it a historic shrine, where Representative Johnson's picture hangs.[3]

When Lyndon was growing up in Blanco County, this history was palpable, real. Adults, referring to the "war," meant not the First World War or even the War between the States but the Texas Revolt and Mexican War. He and his playmates tearfully reenacted in detail the defense of the Alamo and at the age of six Lyndon memorized a poem about the Alamo to recite at a Confederate reunion. The event was cancelled but Johnson remembered the poem his whole life and years later bellowed it out from memory for startled White House staff and guests:

> Santa Anna came rumbling as a storm might come
> There was rumble of cannon; there was rattle of blade;
> There was cavalry, infantry, bugle and drum—
> Full seven thousand in pomp and parade,
> The chivalry, flower of Mexico;
> And a gaunt two hundred in the Alamo!
>
> And thirty lay sick, and some were shot through;
> For the siege had been bitter, and bloody, and long,

"Surrender or die! Men, what will you do!"
And Travis, great Travis, drew his sword, quick and strong,
Drew a line at his feet . . . "Will you come? Will you go?"
I drew with my wounded, in the Alamo.[4]

Equally important in the Texas saga was the cowboy. Lyndon loved to hear his grandfather, Sam Ealy Johnson, recount his cowboy days on the cattle trail from the Texas hill country to Abiline, Kansas. He spoke of intrepid, heroic men and the brave women back home such as his wife Eliza Bunton Johnson who hid under a trap door, a handkerchief in her baby's mouth, while Indians ransacked above. The bill establishing the Texas Rangers had been adopted with the help of Congressman John Bunton, and Eliza's brother, Joe Bunton, (Johnson's great uncle) was one of these legendary Rangers.[5]

Johnson identified with these victorious conquerors of the west but populism acquainted him with the honorable underdog. Sam Ealy Johnson, Sr., a populist as well as a cowboy, talked (according to his grandson) "about the plight of the tenant farmer, the necessity for workers to have protection for bargaining . . . particularly the red schoolhouse and the tenant purchase program where a worker could attain something on his own." Johnson's parents admired William Jennings Bryan "extravagantly" and his father was generally a farm liberal calling for rural education and transportation and government stabilization of crop prices. He supported Wright Patman's anti–Ku Klux Klan Bill (making it a prison offense to wear a mask). Although Sam, Jr., occasionally bent to the prevailing political winds (as when he abstained from voting on the White Primary Bill), he usually followed his ideals. Years later his son remarked, "He was trying to better humanity. He didn't have much to show for it." Lyndon, while admiring the populist-reformist spirit also admired Senator Joseph Bailey, whom his father had opposed, and Uncle Clarence Martin, a conservative Democratic judge who had defeated Sam, Sr., in 1892. Eventually Lyndon would buy the Martin ranch and there establish himself as part of the rancher elite that his father never achieved and his grandfather had criticized.[6]

The agrarian reform legacy both attracted and repelled young Lyndon but it did not acquaint him with the grievances of rural *Tejanos*. Populists ignored or resented Hispanic tenant farmers. *Tejanos* formed their own organizations, such as the *Liga Protectora Mexicana*, founded in San Antonio in 1917, which gave legal aid to farmers and farm workers and lobbied in the state legislature on their behalf. Few Mexican Americans lived in Johnson's native hill country, the central heartland of Texas, a land of independent Anglo- and German-American yeoman farmers eking out livings on small tracts of thin soil.[7]

At Southwest Texas State Teacher's College, the hill country college, Johnson majored in history, taking U.S. history surveys, U.S. diplomatic history, advanced American history, and, of course, Texas history. Johnson met few Mexican Americans except for the janitors he worked with while a student employee. He never commented on the discrimination in the college town of San Marcos.

Rather, he dated his first encounter with prejudice from his stay in Cotulla, where the Anglo minority obviously segregated the Mexican majority. Nevertheless, into the 1940s San Marcos Mexican Americans were denied service at several restaurants and drugstores. Mexican American women could not use the restroom at the courthouse, the Mexican schools were inferior, and the southside Hispanic neighborhood had no sewers. Johnson, like most students, focused on campus activities and did not notice this situation. Unusually ambitious, he worked his way up from assistant janitor to presidential secretary. (Cotulla superintendent W. T. Donaho came to the college and in Johnson's words "offered me a job at $125 a month to teach at the Mexican school" in large part because the twenty-year-old college junior had been recommended by Southwest Texas president C. E. Evans.) Johnson had also been alerted to the position by his cousin Margaret Johnson who taught in Los Angeles, Texas, near Cotulla.[8] As principal he would supervise five teachers, teach sixth and seventh grade history, and manage the building. He would come to Cotulla with great drive to impress the local leaders, much compassion for the powerless, a burning love of history, and little knowledge of Mexican Americans.

The attitudes of the Mexican American students and the Anglo-American administrators of 1928 were shaped, to a large extent, by the region's heritage. Unlike Johnson's hill country, Cotulla (La Salle County), Texas is located on the Nueces River in an area traditionally known as the Brush Country, south of San Antonio and north of the Mexican border counties, a rangeland of cowboys, sagebrush, and mesquite, of a sparse, often violent population.[9] In the decades following the Mexican War many Mexican-Texan ranchers fled or lost their lands and became farm laborers or renegades. Marauding bands of Anglos and *Mexicanos* alike stole horses and cattle and waged vendettas. Texas Rangers such as King Fisher "ranged from the Nueces to the Chicon, from Eagle Pass to Carrizo Springs, and often down . . . on the Nueces by Cotulla." They often applied a double standard of justice to Mexican Texans. One time a boy asked King how many men he had killed in the line of duty. The Ranger replied, "Seven." "I thought it must be more than that," the boy answered. "I don't count Mexicans," King Fisher explained.[10] One of the most famous renegades to cross the Brush Country was Gregorio Cortez, denounced as a murderer by the authorities but extolled as a rebel hero in *corridos* (Mexican ballads). In 1901 he boldly walked into Cotulla, knowing that a posse was searching for him in the nearby countryside. Several Mexican American women aided him before he set off again.[11]

The population grew steadily after the introduction of a railroad line in 1879 and gradually became a settled ranching center. Most of the Mexican American residents worked on the larger ranches as laborers. At the La Mota "spread" in the 1890s the Burks owned a spacious clapboard house while their staff lived in *jacales*, shacks made of sticks and grass.[12]

At this time the Baptist Church established a mission among the Mexican Americans of La Salle County. It was headed by Rev. J. F. Kimball, whose son Henry would marry Johnson's cousin Margaret Johnson and whose daughter Ora would marry J. W. Martin, later a La Salle County judge and prominent Cotullan. Reverend Kimball reported on 28 November 1885:

I have baptized six: four whites and two Mexicans. The two Mexicans are more than ordinary people of their race—the man reads well in his own language, the woman does not read, but in her eye are the manifestations of independent thought. . . . Brethren, while the number gathered into the fold . . . seems to be small, the outlook for a grand work is bright. . . . It will not do to let this work stop once you have begun it. Press rapidly on to the day when it will have become self-sustaining.[13]

In the early 1900s with the advent of irrigation much of the rangeland came under cultivation. Onion, spinich, and other crops were shipped north and La Salle County became part of the new Winter Garden area, roughly six counties between San Antonio and Laredo. Many Mexicans immigrated to the region, attracted by the promise of jobs and fleeing the upheaval of the Mexican Revolution (1910–1920). In 1930, the economist Paul Taylor calculated an average Winter Garden laborer's annual wage at $375 for an adult male, $600 for a family of four. Years later Lyndon Johnson told Ambassador W. Averell Harriman of having seen "the Mexican children going through a garbage pile, shaking the coffee grounds from the grapefruit rinds and sucking the rinds for the juice that was left."[14]

Many Anglos, seeing the west as a land of opportunity, blamed *La Raza* for its problems. The early Anglo settlers and their descendants firmly believed that the region would not have prospered under Mexican control, that Mexican-heritage people were inferior, lacking in ambition and skill, that the Texans had beaten the Mexicans "fair and square" and deserved the rewards. As one Winter Garden resident said in the late 1920s, "They were here before we were and they're working for us. . . . We will always need someone to do menial work. They will not be landowners; they don't save."[15] Differences of race and religion exacerbated the problem, especially in the 1920s as the Mexican American population grew. The Ku Klux Klan reemerged. In 1922 a Mexican American was lynched in Pearsall, home of the Winter Garden Fair, just thirty miles from Cotulla. (Johnson would teach in Pearsall's Anglo school fewer than ten years later.) As one farm woman said, "We feel toward Mexicans like the old southerners toward the Negroes." A merchant lamented the situation, however: "The Mexicans are Catholics and people here seem to think that because of that they aren't worth considering."[16]

One of the most famous La Salle County residents, O. Henry, often used Latin culture in his stories for local color. His portrayals reflected the prejudices of the region and the decade, as in the poem "Tamales":

> This is the Mexican
> Don José Calderón
> One of God's countrymen

Land of the Buzzard,
Cheap silver dollar, and
Cacti and murderers
Why has he left this land,
Land of the lazy man,
Land of the pulque
Land of the bullfight,
Fleas and revolution.

This is the reason
Hark to the wherefore;
Listen and tremble.
One of his ancestors,
Ancient and garlicky,
Probably grandfather,
Died with his boots on,
Killed by the Texans,
Texans with big guns
At San Jacinto.

. . . Dire is the vengeance
Don José Calderón.
For the slight thing we did
Killing your grandfather.
What boots it if we killed
Only one greaser,
Don José Calderón?
This is your deep revenge.
You have greased all of us,
Greased a whole nation
With your Tamales,
Don José Calderón . . . [17]

Beginning in the 1920s *La Raza* permanently outnumbered the Anglo-Americans throughout the Winter Garden–Brush Country area. About 79 percent of Cotulla's population of 3,000 was Mexican American by 1928. The ruling minority, in order to preserve its position and buttressed by its sense of superiority, created a segregated society. Each group had its own community organizations, social events, and churches. Anglos called Hispanics by their first name while the latter were expected to use "Mr." with Anglos, who could visit Mexican American bars and restaurants. The reverse was prohibited unless the *Mexicano* ate in the kitchen. A restaurant owner explained his policies when a well-educated Mexican American professor demanded service: "My Mexican boy asked me what to do. I told him not to serve him: all Mexicans look alike to me. It isn't a question of cleanliness or education, but race. I was told he took it up in Austin (with the State authorities), but I never heard any more of it." [18]

Cotulla Mexican Americans tried to improve their situation through mutual aid organizations and consulate commissions (both of which were covered in *La Prensa* of San Antonio, the largest Spanish-language newspaper in the country) but refrained from overtly challenging the discrimination in the face of an entrenched Anglo authority and threats by the Ku Klux Klan. Some dissatisfied Mexican Americans undoubtedly left Cotulla; others may have surreptitiously joined the Wobblies or various socialist labor groups that recruited among south Texas *Mexicanos*.[19]

The Cotulla school system fit the pattern uncovered by researcher Herschel T. Manuel: ''As we get back from the border . . . there is a noticeable tendency toward at least a partial segregation—except where the Mexican population is relatively small.''[20] Local residents offered several rationales. Dorothy Territo Nichols, who attended Cotulla High School while Johnson taught at Welhausen and later became one of his most loyal and important office workers, recalled: ''Any Mexican student who could speak English and wanted to could attend this school I went to and some of them did . . . but only the higher-class Mexicans sent their children there, usually. . . . Many of them didn't have English as they started them out in the Mexican school.'' Beryle Rutledge Rock, a Cotulla teacher beginning in 1929, described the schools as segregated.:

It was believed that the Latin Americans required a different type of instruction from that of the Anglo-American children. Therefore, two elementary schools were established, the one, exclusively for the Latins and the other, the Amanda Burks School, whose enrollment was limited to Anglo-Americans.

Other reasons often given included the irregular attendance of Mexican American children, that public opinion dictated it, that Anglo schools were overcrowded, that children with language difficulty would receive special help and individual attention, that Mexican American children needed to learn health habits before mixing with Anglo children. These rationales were seconded by studies such as the 1923 University of Texas report that said: ''In many instances, it must be admitted, separate schools are better for both the Mexicans and Americans. That is true in most of the cases where separate schools for the Mexicans have already been established.''[21]

These assumptions failed to withstand close scrutiny. Public sentiment often overruled economic and pedagogical common sense. The smaller systems, least able to afford them, often established two- or three-tiered systems with separate, duplicated facilities for Anglos, *Mexicanos*, and blacks (if any). These districts resembled some of the deep South, although custom, not law, dictated the segregation of *La Raza*. Separation most often occurred in the lower grades, with most Mexican Americans quitting school after a few years. School officials seldom used any standard other than race for dividing the children and those that did test for English and reading competency only tested the Hispanic children. The segregation extended into nonacademic activities such as sports and playground use. While Mexican American children were separated ostensibly for language reasons, German, Czech, Italian, and other foreign-language speakers experienced no such segregation. The social scientist George I. Sánchez summed up the situation:

In all the segregated schools and classes that I have surveyed or observed in more than twenty-five years of experience, I have never found one in which the school personnel, services, and facilities squared up to the implied special offerings upon which the whole idea of segregation . . . rests. . . . Virtually without exception, a segregated school is an inferior school.[22]

Cotulla's "American" school, Amanda Burks, had no Spanish-surname students in the first three grades and few in the upper grades for the years 1927–1929, and the town's only high school had only a handful of Hispanic students. One mother refused to send her child to an Anglo school because:

I don't want to send my little girl over there and have somebody slap her just because she is Mexican. Why can't we have children just as bright as any if they just give us the opportunity. It isn't better to separate. In San Antonio they do not separate, and the children learn the language better.

Another woman recalled attending nearby Pearsall High School (Johnson's next teaching assignment after Cotulla):

We were only six *Mexicanos* in my class. Most families could not send their kids to high school because it cost a lot of money, like for books, clothes, etc. *Mexicanos* did not participate in anything like clubs, and were not represented in anything like being class officers, queens, sweethearts, you know, all that stuff that kids like so much. Well, to belong to any club or to vote in the class, one had to pay a fee. . . . We couldn't afford the extra costs. Besides, the gringos didn't make bones about showing their dislike for us. They snubbed us at all times. We were not wanted there. . . . We were a minority. So we just studied together and survived as best we could. Many would drop out because they couldn't bear the situation.[23]

Cotulla, with over half of the school-age population in La Salle County, had only about one-third of the county's assessed valuation. The school districts applied for state aid based on the "scholastic" or total school-age population rather than on actual attendance figures. Thus, the officials received money for every child but spent it as they saw fit. One Mexican American woman noted bitterly: "In the Mexican schools they have young, inexperienced teachers who are sometimes uninterested. They have inadequate equipment. They are just taking the money received for the Mexicans and spending it for the American school." Johnson bemoaned the situation: "We had only five teachers here, we had no lunch facilities. We had no school buses . . . we did not have money to buy our playground equipment. . . . I took my first month's salary and invested it in those things for my children." Local employers often resisted improvements in the education of Mexican Americans, as noted by a merchant:

They seem to be afraid that if they [sic] learn, they can't handle them as well as they do now. They seem afraid they will unionize and ask higher wages. Some farmers are afraid that if the Mexicans are educated they will want to buy land. Well, why not? They are entitled to it.[24]

Johnson's preparation resembled that of most of the Mexican school staff. Hired at the end of his junior year in college, he was typical in that he was a less experienced teacher than those at Amanda Burks. The better teachers from Welhausen were "promoted" to the Anglo school, as in the case of Johnson using Welhausen as a stepping stone to the job in Pearsall. Such was the pattern throughout Texas in school systems that separated Anglo and Mexican American children.

Most of the Winter Garden–area teachers came from small teachers' colleges, whose graduates commanded lower salaries than those from the University of Texas, had less interest in urban teaching, and accepted the traditional small-town social mores more readily. Lyndon Johnson fit this pattern, identifying with the leadership in small-town society, whether as an aide to President Evans at Southwest Texas State or as an employee of Superintendent Donaho in Cotulla. Donaho wrote:

He is a tireless worker, cooperative at all times, open to suggestions, always pleasant, more than willing to carry out the policies of the school regardless of personal opinion. He is a good mixer and well liked. . . . He is one of the very best men that I have ever had with me.[25]

In addition to supervising him, Donaho taught Johnson several extension courses, including "educational psychology" and "race relations." Doubtless the superintendent upheld the notion of a dual school system, perhaps citing educational research of the 1920s, much of which concluded that Mexican American children were of inferior intelligence.[26] Johnson had learned nothing to the contrary at his San Marcos college, which had no pioneering social scientists such as O. Douglas Weeks and Herschel Manuel at the University of Texas who questioned the prevailing attitudes. Writing in 1930, Dr. Manuel said:

The attitude in general that the Mexican is considered inferior to the non-Mexican is not hard to find. It is so pronounced and so much a part of the general knowledge in the state that it seems superfluous to cite evidence that it exists. To Texas readers one could almost say "ask yourself" or "consult your own experience."[27]

Although anxious to please the local leaders, Johnson also remembered his reformist roots and sympathized with his students. Years later he explained their plight in moving terms in his voting rights speech:

They knew in their youth the pain in prejudice. They never seemed to know why people disliked them. But they knew it was so, because I saw it in their eyes. I often walked home late in the afternoon, after classes were finished, wishing there was more that I could do. But all I knew was to teach them the little I knew, hoping that it might help them against the hardships that lay ahead. . . . Somehow you never forget what poverty and hatred can do when you see its scars on the hopeful face of a young child.[28]

Principal Johnson came into town like a whirlwind, organizing a music group, a baseball team and league, and a debating team even though "they couldn't talk English and I couldn't talk Spanish." Like most Mexican school teachers, Johnson religiously enforced the "English-only" rule, both in the school and on the playground. Considered a strict, fair, but sometimes high-tempered teacher, he spanked chronic offenders who spoke Spanish. Even though he himself had no experience learning a second language, the new principal was convinced that only by using English exclusively could these students learn English effectively and advance to high school. He was merely implementing ideas long held by Texas teachers and supported by state laws since 1905. When one boy had an unusually difficult time with English, Johnson took him home to Johnson City where Johnson and his mother tutored the student until he could pass. In his enthusiasm Johnson ignored the fact that the total exclusion of Spanish in a segregated setting was counterproductive. Few Welhausen students succeeded in high school or even in the upper grades of elementary school. Compassionate on an individual level, he nonetheless enforced an oppressive rule.[29]

Mexican American students who found that their language was unacceptable and "wrong" also learned history through purely Anglo eyes, which often depicted Mexicans as the enemy. Johnson reinforced this view, not realizing the confusion it might cause in young minds. He extolled the Anglo defenders of the Alamo: After all, that same year an Austin newspaper published an article that began:

Santa Anna took the Alamo
That was 1836.
Sam Johnson saved the Alamo.
That was 1905.

Johnson overlooked the Mexican Texans who fought on both sides and in general he lauded the Anglo-American victors, ignorant of the role of Mexican Americans in a Texas history that predated the Anglo-Texans by nearly 200 years. As such, Johnson was only reflecting the views of the times, when as distinguished a Texas as Walter Prescott Webb, president of the American Historical Association, could write in his *The Texas Rangers* (1935):

Without disparagement it may be said that there is a cruel streak in the Mexican nature, or so the history of Texas would lead one to believe. This cruelty may be a heritage from the Spanish of the Inquisition; it may, and doubtlessly should be attributed partly to the Indian blood. . . . As a warrior he was, on the whole, inferior to the Comanche and wholly unequal to the Texan. . . . For making promises—and for breaking them—he had no peer.[30]

Before and after his teaching stint Johnson edited the college paper where he (or one of his staffers) editorialized: "The wonderful battle when the great Sam Houston and his dauntless little band made their valiant stand against the Mexican oppressors. . . . No paens of praise, no showers of appreciation . . . are too great for those heroes of that trying time." He criticized "debunkers" of historical figures: "In biography we wish to see our famous men and women as they were and feel that power and strength and beauty of their lives. . . . Let us have our heroes. Let us continue to believe . . . that it lies within human ability to overcome temptations and trials. . . . "[31] The indignant history major did not pursue a logical corollary, namely that in order to have heroes one may also need villains, as in the form of "Mexican oppressors." The assigned history text in Cotulla elementary schools, *The Beginner's History of Our Country*, called Mexico's revolutionary leaders "bandits" and explained the Texas revolt of 1836 in simple terms:

The Mexican government at first encouraged the coming of the settlers, making rich grants of lands to the pioneers who came. The newcomers, however, were different in language, customs and religion from the Mexicans. They [sic] loved liberty, and the government of Mexico was harsh and tyrannical.[32]

This version ignores the illegal actions of the newcomers, particularly establishing slavery, and overlooks the fact that throughout Mexico loyal citizens rebelled against the Santa Anna administration.

Johnson, like other Anglo-Texans, was ignorant of the numerous Mexican activities in Cotulla. The Cotulla *Record* did not mention one Mexican American event during Johnson's tenure. Nevertheless, in 1928–1929, several large weddings attracted distant friends and relatives. The local mutual aid society met with the mayor asking the city to expand the Mexican cemetery. Those present pledged to collect funds and the mayor offered to put in pipes and other improvements in the lot designated. A drama in four acts, *El Molino Rugiente* was written, directed, and staged with a chorus and orchestra by Gilberto Leyva in April 1929. Various Cotulla youngsters performed. *La Prensa* of San Antonio, which reported on all of these Cotulla Hispanic activities, called the production "an important, stimulating cultural factor." In June 1929 the *Comisión Honorífica* of Cotulla invited the Mexican Consul in Laredo, Rafael de la Colima, to come and explain revisions in the immigration law. He spoke at the "Mexican" school and received an enthusiastic response from the audience of about 1,500. Although *La Raza*'s culture was unappreciated by the local leaders, two major folklorists took note of it. J. Frank Dobie used the tales from ranch hands at La Mota ranch for his 1931 book *Coronado's Children*; in 1934, John Lomax, under the auspices of the Library of Congress, recorded in Cotulla *Los Pastores*, a Christmas musical play performed by Franquilino Mirando and company.[33]

Johnson described the United States as a land of opportunity, where anyone, by working and studying diligently, had the possibility of becoming president.

The young teacher had childhood friends who, he knew, would never rise above the subsistence level, simply because they lacked the necessary education. He failed to mention the many other barriers facing *La Raza*. They were prevented from voting until the late 1940s by the poll tax and confusion over the white man's primary and whether it excluded Mexican Americans as well as blacks. No distinction was made, politically or socially, between immigrants and native-born Mexican Texans, so the newcomers had little incentive to become naturalized citizens. One Winter Garden resident complained about the Anglo-dominated courts of the late 1920s:

If we go to court it is no use. If there is a dispute between two Mexicans the courts are all right, but if it is between a Mexican and an American it is different; the American gets the best of it some way. You never see them sending an American to the penitentiary for killing a Mexican.[34]

Whatever doubts Johnson may have had, he kept to himself, exuding a spirit of boosterism to his students. A sensitive and caring teacher, Johnson was bothered by the pervasive discrimination and poverty. His drive to succeed and to please the authorities (who, after all, were teaching him) combined with his pragmatic nature. Thus he emphasized the work ethic as an explanation and solution.

The Cotulla Mexican school suffered from high attrition, as in 1936 when 24 percent of the student population was enrolled in first grade and only 5 percent in seventh grade.[35]

Thus, Johnson's students were a dedicated minority who had managed to avoid child labor in the fields and stay in school. Several agreed with César Ortiz Tinoco who said that Johnson was "one of the few teachers . . . who made me think: most teachers just make one study." Although a life-long inspiration to a few, Johnson had difficulty reaching the others and keeping them in school. He blamed this on the language barrier, on their extreme poverty, and on their low self-esteem. He did not mention that many employers were uninterested, even hostile to Mexican American educational improvement. As a distant relative of the prominent Martin family and a young man hoping eventually to have a ranch of his own, he may have ignored this bothersome issue. One teacher in neighboring Dimmit County expressed her ambivalent position, caught between her desire to help her pupils and her understanding of societal expectations:

I have wondered why they don't enforce the attendance law. I have seen numbers who have never been to school. We now have more than we can do justice to. We don't have time to do as good work as in the American school. If they went to school, it would raise their standard of living, but of course onion work is what we have for them to do.

Many Mexican American parents in La Salle County blamed themselves in part for the problem, saying that they needed the children to help earn money in the fields. At the same time, they criticized the attendance system and the inadequate teaching:

In Mexico the instruction is in their own language and they have to go to school.

The Mexicans like the Catholic school better. It takes care of the children and takes more interest and the discipline is better. We want a Mexican or a Texas-Mexican teacher in the public school who will have the feeling for the Mexicans and take more interest in them. The board says they haven't enough money but they always want a $50 a month teacher.

We sometimes kick about the teacher teaching in English, but the school board said they would have to pay too much to get a Mexican teacher to teach in English. The teachers don't teach my children. They have been to school several years and they don't learn anything. The Americans say we don't want education. But we pay our own teachers because we want to learn.[36]

Indeed, several towns in the area set up private bilingual schools that came and went as the tenuous finances dictated.[37]

In 1948 the Texas Supreme Court, prodded by Mexican American civic organizations, ruled segregated schools for Mexican Americans unconstitutional, which led to the integration of the Cotulla elementary schools.[38] The defendants—administrators of the Bastrop school district—used the same justifications as many Cotulla residents: that the separation was purely for pedagogical reasons and that there had always been some Mexican Americans enrolled in the so-called Anglo-American school The court ruled, however, that Mexican Americans had been discriminated against as a class, that the grouping of Spanish-surname students together may be prima facie evidence of segregation, and that the ostensible free choice of schools was often undermined by social or economic pressure to conform and attend the Mexican school.[39]

Meanwhile, as Johnson's career blossomed and he became a well-known political figure, he maintained his Cotulla ties. He aided former students and the Hispanic community in general. In 1939 Congressman Johnson received a letter from Felipe González inviting him to the Cotulla High School graduation. Johnson replied that of course he remembered Felipe and sent him the Federal Writers' Project book *Washington: Capitol and City*. That September Felipe's sister Manuela wrote to Johnson that she gave Felipe $252 for a business course in San Antonio and asked the congressman to encourage his former student. Johnson (or his staff) wrote: "Always remember that, as I used to count on you in school days, I still count on you to do your best and put your whole self into your work, and make more than the average success."[40] (Felipe eventually became chief auditor for the Fourth Army Headquarters.) By 1959 several of the former students had formed an informal group of Johnson Cotulla alumni and in 1962 Johnson wrote to Felipe González's brother for a list of the students.[41]

Johnson also maintained his friendship with Cotulla leaders. The honorable W. A. Kerr congratulated Congressman Johnson on his 1937 victory, saying "Your many friends in Cotulla were well pleased with your successful race." Johnson's cousin Margaret Johnson Kimball headed the 1941 Johnson Senate campaign in Cotulla and in 1960 Vice President and Mrs. Johnson attended the Cotulla wedding of Margaret Johnson, Kimball's daughter, who was also Judge Martin's niece. (The bride entered on Johnson's arm.) Just two years earlier, Martin, as the chief La Salle County official, had declared that the county had no relief funds for 300 local unemployed Mexican American families. Grocers such as M. T. Ramírez were over $100 in debt. ''What work is available *braceros* (immigrant contract laborers) and wet-backs are hired,'' said Ramírez. According to Cotulla lawyer John Wildenthal, Jr.:

The Commissioners, court and several leading citizens obtained some job offers to show that the food program is unnecessary and to provide work. . . . Several townspeople have two or three days of yardwork available and they cannot understand why farmworkers need more work.

Wildenthal said that the Mexican Americans were particularly annoyed at the La Salle County ranchers who lobbied for government aid for their cattle but resisted aid for farm workers. Finally, adverse publicity and requests from other public officials such as Senator Johnson led the Cotullans to apply.[42]

In spite of his busy life as president, Johnson kept a lively interest in Cotulla education and took time from his busy schedule to greet a group of contemporary Cotulla students who presented him with a pen drawing of Welhausen school. For education week, 1966, he visited the school and said, ''I learned far more than I taught. The greatest lesson was this one: nothing at all matters more than trained intelligence.''[43] Although he did acknowledge that ''Right here I learned my first lesson in . . . poverty and prejudice,'' he did not elaborate, perhaps so as not to offend his long-time Anglo supporters, although in a private reminiscence he remarked sadly that the Anglos used to treat the Mexican Americans ''just worse than you'd treat a dog.'' As president he reevaluated the teaching methods of the 1920s and 1930s in that his Elementary and Secondary Education Act (ESEA) included an unprecedented provision for bilingual education, a reversal of the punitive English-only methods that he himself had employed. Johnson's Horatio Alger view of education as the great equalizer by now had been modified to consider other factors such as discrimination and bad teaching methods. (The Mexican American role in the drafting of ESEA merits study.)

Nevertheless, Johnson never made a concerted effort to analyze the causes of South Texas discrimination and stratification. He sympathized with *La Raza*'s plight but also strove successfully to become part of the rancher elite and clung to his traditional version of Texas history. (Johnson joined the Texas State Historical Association in 1951 and remained an active member, serving on its board of advisers in 1955.) In 1964 President Johnson said, ''In my country, we were very proud of what we called the Texas Rangers'' and proceeded to tell an old Texas tale:

One of our cowpunching friends took some cattle up to Kansas City to sell and one of the fellows out in the stockyards said to him . . . ''Please tell me what is really the difference between a Sheriff and a Texas Ranger?'' ''Well, the Ranger is the one that when you plug him, when you hit him, he just keeps on going.''

Johnson especially admired Captain L. H. McNelly. In 1875 he took thirty of his Rangers into Mexico. (At one point his men killed all the adult males at the wrong ranch.) He fought the Mexican forces as long as he could and ignored an order by the U.S. Army for him to return to Texas. In 1965 Johnson wrote a foreword to a new edition of *The Texas Rangers*, extolling them in general and McNelly in particular. Although Johnson's own father had supported a bill by Representative J. T. Canales censuring and limiting the autonomy of the Rangers, his son preferred a more grandiose saga. (The reporter Edward P. Morgan observed in 1966, ''There are times when Lyndon Johnson gives the appearance of an old-fashioned western range sheriff—alert, narrow-eyed, suspicious of strange faces, and sudden movement, cruel in his methods of protecting his home country.'')[44]

By the 1960s, however, some Chicanos, notably José Angel Gutiérrez of Crystal City (in the heart of the Winter Garden area) had devised critiques of the local power structure. Gutiérrez compared this region, with its small group controlling an impoverished majority, to the Latin American *hacienda* system. As such the region was ripe for revolt, which came to Crystal City beginning in 1963. Among the demands by the high school students were:

Have Texas history books revised. We want new text books with the history of *Los Mexicanos*. . . . We also want the school books revised to reflect the contributions of Mexicans and Mexican Americans to the United States society, to make us aware of the injustices that we, Mexican Americans as a people have suffered in an ''Anglo'' dominated society.

Eventually the Mexican American majority gained control of the school system and most city offices in Crystal City. Throughout South Texas, in the wake of Crystal City and encouraged in part by Johnson's civil rights legislation, Chicanos organized and obtained city and school posts. Gutiérrez was even elected judge, a turnabout from the likes of Judge Martin. As late as 1964 Cotulla was run entirely by the Anglo-American minority, but by 1967 *La Raza* had elected a Mexican American mayor. Nevertheless, except for cooperatives established in Crystal City, Winter Garden–area economic power remained largely in the hands of a few Anglos, many of them Johnson's long-time supporters who were one with Johnson in their adulation of the Texas Rangers and the Alamo.[45] Thus, Johnson's inner conflict between ambition and compassion was reflected in this conflict between the heirs of two different Texas heritages: the established Anglo elite and the rising Chicano majority. Hubert Humphrey observed correctly that ''He was really the history of this country, with all of the turmoil, the bombast, the sentiments, the passions.''[46]

NOTES

1. U.S., President, *Public Papers of the Presidents of the United States* (Washington, D.C.: Office of the Federal Register, National Archives and Records Service, 1953-), Lyndon B. Johnson, 1965, 286; Merle Miller, *Lyndon: An Oral Biography* (New York: Putnam, 1980), 11.

2. Baines Scrapbook, Papers of Rebeka Baines Johnson, LBJ Library; Robert Caro, *The Years of Lyndon Johnson: The Path to Power* (New York: Alfred A. Knopf, 1982), 42; Ronnie Dugger, *The Politician: The Life and Times of Lyndon Johnson* (New York: W. W. Norton, 1982), 25-28.

3. Dugger, *The Politician*, 299-300; Alfred Steinberg, *Sam Johnson's Boy* (New York: Macmillan, 1968), 16; William S. White, *The Professional: Lyndon B. Johnson* (Boston: Houghton Mifflin, 1964), 89; Miller, *Lyndon: An Oral Biography*, 18.

4. Steinberg, *Sam Johnson's Boy*, 16; Caro, *The Path to Power*, 74; Dugger, *The Politician*, 34.

5. Doris Kearns, *Lyndon Johnson and the American Dream* (New York: Harper & Row, 1976), 28-31; Steinberg, *Sam Johnson's Boy*, 24; Caro, *The Years of Lyndon Johnson*, 4-5, 20.

6. Dugger, *The Politician*, 91-92, 53-56, 71; Rebekah Baines Johnson, Scrapbook, 30; Steinberg, *San Johnson's Boy*, 29.

7. Roscoe Martin, *The People's Party in Texas* (Austin: University of Texas Press, 1933), 99-102; Ralph Guzmán, *The Political Socialization of the Mexican American People* (New York: Ayer, 1976), 42-43; Julie Leininger Pycior, "*La Raza* Organizes: Mexican American Life in San Antonio as Reflected in *Mutualista* Activities, 1915-1930" (Ph.D. diss., University of Notre Dame, 1979), Chapter 6, "*La Liga Protectora Mexicana*"; Bill Porterfield, *LBJ Country* (Garden City, N.Y.: Doubleday, 1965), 32-33; White, *The Professional*, 87, 93-96; Eldon S. Branda, ed., *The Handbook of Texas: A Supplement* (Austin: Texas State Historical Association, 1976), 393.

8. William Pool, Emmie Cradlock, and David E. Conrad, *Lyndon Baines Johnson: The Formative Years* (San Marcos: Southwest Texas State Press, 1965), 97, 99; Alonso Perales, *Are We Good Neighbors?* (San Antonio: Artes Gráficas, 1948; reprint ed., New York: Arno Press, 1974), 213-222; Nan James Mitchell, "An Evaluation of Provisions for the Education of Spanish-Speaking Children in San Marcos, Texas" (Master's thesis University of Texas, 1946); Charla Dean McCoy, "The Education President: Lyndon Baines Johnson's Public Statements on Instruction and the Teaching Profession" (Ph.D. diss., University of Texas, 1975), 22-23, 48; Annette Martin Ludeman, *La Salle County* (Quana, Texas: Nortex Press, 1975), 124.

9. Douglass F. Foley and Clarice Mota, Donald F. Post, Ignacio Lozano, *From Peones to Políticos: Ethnic Relations in a South Texas Town, 1900-1970* (Austin: Center for Mexican American Studies, 1977), x-xi; Pauline Kibbe, *Latin Americans in Texas* (Albuquerque: University of New Mexico Press, 1946; reprint ed., New York: Arno Press, 1974), 143; Walter Prescott Webb and H. Bailey Carroll, eds., *The Handbook of Texas* (Austin: Texas State Historical Association, 1952), I: 424, 649; II: 31, 351; Donald Meinig, *Imperial Texas, An Interpretive Essay in Cultural Geography* (Austin: University of Texas Press, 1969), 84.

10. George Durham, *Taming the Nueces Strip: The Story of McNelly's Rangers* (Austin: University of Texas Press, 1962), viii, 42-43; O. Clark Fisher, "The Life and Times of

King Fisher," *Southwestern Historical Quarterly* 64 (October 1960): 238; Cecil Robinson, *With the Ears of Strangers: The Mexican in American Literature* (Tucson: University of Arizona Press, 1973), 166. For details of the Nueces-area conflict see John Nance, *After San Jacinto: The Texas-Mexican Frontier, 1836–1841* (Austin: University of Texas Press, 1962).

11. Stanley D. Castro, *The Settlement of the Cibolo-Nueces Strip: A Partial History of La Salle County* (Hillsboro, Tex.: Hill Junior College, 1969), 39; Américo Paredes, *"With His Pistol in His Hand": A Border Ballad and Its Hero* (Austin: University of Texas Press, 1973), 78–82.

12. Paul Taylor, *Mexican Americans in the United States: Dimmit County, Winter Garden District, South Texas* (Berkeley: University of California Press, 1930), 362; Ludeman, *La Salle County*, 6, 131, 143; J. Frank Dobie, *Coronado's Children: Tales of Lost Mines and Buried Treasure* (New York: Literary Guild, 1931), 70–80; Foley et al., *From Peones to Políticos*, 53–54.

13. Annette Martin Ludeman, *Pioneering in the Faith* (Wichita Falls, Texas: Quanah Press, 1973), 6–10; Ludeman, *La Salle County*, 124.

14. Taylor, *Dimmit County*, 362, 488; Kibbe, *Latin Americans in Texas*, 195–197; La Salle County Scrapbook, Barker Texas History Archives, University of Texas; Stanford P. Dyer, "Lyndon B. Johnson and the Politics of Civil Rights, 1935–1960: The Art of 'Moderate Leadership.' " (Ph.D. diss., Texas A&M University, 1978), 7, 12, 14.

15. Foley et al., *From Peones to Políticos*, 45–48; Walter E. Smith, *"Mexicano Resistance to Schooled Ethnicity"* (Ph.D. diss., University of Texas, 1978), 82; Taylor, *Dimmit County*, 370.

16. Everett R. Clinchy, Jr., *Equality of Opportunity for Latin Americans in Texas* (New York: Arno Press, 1974), 37; Webb and Carroll, *The Handbook of Texas*, II: 351; Taylor, *Dimmit County*, 379; Foley et al., *From Peones to Políticos*, 16–17; Howard B. Furer, ed., *Lyndon B. Johnson* (Dobbs Ferry, N.Y.: Oceana Publications, 1974), 2.

17. Robinson, *With the Ears of Strangers*, 170–172.

18. Pool et al., *The Formative Years*, 42–44; Smith, *"Mexicano* Resistance to Schooled Ethnicity," 466.

19. Emilio Zamora, "Chicano Socialist Labor Activity in Texas, 1900–1920," *Aztlán* 6 (Summer 1975): 221–236; Clinchy, *Equality of Opportunity for Latin Americans in Texas*, 49; Smith, *"Mexicano* Resistance to Schooled Ethnicity," 466.

20. Herschel T. Manuel, *The Education of Mexican and Spanish-speaking Children in Texas* (Austin: University of Texas Press, 1930), 76; Virgil E. Stickland and George I. Sánchez, "A Study of the Educational Opportunities Provided Spanish-speaking Children," n.d., Latin American Collection, University of Texas, 5.

21. Transcript, Dorothy Territo Nichols Oral History, 18 February 1975 by Michael Gillette, 27, LBJ Library; Beryle Rutledge Rock, "Children's Achievement in the Amanda Burks Elementary School," (Master's thesis, University of Texas, 1951), 4–5; Clinchy, *Equality of Opportunity for Latin Americans in Texas*, 126–127; Foley et al., *From Peones to Políticos*, 66–67, 111.

22. George I. Sánchez, "Concerning the Segregation of Spanish-speaking Children in the Public Schools," *University of Texas Inter-Americans Education Occasional Papers* 9 (1951): 28–29; Strickland and Sánchez, "Educational Opportunities," 1–2, 7, 9–10.

23. Taylor, *Dimmit County*, 457; Foley et al., *From Peones to Políticos*, 108–110; "Texas Teacher's Daily Register . . . Cotulla School Number One" and "Texas Teacher's Daily Register . . . Cotulla High School," 1927–1929, Board of Education, Cotulla,

Texas; Lura N. Rouse, "A Study of the Education of Spanish-speaking Children in Dimmit County, Texas" (Master's thesis, University of Texas, 1948), 30–34, 74–80.

24. McCoy, "The Education President," 24; Pool et al., *The Formative Years*, 142; Taylor, *Dimmit County*, 383–384, 373, 378, 457; Strickland and Sánchez, "Educational Opportunities," 10–11; Manuel, *The Education of Mexican and Spanish-speaking Children in Texas*, 61; Foley et al., *From Peones to Políticos*, 38; Joe Young, "An Administrative Survey of the Public Schools of La Salle County, Texas" (Master's thesis University of Texas, 1939), 41, 46–47, 50, 55–56; Manuel Gamio, *Mexican Immigration to the United States* (Chicago: University of Chicago Press, 1931; reprint ed., New York: Dover Press, 1971), 222–223.

25. Young, "The Public Schools of La Salle County", 400–401; Strickland and Sánchez, "Educational Opportunities," 10; Manuel, *The Education of Mexican and Spanish-speaking Children in Texas*, 68; letter of reference, W. T. Donaho, 21 February 1929, Dorothy Territo Office Files, "LBJA" Biography File, Papers of Lyndon B. Johnson as Congressman, LBJ Library.

26. Clinchy, *Equality of Opportunity for Latin Americans in Texas*, 46–47, 119; Gamio, *Mexican Immigration*, 73. A typical article was "The Intelligence of Mexican American School Children" by Thomas R. Garth. After testing 1,004 Mexican American pupils in Texas, New Mexico, and Colorado, the author concluded that these students had lower native intelligence than "American" children; he did not question the efficacy of the test itself (*School and Society* 27 (1923): F91–F94.)

27. Manuel, *The Education of Mexican and Spanish-speaking Children in Texas*, 20.

28. McCoy, "The Education President," 24; Miller, *Lyndon: An Oral Biography*, 31; *Public Papers*, Lyndon B. Johnson, 286.

29. Pool et al., *The Formative Years*, 141, 144; Steinberg, *Sam Johnson's Boy*, 47; Smith, "*Mexicano* Resistance to Schooled Ethnicity," 78, 101–102; Manuel, *The Education of Mexican and Spanish-speaking Children in Texas*, 150. At the same time that Texas lacked bilingual teachers for its Hispanic population, 90 percent of whom entered school in 1929 with no knowledge of English, those Mexican Americans who managed to obtain teaching degrees were often denied jobs due to racial prejudice (McCoy, "The Education President," 39, 164).

30. Walter Prescott Webb, *The Texas Rangers* (Boston: Houghton Mifflin, 1935, 14; McCoy, "The Education President," 39; Steinberg, *Sam Johnson's Boy*, 47, 16, 20, 24; Miller, *Lyndon: An Oral Biography*, 18; Julian Samora, Albert Peña, Jr., and Joe Bernal, *Gunpowder Justice* (Notre Dame: University of Notre Dame Press, 1979), 2, 66–67; Dugger, *The Politician*, 32.

31. College editorials, "LBJA" Statements File, 25 April 1928, 7 July 1929, LBJ Library; *Southwestern Historical Quarterly* 58 (April 1954): 143, 148; 61 (April 1957): 147, 151.

32. Harry F. Estill, *The Beginner's History of Our Country* (n.d., n.p.), 241, 310.

33. *San Antonio Express Magazine* (11 October 1954); Foley et al., *From Peones to Políticos*, 40; Cotulla *Record*, 1 January 1929 and January–December 1929, inclusive. *La Prensa*, 30 January 1929; 2 January 1930; 7 January 1930, also January 1929-January 1930, inclusive; Dobie, *Coronado's Children*, 70–80.

34. Miller, *Lyndon: An Oral Biography*, 33; Steinberg, *Sam Johnson's Boy*, 47; Donald Post, "Ethnic Competition for Control of Schools in Two Texas Towns" (Ph.D. diss., University of Texas, 1975), introduction; Taylor, 388–399, 403–404, 408, 411.

35. Ludeman, *La Salle County*, photograph of Johnson and his class, 1928; Young,

"The Public Schools of La Salle County," 26–27, 41–42; "Daily Register . . . Cotulla School #2," 1926–1928; U.S., Department of Commerce, Bureau of the Census, Twelfth Census of the United States, 1900: *Population*, 2 (Washington, D.C.: Government Printing Office, 1932): 1010. Manuel, *The Education of Mexican and Spanish-speaking Children in Texas*, 163. Lyle Saunders, "The Spanish-speaking Population of Texas," *University of Texas Inter-American Occasional Papers* 5 (1949): 13, points out the many flaws and undercounting of Mexican-Texans by the Census Bureau.

36. Taylor, *Dimmit County*, 38, 43, 85, 381, 453.

37. Smith, "*Mexicano* Resistance to Schooled Ethnicity," 4–6; Caro, *Years of Lyndon Johnson*, 169.

38. Beryle Rutledge Rock, "Children's Achievement in the Amanda Burks Elementary School" (Master's thesis, University of Texas, 1951), 4–6.

39. Smith, "*Mexicano* Resistance to Schooled Ethnicity," 98–99; Strickland and Sánchez, "Educational Opportunities," 14–15; Sánchez, "Concerning the Segregation of Spanish-speaking Children," 16–22.

40. Felipe González to Lyndon Johnson, 12 May 1939; Lyndon Johnson to Felipe González, 15 May 1939; Manuela González to Lyndon Johnson, 15 October 1939; Lyndon Johnson to Felipe González, 20 October 1939, "LBJA" Select Files, LBJ Library.

41. Lyndon Johnson to Pedro González, 31 July 1962, "LBJA" Select Files, LBJ Library; Bill Davison, "Texas Political Powerhouse . . . Lyndon Johnson," *Look* (4 August 1959).

42. Correspondence, "Cotulla," January-February 1959, Senate Files, Papers of Lyndon B. Johnson as Senator, LBJ Library; Ludeman, *La Salle County*, last chapter, passim.

43. Lyndon Baines Johnson, Cotulla, Texas, 7 November 1966, Statements File, LBJ Library.

44. *Southwest Historical Quarterly* 55 (April 1951): 143, 148; 61 (April 1957): 146, 151; 66 (July 1962): 133, 137; Dugger, *The Politician*, 25, 41.

45. José Angel Gutiérrez, *La Raza and Revolution* (San Francisco: R. and E. Publishers, 1972), 24–27; Meinig, *Imperial Texas*, p. 10; Ludeman, *La Salle County*, 36, 43. For an account of the Crystal City revolt and the formation of La Raza Unida Party, see J. S. Shockley, *Chicano Revolt in a Texas Town* (Notre Dame: University of Notre Dame Press, 1974). Cotulla *Record*, June 1981, for example, describes Chicano involvement in official city activities.

46. Miller, *Lyndon: An Oral Biography*, xvi.

9

LBJ and Supreme Court Politics in the Light of History

David M. O'Brien

The presidential impulse to pack the Court with politically compatible justices is irresistible.[1] In this respect, Lyndon Baines Johnson was no different from any other president. His appointments of Abe Fortas in 1965 and Thurgood Marshall in 1967 were deeply personal and politically strategic. Yet LBJ's contributions to constitutional politics have been marred by charges of "political cronyism"—that, in other words, he went beyond the mere political favoritism practiced by other presidents.

In the light of history, however, LBJ's appointments appear less than pure cronyism and something more than simple political favoritism. His advisory relationship with Justice Fortas, moreover, was neither unprecedented nor unusual, although it, perhaps, pushed to the limits the propriety of justices' off-the-bench activities.

The myth occasionally circulates that judicial appointments should be made strictly on merit. Attorney General Ramsey Clark, for one, told President Johnson that, "I think a most significant contribution to American government would be the non-political appointment of judges."[2] Both of LBJ's appointments to the Court were political, of course, as those of all other presidents. Like other presidents, LBJ sought to infuse his own political philosophy into the Court. For his first appointment, he turned not merely to his trusted friend and adviser, but to a first-rate legal mind, not a second- or third-rate mind, as some presidents have done. Far from cronyism, his second appointment demonstrates political leadership, vision, and a courageous attempt to represent the country within the Court, by naming the first black, Thurgood Marshall, to the high bench.

The myth of merit is perpetuated by jurists and scholars. Justice Felix Frankfurter, for instance, insisted that President John Kennedy and his Attorney General Robert Kennedy chose inferior judges. He once said, "What does Bobby understand about the Supreme Court? He understands about as much about it as you understand about the undiscovered 76th star in the galaxy. . . . He said Arthur Goldberg was a scholarly lawyer. I wonder where he got that notion from.'' What perturbed Frankfurter was that the Kennedy administration did ''not adequately appreciate the Supreme Court's role in the country's life and the functions that are entrusted to the Supreme Court and the qualities both intellectual and moral that are necessary to the discharge of its functions.'' Distinguished individuals were accordingly passed over, in Frankfurter's opinion, and appointed instead were such ''wholly inexperienced men as Goldberg and White, without familiarity with the jurisdiction or the jurisprudence of the Court either as practitioners or scholars or judges.''[3]

The reality is that every judicial appointment is political. Merit competes with other political considerations such as personal and ideological compatibility; the forces of support or opposition within Congress and the White House; and demands for representative appointments based on geography, religion, race, gender, and ethnicity.

The Supreme Court is not a meritocracy for basically two reasons: the difficulties of defining merit and the politics of judicial selection. Any definition of ''judicial merit'' is artificial. Henry Abraham, a leading scholar on the appointment of justices, proposes as a model of ''judicial merit'' a sextet: demonstrated judicial temperament; professional expertise and competence; absolute personal as well as professional integrity; an able, agile, lucid mind; appropriate professional educational background or training; and the ability to communicate clearly, both orally and in writing.[4] But justices themselves have difficulty defining merit and qualities such as ''judicial temperament.'' Judicial merit is perhaps reducible only to that standard of ''obscenity'' offered by Justice Potter Stewart: ''I know it when I see it.''[5]

Judicial selection, as Justice Harlan Stone put it, is like a ''lottery'' from a pool of more or less qualified individuals. Stone's close friend, Harvard law professor and political scientist Thomas Reed Powell, was even more blunt: ''The selection of Supreme Court Justices is pretty much a matter of chance.''[6] Political associations and personal friendships often determine the fate of candidates for the Court.

Meritorious individuals are thus passed over. Paul Freund, a respected Harvard law professor and clerk for Justice Brandeis in 1932, is one who was denied a deserved seat on the high bench. During the Kennedy administration, Freund was offered the solicitor generalship but declined. The Kennedys were accordingly unwilling to give him a life-time appointment to the Court. As Attorney General Robert Kennedy explained, when discussing why Freund and others were not nominated, ''Some of these other people we didn't know, and we did know that Byron White had ability and that Arthur Goldberg had ability. We'd worked with them, they'd worked with us, so why not appoint them rather than somebody that someone else said was good but that neither my brother nor I knew? That was the basis of it.''[7] Insiders in the Johnson White House and others continued to push for Freund's appointment. Even though he was then in his sixties, Freund, insisted presidential adviser James Rowe, "is, without question, easily the most qualified man in the United States to sit on the Supreme Court."[8] When he was seventy (well beyond the age of appointment) his nomination for Justice William Douglas' seat in 1975 was again urged on the ground that any appointment by the unelected "accidental President" Gerald Ford would be controversial. Freund's "nomination would be perceived as apolitical" and he would serve, if even for a short time, with distinction.[9] Freund was nonetheless passed over again.

The appointment of justices is constrained by the Constitution and the competitive politics of the nomination and confirmation process. Article II, Section 2 of the Constitution stipulates that the president "shall nominate, and by and with the Advice and Consent of the Senate, shall appoint" members of the federal judiciary. The Senate's power to reject nominees is the crucial obstacle that a president must overcome. Twenty-five of the 128 nominations to the Court have fallen prey to partisan politics, either due to the nominee's political views or because the Senate wanted to deny "lame duck" presidents appointments to the high Court. LBJ's promotion of Justice Fortas to chief justice in 1968 was one of those defeated by partisan politics.

The appointment process has basically become a bargaining process in which the influence of the Senate is greater over lower court judgeships and that of the president over nominations to the Supreme Court. At the level of federal district courts, in Attorney General Kennedy's words: "Basically, it's senatorial appointment with the advice and consent of the president."[10] Presidents have greater discretion at the level of circuit courts of appeals, whose jurisdiction spans several states. They may play senators off against each other by claiming the need for representation of different political parties, geographical regions, religions, races, and the like within a circuit. "In the case of the Supreme Court Justices," President Herbert Hoover's Attorney General William Mitchell observed, "with the whole country to choose from, the senators from one state or another are in no position even if they were so inclined, to attempt a controlling influence. Such an appointment is not a local matter, and the entire nation has an equal interest and responsibility."[11]

Packing the Court has thus come to mean not merely filling the bench with political associates and ideological kin, but accommodating demands for other kinds of symbolic political representation as well. Just as some people maintain that merit rather than political favoritism should govern appointments, there are those, like Justice Stone, who lament that "the view has come to prevail that in addition to political considerations, considerations of race, religion, and sectional interests should influence the appointment."[12] Yet neither merit nor representative factors such as geography, religion, race, and gender control judicial appointments. Rather, they are simply competing political considerations in presidential attempts to pack the Court. How different presidents weigh those competing considerations is what is important.

In historical perspective, religion, race, and gender have been barriers, rather than bases for appointments to the Court. The overwhelming majority (92) of the 103 justices have come from established Protestant religions. The remaining eleven included six Catholics and five Jews. LBJ was the last president to appoint a Jew to the Court and none have sat on the high bench since Justice Fortas stepped down. And there were no nonwhites until LBJ broke the color barrier with his second appointment.

What remains significant about LBJ's Court-packing is not simply that he appreciated the symbolic importance of representative appointments for both the Court and the country. He did, but those considerations did not entirely control his appointments. Religon did not enter into his first nomination, whereas race was paramount in his second. Neither appointment sacrificed LBJ's basic concern with appointing unquestionably capable individuals with whom he had ideological and personal affinity, and whom he trusted to advance his vision of constitutional politics. Unlike his immediate predecessors and successors in the Oval Office, LBJ was not disappointed with his appointments to the Court.

RELIGION AND RACE

Religion has political symbolism, but played little role in judicial selection until the twentieth century. The so-called Catholic seat and Jewish seat were created accidentally, rather than due to presidential efforts to give the Court religious balance. Representation, of course, is purely symbolic. Catholics and Jews do not have well-defined positions, for example, on statutory interpretation. Nor does the appointment of a Catholic or a Jew guarantee that the views of either faith will be reflected in the voting of representative justices. Justice William Brennan, a Catholic, did not heed Church teachings when voting in *Roe* v. *Wade* (1973) to uphold a woman's right to obtain an abortion. Religious and racial considerations, moreover, appear "highly indefensible and dangerous" to the extent that more qualified individuals are passed over. Such considerations, Frankfurter contended, are "not only irrelevant for appointments to the bench, but mischievously irrelevant—that to appoint men on the score of race and religion [is] playing with fire."[13]

After the appointment of Louis Brandeis in 1916, there developed an expectation of a Jewish seat. With the confirmation of Benjamin Cardozo in 1932 and then his replacement by Felix Frankfurter, two Jewish justices sat on the Court until Brandeis retired in 1939. When Frankfurter stepped down in 1962, the Jewish factor mattered, and President Kennedy named Arthur Goldberg, his secretary of labor. Three years later LBJ persuaded Goldberg to become ambassador to the United Nations, and his vacancy was filled by Fortas.

Although politically symbolic, religious representation on the Court never amounted to a quota system. Catholics and Jews were more often selected because of personal and ideological compatibility with the president. This was especially true of LBJ's appointment of Fortas.

"The question of whether or not this appointee should be Jewish concerns me," Attorney General Nicholas Katzenbach told the president, adding:

I think most Jews share with me the feeling that you should not seek a Jewish appointment for the "Jewish seat" on the court. It is somewhat offensive to think of religion as a qualification, and you will recall that after Mr. Justice Murphy's death there was not a Catholic on the Court for a period of eight years. . . . On balance, I think, if you appoint a Jew he should be so outstanding as to be selected clearly on his own merits as an individual.[14]

Johnson was intent on appointing Fortas, regardless of his religion. The two had known each other since the New Deal, both shared a political vision and LBJ (like so many others) admired Fortas' quick, analytical mind and personal integrity. In 1964 LBJ had unsuccessfully urged Fortas to become attorney general. Fortas also initially declined appointment to the Court. He told the president, "I want a few more years of activity."[15] But Fortas finally reluctantly agreed to enter the marble temple.

"The time has come" for the appointment of a black to the Court, LBJ's advisers assured him in 1967.[16] The symbolism of appointing a black was never lost on the president, nor had LBJ's commitment to appointing Thurgood Marshall ever waned. As director of the NAACP Counsel of Legal Defense and Education Fund, Marshall gained national recognition arguing the landmark school desegregation case, *Brown* v. *Board of Education* (1954). In 1961, Kennedy named him to the court of appeals for the second circuit. Subsequently, Johnson convinced him to give up the judgeship and become his solicitor general. LBJ wanted "that image, number one" of a black solicitor general, recalls Justice Marshall. LBJ told him at the time, "You know this has nothing to do with any Supreme Court appointment. I want that distinctly understood. There's no quid pro here at all. You do your job. If you don't do it, you go out. If you do it, you stay here. And that's all there is to it."[17] That, of course, was not all there was to it. The solicitor generalship offers experience in representing the government before the Court and a strategic basis for elevation to the high bench. As Cornelius Vanderbilt, Jr., recognized, when congratulating the president on the appointment, "This is *great* news! Also it is *very* clever politics."[18]

Marshall was not the first black to be seriously considered for the Court. Twenty years earlier rumors circulated that William Hastie might be named. Dean of Howard University Law School and later a court of appeals judge, Hastie was given more serious consideration during the Kennedy administration. Attorney General Kennedy recalls that Hastie was his first choice for the vacancy eventually filled by Byron White. Kennedy talked with both Chief Justice Earl Warren and Justice Douglas about the nomination. Warren "was violently opposed to having Hastie on the Court," according to Kennedy. "He's not a liberal, and he'll be opposed to all the measures that we are interested in, and he would just be completely unsatisfactory."[19] "Hastie is a very fine person,"

Douglas observed, but "he is sort of a pedestrian type of person, very conservative."[20] Based on merit, presidential adviser Jim Rowe and others argued that Hastie deserved the appointment, since he was "much more of a legal scholar than Marshall."[21] The Kennedys decided against the nomination. They had just suffered defeat of their proposed Department of Housing and Urban Development due to the "political error" of announcing that, if the department were established, Robert Weaver would be named as secretary and become the first black cabinet member.[22] Such opposition to the naming of blacks to prominent government posts reinforced Johnson's commitment to appoint Marshall. There were other leading blacks, but LBJ felt that Marshall had paid his political dues, and the appointment was undeniably politically symbolic, if not crucial for the country.

THE LBJ-FORTAS CONTROVERSY

The myth of the cult of the robe—that justices are "legal monks" removed from political life—has been perpetuated by justices, like Frankfurter, who hypocritically proclaim, "When a priest enters a monastery, he must leave—or ought to leave—all sorts of worldly desires behind him. And this Court has no excuse for being unless it's a monastery."[23]

The reality is that justices are political actors and find it more or less hard to refrain from outside political activities. Off-the-bench activities are the norm. More than seventy of those who have sat on the Court advised presidents and congressmen about matters of domestic and foreign policy, patronage appointments, judgeships, and legislation affecting the judiciary. Even more justices have made their views on public policy known through speeches and publications.[24]

Still, is it not wrong for justices and presidents to consult with each other? The traditional view was well expressed by North Carolina's Senator Sam Ervin, during the confirmation hearing on the nomination of Fortas as chief justice in 1968:[25]

I just think it is the height of impropriety for a Supreme Court justice, no matter how close he may have been to the President, to advise him or consult with him on matters, public matters that properly belong within the realm of the executive branch of Government, and which may wind up in the form of litigation before the Court.

History, however, is replete with justices advising presidents, and standards of judicial propriety have evolved. Ultimately, what is crucial is whether off-the-bench activities bring the Court into a political controversy. Fortas' relationship with LBJ and the battle over his confirmation as chief justice illustrate the politics of off-the-bench activities.

Fortas' relationship with LBJ was by no means unprecedented. Their relationship stemmed from the days of the New Deal and was shaped by the experience of those associated with the inner circle of Democratic politics dating back to Franklin Roosevelt's administration. After graduating and teaching for a year at Yale Law School, Fortas went to Washington in 1934 as an assistant at the Securities and Exchange Commission. The commitment and interaction among New Deal lawyers left an indelible imprint on Fortas, no less than on Johnson who saw himself as FDR's protege.

The off-the-bench activities of the Roosevelt Court established a model for the Fortas-Johnson relationship. In his first term, FDR relied on advice from Brandeis, who had been an adviser to President Woodrow Wilson. "I need Brandeis everywhere," Wilson observed, "but I must leave him somewhere."[26] A respected "prophet of reform," Brandeis stood as a "judicial idol" for New Deal lawyers. During the early years of the New Deal, as political scientist Bruce Murphy has shown, Brandeis used Frankfurter as his "scribe," his intermediary for promoting his ideas in the Roosevelt administration.[27] But the "Brandeis-Frankfurter connection" was neither secret nor deemed newsworthy or improper within Washington political circles.[28]

When Roosevelt filled vacancies on the Court, he continued to feel free to turn to his appointees for advice. Shortly after leaving his post as solicitor general, Justice Stanley Reed sent a note requesting a meeting with the president that reveals the attitude of the Roosevelt Court toward their president. "If it is not too much of an intrusion [our meeting] will help me to maintain, in some degree, my understanding of your objective."[29] After Frankfurter joined the Court, he continued his advisory relationship, though his constant meddling sometimes backfired. Frankfurter also competed for influence with others on the Court. Justices Harlan Stone, Hugo Black, and William Douglas advised the president on judicial appointments and other matters of public policy. Justice Frank Murphy frequently met with FDR to discuss the war in the Pacific; and Jimmy Byrnes, during his brief stay on the bench, continued to offer advice on the constitutionality of legislation.[30] Unlike Frankfurter, after FDR's death, Douglas continued to advise Presidents Truman, Kennedy, and Johnson on concerns ranging from saving the redwoods in the west and protecting the environment to increased Soviet influence in the Middle East and the wisdom of diplomatic recognition of China.[31] When a president like FDR and justices find commonality of purpose and personal and ideological compatibility, consultations are inevitable and questions of propriety overlooked.

Johnson's relationship with Fortas was more intimate and extensive than that of FDR and his Court. The president counted Fortas among his elite group of foreign policy advisers. Regularly joining White House meetings on the Vietnam War, Fortas attended more cabinet meetings than the man he replaced on the bench, U.N. Ambassador Arthur Goldberg, who was one of the few "doves" in the administration.[32]

"Should we get out of Vietnam?" That was the central question at the November 2, 1967 meeting of the foreign policy advisers (and a question continually debated throughout LBJ's term). "The public would be outraged if we got out,"

Fortas observed. "What about our course in North Vietnam?" The president asked, "Should we continue as is; go further, moderate it; eliminate the bombing?" Both "hawks" on the war, "Fortas and Clark Clifford recommended continued bombing as we are doing." Less than a year later in the spring of 1968 the North Vietnamese successfully penetrated South Vietnam in the so-called Tet offensive. General William Westmoreland demanded more troops. Goldberg pressed for a bombing halt and a more vigorous initiative at peace negotiations. Protest against the Vietnam War was steadily mounting. LBJ was at the crossroads of a major decision affecting the war and his presidency. At a March meeting, Goldberg pushed for direct talks with Hanoi and for a "cessation of the bombing" of North Vietnam. Fortas opposed a pause in the bombing. He urged the president to explain in a speech to the American people the need for troop reinforcement and our "strength and resoluteness" in the war. Fewer than ten days later, Johnson announced the most critical decision of his presidency. Bombing would continue but only in the area south of Hanoi, where the North Vietnamese had a large military force and from where they were invading South Vietnam. He thus opened the possibility for negotiations with the Hanoi government but also announced his decision not to seek reelection.[33]

Fortas was no less active in the formulation of domestic policy. He attended meetings on fiscal policy, labor legislation, election reform, and campaign financing, often offering his views on matters that would eventually come before the courts.[34] Senator Thruston Morton recalls a telephone call to learn LBJ's position on pending legislation and being told, "Well, the president is away, but Mr. Justice Fortas is here and he's managing the bill for the White House."[35] Fortas also helped write LBJ's speeches and messages to Congress on civil rights and criminal justice reform and recommended individuals for appointments as attorney general and to federal judgeships.

Fortas' nomination as chief justice was defeated, but not primarily due to his advising LBJ. Even after it was revealed that he accepted $15,000 for teaching a seminar on "Law and the Social Environment" at American University, the public supported confirmation by a two-to-one margin.[36] Several factors contributed to his defeat. Johnson overestimated his influence after announcing that he would not seek reelection. Anticipating Richard Nixon's victory in the 1968 election, Republican senators wanted to deny LBJ any appointments to the Court. White House advisers also told LBJ that it was a mistake to name another close personal friend, Homer Thornberry, to the vacancy created by Fortas' promotion.[37]

Senate opposition primarily focused on Fortas' judicial record and his support of the Warren Court's "liberal jurisprudence." As Virginia's Senator Harry F. Byrd explained, "The Warren Court has usurped authority to which it is not entitled and is not serving the best interests of our nation. Mr. Fortas appears to have embraced the Warren philosophy, which philosophy I strongly oppose."[38] In Senator James Eastland's words: "The main thrust of Justice Fortas' philosophy as expressed in his opinions is to tear down those ideas, ideals, and institutions that have made this country great. . . . ''[39]

Defeat, Fortas told Warren, ultimately came from the "bitter, corrosive opposition to all that has been happening in the Court and the country: the racial progress, and the insistence upon increased regard for human rights and dignity in the field of criminal law. Other elements contribute to the mix, but it's my guess that they are minor.''[40] Shortly before he asked LBJ to withdraw his nomination, Fortas explained to Justice John Marshall Harlan that he had "not been a governmental 'busybody' '' and had "never 'volunteered' suggestions or participation in the affairs of state. On the other hand, I felt that I had no alternative to complying with the president's request for participation in the matters where he sought my help—or more precisely, sought the comfort of hearing my summation before his decision. That's about what it amounted to in the case of President Johnson–Justice Fortas.'' He had no regrets about his off-the-bench activities and could not believe that he "injured the Court as an institution.''[41]

Less than a year later, Fortas resigned from the Court. He did so because of further publicity that he had acepted $20,000 in 1965 as an adviser to the Wolfson Family Foundation, a foundation devoted to community relations and racial and religious cooperation. Fortas had terminated his relationship with the foundation during his first year on the Court and had returned the $20,000. He conceded "no wrong doing.'' But, Fortas told Warren, "the public controversy relating to my association with the Foundation is likely to continue and adversely affect the work and position of the Court.'' The Court's prestige, he concluded, "prompts my resignation which, I hope, by terminating the public controversy, will permit the Court to proceed with its work without harassment of debate concerning one of its members.''[42]

CONCLUSION

Like other presidents, LBJ sought to infuse his own political philosophy into the Court and thereby influence the direction of public policy and constitutional politics. Although he had only two opportunities to make appointments to the Supreme Court, LBJ was largely successful in his attempt at Court packing, unlike many other presidents who have tried and failed. In his four years on the Court, Fortas joined the majority of the Warren Court in some of landmark rulings that expanded the protections of the Bill of Rights for all Americans. During his brief tenure, he delivered forty opinions (about eight a year) for the Court announcing its decisions. Among those opinions, two stand out: *In re Gault* (1967), extending procedural guarantees of the Bill of Rights to defendants in juvenile courts; and "the black arm band case,'' *Tinker* v. *Des Moines Community School District* (1969), in which the Court upheld under the First Amendment the right of students to wear armbands in protest of the Vietnam War and recognized the important principle of constitutionally protected symbolic speech. Justice Marshall, now in his nineteenth year on the Court, also joined those rulings of the Warren and Burger Courts that have extended basic constitutional rights and civil liberties. But even more important, Justice Marshall has stood as a symbol of the need, both for the Court and the country, for some measure of democratic representation on the highest court in the land.

Public perception and acceptance of the legitimacy of the Court are no less crucial than who sits on the high bench. Constitutional law is a kind of dialogue between the Court and the country. And the great struggles of constitutional politics are determined as much by what is possible in a system of free government and pluralistic society as by what the Court says about the Constitution. LBJ understood this important fact of our system of constitutional politics in his appointments to the high Court, just as did Justice Fortas when he resigned from the Court—resigned not because his relationship with LBJ was illegal, improper, or unprecedented, but so that the Court's prestige would not further suffer from partisan attacks and that it might continue its struggle to vindicate the substantive value choices of human dignity and free government embedded in the Constitution.

NOTES

1. For a further discussion, see David M. O'Brien, *Storm Center: The Supreme Court in American Politics* (New York: W. W. Norton & Company, 1986), Chapter 2.

2. Memorandum to the President, 6 January 1965, John Macy Papers, Box 726, "Judgeships File," LBJ Library.

3. Justice Felix Frankfurter Oral History, 52–53 Kennedy Presidential Library (hereafter cited as KPL). See also Letter, 15 May 1964, Charles Wyzanski Papers, Box 1, File 26, Harvard Law School (hereafter cited as HLS).

4. Henry J. Abraham, "A Bench Happily Filled: Some Historical Reflections on the Supreme Court Appointment Process," *Judicature* 66 (1983): 282, 286.

5. *Jacobellis* v. *Ohio*, 378 U.S. 184, 197 (1964).

6. Letter, 9 October 1928, Harlan F. Stone Papers, Box 24, Library of Congress (hereafter cited as LC).

7. Robert Kennedy Oral History, 620–621, KPL.

8. Memorandum, 18 May 1967, WHCF-FG, Box 535, LBJ Library.

9. Letter, 13 November 1975, WHCF-FG, Box 51, Ford Presidential Library (hereafter cited as FPL).

10. Kennedy Oral History, 603, KPL. See also, WHCF-FG, Boxes 505 and 530, KPL.

11. W. Mitchell, "Appointment of Federal Judges," *American Bar Association Journal* 17 (1931): 569. See also WHCF, Box 441, Hoover Presidential Library.

12. Letter to Thomas Reed Powell, 15 October 1928: Stone Papers, Box 24, LC.

13. Letters, 22 November 1954 and 10 September 1941, Charles Wyzanski Papers, Box 1, Files 13 and 18, HLS.

14. Memorandum for the President, Supreme Court Vacancy, Ramsey Clark Papers, "Judgeships File," LBJ Library.

15. Letter to the President, 19 July 1965, WHCF-FG, Box 535, LBJ Library.

16. Letter from Paul Carrington to Joseph Califano, 13 March 1967, Records of Department of Justice, National Archives and Record Service.

17. Justice Thurgood Marshall Oral History, 7, LBJ Library.

18. Letter, 13 June 1967, Macy Papers, Box 365, Marshall File, LBJ Library.

19. Kennedy Oral History, 614–615, KPL.

20. Interview with Justice William O. Douglas, 155, Seeley G. Mudd Library, Princeton University (hereafter cited as MLPU).

21. Letter, 21 June 1965, WHCF-FG, Box 535, LBJ Library.

22. John Macy Oral History, 31–33, LBJ Library.

23. From the *Diaries of Felix Frankfurter*, J. Lash, ed. (New York: W. W. Norton, 1974), 155.

24. This is based on the definitive study of extrajudicial activities by William Cibes, "Extra-Judicial Activities of Justices of the United States Supreme Court, 1790–1960" (Ph.D. diss., Princeton University, 1975) (based on public and presidential papers), and the author's own study of papers of fifty-five justices and those of six presidents, as discussed in O'Brien, *Storm Center*.

25. Senate Committee on the Judiciary, *On the Nomination of Abe Fortas of Tennessee to the Chief Justice of the United States*, 90th Cong., 2d. Sess., 1968, 1303.

26. A. Lief, *Brandeis: The Personal History of an American Ideal* (Harrisburg, Pa.: Telegraph Press, 1936), 409.

27. B. Murphy, *The Brandeis/Frankfurter Connection* (New York: Oxford University Press, 1982).

28. Based on conversations with former solicitor general and dean of Harvard Law School, Erwin Griswold (1983), and Washington lawyer-lobbyist Thomas "Tommy the Cork" Corcoran (1982).

29. Note the President, 26 October 1938; PPF, Box 4877, Roosevelt Presidential Library (hereafter cited as RPL).

30. Justice Murphy's notes on his meetings with President Roosevelt during 1940–1943 are in the Eugene Gressman papers, Bentley Historical Library, University of Michigan, and Justice Byrnes' memoranda to the president and other White House advisers are in Byrnes Papers, Clemson University. See also Alpha Files, Boxes 607, 4877 and 6389, and PSF, Box 186, RPL.

31. See WHCF-PSF, Boxes 118 and 284; PPF, Box 504, Truman Presidential Library (hereafter cited as TPL). Kennedy Interview and Kennedy Papers, Box 16, KPL. WHCF-Name Series, Letter, 22 March 1966; WH-Famous Names, Letter, 25 February 1964; WHCF-FG, 535 and 505/9, LBJ Library.

32. Goldberg attended fewer than half of the Cabinet meetings held during his first two and one-half years as ambassador to the United Nations. Memoranda and other materials in WHCF-OF, Goldberg File, LBJ Library.

33. Memo from Jim Jones to the President, 2 November 1967, WH-Notes File; Meetings Notes File, 2 November 1967; 2 and 27 March 1968, Meetings Notes Files, LBJ Library.

34. Diary Backup, Boxes 43, 60, 63 and 66, LBJ Library.

35. WHCF, Fortas/ Thornberry Series, Box 1, JPL: Diary Backup, Box 45, WHCF-Name File (Douglas); and Macy Papers (Fortas File), LBJ Library.

36. Memorandum to Temple, WHCF, "Fortas-Thornberry Series," Chron. File, and Letter, 9 September 1969; Christopher Papers, Box 18, LBJ Library.

37. Clifford Oral History, Tape 4, 29; Porter Oral History, 28–34; Macy Oral History, 726; and Temple Oral History, LBJ Library.

38. Letter, 6 September 1968, WHCF, "Fortas-Thornberry Series," Chron. File, LBJ Library.

39. Senate Judiciary Committee, *Report on the Nomination of Abe Fortas*, 90th Cong., 2d Sess., 1968.

40. Letter, 25 July 1968, Warren Papers, Box 352, LC.

41. Letter, 24 July 1968; Harlan Papers, Box 531, MLPU.

42. Letter, 14 May 1969; Harlan Papers, Box 606, MLPU; and Warren Papers (Statement of Wolfson), Box 353, LC.

10

Abe Fortas: Presidential Adviser

Bruce Murphy

For most Americans today, their memory of Justice Abe Fortas, if they even have one, is negative. How tragic and ironic for the man who at age twenty-three was being characterized by journalists as "the symbol of the New Deal" to be remembered now as the only Supreme Court justice in history to resign under fire.[1] And how equally ironic that the man who put him in that position initially, who in William O. Douglas' words "ambushed" Fortas for the Supreme Court, was one of the men who loved him the most—his closest political friend and ally, Lyndon Baines Johnson.[2]

Indeed, Washingtonians and journalists generally cite four ways that Fortas failed liberal America. In the words of Victor Navasky, writing shortly after the tragic resignation from the Court:

Washington is an ungenerous town. Some of its younger inhabitants consider Abe Fortas a "war criminal" because he has not yet repudiated the hawkish advice he allegedly gave LBJ on the war. Liberals blame him for consulting with the president at all, and for the indiscretion which caused him to resign, thereby upsetting the balance of the old Warren Court in Nixon's favor.... [And] public interest lawyers consider Fortas's greatest sin to be the work he did on behalf of such clients as Phillip Morris cigarettes before he arrived on the Court.[3]

It seems that no matter what book on Vietnam you read, Fortas is portrayed as a war hawkish Rasputin behind the Johnson throne and one of the "architects" of the conflict.[4]

This chapter will focus on the nature of Fortas' role in the Vietnam advising process in the hopes of drawing some tentative conclusions about the validity of this charge against him. In addition, I hope to use these historical data to draw some larger theoretical conclusions about the nature of outside advisers to presidents.

Because of the critical nature of the charges against Fortas, it is worth beginning with a word about the premise of this chapter with respect to the nature of the war as a policy. Some have argued that Vietnam was a failed policy. However, others still argue that it not only had its limited successes, but could have been even more successful. This debate will be left to others. I will start from a more neutral position for purposes of this analysis that the war was unproductive in its geopolitical, military, and psychological impact. The phrase: "Let's not have another Vietnam," has certainly become part of this nation's lexicon.

This being the case, how might the unproductive policy of the war have been avoided or been made more productive? Politically speaking, was this a failure of the advisory process or the president or both? Lawrence Berman uses this question quite effectively to explore the 28 July 1965 50,000 troop escalation and concludes, "In the final analysis the president and not his advisers must accept most of the blame. Johnson was the cause of his ultimate undoing."[5] Since Fortas played little or no role in this initial decision, my focus is now on the nature of his role for the rest of the course of the war.

Since Fortas is accused of being an architect of the war, my questions will be threefold. First, what is the proper role of an outside adviser to the president? Next, what specifically was the nature of Abe Fortas' work with Lyndon Johnson on Vietnam? And, finally, by applying the first section to the second, how did this advisory interaction solely on the question of the war measure up to the theoretical demands of the relationship? I hope that in answering the final question we will have a sense of the level of blame one can assess to Fortas on this policy.

OUTSIDE PRESIDENTIAL ADVISERS: THE THEORY

Let's turn now to a short discussion of the nature of outside presidential advising. First, there is the matter of a definition. Here an "outside" adviser to the president will be used to describe someone offering the president some combination of information or opinion who is not then in the normal executive branch advising channels. The limited body of literature on the presidential advising structure makes clear the importance of such "outsiders" to provide a sort of "reality check" for the chief executive.[6] Many, including most notably George Reedy, have noted the tendency of the modern president to surround himself with "yes men" on the staff who tend to isolate him from the main stream of American thinking on an issue.[7] It is an isolation that, as Irving Janis has noted, can become almost a mindless "group think" during times of crises, resulting in tragic mistakes of policy.[8] And it is an isolation that many, such as Richard Neustadt and Jonathan Schell, have noted has become even more profound a prospect as the president has gained sole control over the nuclear military arsenal.[9] Theodore Sorensen discusses the need for:

independent, unofficial sources of advice for the same reasons he needs independent, unofficial sources of information. Outside advisers may be more objective. Their contact with affected groups may be closer. They may be people whose counsel the president trusts, but who are unable to accept government service for financial or personal reasons. They may be people who are frank with the president because, to use Corwin's phrase, their "daily political salt did not come from the president's table." [10]

For this reason, Franklin D. Roosevelt made it a practice in running his administration to constantly crosscheck his institutional advisers by consulting with a select group of outsiders, such as Bernard Baruch, or even freewheeling insiders with formal portfolios in other areas, such as Raymond Moley and Thomas Corcoran. In this fashion, he could ensure not only the correctness of the results of his formal advisory process, but also sense the political problems that might arise down the road from their promulgation.

As it happened, several of those advisers on select issues were members of the Supreme Court of the United States. Disdaining the commonly held public myth of "Caesar's wife," nonpoliticians on the Court—Louis D. Brandeis, Felix Frankfurter, and William O. Douglas, among others—did not hesitate to offer their views, sometimes even in response to presidential requests, on a wide number of policies ranging from administration appointments, law making, economic policy, and foreign affairs. [11] Of course, the nature of this sort of outside advisory relationship may raise grave problems of ethics and limit the justice's maneuverability, as I have argued elsewhere. [12]

But there is something more that is implied in the nature of the term *outside adviser*. In seeking a reality check, the president wants and needs someone to tell him whether the normal bureaucratic processes have provided correct and/or meritorious advice. The fear would be that the normal institutional dynamics of the White House and the executive branch might lead to a situation in which key questions are not asked, key options are not considered, or maybe even key recommendations are not presented to the president out of fear that "the boss" will not like the news. Thus, a key element implied in the concept of "outside advising" is the word "independent."

Too many of the president's institutional advisers do not have the incentive or are too much at risk to provide such outside advice. One must consider one's own vulnerability, one's competence to speak, and what might be in it for him if such a role is to be played. What is needed is someone with the capacity—either by reason of a long-standing relationship with the president, or a status that cannot be affected by the president's whims (that is, he cannot be fired or does not care if the president never calls him again in the future)—to provide a freewheeling, open, and honest assessment of the current conditions. In this fashion, one can truly provide outside advice.

Then, too, the concept of "independent outside advice" involves far more than the adviser's "capacity to give." It also involves the president's "capacity to receive." Does the president want to hear news that is bad or contrary to his own preconceived notions? Is the president strong enough to hear criticism or, even more important, to heed it enough to act upon it? A president must be what James David Barber termed an "active positive" personality, with an ego strong enough to take bad medicine, to seek out other alternatives that might not be in his best political short-run interests.[13] Alexander George, in examining the foreign policy advising process, sees a series of nine types of "possible (and possibly dangerous) malfunctions of the advisory process." Among them are:

> when the decision maker and his advisers agree too readily on the nature of the problem facing them and on a response to it, . . . when advisers and policy advocates take different positions and debate them before the executive, but their disagreements do not cover the full range of relevant hypotheses and alternative options, . . . when advisers to the executive thrash out their disagreements over policy without the executive's knowledge and confront him with a unanimous recommendation, . . . [and] when the executive, faced with an important problem to decide is dependent upon a single channel of information.

To solve this process George advocates a "formal options" system by which the president imposes a certain amount of hierarchical coordination and control from above, supplemented by a "multiple advocacy" of advisers.[14]

Realizing the importance of the combined capacities to give and receive the provision of properly independent outside advice, then, would seem to involve at least three elements: either proximity or competence (preferably both), timing, and role. The first element—proximity of the adviser to the president—would indicate that the president must have a certain amount of dear friends whom he considers "peers." These would be individuals who might freely tell him to "go soak his head" if the occasion demanded, without fear of the negative consequences. In the absence of this, a large amount of expertise on a given issue—one that the president might heed—would well serve as a substitute condition. Of course, it might also be true that the "peer" could be an expert on some subjects but not others, whether or not the president chooses to recognize that fact.

Then there is the nature of the "timing" of the advice sought. Has the decision already been made by the administration or at least been so well framed in the president's mind that nothing said by the outside adviser can change the fact except to make alterations at the margins. If the policy has not already been "locked in," there is a chance that the independent nature of the outside advice can have an impact. If it has, then the question would be more one of implementation rather than first consideration of direction.

Finally, there is the question of what "role" an adviser of any type might adopt with the president. The nature of one's role would largely dictate the nature of the advice preferred. Imagine for a minute the sort of advice a man might seek and receive on whether he should divorce his wife (assuming that all communication with the "insider," the wife, had broken down). He could go to the experts. The marriage counsellor would tell him about the need for better communication and more meetings down the road. The clergy might tell him about passages to read from the scriptures. The psychiatrist would tell him about the failures of his childhood or his toilet training. And the lawyer would tell him about legal fees. He could go to the pseudo experts—the advice columnists—who might ask other readers for assistance. Or the bartender might talk about where his three marriages went wrong. He could go to his peers. The relative might ask about the effect on the kids. The mistress might say she had waited years to hear this. But the friend is likely to say, "Yeah, she's a bitch. Glad you're going to dump her." All in all, what the man hears depends on whom he asks and how much he wants to listen. One can imagine a similar range of options on the war depending on the nature of the role adopted by the adviser—representative of the military, of the political elite, of the press, of the public, or just a friend representing the president's own interests.

All in all, the nature of the advisory interaction between an outsider and a president is an idiosyncratic one depending on the president, the adviser, and the issue involved. Perhaps it was Fortas who best described "the qualities most requisite in a presidential adviser." They are

the courage to assert one's views and the capacity for humility. An adviser must be able and willing to subordinate himself to the role—most obviously, with a discretion that assures the absolute confidentiality of the relationship. At the same time, he must be steadfast in stating his own views forthrightly and willing to accept decisions contrary to those views. He must be willing sometimes to accept public blame for decisions which he did not make and to go on functioning in the context of policies with which he did not agree. As for specific skills, the most important is not only a broad background of experience and the ability clearly and neatly to express his views, but also the ability to listen, to distill the statements of others, and to summarize facts and opinions with an objectivity undistorted by his own personal views. Since the president has to act on a distillate of data and opinion, an essential advisory task is to aid the process by making sure that the distillate is true to the ingredients. I stress humility in all this for one reason. A presidential adviser always has to realize that a president, if he does his job, makes his decision on the basis of a huge variety of factors and values. . . . [The adviser] must therefore realize that his own conclusions are based on data far more limited than what is available to the president and on less than all of the value factors that a president must consider. He also must realize that he is the adviser—the helper—that he is not the president.[15]

At this point it is worthwhile to look at the nature of the relationship between Abe Fortas and Lyndon Johnson on the question of Vietnam. How much of a "reality check," that is, how much independent outside advice was provided from the outside by the Supreme Court justice. Only by looking at this question can we judge how much of an "architect" Fortas was for the war.

FORTAS AND JOHNSON: A BRIEF HISTORY

By 1965 the friendship of Abe Fortas and Lyndon Johnson had dated back nearly thirty years. Over those decades, beginning when Johnson was a lowly congressman from Texas and Fortas the undersecretary of the interior, the two men had a certain pragmatic commonality of political interests that put them on the same side of many issues. But it was Fortas who did most of the favors in the relationship. And Johnson, a man who never liked to owe anyone, never forgot the fact that it was Fortas who had helped to craft the legal arguments in 1948 that put him in the Senate. During the 1950s, while Fortas served as an informal member of a "Court of Last Resort" considering issues and political strategies for then Senate Majority Leader Johnson, the relationship strengthened.

Thus, it was not surprising in 1963 upon ascending to the White House that Johnson made one of his earliest calls for advice and support to the Washington lawyer who had done so much for him in the past. And it was not surprising either that when the opportunity first presented itself the president put, or rather forced, Fortas on the Supreme Court of the United States. Finally, it was not surprising, given the long-standing nature of the relationship, that this new position in no way affected the close advisory capacity between them. Hundreds of phone calls passed between them, and scores of one-on-one and formal meetings engaged them on such diverse subjects as judicial and executive appointments, criminal justice policy, speeches to be delivered, the Detroit riots, and a pending railroad strike. Neither man had any trouble with the frequent calls from the White House. For all intents and purposes, things between them were the same as they had always been. Fortas thus had the opportunity with the president that Felix Frankfurter had always craved—he was one of the president's "inner circle," a member of his "kitchen cabinet" to be consulted freely on all issues, no matter what subject, if they happened to be perplexing the president.[16]

When questioned about the nature of his role with the president by the Senate Judiciary Committee in the 1968 confirmation proceedings for chief justice, Fortas was suitably vague:

It is well known that the president and I have been associated, mostly as lawyer and client, for a great many years. The president does me the honor of having confidence in my ability, apparently, to analyze a situation and to state the pros and cons. In every situation where I have called to the White House for this purpose, so far as I can recall my function—the president runs conferences, as I am sure all of you know—my function has been to listen to what is said. The president has called on me last. And it is my function, then, to sum up the arguments on the one side, the considerations on the other side. Mr. Chairman, it would be very misleading to allow the impression to prevail that this is a matter of frequency. It occurs very seldom. And it has occurred only in matters that are very perplexing and that are of critical importance to the president, where he wants some additional assistance. That has been the extent of my role.[17]

It sounded good, but in fact, the truth was somewhat different from this portrait. The periods of consultation were far greater than portrayed, and the opportunity to "sum up" was far less neutral than Fortas would have you believe, given a man of his legal skills. Then, too, there was the additional discrepancy brought on by the fact that Fortas did far more than "sum up" when it came to Vietnam or any other issue plaguing Lyndon Johnson.

Johnson, however, seemed to see the Fortas role quite differently, and told Zbigniew Brzezinski that in no uncertain terms:

> The president once said to me that the only people in whom he could really have confidence in terms of good solid judgments in international affairs were [Abe] Fortas and [Clark] Clifford, that these were the only people who gave him solid, sound advice, and these were the only people who were not taken in by circumstances or events or even other individuals. In this particular instance, the president said that [Anatoly] Dobrynin, the Soviet ambassador is an extremely effective person in taking people in. And he recounted some story to the effect that the Soviet ambassador can influence people on the Hill, he can even influence [Robert] McNamara, he can even influence [Dean] Rusk, and the only people who aren't taken in are Clifford and Fortas.[18]

JOHNSON, FORTAS, AND VIETNAM

What then was the nature of the role adopted by Fortas when the president consulted him about Vietnam? Men with disparate enough views on the war as Associate Justice William O. Douglas and former Undersecretary of the Air Force Townsend Hoopes agreed that Fortas' role here was indispensable. Douglas writes in his memoirs about the justice's unique ability to tap the president's "innermost desire": "Though Lyndon was not at home with the 'intellectuals,' over the years he became very dependent on Abe Fortas for all his decisions. Not that he always followed Abe's advice; he often did not. But he had such confidence in Abe that he was crippled without him."[19] To that, Hoopes adds in his memoirs of the meetings on Vietnam that were headed by the president and attended by Abe Fortas, Fortas continued to play the curious role he had assumed on other occasions in the running debate on Vietnam—as spokesman for those private thoughts of Lyndon Johnson that the president did not wish to express directly.[20]

Fortas himself argued, however, that this role did not start with the initial decision to send 50,000 more troops to the war in July 1965:

> On Vietnam my intensive thinking about it was *after* we had a lot of men in there. I find myself thinking back and saying, "If only he had asked me before, I'd have said don't send ground troops in there." But I don't know if that's what I *would* have said—that's *post hoc*. I never had occasion to center on the problem. I was well after the Tonkin gulf. I kept no notes. With ground troops in there the question changed.[21]

As the American fortunes declined in the war, however, Fortas moved from what was initially a peripheral position as Johnson's adviser when the 1965 escalation occurred, to a position of preeminence. One indication of this fact comes in the number of formal meetings at the White House on the war attended by the justice. Only three invitations came in the twenty-six months after the July escalation. However, in the period from October 1967 to June 1968, when things were going exceedingly badly for the president, Fortas was present at ten formal White House meetings. This of course does not take into consideration what was surely a large number of personal and telephone conversations between the two men on this perplexing issue.[22]

When Fortas was given an opportunity to express his views on the war, he made little doubt about his hawkish views. Invited by the president to respond to Robert McNamara's proposal in late 1967 for a new bombing halt, Fortas wrote in his own memorandum to Johnson:

Our duty is to do what we consider right—not what we consider (on a highly dubious basis with which I do not agree) the "American people" want. I repeat that I believe they do not want us to achieve less than our objectives—namely to prevent North Vietnamese domination of South Vietnam by military force or subversion; and to continue to exert such influence as we reasonably can in Asia to prevent an ultimate communist takeover.[23]

Having heard this same advice from Fortas and Washington attorney Clark Clifford two years earlier when McNamara successfully argued the case for a bombing pause only to see it have no effect on the progress of the war, this time Lyndon Johnson was persuaded against another bombing pause.

Fortas' role with the president on the war centered on the dual issues of building support for Johnson's policy here and the public relations aspects of how to sell future policies to the public. Despite the fact that Fortas had lived in the nation's capital nearly all of his professional life, he had an unfailing confidence in his own ability to interpret what "the public" wanted. Of course, the public's desires always seemed to be what Lyndon Johnson wanted to hear. Typical of this advice was a two-page, unsigned memorandum written by the justice for the president's eyes. Here, Fortas laid out the strategy for winning what he saw as the real war—the "propaganda battle" to build American support.[24] So obvious was the intent of this and other memoranda that White House personnel took to filing them in the "public relations activities" files of the section on Vietnam.

Near the end of Johnson's presidency, Fortas' advisory posture with the president had pushed him to the extreme of American policy making on the war. While nearly all of the president's advisers in March 1968 were pushing either for complete withdrawal from the war or searching for some diplomatic solution to the conflict, the justice wrote a memo to the president taking a very different tack. After outlining a multipoint strategy for expanding the conflict, he argued that the war should be brought "home to North Vietnam." The question was now, he argued, how far the war could be widened without actually launching an American invasion of the north. However, no one other than the president seemed to give this memo much attention when it was circulated among the top advisers.[25]

Since Fortas had been lumped for so long with the Washington lawyer, Clark

Clifford, in the nature of his advice on the war, this interaction provides an interesting counterpose to the relationship with the justice. Outside of government Clifford was virtually indistinguishable from Fortas in the hawkish and supportive nature of his advice. This, in fact, represented a continuation of long-held views about the need for a strong U.S. effort—even militarily—to contain communist aggression. As of January 1968, the *New York Times* labelled him as a man who "most explicitly believes that the way out of Vietnam lies not through bombing pauses or peace overtures, but through military pressure that will bring North Vietnam to its knees."[26] However, upon replacing Robert McNamara as secretary of defense in March 1968 and becoming exposed on a daily basis to all of the government's information on the war as well as taking on new formal responsibilities, Clifford's position on the war changed 180 degrees.

Now, through a series of questions and maneuvers, including the convening of the second "wise men" meeting, that have been documented in his classic *Foreign Affairs* article, he was actively prodding the president to seek a bombing halt, a negotiated settlement, and disengagement from the war.[27] The result of the new advisory maneuvers was the 31 March speech seeking negotiated peace, limiting the bombing runs, and the president's decision not to run for reelection. In many ways, then, Clifford was now providing "outside independent advice" while now technically an administration insider—and doing so at the very time that the other "outsider," Fortas, was recommending even at this late date the need to "bring [the war] home to North Vietnam." The result for Clifford's relationship with Johnson was quite profound. As he later told journalist Stanley Karnow, "The bloom was off our relationship."[28]

But if Clifford became the "inside-outsider," then Fortas remained the obverse, the "outside-insider." In many ways, he was simply too close to the president on this matter to give a proper "reality check." Throughout, his views on the war were virtually indistinguishable from the president's. Rather than providing alternative analyses, he was more concerned with telling the president how to win the propaganda war—how to sell the conflict to an increasingly skeptical public. Rather than looking for ways to limit or end the degenerating policy, even at the end he was looking for ways to justify expanding the conflict. He never looked for new slants, only ways to protect the president's slant.

CONCLUSION

Using all of our earlier criteria describing "independent outside advisers" one can see the reasons for such a failure. First, Johnson was well known as not having a "capacity to receive" critical opinions on any policy. To him, it seems, loyalty was to be valued above all things. He may have wanted to know what the alternative arguments would be, in a devil's advocate fashion, but only for the purpose of anticipating negative arguments rather than rethinking his programs. But then the fault here was not all the president's—for on this policy

Fortas seems to have been incapable of giving independent advice. He was neither an expert on the subject nor far enough removed from the president to be unaffected by the outside negative pressures upon him. Faced with a dear friend who was being exposed to critical public opinion on all sides, his natural reaction was to defend, rather than to question. Fortas had no stake in the policy, except of course to protect his friend the president.

But for me the key to understanding the nature of Fortas' actions here is to look once more at the nature of his role with the president when consulted on the war. With the close nature of their personal relationship, the opportunity was here for Fortas to act as a peer and tell Johnson quite honestly what he thought of the war, not thinking of the consequences. Instead, Fortas played a combined role of friend and lawyer. As a friend, he was more of a supporter, a confidante, a sounding board—never testing policies but only allowing the president to hear his own views and arguments sounded out. And as a lawyer, he had the appearance of competence on any issue while acting as an advocate. Once his "client," the president, set the policy, Fortas as "lawyer" told him how to do it. In many ways, then, to finish with the analogical question of whether he was an "architect" of the war, Fortas served not as the architect or original conceiver of the plan, but more as the draftsman who helps to sharpen that conception on the paper for others to see and consider. Here, one's degrees of freedom are more limited to questions of whether the plan is feasible and how to make the plan look as good as possible to the outside eye. But the general concept remains in place. Fortas' posture was more "to protect and serve," rather than to question and critique.

In all respects, then, it seems that Fortas was too much the Johnson insider to test the plan. This was far from being a model of an outside adviser, with independent actors, close to the president and early in the decision-making process, adopting a critical role in fully testing the program. Instead, this was a model of an outside reinforcer—a close friend, perhaps too close, coming in late in the process, taking a defensive posture, and adopting the role of supporter and advocate. The independent quality of the advice here is totally lacking.

Should he be faulted, then, for the war? Only in the sense that he was one of the few people Johnson was listening to—although given Clifford's experience one wonders how long that might have lasted had he changed his views. Even close presidential friends such as former Congresswoman Helen Gahagen Douglas understood the importance of Fortas to Lyndon Johnson. Douglas recalled a meeting toward the end of the presidency in the White House with Mrs. Johnson: "The few minutes we spent with Lady Bird confirmed this impression [that the president was suffering]. She spoke of the president's torment and unhappiness over the war . . . and of what solace the friendship of Abe and Carol Fortas had been to him and to her."[29]

Perhaps, then, if he had been more forceful in advocating the other side it might have affected the president's views. So the error here was one of a "missed opportunity," with no one that close to the president telling him to look again.

But I wonder how many of us, faced with a friend of over thirty years in desperate trouble with no simple way out, might not have acted in the same manner. And when one makes that friend a president, the policy a war with lives already lost, and the situation one in which history and a nation are scrutinizing every move, it becomes even more difficult to assess. We are left only to wonder how history might have changed had Abe Fortas acted differently.

NOTES

1. Beverly Smith, "Uncle Sam Grows Younger," *The American Magazine* (February 1934), 122.

2. William O. Douglas, *The Court Years: 1939–1975, The Autobiography of William O. Douglas* (New York: Random House, 1980), 319.

3. Victor Navasky, "In Washington, You Just Don't Not Return a Call from Abe Fortas," *The New York Times Magazine*, 1 August 1971, 32.

4. See, for example, Stanley Karnow, *Vietnam: A History* (New York: The Viking Press, 1983), 420.

5. Lawrence Berman, *Planning a Tragedy: The Americanization of the War in Vietnam* (New York: W. W. Norton and Company, 1982), 145.

6. A fine volume containing some of these works is Thomas E. Cronin and Sanford D. Greenberg, *The Presidential Advisory System* (New York: Harper & Row, 1969), Part II.

7. George Reedy, *The Twilight of the Presidency* (New York: World, 1970).

8. Irving L. Janis, *Groupthink* (Boston: Houghton Mifflin Company, 1982).

9. Richard E. Neustadt, *Presidential Power: The Politics of Leadership from FDR to Carter* (New York: John Wiley and Sons, 1960 and 1980), Chapter 10.

10. Theodore C. Sorensen, "Presidential Advisers," in Cronin and Greenberg, *Presidential Advisory System*, 9.

11. See Bruce Allen Murphy, *The Brandeis/Frankfurter Connection: The Secret Political Activities of Two Supreme Court Justices* (New York: Oxford University Press, 1982).

12. Bruce Allen Murphy, "Brandeis, FDR, and the Ethics of Judicial Advising," in Wilbur J. Cohen, ed., *The Roosevelt New Deal: A Program Assessment Fifty Years After* (Austin: Lyndon Baines Johnson Library, 1986).

13. James David Barber, *Presidential Character: Predicting Performance in the White House* (Englewood Cliffs, N.J.: Prentice-Hall, 1977).

14. Alexander George, *Presidential Decisionmaking in Foreign Policy: The Effective Use of Information and Advice* (Boulder, Colo.: Westview Press, 1980), 121–136, 191–208.

15. Abe Fortas, "The Presidency as I Have Seen It," in Emmet Hughes, *The Living Presidency* (New York: Coward, McCann, and Geoghegan, 1972), 334.

16. For more, see Bruce Allen Murphy, *Abe Fortas: A Political Biography* (New York: William Morrow and Company, 1988).

17. Nominations of Abe Fortas and Homer Thornberry, Hearings before the Committee on the Judiciary, U.S. Senate, 90th Congress, 2d Sess., at 104 (1968).

18. Zbigniew Brzezinski Oral History, LBJ Library, 24.

19. Douglas, *The Court Years*, 188, 336–337.

20. Townsend Hoopes, *The Limits of Intervention* (New York: David McKay Company, 1969), 217.

21. Navasky, "You Don't Not Call," 33.

22. Count taken from Johnson administration's White House Diary, LBJ Library.

23. Memo, Fortas to Johnson, 5 November 1967, quoted in Lyndon Baines Johnson, *The Vantage Point: Perspectives of the Presidency 1963–1969* (New York: Holt, Rinehart and Winston, 1971), 374.

24. Fortas to Johnson, undated, "Public Relations Activities," Vietnam Country Files, Box 99, 7E (1)b, Feb. 1967-Oct. 1967, National Security Files, LBJ Library.

25. Memo, Fortas to Johnson, 19 February 1968, retyped on 12 March 1968, Fortas-Thornberry Materials, Box 1, LBJ Library.

26. Patrick Andrews, "The New Defense Secretary Thinks Like the President," *New York Times Magazine*, 28 January 1968, 20–21.

27. Clark Clifford, "A Viet Nam Reappraisal," *Foreign Affairs* (July 1969). See also, Karnow, *Vietnam*, 552–566.

28. Karnow, *Vietnam*, 560.

29. Helen Gahagen Douglas Oral History, LBJ Library, II, 13.

11

Lyndon Johnson and the Civil Rights Revolution: A Panel Discussion

Editors' note: The following panel discussion involves what is arguably the most enduring of President Johnson's legacies—civil rights. The discussion is broad, ranging from matters of presidential style to legislative strategy. Johnson's attitude toward civil rights is also explored, as the participants trace the evolution of his thinking from his tenure in the Senate, to the vice presidency, and finally to the presidency. The moderator is Louis Martin, who was deputy chairman of the Democratic National Committee in the 1960s and a Johnson political intimate. Other discussants include two former attorneys general, Ramsey Clark and Nicholas deB. Katzenbach, and three well-known civil rights activists, James Farmer and Floyd B. McKissick, Sr., two former national directors of CORE (Congress of Racial Equality), and Joseph L. Rauh, Jr., a former national chairman of the Americans for Democratic Action.

MODERATOR: LOUIS E. MARTIN

Thank you Mr. Chairman. I am delighted and honored to be here and ever since I learned the identities of the panelists, I have been looking forward with considerable excitement to this panel on civil rights. I knew these gentlemen in the 1960s when they were fighting to remove some of the warts on the face of America. Each of them interacted in one way or another with President Lyndon B. Johnson. They shared his conviction that the abuses of civil rights, so pervasive, so widespread in so many areas, were morally wrong and imperiled the national interest.

At the Democratic Convention in Los Angeles in 1960 when LBJ was nominated as the candidate for vice president, some black leaders and some liberal whites expressed outrage. LBJ was upset with the protest. The late Frank Reeves, a lawyer who was District of Columbia delegate to the Convention, told me that LBJ asked him to meet with the black delegates at the convention. According to Frank, LBJ defended his civil rights record in an eloquent and emotional speech. Among other things, he told the black delegates, "I'll do more for you in four years than anyone else has done for you in one hundred years." And he was a man of his word.

The panelists from whom you are about to hear were intimately involved in the civil rights struggle, worked intimately with the president, and they helped write every chapter in American history. Let us hear from them.

RAMSEY CLARK

For longer than I can remember, I've been so critical of every aspect of government activity, particularly in the foreign field, but also in the domestic and particularly in civil rights, that as I thought over what I should say this afternoon I felt myself slipping out of character. I even became concerned that I might have an identity crisis. But it felt good. It really did.

When I recall President Lyndon Johnson and this consuming issue of that period, civil rights, I feel better about it than anything I've been involved in in my lifetime. There was a purity about it, I believe, in terms of commitment to principle, the ideal of equality, less fettered by political consideration than in any other activity of government or out of government that I have been involved in. His period in the White House in civil rights was a period of stunning change. I'll speak so optimistically about this. I need to preface it by saying I don't think we solved the problems of race in America. I think they are profound and pervasive still today here at home and a threat to life on the planet, but I believe that there was a clarity of vision and a purity of purpose that was real and profound.

The absolutely stunning effect of the murder of John Kennedy was overcome, I think, in very large part by the spirit of idealism that was generated by the civil rights movement, which to me was the noblest quest of [the] American people in our time. President Johnson [had an] absolute commitment to the enactment of the 1964 Civil Rights Act. He was a master at the Congress, and it was no easy task to get through what would be seen by any political science analyst as a pretty radical piece of legislation. Many lawyers were appalled at some of the things it sought to do. But President Johnson's commitment was profound and total.

In early 1965 he was the one that was prodding us to get a Voting Rights Act out, and he was the one who was angry that we had been unable to develop the formulas we needed before the march from Selma [to] Montgomery. He wanted to provide leadership. I doubt if he ever had a more fulfilling moment in his life than the moment in the rotunda in the Capitol with the big six as we called them then—A. Phillip Randolph, Whitney Young, Roy Wilkins, Jim Farmer, and Martin Luther King, Jr., and the great John Lewis. The big six and he signed the Voting Rights Act of 1965—the most exciting experiment in democracy in our history, revolutionary in its impact so that now the problems we have are a Julian Bond and a John Lewis running against each other.

[In August 1965] Watts, south central Los Angeles, broke out in rioting. Hundreds of cars burned. Thirty people plus [were] killed. Tens of millions of dollars of damage [was done]. A stunning phenomenon. I subscribe to the view that Ronald Reagan's political ascendency began with the Watts riots. The following year he defeated a very popular, very able governor, Pat Brown. The fear that gripped California, the sale of guns that immediately followed that, the division in the country, the racism—Lyndon Johnson was as astute a judge of human nature as I would ever hope to meet, and I think he could see as clearly as Ronald Reagan or anybody else the effect of the Watts riots on the American people, the fear that it caused and the hatred that flowed from the fear. And yet he was the most insistent person that we send up new civil rights legislation that he announced at the beginning of the legislative session in 1966. It would have been very, very easy to follow a different political course at that time. He was the one—I'll be interested to see if anyone tries to contradict this—that insisted and finally surprised at least me and as far as I know nearly everybody else when in his address to the Congress he used the phrase, "We shall overcome." He didn't have to say that, but as a signal its impact was profound.

He put his mind and his inexhaustible energy into the effort. Open housing— I mean you're going from preaching to meddling then. You talk about where people live and who lives next door and all the rest. And he pressed it. He pressed it even after the Newark and Detroit riots. He pressed it until the Congress enacted the 1968 Civil Rights Act with chapters that touched on every major deprivation of civil rights in our country in ways that sought to be more effective than any we had seen before. We know how slow and ponderous the efforts had been. Ten years after *Brown* v. *Board*, 1 percent of the children in the public schools of the eleven states that had comprised the Confederacy were in desegregated schools by HEW [Health, Education and Welfare] standards—95 percent or less of one race. We sought guidelines, and he fought to the end.

But to me, I think perhaps the most convincing and profound manifestation of his commitment throughout this period to the idea of equality was during Resurrection City, as it was called, the poor people's campaign. Martin Luther King had planned what I think was the most imaginative of all the creative efforts of his life—an authentic effort to bring the poor people of the country from the Coghill Indian Reservation in the state of Washington from Marks, Mississippi, and all the other places—to bring them by wagon, any other way you had to get there—the poor people of America to the nation's capital to camp at the foot of Lincoln on the mall between the Washington Monument and the Lincoln Memorial. And the reaction of the nation was sad, even shocking, to see the pretty little white children there holding their parents' hands, to see raw poverty and the violence of it.

Resurrection City was exposing the misery of poverty and discrimination in our society in a dramatic way. It was affecting hearings by Senator John McLellan and others. It was affecting the 1968 political season. I was constantly being told you've got to sweep those people out. You're defeating the Democrats in 1968. President Johnson invited me over to lunch one afternoon, and the two of us just sat in the garden in the White House. It was a pretty spring day, late spring, and he said, "Ramsey, you're my lawyer and I only want you to do what's right and you know how I feel about civil rights, but I have a long political involvement and you haven't, and I only want you to know that many people are saying that this demonstration is destroying the Democrats' chance for election in 1968." That all sounds pretty strange and remote right now, but it was very intense and real then. And he said, "That's all I wanted to say, and you do what's right." And the poor people maintained their camp until they decided to leave, and there was no violence and there was no police action and nobody got hit in the head.

And the most glorious moment of pure joy that I ever saw at the end of a time was the reception that the civil rights leaders gave to Lyndon Johnson in December of 1968—it could have been in January of 1969—where you could feel the genuineness of the belief of black America and its leadership in what he had done. I think he truly believed this, and I think that it was true.

JAMES FARMER

As I was reflecting on my relationship with President Lyndon Baines Johnson, I thought I might touch upon his style and my perception of the man and what was happening with the movement when he came to the White House.

I was impressed with his style. Shortly after he became president, in fact three days after the assassination of President John F. Kennedy, I got a call from President Johnson. I had never been called by a president before and certainly not at home. The call and the voice said, "Is this Mr. Farmer?" and I said, "Yes." "Mr. James Farmer?" and I said, "Yes." "Hold the line for the president." I started to ask myself the usual question, "The president of what?" But Lyndon Johnson's voice come on the phone, and he identified himself, "This is Lyndon Johnson and I want you to know I remember when you were in my office when I was vice president. We had a long chat and a good one, and you made a suggestion to me and I followed through on the suggestion and I appreciated the suggestion. And I asked you to do something for me and you followed through on that, and I want you to know that and I appreciated it very much. Now I'm going to need your help in the days and weeks and months and hopefully the years that lie ahead, and I hope I'll have your help." I said, "Well, Mr. President, if we're going the same way, we of course can walk together." You know I was flattered. I had heard of the Johnson "treatment" and now I was experiencing it. It was beyond my fondest dreams. Then he said, "We've got to sit down and talk, so next time you're in Washington drop by and see me."

Well, I called a political friend of mine and asked, "What does it mean when the president of the United States says, 'Drop by and see me?' " And he said, of course, "The president does not just say 'Drop by and see me.' " "But he just did," I replied. He said, "Well, call his appointment secretary after a reasonable period of time and make an early appointment at his convenience." Which I did.

And the meeting was a lengthy one when I saw the president in the Oval Office. There was warmth there—you know, the old Texas handshake. He almost pulled my arm out of the socket shaking hands. There was no wall between us. We were Texans and he said, "What part of Texas do you come from?" I told him, "Marshall." "Doggone," he said, "do you realize that's Lady Bird's home town," and that her father owned a filling station on such and such street and avenue. I didn't remember where that was, of course, but we chatted.

And as we talked, his phone was constantly ringing, or he was making phone calls to senators, twisting their arms, cajoling, threatening, lining up votes for the Civil Rights Act. And I was taking it all in. I suspected that a part of it was for my benefit—to convince me he was really fighting for it. And he *was* fighting for it indeed. During a lull in the phone calls I asked him, "Well, Mr. President, how did you get to be this way?" "What do you mean?" [he replied]. I reminded him that his voting record had not been all that good in the Congress through the years. Now he was fighting hard to get the Civil Rights Bill passed, enacted into law. He said, "I will answer that by quoting a good friend of yours and you will remember the quotation, 'Free at last, free at last. Thank God almighty, I'm free at last.' " And he of course was referring to the fact that he was now president of the United States and he could act out [of] his own conscience and his own feelings.

That was the style of Lyndon Johnson. He told me that whenever we had a problem in this movement or wanted to talk to him, call; the call would get through to him. Write and the letter would get through to him. And it did. In fact, it was embarrassing once when a member of my staff sent a wire to the president I didn't know had been sent. It was over my name. The president called me at home and my wife told the White House if they called National Airport they would probably catch me walking in there at that moment because I had a flight leaving shortly. And they did. I was paged. And he said, "Mr. Farmer, I want you to know I got your wire, and I started work on it right away." I didn't have the vaguest notion what the wire was all about and tried to avoid sounding stupid. He sensed right away that I didn't know what he was talking about. He said, "I just spoke to the president of Mexico and told him it's not right for those wetbacks to swim across the river and take our people's jobs and so we're going to do something about it."

That went on for some months. It went on indeed until early 1965 or late 1964 when priorities shifted. I fell out of favor with the president for a number of reasons. One reason was the movement had changed. It had become more raucous. When Johnson became president, the movement was shifting its focus from purely southern to national, meaning northern. It was also becoming less and less of a middle-class movement and beginning to encompass the poor folk of the streets in the northern cities. And that meant it was moving from being a movement of means-oriented idealists to being more a movement of the masses of ends-oriented militants who were saying increasingly we will win this freedom by any means necessary. It meant that those of us who were leaders were astride limitless energies and ambiguous energies. We were not really in control. We were not calling the shots. I think the president did not fully understand that. And when demonstrations went on such as the one in Atlantic City in 1964, he did not understand and thought we were demonstrating against him. The demonstration was for the Mississippi Freedom Democratic Party, and I think that the president thought that this was a slap in the presidential face.

He also was upset when CORE [Congress of Racial Equality] and SNCC [Student Non-violent Coordinating Committee] refused to go along with a moratorium on demonstrations when it was clear that [Barry] Goldwater was the Republican nominee and he would be running against Goldwater. The civil rights leaders were considering a moratorium. All had agreed to it, except me. SNCC then supported me. This was difficult for the president to understand. But we had our political problems too. We were trying to bring the poor into the movement. We were trying to develop a discipline which would harness their tremendous energies at the same time as he was building a war against poverty. But we did not have enough communication then.

The president's sincerity was beyond question. His sentiment was for the people. He desperately wanted to be the first American president to deal with the problem of civil rights and to get it behind us, so we could be a united country. And I simply wish that he and the activist wings of the movement had remained close throughout his tenure in office. I think that partnership could have speeded up the movement and perhaps we could have been even farther ahead than we are now.

NICHOLAS deB. KATZENBACH

It wasn't always easy with President Johnson to know what it was he sincerely felt from his gut and what it was that was part of the game he loved to play of politics. But there were two things that I know he believed with absolute and complete sincerity. One was that this country had to treat the races—and the world had to treat the races—without any kind of discrimination at all. That was something he felt very deeply. And the other thing that he felt very deeply was that everybody in this world was entitled to be educated. And on those two things I never had the slightest doubt about his sincerity that came from his heart and that it was unwavering and totally committed.

Indeed, the first contact that I had [with him was during] the Kennedy administration [when Johnson was] vice president, and the subject was civil rights. [Our meeting involved] a rewrite of the executive order with respect to government contractors in order to tighten it up and toughen it up and to make it more effective, and he was working with Bill Moyers. He wanted to get it out. He wanted to get it out in a hurry. He wanted to make clear—it was his responsibility as vice president—he wanted this to be tougher and more effective than it had been before.

I also want to say some words about the 1964 Civil Rights Act in particular. It's necessary to understand that with respect to the Act—and the then vice president was active in formulating some of the principles of that Act—that when it went down to the House of Representatives, we were aware of the fact that it could not pass unless it had bipartisan support in committee and in the House. We went down and spoke to Congressman Bill McCulloch who I don't think in his long years in Congress had ever had a black in his district. He said that he would support a reasonable bill, but that in return for his support we must promise that we would not sell the House of Representatives out in the Senate. The 1957 and the 1960 Acts, both of which President Johnson then in the Senate had been involved with—in each case you had a bill that had come from the House with some strength that had to be watered down in the Senate in order to get it enacted. I say this as background, because when we did get it through the House with bipartisan support, it was passed after President Kennedy's death. President Johnson was in the White House.

Three or four days after that I went over to a reception at the White House. He grabbed me and said, "How are you going to deal with the Civil Rights Act in the Senate?" I said, "Well, we're going to get cloture, Mr. President." And he said, "Wait a minute," and he pulled up two chairs and we were sitting in the big hall in the White House, in the entry hall. I think it was a diplomatic reception. There were people all around us and the two of us were sitting there and he says, "You can't get cloture." And I said, "Mr. President, I think we can." So we began discussing the Senate votes, and it was something I had spent a lot of time on, I think somewhat to his surprise. I suspect as Bobby's [Attorney General Robert F. Kennedy] deputy I was somewhat suspect anyhow, but I had done my homework on this and I thought it was possible to get cloture, and we went through the votes that we had to get. And I said, "We have to get seven of these eleven votes, and if we can do that then we can get cloture." And he said, "I don't think it's possible."

He was asked at a press conference two, three days later, "What are you going to do with the Civil Rights Bill?" He said, "We're going to get cloture." And when Lyndon Johnson, with all his experience in the Senate said, "We're going to get cloture," that made it believable. And Nick Katzenbach said it, and nobody believed it.

And he went to work on those eleven votes. I don't know what he did. He never told me. All that I know is that Carl Hayden, who had spent more years than most of us lived in the Senate [and] who was president pro tem of the Senate at that time, went into the backroom when the votes were counted because he had always, coming from a small state, been absolutely committed that he would never vote for cloture. And we had the votes and it came out that he had voted against it. And I asked President Johnson later, "Why did he go into the back room that way?" President Johnson said, "He promised me that if his was the deciding vote, he was going to vote for cloture." I'm not sure how many dams were built or how many other public works occurred, but we did get cloture.

He signed the bill. As Ramsey said, he was pleased and proud on that occasion and then he said, "What are we going to do next year in civil rights?" And I said, "Jesus Christ, Mr. President, we just spent two years on this bill and practically nothing else happened." He said, "What are we going to do? Let's get a bill. Let's get a voting rights bill." And so that's what we did with a great deal of help from Bull Conner [Birmingham, Alabama, chief of police] and Sheriff [Jim] Clark [of Selma, Alabama] and other heros of the south, we succeeded in getting it.

But I do want to say one other anecdote on that. The Voting Rights Bill was much easier obviously having gotten the 1964 Civil Rights Act, and also it was interesting that nobody in the Senate, none of the people who were on the southern side of that, [Georgia Senator] Dick Russell and others, none of them were prepared to defend denying the vote to blacks. Not a person there was willing to do that. They would defend things like literacy tests which were so badly abused, but they never would defend not getting the vote. So that made it somewhat easier.

But I will tell this story. There were a lot of demonstrations going on at that time in the south, in the north; everywhere [there was] a lot of dissatisfaction with the situation with respect to civil rights. And George Wallace came up to Washington one Saturday to visit the president of the United States, and there was a big bunch of demonstrators outside the White House. This was just before the Voting Rights Bill went down, and I went over to see the president just before that. He said, "Write down eight points, eight things I can ask him to do." I said, "What kind of things do you want?" He said, "I don't care what they are as there is something he ought to do." I said, "Are there things that you want him to do *really*?" He said, "No, I don't care. Just give me some things in writing that I can ask him to do." So he had this. I scribbled it out on a yellow sheet of paper. We sat there. Wallace came in and typical of LBJ, [as] he was greeting the governor, . . . he turned to Secret Service man Lem Billings who came from Alabama. He said, "Lem, come over here I want you to meet your governor." He got Wallace into that mood, and then he began getting into civil rights. He said, "George, you see all those people demonstrating outside the White House?" "Yes, Mr. President, isn't that terrible, just awful." And the president said, "We ought to put a stop to that George." "I couldn't agree with you more, Mr. President." He said, "You know George they've got all those cameras out there, all those television crews. Why don't you and I go out there right now and tell them that you have decided—he looked down on the sheet of paper—you have decided to desegregate every school in Alabama."

And Wallace said, "I-I-I can't do that. That's the school boards that control that." And the president says, "Don't you kid me (he used another word actually). George you run the state of Alabama." And then Wallace was sitting there miffed, really upset by this, and so the president said, and this was so typical of President Johnson, he said, "How do you feel about Vietnam, George?" And he'd take him off and he put him back and he played him like a violin, and George Wallace left. He didn't meet the press. He left by a back door. He didn't want to meet the press.

And the president went out and talked to the press . . . because he told them that he met with Governor Wallace and that they had gone over things. Then he said that he told him that we're going to introduce a new Civil Rights Bill. And he said, I have the attorney general here and he's going to brief you on it. The cameras were grinding. And I said, "Mr. President this is meant to be a background briefing." So he said with the cameras still grinding, "This is on background; now you turn off those cameras." So it was a background briefing from some source the next day who had appeared on television the night before saying this is a background briefing.

Let me conclude by just echoing what has been said and what I said at the outset. President Johnson believed deeply in racial equality. He believed it I think as a moral principle, and he believed it as a political principle. And when I say he believed it as a political principle, he once said to me, "You know segregation is absolutely crazy." He said, "Eighty percent of the world is not white, and we have to live in this world as we have to live with everybody else in it." So let me conclude with that, by simply saying that I was very honored to be a part of that and to have the leadership in civil rights which Lyndon B. Johnson gave.

FLOYD B. MCKISSICK

I would like to go back and put things in focus as in regards to President Lyndon Baines Johnson. It is difficult to describe a man and his times without truly understanding the man and without truly focusing upon the times in which he lived. As far as Lyndon Baines Johnson is concerned in 1960, I was convinced of that man's character, his stamina, before most people were. I was associated with the NAACP [National Association for the Advancement of Colored People]. Clarence Mitchell [of the NAACP] taught me a lot about politics on the Hill in Washington. And I had the opportunity to meet Senator Johnson. Senator Johnson did not have a good record. Through Adam Clayton Powell [New York congressman] again I had the opportunity to associate [with Johnson] and most times not on record, but in the rotunda running from one room to the other to deal with matters of importance as of that time.

In February, mind you in February of 1960, Senator Johnson at that time told a group where there were no cameras and nobody was recording anything that the time had come. Clarence Mitchell was there, as you well know. And he

[said], "We're going to get this Civil Rights Bill of 1960 through." He said, "You know I'm going to have to go against the south to do it." And many blacks at that time said, "You know he ain't going to do that. I been knowin' white folks a long time and he's a southerner. Hubert Humphrey's over here and he ain't done it, but I don't believe that Lyndon Baines Johnson is going to go against [Richard] Russell, who had organized to filibuster against the 1960 bill—and this was the bill that had sent registrars into the south as we had been active on voter registration campaigns.

The [stage] was set when Lyndon Baines Johnson had to publicly declare himself, and he announced that he would keep the Senate running day and night to get this Civil Rights Bill passed. That's the first time in history that a white man, black or white, from the north or south, had made such a declaration. This was not when he was president. Many said, "Johnson was a smart politician, no doubt about that. He knew how to talk to the devil and make him change his program and if not change it, he'd postpone it for two or three days at any rate." He could do that. He knew how to do it. And he [said], "I'm going to get this thing done." And he was the first man who said, "We will put cots on the Senate floor if we have to." And it actually occurred that in March the Senate put cots on the floor. Many of you forgot about this. There's no question about whether he was sincere. Cots were on the floor. And they ran a filibuster. And Lister Hill of Alabama—those three great southerners now, Lister Hill of Alabama, [John] Stennis of Mississippi, and Russell—and here was Lyndon Baines Johnson fighting them. The solid south was no longer solid. And he proved that civil rights was the thing. He fought that bill all the way through, and that bill finally passed in April of that year.

And while this bill was being passed, I never had a chance to meet him and get to know him, except that we knew each other and every now and then he would see me because he would remember me because we had talked about the blues one time, talking about John Lee Hooker. I told him John Lee Hooker was from Alabama. And he said he would put Lightning Hopkins up against him any time because his blues had a better beat. He was that kind of man.

So in 1960, Lyndon Baines Johnson knew that he had to make a break. I think that. I sort of feel as a minister that if you go back to the Book of Esther there and you see that verse that [Mordechai] was saying "Who knows but you were not sent to the kingdom but for a time as this." Because I doubt whether any other southerner had the capacity, the endurance, the tenacity, and ability of persuasion to put through the Civil Rights Act of 1960 other than a Lyndon Baines Johnson under [Dwight] Eisenhower who was then president. Therefore, I come to the conclusion that what he was going to do, and the "We shall overcome" speech is really just a conclusion of what the man had in mind and what he was doing. Because he went out in front and much of this was not known. Even he fought one allegation from one nice little southern lady wearing tennis shoes who said, "If you, Mr. Johnson, keep the Senate on the floor all days and all nights, don't you recognize that you may be responsible for the death of some of the elderly men.'' And he made the remark that this civil rights legislation must go on.

Now, I want to give a caveat, and then I will stop and let you all talk. As a militant, and as Farmer said, the nation was in a change. The civil rights movement, I [believe stopped] with the march on Washington. I did not believe that the march on Washington had served [anything] but to pacify to a great extent or to satisfy to a great extent the needs of middle-class blacks and it afforded opportunities for blacks. But those who were still the residuals of slavery—and we've got the residuals of slavery still here today—we can't erase the residuals by just passing a Civil Rights Act telling them that they can vote. You know, ''You're free,'' so you stand up in the street and you shout you're free, but what can you do with your freedom? You got no job. You can eat at Woolworth's, but you can't pay for a cup of coffee if you went to the counter. So our problem had been partially solved. There was a need to carry the Great Society programs forward.

In conclusion, I would like to say that the legacy of Lyndon Baines Johnson lives on. It is easier for a southerner now to do things that he never did before. It's easier for a white southerner to assert himself. No, it was not difficult for many whites to attest to be friends, in a quiet room in the back, but they couldn't be friends up front. So I think Lyndon Baines Johnson did a lot to free not only blacks, but he did a lot to free white men to exert themselves in prominent places in politics as well as in every sphere of American life to carry on. His legacy continues and someone says, ''What did the poverty program [do]?'' And they analyze it now and they say the poverty program didn't do a lot of things. I'm here to say that the poverty program, if we truly analyze that legacy [did succeed]. The point of it is we still have an unfinished job to do and that job was merely started, but the legacy of Johnson lives on and we should commend and always remember what he did.

JOSEPH L. RAUH

As the last speaker from the geriatric ward, I guess I do have a slightly different view of some of the matters, but in order so I don't get misinterpreted, I will start with where I'm going to finish. President Johnson was the greatest civil rights president of all times.

Now, having said that, I can go back. I had a casual acquaintance with the president way back in 1941 when he was a New Deal congressman, and in 1948, Tommy Corcoran [an adviser to President Roosevelt] got about ten of the young lawyers in Washington to handle Lyndon's case against Colt Stevenson [Johnson's opponent in a Texas Senate campaign] when he had gotten elected by the margin of seventy-seven votes and even those seventy-seven Stevenson claimed had been stolen. So we had a battery of lawyers and I didn't do very much, but I started my career with Johnson with a telegram, an effusive telegram, from him saying I was a gentleman and a scholar and he would never have won this without me—which was nonsense. But it was a great thing to have that telegram through all the fights we went through after that. It would hardly have foreshadowed the battles that occurred after that.

Well, I start with the summer of 1956. A dream Civil Rights Bill came over from the House of Representatives. It provided for the enforcement of the school desegregation case [*Brown* v. *Board of Education*] which had been as you know passed two years earlier. Well, it was too late to pass the bill, Majority Leader Lyndon Johnson thought. So he said, "We're not going to bring the bill up." The two leaders of the civil rights bloc in the Senate were Paul Douglas and Hubert Humphrey. Hubert Humphrey was running for vice president, and he sure didn't want this thing brought up, and that was perfectly understandable. Douglas, however, was rather headstrong and had been sort of the opposite number of Johnson in the Senate, [and he] insisted on a motion to bring it up. Now, we could have just lost it easy. But Lyndon Johnson was determined to show who was running the Senate, so he insisted on the roll call. We got three Republicans and three Democrats. It was so humiliating for the civil rights movement that Douglas, when he went to the elevator, said to his assistant, "Press the button for senators. Let's pretend I am one." You couldn't have gotten the bill through. There was no way to get that bill through in June 1956 when you were going to have a Democratic Convention the next [month]. But he didn't have to give us quite as big a shock as he did.

Next year, [the] same bill comes over from the House. Majority Leader Johnson couldn't just shelve that. I think what he did was politically the most brilliant performance I have ever seen in the Senate. He had to be for civil rights, and he also had to be for something on the southerners. So what did he do? He took everything out of the bill except voting rights. He took what was then known as Part III out of the bill. He got [George] Aiken and [Clinton] Anderson, two moderates of both parties, to move to delete it, and he beat us badly on that. Then he weakened the voting rights [provision], which was all that was left, with a thing called the jury trial amendment. The only thing is he was absolutely right on the jury trial amendment, because there should be a jury trial for some forms of contempt. At any rate, then he lets this bill through, which we felt had been weakened terribly, but he got it through. So look at what he had been able to do as a great politician. For the southerners, they could go home and claim they won because he took out everything that supported the Supreme Court decision on desegregation. So the southerners went home and said, "We won, we beat those northerners. There's nothing in this bill about desegregation. The Supreme Court's decision is repudiated." The northerners, whom he was appealing to, they said, "Isn't it wonderful. For the first time in eighty-seven years, we have a Civil Rights Bill to protect the right to vote." He had it both coming and going.

It was so brilliant that he had the Republicans squirming, absolutely squirming in the Senate. And indeed Vice President [Richard] Nixon and Attorney General [William] Rogers came up to our group—Clarence [Mitchell] and me and a couple of others—and said this bill is so bad we ought to defeat it. And Nixon went so far as to get a stooge of his who later he gave a job in his administration who was then the head of the ACLU [American Civil Liberties Union] office in Washington, he got him to come out against the bill and say the ACLU's opposed to the bill.

Well, this was a real dilemma for the civil rights movement. A great bill had come over from the House. A very weak bill was there. What were we going to do? We could have killed the bill if you took the people who were opposed to any bill and if you took the civil rights groups opposed and we could have killed the bill. But a great man, Roy Wilkins—he and Clarence ran the NAACP and they were both great men—Roy called a meeting of the civil rights people, and we decided: Of course you've got to pass this bill. Eighty-seven years without a single piece of legislation and you're going to turn one down. No matter how weak it is. Well, anyway the bill was passed, and I think it was a right decision and I think it ended this idea that you couldn't pass a bill.

One of my friends [Johnson Counsel] Harry McPherson writes in his book that I fought against accepting it, and I think I understand why he would do that. He just assumed that after all the fights that we had had with Johnson not to weaken the bill, how much we must have been against the bill. Only, as I told him at the time of his book, he was wrong. And thank God for Roy Wilkins [who] felt we had to have that bill.

You come to 1960, and Floyd, I guess I just have to disagree. The 1960 bill was of no significance. It was so weak that you had to have the 1964 and 1965 bills. I can't agree with you. There were no registrars in that bill. What they did was to set up a few referees in litigation which the registrar system was to get away from. And I really don't feel that that was a particularly significant civil rights thing although again it was signed by Eisenhower and so we had [two Civil Rights Acts] when Lyndon Johnson is elected vice president.

I believe that this is the change that happened. I believe that Lyndon Johnson was a prisoner of his constituency in the 1950s. That's why he had to weaken the bills. That's why these things happened, and why we were opposed to them. I believe that once he had a national constituency as vice president, then as president, the thing was wholly different. It seems to me that what happened was that when he had a national constituency it was politically possible to do these things. He became our champion, with his heart wanting to be our champion. That doesn't in any way change my opinions that [he] was our great opponent of the 1950s. It is that when you get in our political system that this is a wonderful thing. As he got a national constituency, he acted for that national constituency. He acted for that national constituency and his very actions changed his own view, until he was the number one champion of civil rights in America.

And you can see it in the 1963–1964 bill and the 1965 bill. In the 1963 bill, it started with [John F.] Kennedy. It actually starts in Birmingham when the dogs are after the kids and all of those terrible things that happened. President Kennedy said to us when he set up his bill, ''Bull Conner did more for civil rights than anybody in this room." And, of course, there was King and Wilkins and maybe they thought that was a little exaggeration, but anyway it was fun. In the 1963 bill, there was a difference of theories. Nick Katzenbach stated their theory, and I understand it. But just to say what the difference of theories was. The administration theory was: Get a bill that you can get through and hang on to it for dear life. Our theory was: Get the most you can to start with and hang on for dear life. I'm not going to argue the theory. I'm just going to say the nice thing that Nick said in the other room before we came on here. He said, "Joe, you and I had our differences right through on that bill, but we both won." And I think that's really what did occur.

When Kennedy was assassinated, we were losing. The thing was stalled in the [House] Rules Committee. We were having one hell of a time. President Johnson picked it up from the floor there and got it through the House brilliantly. Clarence Mitchell and I were sitting in the gallery of the House the last couple of days as the thing clearly came through. And we were so happy and we were so relaxed, and we didn't have a thing to do, and I got the call to the two of us that said, "Call the White House." And I obviously would do what I was told. And the president said to me, "What are you guys doing about the Senate?" And we hadn't even . . . it was two days from getting it through the House and I b-b-b-b and nothing came out. We weren't doing anything about it. He barked out orders about a mile a minute. He said, "Now you and Clarence go over and see Mike Mansfield," who was the majority leader, his successor, "and this is what you tell him." He said, "You tell Mike Mansfield that I don't want another piece of legislation until this is passed. The way we're going to beat the filibuster is just letting it lie there forever." I don't know if this is before or after he told you you couldn't get cloture, but anyway he was telling us that you could get cloture and he told us to tell Mansfield—imagine here is the president of the United States telling two civil rights leaders to tell the majority leader what to do—whatever the orders were they were carried out. At any rate, I think that was the most crucial decision on civil rights in legislative history, in his willingness to say—most presidents don't like a filibuster because they got something else they want—he says there's nothing else I want right now. I'm willing to wait if it takes 'til next year and have the Senate go. That decision, I think is why we broke the filibuster and got the 1964 law, and I believe he got wonderful things.

Great politician that he was, he really brought us into a great controversy again. Lyndon Johnson was a very forgiving person. He forgave me all my sins for opposition in previous times when he became president. He even took me along to the funeral for [New York] Senator Herbert Lehman on his plane. And when I walked in with Johnson, there was more surprise at me than at the president being there, just because we had been at odds so often. But this was the kind of forgiving person he was. Well anyway, the forgiveness didn't last too long because I was the counsel for the Mississippi Freedom Democratic Party [which posed a challenge to the seating of the "regular" delegation] to which Jim Farmer referred. The president was a great politician, but sometimes he was a little overexcited. He really thought Goldwater had a chance. He really thought that there would be a terrible backlash through the Mississippi Freedom Democratic Party, and he had to sort of clamp it down. And there was a little bit of a Robert Warwick "Every man has his price" with President Johnson. He got two people diabolically to tell me to stop it. One was my only real important client, Walter Reuther [head of the United Auto Workers], the other was my only really important friend in politics, Hubert Humphrey. And he got both of them to keep calling me and telling me to stop it. And indeed Hubert said to me, "I know, Joe, you've got to go on, but what do I tell the president?" And here's Hubert who's running for vice president and the poor guy has to tell the president something. I just said, "Well you tell him I'm just a son-of-a-bitch nobody can do anything with." And Hubert said, "The president won't like that as an answer." Well, anyway, the thing was compromised, there was no backlash. The president won in a landslide. I've always thought that the compromise that was worked out there was a very good one. What we got was an ouster of the regulars—you see we had a black delegation from Mississippi called the Mississippi Freedom Democratic Party. What we won was the ouster of the regulars who wouldn't take a loyalty oath to the party. We also got two delegates, which we didn't take because we didn't accept the compromise. I think we should have. We got a promise for the future. And that was the most important thing because when Aaron Henry and Fanny Lou Hamer walked in as the heads of the delegation from Mississippi in 1968, it broke the whole idea—when you think today of the whole democratic structure of our conventions—you realize what the president's compromise at that time had done. Again it was a matter of political genius in my opinion.

Well, at any rate, I guess I'll say again as I started that Lyndon Johnson was the greatest civil rights president in history. He may not [have been] when he started, and I do not believe that he did, when he started, burn with the most force for civil rights. I think as he did these things he became our forceful champion. He got without any doubt the most done of any president of the United States in this field. I believe there are millions of women, Hispanics, handicapped, gays, who must realize that all of the civil rights revolutions in other fields followed the black revolution. The feminists' movement, the Hispanics, the handicapped, the aged, the gays, all of this follows what President Johnson did in the area of blacks. So I think that all over the United States there are millions of people, not just blacks, others who had legal revolutions following that, who owe President Johnson their feelings. What they have today in the legal world President Johnson got for them.

III

ECONOMIC POLICY

12

LBJ, the Council of Economic Advisers, and the Burden of New Deal Liberalism

Donald K. Pickens

The United States has always been the home of contradiction and paradox where the ideal and the actual exist in an uneasy relationship. U.S. history is an exercise in middle-class utopianism. The American ideal of the good society has always held the utopian ends of perpetual peace, guaranteed abundance, and conditioned virtue. Historically, middle-class means have been employed in realizing those ends.[1]

The eighteenth-century founding fathers created the ideal of a good society—based on republican materialism—as the material stake-in-society thesis. This good society contained such republican notions as a self-determined government, with constitutional checks and balances, physically close to a homogeneous population in a geographically limited area. Naturally, the actual course of American history has repeatedly challenged these asumptions, particularly during the Johnson administration. Yet the vision remained of a middle-class utopia where economically independent men could meet and function as political equals. As realists, eighteenth-century American leaders divided society into the "haves" and the "have nots"; they feared the social dangers of a permanent proletariat. The solution was an expanding economy or economic growth, the historic hope of the American experience.

Both intellectually and environmentally Americans expected more. They worked hard to turn dreams of abundance into social realities. Resources, however historically defined, supported democratic or mass expectation. American nationalism became attuned to this mass yearning for material improvement by blending the form of government (republican) with the ideal of the good society (upward mobility for all). This historical process of changing all of society into a vast middle class was assumed to be automatic, given human nature and the naturalness of American institutions. The result was cultural politics, the dispute over the best method for realizing the good society.[2] By the twentieth century the issue, often unarticulated, was one of finding limits to this historic process of increased cultural expectations. Two factors changed this native optimism about abundance providing economic growth for all.

The first factor was the "discovery of society," the complex story of how the social sciences and the rise of antiformalism in social philosophy destroyed the moral absolutes and romantic individualism of the nineteenth century. Some social theorists, for example, William Graham Sumner, stressed the finiteness of resources that dictated the limits in realizing a democratic society, while other thinkers, such as Simon Patten, emphasized society's power to create mass abundance out of nature's scarcity. In light of the democratic contour of American history, the intellectual emphasis was that social institutions shaped malleable human nature. People became limited, or determined, by what they experienced.

The Great Depression of 1929 was the second factor of change.[3] A genuine fear of economic maturity, of a frontierless America, affected both politicians and intellectuals.[4] A number of significant Americans, in and out of political power, believed that automatic economic growth was not possible. New approaches, new techniques would be used. American liberalism made its final break from its nineteenth-century legacy of laissez-faire public policy. And in the subsequent upheavals of depression, New Deal, war, hot and cold, the national Democratic party became the party of a new liberalism based on an activist statism and planning. This development is common historical knowledge but necessary background to understanding the complex relationship of Lyndon B. Johnson to the Council of Economic Advisers and to New Deal liberalism.

The thesis of this chapter is that Lyndon Johnson was not the "wrong man from the wrong place at the wrong time under the wrong circumstances."[5] If he had been, the result would have been not a tragedy but merely an uncomfortable anomaly of the historical process. To the contrary, there was a sort of Hegelian grandeur or "inevitability" to Johnson's life and career.[6]

Historians are divided about LBJ's relationship to ideology. One historian asked, "What role did ideology play in Johnson's political career?"[7] Another scholar replied, "The ideology of Lyndon Johnson is not easy to capsulize."[8] The Roosevelt–New Deal legacy provided him with a certain ideological legitimacy.[9] The Great Depression[10] and the struggle against totalitarianism during World War II shaped Johnson's value system as a person and as a politician.[11] Unfortunately during his presidency, cultural developments beyond his control created militant groups who questioned the validity of the New Deal legacy (fused during the Truman and Eisenhower years) of a domestic welfare state and global policy of interventionism. Heir to the Munich–Pearl Harbor syndrome, Johnson's foreign policy was Cold War orthodoxy, maintaining the ramparts of democracy.[12]

Before examining these various elements, it is necessary to note an important addition to the FDR–New Deal agenda for post–1945 liberals. In addition to unemployment, economic growth, and poverty, the issue of "quality of life" became an issue for the heirs of the New Deal, both Kennedy and Johnson partisans. As Herbert Stein observed, "Therefore, those who held this view were quite prepared to alter the pattern of production that resulted from consumers' expenditures whenever they thought some better purpose would be served by government intervention."[13] Influenced by the "Galbraithian" rejection of the notion of consumers' sovereignty, the Kennedy people held key administrative positions during the Johnson years until about 1967. On a personal level, Johnson wanted their approval; hence, John Kenneth Galbraith warned him that "the whole liberal community" would be watching his performance.[14] Johnson's celebrated politics of consensus was only possible under the rubric of economic growth. Johnson's response to these factors was critical to the future of New Deal–inspired liberalism.

The FDR–New Deal connection had its difficulties for LBJ and for liberals generally. Privately, New Dealers worried about economic maturity, a frontier-less economy, while publicly they praised the "can do" spirit of the American people, largely a result of the World War II experience, translating it into hymns of productivity.[15] New Dealers embraced the pluralistic solution, interest group liberalism, while defending the general proposition of the capitalist ideology. Roosevelt's style and limited statism changed the context of American liberal-ism.[16] Influenced by government policies or war, expectations continued to rise at a Malthusian rate. "Public authority was left to grapple with this alienating gap between expectation and reality."[17]

The Employment Act of 1946 was the classic result of this evolution in American reform. While not guaranteeing full employment—"a job for every-one"—the law did commit the federal government to creating conditions for growth in the economy. The Council of Economic Advisers would provide the expert knowledge for preventing economic maturity and a postwar depression.[18] Meanwhile, as the Employment Act of 1946 expressed one part of the New Deal, the World War II experience provided the context for a global New Deal. Given *A Second Chance*,[19] internationalists, now supported by reformers con-cerned about economic growth at home and abroad, launched a campaign to make the world safe for democracy and to increase American productivity. The Great Depression and the war experience greatly influenced New Deal liberals. From 1940 to 1946, people such as Dean Acheson, Fred Vinson, and President Truman argued that collective security in the postwar world needed an American economy that would realize expanded foreign markets and avoid economic stag-nation at home.[20] All men everywhere could share in American expectations.

The emerging Cold War contributed to this process of New Deal liberalism. Whatever its origins, the Cold War made government spending, deficit or not, respectable.[21] After the Truman years, the cliché "guns and butter" became an operational norm.[22] During the Eisenhower administration, it was the liberals' rallying cry as New Deal liberalism evolved into Cold War liberal statism or a form of neomercantilism. In this policy of "reactionary Keynesianism," both domestic "do-gooders" and military "hard liners" shared an institutional and policy home in governmental spending.[23] This Keynesian fiscal policy stressed the reduction of corporate and personal income tax and increased tax credits to maintain high aggregate demand and profits. Redistributive taxation and social spending were not necessary or desirable.[24]

Meanwhile hampered by charges of losing the Cold War, John Kennedy, a magnificent example of the Cold War liberal as "imperial president," wanted to get this country moving. "Consequently, the virtues of economic growth had become as much a sine qua non for liberals as balanced budgets continued to be for conservatives, with the methodology for stimulating production the most debatable point."[25] Unfortunately, the hard liners more often than not carried the day. Military expenditures did increase, often with disastrous long range results.[26] In the short run they did provide jobs in the increasingly important political area of the Sun Belt, the geographical arc from Miami to Los Angeles via Houston and Dallas.[27] Aside from the questions of post–1929 American reform, did the New Deal really solve the problems of unemployment and the fear of economic maturity? Having exorcised the spectres of the 1930s via the "new economics,"[28] the cultural myth of the postwar society "became the all-encompassing ideally self-correcting, providentially automatic political process."[29] By that means, administration replaced ideology for the Kennedy and Johnson Democrats.

Although the story of how LBJ became a presidential candidate in 1960 is well known, it should be stressed that his campaign was not an exercise in political vanity. Considering his senatorial career based on personal ability and being from the "deep west," Johnson always sought a national political career. The growing electoral importance of Texas (plus his personal importance as senator) made Johnson's placement on the 1960 ticket not only a stroke of necessity but a valuable gesture of unity and consensus within the Democratic party. In the end JFK's death made LBJ president.

The outline for the Great Society and an interventionist foreign policy were already in place before Kennedy died.[30] In the few weeks after Kennedy's assassination, Johnson embraced domestic and foreign policies that set the tone for the remainder of his presidency. Within a week, Johnson heard the chairman of the Council of Economic Advisers, Walter Heller, speak of Kennedy's domestic program for the campaign of 1964.[31] Partly formed by the CEA, the ideas—welfare programs with public participation—became the Great Society. Even earlier, on 24 November 1963, after a depressing briefing from Henry Cabot Lodge, Johnson stressed that the United States would give full support to South Vietnam's struggle against the North. For like Kennedy, Johnson believed that America must be bold in foreign policy to reassure allies and silence conservative congressional critics. Because of his political experience and the Cold War political culture, Johnson inevitably supported these foreign and domestic policies. "I am not going to be the president who saw Southeast Asia go the way China went," said Lyndon Johnson.[32] And he *really* meant it. The Democratic party was not going to "lose" another China. A simple-minded historical judgment to be sure, but it was one that LBJ truly thought many Americans believed. For years some Republicans analyzed Cold War foreign policy in those terms.

LBJ did not create the "guns and butter" formula. Its historical roots go back at least to the days of Theodore Roosevelt, but the New Deal and fighting World War II gave large philosophical and institutional support to the concept. "What self-determination was to Woodrow Wilson, a healthy Gross National Product was to Lyndon Johnson—the assurance of peace with justice."[33] In July 1964 Johnson confidently told business and labor leaders that his administration was the first "in a century unmarred by economic recession or depression." And even in 1968 after four years of foreign war and domestic riot, he saw power in the economy: "Today the war in Vietnam is costing us 3 percent of our total production. That is a burden a wealthy people can bear. It represents less than one year's growth in our total output."[34] His famed politics of consensus moved and had its being in economic growth. "So long as the economic pie continues to grow," Johnson argued, "there will be few disputes about its distribution among labor, business, and other groups."[35] This basic assumption in domestic reform also operated in foreign policy: All societies (or cultures) desire and have the same values. Little wonder that at one time the Mekong River was to be the site for a Far Eastern TVA. Johnson was not alone in these beliefs. For example, Robert McNamara casually dismissed the economic miscalculation about the war cost with the remark, "Do you really think that had I estimated the cost of the war correctly, Congress would have given any more for schools and housing?"[36]

Full employment, not a balanced budget, was the politically popular policy— more for everyone, be he defense contractor or ghetto poor. At the same time, in a modern industrial society, poverty is an intolerable condition rather than an established fact.[37] A national commitment expressed as a federal program could solve or ameliorate poverty.[38] The idea was Johnson's morning star.

LBJ AND THE CEA

With these remarks as background, as context, attention might be directed to LBJ's relationship with the Council of Economic Advisers, a creature of the Employment Act of 1946. At its inception the council was a classic example of government by experts in which economists could correctly anticipate economic tomorrows and thereby ease the burden of governing a complex economy. Understandably, the CEA became an instrument of presidential will, a part of any administrative team.[39] Out of their own personal motives and ambitions[40] activist economists contributed to this evolution.

In the ideological rush from the New Frontier to the Great Society, an important factor was ignored or forgotten. The economic situations of 1939 and 1963 were not the same. In 1939, the economy's slack was significant; unemployment was high, industrial capacity underused. Increased government spending (for defense and war preparedness) served the dual functions of defending the nation and providing jobs. Coupled with the later economic success in fighting World War II, government expenditures in foreign aid and defense moved the economy toward full employment. It was not the failure but the success of the American economy that gave LBJ his major problems. As previously noted, for political and ideological reasons, Johnson wanted the nation to move forward, destroying both domestic poverty and ultimately foreign poverty, the origins of international communism. With production and distribution patterns as they were—with no significant chance or desire to change them—the economy was very quickly primed for an explosion of inflation.[42] "Success" made a failure of Johnson's presidency.[43]

Walter Heller was chairman of the CEA when LBJ became president. An active and charming individual, Heller saw his role as advisory and educational. Unafraid of political criticism, Heller sought a close identity with Johnson, both the man and his policies.[44] Heller was (and is currently) a Keynesian economist.[45] His political and economic outlook was similar to Johnson's vision: "An expanding economy enables the nation to declare social dividends out of growing output and income instead of having to wrench resources away from one group to give them to another and thus enables presidents to press ahead with a minimum of social tension and political dissent."[46] Although the Johnson administration by 1968 was saying "once Vietnam is over,"[47] Heller believed that, "In an economic sense, the president is dead right: the country *can* have both guns and butter when military outlays claim less than 10 percent of the country's huge annual output, a smaller proportion than in the peace time years 1955–60."[48] As chairman and economist Heller expressed a major professional concern about unemployment more than inflation. He often invoked the engaging public optimism inherited from New Deal liberalism: "The significance of the great expansion of the 1960s was not only in its striking statistics of unemployment, income and growth but its glowing promise of things to come."[49] The glowing promise was realizable under the rubric of a New Deal–Keynesian formula: "Public expenditure programs will play a large part in pushing out the social and scientific frontier that will define our economy's limits in the future."[50]

His successors to the chairmanship during the Johnson years, Gardner Ackley and Arthur Okun, followed in the same general policy footsteps.[51] For example, in mid–1965, Ackley was confident that the guns-butter formula of Cold War liberalism was not only possible but maybe desirable: "We are certainly not saying that a Vietnam crisis is just what the doctor ordered for the American economy in the next twelve months. But, on a coldly objective analysis, the overall effects are most likely to be favorable to our prosperity."[52] It was a mistaken assumption. By the time Arthur Okun became chairman, a note of despair was being expressed: "The economy will finally get its much needed cooling off. This looks as certain as an economic forecast can be." Soon the haunting refrain of Keynesian concern was in the background, for Okun wrote to Johnson that the "economy will slow down too much."[53] By political choice and individual selection, Johnson's CEA was an activist agency via a Keynesian fiscal policy.[54]

The CEA misjudged only four times, but *what* four times they were! In 1962, the economy was sluggish, which the CEA did not recognize until May of that year. Then in late 1965 and early 1966 the agency failed to anticipate correctly the economic force of the Vietnam War. "The basic price environment was still one of stability, however, and little of general inflation was seen. These projections were based on a then anticipated slow buildup of defense purchases."[55] The problem of government was one of degree and not of kind. In December 1965 Ackley wrote that "*economic gains this year were even stronger than previously indicated*. Of course," he continued, "the substantially higher-than-planned level of defense spending is a major factor in the results."[56] The year 1966 continued to be a bad one for forecasting and 1968 was simply a disaster.

Despite a temptation to score clever remarks of hindsight at the expense of the past, one must note that the experiences of the Council of Economic Advisers have more elements of tragedy than comedy, of sorrow than pratfalls. In advising LBJ on realizing the objectives of New Deal liberalism, the council worked very hard. As the archives indicate, the memos, etc., were judicious and informative. Yet Johnson betrayed the council as he betrayed himself, thinking always that domestic reform and an aggressive foreign policy could be achieved out of the endless manipulations of tax policy, government expenditures, and easy credit.

The historical issue of LBJ's relationship to the CEA remains. For example, the LBJ materials in Austin are full of CEA activity. Nearly daily, Heller, Ackley, and Okun, each in his turn, kept the president informed. Johnson responded with public praise for his council and took a personal interest in staffing the agency.[57] The council from the beginning of Johnson's term worried about securing twin goals of domestic economic uplift and a strong national presence in foreign affairs. It was in close touch with the Treasury and similar departments in the government.[58] For example, the CEA worked closely with the Committee for the Economic Impact of Defense and Disarmament until September 1967, "when its more general concerns gave way to the specific interests of the Cabinet Committee on Post-Vietnam Planning."[59] Ah! there's the rub. Vietnam.

The war simply destroyed the council's effectiveness. The military-economic dynamics of the war shoved the agency aside. Assuming that the war in Vietnam would be over by 30 June 1967, President Johnson ignored the CEA's advice for a tax increase. He lied to key congressmen and business leaders about the real cost of the war, and they, in turn, told him not to push for a tax increase, information LBJ forwarded to the CEA. As a result of this internal administrative mendacity, the deficit for fiscal 1967 was $9.8 billion. The deficit for fiscal 1968 was $27 billion.[60] As the war effort increased, the council's role became a minor one. Not until late 1967 when General Westmoreland asked for additional troops did President Johnson, for the first time, send the request to the CEA for a judgment about its economic impact. The council's judgment was negative.[61]

From 1965 to 1967 the CEA was not at the center of power. The CEA was not alone in this situation. As for the future, "the only guidance we could get on that unpredictability was the sale of effort that the Defense Department and Joint Chiefs outlined," observed Henry Fowler in 1969.[62]

In 1965 the future looked promising, but it was a bad year for the CEA's contributions to Johnson's Great Society. December brought not only Christmas but also crisis. The Federal Reserve Board raised the discount rate. LBJ and the CEA were caught off balance. Publicly, Johnson was the voice of sweet reason: "My view and the view of the secretary of the treasury and the Council of Economic Advisers is that the decision on interest rates should be a coordinated policy decision in January when the nature and impact of the administration's budgetary and Viet-Nam decisions are known. This view was apparently shared by three of the seven board members."[63] In Cold War liberal rhetoric, Willard Wirtz, secretary of labor, responded that, "There can be no tolerance for the suggestion that expansion of the economy must be slowed down . . . while there is still so much to be done."[64] Meanwhile, quietly and without consulting with the CEA, the Defense Department prepared a request of $12.8 billion for a supplementary military appropriation. In January 1966 defense asked Congress for the money and from that day forward until mid–1968 when Johnson admitted to himself (and to his advisers) that Vietnam was a political and military disaster, the government's economic policies were under the military's control.[65]

Under the pressure of Vietnam, the war on poverty, "the climax of more than a half century of liberal reform," retreated.[66] On 27 January 1966, President Johnson publicly but obliquely expressed the issues discussed in this chapter. First he claimed that with only 1.5 percent of the gross national product going to the effort in Vietnam, "Our prosperity does not depend on our military effort." He then recognized the possibility of inflation "in an economy approaching full use of its resources, the new requirement of Vietnam makes our task of maintaining price stability more difficult." The answer therefore was to "sacrifice the luxury of the tax reduction. We must hold the expansion of our civilian Great Society programs below what would have been possible without Vietnam."[67] Years later from Johnson's *Vantage Point*, he ignored the CEA's advice and role in his administration.[68]

At the time, the council urged a tax increase to answer the increased military pressure in Vietnam. The increase came two and a half years too late.[69] Saving a dispirited Great Society was still a desire: "If a moderate expenditure cutback can achieve the tax bill, it would offer the best possible protection for social programs."[70] But the reality remained that "any significant change in the Vietnam situation—for better or for worse—would create a new ball game in fiscal policy."[71] The difficult political task was carefully tuning the economy down.

Vietnam was, of course, a constant factor. Secretary Rusk or McNamara reported on its status but without any discussion of policy. Very rarely would the cabinet meeting become a time at which a cabinet officer would say, "Mr. President, I think we're on the wrong track."[72] The Council of Economic Advisers was equally silent. Consensus politics with its major elements of secrecy was imposed from the top, the presidency, down through the governmental structure. It was a fine technique when peace existed and the economy grew and hard choices were few, but after December 1965 it came apart.

Johnson's Great Society suffered as postwar liberalism with its elements of New Deal idealism and New Frontier expectations became "cost-free liberalism," assuming that improvements would be financed out of economic growth. Such a liberalism shared the same fate as the illusory "peace dividend" discussed by reformers during the Vietnam War.[73]

In summary, the Vietnam adventure was a hot economic ending to one phase of the Cold War. The first twenty-five years of the Cold War made it by far the most expensive in U.S. history.[74] Yet President Johnson was correct in believing that the Vietnam military effort was not an economic necessity to America's well-being. In fact, the "guns" really damaged the opportunity for more "butter."[75] While some scholars have praised Johnson's political economy (some real achievements despite Vietnam), the story is tragic.[76] The conventional wisdom of New Deal–Cold War liberalism was just too burdensome for the Johnson administration.

In the dialectical irony that is history, LBJ's excesses and successes damaged the Rooseveltian legacy. Johnson's particular use of the New Deal legacy discredited it in the eyes of many people. Liberalism lost its credibility to speak for civic virtues. In his own way LBJ cast a shadow on FDR.[77] LBJ and his presidency became "captives rather than heirs of the past."[78] Future administrations did not improve the historic standing of New Deal liberalism. Nixon, Ford, Carter—their presidencies meant finite economic possibilities as inflation reduced the historic reputation of New Deal reformism.[79] In another jest of history, supply-siders of the late 1970s claimed the Keynesian fiscal revolution to save American "production" from the demand-siders of Kennedy-Johnson liberalism.[80] Even now, as he destroys the domestic and foreign policy achievements of the last fifty years, President Reagan invokes the name of FDR on occasion. The burden of New Deal liberalism has lost institutional and ideological weight.

NOTES

1. Donald K. Pickens, "The Expanding Economy: An Overview of United States History as an Exercise in Middle Class Utopianism," *Journal of the American Studies Association of Texas* 4 (1973): 30–38. See Thomas C. Cochran, "The Paradox of American Economic Growth," *The Journal of American History* 61 (March 1975): 925–943 for a counterargument.

2. For background see Robert Kelley, "Ideology and Political Culture from Jefferson to Nixon," *American Historical Review* 82 (1977): 531–562.

3. Richard S. Kirkendall, "The Great Depression: Another Watershed in American History?" in John Braeman et al., eds., *Change and Continuity in Twentieth-Century*

America (New York: Harper Colophon, 1966), makes a good case against the watershed analogue but understates the intellectual and ideological significance of the event.

4. Steven Kesselman, "The Frontier Thesis and the Great Depression," *Journal of the History of Ideas* 29 (April-June 1968), and Theodore Rosenof, *Dogma, Depression and the Debate of Political Leaders Over Economic Recovery* (Port Washington, N.Y.: Kennikat Press, 1975). For two differing perspectives on the 1930s see Richard H. Pells, *Radical Visions and American Dreams* (New York: Harper & Row, 1973), and Charles R. Hearn, *The American Dream in the Great Depression* (Westport, Conn.: Greenwood Press, 1977).

5. Eric F. Goldman, *The Tragedy of Lyndon Johnson* (New York: Knopf, 1969), 531.

6. Tom Wicker, *JFK and LBJ, The Influence of Personality Upon Politics* (Baltimore: Penguin Books, 1968), 16.

7. Robert A. Divine, "The Johnson Literature," in Robert A. Divine, ed., *Exploring the Johnson Years* (Austin: University of Texas Press, 1981), 6.

8. Vaughn Davis Bornet, *The Presidency of Lyndon B. Johnson* (Lawrence: University Press of Kansas, 1983), 339.

9. Alonzo L. Hamby provides valuable background to this relationship in his "The Vital Center, the Fair Deal, and the Quest for a Liberal Political Economy," *American Historical Review* 77 (June 1972) and "The Liberals, Truman, and F. D. R. as Symbol and Myth," *The Journal of American History* 56 (March 1970).

10. Herbert Stein, *Presidential Economics, The Making of Economic Policy from Roosevelt to Reagan and Beyond* (New York: Simon and Schuster, 1984), 29.

11. T. Harry Williams, "Huey, Lyndon and Southern Radicalism," *The Journal of American History* 60 (September 1973): 292. For a different and more critical judgment see Otis L. Graham, Jr., *Toward the Planned Society, Roosevelt to Nixon* (New York: Oxford University Press, 1976), 186–187. "A vital government," Johnson wrote, "cannot accept stalemate in any area—foreign or domestic. It must seek the national solution, vigorously and courageously and confidently." Lyndon B. Johnson, "My Political Philosophy," *The Texas Quarterly* 1 (Winter 1958): 21.

12. The intellectual ease with which Johnson accepted this orthodoxy can be understood by the analysis presented in Leslie K. Adler's and Thomas G. Paterson's article, "Red Fascism: The Merger of Nazi Germany and Soviet Russia in the American Image of Totalitarianism, 1930s–1950s," *American Historical Review* 70 (April 1970).

13. Stein, *Presidential Economics*, 95.

14. Bornet, *The Presidency of LBJ*, 10, 26; see also Mark I. Gelfand, "The War on Poverty," in Divine, ed., *Exploring the Johnson Years*, 134.

15. John Morton Blum, *V Was for Victory: Politics and Culture During World War II* (New York: Harcourt Brace Jovanovich, 1976), 328–331, analyzes how Keynesianism "won" the war and secured the "peace" of economic growth.

16. Theodore J. Lowi, *The End of Liberalism* (New York: W. W. Norton, 1969), 47; James T. Patterson, *Congressional Conservatism and the New Deal* (Lexington: University of Kentucky Press, 1967), 133–134. Elliot A. Rosen, *Hoover, Roosevelt, and the Brain Trust* (New York: Columbia University Press, 1977) is a recent positive judgment of FDR as reformer.

17. Lowi, *The End of Liberalism*, 69–70. John Brooks, *The Great Leap* (New York: Harper Colophon, 1968) is instructive about this increase in expectations.

18. Stephen K. Bailey, *Congress Makes a Law* (New York: Columbia University

Press, 1950), 9–10. For an intellectual origin of the 1946 law see James Tobin, "Hansen and Public Policy," *The Quarterly Journal of Economics* 90 (February 1976): 32–37.

19. Robert Divine, *Second Chance, The Triumph of Internationalism in America During World War II* (New York: Atheneum, 1967). For a conservative critique see Ronald Radosh, *Prophets on the Right* (New York: Simon and Schuster, 1975), and for a different valuation see Thomas G. Paterson, ed., *Cold War Critics* (Chicago: Quadrangle Books, 1971).

20. Bruce M. Russett and Elizabeth C. Hanson, *Interest and Ideology, The Foreign Policy of American Businessmen* (San Francisco: W. H. Freeman and Company, 1973), 53, 131.

21. A handy summary of the issues is Lloyd G. Gardner, Arthur Schlesinger, Jr., and Hans J. Morgenthau, *The Origins of the Cold War* (Waltham, Mass.: Ginn and Company, 1970).

22. For background see Donald K. Pickens, "Truman Council of Economic Advisers and the Legacy of New Deal Liberalism" in William F. Levantrosser, ed., *Harry S. Truman, The Man from Independence* (Westport, Conn.: Greenwood Press, 1986), 245–263.

23. Herbert Stein, *Fiscal Revolution in America* (Chicago: University of Chicago Press, 1969). For a specific example of this development see Donald J. Mrozek, "The Truman Administration and the Enlistment of the Aviation Industry in Postwar Defense," *Business History Review* 48 (Spring 1974): 88. Michael Harrington, "A Reactionary Keynesianism," *Encounter* 26 (March 1966): 50–52.

24. Robert Lekachman, *Inflation* (New York: Vintage Books, 1973), 90.

25. Herbert S. Parmet, *The Democrats, The Years Since F.D.R.* (New York: Macmillan, 1976), 195. Parmet's speech "John F. Kennedy and the Politics of the New Economics" at the Organization of American Historians, 13 April 1978 was highly instructive. See also Graham, *Toward a Planned Society*, 93–94, 130. For the foreign policy consequence of economic growth see David Bruner and Thomas R. West, *The Torch Is Passed, The Kennedy Brothers and American Liberalism* (New York: Atheneum, 1984): 92–93.

26. See, for example, the books of Seymour Melman, particularly his *The Permanent War Economy, American Capitalism in Decline* (New York: Simon and Schuster, 1974).

27. Given the Cold War, "short run Keynesian theory cut loose from a larger historical perspective is consistent with a predilection to accept and preserve an existing institutional structure." Richard X. Chase, "Keynes and United States Keynesianism: A Lack of Historical Perspective and the Decline of the New Economics," *Journal of Economic Issues* 9 (September 1975): 451.

28. See J. Ronnie Davis, *The New Economics and the Old Economics* (Ames: Iowa State University Press, 1971), for a good historical background.

29. Lowi, *The End of Liberalism*, 54. Based on the analysis presented in this essay, "The New Economics, premised on the continued necessity for 'full employment' must as a consequence accept continuing economic growth as a logical imperative." Chase, "Keynes and United States Keynesianism," 454.

30. James L. Sundquist, *Politics and Policy: The Eisenhower, Kennedy and Johnson Years* (Washington, D.C.: Brookings Institution, 1968), 112, 138–145. Jim F. Heath's fine book, *Decade of Disillusionment* (Bloomington: Indiana University Press, 1976), 185–186, 295, effectively explains the relationships between the two presidencies.

31. Walter Heller, "Memorandum for the President. Subject: The Services of Your Council of Economic Advisers," 1 December 1963. LBJ Library.

32. As quoted in Wicker, *JFK and LBJ*, 208.

33. Doris Kearns, *Lyndon Johnson and the American Dream* (New York: Harper & Row, 1976), 97.

34. "Remarks to Businessmen, 23 July 1964" and "Remarks to Labor Leaders, July 24, 1964," *Public Papers of the Presidents, Lyndon B. Johnson*, vol. 1 (1963–1964), 882. The second quote is in "The Economic Report of the President, February 1, 1968," ibid., vol. 1 (1968–1969), 145.

35. Kearns, *LBJ and the American Dream*, 187.

36. As quoted in David Halberstam, *The Best and the Brightest* (New York: Random House, 1972), 610.

37. Lowi, *The End of Liberalism*, 215., See also Robert H. Bremmer, "Poverty in Perspective," *Change and Continuity in Twentieth-Century America*, 263–280. For background see James T. Patterson, *America's Struggle Against Poverty, 1900–1980* (Cambridge, Mass.: Harvard University Press, 1981).

38. Bornet, *The Presidency of LBJ*, 347.

39. Robert W. Stevens, *Vain Hopes, Grim Realities: The Economic Consequences of the Vietnam War* (New York: New Viewpoints, 1976), 45, 209.

40. *The Administrative History of the Council of Economic Advisers* 1, 1–4, LBJ Library.

41. Ibid., vol. 1, "Chapter Five CEA's Role in Major Program Areas."

42. Heath, *Decade of Disillusionment*, 292 gives an example of that policy and Kennedy's statement, "In short, our primary challenge is not how to divide the economic pie, but how to enlarge it," quoted by Hobart Rowen, *The Free Enterprisers, Kennedy, Johnson and the Business Establishment* (New York: G. P. Putnam's Sons, 1964), 114. It indicates a limiting legacy from New Deal liberalism.

43. Melman, *The Permanent War Economy*, 70, 79, 83, 97.

44. Ibid., 21, 37, 166–167. Sar A. Levitan, *The Great Society's Poor Law: A New Approach to Poverty* (Baltimore: Johns Hopkins University Press, 1969), 13–18. For additional examples of influence see Joseph A. Peckman Oral History, 19 February 1969, 24–25, LBJ Library.

45. A good example is Heller's memo to LBJ, 14 December 1963, titled, "The Unemployment Cost of Budget Cutting," *The Administrative History of the CEA*. A summary of his thought can be found in Milton Friedman and Walter W. Heller, *Monetary vs. Fiscal Policy* (New York: W. W. Norton, 1969). Walter W. Heller, ed., *Perspectives on Economic Growth* (New York: Vintage Books, 1968) is a good indication of his thinking as well as the other economists associated with the CEA.

46. Walter W. Heller, "President Johnson and the Economy," in James McGregor Burns, ed., *To Heal and to Build* (New York: McGraw-Hill, 1968), 153.

47. Ibid., 154.

48. Ibid., 164.

49. Walter W. Heller, *New Dimensions of Political Economy* (Cambridge, Mass.: Harvard University Press, 1966), 58.

50. Ibid., 109.

51. Examples of their thinking are in Arthur M. Okun, ed., *The Battle Against Unemployment* (New York: W. W. Norton, 1965) and Gardner Ackley, "The Contribution of Economists to Policy Formation," *The Journal of Finance* 21 (May 1966): 169–177.

52. Memo to LBJ from Gardner Ackley, 30 July 1965 on the "Economic Aspects of Vietnam," *The Administrative History of the CEA*.

53. Memo to LBJ from Arthur Okun, 24 July 1968, Papers of LBJ, FG 11-3, Box 61, LBJ Library.

54. *The Administrative History of the CEA*, vol. 1, Chapter 2, "The CEA Role in Fiscal Policy."

55. Ibid.

56. Confidential Memo to LBJ from Gardner Ackley, 22 December 1965, Papers of LBJ FG 11-3, Box 58, LBJ Library.

57. *Public Papers of the Presidents, Lyndon B. Johnson* contains many examples of Johnsonian love and admiration for the CEA. See vol. 1, 1964, 609, 824, 825, 959; vol. 3, 1966, 83, 128; vol. 1, 1968, 126.

58. Joseph Barr Oral History, 25 August 1969, LBJ Library.

59. *The Administrative History of the CEA*, vol. 1, Chapter 5, "Economics of Defense and Disarmament."

60. Halberstam, *The Best and the Brightest*, 608. See also p. 144. Doris Kearn's article "Lyndon Johnson's Political Personality," *Political Science Quarterly* 89 (Fall 1976): 385–409 is highly informative about why, politically, institutionally, personally, LBJ lied.

61. Ibid., 610.

62. Henry Fowler Oral History, 10 June 1969, LBJ Library.

63. Statement by the President on the Raising of the Discount Rate by the Federal Reserve Board, December 15, 1965," *Public Papers of the Presidents, Lyndon B. Johnson*, vol. 2, 1965, 1137. See also G. L. Bach, *Making Monetary and Fiscal Policy* (Washington, D.C.: Brookings Institution, 1971), 122.

64. As quoted in Stevens, *Vain Hopes, Grim Realities*, 210.

65. According to Melman, *The Permanent War Economy*, 150–151, it was a climax of a long historical process. For the immediate context see Halberstam, *The Best and the Brightest*, 544–545.

66. Mark I. Gelfand, "The War on Poverty," in Divine, ed., *Exploring the Johnson Years*, 126.

67. The first two quotes are in the "Annual Message to the Congress: The Economic Report of the President, 27 January 1966," *Public Papers of the President, Lyndon B. Johnson*. vol. 3, 1966, 97, 109. The last quote is from "Remarks at the Signing of the Economic Report for 1966," ibid., 95. See also Stevens, *Vain Hopes, Grim Realities*, 56–60.

68. LBJ's book simply does not discuss the CEA in any meaningful manner. To be sure, he puts his own pespective on events discussed in this chapter but he never recognizes the historic factors creating his major difficulties. In his chapter, "Bite the Bullet," 448–461, he denies having lied to businessmen and Congress about the high cost of Vietnam.

69. Bornet, *The Presidency of LBJ*, 244.

70. Memo to LBJ from Arthur Okun, 27 April 1968, *The Administrative History of the CEA*, vol. 2.

71. Ibid., 13 May 1968.

72. Alexander Trowbridge, former Secretary of Commerce, Oral History, 19 February 1969, LBJ Library.

73. Bornet, *The Presidency of LBJ*, 103.

74. James L. Clayton, "The Fiscal Cost of the Cold War to the United States: The

First 25 Years, 1947–1971,'' *The Western Political Science Quarterly* 25 (September 1972): 393.

75. Ibid., 395. Seymour Melman supports the same position. See *The Permanent War Economy*, 260–300. Both Clayton and Melman accept the industrialism versus militarism argument inherited from such "conservative" thinkers as William Graham Sumner and Thorstein Veblen.

76. Sar A. Levitan and Robert Taggart, *The Promise of Greatness* (Cambridge, Mass.: Harvard University Press, 1976) is a good analysis of LBJ's positive contribution to American life.

77. William E. Leuchtenburg, *In The Shadow of F.D.R.: From Harry Truman to Ronald Reagan* (Ithaca, N.Y.: Cornell University Press, 1983), 160.

78. Divine, "The Johnson Literature," *Exploring the Johnson Years*, vol. 16; Burner and West, *The Torch Is Passed*, 261, 268.

79. Garry Wills, "Carter and the End of Liberalism, *The New York Review of Books* 24 (May 12, 1977): 16–20 is a brilliant summary of this historic development. See also Paul N. Goldstone, *The Collapse of the Liberal Empire: Science and Revolution in the Twentieth Century* (New Haven, Conn.: Yale University Presss, 1977) and Donald K. Pickens, "Infinite Desires in a Finite World," *Social Science Quarterly* 57 (September 1976): 466–472. Today, middle- and upper-class interests recognize the New Deal merit of liberal spending programs. See Everett C. Ladd, Jr., "Liberalism Upside Down: The Immersion of the New Deal Order," *Political Science Quarterly* 89 (Winter 1976–1977): 577–600. The New Deal legacy is now the status quo.

80. Stein, *Presidential Economics*, 107.

13

Lyndon B. Johnson and the 1964–1968 Revenue Acts: Congressional Politics and "Fiscal Chickens Coming Home to Roost"

Phillip M. Simpson

The central thesis of this chapter is that the executive-congressional politics of the 1964 Revenue Act fundamentally shaped the politics of the 1968 Revenue and Expenditure Control Act. These two great tax policy debates of the 1960s bring into clear relief the built-in dilemmas of "new economics," as well as the tensions, conflicts, and choices of the Johnson presidency itself.

The centerpiece of President Kennedy's economic policy was a tax cut, which he embraced in early 1963 after a two-year debate in the administration and Congress over the need for such a cut. The House Ways and Means Committee and its prestigious Chairman, Wilbur D. Mills (D-Ark.), were eventually transformed by Kennedy into a formidable tax policy juggernaut that was moving the tax cut to congressional acceptance when Kennedy was cut down.[1]

Conservatives of both political parties were generally opposed to extensive growth in either the federal government or the deficit, and they favored tax reduction as a "free enterprise way" of stimulating economic growth without inflation. Kennedy successfully clothed the liberal innovative tax policy in conservative economically orthodox garb in order to gain the support of conservative congressional Democrats, especially Mills and Ways and Means.[2] Kennedy deemphasized the planned deficit feature of the tax cut, promised a tight lid on government spending, emphasized the wastes of unemployment and unused economic potential, and restated his belief in the operation of free market processes.[3] Led by the powerful Mills, Ways and Means and the House fell behind the Kennedy program in near party-line votes. House committee and floor consideration of the Kennedy tax cut centered on Republican attempts to trim the impact of a stimulative deficit and tie the liberal Democrats to spending ceilings they did not want.[4] In a Kennedy-Mills maneuver that would dramatically affect the politics of the 1968 Revenue and Expenditure Control Act, Mills offered and won acceptance of a softer "sense of the Congress" declaration, which embodied the rhetorical-symbolic wedding of "new economics" and "puritan ethic, economic orthodoxy." The declaration committed the government to balancing the budget, debt reduction, and restrained government spending.[5] Before the decade ran its course, the conservative Republicans had formed a loud "I told you so" chorus, and Wilbur Mills fought for the integrity of the "sense of Congress declaration" in a heated battle with fellow southerner Lyndon B. Johnson over the 1967–1968 surcharge.

With House passage, the Senate Finance Committee held hearings on the bill. It was clear to Kennedy and his congressional coalition that the chairman of the Senate Finance Committee, Senator Harry F. Byrd (D-Va.), a major exponent of "fiscal frugality,' would not cooperate in expediting the measure. This is essentially where the tax cut stood when Kennedy was murdered.[6]

Johnson embraced the tax cut policy, but decided not to push for action on the tax bill in 1963.[7] Instead, the new president made a "deal" over lunch with Senator Byrd that ensured action early in January 1964. Johnson promised to keep the administrative budget for FY 1965 below the $98 billion level and then send it to the Congress before final Senate action on the tax bill. Byrd would then step aside to let Russell Long manage the bill. Johnson initiated a well-publicized economy drive in order to hold the budget down to a level even lower than that suggested by House Republicans. Johnson was in effect proposing to reduce the deficit for 1965 by over half of the Kennedy $10 billion.[8]

The Senate Finance committee bill was viewed as "strikingly similar" to the House version, with the exception of the deletion of Mills' "sense of the Congress" declaration. That provision, it was felt, was now unnecessary in view of the many administration promises to hold down spending.[9]

The "Johnson treatment," the widely publicized economy drive, the reduction of the forecasted deficit for FY 1965, and the emotional push of the Kennedy death produced a bipartisan Senate vote in support of the bill. The tenor of Senate debate indicated that most were highly pleased with Johnson's willingness to make hard commitments on spending/deficits where Kennedy had made only verbal promises.[10]

The Conference Committee produced House Report 1149 containing an $11.5 billion tax cut. House conferees, led by Mills, succeeded in reinserting the "sense of the Congress declaration" on spending and deficits. The bill generally reflected the House profile. With House Republican opposition greatly lessened, the House adopted the tax cut bill on 24 February 1964, in a 326–83 vote, with 23 members not voting. A total of 108 Republicans joined 218 Democrats in support of the measure. President Johnson was everywhere, and Wilbur Mills acknowledged this in floor debate. The Senate adopted the measure the next day in a bipartisan margin of 74–19 with 7 not voting, and Johnson signed the bill into law on 26 February 1964.[11]

Between adoption of the 1964 tax cut and January 1967, the Johnson administration was forced to alter its economic policy focus from stagnation to inflation.

In that more simple era devoid of "stagflation," the policy choices offered by "new economics" seemed simple enough: raise taxes, slow demand, restrain government spending, or some combination of these in conjunction with various monetary/fiscal thrusts. However, the political dictates of demand restraint "new economics" were immeasurably complicated by the Vietnam War expansion, the development of Great Society activism and growth in the federal government, and political bargains struck between President Johnson and the Congress in ensuring pasage of the 1964 tax cut. Just as Johnson's intentions for peace in campaign 1964 turned to wider war, allusions made in the tax cut policy of 1963–1964 to fiscal frugality and restraint in government growth turned to growth in federal government activism practically unprecedented in the twentieth century. Even with Johnson's political power base in the now famous eighty-ninth Congress, the triple tensions of wider war, increased federal activism at home, and the nature of past fiscal promises were bound to produce political disintegration from both left and right. In fiscal and economic policy, these various tensions were joined in the fight to raise (or not to raise) taxes in 1967–1968.

The stresses in the American economy that developed in 1965 and 1966, especially the increases in wholesale and consumer prices, had a complex of causal factors: (a) the increase in Vietnam spending, (b) the increase in Great Society outlays, (c) federal fiscal and monetary conditions that were stimulatory in nature, (d) federal deficit financing, and (e) lack of restraint in the private sector, which added a "cost-push" dimension to "demand-pull" inflation.[12]

The Committee for Economic Development maintains that the rapid increase in Vietnam spending was "superimposed on an economy in which there was little slack in 1965."[13] Defense outlays increased between 1965 and 1968, and Johnson at the same time began pursuing the "Great Society" at home in a belief that we could have both "guns and butter."[14] Early on, Johnson could practice the politics of consensus, fight Vietnam, increase social services, lower taxes—all within the context of a growing economy. By late 1965, this harmony was coming to an end. In December 1965, the "Triad" (Treasury, BOB, and CEA) "recommended that all major budgetary, tax, and monetary decisions be deferred in order to create a coordinated monetary-fiscal package designed to meet the economy's needs for non-inflationary expansion." Gardner Ackley, CEA chief, advised Johnson in mid-December 1965 to increase taxes in light of projected budget increases. Johnson ignored this advice, but did follow suit in 1966 with the "bits and pieces" tax program that reduced purchasing power by about $10 billion.[15]

Why did Johnson resist so long in calling for the surcharge in 1967? There are several explanations, all of which are plausible, and all are probably correct to some extent: (a) Johnson was afraid that austerity would kill the Great Society, (b) Johnson feared that Congress would turn down such a request, (c) Johnson was uncertain about economic trends and the Vietnam War, and (d) Johnson received mixed advice from his economic policy team.[16]

By late 1966 the administration, though still divided, was ready to at least place the surcharge proposal on the congressional agenda. On 10 January 1967, President Johnson went before a joint session of Congress to propose an across-the-board tax increase. The president used primarily an economic justification, singling out concern about the growth in prices and interest rates. It was clear when President Johnson presented his tax increases that the administration was not yet ready to give the tax increase the push that would be necessary for congressional approval.[17] Why the delay? The Johnson administration delayed submitting a request as a result of this economic uncertainty plus the aforementioned factors. The president was attempting simply to hedge his bets.

By August 1967 the president's economic advisers had concluded that "economic growth has resumed and the economy is picking up speed." At the same time, the president sent 45,000 more troops to Vietnam. The conclusion was that we needed the "movement of fiscal policy toward restraint in order to safeguard prosperity."[18]

In a special message to the Congress on 3 August 1967, the president proposed an enlarged tax increase and ordered each department to make all possible reductions. At the same time, he pressed Congress not to appropriate more money than he was asking. What about the "Great Society"? President Johnson made it clear that he thought the march should continue.[19] The Ways and Means Committee, in compliance with the president's request, began hearings on the tax proposal in August 1967. The most important witnesses were President Johnson's "quadriad" of economic advisers, and they carried most of the burden in the long struggle to get a tax increase. Treasury Secretary Henry Fowler outlined five arguments for the imposition of the tax: (a) to meet the costs of Vietnam, (b) to hold down the deficit, (c) to avoid high interest rates and tight money, (d) to protect economic growth and price stability, and (e) to protect our balance of international payments posture.[20]

As the hearings progressed, the deep division between the administration and the Ways and Means Committee became clear. Most importantly, the leadership of the committee, Chairman Mills and ranking minority member John Byrnes, joined the same side of the policy fence in pressing for expenditure reduction before acting on any tax increase. Mills had finally accepted Thomas B. Curtis' 1963–1964 argument that tax policy should be predicated on what the latter had called "expenditure reform." In essence, Mills had taken very seriously the arguments advanced by Kennedy and Johnson in 1963 and 1964 that the approach to economic growth was through the private economy. What he saw now was a violation of that pledge, as evidenced by the increase in government spending and activity, the Vietnam War notwithstanding. Mills also believed that much of the inflation was of the "cost-push" variety—the source was increased cost administered by labor or business—and would not be stopped by attacking aggregate demand.[21]

The hearings drew to a close in September 1967. The direction of committee thinking was clear: no spending reduction initiated by the administration, no tax increase. On 3 October 1967 the committee formalized its position by adopting a resolution that laid the tax program on the table. All ten Republicans joined ten Democrats, including Chairman Mills, in support of the motion. Chairman Mills, with this solid support behind him, began to personally lead the battle with the administration over the future direction of fiscal policy.[22] His (and the committee's) expectation of the administration was clear: The "control of spending is a prerequisite for my even considering a tax increase." "We want to pause," he said, "in this headlong rush toward bigger government."[23] President Johnson said that Mills and House Minority Leader Gerald Ford, who joined Mills, would "live to rue the day" they decided to table the bill.[24]

The remainder of 1967 saw the struggle between the Ways and Means Committee and Johnson intensify, as the committee held up action in order to squeeze unspecified cuts from the administration. The administration only very reluctantly fell in line with committee expectations, and the "tug of war" that ensued was often frustrating and bitter. If reduction had to come—as the Ways and Means Committee and Mills demanded—the executive expected the Congress to do the unpopular slashing.

Despite President Johnson's desire to lay the burden of cutting the budget on Congress, his administration had revised the earlier proposal by November 1967. The Ways and Means Committee agreed to meet on 29 November 1967 to hear testimony from Fowler, Schultze, and Martin. The hearings took on added significance because of the British devaluation of the pound sterling in November, placing new stress on the dollar. The administration plan was unveiled: The tax increase proposals of August were repeated, but a second section with statutory reductions in spending was included. The Ways and Means Committee, through the action of Chairman Mills with the concurrence of Byrnes, adjourned the hearing without taking any action. The committee's leadership was not satisfied with the amount of spending reduction suggested.[25]

In proposing specific budget reductions, both the administration and the committee realized that such a proposal was also a direct concern of the House Appropriations Committee. Mills said he would be "very, very loath to get into the jurisdiction of any other committee."[26] For this reason, Mills suggested that the administration propose the package to the House Appropriations Committee. The administration did so, and the second section of the proposal, which contained the spending reductions, became law in December 1967.[27]

As 1967 came to an end, the impasse between the administration and the Ways and Means Committee had not been broached. President Johnson expressed the belief that the passage of the $4 billion plus reduction in December 1967 was enough to justify the tax increase and to satisfy the demands of the Ways and Means Committee. Chairman Mills, however, indicated that he would not end the drive to enact further spending reductions. His one concession to the administration was to promise that the committee would again consider the tax proposal in January 1968.[28] The first half of 1968 was a period in which the major differences between the administration and Congress over fiscal policy were resolved. The Ways and Means Committee, under the stern personal direction of Mills, held out until the very last, thus helping to force reductions in government spending.

Ways and Means Committee met to hear administration testimony in January 1968. The "quadriad" (Fowler, Schultze, Ackley, and Martin) went before the Committee to carry President Johnson's general appeal through specific arguments. Fowler struck out at the budget slashers. It was clear that the committee (and Mills) was not yet willing to give in. Mills perceived the Ways and Means Committee as a court in a trial, with himself as the people's attorney, in a battle between the "federal government . . . [and] . . . the taxpayer." The American people, he asserted, did not like tax increases, especially if the government did not have its "house in order." The Chairman restated his position that he was trying to be consistent with the pledge of the 1964 Revenue Act in reducing the role of government and easing the heavy burden of taxation.[29]

Mills stated that it would be possible for the committee to proceed with consideration of that part of the proposal that sought to continue excise taxes at existing rates and accelerate selected income tax payments, which the House approved in February 1968. The simple move to continue excise taxes at existing rates took on new importance, as the Senate amended the measure to include the surtax request and spending reduction. The committee made clear that its action did not assure the death of the tax surcharge.[30]

Mills mentioned in floor debate three factors that could influence his decision to delay the surcharge or act on the measure: an acceleration of Vietnam expenditures, the development of "demand-pull" rather than "cost-push" inflation, and a worsening of the international financial situation. In the Senate, the fiscal package of a tax increase (with the surcharge) and spending cuts was approved.[31] In hearings before the Senate Finance Committee, Fowler reiterated the necessity for having the tax surcharge in addition to the excise tax and acceleration of payments action. Fowler made it clear that, in spite of his attention to the "normal process" of getting the surtax, he and the administration would welcome any action (by the Senate committee or otherwise) that would increase taxes. At the same time the Senate Finance Committee was considering the possibility of the surtax addition, the United States faced a critical situation in the international gold market.[32] This was the "trigger" to congressional action "according to most observers," as two "fiscal conservatives," Senator George Smathers and Senator John J. Williams (R-Del. and the ranking Republican on the Senate Finance Committee), moved in the Senate Finance Committee to adopt a spending-taxing package that included the surtax.[33] The move was defeated in committee, but was revived and passed on the Senate floor. The administration supported the Smathers-Williams proposal (or was at least silent), hoping thereby to dislodge the tax proposal. The administration supposedly thought it could compromise away the spending cuts in conference. There was some speculation that Mills was also behind the Senate amendment, because he would have control over both the increase and the cuts in the conference committee.

Senator Williams had "gambled that we'd have a friend in the House and we did."

During the Senate debate on the fiscal program, President Johnson made an earnest plea for action and, at the same time, withdrew from the presidential race. The president's conciliatory theme carried over into his appeal for a tax hike. The president seemed to be saying that he would accept a reasonable spending limitation in return for the tax increase.[34]

Most of April and some of May 1968 were consumed by a deadlock in conference committee. Complex negotiations and bargaining between Senate and House leadership and the administration finally produced agreement on 9 May 1968. Throughout much of April, the conferees jockeyed over a possible compromise. In the final analysis, the House Appropriations Committee, chaired by George Mahon (D-Tex.), was to play the key role in reaching a compromise agreement. On 30 April 1968 President Johnson met with key congressmen involved in the disagreement, including Mills and Mahon. Agreement between the administration and the Appropriations Committee was ostensibly reached over long- and short-run spending reduction in a mix that was to be labelled the "10-8-4." That is, the cuts were to be $10 billion in appropriations requested in January 1968, $8 billion reduction in past appropriations, and a $4 billion reduction in 1969 fiscal year spending. Mills, still holding out for an unspecified amount, remained silent on the proposal. The House Appropriations Committee formalized its support for the formula on 1 May 1968, by a twenty to zero vote, with committee Republicans abstaining. Mahon thought that this move would "break the deadlock" between the president and Congress. This is just what happened. This action by Appropriations would free Mills of jurisdictional concern. He could add the spending restraints with the knowledge that he had the general backing of the powerful Appropriations Committee. In addition, the "10-8-4" formula was a step in the direction of a restriction on long-term obligational spending and not just a deferral in 1969 spending.[35]

The Ways and Means Committee, under LBJ's pressure, was called into session in May 1968 to consider the tax proposal. By a bipartisan vote of seventeen to six the committee approved the "10-8-4" formula. The committee, according to the resolution, "acted in the light of existing critical domestic and international fiscal situations." On 9 May 1968 the conferees reached agreement and a "10-8-6" formula was accepted—more cuts than LBJ wanted.[36]

In May 1968, proponents of the conference report got the crucial endorsement they had been waiting for from President Johnson. Johnson expressed "regret" about the $6 billion spending cut, but feared the "gates of economic chaos" would open without the bill.[37] The House took up the conference report on 20 June 1968. The bill had the formidable backing of both the Democratic and Republican leadership in Congress and the endorsement of the president. Mills made clear that he had finally bought the administration argument about "demand-pull" inflation, and he spoke for the measure because of what it would do to and for the economy. One congressman's argument pretty well reflected the House: "The guns and butter argument has been going on since nearly the beginning of the war in Vietnam," and now "the chickens are coming home to roost." The House accepted the conference report by a 268-to-150 vote margin.[38]

The Senate took up the package on the following day, 21 June 1968. Senator Smathers, the second ranking Democrat on the Senate Finance Committee, in introducing the bill used the same economic arguments reflected by Mills in the House. Senator Williams, the ranking Republican on the Senate Finance Committee, spoke for the measure in economic terms, urging passage because the Senate had no "choice." The Senate voted to accept the conference report by a safe margin of sixty-four to sixteen.[39]

The measure (the 1968 Revenue and Expenditure Control Act), which had now passed the House and Senate, had three titles. Title I contained the tax increases proposed by the administration. Title II contained specific limitations on federal spending and the federal work force. The last title simply made some minor changes in the social security laws.[40] On 28 June 1968 President Johnson signed the 1968 Revenue and Expenditure Control Act into law. The president saw the matter for what it was—the other side of the "new economics" application from what it had been in 1964. In 1964, he said, "we put our foot on the accelerator" and in 1968, "we applied the fiscal brakes." The president thought that the bill was our "insurance policy" to "protect our prosperity."[41] Many would also say that the "new economics" had also passed a critical test, or, alternately, a conservative trap had been successfully sprung on a liberal president.

CONCLUSIONS

It is clear from this chapter that the roots of tax and fiscal policy difficulties in 1967–1968 were embedded in the politics that produced the 1964 tax cut. In order to build a coalition behind "new economics" stimulation in 1964, Johnson stressed the conservative values of frugality, free enterprise growth, lean government, and balanced budgets even more than had Kennedy. In securing congressional support, both administrations had talked powerful congressmen—especially Wilbur Mills—into supporting their position (thus bringing reluctant congressmen along with them) based on what appeared to be fiscally conservative and "free enterprise" growth commitments. After three years of Great Society activism and broken pledges on Vietnam, Mills and others in Congress saw standing down Johnson's budgetary and fiscal policies as a matter of integrity. The Republican leadership, especially in the House, felt very much vindicated in their initial opposition to the 1964 tax cuts as events of 1966–1968 unfolded.

Just as some liberal groups were alienated by what they considered to be Lyndon Johnson's reneging on pledges of peace in Vietnam in campaign 1964, so were some conservative groups (Mills, southern Democrats generally, and the Republican party in Congress) alienated by what they saw as deception in the area of fiscal, tax, and economic policy.

Johnson's clear tendency was to overstate cases in order to get votes, either at the public or congressional level. Thus, Johnson's consensus building had an element of "overkill" that suggested to many a quality of deceit and dishonesty, correctly or not. These factors were exacerbated by the inherent nature of "new economics" theories of the 1960s. The view that "less is more" (less taxes mean more growth) would only work within the context of a certain level of government spending, or even deficits. The problem was one of convincing old-line fiscal conservatives that less taxes *should not* be matched by actually having less government. It was very tempting to get votes in 1963–1964 by promising less government or at least more efficient government. But the promise, when made, undermined the very theoretical propositions then being fed to JFK and LBJ by their economic policy teams. Good intentions must be based upon argumentation developed in an open, free, democratic debate if possible. Perhaps if these dictates had been followed more closely in both war and fiscal and domestic policies, we could have avoided much of the dismantling of the progressive state under the Reagan presidency. Certainly our failure in Vietnam and the stagflation of the 1970s might very well relegate the Democratic party to minority status. This is hardly the monument Lyndon B. Johnson would have wanted to leave to history.

NOTES

1. Phillip M. Simpson, "John F. Kennedy and the 1964 Revenue Act: The Politics of Formulation and Legitimation" (Paper delivered at the Hofstra University Conference on John F. Kennedy, Hempstead, New York, March 1985).

2. Phillip M. Simpson, "Macro-Economic Decision-Making: The 1964 and 1968 Revenue Acts" (Ph.D. diss., University of Arizona, 1971), 156 and Chapters 4 and 5.

3. *Public Papers of the Presidents: John F. Kennedy*, Address before the Nineteenth Washington Conference of the Advertising Council, 13 March 1963.

4. *Congressional Quarterly Almanac*, 1963, CQ Service, Washington, D.C., 483; *New York Times*, 11 September 1963.

5. *Public Papers of the Presidents: John F. Kennedy*, Letter to the Chairman, House Ways and Means Committee on Tax Reduction, 21 August 1963, 637–639; House Committee on Ways and Means, *House Report 749*, 88th Cong., 1st Sess., 1963.

6. Senate Finance Committee, *Hearings on the President's 1963 Tax Proposals*, 88th Cong., 1st Sess., 1963, Parts 1–5.

7. Jack Bell, *The Johnson Treatment* (New York: Harper & Row, 1965), 90–91; "Lyndon B. Johnson: Tragedy and Transition," A nationally televised interview conducted by Walter Cronkite, CBS Television, 2 May 1970.

8. *New York Times*, 6 December 1963; Lyndon B. Johnson, *The Vantage Point* (New York: Holt, Rinehart and Winston, 1971), 36.

9. Senate Finance Committee, *Senate Report 830*, 88th Cong., 2d Sess., 1964, 8; *Congressional Quarterly Almanac*, 1963, 526–532.

10. *Congressional Record*, 88th Cong., 2d Sess., 1964, 110, Part 2: 1745.

11. House Ways and Means Committee, *House Report 1149*, 88th Cong., 2d Sess., 1964, 18; *Congressional Quarterly Almanac*, 1964, 539–540; *Congressional Record*, 88th Cong., 2d Sess., 1964, 110, Part 3: 3582, 3563, 3692.

12. Council of Economic Advisers, *Economic Indicators*, prepared for the Joint Economic Committee of the United States Congress, 1957–1968.

13. Committee for Economic Development Research and Policy Committee, "The National Economy and the Vietnam War," April 1968, 18.

14. *Public Papers of the Presidents: Lyndon B. Johnson*, Annual Message to the Congress on the State of the Union, 12 January 1966, 3.

15. John W. Sloan, "President Johnson, the Council of Economic Advisers, and the Failure to Raise Taxes in 1966 and 1967," *Presidential Studies Quarterly* 15, no. 1 (Winter 1985): 91–92.

16. Ibid.

17. *Public Papers of the Presidents: Lyndon B. Johnson*, The President's Annual Message to the Congress on the State of the Union, 10 January, 1967, 8.

18. House Ways and Means Committee, *Hearings on the Tax Proposals of the President*, 89th Cong., 2d Sess., 1966, 736, Part 1, 49.

19. *Public Papers of the Presidents: Lyndon B. Johnson*, Special Message to the Congress on the State of the Budget and the Economy, 3 August 1967, 733–740.

20. House Ways and Means Committee, *Hearings on the Tax Proposals of the President*, 89th Cong., 2d Sess., 1966, Part 1, 15–30.

21. Ibid; Wilbur D. Mills, Address at a Convention of the Arkansas Farm Bureau Federation, Hot Springs, Arkansas, 20 November 1967.

22. *Congressional Quarterly Almanac*, 1967, 653.

23. *New York Times*, 7 October 1967.

24. *Public Papers of the Presidents: Lyndon B. Johnson*, The President's News Conference of 7 November 1967, 1050.

25. House Ways and Means Committee, *Continuation of Hearings on the President's Surtax Proposal*, 90th Cong., 1st Sess., 1967, 9–200.

26. Ibid., 190.

27. Ibid., 200; *Public Papers of the Presidents: Lyndon B. Johnson*, Statement of the President after Signing the Joint Resolution Providing for Continuing Appropriations Fiscal Year 1968, 19 December 1967, 1174.

28. Ibid.; *New York Times*, 16 December 1967.

29. House Ways and Means Committee, *Continuation of Hearings on the President's 1967 Surtax Proposal*, 90th Cong., 2d Sess., 1968, 3–162.

30. Ibid., 1; *Congressional Record*, 90th Cong., 2d Sess., 1968, 114, Part. 4: 4713.

31. *Congressional Record*, 90th Cong., 2d Sess., 1968, 114, Part 4: 4704–4795, 4709.

32. Senate Finance Committee, *Hearings on the Tax Adjustment Act of 1968*, 90th Cong., 2d Sess., 1, 132, 68.

33. *Congressional Quarterly Almanac*, 1968, 263–270; *Congressional Record*, 90th Cong., 2d Sess., 1968, 113, Part 6: 7722, 8567.

34. *Public Papers of the Presidents: Lyndon B. Johnson*, The President's Address to the Nation Announcing Steps to Halt the Vietnam War and Reporting His Decision Not to Seek Reelection, 31 March 1968, 472.

35. *New York Times*, 5 May 1968; *Congressional Quarterly Almanac*, 1968, 274.

36. *Congressional Quarterly Almanac*, 1968, 274.

37. *Public Papers of the Presidents: Lyndon B. Johnson*, The President's News Conference at the LBJ Ranch, 30 May 1968, 674.

38. *Congressional Record*, 90th Cong., 2d Sess., 1968, 144, Part 14: 17960–18087.

39. Ibid., 18152–18180.

40. House Ways and Means Committee, *House Report 1533*, 90th Cong., 2d Sess., 1968.

41. *Public Papers of the Presidents: Lyndon B. Johnson*, Statement by the President Upon Signing the Tax Bill, 28 June 1968, 754–755.

14

The Vietnam War and Inflation Revisited

Tom Riddell

It is more than a decade since the end of the Vietnam War. Enough time has passed to sort out the historical record concerning the war and its economic impacts. Like all wars, though, there will continue to be controversy over interpretations of it and its effects. Most analysts note that the war led to a critical reevaluation of American foreign policy and produced caution toward military intervention. There is also widespread recognition of the economic costs of the war and its responsibility for stimulating inflation in the 1960s. But in the 1980s President Ronald Reagan, seeking to reinterpret the history of the war, labelled it a "noble cause" and tried to jettison the "Vietnam syndrome." Some economists, also echoing positions from the war years, recently suggested that the economic burden of the war was trivial.

John F. Walker and Harold G. Vatter, playing the revisionists, "argue that most of the facts asserted in the conventional wisdom regarding the alleged Vietnam War origins of the current inflationary period are wrong," that the war cannot be held responsible for increased inflation in any year but 1968, and that the macroeconomic impact of the war was short lived and minimal.[1] In this chapter, I will confront this challenge and reexamine the economic consequences of the Vietnam War and whether it caused an acceleration of inflation in the late 1960s. Such analysis should contribute to our understanding of recent economic history and of the possible economic effects of military expansions—which could presumably inform current and future economic policy.

INFLATION IN THE 1960s

Table 14.1 presents data on various measurements of annual rates of inflation from 1960 to 1971. These data demonstrate the source of the conclusion by most

Table 14.1
Inflation During the Vietnam War Period, 1960 to 1971

Year	Change in Consumer Price Index, December to December, Unadjusted	Change in CPI, Year-to-Year, Adjusted	Change in Producer Price Index, December to December, Unadjusted	Change in PPI, Year-to-Year, Adjusted	Annual Change in GNP Implicit Price Deflator
1960	1.5	1.6	1.8	0.8	1.6
1961	0.7	1.0	-0.5	0.0	0.9
1962	1.2	1.1	0.1	0.3	1.8
1963	1.6	1.2	-0.2	-0.3	1.5
1964	1.2	1.3	0.5	0.4	1.5
1965	1.9	1.7	3.3	1.7	2.2
1966	3.4	2.9	2.2	3.2	3.2
1967	3.0	2.9	1.6	1.2	3.0
1968	4.7	4.2	3.1	2.8	4.4
1969	6.1	5.4	4.8	3.7	5.1
1970	5.5	5.9	2.2	3.5	5.4
1971	3.4	4.3	3.2	3.1	5.0

Source: Economic Report of the President, 1982, 237, 295, 302.

professional economists and the public that the acceleration of inflation was linked with the Vietnam War.

For the period 1960–1964, all of these price indices show relatively low and stable rates of inflation in a range of less than 1 percent to less than 2 percent. The annual change in the CPI (from December to December and unadjusted) never exceeded 1.6 percent in the first half of the decade and averaged 1.2 percent. The changes in the adjusted, year-to-year CPI also averaged 1.2 percent. Both measures of the producer price index had average annual increases over the period of less than 1 percent. The GNP price deflator increased at an average annual rate of 1.5 percent. These trends continued the low rates of inflation experienced in the late 1950s. But with the escalation of the Vietnam War in 1965, there was an acceleration in the rates of increase in all of these measures of price levels.

From December 1964 to December 1965, the unadjusted CPI increased by 1.9 percent, up from 1.2 percent the previous year. This was followed by an increase of 3.4 percent in 1966, 3 percent in 1967, 4.7 percent in 1968, and 6.1 percent in 1969. A similar pattern of accelerating inflation emerges in the year-to-year, adjusted CPI changes. The annual percentage increases in the GNP price deflator also accelerated from 1965 to 1969—2.2 to 5.1 percent. In the two series for producer prices, there were marked jumps in the annual rates of change in 1965 and 1966, a slow down in their rate of increase in 1967 (due to a "growth recession"), and renewed acceleration in 1968 and 1969.

Walker and Vatter contend that the data on inflation do not demonstrate an acceleration in inflation until 1968.[2] They base this conclusion on an analysis of quarterly changes at annual rates for the CPI and the PPI and on the assertion that any changes in the price indices of less than 3 percent are not significant.

While the quarterly data show variance in the rate of inflation during the period of the Vietnam escalation, I would argue that they do not provide adequate information on the trend in the rate of inflation in the period prior to the escalation or during it. For this purpose, the changes in the annual rates of inflation are superior, as is demonstrated in the use of such data in most economic discourse. Walker and Vatter refer to a statement in an introductory economics textbook about the 2 to 3 percent margin of error in the CPI and conclude that any change in it of less than 3 percent amounts to "no inflation."[3] Walker and Vatter transpose this *range* of uncertainty to 3 percent as the standard and use it as an absolute test of the existence of inflation. The fact that the CPI is based on a survey and has a margin of error does not mean that it cannot be used to identify patterns of change in consumer prices. It is a consistently measured series over time, and economists rely on statistical techniques to ensure its ability to reflect trends in the prices of goods and services. If economists were not allowed a 3 percent margin of error, there is not much that we could say about the economy with any degree of confidence.

THE TIMING AND IMPACT OF THE VIETNAM WAR ESCALATION

Both economic theory and history suggest the conclusion that wars may have an inflationary impact on the economy. In all of its major wars, the United States has experienced increased rates of inflation.[4] The connection between war spending and inflation is based on both conventional micro- and macroeconomic theory. Increased war spending stimulates the demand for labor and raw materials used in war production. Increased price pressures develop for these factors of production in proportion to the tightness of their markets. The macroeconomic effect results from the stimulation of aggregate demand in the economy as a whole. Government spending to prosecute the war effort is added onto total spending in the economy. The new spending creates demand for war goods, as well as higher incomes throughout the economy that will be spent on nonmilitary goods and services. The increased demand for both military and consumer products contributes to inflationary pressures in the economy. The inflationary impact of the war will depend on the state of the economy, the manner by which it is financed, and wartime economic policy. If the economy is close to full employment, *ceteris paribus*, increased war spending will have a larger inflationary impact. If the war is financed by printing money or by the Federal Reserve lending directly to the Treasury, there will be higher inflation. If the government does not increase taxes to pay for the war, the inflationary impact of the war will not be checked.

The issue here is whether the Vietnam War caused increased inflation in the 1960s. The analysis will rest on an investigation of the impact of the war (taking into account the magnitude and timing of the buildup for the war), the state of the economy at the time, how it was financed, and wartime economic policy.

To examine the impact of the war, we must identify the period of time when the war made extra demands on the resources of the society. Walker and Vatter suggest a period of escalation from fourth quarter 1965 to second quarter 1967 using quarterly data and 1966–1967 using annual data; their definition of escalation is that period of time during which national defense purchases of goods and services as a percentage of GNP increased.[5] There are two problems with this definition—one of substance and one of measurement.

U.S. involvement in the war was an extraordinary occurrence in the history of the country. In this light, the effect of war spending lasted for the entire period of time during which the war was making an extra claim on the society's resources. Table 14.2 presents information on the annual costs of the war from FY 1965 to FY 1975. The full costs of all forces, equipment, and materials used in the war amounted to over $140 billion; and the incremental costs of fighting the war over and above the normal costs of using baseline forces in peace time were over $110 billion.[6] While it is true that the war placed accelerating demands on resources during the 1966–1967 period, it is also true that the war made an extra claim on resources throughout its tenure (subject to countervailing fiscal policies). Walker and Vatter focus only on the period of escalation. Whether inflation is engendered by an *escalation* is certainly a relevant question; but it is not the only question in determining the inflationary impact of a war.

Furthermore, from an examination of the data they present, as well as Table 14.2, it is possible to identify a different and longer period of escalation. Table 14.2 shows war spending increasing in every fiscal year from 1966 through 1969. Walker and Vatter note that defense purchases as a percentage of GNP were 7.1 percent in third quarter 1965, increased to 7.4 percent in fourth quarter 1965, and then increased in every quarter to 9.0 percent in second quarter 1967. In third quarter 1967, they decreased to 8.6 percent, bringing the "escalation" to a close. However, there are two important qualifications to this dating of the escalation. In fourth quarter 1967, defense purchases went back up to 9.0 percent of GNP, increased again to 9.1 percent in first quarter 1968, and returned to 9.0 percent in second quarter 1968. The dating by Walker and Vatter of the end of the escalation seems to be at least questionable and certainly arbitrary. Based on these figures, it could be argued that the escalation lasted into 1968; only after second quarter 1968 were there consistent decreases in defense purchases as a percentage of GNP.[7] In fact, one could argue that the escalation lasted until defense purchases as a percentage of GNP went back to their prewar level. By this criterion, the escalation would last until third quarter 1970 based on quarterly data and 1971 on annual data. (It was 7.2 percent in 1965, 9.0 percent in 1967, 7.5 percent in 1970, and 6.6 percent in 1971.)

The history of the war itself also substantiates the conclusion that Walker and Vatter incorrectly specify the timing of the escalation. Spending on the war reached its peaks in FY 1968 and FY 1969. Recalling the initial escalation of

Table 14.2

The Estimated Incremental and Full Costs of Direct American Military Involvement in Indochina, Fiscal Years 1965–1975 (Billions of Current Dollars)

Fiscal Year [*]	Incremental Costs [a]	Full Costs [a]
1965	$ .1 [b]	$ .1 [b]
1966	5.8	5.8
1967	18.4	20.1
1968	20.0	26.5
1969	21.5	28.8
1970	17.4	23.1
1971	11.5	14.7
1972	7.3	9.3
1973	6.2 [c]	7.9 [c]
1974	4.1 [d]	5.0 [d]
1975	2.0 [d]	2.5 [d]
TOTALS	$114.3	$143.8

[*] The U.S. Government Fiscal Year for all these years was from July 1 through June 30, e.g., Fiscal Year 1965 was from July 1, 1964 to June 30, 1965.

[a] Full costs cover all forces, baseline and additional, and equipment and materials used in the war. Incremental costs cover the added costs of fighting the war over and above the normal costs of operating the baseline force in peacetime. These are the two methods of cost accounting for the war supplied by the Pentagon.

[b] The figures for Fiscal Year 1965 are most likely too low to cover the build-up of troops in 1964-1965 and the stepped-up air activity in response to the Gulf of Tonkin incident (August 1964) and the Pleiku attacks (February 1965).

[c] These are estimates based on the original and revised budget submissions of the Department of Defense. They reflect the combined effects of the United States response to the Spring 1972 offensive of the North Vietnamese, the American bombing of North Vietnam in December 1972, and the cease-fire obtained at the end of January 1973.

[d] Estimates based on the costs of U.S. military assistance to Indo-China and the continued presence of U.S. air and naval forces in Southeast Asia.

Sources: Tom Riddell,"A Political Economy of the American War in Indo-China: Its Costs and Consequences" (Ph.D. diss., The American University, 1975), 98-99; and U.S. Department of Defense (Comptroller), The Economics of Defense Spending (Washington, D.C.: U.S. Government Printing Office, 1972), 149.

direct American military involvement in the war, the Gulf of Tonkin incident took place in August 1964 and was followed by an intensification of U.S. bombing of North Vietnam and by a massive increase in the number of American military personnel in Vietnam. From August 1964 to May 1965 (during FY 1965), an additional 50,000 troops were sent to Vietnam.

At the end of July 1965, President Johnson announced that the administration needed additional funds to wage conflict and that a further supplemental appropriation would be required in January 1966. By the end of 1965, 100,000 people were added to U.S. forces in Vietnam, bringing the total to more than 180,000.

Table 14.3
Indicators of Defense Activity, Annual Amounts (Billions of Current Dollars 1964 to 1970)

Year	National Defense Purchases of Goods and Services	Defense Department Military Prime Contract Awards	Defense Department Gross Obligations Incurred, Total
1964	49.0	26.6	55.0
1965	49.4	29.9	58.3
1966	60.3	40.2	73.2
1967	71.5	42.4	81.8
1968	76.9	42.3	87.0
1969	76.3	35.2	81.3
1970	73.5	33.5	80.0

Year	Defense Department Gross Obligations Incurred, Procurement	Manufacturers' New Orders, Defense Products Industries	Defense Department Progress Payments Outstanding
1964	15.6	27.4	3.2
1965	16.6	32.2	3.9
1966	23.6	39.1	5.5
1967	26.5	44.9	7.5
1968	28.3	46.7	8.5
1969	20.9	43.1	9.8
1970	20.1	42.9	9.4

Sources: U.S. Department of Commerce, Bureau of Economic Analysis, Defense Indicators, November, 1972, 36; October, 1976, 31; October, 1977, 31 and 33; and November, 1977, 31 and 33.

By the end of 1966, there were 385,000 U.S. military personnel in Vietnam. The number continued increasing until the end of 1968 when the total reached 538,000.[8] The timing of the escalation has much longer boundaries than identified by Walker and Vatter. Instead, the period of escalation lasted from 1965 through second quarter 1969 (the end of FY 1969).

THE ECONOMIC IMPACT OF THE WAR

The most critical error that the revisionists make in their argument that the war had little to do with increased rates of inflation during 1965–1967 stems from their usage of only one measurement of the impact of the war on the economy. The variable they use is national defense purchases of goods and services by the federal government.

Table 14.3 presents some of the data that the revisionists ignore. National defense purchases record payments made by the federal government to individuals and businesses; it is a *final* indicator of defense activity in the economy. Progress payments outstanding represent early payments by the Department of Defense to contractors for work in progress; it is an *intermediate* indicator of defense activity. The other measurements in Table 14.3 are all *advance* indicators. They measure the volume of commitments and contracts that DOD makes

Table 14.4
Annual Rates of Change in Defense Indicators, 1965 to 1969

Year	GNP, Current Dollars	National Defense Purchases of Goods & Services	Military Prime Contract Awards	Manufacturers' New Orders, Defense Pro- ducts Industries	Department of Defense, Gross Obligations Incurred
1965	8.4%	.8%	12.5%	17.5%	6.0%
1966	9.4%	22.1%	34.0%	21.4%	25.5%
1967	5.8%	18.6%	5.5%	14.8%	11.8%
1968	9.2%	7.6%	-.3%	4.0%	6.3%
1969	8.1%	-.8%	-4.8%	-7.7%	-6.6%

	Department of Defense, Gross Obligations Incurred, Procurement	Defense Department Progress Payments Outstanding
1965	6.4%	21.9%
1966	41.8%	41.0%
1967	12.5%	36.4%
1968	6.6%	13.3%
1969	-25.9%	15.3%

Source: Economic Report of the President, 1982, 233 for GNP growth rate.
All others from Table 3. Percentage changes all calculated.

with the private sector for military goods and services. Military prime contracts, gross obligations incurred, and manufacturers' new orders all register activity undertaken in the private sector at the behest of the federal government and in advance of actual payment for the work completed. Consequently, during periods of military buildups, the advance indicators are the first to signal the impact of the increased demand for military goods and services in the economy.[9]

An examination of the relative changes in these measurements of defense activity compared to changes in GNP during the period 1965–1969 provides information about the timing of the impact of increased military spending on the economy. Table 14.4 presents the annual rates of change for these defense indicators. All of the indicators, with the exception of gross obligations incurred, total, decreased in 1964. In 1965, along with the escalation of the war, all of the indicators increased. The advance indicators all increased by much more than national defense purchases, which increased by only .8 percent. Military prime contracts (12.5 percent), manufacturers' new orders in the defense products industries (17.5 percent), and progress payments outstanding (21.9 percent) all increased at a rate significantly in excess of the growth rate of current GNP (8.4 percent). The other advance indicators registered increases only slightly below the increase in GNP. In 1966, the pace of the buildup accelerated. The annual rates of increase in all of the indicators were larger than the rate of increase in GNP—with the increases in most of the advance indicators being the largest of all. The buildup slowed down somewhat in 1967, but the rate of increase of defense purchases, manufacturers' new orders, gross obligations incurred, and progress payments outstanding were all larger than the growth rate of GNP. In 1968, the indicators (with the exception of progress payments) showed the beginning of the end of the escalation period. Military prime contracts actually decreased; and defense purchases, manufacturers' new orders, and gross obligations incurred (total and procurement) continued their increase but at a rate below that of GNP. The indicators for 1969 (except progress payments) all decreased.

The leading indicators point to the acceleration of defense activity in 1965. This activity took place primarily in the private sector as military contractors expanded their inventories and their demands for raw materials and personnel. The impact of the escalation was intensified in 1966 and 1967; in fact, increased military purchases accounted for 16.8 percent and 25.9 percent respectively of the increases in GNP for these two years. The end of the escalating economic effect of the war is somewhat more problematic. The leading indicators indicate a deceleration in 1968; but the data on war spending (Table 14.2) show a continued increase through FY 1969. Although it is not an unarguable proposition, I would date the period of escalation from second quarter 1965 through second quarter 1969. This was the period during which military activity in the private sector and actual spending for the war were increasing.

The general effects of wartime escalations—increased demand for resources, a stimulus to aggregate demand, and the timing of the impact—all lend support to the hypothesis that the war stimulated inflation in 1965, 1966, and 1967.

The war increased demand for raw materials, metals, and industrial products. The impact on prices is indicated in a comparison of the wholesale price indices for all commodities, metal and metal products, and machinery and equipment. For the period 1960–1964, all of these indices declined or increased minimally. In 1965 and 1966, with the beginning of the war, all showed substantial increases. From 1965 through 1968, the wholesale price index for all commodities increased by 8.2 percent. The index for metals and metal products increased by 9.2 percent, and the index for machinery and equipment increased by 11.2 percent. Tightened labor markets due to economic expansion and the drain of the military draft led to accelerated wage increases after 1965. The annual increase in average hourly compensation averaged just under 4.0 percent for the 1960–1965 period. But in 1966 average compensation increased by 6.1 percent; and the average annual increase through 1971 was about 7 percent. The bargaining position of labor unions reflected tight labor markets. From 1961 to 1964, negotiated settlements produced average annual increases in hourly wages of about 3 percent. But beginning in 1965, the annual increases in negotiated wages began to accelerate. The increase in 1965 was 3.7 percent and accelerated to an average annual increase of 6.6 percent from 1966 through 1970. In addition to these price and wage pressures from the extra demands of the war, the context of the economy, the financing of the war, and wartime economic policy contribute to an inter-

Table 14.5
Measures of the General State of the Economy, 1964–1970

Year	Actual/Potential GNP	Rate of Unem-ployment	Capacity Utilization Rate, Manufacturing
1964	98.2	5.2	85.6
1965	100.1	4.5	89.6
1966	102.1	3.8	91.1
1967	101.2	3.8	86.9
1968	101.9	3.6	87.1
1969	101.0	3.5	86.2
1970	97.2	4.9	79.3

Sources: Actual/potential GNP from U.S. Department of Commerce, Bureau of
Economic Analysis, Survey of Current Business, April 1982, 25.
Unemployment rate and capacity utilization rate from Economic Report
of the President, 1982, 266 and 283.

pretation of the culpability of the war in stimulating inflation throughout the economy.

The closer the economy is to full employment, the more inflationary the impact of a war is likely to be. Table 14.5 contains data indicating the relationship between actual and potential GNP for 1964–1970, along with other measurements of the general state of the economy. In 1965, the ratio of actual to potential GNP was 100.1 and the economy continued to operate above capacity through 1969. Similarly, the unemployment rate was relatively low, given post–World War II experience, and had been decreasing since 1961. In 1965, the capacity utilization rate for manufacturing was at its highest level since World War II (in excess of rates during the Korean War). These data indicate an economy operating near or above its capacity and in which unanticipated increases in aggregate demand could be expected to stimulate inflationary pressures. The war, more-over, coincided with a tax cut to stimulate the economy and the launching of a campaign against poverty. From 1965 to 1969, actual GNP exceeded potential GNP, the capacity utilization rate for manufacturing remained in the high eighties, and the unemployment rate continued to decrease to 3.5 percent (the lowest it had been since World War II except for the Korean War years). The war escalation took place in an expanding economy. It was in this context that the extraordinary stimulus of the war contributed to inflationary pressures in the mid–1960s.

To demonstrate that the war was a source of inflation, it must also be shown that the manner in which it was financed accommodated increased war spending and that wartime economic policy did not take purchasing power away from other sectors of the economy. Revisionists argue that during the war "tax in-creases" did reduce inflationary pressures, that other federal spending was re-duced, and that monetary policy was not excessively expansionary.[10] They identify two sources of tax increases during the period third quarter 1965 to second quarter 1968. The first was the combination of increasing tax collections in a progressive tax system during a period of rising incomes and scheduled increases in social insurance taxes. The second was the 1968 surtax passed by Congress to help finance the war and relieve inflationary pressures in the economy. However, the surtax was not passed until third quarter 1968; and afterward the federal taxes' share of GNP actually decreased. Until the passage of the surtax, tax rates did not change during the first three years of the war; and there was no significant decrease in personal consumption expenditures and disposable personal income as a percent of GNP, which would signal the contractionary effect of increased taxes.[11] Also, the impact of increased social insurance taxes is not so clear.

Walker and Vatter argue that the increases in social insurance taxes were in excess of increased social insurance benefits and consequently that this "is unequivocally anti-inflationary."[12] They are correct in arguing that social insurance tax collections were increasing; their share of total federal receipts grew from 19.1 percent in 1965 to 23.0 percent in 1970.[13] Social insurance contributions accounted for about 80 percent of federal trust funds receipts, and throughout the duration of the war these trust funds experienced surpluses. These surpluses are anti-inflationary only if they are not made available to other agents of demand in the economy. However, they were made available to the Treasury through the only thing that the Social Security Administration, for example, is allowed to do with its surpluses: purchase U.S. Treasury securities. The amount of federal debt held by other government accounts actually increased more than the amount of debt held by the Federal Reserve during the 1965–1969 period. From December 1965 to December 1969, total federal debt increased by $47.3 billion. The Fed's holdings increased by $16.4 billion, the private sector increased its holdings by $1.5 billion, and other government agencies increased their holdings by $29.3 billion.[14] This diminished the potentially anti-inflationary impact of increased social insurance taxes.

In fact, the contribution of the federal trust funds surpluses helped to finance increased war spending. When the Fed lends to the Treasury, it creates money. When other federal agencies lend funds to the Treasury, it does not directly create money because it merely transfers purchasing power from the public to the Treasury. However, if the receipts are withheld from circulation, it could have a contractionary effect on the money supply. Walker and Vatter present data to show that the possible monetary impacts of the war were minimal and that there was no excessive money creation in the escalation period.[15] In addition to their neglect of the increase in federal debt held by government agencies other than the Fed, the data on the growth of the money supply could be interpreted in a different way. From 1960 to 1964, the money supply had been increasing at an annual rate of less than 3 percent. However, with an increasing federal debt, the rate of increase of M1 accelerated to 4.7 percent in 1965. In 1966, as a result of a Fed decision to tighten up on monetary policy in response to the inflationary effects of the war, M1 grew at a rate of only 2.5 percent. When the

Fed's attempt at contraction was abandoned, money supply growth took off to rates of 6.6 percent in 1967 and 7.7 percent in 1968.[16]

Walker and Vatter also argue that federal nondefense purchases helped to reduce the inflationary impact of the war because they decreased as a percentage of GNP during the escalation. Regardless of the period of escalation, they are correct. But the contribution to reduced aggregate demand was minimal, as the GNP share of federal nondefense purchases decreased from 2.6 to 2.4 percent— a 7.7 percent fall in its share—whereas the share of defense purchase increased during the war buildup by 28.2 percent.

There is one additional factor that must be analyzed in assessing the inflationary impact of the war: the role of wartime economic policy or, rather, the failure of economic policy makers to institute any effective constraints on aggregate demand. As Keith M. Carlson, writing in the *Federal Reserve Bank of St. Louis Review* in February 1967, pointed out:

At times of high employment and near-capacity levels of output, a resource transfer from civilian to military use is normally effected by either tax increases or a system of Government controls. Neither route was followed with respect to the Vietnam buildup in late 1965 and 1966. Instead a price mechanism was utilized to effect the resource transfer, i.e., the Federal Government bid away goods and services from civilian use for the war effort. Overall price increases thus operated as a silent tax in the absence of more restrictive fiscal or monetary actions.[17]

The question thus becomes: What was the economic policy response to the war and why did it fail?

THE ECONOMIC POLICY FAILURE DURING THE WAR

Walker and Vatter dismiss the relevance of wartime economic policy with a reference to the 1966 annual report of the Council of Economic Advisers. In this report, the CEA noted that the economy had reached the targeted unemployment rate goal of 4 percent, that it seemed possible that the economy could tolerate this high rate of employment, but that the risk of inflation was greater. From this, Walker and Vatter conclude that "the government's policy was to produce inflation in the late 1960s. That policy was not based on war but on a desire to lower unemployment and to test the technical characteristics of the system. This approach makes the war irrelevant. If the demand increase had not been for war it would have been for something else."[18] The comments from the CEA do show that the policy objective was not to create inflation, but rather a sensitivity to the potential for inflation. Besides, the CEA does not make economic policy. A better method of examining the role of economic policy and its relationship to the war involves the context in which it was being set and the actual decisions that were made.

There are two questions relevant to an assessment of economic policy during the war. One concerns the awareness of policy makers of the inflationary effects of the war. The other concerns the lack of an effective policy to counter those impacts. Both economic theory and history suggest that wars induce inflation. In all its previous wars, the United States adopted a variety of measures to dampen inflation. These have included increased individual and corporate income taxes, excise taxes, wage and price controls, and rationing.[19]

In the case of the Vietnam War, the government failed to adopt appropriate and sufficient wartime policies to reduce inflationary pressures. This failure was primarily a result of the politics of the war. The war escalated slowly and was initially referred to as the Vietnam "conflict." Initial cost estimates for the war were outrageously low. President Johnson was reluctant to engage in a public debate about economic restraint due to the war and, concurrently, about the war itself. Furthermore, Johnson wanted to preserve his commitment to the Great Society from any budget restraint associated with increased spending for the war.[20]

The war began without a formal declaration. The administration introduced increased numbers of troops into Vietnam gradually. And it consistently underestimated war costs in its budget submissions to Congress. Johnson decided on a path of slow escalation, but one that included flexibility.[21] During fiscal years 1965, 1966, and 1967, the original budget requests for the war were eventually exceeded by more than 100 percent in supplemental requests for funds.[22] Since there was no "war" and since the original requests for funds did not foresee a massive increase in spending for the war, the Johnson administration did not need to introduce any comprehensive wartime economic policy measures.

Nevertheless, there were a number of responses to the increased inflationary pressures brought about by prosperity and the effect of the Vietnam escalation. Table 14.6 contains a summary of policy measures or proposals to restrain demand in the economy from 1965 through 1968. One of the first instances of an administration concern with the inflationary effects of the war was a December 1965 CEA recommendation to Johnson that he consider a tax increase to help pay for the war.[23] But Johnson refused because he did not want to adopt wartime economic measures for fear of touching off a debate on the war or of losing some of his Great Society programs.[24] Throughout the remainder of 1966 and 1967, mild policies of restraint were utilized. Johnson relied on the CEA's wage-price guideposts and patriotic appeals to dampen inflationary wage and price movements. Scheduled reductions in federal excise taxes on telephone service and automobiles were rescinded and collections of some federal taxes were accelerated. In his *Economic Report of the President* for 1967, Johnson suggested that he might call for an income tax surtax to restrain the economy. Finally, in August 1967 he formally proposed a 10 percent surcharge on income taxes. Congressional hearings were held on this proposal in August, September, and November 1967 and in January 1968. In these hearings, virtually all of the administration officials and others who testified acknowledged the responsibility of the war in making the surtax necessary. But the proposal stalled over congres-

Table 14.6

Economic Policy Responses to the Impact of the Vietnam War, 1965 to 1968

Date	Policy Action
December 1965	Federal Reserve raises discount rate from 4 percent to 4 1/2 percent.
December 1965	Council of Economic Advisers sends tax increase request to Johnson, which he rejects.
January 1966	President Johnson proposes accelerated corporate and individual income tax collections and a revision of the scheduled eliminations of the federal automobile and telephone excise taxes.
March 1966	Johnson holds meetings with congressional and business leaders in which they back his reluctance to raise taxes to finance the war.
September 1966	Federal Reserve sends letter to commercial banks urging restraint in business loans.
September 1966	Johnson announces restraint on federal non-defense spending and requests a sixteen-month suspension of the 7 percent investment tax credit and of accelerated depreciation on business construction.
Fall 1966	Administration fails to release a Midyear Review of the Budget.
January 1967	Johnson proposes a 6 percent income tax surcharge on corporate and individual incomes.
March 1967	Johnson requests the reinstitution of the 7 percent investment tax credit.
August 1967	Johnson firms up his tax surcharge request and asks for a 10 percent surcharge on income taxes.
January 1968	Johnson proposes broad series of measures to directly control increasingly difficult balance of payments problems.
March 1968	Johnson holds another series of meetings with business leaders in which the economic impact of the war is more forthrightly discussed than previously.
March 1968	Lyndon Johnson withdraws from the approaching 1968 Presidential election and announces steps to negotiate an end to the war.
June 1968	Congress finally enacts the 10 percent income tax surcharge to help finance the increasing costs of the war.

Sources: _Economic Reports of the President_, 1965 to 1970; and Riddell, "A Political Economy of the American War in Indo-China," 333-334.

sional desires to cut nondefense federal spending and Johnson's unwillingness to compromise over his Great Society programs. In early 1968, the economic environment deteriorated with accelerating inflation, a massive increase in the budget deficit, and an international monetary crisis. At this point, congressional leaders and administration officials worked out a compromise that called for the income tax surcharge in return for a commitment to cut nondefense federal spending by $6 billion in the FY 1969 budget. The surtax finally became law on 28 June 1968.

Some measures of economic restraint were used during the escalation period, but they were inadequate. Why? The war was escalated slowly and by stealth. However, within the administration there were predictions and plans for a much longer and costlier war. Yet, in public, the posture was confidence in a contained, successful, and "cheap" conflict. As Johnson himself quotes one of his major advisers, McGeorge Bundy, in his memoirs: "At its very best the struggle in Vietnam will be long. It seems important to us that this fundamental fact be made clear and our understanding of it made clear to our own people. . . . [T]here is no shortcut to success in Vietnam."[25] This evaluation of the reality of U.S. involvement in Vietnam and where it was likely to lead was not shared with the public (at least not until the Pentagon Papers were published). Consequently, there was no public reason to ask for typical wartime economic measures. The lack of adequate economic policy measures and a war stimulus that was larger and would last longer than was admitted in public went hand in hand. As Walter Heller has put it, there was "an unwillingness to loose the flood of debate on Vietnam for which a tax proposal would provide the tempting occasion."[26] And Lyndon Johnson wanted very much to protect his Great Society: "We are a rich nation and can afford to make progress at home while meeting our obligations abroad—in fact, we can afford no other course if we are to remain strong. For this reason, I have not halted progress in new and vital Great Society programs in order to finance the costs of our efforts in Southeast Asia."[27]

Throughout 1965, 1966, and 1967, it would be guns and butter. Not until late 1967 and 1968 did the debate about the war and wartime economic policy get the public airing it deserved given the economic impacts of the war. In fact, Johnson himself reaped the harvest of secrecy when he renounced the presidency in March 1968 as a result of the political and economic ramifications of his conduct of the war.

Charles Schultze, director of the Bureau of the Budget during the Johnson administration, summarized this policy failure in congressional testimony in 1970 on the economic effects of the war:

Our earlier inflation is in part due to the fact that we wouldn't cover the financial costs of the war in taxes and finally in turn, one of the reasons we wouldn't cover the financial cost of the war in taxes was because it was basically an unpopular war. . . . [T]he inflation that we are trying to stop originated from a combination of the Vietnam War on the one hand and our political inability to finance it on the other.[28]

The Vietnam War stimulated inflation in the mid- and late 1960s. This result was a combination of the economic impact of the war, the state of the economy at that time, the manner in which the war was financed, and the conduct of economic policy. Given the structure of the economy and the institutional power of large corporations and labor unions, this inflation produced further cost-push sources of inflation. This inflationary experience laid the foundation for the increased difficulties with inflation in the 1970s—the price-wage spiral, the productivity crisis, energy price increases, excessive monetary growth and easy credit, and so on.

CONCLUSION

Walker and Vatter concluded in their analysis that the Vietnam War was an "economically trivial event" and posed the question of what the effect would be if the nation really engaged in a massive military escalation: "The profession needs to tell the nation that the economic barrier to war, its appalling economic costs, has been destroyed by the tremendous size of our economy. Consequently, we'd better erect stronger political and social barriers or we will have more war."[29]

I have shown that the Vietnam War was by no means a trivial economic event. It increased the percentage of the nation's resources going to defense purposes by only 2 percent of GNP, but it also lasted for almost a decade and cost the Treasury almost $150 billion. It induced accelerated inflation. The nation continues to bear the economic costs of that war in interest payments on the debt incurred during the war, programs for Vietnam veterans, and lost output from disabled and disoriented veterans. There were and are economic burdens of the Vietnam War—to go along with the political, social, and cultural upheavals it unleashed in the United States in the 1960s and 1970s. It is a lesson that economists bear a responsibility for sharing.

NOTES

1. John F. Walker and Harold G. Vatter, "The Princess and the Pea: or The Alleged Vietnam War Origins of the Current Inflation," *Journal of Economic Issues* 16 (June 1982): 597–599.

2. Ibid., 599, 604.

3. Ibid., 598–599.

4. Tom Riddell, "A Political Economy of the American War in Indo-China: Its Costs and Consequences" (Ph.D. diss., American University, 1975), 209–211.

5. Walker and Vatter, "The Princess and the Pea," 598.

6. These direct budgetary costs are all in current dollars. Estimates for all of the economic costs of the war, including foreign and military assistance, future veterans' benefits, losses from deaths and injuries, interest on the debt, etc., have placed the total at close to $700 billion. See Tom Riddell, "The $676 Billion Quagmire," *The Progressive* 37 (October 1973): 33–37.

7. U.S. Department of Commerce, Bureau of Economic Analysis, *Defense Indicators* (Washington, D.C.: U.S. Government Printing Office, 1977), 32.

8. General W. C. Westmoreland, "Report on Operations in South Vietnam, January 1964–June 1968" in Admiral U.S.G. Sharp and General W. C. Westmoreland, *Report on the War in Vietnam* (Washington, D.C.: U.S. Government Printing Office, 1968), 95–109.

9. Murray L. Weidenbaum, "The Inflationary Impact of the Federal Budget," *Financial Analysts Journal* (July-August 1966) in Joint Economic Committee, U.S. Congress, *Economic Effect of Vietnam Spending*, 2 vols. (Washington, D.C.: U.S. Government Printing Office, 1967), 2: 498–501; and Murray L. Weidenbaum, "Impact

of Vietnam War on American Economy'' in Joint Economic Committee, *Economic Effect of Vietnam Spending*, 1:193–236.

10. Walker and Vatter, ''The Princess and the Pea,'' 600–604.

11. Charles Garrison and Anne Mayhew, ''The Alleged Vietnam War Origins of the Current Inflation: A Comment,'' *Journal of Economic Issues* 17 (March 1983): 175–186.

12. Walker and Vatter, ''The Princess and the Pea,'' 606.

13. Office of Management and Budget, Budget Review Division, Fiscal Analysis Branch, *Federal Government Finances, 1983 Budget Data* (Washington, D.C.: U.S. Government Printing Office, 1982).

14. *Economic Report of the President* (Washington, D.C.: U.S. Government Printing Office, 1971), 277.

15. Walker and Vatter, ''The Princess and the Pea,'' 602–604.

16. *Economic Report of the President* (Washington, D.C.: U.S. Government Printing Office, 1982), 303.

17. Keith M. Carlson, ''The Federal Budget and Economic Stabilization,'' *Federal Reserve Bank of St. Louis Review* (February 1967) in Joint Economic Committee, *Economic Effect of Vietnam Spending*, 2: 588–589.

18. John F. Walker and Harold G. Vatter, ''Demonstrating the Undemonstrable: A Reply to Garrison and Mayhew,'' *Journal of Economic Issues* 17 (March 1983): 186–196.

19. Riddell, *A Political Economy of the American War in Indo-China*, 320–330.

20. Ibid., Chapter 5.

21. Lyndon B. Johnson, *The Vantage Point* (New York: Popular Library, 1971), 142–146.

22. Joint Economic Committee, *Economic Effect of Vietnam Spending*, 1:70–99, 175–192, 360–361.

23. Gardner Ackley, ''LBJ's Game Plan,'' *The Atlantic* 230 (December 1972), 46–50.

24. David Halberstam, *The Best and the Brightest* (New York: Random House, 1972), 606.

25. Quoted in Johnson, *The Vantage Point*, 127.

26. Walter Heller, *New Dimensions of Political Economy* (New York: W. W. Norton and Company, 1967), 94.

27. *Budget of the United States Government, Fiscal Year 1967* (Washington, D.C.: U.S. Government Printing Office, 1966), 7.

28. Charles Schultze, Statement to the Senate Foreign Relations Committee, U.S. Congress, *Hearings, Impact of the War in Southeast Asia on the U.S. Economy* (Washington, D.C.: U.S. Government Printing Office, 1970), 232–233.

29. Walker and Vatter, ''Demonstrating the Undemonstrable,'' 195.

15

Lyndon Johnson and the Limits of American Resources

John E. Ullmann

The Johnson administration is now some twenty years in the past. This is sufficiently long to make judgments on its role as a watershed in American history and development and sufficiently short to formulate significant inferences for our current situation. As Winston Churchill said in 1936, during his time of political isolation, "The use of recriminating about the past is to enforce effective action at the present."[1]

American presidencies have a major role in shaping the perception of the country by its own citizens and the rest of the world and yet there is also an important constant factor in this perception. There surely can be little quarrel with the proposition that a positive evaluation of the United States comprises in the first place a well-functioning economy that provides a good life to a large proportion of its citizens and is able, therefore, to sustain a substantial private sector, a generally libertarian atmosphere, and a widely shared sense of progress. All of these are the elements of a competent performance on the part of capitalism—fostering a perception of still higher potential—and thus impart acceptability to the system. Furthermore, the example of such success encourages and, in view of the sheer size and impact of the United States, largely makes feasible the viability of similar systems and objectives elsewhere, without the repressions to which governments of all persuasions generally resort when their blunders catch up with them. The deepening shadows that now hang over all these components of national success are in a real sense traceable to the dysfunctions first engendered and predicted during the Johnson administration, most particularly in connection with its escalation of the Vietnam War.

This is not to say that these protracted ill effects were all directly caused by the policies and events of the Johnson years; timing is certainly not the same as causality. However, in this connection it is not necessary to show that every major economic indicator turned downward immediately. In a huge economy like that of the United States, there are long time lags. Nevertheless, some crucial measures showed exactly such changes for the worse. Moreover, the performance of an economy must not be judged merely against its own current trends. Rather, it must also be viewed against the goals it has set for itself and against its potential. The latter may be difficult to assess, but there have been few times in American history when the nation's plans for its betterment had been more clearly articulated. At any rate, by 1968, the political atmosphere had so changed as to make the remedies proposed then and subsequently, impossible to implement.

The reasons for these troubles are, in detail, as varied as the issues then before the country and the world, but one factor is clearly common to most of them: During the Johnson administration, the United States reached the limits of the reach of its economy, of its foreign and military policy, and of its ability to cope with, let alone alleviate, its gathering domestic difficulties.

For a long time, especially following World War II and continuing to the early sixties, the United States had an international good name unlike that ever possessed by another country. Its aura and record of generosity, humanitarianism, liberty, scientific and technical progress, cultural innovations, and general well-being served as an inspiration and objective to hundreds of millions all over the world, and not just to those stuck in obvious tyrannies and economic disaster areas. To be sure, all these perceptions and images can yield to higher criticism, but that made them no less real. Their decline is itself a melancholy judgment on the changing role the United States now plays in the world and first started to play in a significant, serious, and irreversible manner during the Johnson presidency.

Except as noted later, in a military sense where they usually make themselves painfully clear, the limits of national capability and effort tend to be matters of public perception rather than objective reality, as well as of the willingness of people to put up with the demands of their government. Unfortunately, the transgression of the limits may not be generally recognized while it is taking place. For instance, food shortages, higher taxes, and inflation are clearly noticeable, but only the latter was a significant factor in Johnson's time, higher taxes being deliberately avoided. Such other limits as those in the growing industrial decline were noticed by only a very few students of the problem and ignored or dismissed by everybody else. What was surprising in Johnson's time was not a growing body of opinion that thought the war was not justifiable or worth the effort, but that such extensive national damage could be inflicted before a refusal to proceed further became insistent enough to prompt a major change of policy. In short, as is usual in such situations, there was a growing conflict between the rising opposition and leaders still determined to take their misjudgments to some apocalyptic conclusion.

For the United States, a failure to recognize limits had a devastating and demoralizing effect on economic and social development just at a time of far-reaching plans and programs for societal improvement, as well as on the industrial structure and on foreign and military policy. Yet it is a constant feature of such limits that the leaders who go beyond them refuse to recognize them, and, as his own expressed views show, Lyndon Johnson was no exception to this rule.

The notion of limits did not sit well with Lyndon Johnson. Confronted once during an interview with the guns versus butter problem he said that this was like asking him to support one of his daughters but not the other. Yet this was in 1967, by which time the choice had clearly been made in favor of guns.

To get the full reach of Lyndon Johnson's vision of the national agenda, it is useful to reread his 1965 State of the Union address. He started by noting the "brutal and bitter conflict in Vietnam" and that this "just must be the center of our concerns." But then he said: "This nation is mighty enough—its society is healthy enough—its people are strong enough—to pursue our goals in the rest of the world and build a great society here at home."[2] The rest of his address oscillated between the last two phrases to such an extent that one can do a cut-and-paste job in which the peace and war paragraphs each make up a separate speech—a kind of oratorical confrontation between two Lyndon Johnsons, or between Prospero and Caliban.

The range of his program is best shown in his own words:

I recommend that you provide the resources to carry forward with full vigor the great health and education programs that you enacted into law last year.

I recommend that we prosecute with vigor and determination our war on poverty.

I recommend that you give a new and daring direction to our foreign aid program, designed to make a maximum attack on hunger and disease and ignorance in those countries that are determined to help themselves—and to help those nations that are trying to control population growth.

I recommend that you make it possible to expand trade between the United States and Eastern Europe and the Soviet Union.

I recommend to you a program to rebuild completely, on a scale never before attempted, entire central and slum areas of several of our cities in America.

I recommend that you attack the wasteful and degrading poisoning of our rivers—and as the cornerstone of this effort clean completely entire large river basins.

I recommend that you meet the growing menace of crime in the streets by building up law enforcement and by revitalizing the entire federal system from prevention to probation.

I recommend that you take additional steps to ensure equal justice to all of our people by effectively enforcing nondiscrimination in federal and state jury selection; by making it a serious federal crime to obstruct public and private efforts to secure civil rights, and by outlawing discrimination in the sale or rental of housing.[3]

Underlying this program was a remarkable degree of faith in the sense of fairness and generosity of his listeners and their constituents. As he put it:

I have come here to recommend that you—the representatives of the richest nation on earth—you the elected servants of the people who live in abundance unmatched on this globe—you bring the most urgent decencies of life to all of your fellow Americans.

There are men who cry out: We must sacrifice. Well let us rather ask them: Who will they sacrifice? Are they going to sacrifice the children who seek the learning, or the sick who need medical care, or the families who dwell in squalor that are now brightened by the hope of home? Will they sacrifice opportunity for the distressed—the beauty of our land, the hope of our poor? . . .

We will not heed those who wring it from the hopes of the unfortunate here in a land of plenty. But if there are some who do not believe this, then, in the name of justice, let them call for the contribution of those who live in the fullness of our blessing rather than try to strip it from the hands of those that are most in need.

And let no one think that the unfortunate and the oppressed of this land sit stifled and alone in their hope tonight. Hundreds of their servants and their protectors sit before me tonight here in this great chamber.[4]

INDUSTRIAL LIMITS AND DECLINE

To understand the way in which the limits of American industrial strength manifested themselves and then led to the, by now, universally acknowledged decline of American industry, it is necessary to review the ways in which military overemphasis depletes and impairs an industrial economy. First, it preempts capital resources. Investments are made in military efforts and not in industry. Second, it preempts scientific and technical resources and thus deprives industry of those innovations on which it depends in order to stay competitive. The fact that there has been no clear ''capital shortage'' is no answer; it only means that because there have been few or wrong types of innovation, there simply are not many useful investment opportunities in industry.

The third factor is less often cited but it may be the gravest of the three in the long run. The way military resources in general and the related industries in particular are organized, and the patriotic excuses advanced for their dysfunctions, make acceptable a degree of inefficiency and waste on a hitherto unknown scale. That kind of operation soon becomes contagious; bad management drives out good in a novel sort of Gresham's law. Society loses its capacity for technical-managerial competence and its ability to carry out any major project, public and (increasingly) private, without turning it into a racket.[5]

The decline of American industry shows itself in many ways. From what was, in Johnson's time, still a minor but growing incursion, the market share of imported cars marches inexorably toward the one-third mark. Shoe manufacturing and shipbuilding were in trouble then and are practically extinct now, except for Navy orders for the latter where, as for example, in the Aegis cruiser program, waste and poor design are almost routine. The United States first became a net importer of steel in 1963, and the gap has widened steadily since. Indeed, if one examines the ratios of exports to imports in every major industry group except food, then, taking 1965 as a benchmark, everyone of them has decreased, i.e., turned more unfavorable, with the United States becoming a net importer of several major ones, like machine tools. The problems of that industry were, in fact, extensively discussed in the Johnson years because of its essential role in keeping the rest of industry up to date.[6]

Another trouble spot was electronics, in which it became obvious that the United States was about to miss some rather important buses if its technical efforts did not give speedy attention to the gathering competitive pressures. It was also clear that such a response would be an excellent way of employing engineers and others when and as military work was phased out.[7] In 1964, a study directed by the present writer, *Conversion Prospects of the Defense Electronics Industry*, dealt in detail with the need to respond to the burgeoning opportunities.[8] Proposals for a change of policy fell on deaf ears, however, as the lethal gadgetry of the war preempted the resources that might have been used.[9]

By 1969, Japanese industrial ascendancy was an accomplished fact; Japan, which did not participate in the military potlatch, had managed to do most of the commercial development of consumer products and so, by the middle 1960s, manufacture of radios in the United States was ending and that of television sets was not far behind. Computer elements, especially chips, were soon to follow, even though computers themselves continue to be made in the United States or, anyway, assembled. Nobody expected the United States to compete with drastically lower wages, but there was a time when this was unnecessary; throughout its industrial development, technical and production skills in the United States had been equal to the task of keeping American products in the forefront, even though the workers fared much better economically. What happened by the late 1960s was that the skills were going to military purposes, including such well-known weapon lemons of the time as the F–111 fighter-bomber and the C5A transport, thus establishing a technical-industrial Rake's Progress that led inevitably to the $300 claw hammers and $640 toilet seats of our time.

A clear indication of what was going wrong is presented by the trends in technical and scientific research and development at the time. From 1953 to 1961, federal spending on R&D had increased by about 14 percent a year. This slowed down and finally leveled off by 1968, as the Vietnam War made its demands. There was little increase in the following decade; the war itself, after all, went on till 1974. Industrial spending for R&D likewise leveled off, falling by some 20 percent in relation to sales.[10]

There was a qualitative change as well. The military purposes that were most strongly supported diverted energies from nonmilitary projects that had been strongly favored. Just as the Great Society was an exciting prospect for social scientists, other scientists and engineers had had visions of important new ventures. In the early 1960s, there were hydrogen-oxygen fuel cells powerful enough to run an agricultural tractor. Intensive work was going on in sea water desalination, solar power and other renewable energy methods, fusion power, and possible new automotive power systems. There were corresponding hopes in the life sciences.

As resources went elsewhere, all these efforts were starved of resources;

scientists and engineers who took up some of the energy-related concepts again in the energy crises of the 1970s encountered a hiatus in the literature that bore a painful resemblance to Rip Van Winkle's sleep. One "bottom line" of that time of trouble is to be found in the so-called patent balance, i.e., a comparison of the number of foreign patents issued to Americans with U.S. patents issued to foreigners. It has been highly favorable for decades but between 1968 and 1974 the surplus shrank by 30 percent.[11]

All this, incidentally, sheds a melancholy light on the "spinoff" of military technology that was and still is often cited as in some way justifying it. The cases of successful transplants of this sort are few and far between. Jet planes and radar are among the few examples. Yet the 1960s clearly show the failure of that comfortable rationalization, not only in the obvious fact that successful commercial product development was rapidly becoming the province of non-militarized competitors like Japan and West Germany, but also in two conspicuous failures having to do with radar itself, where American technology was far advanced. As jets took over air service in the late 1950s, clear air turbulence (CAT) and the need for a good air traffic control system were soon recognized as problems. Some ideas for CAT warning systems were discussed, but never adequately supported. Aside from a warning system for wind shear at airports, currently being introduced at a glacial pace, we still are without one. As to traffic control, one idea of the 1960s was to convert an early warning system for hostile aircraft into a traffic control system. However, it was soon noted that defense systems are supposed to *produce* collisions (i.e., interceptions), not avoid them; here too, occasional disasters notwithstanding, we lack an adequate control structure. The forebears of AWACS planes and Star Wars fantasies (such as the ABM proposals of the time) took the resources that might have been available.[12]

History has also not been kind to the other rationalizations of technical-industrial decline that surfaced in those years. Thus, a move into services instead of manufacturing brings with itself a society with inevitably poor productivity, with badly paid jobs for most of those in them. A concentration on high-tech is futile when commercial product development is systematically mishandled and when it is manifestly impossible to keep foreign competitors in their places. The so-called information age that was to replace the industrial one is also a mirage. Information in business is not a free good and must be functionally and economically justified; otherwise, all it does is increase overhead.

A detailed exploration of these issues and of the many other excuses offered is beyond our scope, but the evidence is overwhelming that the current industrial decline traces back to the needs of the Vietnam War and specifically to its effects on the nation's scientific and technical resources.[13] It is no consolation that as a percentage of gross national product the resources devoted to the military sector appeared to some as relatively modest.[14] When they include a huge share of scientific-technical effort, i.e., of what is literally the way to the national future, they exercise an adverse leverage totally out of proportion to the money amounts involved.

In relation to its gross national product, Japan spends about one-seventh of U.S. expenditures, and accusations that it was having a "free ride" first surfaced significantly in the Vietnam era. However, Japanese military efforts are small only in relation to American ones; the Japanese Defense Agency has the eighth largest military establishment in the world and its firepower is now estimated as being higher than that of the Imperial army at its peak. Japan, like most American allies, plans its military efforts in relation to what it perceives to be its security needs and the range of missions of its armed forces and does not share the absolutist bipolar view of the world that has been a constant in American politics in the last four decades. Japan trains somewhat more engineers than the United States and most of them go into commercial work; at least a third and probably more of American ones go into the military sector. The growth in the scientific content of weaponry that requires their talents likewise goes back to the Kennedy-Johnson years.[15]

It is clear, then, that the excuses offered for the troubles of recent decades have not stood up, which does not mean that they are not alive and well in the at least equally deluded atmosphere of today. What *has* stood up is the rather elementary principle that one cannot be everywhere at once and that at a given time, there are always limits.

SOCIOECONOMIC LIMITS AND DECLINE

The industrial decline was paralleled by declines in other areas of national concern, especially those that Lyndon Johnson had sought to bring to the forefront of national attention. There was, first of all, the mere fact of what was spent for what in the federal budgets. War costs went from $103 million in 1965, when escalation started in earnest, to $5.8 billion in 1966, $20 billion in 1967, $26.5 billion in 1968, and $28.8 billion in fiscal 1969, i.e., in Johnson's last budget.[16] By contrast, expenditures for Medicare and Medicaid, two of Johnson's most innovative programs, totaled about $16 billion for his entire administration. This was, to be sure, due in part to the much lower cost of medical care in those days, but to hear some of the critics tell it, the Johnson administration spent huge sums on these projects rather than on the war.

Though much attention has been focused on such new housing programs as model cities, government spending at all levels on housing only increased from $2 billion to $2.8 billion a year in 1964–1968; however, the tax savings from the deduction for mortgage interest and local taxes in the federal personal income tax went from $2.7 billion to $4.8 billion a year, i.e., they increased at a rate 27 percent greater.[17] Expenditures related to other parts of Johnson's agenda were likewise minor, certainly when compared to the war budgets.

Nevertheless, these programs and others like them have been excoriated ever since as "throwing money at a problem," as if much more had not then been and is not now being thrown at war and its instruments. The real problem was simply that not only was the money not forthcoming but that the nation's attention was focused elsewhere.

The administration was preoccupied with the war and supporters of the new programs soon realized that the war stood in the way of effective action. For many of them, this meant focusing their own attention and activities on ending the war and so their interests too had to shift. Instead of seeing how the far-reaching programs envisaged could be carried through with the skill and tact they required, they had to worry about the survival of the programs. Some programs expired, of course, and others were allowed to linger a while longer, which guaranteed unfulfillable expectations and resulting frustrations and little in the way of results.

The economic limits as such also encompassed the balance of payments problem, which first became serious under the Johnson administration, although much as today, there were people who tried to ignore it. Military expenditures abroad, including Vietnam, were the major reason for the problem; exports still exceeded imports, although the margin was shrinking rapidly. Instead of recognizing this, the Johnson administration once floated a trial balloon to raise passport fees drastically (to as much as $500) in order to discourage foreign travel and thus reduce the negative balance in tourism.

The principal element in Johnson's economic policy was, however, the financing of his military expenditures by debt. Years later, Wilbur Mills, who was then chairman of the House Ways and Means Committee, admitted that this was deliberate. By 1968, the federal budget deficit had risen to $27 billion, i.e., to about the cost of the war. Personal income tax receipts then stood at about $70 billion, which would have meant a tax surcharge of 38.6 percent to balance the budget. Including the corporate tax receipts of about $32 billion as a base would have required an extra 26.5 percent for all.[18] In short, there was a perceived limit to what people would stand, even though then, just as now, people believed that the problem could be met by leaving the whole mess to their descendants and by depriving the poor. In Johnson's case what happened was the dollar crash of 1971, preceded and followed by that particular combination of inflation and stagnation that began to be known as stagflation.

Perhaps the best, albeit most distressing way to sum up this change for the worse in the political atmosphere is to note that discussions of the "affluent society" in the fifties and early sixties were replaced by the early 1970s by the "politics of falling expectations." It is true that this change was in part due to the energy crisis, but the scientific-technical preemptions of the Vietnam War were one of the principal causes of American inability to deal adequately with the problem. Socioeconomic deterioration has continued as the expansion of economic opportunity envisaged by Johnson gave way to what is becoming a two-tier society in which later arrivals at jobs get much less money and fewer fringes than earlier ones. In other words, for the first time in American history, the rising generation will be materially worse off on the whole than its elders. There is a growing lower tier of Americans, including a large and seemingly permanent underclass, so alienated and shut out that, fortunately for the current ascendancy in American politics, it no longer participates significantly in the nation's governance. At a time when a third of American children are raised in poverty, the last word should perhaps belong to another Johnson, the eminent Dr. Samuel: "Where a great proportion of the people are suffered to languish in helpless misery, that country must be ill policed and wretchedly governed; a decent provision for the poor is the true test of civilization."[19]

MILITARY LIMITS AND FOREIGN POLICY

Limits in foreign and military policy and related actions showed themselves in two major ways. By becoming involved in a large land war in Asia, the United States exceeded the reach of its military power and instead became locked into a futile spiral of escalation. But perhaps even more important for American foreign policy, the United States, bogged down in an Asian quagmire, found itself unable to manage crises in other parts of the world no less crucial to the American national interest. Thus, the United States stood by helplessly in the face of the growing carnage occasioned by the Biafran secession and even more helplessly in May and June 1967 as the Middle East tumbled inexorably toward another war.

The limits of U.S. foreign and military policies manifested themselves explicitly in 1968, when the escalation process came to a halt; it was to be six more years before the real end, but the refusal in spring 1968 to furnish the 206,000 more troops demanded by U.S. military leaders was the turning point. The then under-secretary of the air force, Townsend Hoopes, has given an account of the increasing isolation and self-deception among the small coterie of foreign and military policy advisers who made the central decisions on the conduct of the war.[20]

However, when General Earl Wheeler went to Vietnam following the Tet offensive and came back with the demand for what would have been a one-third increase in U.S. troops, the serious defections among presidential advisers started. According to Hoopes, Clark Clifford, McGeorge Bundy, and Dean Acheson in particular had a change of heart and Acheson's newly acquired dovelike markings proved especially decisive. More elements of Congress, the press, business, and academia began to pull away from the stereotyped pose of the escalators whose strategy basically called for unlimited efforts to attain limited ends. At the end, there was a rather pathetic atmosphere of Haydn's *Farewell Symphony* about it all.

The change of heart among these decision makers had a special significance for Lyndon Johnson. A variety of personal feelings of inferiority in relation to John F. Kennedy had caused him to stress continuity in foreign policy in which his own expertise was limited compared with his grasp of domestic issues. How justified this was is debatable; Johnson, after all, had been Senate leader and chairman of its Preparedness Investigations Subcommittee. Still, as Max Frankel put it years later in an obituary on him:

So he clung to the Kennedy men and boasted of their Ph.D. degrees and he was afraid, even after his landslide election in 1964, to bring his own men to the capital. And he could not comprehend, to the moment of death, how so many Kennedy partisans around the country could turn against him because of a war in which he felt he had taken the counsel of his predecessor's Cabinet and aides.[21]

Johnson thus could not reconcile what has been the bane of the Democratic party for the past four decades. It has a peacefully inclined wing and a warlike one. The problem is that the members of the latter generally prevail over the former, whereupon the doves (to use a term that is itself a Vietnam legacy) try to split the difference in some way. They forget, of course, that when Americans want to vote for hawks, Republicans furnish them with a host of candidates; though there were Republican opponents of the Vietnam War, their party overwhelmingly supported it while the Democrats were split. Johnson seems to have viewed the Democratic party as being composed only of the southern conservative wing familiar to him and a homogenous northern one without being aware of the great split within the latter between Cold Warriors and others. Eventually, of course, the Republicans were able to exploit for their own benefit the growing popular desire to end the war even though they had strongly supported it while a large number of their political adversaries had not.

THE LEGACY

Violating the limits of its resources during the Johnson years has set the tone for much of the national agenda of the United States ever since. First and most obviously, can anyone imagine a candidate of either major party for *any* office, let alone the presidency, setting forth an agenda such as the one cited above from the 1965 State of the Union address? To the contrary, even Democratic candidates feel impelled to show their machismo and turn their back not only on repairing the obvious social damage but on what has come to be called the "Vietnam syndrome." For a time this meant that potential interventions, as in Angola or early on in Nicaragua, faced greater opposition but that stage has clearly passed. The Iran-Contra affair, support for rebels in Angola and, more covertly, Mozambique, and the Gulf patrols make that point rather clearly.

This may be a far cry from the role the United States envisaged for itself in the Johnson years, as a global gendarme standing by itself against both the Soviet Union *and* China, but given the realities of the economic situation, as well as political common sense, it is bad enough. Certainly, there is no disposition to accept the view first put forth in 1966 by Senator J. W. Fulbright (D-Ark.), after he had broken with Johnson over the war, that "most of what goes on in the world is either none of our business or, in any case, beyond our wisdom and our resources" and "we are still acting like Boy Scouts dragging reluctant old ladies across streets they do not want to cross."[22]

Yet the economic realities have caught up in other ways. The then first visible balance of payments problem has gone on until the United States is a net debtor to the world, and its budgetary policies have almost tripled the national debt. Putting wars and arms races on credit, rather than having the political courage to require people to pay enough taxes to pay for them, *if that is what they really want*, originated, as noted, in the Johnson years.

Equally sad is the legacy left to the social scientists and technicians in all fields who were inspired by Johnson's vision of a better future. Only now are some of the major issues being raised again, with action clearly deferred to a more propitious political era that may well be far in the future, as well as sharply constrained by the debt burden.

A poignant summary of the complexity and limits of power is one offered by Johnson himself, shortly before he died: "Presidents quickly realize that while a single act might destroy the world they live in, no single act can make life suddenly better or can turn history around for the good."[23] It was his tragedy that he was involved in such a single act and that a failure to see the limits of his country's reach set it on a path of decline that has not reached its term.

NOTES

1. W. Churchill, Speech in the House of Commons, 29 May 1936.

2. State of the Union Address, January 1965.

3. Ibid.

4. Ibid.

5. J. E. Ullmann, *The Prospects of American Industrial Recovery* (Westport, Conn.: Greenwood Press, 1985), esp. Chapters 1, 3, and 9. See also S. Melman, *Pentagon Capitalism* (New York: McGraw-Hill, 1970), esp. Chapter 1 and J. F. Gorgol and I. Kleinfeld, *The Military-Industrial Firm* (New York: Praeger, 1972).

6. Ullmann, *Prospects*, 8–12, 20–24, 160–171.

7. J. E. Ullmann, "Occupational Conversion" in U.S. Congress, Senate, Subcommittee on Employment and Manpower, *Convertibility of Space and Defense Resources to Civilian Needs: A Search for New Employment Potentials*, 88th Cong., 2d Sess. (Washington, D.C.: U.S. Government Printing Office, 1964), 675–692.

8. J. E. Ullmann, ed., *Conversion Prospects of the Defense Electronics Industry* (Hempstead, N.Y.: Hofstra Yearbooks of Business, 1964). See also a second edition, *Potential Civilian Markets for the Defense Electronics Industry* (New York: Praeger, 1970).

9. J. E. Ullmann, "Conversion and the Import Problem: A Confluence of Opportunities," *IEEE Spectrum*, 7 (April 1970): 55. This article was a more formal version of "The Sun Keeps on Rising or Uncle Casey at Bat," a paper presented to the Computer Elements Committee of the Institute of Electrical and Electronic Engineers in March 1969.

10. National Science Board, *Science Indicators 1974* (Washington, D.C., 1975), 4, 5, 16, 33. For a recent interpretation of these trends and their current state, see "Now R&D Is Corporate America's Answer to Japan Inc.," *Business Week*, 23 June 1986, 134. The article is not optimistic as to a speedy reversal of decline. For an earlier discussion

of these issues, see J. E. Ullmann, "Tides and Shallows," in L. Benton, ed., *Management for the Future* (New York: McGraw-Hill, 1978), 283–297.

11. National Science Board, *Science Indicators 1974*, 106.

12. Ullmann, *Conversion*, 215–250.

13. Ullmann, *Prospects*, 20–24.

14. For a notably complacent view of the issues, see M. Weidenbaum, *The Economics of Peacetime Defense* (New York: Praeger, 1974).

15. Ullmann, *Prospects*, 45–47, 216–218.

16. Office of Management and Budget, *Budget of the United States 1969* (Washington, D.C.: U.S. Government Printing Office, 1968).

17. E. W. Mills, "Taxation and the Financing of Suburbia," in J. E. Ullmann, ed., *Suburban Economic Network* (New York: Praeger, 1977), 48.

18. D. Halberstam, *The Best and the Brightest* (New York: Random House, 1969), 606–609; U.S. Department of Commerce, *1969 Statistical Abstract of the United States* (Washington, D.C.: U.S. Government Printing Office, 1969), 378.

19. J. Boswell, *The Life of Samuel Johnson, Ll.D.*, vol. II (New York: E. P. Dutton, 1949), 395–396.

20. Townsend Hoopes, *The Limits of Intervention* (New York: David McKay, 1969); see also J. E. Ullmann, "The Expert Mismanagement of the Vietnam War," *War/Peace Report* (February 1970): 10.

21. Max Frankel, "A Personal Politician," *New York Times*, 23 January 1973.

22. J. W. Fulbright, *The Arrogance of Power* (New York: Vintage, 1966), 18.

23. *New York Times*, 23 January 1973.

IV

FOREIGN POLICY AND DIPLOMACY

16

Senate Majority Leader Lyndon B. Johnson: The Formosa and Middle East Resolutions

Thomas M. Gaskin

Who were the greatest senators in the history of the United States? Daniel Webster, John C. Calhoun, Henry Clay, Robert Taft, and Bob LaFollette were the men chosen in 1957 by a Senate committee appointed by Lyndon Johnson.[1] Today, if additional senators were selected to join this hall of fame, Lyndon Johnson would undoubtedly be high on the list. The consummate politician, few other senators have equaled Senator Johnson's reputation as a legislative genius.[2] This reputation as a master of the Senate rests primarily on his accomplishments as a domestic politician. Researchers have given Senator Johnson little credit for more than a vague knowledge of U.S. foreign policy. For instance, Philip Geyelin writes in his book *Lyndon B. Johnson and the World*, "He had no taste and scant preparation for the deep waters of foreign policy. . . ."[3] Similarly, Tom Wicker, the author of *JFK and LBJ: The Influence of Personality upon Politics*, notes, "Johnson had little or no experience in the conduct of foreign affairs. . . ."[4] More recently in discussing Johnson's congressional career, Ronnie Dugger concludes, "Lyndon Johnson was principally a domestic politician, and his foreign policy was neither subtle nor profoundly well informed."[5] Despite these criticisms, an examination of Majority Leader Lyndon Johnson's role in the congressional passage of the Formosa Resolution in 1955 and the Middle East Resolution in 1957 reveals that he was increasingly involved with the foreign policy issues of the day and that he played an important role in shaping those policies, especially after Senator Walter George retired from the Senate.

Democratic successes in the 1954 congressional elections elevated Senator Johnson from minority to majority leader status in the Senate; they also intensified President Eisenhower's desire for bipartisan cooperation. Disgusted with many members of the Republican party who opposed his policies, Eisenhower was particularly furious with Senator William Knowland, majority leader in the eighty-third Congress, and about whom Eisenhower had written, "It is a pity that his wisdom, his judgment, his tact, and his sense of humor lag so far behind his ambition."[6] With Knowland's loyalty suspect and the Democrats in control of Congress, Eisenhower needed Democratic support more than ever. Less than forty-eight hours after the results of the election were clear, President Eisenhower invited the Democratic and Republican congressional leaders to meet with him and Secretary of State John Foster Dulles for a review of foreign policy.[7] Hailing the upcoming meeting with the president as "a step in true bipartisanship," Johnson reminded that "there has got to be more than just a review of tactics and decisions that have already been made."[8]

Eisenhower opened the 17 November 1954 meeting by emphasizing "that in the field of foreign policy and national security, he [Eisenhower] was without reservation anxious to establish new and even better patterns of bipartisanship, that he intended to consult in advance on policy matters, though occasionally there would not be time for consultation. . . . Such urgent actions however, would be in conformity with general policies discussed in advance."[9] A month later, in another bipartisan congressional meeting, after a complete review was made of foreign relations, the budget, foreign trade, national defense, and mutual security, Eisenhower reiterated it was "his great hope that all of these programs would always be considered in an honest bipartisan way. He [Eisenhower] also recognized that the initiative in these areas was not a monopoly of the executive branch and he would give full attention to things begun in Congress."[10] Furthermore, he promised that congressional Democrats would participate in the shaping of foreign and defense policies.[11]

Thus, when Lyndon Johnson assumed his new duties as Senate majority leader in 1955, he faced a dilemma. He had attended the bipartisan meetings with the president and was aware of Eisenhower's desire to gain Democratic congressional backing on foreign policy matters. Yet Paul M. Butler, the national chairman of the Democratic party, wanted a vigorous, partisan attack against Eisenhower and his policies, as did liberal Democrats in the Senate.[12] Johnson's position of power depended on a single vote, that of independent Wayne Morse of Oregon. It was obvious that Eisenhower was going to be difficult to defeat in 1956, and an open battle with the president might lose the slim majority the Democrats enjoyed in the Senate.[13] William S. White, Johnson's *New York Times* journalist friend, stated the majority leader's problem clearly: "How much bipartisanship, on what, and when and under what circumstances?"[14]

In 1955 Senator Johnson was inclined to accept President Eisenhower's offer of increased participation by the Democrats in the area of foreign policy for three reasons. The first reason had to do with the senator who sat next to the new majority leader in the upper house, Walter Franklin George. The Georgia senator in length of service was the senior member of the Senate. Because he was a respected supporter of bipartisanship, President Eisenhower and Secretary of State Dulles convinced Senator George to become chairman of the Senate Foreign Relations Committee rather than chairman of the Finance Committee.[15]

During the eighty-fourth Congress, Senator George became the embodiment of bipartisanship—the Republican administration's Arthur Vandenburg.[16] Senator Johnson may have been the majority leader, but he relied on Senator George for advice and direction concerning foreign policy matters, saying that "he would no more think of interfering in George's sphere of foreign policy than he would propose to try to tell a Texas uncle how to run a ranch."[17]

Senators Johnson and George did consult frequently, but it is clear that George did not have to convince Johnson to support a bipartisan approach to foreign policy.[18] Admittedly, Johnson had told his colleagues, "I've got the committee chairmen and I could make him [the president] sweat," but his experience as a congressman during World War II and the Cold War had convinced him that Eisenhower needed support and latitude in protecting American interests abroad.[19] Johnson was not going to be the Henry Cabot Lodge, Sr., of his day.[20]

Besides Senator George's enthusiasm for bipartisanship and Johnson's own internationalist beliefs, a third reason why he supported Eisenhower's foreign policy was the desire to exploit the divisions in the Republican party. George Reedy, an aide to Johnson in the 1950s, described the Johnson strategy:

It consisted in persuading the public that the Democrats were constantly coming to President Eisenhower's rescue against troglodyte Republican senators who sought to shackle this great and good man. . . . All Johnson had to do was to keep pushing foreign policy issues to the fore until there was general acceptance of the notion that his chief mission in life was to rescue the general from scheming politicians.[21]

How Senators Johnson and George used bipartisanship as a shibboleth to encourage Democratic party unity and at the same time to exacerbate differences among the Republicans can most easily be seen during the 1955 Formosa crisis.

When the Chinese Communists made threatening gestures in late 1954 and early 1955 to invade Quemoy and Matsu and then to attack Formosa, Eisenhower told his press secretary, Jim Hagerty, that he "had made up his mind to not let the ChiComs get away with murder in the China Sea."[22] The president then took the unprecedented step of asking Congress to pass a resolution authorizing him to use U.S. armed forces to protect Formosa, the Pescadores, and "related positions and territories."[23] Intending to bolster the morale of the Chinese nationals and to clearly let the Chinese communists know the U.S. government's position, the resolution was also meant to avoid the mistake Truman made in Korea of not consulting Congress before sending the U.S. military into action.[24] Dulles worked with Senator George and Asian specialist Senator Mike Mansfield to get the resolution through the Senate in late January by a resounding eighty-three–to-three vote.[25]

On 10 January, nine days before Eisenhower and Dulles first discussed the need for the congressional resolution, Johnson was heading for the Mayo Clinic in Rochester, Minnesota, to have a kidney stone removed. He would be away from the Senate during the time the Formosa Resolution was introduced, while the Armed Services and Foreign Relations Committees held hearings on the resolution, and when the vote was taken.[26] Bobby Baker, secretary for the majority, helped keep Johnson informed of the progress of the administration's proposal.[27] After the resolution was accepted by the Senate, Johnson wrote Senator Styles Bridges, "I had to follow the progress of the Formosa resolution at a great distance and through meager newspaper accounts, but it sounds as though everything came out all right in the end. That was a tough one, and I am glad that the final vote went as high as it did."[28]

Johnson called the passage of the resolution "a tough one" because he knew many Democratic senators were critical of it. Senator Hubert Humphrey insisted there was "a remarkable difference of opinion in the Senate, away beyond the difference shown by the vote on the resolution. . . ."[29] Disgruntled Senator Wayne Morse wrote a friend, "It made me most unhappy to find out that so many would like to have joined me in opposing the Resolution . . . , but they simply had to go along with the Democratic leadership."[30] Several amendments were introduced to limit what Morse called "a predatory authorization" to wage war.[31] One amendment by Herbert Lehman would have limited Eisenhower to protect only Formosa and the Pescadores. The vote was seventy-four to thirteen against the change, with Senators Kennedy and Johnson both being in the hospital and pairing their vote, Kennedy for the amendment and Johnson against.[32]

The Formosa Resolution kept President Eisenhower's options open. By the spring of 1955 the Formosa crisis had eased. In April the Chinese communists offered to negotiate, and by late summer the threat of war in the Far East had ceased to be an immediate concern. Eisenhower's leadership during the Quemoy-Matsu crisis has been described as "a *tour de force*, one of the great triumphs of his long career."[33] If it was, Senator George deserved much of the credit. Senator George had steered the resolution through the Senate Foreign Relations Committee and the Senate without amendment, and he had delivered a dramatic speech allaying any doubts senators might have had about the resolution.[34] Senator Johnson's role was less significant. Clearly a backer of the resolution, his illness kept him from actively lobbying for its passage; nonetheless, he strove to keep abreast of the progress of the administration's proposal. Senator George's leadership during the Formosa crisis made him the Democratic party's foreign policy spokesman in the Senate.

THE MIDDLE EAST

Two years later President Eisenhower once again asked Congress for authority to intervene in a distant land, this time in the Middle East. Majority Leader Johnson determined the fate of the resolution in the Senate and, in the process, became a national spokesman on foreign affairs.

On New Year's Day 1957 Eisenhower explained in a bipartisan legislative meeting that "the United States just cannot leave a vacuum in the Middle East and assume that Russia will stay out."[35] Consequently, he informed the assembled legislators that he was going to ask Congress for authority to send economic and military assistance to the Middle East and U.S. troops if a nation in that area asked for them. At the end of the meeting Eisenhower told the congressmen, "These critical times and situations like the one in the Middle East require us to work closely together if America's objectives are to be achieved."[36] Then talking directly to Johnson and Sam Rayburn, the President remarked, "You know you are as welcome in this house—in this office as anyone . . . the Congress is under Democratic control, and you as official leaders have the right and you have the duty to call on me when you think something necessary, just as I have the duty to call it to your attention when I think something is needed."[37] As in late 1954, Eisenhower was emphasizing his willingness to work with the Democrats in establishing a bipartisan foreign policy. Based on the support the Senate Democratic leadership had given the Formosa Resolution, Eisenhower and Dulles might have expected similar backing for the Middle East Resolution.

The situation was entirely different in 1957. The seventy-eight-year-old Senator George had announced his decision in May 1956 not to run for reelection because of health reasons and the strain of campaigning.[38] The unmentioned and deciding factor in determining Senator George's retirement from the Senate was that his preoccupation with international affairs had made his defeat by Herman Talmadge a certainty in the 1956 election.[39] Senator George had been seeking a position in the Eisenhower administration as a "graceful way of retiring," and with Johnson's encouragement, Eisenhower did offer George the post of special ambassador to work for the development of the Atlantic Community.[40] In the Senate, Johnson lauded Senator George as a national and world figure. He reminded his colleagues, "Walter George is to me more than a towering figure of statesmanship. He is also one of my closest and most dearly beloved personal friends. For the past few years we have sat side by side in the Senate. He has always given me the advice and counsel of a wise father. Without him I do not believe I would have done as well as I have."[41]

Although Senator George remained in the Senate until January 1957, his position of power was diminished by his decision not to run for reelection. Senator George told Secretary Dulles that he was afraid that Dulles and Eisenhower "would have trouble with Senator Johnson, that he [George] . . . had in the past been able to exert a sobering influence upon Senator Johnson and to stop him from doing some of the political things in the field of foreign relations which he had wanted to do, He was not sure what would happen now that . . . [his] influence was removed."[42]

A second difference in 1957, as compared to the Formosa crisis, was that many senators were skeptical that the situation in the Middle East was at the boiling point. By January 1957 a cease fire had been in place for several months. Johnson was ready to unite behind the president during a crisis, but not if the threat was only imaginary.[43] Critics noted that it was Arab nationalism, not communism, that threatened nations in the Middle East that were most closely allied to the United States. Also they pointed out that Egypt and Syria, the two countries whose independence was endangered by communism, were least likely to request aid from the United States.[44]

A third factor that mitigated against Johnson supporting the Middle East Resolution was that he felt that Dulles had mishandled American interests in the area. In June 1956 at a bipartisan congressional meeting Johnson had declared his opposition to helping Egypt build the Aswan Dam.[45] Nasser's later refusal of the American loan reinforced in Johnson's mind the mistake of making the original offer. After the Egyptians nationalized the canal and Britain and France threatened to use force against Nasser, Johnson told Eisenhower and Dulles in another bipartisan meeting that he had studied the situation and there were two alternatives: Try to solve the problem peacefully by having an international authority acquire title to the canal or to support our allies. When the United States did not support Israel, Britain, and France, Johnson was disappointed and disillusioned.

On 5 January 1957, before a joint session of Congress, Eisenhower presented his Middle East Doctrine. Johnson responded to the request by saying, "Congress will examine the proposal carefully and thoroughly to determine whether the action is justified, prudent, and in accord with the best information available."[46] Before hearings on the resolution were held by the Senate Armed Services Committee, of which Johnson was a member, and the Senate Foreign Relations Committee, Johnson and Rayburn attempted to clear with Dulles a substitute resolution that would have eliminated the economic aid provisions from the Eisenhower proposal.[47] When Dulles refused the simplified substitute, the Democrats in the Committee hearing, with Johnson's encouragement, proceeded to adopt an amended resolution saying that the United States "is prepared" to use force to repel communist aggression if the president determined the need; funds for economic and military assistance to Middle East nations had to come from existing economic funds; and Congress would have fifteen days' notice before economic aid was granted under the provisions of the resolution.[48] Johnson justified the Senate's right to make changes in the president's resolution in a speech before his colleagues: "The Congress has a responsibility to examine the facts; weigh them in the light of past experience; to determine whether a policy is justified; to decide whether there are constructive alternatives; to unify the country by selecting alternatives if they are justified."[49]

The amendments were acceptable to Eisenhower; however, the passage of the resolution snagged on the Israelis' failure to withdraw from Egyptian territory. The president threatened to support economic sanctions against Israel in the United Nations if Israel did not leave Gaza.[50] Johnson wrote Dulles a letter urging the secretary to "instruct" the U.S. delegation to the UN to oppose sanctions.[51] Later in a February bipartisan meeting with Eisenhower and Dulles, Johnson reiterated his opposition to sanctions, adding "that there are some times when the Congress must . . . express its viewpoint."[52] Privately Johnson let it be known that if the administration allowed sanctions to be placed on Israel, the Middle East Resolution was dead.[53] When Israel announced on 1 March that it would withdraw from Egypt, the Middle East Resolution moved once again through the Senate. On 5 March the resolution was passed by the Senate seventy-two to nineteen and four days later was signed into law.[54] On the day the Senate voted Johnson cautioned Secretary Dulles, "treat this as a victory. . . ."[55]

The victory was clearly Senator Johnson's. He had demonstrated that he was the heir to the position that Senator George had held as the primary spokesman in the Senate on foreign policy issues. He had also sent a message to Eisenhower that he would not be as easy to get along with as Senator George had been. Rather than just a domestic politician he had shown that he was and would be intimately involved with the shaping of the nation's international relations. Thruston Morton, assistant secretary of state in charge of congressional relations during the mid–1950s, best sums up majority leader Johnson's transformation:

When I worked with him when I was in the State Department, he was very careful to touch all bases. . . . He'd say, "Well, come on up here, and let's touch some bases." And he'd ask Senator George . . . Senator Russell . . . he'd ask the leaders of the Senate in to sit down and I'd explain it [foreign policy] to them. Then as time went on, I noticed that he got more and more confidence. . . . He finally got to the point where . . . these so-called old-timers of the Senate, and they were great men . . . relied on his judgment. . . . I don't think any man in history—any leader of either party in history, any leader in the Senate was more effective than was LBJ.[56]

NOTES

1. David Leon Chandler, *The Natural Superiority of Southern Politicians, a Revisionist History* (Garden City, N.Y.: Doubleday & Company, 1977), 254.

2. Ralph K. Huitt describes Johnson as "the most skillful and successful [Senate Democratic leader] in the memory of living observers." "Democratic Party Leadership in the Senate," *The American Political Science Review* 55 (1961); 337. Doris Kearns, although critical of Senator Johnson's emasculation of the Senate, writes, "There can be no doubt that Lyndon Johnson was among the most effective and powerful leaders in the history of the United States Senate." *Lyndon Johnson and the American Dream* (New York: Harper & Row, 1976), 158. George Reedy unabashedly claims that history will judge Senator Johnson "as one of the most successful—if not the most successful—of Senate leaders." *Lyndon B. Johnson: A Memoir* (New York: Andrews and McMeel, 1982), 88.

3. Philip Geyelin, *Lyndon B. Johnson and the World* (New York: Frederick A. Praeger, 1966), 15.

4. Tom Wicker, *JFK and LBJ: The Influence of Personality Upon Politics* (New York: Penguin Books, 1968), 153.

5. Ronnie Dugger, *The Politician: The Life and Times of Lyndon Johnson. The Drive for Power from the Frontier to Master of the Senate* (New York: W. W. Norton Company, 1982), 220.

6. Dwight D. Eisenhower, *Mandate for Change, 1953–56* (Garden City, N.Y.: Doubleday & Company, 1963), 193. Stephen E. Ambrose, *Eisenhower: The President*, vol. 2 (New York: Simon and Schuster, 1984), 164.

7. W. H. Lawrence, "Eisenhower Calls Bipartisan Talks on Foreign Policy," *New York Times*, 6 November 1954.

8. Eisenhower Holds Key to Teamwork, Democrats Warn," *New York Times*, 7 November 1954.

9. Arthur Minnich, "Memorandum of Bipartisanship Briefing of Congressional Leaders on Foreign Policy," 17 November 1954, Legislative Meeting Series 1954 (5), Whitman Legislative Meeting Series, Eisenhower Library.

10. Arthur Minnich, "Bipartisanship Leadership Meeting," 14 December 1954, Legislative Meeting Series 1954 (5), Whitman Legislative Meeting Series, Eisenhower Library.

11. Ibid.; William S. White, "President Grants Democrats Voice in High Policies," *New York Times*, 15 December 1954.

12. Rowland Evans and Robert Novak, *Lyndon B. Johnson: The Exercise of Power* (New York: New American Library, 1966), 145–146. Alfred Steinberg, *Sam Johnson's Boy: A Close-Up of the President from Texas* (New York: Macmillan, 1968), 394. William S. White, "Congress to Open Today in Harmony with White House," *New York Times*, 5 January 1955.

13. Booth Mooney, *The Politicians, 1954–60* (Philadelphia: J. P. Lippincott Company, 1970), 214.

14. William S. White, "Bipartisanship Poses Question in Congress," *New York Times*, 9 January 1955, sec. 4.

15. Memorandum of Conversation, Senator George and John Foster Dulles, 17 November 1954, Senator W. F. George, January 1954 to December 1956 (4), Subject Series, John Foster Dulles Papers, Eisenhower Library.

16. William S. White, "Senator George—Monumental, Determined," *New York Times Magazine*, 13 March 1955, 12.

17. Chandler, *Natural Superiority*, 329. Walter Jenkins, Johnson aide, also stressed his employer's reliance on Senator George in the foreign policy field. Walter Jenkins letter to author, 23 April 1984.

18. Malcolm E. Jewell, *Senatorial Politics and Foreign Policy* (Westport, Conn.: Greenwood Press, 1962), 76.

19. Evans and Novak, *Exercise of Power*, 169. Harry McPherson, *A Political Education* (Boston: Little, Brown and Company, 1972), 107, 110. Johnson drew the analogy between Eisenhower and the pilot of a plane Johnson was in over New Guinea that was attacked by Japanese Zeroes: "He was our pilot—our only pilot—and I wasn't going to argue with him as long as he fought the enemy." Address by Democratic Members of the U.S. Senate before the American Society of Newspaper Editors, 17 April 1953, Statements of Lyndon B. Johnson, LBJ Library.

20. McPherson, *A Political Education*, 111.

21. Reedy, *Lyndon B. Johnson: A Memoir*, 85.

22. Quoted in Ambrose, *Eisenhower*, 233.

23. Ibid., 232. Eisenhower, *Mandate for Change*, 469.

24. Ambrose, *Eisenhower*, 232.

25. John Rourke, *Congress and the Presidency in U.S. Foreign Policymaking, A Study of Interaction and Influence, 1945–1982* (Boulder, Colo.: Westview Press, 1983), 86–87.

26. According to Booth Mooney in *The Politicians*, 216–217, Johnson was the prime supporter of the Formosa Resolution in the Senate. Supposedly he had to convince Senator

George, who had "some reservations about certain provisions," by flattering, cajoling and appealing to his fellow southerner's sense of "old fashion and honest spirit of patriotism." I have found no evidence to support Mooney's claim.

27. Baker to Lyndon Johnson, 26 January 1955, "Robert C. Baker (1953–57)," Prepresidential Confidential File, LBJ Library.

28. Lyndon Johnson to Styles Bridges, 2 February 1955, "Styles Bridges," LBJA Congressional File, LBJ Library.

29. Senate Committee on Foreign Relations, *Hearings on Mutual Defense Treaty with the Republic of China* (Executive Session), 48th Cong., 1956, 1st Sess., 78–79.

30. Gary Reichard, "Divisions and Dissent: Democrats and Foreign Policy, 1952–56," *Political Science Quarterly*, 93 (Spring 1978): 63.

31. Eisenhower, *Mandate for Change*, 468.

32. Ibid., 468–469.

33. Ambrose, *Eisenhower*, 245.

34. President Eisenhower did acknowledge in a public letter Senator George's invaluable help in directing the resolution through the Senate: "Personally I thought your leadership in the hearing on the Formosa Resolution was superb. I send you both my congratulations and grateful thanks." "Ike Praises George on Formosa Handling," *Atlanta Journal*, 6 February 1955. Senator George's speech is described in Doris Fleeson, "Walter George Wraps up Senate Debate on Issues of the Eisenhower Resolution," *Atlanta Journal*, 31 January 1955.

35. Bipartisan Congressional Leadership Meeting, Arthur Minnich, 1 January 1957, Legislative Leaders Meetings 1957 (1) (January-February), Whitman Legislative Meeting Series, Eisenhower Library.

36. Concluding Remarks of President at Bipartisan Meeting, 1 January 1957, January 1957 Diary Staff Memos, Whitman, DDE Diary Series, Eisenhower Library.

37. Ibid., 2.

38. Ken Turner, "Would Not Shirk Duty, Senator Says to Bid," *Atlanta Journal*, 9 May 1956.

39. Val G. Mixon, "The Foreign Policy Statesmanship of Senator Walter F. George: 1955–56," *West Georgia College Review* 6 (May 1973): 39.

40. Rourke, *Congress and the Presidency*, 91; Turner, "Would Not Shirk Duty."

41. *Congressional Record*, 84th Cong., 2d Sess., 9 May 1956, 102, Part 6: 7778.

42. Memorandum of Conversation with Senator George, 11 August 1956, Senator Walter F. George, January 1954 to December 1956 (Memos of Conversations) (1), John Foster Dulles Papers, Subject Series, Eisenhower Library.

43. George Reedy, Oral History, no. 10, 14 October 1983, 6–7, Michael Gillette, interviewer, LBJ Library.

44. Robert Divine, *Eisenhower and the Cold War* (New York: Oxford University Press, 1981), 91–92.

45. Steinberg, *Sam Johnson's Boy*, 458.

46. William S. White, "Congress Is Cool to Plan, But Is Likely to Accede," *New York Times*, 6 January 1957.

47. Evans and Novak, *Exercise of Power*, 176.

48. " 'Eisenhower Doctrine' for the Middle East," *Congressional Quarterly Almanac*, 85th Cong., 1st Sess., vol. 13 (Washington, D.C.: Congressional Quarterly), 577.

49. "Excerpts from Mansfield Johnson Speeches on the Mideast," *New York Times*, 30 January 1957.

50. Ambrose, *Eisenhower*, 385.

51. Evans and Novak, *Exercise of Power*, 178.

52. Bipartisan Congressional Meeting, 20 February 1957, Legislative Leaders Meeting 1957 (1) (January-February), Whitman Legislative Meeting Series, Eisenhower Library.

53. Evans and Novak, *Exercise of Power*, 179.

54. Ibid.; Dwight D. Eisenhower, *Waging Peace, 1956–61* (Garden City, N.Y.: Doubleday & Company, 1965), 182.

55. Telephone Call to Senator Johnson, 5 February 1957, Memoranda of Telephone Conversations, March 1957–April 30, 1957 (4), Papers of John Foster Dulles, Telephone Conversation Series, Eisenhower Library.

56. Thruston Morton Oral History, 26 February 1969, 6–7, Joe B. Frantz, interviewer, LBJ Library.

17

Lyndon Johnson as Diplomat in Chief

Elmer Plischke

On 22 November 1963, that fateful day in Dallas, when Lyndon Johnson took the oath of office as president, he was invested with all of the multidimensional roles of the presidency. They embraced not only those of chief executive, commander in chief, political leader of the nation, custodian of the national interest, and steward of peace and stability, but also that of diplomat in chief—which Clinton Rossiter characterized as "the most important and exacting of all those we call upon the president to play."[1] As with other presidents, this role—prescribed in basic terms by the Constitution and amplified by law and precedent—catapulted him to the pinnacle of leadership in making and implementing the foreign policy of the nation, but his particular statecraft was modulated by his perceptions of the presidency and the diplomatic establishment, his innate qualities, the deputies he relied upon, his style, and the unfolding of events.

Almost immediately, on 24–25 November, when a phalanx of foreign dignitaries deluged Washington to attend the Kennedy funeral, Johnson was thrust into his first major summit experience. Some 220 of the world's leaders—representing ninety-two countries, five international organizations, and the Vatican—gathered in the nation's capital. These included the emperor of Ethiopia; the king of Belgium; the queen of Greece; the grand duke of Luxembourg; several crown princes and princesses; the presidents of France, West Germany, Ireland, Israel, the Philippines, and South Korea; former presidents of two Latin American republics; the vice president of Spain; the chancellor, prime minister, or foreign minister of eighteen countries; and dozens of other ranking officials such as cabinet members, leaders of national parliaments, and the like. Taking advantage of this unique assemblage, in two days the new president conferred privately with the leaders of at least nine countries, including five of our NATO allies and Anastas Mikoyan (deputy premier of the Soviet Union with whom

Johnson conferred for nearly an hour), and he met jointly with 100 representatives of the Latin American countries to reaffirm support of the Alliance for Progress.[2]

He fell heir to well-established precedents in summitry. Some of these were first employed by President Washington, others were added in the twentieth century, and all were amplified and refined from time to time.[3] These basic techniques include presidential personal communications with other world leaders, commissioning special envoys as presidential personal diplomatic surrogates, hosting foreign chiefs of state and heads of government that visit the United States, presidential foreign visits and trips, and participation in summit meetings and conferences convened both in the United States and abroad.

Johnson's previous political career—as a member of Congress for nearly a quarter century, and for thirty-five months as vice president—had introduced him to some of these summitry techniques. As a ranking member of Congress he traveled abroad on legislative business, such as his trip to London to discuss NATO nuclear proposals in 1960. Two years earlier President Eisenhower requested him to go to Mexico as his special envoy to discuss continental problems with President-elect Adolfo Lopez Mateos. He also met with foreign leaders who came to the United States, including Soviet Deputy Premier Frol R. Kozlov (who visited Washington and lunched with Johnson and Senate Foreign Relations Committee members) and President Lopez Mateos (who came on a state visit and was treated to a barbeque reception at the Johnson Texas ranch) in 1959, and West German Chancellor Konrad Adenauer (who was also entertained at his Texas ranch) the following year.[4]

Aside from participating in sessions of the National Security Council and chairing the National Space Council, for three years he provided the traditional vice presidential ceremonial functions for visiting summit dignitaries and also fulfilled several special ceremonial assignments abroad. He was sent to represent the United States at the independence anniversary celebration of Senegal in April 1961, which was followed by a briefing in Geneva on nuclear test ban talks and attendance at the ceremonies celebrating the fifteenth anniversary of the NATO supreme headquarters. In addition, he went to Sweden to attend the funeral of Dag Hammarskjöld in 1961 and to Rome for Pope John's funeral the following year, and he attended the inauguration of Juan Bosch as president of the Dominican Republic in 1963.[5]

Most important, President Kennedy commissioned Johnson as his personal emissary to undertake a number of overseas fact-finding and goodwill missions.[6] The first and most comprehensive—which Rowland Evans and Robert Novak called "the high point" of his vice presidential travels—took him to Asia in May 1961 for a sweeping tour of six countries: South Vietnam, the Philippines, Taiwan, Thailand, India, and Pakistan.[7] Traveling 28,000 miles in thirteen days, his mission was to meet with their leaders "on the highest level" and assess the deteriorating political situation in Southeast Asia, which he called one of "the most challenging trips that I have ever taken."[8] When the Berlin Wall was erected later that year, he headed a delegation to that beleaguered city to reassure

the Berlin and West German governments of continued United States commitment to preserve a free Berlin and to deliver a presidential letter to Mayor Willy
Brandt.[9]

In 1963 he made two goodwill trips to eight north European countries. In
September he spent two weeks in the five Nordic nations, as the highest ranking
American official ever to visit those countries, and early in November he undertook a tour of the Benelux powers. Just two weeks later, as president, he
met the corps of leaders from all over the world that descended upon Washington.
It has been estimated that, as vice president, he launched forth on a subsummit
trip on the average of every three months, that he visited dozens of foreign
countries, and that he shook hundreds of thousands of hands.[10] These ventures
abroad probably provided him the greatest gratification of all his vice presidential
foreign relations responsibilities.[11]

When he was sworn in as president, therefore, not only were all the major
techniques of summitry established presidential practice, but—as subsummi-
teer—Johnson had already participated personally in many of them. Later, as
president, he employed them all during his five years in the White House and
added some touches of his own. He communicated in writing, by telephone,
and by hot line. He received and conferred with dozens of foreign leaders who
came to the United States on a variety of summit visits. He undertook eleven
trips abroad during which he visited nineteen countries and the Vatican. And he
engaged personally in twenty-two meetings and conferences. Like other presidents his personal diplomacy reflected the summit momentum that had previously
been established but also the particular milieu of his times, especially the Cold
War, the festering Berlin problem, the Six Day War in the Middle East, troubles
in Cyprus, the Caribbean, and elsewhere, and the Vietnam War.

SUMMIT COMMUNICATIONS

Since George Washington sent the first presidential letter to a foreign leader
when, in 1789, only seven months after his inauguration, he wrote to the sultan
of Morocco, presidents have written thousands of messages to other chiefs of
state and government. Lyndon Johnson was no exception. Like his predecessors
he transmitted and received summit invitations and the customary congratulatory,
condolence, greeting, and other ceremonial messages that flow among the capitals
of the world, and he also communicated directly with their leaders concerning
policy issues, diplomatic problems, and crises.

For example, he engaged in exchanges with Prime Minister Harold Wilson
(Great Britain) and Chancellor Ludwig Erhard (West Germany) to prevent a
possible breakdown in the financial foundation of NATO (1966), with President
Gustavo Diaz Ordaz (Mexico) on the lower Rio Grande salinity issue and to
offer rehabilitation assistance following a hurricane (1966), with President
Charles de Gaulle pertaining to French withdrawal from NATO (1966) and
France's financial crisis (1968), with Chancellor Kurt Kiesinger (West Germany)

concerning the Berlin question (1968), with British, Italian, and West German leaders to resolve an international gold crisis (1968), and with the leaders of Vietnam regarding the war in Southeast Asia. Reflecting only a fragment of his personal correspondence, *Public Papers of the Presidents of the United States* for the Johnson years presents some sixty presidential messages transmitted to the Pope and the leaders of the European community, the Organization of African Unity, and thirty-six foreign countries primarily in Europe, Asia, and the Pacific. But these, put immediately into the public domain, constitute the mere tip of the iceberg.[12]

Initiated by Presidents Eisenhower and Kennedy, Lyndon Johnson continued a running flow of correspondence with the leaders of the Soviet government. The series was initiated by him on 26 November 1963 and, according to his memoirs, he decided early the following year "to maintain fairly regular contact" with the Kremlin. He reported that these messages exchanged views "on matters as diverse as the situation in Laos and the possibility of using nuclear power to produce fresh water from salt water."[13] Some communications discussed generalities on settling territorial disputes and working together to resolve bipartite and regional problems and to maintain the peace. Others dealt with more concrete matters—negotiating an East-West nonaggression pact, curbing the strategic arms race, the nuclear test ban, the Six Day War in the Middle East, and the Soviet invasion of Czechoslovakia.[14]

President Johnson also communicated in writing with other leaders in times of international crises. Twice he intervened to prevent the outbreak of hostilities. In June 1964 he wrote to President Ismet Inonu of Turkey, seeking to forestall its invasion of Cyprus and avoid a Greek-Turkish war.[15] In May 1967, immediately prior to the Six Day War, he called Prime Minister Levi Eshkol to restrain Israel, to President Gamal Abdel Nasser to assure him of U.S. friendship for Egypt, and to Aleksei N. Kosygin suggesting a joint U.S.-Soviet effort to ameliorate the Arab-Israeli conflict.[16] Once civil disturbances or hostilities broke out in such crises, however, he employed other means of communication.

During the Vietnam War, it has been estimated that between 1965 and 1967 the White House initiated more than two thousand attempts to produce serious, substantive peace talks with North Vietnam leaders.[17] President Johnson has revealed that a good many others—as third parties—sought to provide neutral channels of communication between Washington and Hanoi, or to facilitate methods of direct negotiation, and that they and the United States endeavored to launch contacts with North Vietnam through half a dozen neutral sites, including Beijing, Moscow, Paris, Prague, Rangoon, and Rome.[18] He also added that by these processes the White House was "in touch regularly with Hanoi either directly or indirectly from early 1965 to the opening of the Paris peace talks in May 1968."[19]

Moreover, on 8 February and 6 April 1967, the president wrote directly to Ho Chi Minh. His messages were delivered to the North Vietnam embassy in

Moscow. He suggested that emissaries of the two governments meet in secret to try to negotiate a peace settlement. President Ho Chi Minh responded by charging the United States with maneuvering to conceal aggression and indicated that his government would not meet with Americans until certain nonnegotiable preconditions were fulfilled. In his second letter, President Johnson reaffirmed his offer to negotiate and appealed for the implementation of the multipartite Geneva accords, which the North Vietnam leader ignored.[20] Commentator Hugh Sidey has recounted that the president claimed "he had never known a man with whom he could not find some area of understanding if the two could sit down and talk face to face."[21] Nevertheless, the tortuous road to achieve negotiations in Paris took years, and even then the war escalated and a ceasefire was not consummated until the fifth year of the Nixon administration.

In addition to his written messages, President Johnson communicated with other summit leaders via the telephone and the Washington-Moscow hot line. For several decades it was not uncommon for the president to telephone the leaders of Canada, friendly European powers, and other nations to discuss matters of urgency on a personalized basis. To deal with the Panama Canal crisis early in 1964, after diplomatic relations were severed by the Panamanian government, President Johnson immediately telephoned President Roberto Chiari, appealing for the restoration of order and indicating that he was sending a special emissary to negotiate a settlement.[22] The following year columnist Drew Pearson reported that the president used the telephone so much that some aides regarded it "as an extension of his right ear," that he would not hesitate to pick up the phone and place a call "anywhere in the world," that he called British Prime Minister Harold Wilson frequently (even though he had available a direct teletype connection between the White House and No. 10 Downing Street), and that he maintained intimate telephone contact with Canadian Prime Minister Lester Pearson. When he met with the latter to sign the Roosevelt Campobello International Park Agreement in 1964, in a toast he told the Canadian leader, "Whenever we have anything to say to each other let us just pick up the telephone and say it, whether it be to discuss a problem or simply to ask, 'How are you getting along up there?' " As a consequence Drew Pearson concluded that Lyndon Johnson had launched the era of telephonic summitry.[23]

Johnson also was the first president to use the hot line—a special teletype circuit linking Washington and Moscow (called Molink), established in 1963—for communicating instantaneously with Soviet leaders. During the Six Day War between Israel and the Arab countries, 5–10 June 1967, this hot line served as the primary communications link between the White House and the Kremlin to contain and resolve the crisis. It was first activated on 5 June by Premier Kosygin, who expressed concern over the fighting and sought assurances that the United States would not intervene. It was also activated on 8 June by President Johnson to inform the Soviet leader of American reaction to the Israeli attack on the American communications ship *Liberty*, and was resorted to again by the Kremlin two days later when Kosygin stipulated that if Israel did not cease its military operations immediately, the Soviet Union would take "necessary actions, including military," thereby threatening to escalate the war.

During these crucial six days more than a dozen messages crackled over the hot line as, according to one presidential adviser, "we moved very close to the precipice," and causing Lester Velie to observe, "Thus, for a brief moment the fate of the world hung on a thin hot line." Later Louis Heren concluded that this experience demonstrated that Johnson "understood the superpower game and was capable of playing it with determination and caution." At their Glassboro meeting (1968), Kosygin confided to the president that together they had "accomplished more on that one day [10 June] than others could accomplish in three years," and in his memoirs the president declared, "The hot line proved a powerful tool not merely, or even mainly, because communications were so rapid. The overriding importance of the hot line was that it engaged immediately the heads of government and their top advisers, forcing prompt attention and decisions."[24]

Thus, President Johnson became an active and in some respects an avid summit communicator. Although his exchanges with the Kremlin may not have been as numerous or as personalized as those of Franklin Roosevelt with Winston Churchill and Joseph Stalin, or as lengthy as the Eisenhower-Kremlin messages in the 1950s during the five-year interval between the Geneva and Paris Four-Power Summit Conferences, or as momentous as those of Kennedy during the Cuban missile crisis in 1962, they nevertheless were frequent, occasionally initiatory rather than merely reactive, and sometimes crucial. By disposition and necessity, therefore, Lyndon Johnson continued the momentum of personal communication established by his predecessors and, in certain respects, he was persuaded to innovate.

SPECIAL SUMMIT SURROGATES

Special presidential diplomatic representatives—called secret agents in early American history—have been employed as personal surrogates by presidents since the days of Washington. It has been estimated that by the time of World War I some 500 to 600 had been commissioned.[25] During recent decades two dozen or more have been used in a single year and, while their total number and the quantity of their missions can only be surmised, during his administration in all probability President Johnson appointed well over 125.

Such special envoys are designated, without Senate confirmation, to represent the president at the highest level. The emissary's authority and duties are determined by the chief executive to whom the appointee is personally responsible, and he reports directly to the White House. The president may rely upon a former president, the vice president, the first lady, the secretary of state or some other cabinet officer, a member of the White House staff or the diplomatic establishment, or an outsider to function in this capacity. Often the special agent is used for a specific mission, usually of relatively short duration, but some serve for extended periods, sometimes in a series of either related or disparate missions.[26]

President Johnson used various types of special emissaries, including President Truman, the first lady, and Vice President Hubert Humphrey. For example, Truman and Lady Bird Johnson headed the American delegation to represent the United States at the funeral of King Paul of Greece (1964).[27] Beginning in 1965 Vice President Humphrey was available for such ceremonial functions as attending the funeral of India's Prime Minister Lal Bahadur Shastri (where he spoke with Kosygin for two hours in 1966), the inaugurals of Joaquin Balaguer of the Dominican Republic (1966) and President Park Chung Hee of Korea (1967). In June 1965 he conferred with President de Gaulle in Paris. President Johnson also sent him on a series of subsummit tours of Asia and Africa—a goodwill five-day trip to four Asian allies (1965), a fourteen-day fact-finding mission to nine Asian and Pacific countries (accompanied by Averell Harriman and McGeorge Bundy, following the Honolulu summit meeting, 1966), a nine-day trip to attend the inauguration of President Nguyen Van Thieu in South Vietnam and undertake visits to Malaysia and Indonesia (1967), and a twelve-day goodwill sweep of nine African countries (1968).[28]

Aside from appointing a good many other special envoys for occasional ceremonial and similar ad hoc missions—such as sending Robert Anderson (former secretary of the treasury) and George Ball (then under secretary of state) as confidential spokesmen to improve White House relations with de Gaulle (1964) and Chief Justice Earl Warren to lead the U.S. delegation at funeral services for Winston Churchill (1965)—President Johnson relied on them particularly for consultation and negotiation to prevent and/or resolve crises, and in a few cases he used them as roving diplomats.[29] To illustrate, he sent George Ball to Cyprus, Greece, and Turkey to forestall the outbreak of war (1964) and later commissioned Cyrus Vance (then special aide to the president) as a shuttle legate to mediate a settlement of this dispute (1967). The following February Vance was sent to South Korea to seek a solution to the crisis over the seizure of the *Pueblo* by the North Koreans.[30] During the Middle East conflict of 1967, prior to the outbreak of the Six Day War, in addition to transmitting his personal letters referred to earlier, the president employed Secretary of State Dean Rusk, Ambassador Charles Bohlen, Robert Anderson, and Ambassador Arthur Goldberg (in the United Nations) as his primary emissaries to prevent resort to hostilities.[31]

During the crises that involved the United States as a direct participant, President Johnson relied heavily on selected individuals and teams of special agents for a variety of important functions. At the time of the Panamanian uprising in 1964, initiated by student demonstrations and rioting, he sent Thomas C. Mann (newly appointed assistant secretary of state for Inter-American Affairs) as his personal representative to head a five-man delegation to talk with Panamanian leaders. Subsequently he commissioned Edwin M. Martin (former assistant secretary of state and newly appointed ambassador to Argentina) to continue on-the-spot negotiations, and several months later he named Robert Anderson, assisted by Jack Vaughn (newly appointed ambassador to Panama), to work out a settlement.[32]

When civil strife erupted in the Dominican Republic the following year and U.S. citizens were held to be in jeopardy, the president relied again on special agents to resolve the conflict. The first delegation, headed by John Bartlow Martin (former ambassador to the Dominican Republic), was sent to observe and report. The second mission, consisting of Mann (undersecretary of state), Bundy (special assistant to the president), Vance (deputy secretary of defense), and Vaughn (assistant secretary of state), was sent to seek a diplomatic solution. The third, which eventually succeeded, constituted a special committee of the Organization of American States, including Ellsworth Bunker (who had previously held several ambassadorial appointments), accompanied by ranking diplomats from Brazil and El Salvador.[33]

In dealing with problems of fact-finding, establishing diplomatic contacts, and informing allied and other governments of U.S. policy and actions during the Vietnam War, President Johnson relied on another group of special envoys. These ranged from such personal aides as Walt Rostow and his successor McGeorge Bundy, Dean Rusk, Averell Harriman, and Arthur Goldberg to the occasional missions of Vice President Humphrey, Henry Kissinger (who provided a conduit through two Frenchmen who had contacts in Hanoi), and William Sullivan (ambassador to Laos), who served as intermediary with Harry S. Ashmore and William C. Baggs, U.S. journalists who met with Ho Chi Minh in 1968.[34]

When he launched his highly publicized peace offensive to accompany a thirty-seven–day Vietnam bombing pause commencing the day before Christmas in 1965, the president saturated the world with personal letters to many heads of state and government, delegated Secretary of State Rusk to talk with numerous ambassadors and foreign ministers both in Washington and abroad, and dispatched Vice President Humphrey to carrry his message to the Far East, Ambassador Goldberg to Rome, Paris, London, and other European capitals, Assistant Secretary of State G. Mennen Williams to more than a dozen African nations, Assistant Secretary of State Mann to Latin America, and presidential assistant Bundy to Canada, while Ambassador-at-Large Harriman visited Warsaw and Belgrade and then circled the globe. The president, consequently, put into action a comprehensive process of diplomatic exchanges and consultation, with the White House captaining this massive venture in summitry, which Johnson called "one of the most widespread diplomatic campaigns of my presidency."[35] Most crucial, eventually, was his designation of Harriman and Vance as his personal emissaries to represent the United States in negotiations with North Vietnamese at the unproductive Paris Peace Conference from May 1968 to the end of his administration.[36]

Thus, Lyndon Johnson relied upon a substantial cadre of personal surrogates dispatched on scores of assignments throughout the world. To provide himself with top-level roving emissaries, he also appointed Harriman, Bunker, Henry Cabot Lodge, and George McGhee as ambassadors-at-large, to be available on a continuing basis.[37] It may be concluded, therefore, that he held much of U.S. crisis diplomacy close to the chest, with firm White House management and control. According to Jack Valenti, the president indicated, "We may go to hell in a hack and sink the ship tomorrow, but I'm going to be up there with the wheel in my hand."[38] He utilized special presidential emissaries freely and, except for some ceremonial functions, they were largely contemporary office holders and professional diplomats. Aside from his natural dependence on his national security adviser and secretary of state, he placed greatest reliance for crucial special missions on Harriman, who had amassed a noteworthy record in this capacity under three previous presidents—Franklin Roosevelt, Truman, and Kennedy—and of whom Henry Brandon of the *New York Times* wrote, "He is the diplomat and statesman par excellence."[39]

SUMMIT VISITS TO THE UNITED STATES

In this age of mass communications, rapid and easy travel, proliferation of states and their international concerns, and saturation public relations, it is not surprising to see government leaders criss-crossing the globe to consult one another. Shortly after the birth of the United States, in 1805 Sidi Soliman Melli Milli, the Bashaw of Tunis, came to this country on official business. Two decades later the Marquis de Lafayette was invited, under congressional authorization, to come for a hero's welcome in recognition of his service during the Revolutionary War. Technically speaking, however, the earliest summit visits—involving heads of state and government—brought King Kalakaua of Hawaii to Washington in 1874 and Emperor Dom Pedro I of Brazil two years later. Such visits remained exceptional until the 1930s, but they have since become commonplace.[40]

A few weeks after he took the oath as president and hosted those who came to attend the Kennedy funeral, late in December 1963 Chancellor Ludwig Erhard of West Germany—whose visit was scheduled for months but had to be postponed—came for a two-day session with the president at his Texas ranch. This provided an opportunity for the two leaders to discuss U.S.-German relations and NATO budgetary problems and to initiate Johnson's efforts in personal diplomacy.[41] According to Jack Valenti, this reflected the president's idea that "the better you know people the better you understand them" and that the president "should have as much personal contact as possible with foreign heads of state and their envoys." Valenti also reports that President Johnson boasted that he had seen thirty chiefs of state and government in his first eight months, compared with Eisenhower's record of seeing only seventy in eight years.[42]

During the next five years foreign dignitaries came to this country on 106 summit visits, averaging twenty-four per year throughout his tenure. This represents a ratio of nearly one visitor every two weeks, the largest quantity for

Table 17.1
Summit Visits to United States (22 November 1963–20 January 1969)

A. Visits Per Year

Year	No.	%
1963	18	14.52
1964	21	16.93
1965	10	8.06
1966	12	9.68
1967	37	29.84
1968	26	20.97
1969	0	0.00
Total	124	100.00

B. Number of Days Per Visit

Days	No.	%
1	34	27.42
2	58	46.77
3	27	21.77
4	4	3.23
5	0	0.00
6	0	0.00
7	1	0.81
	124	100.00

C. Rank of Visitor

Title	No.	%
Monarch: Emperor, King, Queen, Shah, Sultan	17	13.71
President	35	28.22
Prime Minister, Premier, Chancellor	65	52.42
President-elect	3	2.42
Others	4	3.23
Total	124	100.00

D. Type of Visit

Type	No.	%
State Visit	20	16.13
Official Visit	30	24.19
Informal/Unofficial Visit	42	33.87
Ceremonial Visit	19	15.32
Private Visit	7	5.65
Summit Meeting	6	4.84
	124	100.00

Source: Based on Elmer Plischke, Presidential Diplomacy: A Chronology of Summit Visits, Trips, and Meetings (Dobbs Ferry, N.Y.: Oceana, 1986), 97–104, 147.

any president to that time. As indicated in Table 17.1, part A, while the number occurring during the last forty days of 1963 was exceptionally high, the flow receded the next three years but increased substantially in 1967 and 1968. The duration of individual visits was short, with three-fourths lasting but one or two days and only five running for more than three days (see Table 17.1, part B). The longest—lasting seven days—was made by Chancellor Kiesinger of West Germany in 1967.

Nearly a dozen and a half summit visitors were reigning monarchs, including Shah Mohammed Reza Pahlavi of Iran and the kings of Jordan, Kuwait, Nepal, Saudi Arabia, Thailand, and four European allies—Belgium, Denmark, Greece, and Norway. A substantial number (28 percent) were presidents and three were presidents-elect from Latin American countries, but the majority (52 percent) were prime ministers and chancellors (see Table 17.1, part C). The remainder embraced acting President Park Chung Hee of Korea and the leaders of the Communist regimes of Burma, Ghana, and the Soviet Union. The preponderant majority (94 percent) were full-time heads of government.[43]

Analysis of summitry reveals that, on the basis of intent and procedure, there are several distinguishable categories of summit visits: state visits; official, informal and unofficial, ceremonial, and private visits; and meetings or conferences.[44] Approximately one in every six visitors came on a formal state visit during the Johnson administration (see Table 17.1, part D). Generally the most ceremonious and restricted solely to chiefs of state, such visits are undertaken on the invitation of the United States, normally do not exceed but usually number fewer than four per year, and ordinarily last two or three days. These state visitors included seven leaders of European allies, half a dozen monarchs, and the chiefs of such new African states as Chad, Senegal, and Upper Volta.[45] This represented the largest contingent of such visits during the tenure of any president prior to Jimmy Carter.

The preponderant share of President Johnson's summit guests came on some thirty official and forty-two unofficial or informal visits. These involve either heads of state or government, usually minimize ceremony, and emphasize consultation on official business. They differ in that the official visit is initiated by the United States, which bears the essential expenses of the guests, whereas the unofficial may be suggested by either government and expenses are borne by the visitor's government. Aside from the reigning monarchs of Greece, Iran, Jordan, and Morocco, and the presidents of seven republics, those coming on such visits were prime ministers and chancellors, with the largest numbers representing Australia, Canada, West Germany, Great Britain, Italy, and Jordan.

The number of what may be designated ceremonial visits was abnormal during the Johnson years because the first seventeen such summit visitors came on 24–25 November 1963 for President Kennedy's funeral. The only other visits of this type occurred the following year when Prime Minister Pearson of Canada came to Great Falls, Montana, and Blaine, Washington (as part of an exchange of visits),[46] and when Presidents Johnson and Lopez Mateos of Mexico celebrated the settlement of the El Chamizal dispute in El Paso, Texas.[47] The private visits, of which there were seven, were initiated by the visiting dignitary, primarily for personal reasons.

Normally summit visitors center their sojourn on the nation's capital, but in a few cases the president met with them elsewhere, such as Camp David, although he tended to prefer the LBJ Ranch in Texas, and three times he met with the Mexican president in El Paso. As indicated later, he also participated in official summit meetings at Glassboro, New Jersey, and in overseas United States territory (Guam and Hawaii).

The summit visits during the Johnson administration represented sixty-six countries (see Table 17.2). Aside from Mexico and a few other states, the leaders of a dozen of our NATO, Middle East, and Manila Pact allies undertook the largest numbers, aggregating some fifty visits. The number of countries and visits by geographic areas, as indicated in Table 17.2, represents some deviation from the norm, especially in that there were substantially more from Asian/Oceanic countries (no doubt because of the Vietnam War) and, except for Mexico, fewer from Latin American republics. The largest numbers of visitors came from West Germany (eight), Canada, Denmark, and Great Britain (five each), and Australia, Iran, Italy, South Korea, and Mexico (four each). On the

Table 17.2
List of Countries: Visitors to United States and President's Visits Abroad

Country	Foreign Visitors	President's Visits	Country	Foreign Visitors	President's Visits
Afghanistan	1		Laos	2	
Austria	2		Lesotho	1	
Australia	4	2	Liberia	1	
Barbados	1		Madagascar	1	
Belgium	1		Malawi	1	
Bolivia	1		Malaysia	1	1
Brazil	1		Malta	1	
Burma	1		Mauritius	1	
Burundi	1		Mexico	4	3
Cambodia	1		Morocco	1	
Cameroon	1		Nepal	1	
Canada	5	3	New Zealand	2	1
Chad	1		Nicaragua	1	1
China, Republic of	1		Niger	1	
Costa Rica	2	1	Norway	1	
Denmark	5		Pakistan	1	1
El Salvador		1	Paraguay	1	
Ethiopia	2		Philippines	3	1
France	1		Romania	1	
Germany, Fed. Rep.	8	1	Rwanda	1	
Ghana	1		Saudi Arabia	1	
Greece	2		Senegal	1	
Guatemala		1	Singapore	2	
Guyana	2		Somalia	1	
Honduras		1	Surinam		1
India	1		Swaziland	1	
Iran	4		Sweden	1	
Ireland	2		Thailand	2	2
Israel	3		Tunisia	1	
Italy	4	1	Turkey	3	
Ivory Coast	1		U.S.S.R.	1	
Jamaica	3		United Kingdom	5	
Japan	3		Upper Volta	1	
Jordan	3		Urguay		1
Korea, Republic of	4	1	Vatican City		1
Kuwait	1		Vietnam	3	2
			Total	124	27

Geographic Areas	Countries	Visits to U.S.	President's Visits
Africa	17	18	
Asia & Oceana	17	33	9
Europe	15	35	3
Mideast	8	17	
Western Hemisphere	15	21	15
Total	72	124	27

Source: Extracted from Elmer Plischke, Presidential Diplomacy: A Chronology of
          Summit Visits, Trips, and Meetings (Dobbs Ferry, N.Y.: Oceana, 1986),
          Chapters 2 and 4.

other hand, the visit by Prime Minister C. K. Yen of the Republic of China in
1967 was unique in that, unlike the practice of other Asian allies, there were
only two other such visits in more than three decades, despite the fact that the
Republic of China was an ally of the United States for a quarter of a century.[48]
It is interesting, though not surprising, to note the absence of certain countries

from this list, such as the communist states—Cuba, the People's Republic of China, Mongolia, and the Warsaw Pact members, except for Romania and the Soviet Union.

Most of these summit visits ran smoothly. However, some of Johnson's practices—such as shortening the visitor's stay, discouraging the use of reciprocal dinners for the president hosted by the summit guest, the abrupt postponement of visits by Pakistan's President Ayub Khan and India's Prime Minister Shastri because of strained relations in 1965, and his tardiness in appearing at the stag reception given in his honor by King Faisal of Saudi Arabia in 1966—created difficulties but not serious summit impediments.[49]

Among the main conclusions that may be drawn are that, in receiving 124 summit visitors who spent some 250 days in the United States, along with devoting time to planning and preparation, Lyndon Johnson paid a great deal of attention to this aspect of his personal diplomacy. Commenting on his role as chief of protocol during the Kennedy and Johnson administrations, Angier Biddle Duke declared: "For the past thirty-three months I have been planning, programming, and managing the meetings between the president of the United States and nearly eighty world leaders. . . . As a traffic manager for this kind of diplomacy, I have seen suspicions dissolved, fears dispelled, friends reassured, opponents disarmed and even persuaded."[50] Even though no foreign leader came to the United States as frequently as had Prime Minister Mackenzie King (eighteen visits) and Winston Churchill and Konrad Adenauer (nine visits each), by this process of summitry President Johnson established friendly relations with such world leaders as King Hussein I (Jordan), Shah Pahlavi (Iran), Presidents Diaz Ordaz (Mexico), Park (South Korea), and Thieu (South Vietnam), and Chancellor Erhard (West Germany) and Prime Ministers Pearson (Canada) and Wilson (Great Britain)—each of whom came on at least three visits. As a consequence, by means of such visits he was able to maintain widespread and continuing personal contact with a broad spectrum of leadership of the world.

JOHNSON'S TRIPS AND VISITS ABROAD

Four weeks after he was sworn in, President Johnson proclaimed, "I am ready and willing to meet with any of the world leaders at any time there is any indication a meeting would be fruitful and productive."[51] While this revealed his intent, he also said that he disliked going abroad while he had no vice president. When in March 1964 a group of congressmen suggested a meeting with President de Gaulle to improve Franco-American relations, he responded that he would not leave the United States "while the vice presidency is vacant," and he adhered to this determination until Hubert Humphrey was inaugurated as vice president, except for a brief exchange of visits with Canada's Prime Minister Pearson which took him to Vancouver on 16 September 1964.[52] The two leaders met in Great Falls, Montana, flew together over the Columbia River to Vancouver, and then motored back to Blaine, Washington, in one day.[53] In April 1965 the president reiterated his willingness to confer with other world leaders, "I say again that I will talk to any government, anywhere, any time, without conditions, and if any doubt our sincerity, let them test us."[54]

Although history is replete with accounts of political principals traveling abroad on diplomatic affairs, foreign ventures by the president of the United States are a twentieth century innovation. After Theodore Roosevelt first set foot on Panamanian territory in 1906, to inspect the construction of the canal, William Howard Taft participated in an exchange of visits across the border with the Mexican president in 1909, and Woodrow Wilson attended the World War I Peace Conference in Paris ten years later, every president, except Herbert Hoover, has ventured abroad, and the peace has accelerated substantially since World War II.

As indicated in Table 17.3, President Johnson undertook eleven trips abroad and made twenty-seven summit visits. More than half of his trips were to single countries. His longest foreign venture took seventeen days, but the duration of individual summit visits was restricted to one to four days, with half of them, reflecting his style, limited to a single day or less. Like other presidents, he varied the nature of his visits (see Table 17.3, part C). However, an unusually high quantity (60 percent) were to attend bilateral and multilateral summit gatherings, and his combination state visit–summit conference or meeting was unique.[55] Most of the rest were informal or ceremonial. Whereas other presidents set forth on a good many regular state and official visits (aggregating 22 percent over the years), none of Johnson's were so designated.

He traveled to twenty countries—Canada and Mexico each three times; Australia, Thailand, and Vietnam twice; and the rest only once (see Table 17.2). Deviating considerably from the normal pattern, nearly 90 percent of his foreign visits were to Western Hemisphere and Far East countries. He visited no African or Middle East nations and went to only two European states plus the Vatican. So far as the latter are concerned, attendance at Konrad Adenauer's funeral (Johnson's first trip to Europe, in April 1967) enabled him to confer with British, French, and Italian, as well as West German leaders,[56] and during his pickaback visits to Rome and the Vatican on his return from Australia (December 1967) he met with Italian leaders and had an audience with Pope Paul VI.[57]

President Johnson emphasized Western Hemisphere relations by his foreign ventures. His three trips to both Canada and Mexico were largely ceremonial.[58] Of greater significance, in April 1967 he participated in a meeting of the chiefs of state of the American republics at Punta del Este to discuss ways to strengthen the Alliance for Progress and develop an American common market.[59] During his last year in office, he also attended a conference of the presidents of the Central American governments at San Salvador, where he spoke of the "spirit of Central America" and subscribed to a joint declaration concerned with economic and social development, trade, a Central American Bank, and U.S. aid.[60] On his return voyage he stopped off briefly for informal visits in Nicaragua, Costa Rica, Honduras, and Guatemala—all in one day.[61]

Johnson's most important and wide-ranging foreign ventures took him to the

Table 17.3
President Johnson's Trips and Visits Abroad (22 November 1963–20 January 1969)

Trips						
A. Trips Per Year				**B. Types of Trips**		
Year	No.	%			No.	%
1963	0	0.00		To Single Country	7	63.64
1964	1	9.09				
1965	0	0.00		To 2 or More Countries	1	9.09
1966	4	36.36				
1967	5	45.46		Grand Tours	3	27.27
1968	1	9.09				
1969	0	0.00				
Total	11	100.00		Total	11	100.00

Visits							
C. Type of Visit				**D. No. of Days Per Visit** *			
Category	No.	%		Days	No.	%	Total No. of Days
Conference	2	7.41					
Meeting	9	33.33		1	15	55.56	15
State Visit and Conference or Meeting	5	18.52		2	5	18.52	10
Ordinary State Visit	0	0.00		3	3	11.11	9
Official Visit	0	0.00		4	4	14.81	16
Informal Visit	4	14.82					
Ceremonial Visit	5	18.52		Total	27	100.00	50
Audience with Pope	1	3.70					
In Transit Stopover	1	3.70					
Total	27	100.00					

* The duration of visits represents full or partial days.

Source: Based on Elmer Plischke, Presidential Diplomacy: A Chronology of Summit Visits, Trips, and Meetings (Dobbs Ferry, N.Y.: Oceana, 1986), 18–20, 37.

Far East. In October 1966, to meet with the leaders of Asian allies, he undertook his major grand tour and visited seven countries, with stopovers in Hawaii, American Samoa, and Alaska en route, and he attended the Manila Conference. The press intimated that this trip was planned to buttress his waning popularity, enhance his image, and influence forthcoming congressional elections. These may have had a bearing, but he made it clear that he had more serious objectives in mind. He declared that his purpose was "to explore every possibility and every proposal that has been advanced for a solution of the Vietnam conflict and the rehabilitation of that country."[62] President Ferdinand E. Marcos of the Philippines provided the catalyst by calling the Manila Conference to consider the future of Asia, and the rest of the president's voyage was built around this meeting.

Visits to five countries on this trip—New Zealand, Australia, Thailand, Malaysia, and South Korea, the first presidential state visits to these countries—entailed many of the customary ceremonial activities and formal receptions. He attended three state luncheons and dinners, received an honorary degree in Bangkok, and delivered some thirty major addresses. But his primary concern was to align policy respecting the Vietnam War and plan for the future of the Western Pacific area which, in his published report, he called "The Promise of the New Asia." The trip produced what Johnson heralded as a change in basic United States policy toward the Pacific—branding it the crucial area of the era—which the media referred to briefly as the "Johnson Doctrine."

Following the Manila Conference (discussed in the next section), on 26 October he flew to the U.S. base at Cam Ranh Bay in Vietnam, to greet American troops at the war front. He addressed an assembly of seven thousand, commending their performance. An intricate plan was executed to keep his trip secret until his safe return. The next day, in Manila, he delivered an address, transmitted to the White House for rebroadcast to the American people, reporting on the results of the Manila Conference and his trip to Vietnam. During his visit to South Korea he also met with U.S. troops stationed at Camp Stanley.[63] Returning to Washington, he said that he was "much more hopeful" than when he left, and added, "I have seen millions of faces—by one estimate, more than five million. . . . Almost all of them . . . were friendly to the United States of America."[64] He called this the most historic and encouraging journey in his life and, in his memoirs, he concluded optimistically, "Certainly the vision of a new Asia was closer to reality."[65]

The following year, late in December, he set forth on his second trip to Asia, to attend the funeral of Prime Minister Harold E. Holt of Australia. In Canberra he conferred with other attending heads of government, including Presidents Park Chung Hee of South Korea and Nguyen Van Thieu of South Vietnam. He then proceeded on the first presidential whirlwind, globe-girdling tour—labelled a "Johnson extravaganza" by the *Washington Post*—returning via Thailand, Vietnam, Pakistan, and Italy, and he arrived home in time to deliver his Christmas message to the nation. En route there were stops in Hawaii where he delivered an address in a rainstorm, Samoa (Pago Pago) for an impromptu midnight festival of song and dance, Canberra for a 4:40 A.M. reception by Australian leaders, Melbourne for the memorial services and discussions with other world dignitaries, Thailand (Khorat) and Vietnam (Cam Ranh Bay) to greet U.S. servicemen, Pakistan to talk with President Ayub Khan, and Rome to confer with Premier Aldo Moro and spend an hour in audience with the Pope. On this amazing odyssey, planned on short notice, the president traveled 27,300 miles in only four and one-half days, and spent more than half that time in flight.[66]

Once President Johnson tasted the elixir of summit travel and set out on his Asian excursion in 1966, he made eight trips, with twenty-four visits to twenty different countries in fewer than three years. Aside from those to neighboring Canada and Mexico and to attend Chancellor Adenauer's funeral, his foreign ventures centered largely on participating in inter-American summit gatherings and consulting with Vietnam War allies. Unlike President Eisenhower and others, he undertook no goodwill grand tours, nor did he venture to Africa or the Middle East. His audience at the Vatican maintained the continuity of such presidential visits, begun by Woodrow Wilson and continued by every president since Eisenhower.[67] His visits to U.S. troops at Cam Ranh Bay were the first such hazardous excursions in time of hostilities since Franklin Roosevelt went to Casablanca and Sicily in 1943.[68]

Even though he was denied the opportunity of meeting personally with the leaders of North Vietnam to resolve the conflict in Southeast Asia, in his foreign travels he nevertheless focused on what he regarded as urgent public matters, and yet his flexible style enabled him to introduce or modify some summit practices. Enthusiasm for creating a collective policy for the Pacific, with mutual guarantees against aggression, in cooperation with free Asian nations on the basis of equality, while presumably genuine, was short lived—inducing Peregrine Worsthorne of the *London Sunday Telegraph* to claim that Lyndon Johnson had "a taste to play the king and determine the part of the world where he will make his bid for immortality."[69] If this was the president's expectation he was to be disappointed.

SUMMIT CONFERENCES AND MEETINGS

In addition to expressing his willingness to go anywhere, any place, at any time in the cause of peace,[70] President Johnson declared, "The people of the world prefer reasoned agreement to ready attack. That is why we must follow the Prophet Isaiah, saying, 'Come now, let us reason together.' "[71] On the matter of meeting with the Soviet Premier Kosygin, he later repeated this and added, "When they tell me to negotiate, I say 'Amen.' I have been ready to negotiate and sit down at a conference table every hour of every day that I have been president of this country, but I just cannot negotiate with myself."[72]

His willingness to engage personally in summit conferencing is evidenced by his participation in twenty-two conferences and meetings in fewer than five years. As indicated in Table 17.4, all but three of these were bilateral, nearly three-fourths convened abroad, and the preponderant majority (more than 90 percent) were meetings as distinguished from the two that were designated as conferences. The "summit conference" tends to be more carefully prepared and managed, involving prenegotiation of agenda and format, the advance compilation of position papers and draft diplomatic instruments, the fixing of purposes and ground rules, more highly structured delegation staffs and deliberation organization, the keeping of more formal records, and the production of concrete end-products.[73] A final distinguishing factor is the primary presidential role, varying from ceremonial to discussion and negotiation.[74] Table 17.4, part F, indicates that at six

Table 17.4
President Johnson's Participation in Conferences and Meetings (22 November 1963–20 January 1969)

A.	Conferences and Meetings Per Year		B. Type of Gathering		C. Location		D. No. of Days
	No.	%	Conference	Meeting	U.S.	Abroad	
1963	0	0.00	0	0	0	0	0
1964	1	4.55	0	1	0	1	1
1965	0	0.00	0	0	0	0	0
1966	10	45.45	1	9	1	9	26
1967	7	31.82	0	7	2	5	12
1968	4	18.18	1	3	3	1	9
1969	0	0.00	0	0	0	0	0
Total	22		2	20	6	16	48
%		100.00	9.09	90.91	27.27	72.73	

E.	Participants		F. Primary Presidential Role		
	Bilateral	Multilateral	Ceremonial	Discussion	Negotiation
1963	0	0	0	0	0
1964	1	0	1	0	0
1965	0	0	0	0	0
1966	9	1	3	5	2
1967	6	1	1	6	0
1968	3	1	1	3	0
1969	0	0	0	0	0
Total	19	3	6	14	2
%	86.36	13.64	27.27	63.64	9.09

Source: Based on Elmer Plischke, Presidential Diplomacy: A Chronology of Summit Visits, Trips, and Meetings (Dobbs Ferry, N.Y.: Oceana, 1986), 239–41, 253.

gatherings the president's role was essentially ceremonial, whereas at fourteen he engaged in conferral and discussion, and he was called upon to negotiate at only two. This was not unusual, except when compared with the function of Wilson at Paris in 1919 or Roosevelt during World War II.

These summit gatherings of President Johnson were of short duration, with two-thirds running for merely one or two days, and only three—the Punta del Este inter-American conclave and two combined state visits and summit meetings—lasting four days. Counting days and parts of days, all told Johnson's summit conferencing aggregated forty-eight days. Even the Manila Conference lasted fewer than three days—as compared with the 157 days Wilson spent at Paris in 1919, the twenty-four days Roosevelt devoted to the Arcadia Conference, or the seventeen days Truman attended the Potsdam Conference and Carter spent at Camp David to negotiate the Egyptian-Israeli Accords.

Much of Johnson's summit conferencing, both in the United States and abroad, has already been noted, such as his sessions with the leaders of Canada and Mexico, several Far East powers, and the American Republics. Of these sixteen summits, only two were multilateral (the inter-American gatherings), merely one was classified as a conference (that of the Central American presidents), and only one was convened in the United States (the final meeting of the president with Diaz Ordaz, 1968). Unlike other presidents, Johnson participated in no NATO sessions or western Three-Power or Four-Power meetings.

The remaining six summit gatherings consisted of four bilateral meetings with the presidents of South Vietnam and South Korea in American overseas territory, the multipartite Manila Conference, and the president's sole east-west summit meeting with Premier Kosygin. During his last three years, Johnson met with South Vietnam's President Thieu in Honolulu in 1966, Guam in 1967, and Honolulu again in 1968. At the first of these they discussed the war and Vietnam's political future, and issued the "Declaration of Honolulu," which consisted of several parts specifying the purposes of the Vietnam government, the objectives of the United States, and joint commitments. The following year the president flew to Guam to confer with his "Saigon Team" and Vietnam leaders where, for thirty hours, they discussed the newly drafted South Vietnam constitution and other nonmilitary matters, but they reached no major new decisions. Following the cessation of United States bombing of North Vietnam, in mid–1968 the president returned to Honolulu to confer with President Thieu for ten hours. They concentrated especially on the Vietnam peace negotiations then convening in Paris and such subjects as self-determination and the formation of a coalition government.[75] In 1968, the president also met with South Korea's President Park Chung Hee in Honolulu. Confronted with the seizure of the *Pueblo* and other North Korean probes, he reassured the South Korean government of continued U.S. support.[76]

The most historic and portentous conclave that President Johnson attended met in Manila, 24–26 October 1966. This was intended to be the highlight of his 31,500-mile Pacific tour. He and the leaders of Australia, Korea, New Zealand, the Philippines, South Vietnam, and Thailand discussed mutual aims in the Vietnam War. Their deliberations, the results of which were embodied in three documents—a statement titled "Goals of Freedom," a "Declaration of Peace and Progress in Asia and the Pacific," and a joint communique—committed them to resist aggression, build a secure and ordered region, seek conciliation and peace throughout the area, and conquer hunger, illiteracy, and disease. Aside from the advantage of personal behind-the-scenes exchanges and publicity, the prime consequence of this conference was an alleged "Spirit of Manila," but it appears that the underlying purpose of both the conference and the presidential tour 'was to enhance allied unity in Vietnam under U.S. leadership.[77]

Because of President Eisenhower's experience at the aborted Paris east-west, Four-Power Conference (1960) and President Kennedy's sobering talks with Premier Nikita S. Khrushchev in Vienna (1961), initially President Johnson was wary of meeting with Soviet leaders. Following his election in 1964, however, he proposed an exchange of summit visits to be held during the following year, but it was not until June 1967 that he and Premier Kosygin met for two days in

Glassboro, New Jersey.[78] The Soviet leader had come to New York to attend a special session of the UN General Assembly to deal with the Mideast Six Day War. Following an embarrassing minuet of maneuvering, they finally agreed to an impromptu meeting at a "neutral" site—called "Holly Bush," the home of the president of Glassboro State College. Due to prior presidential commitments in Los Angeles on Saturday, the meeting was held in two sessions—on Friday and Sunday, 23 and 25 June.

Except for working luncheons at which they were joined by their advisers, the two leaders talked privately in the small study of the college president, seated at a low table, accompanied only by their interpreters. They conferred for nearly ten hours, and most of this time was devoted to informal conversations. They drafted no official communiques although, as they emerged from their sessions, both leaders issued brief, rather noncommittal oral statements to the press. The only specific agreements reached were to have their deputies continue negotiations in New York, especially on arms control, and "to keep in good communication in the future"—through their foreign ministers, their ambassadors, "and also directly." This last point raised some speculation as to whether it implied subsequent "big two" summit meetings. While the White House press office equivocated respecting the future, this was to be President Johnson's only meeting with the Soviet premier. In Los Angeles, he began referring to a "Spirit of Hollybush," and one editorial writer went so far as to call him ecstatic, but when the leaders reconvened on Sunday and got down to the hard realities of concrete matters, they found their differences to be so profound that accommodation and even policy parallelism rarely exceeded nebulous generalities.[79]

President Johnson, nevertheless, concluded that it was helpful "to sit down and look a man right in the eye and try to reason with him, particularly if he is trying to reason with you."[80] The public learned little of what was actually said at Hollybush, but press analysts regarded the meeting, even if it failed to contribute materially to settling the pressing issues of Vietnam and the Middle East, as serving a number of beneficial purposes. It dissipated some of the propaganda image each of the leaders had of the other and probably eased relations below the surface and engendered a better climate for subsequent discussions. Synthesizing his assessment, the president conceded the obvious—that "one meeting does not make a peace"[81]—but, contrary to what Eisenhower told his cabinet in 1953, he confessed that he had learned that the leaders of the two adversary powers "could sit down together without either losing his nerve or his shirt."[82] Later, after he had announced that he would not seek reelection and even after his successor was chosen, he sought to cap his White House career by initiating a second U.S.-Soviet summit, but this failed to materialize.[83]

Quantitatively, Lyndon Johnson's summit conferencing record exceeded those of his predecessors. He averaged four per year, greater than the ratios of Roosevelt, Truman, and Eisenhower, and overall his meeting record also surpassed that of Kennedy. While initially reluctant to leave the United States because he lacked a vice president, eventually the lure of the summit became overpowering.

His response was a well-orchestrated series of short, relatively safe, and often largely ceremonious meetings, particularly with the leaders of Canada, Mexico, and other Latin American countries. Nevertheless, although he did continue the series of meetings with Soviet leaders that began during World War II, the thrust of his more memorable conferencing focused rather on the powers involved in the Vietnam War and the Pacific.

THE VERDICT

Except for his expressions of willingness to confer with other world leaders, his judgment on the value of the hot line, his comparisons with President Eisenhower, and his comments on specific summit experiences in his press conferences and memoirs, President Johnson was not inclined to analyze the nature and value of presidential diplomacy. Nevertheless, he apparently enjoyed his role as diplomat in chief. Aside from such summit features as the ceremonial goodwill grand tour, participation in NATO and western Big Three and Big Four meetings, and constitutive conferences and formal meetings with Soviet leaders, he proved to be an active summiteer and employed all of the basic techniques developed by his predecessors. He also introduced innovations of his own that, albeit minor, included extensive combination formal state visits and summit meetings abroad, the whirlwind globe-girdling tour, utilization of funerals both in this country and abroad for informal summit conferral, use of the Washington-Moscow hot line, simultaneous global saturation by special emissaries during the Vietnam peace offensive, and frequent, often truncated summit visits to Washington, and sometimes to the informal setting of his LBJ Ranch.

Nuances that characterize his brand of summitry ranged from shortening both visits to the United States and his visits abroad, taking advantage of various ceremonious activities to consult with other leaders, and minimizing presidential negotiation, which he left rather to his secretary of state, diplomats, and technical experts. Although he is not criticized for seeking to be his own secretary of state, he proved to be a summitry enthusiast and therefore, not unlike other presidents, he often served as his own ambassador or relied on high-level personal surrogates.

Despite the complexities of delineating the contemporary public and subsequently determined "expert" image of presidents, certain depictions are associated with him.[84] Whereas Washington is regarded as the "father of his country," Lincoln as the "great emancipator," and Wilson as the exponent of self-determination and "crusader for a better world," Johnson is identified especially with internal social reform and the "Great Society." But he also has been regarded as a "power wielder" and "wheeler-dealer" given to "jawboning" and eager "to press the flesh," and he is widely remembered simply as "LBJ."[85]

One of the common ways of gauging the presidential image, as reflecting contemporary popularity, is by means of public opinion polls. On the basis of cumulative, periodic Gallup polls—which survey the public impression of how he handled the presidency—in terms of average approval ratios throughout his tenure, President Johnson rated lower than any of his predecessors since the 1930s, except for Truman, but, by comparison, his aggregate rating also exceeded that of each of his successors by a margin of 6 percent or more. While his popularity record fluctuated substantially, his extreme highs and lows also generally followed this pattern, although in January 1964 he achieved a higher score than had Eisenhower, and his lowest rating, in August 1968, was overshadowed only by that of Truman.[86]

President Johnson's basic image cycle followed the traditional pattern. He attained his peak soon after he became president, and his popularity gradually diminished during the next five years. So far as foreign affairs are concerned, it rose four points after he returned from his trip to Asia and the Manila Conference in 1966 and by eight points following the Glassboro meeting in 1967, but fell by some three to five points subsequent to the Punta del Este and San Salvador inter-American meetings. Whereas public support normally rallies behind a president when the United States becomes involved in an international crisis, Johnson's record fluctuated, rising substantially at the time of the Dominican crisis (1965) and the Middle East Six Day War (1967), but declining during the Panamanian (1964) and *Pueblo* (1968) crises. His meetings with South Vietnam and Korean leaders in Hawaii and Guam produced mixed results (increasing in two cases and falling in two others), and his summit visits to Canada and Mexico had little impact on his polls.[87]

Among the generalizations that may be drawn are that both advances and declines in presidential stature are relatable to major summit ventures and international crises, and that even though such experiences may evoke favorable commentary in the media, they do not necessarily result in improved presidential popularity ratings. The notion that the public uniformly provides reflexive support for the president's reception of summit visitors, trips abroad, and high-level conclaves cannot be sustained.[88]

Review of some half dozen collective surveys and individual assessments since the 1960s that provide comparative ranking of presidents by historians and other "experts" reveals that Lyndon Johnson is not included in any major list of great presidents. Only one of these assessments lists him as last among the thirteen "strongest Presidents."[89] On the basis of more specific criteria, in a poll of 570 historians, in 1970 Gary M. Maranell ranked him as only sixteenth of thirty-five presidents in "general prestige" (the lowest of those that received a positive score). However, it listed him as fourth in "presidential activeness," eighth in "strength of action," and ninth in "accomplishment of his administration," and, on the other hand, only as twenty-third in "flexibility" and thirty-first in "idealism" (which, in turn, rated him high in "practicality").[90]

In subsequent surveys, in 1982, Johnson was ranked tenth (high in the "above average" category but below the eight "greats" and "near greats") by Robert K. Murray and Tim H. Blessing, based on a nineteen-page questionnaire responded to by nearly 1,000 historians, and he was rated twelfth (high in the mediocre category) in the *Chicago Tribune* survey of approximately fifty "leading historians and political scholars."[91] As with other presidents, such valuations by "experts" vary depending upon that which is assessed, but President Johnson is not included among the "greats" or "near greats," and is ranked below the top third in prestige.

To regard presidents as noteworthy diplomats in chief, however, is quite another proposition. They may be remembered in the annals of American diplomacy for different reasons and for excelling in differing summitry techniques. Nevertheless, no president is perfect, either as chief executive or as diplomat in chief. Even the "greats" are flawed. Though viewed as notable, or at least as memorable, performers at the summit, so far as their qualities and achievements are concerned, none is really the consummate summiteer. Assessment needs to be founded on such tests as innate capability and enthusiasm for the role, innovation, initiative, performance, accomplishment, and long-range legacies. Based on these and related criteria, in terms of foreign policy making and implementation, the American summit hall of fame includes only George Washington and in the twentieth century Theodore Roosevelt, Woodrow Wilson, Franklin Roosevelt, Harry Truman, Dwight Eisenhower, and Richard Nixon—but not Lyndon Johnson. Though active and at times enthusiastic and successful in achieving his declared objectives, he was not outstanding.[92]

It must be concluded that in surveying the various forms of presidential diplomacy, factors other than the degree of personal involvement are essential to assure either popular or subsequent "expert" approval, and that quantity of participation does not necessarily guarantee superior performance or approbation. Nevertheless, the president's authority and influence at the summit and his stature in the long run are conditioned by the image he projects and the prestige he reflects to his countrymen and foreign governments. Coping with the pressure to satisfy as well as to gratify, in part presidents venture to the summit to enable them to be admired and well remembered, and in Lyndon Johnson's case he focused primarily on promoting cooperation and development in the Western Hemisphere and restraining communist expansion in Southeast Asia and ending the Vietnam War honorably.

It has been said that he harbored an almost pathological desire to be judged great,[93] and one of his biographers disclosed that he was well aware that his place in posterity would be established, not by the passage of a tax bill or even a civil rights act, "but by what he does in the world," and that he "was very sensitive to the impression he would create . . . in the world at large."[94] Not unlike other presidents he besought historicity as peace maker. There can be little question that he was concerned with both peace making and peace keeping, and that this motivated his resort to the summit. Reflecting on his role in the presidency and "how inadequate any man is for the office," he confessed in his memoirs:

The magnitude of the job dwarfs every man who aspires to it. Every man who occupies the position has to strain to the utmost of his ability to fill it. I believe that every man who ever occupied it, within his inner self, was humble enough to realize that no living mortal has ever possessed all the required qualifications.[95]

And this applied as much to his functioning as diplomat in chief as to his other presidential roles. It is axiomatic that in the long run the image of a president's summit craftsmanship will depend on the process by which he is judged and by who recounts his ventures to the summit.

NOTES

1. Clinton Rossiter, *The American Presidency*, 2d ed. (New York: Harcourt, Brace and World, 1960), 28.

2. Elmer Plischke, *Diplomat in Chief: The President at the Summit* (New York: Praeger, 1986), 76, 141; for lists of visits, see Elmer Plischke, *Presidential Diplomacy: A Chronology of Summit Visits, Trips, and Meetings* (Dobbs Ferry, N.Y.: Oceana, 1986), 97–98; and Department of State, "Lists of Visits of Foreign Chiefs of State and Heads of Government to the United States, 1789–1978" (Washington, D.C.: Department of State, processed, 1979), 27–29.

3. For a complete list of presidential summit "firsts," see Plischke, *Diplomat in Chief*, 483–485.

4. Factual data concerning these and other summit events are readily available in the contemporary press, news magazines, and such resources as *Facts on File*.

5. For documentation, for example, respecting the Hammarskjöld funeral and the Geneva and NATO visits, see *Public Papers of the Presidents of the United States: John F. Kennedy, 1961*, 632–633, and for attendance at Pope John's funeral, see *Papers of Presidents: Lyndon B. Johnson, 1963–1964*, 129.

6. President Kennedy was well aware of Johnson's restlessness in his role as vice president and sought to use him as his summit deputy for certain missions. See Jack Valenti, *A Very Human President* (New York: Norton, 1975), 306–307; and Merle Miller, *Lyndon: An Oral Biography* (New York: Putnam, 1980), 277.

7. Rowland Evans and Robert Novak, *Lyndon B. Johnson: The Exercise of Power* (New York: New American Library, 1966), 324.

8. Lyndon Baines Johnson, *The Vantage Point: Perspectives of the Presidency, 1963–1969* (New York: Holt, Rinehart and Winston, 1971), 52–54, 222–223. For detail and color, see Eric F. Goldman, *The Tragedy of Lyndon Johnson* (New York: Knopf, 1969), 387–393; also see Evans and Novak, *Lyndon B. Johnson*, 320–324, for analysis of this trip and Johnson's report to President Kennedy, and Miller, *Lyndon: An Oral Biography*, 282–286, for details of Johnson's performance on the trip.

9. Charles E. Bohlen, *Witness to History, 1929–1969* (New York: Norton, 1973), 483–488. Bohlen reported that on this trip the vice president "performed admirably" doing "the right thing at the right time" (485). Also see Evans and Novak, who regarded this Berlin trip as the "most spectacular mission of his vice-presidency," *Lyndon B. Johnson*, 325.

10. Miller, *Lyndon: An Oral Biography*, 280–281.

11. Evans and Novak conclude that Johnson's tenure as vice president was "the most uncomfortable period of his life," because during those three years he "could be close to his own impulsive, bigger-than-life self only when beyond the borders of the United

States," and that "Johnson could stretch his legs and revert to a semblance of the vigorous freewheeler only when he traveled," *Lyndon B. Johnson*, 320, 325.

12. Johnson, *Vantage Point*, 306–311, 318–319, 321; *Papers of Presidents: Lyndon Johnson, 1963–1964*, no. 170, item 5; *1966*, 1036–1037, 1140; *1968–1969*, 718–719.

13. Johnson, *Vantage Point*, 24–25, 468. Johnson's initial letter to Nikita Khrushchev was handed to Deputy Premier Anastas Mikoyan on 26 November 1963; for text of the letter, see *Vantage Point*, 25; Mikoyan had come to Washington to represent the Soviet government at President Kennedy's funeral.

14. Ibid., 25, 290–291, 464–466, 468, 476, 479–481, 485–486, and 602–603 for the text of Johnson's letter to Khrushchev of 18 January 1964. Also see "Khrushchev-Johnson Notes on the Use of Arms," *Current History* 46 (1964): 357–363.

15. George W. Ball, *The Past Has Another Pattern: Memoirs* (New York: Norton, 1982), 350–352.

16. Johnson, *Vantage Point*, 290–291.

17. George C. Herring, *America's Longest War: The United States and Vietnam* (New York: Wiley, 1979), 164. See also David Kraslow and Stuart H. Loory, *The Secret Search for Peace in Vietnam* (New York: Random House, 1968).

18. For lists of major U.S. and third party peace initiatives (with North Vietnam reactions), see Johnson, *Vantage Point*, 579–591.

19. Ibid., 250.

20. The Geneva Accords of 1954 and 1962 concerned Vietnam and Laos. For discussion of these attempts, see Johnson, *Vantage Point*, 252–253, 255–256, 586, with the text of the Johnson–Ho Chi Minh letters on pages 592–596; also *Papers of Presidents: Lyndon Johnson, 1967*, 390–391. For the exchange between Pope Paul and President Johnson, 7–8 February 1967, see *Papers of Presidents: Lyndon Johnson, 1967*, 162 and Johnson, *Vantage Point*, 253.

21. Hugh Sidey, *A Very Personal Presidency: Lyndon Johnson in the White House* (New York: Atheneum, 1968), 221.

22. Johnson, *Vantage Point*, 182–183; *Papers of Presidents, Lyndon Johnson, 1963–1964*, 324–325, 404–406.

23. Drew Pearson, "Washington Merry-Go-Round," *Washington Post*, 26 January 1965. William Jordan reports that Johnson "was an inveterate user of Alexander Graham Bell's instrument" and that he would "look at three television stations at once" while "trying to talk over two or three telephones at the same time." See Miller, *Lyndon: An Oral Biography*, 535. For President Johnson's statement to Prime Minister Pearson, see *Papers of Presidents: Lyndon Johnson, 1963–1964*, 207.

24. Johnson, *Vantage Point*, 287, 298–303, 484; *Papers of Presidents: Lyndon Johnson, 1967*, 615–616; Lester Velie, "The Week the Hot Line Burned," *Reader's Digest* (August 1968): 44; Louis Heren, *No Hail, No Farewell* (New York: Harper & Row, 1970), 164; Hugh Sidey, "Over the Hot Line: The Middle East," *Life* (16 June 1967): 24b; James M. Ennes, Jr., *Assault on the "Liberty": The True Story of the Israeli Attack on an American Intelligence Ship* (New York: Random House, 1979). A summary statement on the establishment and use of the hotline is provided in Plischke, *Diplomat in Chief*, 52–58, and Marjorie M. Whiteman, *Digest of International Law*, vol. 9 (Washington, D.C.: U.S. Government Printing Office, 1968), 860–862. President Johnson also used the hot line in 1968 to inform the Soviet government of the progress of the historic American space flight to the moon; see *Washington Evening Star*, 27 December 1968.

25. On the nature and use of special presidential diplomatic representatives, see Henry

M. Wriston, *Executive Agents in American Foreign Relations* (Baltimore: Johns Hopkins Press, 1929) and "The Special Envoy," *Foreign Affairs* 38 (January 1960): 219–237; and Elmer Plischke, *Conduct of American Diplomacy*, 3d ed. (Princeton, N.J.: Van Nostrand, 1967), 48–49, 92–96.

26. Plischke, *Diplomat in Chief*, 64.

27. See Lady Bird Johnson, *A White House Diary* (New York: Holt, Rinehart and Winston, 1970), 81–85.

28. In Washington he also was empowered to sign an aid agreement under the Food for Peace program with Mohamed Ibrahim Egal of Somalia in 1968; *Facts on File, 1968*, 216. For general commentary on Vice President Humphrey, see Marie D. Natoli, "The Humphrey Vice-Presidency in Retrospect," *Presidential Studies Quarterly* 12 (1982): 603–609.

29. *Facts on File, 1965*, 237–238, *1966*, 9, 19, 271, and *1967*, 301, 487–488; Philip Geyelin, *Lyndon B. Johnson and the World* (New York: Praeger, 1966), 93; and Goldman, *Tragedy of Lyndon Johnson*, 262 for comment on President Johnson's reasons for not sending Vice President Humphrey to Churchill's funeral.

30. Ball, *The Past Has Another Pattern*, 340–359; Cyrus Vance, *Hard Choices: Critical Years in America's Foreign Policy* (New York: Simon and Schuster, 1983), 144, 168, 408. On the *Pueblo* incident also see Heren, *No Hail, No Farewell*, 188, 229; and Miller, *Lyndon: An Oral Biography*, 527–528.

31. Johnson, *Vantage Point*, 287–304.

32. Ibid., 180–184. For commentary on the political ramifications, see Evans and Novak, *Lyndon B. Johnson*, 399–405; Geyelin, *Lyndon B. Johnson and the World*, 100–111; and Goldman, *Tragedy of Lyndon Johnson*, 73–77.

33. Johnson, *Vantage Point*, 187–205. For commentary, see Vaughn Davis Bornet, *The Presidency of Lyndon B. Johnson* (Lawrence: University of Kansas Press, 1983), 174–178; Evans and Novak, *Lyndon B. Johnson*, 510–529; Geyelin, *Lyndon B. Johnson and the World*, 236–258; and Goldman, *Tragedy of Lyndon Johnson*, 394–398.

34. For analysis of Dean Rusk's role as secretary of state, see Warren I. Cohen, *Dean Rusk* (Totowa, N.J.: Cooper Square, 1980); on the roles of Kissinger and Sullivan, see Johnson, *Vantage Point*, 266–267, 498, and Herring, *America's Longest War*, 179–180. For a brief overall survey of Johnson and the Vietnam War, see Plischke, *Diplomat in Chief*, 85–89.

35. Johnson, *Vantage Point*, 238. On this peace offensive via summit surrogates, see also Plischke, *Diplomat in Chief*, 88–89; Ball, *The Past Has Another Pattern*, 404–406; and Evans and Novak, *Lyndon B. Johnson*, 553–556.

36. Johnson, *Vantage Point*, 504–529. For additional commentary on the U.S. delegation to the Paris Peace talks, see Cohen, *Dean Rusk*, 312–316; Henry F. Graff, *The Tuesday Cabinet: Deliberation and Decision on Peace and War under Lyndon B. Johnson* (Englewood Cliffs, N.J.: Prentice-Hall, 1970), 154–163; Herring, *America's Longest War*, 213–216; and Miller, *Lyndon: An Oral Biography*, 517–522. For a comprehensive bibliography of materials on Johnson and the Vietnam War, see *Lyndon B. Johnson: A Bibliography* (Austin: University of Texas Press, 1984), 180–202.

37. The position of ambassador at large was created by law in 1949 and requires Senate approval; appointees serve the president and secretary of state at a high level in whatever missions they assign. For analysis of the office, see Lee H. Burke, *Ambassador at Large: Diplomat Extraordinary* (The Hague: Nijoff, 1972).

38. Valenti, *A Very Human President*, 308.

39. *New York Times*, 5 March 1967. For a summary survey of Harriman's diplomatic career, see Plischke, *Diplomat in Chief*, 101–104.

40. According to the Department of State there were only 23 summit visits to the United States prior to Franklin Roosevelt and 72 during his 13 years in the presidency, 63 while Truman was president, and 115 during the Eisenhower years. For complete lists, see Plischke, *Presidential Diplomacy*, 71–145 and Department of State, "Lists of Visits of Foreign Chiefs of State and Heads of Government to the United States, 1789–1978," 2–22. For the purposes, procedures, and results of summit visits see Plischke, *Diplomat in Chief*, 143–170.

41. For comment on this visit, see Evans and Novak, *Lyndon B. Johnson*, 387–389. For pertinent documents, see *Papers of Presidents: Lyndon Johnson, 1963–1964*, 91–100. This compilation provides published documentation on many such summit visits during the Johnson administration.

42. Valenti, *A Very Human President*, 307.

43. Plischke, *Presidential Diplomacy*, 97–104; for summary statistics, see Table 17.1, Part C, and Table 17.2.

44. For analysis of various types of summit visits, and the development of United States practice, see Plischke, *Diplomat in Chief*, Chapter 4, esp. 134–142.

45. For visits of Haile Selassie and King Faisal, respectively, see *Papers of Presidents: Lyndon Johnson, 1967*, 179–182, and *1966*, 640–644.

46. *Facts on File, 1964*, 305; also see note 53.

47. *Papers of Presidents: Lyndon Johnson, 1963–1964*, 1117–1122.

48. For Prime Minister Yen's visit, see *Papers of Presidents: Lyndon Johnson, 1967*, 518–521, 526–527. The two leaders reaffirmed commitments under the Mutual Defense Treaty of 1954 and their policy to contain communism.

49. For discussion of such incidents during the Johnson administration, see Plischke, *Diplomat in Chief*, 149, 151, and Geyelin, *Lyndon B. Johnson and the World*, 266–270.

50. Angier Biddle Duke, "Protocol and the Conduct of Foreign Affairs," *Department of State Bulletin* 49 (4 November 1963): 700–701.

51. *Papers of Presidents: Lyndon Johnson, 1963–1964*, 65.

52. *Washington Post*, 28 March 1964.

53. *Papers of Presidents: Lyndon Johnson, 1963–1964*, 1074–1077.

54. *Papers of Presidents: Lyndon Johnson, 1965*, 449. For critical comment on such statements, regarding them as posturing and a ploy, see Robert Sherrill, *The Accidental President* (New York: Grossman, 1967), 258–259.

55. To the 1960s only President Truman had made such a combination visit when, in 1947, he was formally received in a state visit by the Brazilian government and he also addressed the Rio Inter-American Conference.

56. *Papers of Presidents: Lyndon Johnson, 1967*, 462–463; also see *Facts on File, 1967*, 139.

57. Johnson, *Vantage Point*, 379–380.

58. Ibid., 292, 348; *Papers of Presidents: Lyndon Johnson, 1966*, 416–424, 875–876, 1428–1430; *1967*, 574–577, 952–962.

59. Johnson, *Vantage Point*, 348–351; *Papers of Presidents: Lyndon Johnson, 1967*, 442–451. Also see Department of State, *Commitment for Progress: The Americas Plan for a Decade of Urgency* (Washington, D.C.: U.S. Government Printing Office, 1967).

60. *Papers of Presidents: Lyndon Johnson, 1968–1969*, 785–797; text of Joint Declaration is given at pages 785–790.

61. *Papers of Presidents: Lyndon Johnson, 1968–1969*, 797–800; also see *Facts on File, 1968*, 265.

62. White House Press Release, 17 October 1966.

63. On this Asian trip, see Johnson, *Vantage Point*, 248–249, 359–364; *Papers of Presidents: Lyndon Johnson, 1966*, 1216–1305, with text of the president's statement to U.S. troops in Vietnam at pages 1269–1270 and text of his broadcast to the American people at pages 1270–1273. Also see Department of State, *The Promise of the New Asia* (Washington, D.C.: U.S. Government Printing Office, 1966) and U.S. Information Service, *Journey to the Pacific* (Washington, D.C.: U.S. Information Service, 1966). Also see Graff, *Tuesday Cabinet*, 119, 145–148; Sidey, *A Very Personal Presidency*, Chapter 6. On the "Johnson Doctrine," see "Towards a Johnson Doctrine," *Round Table 55* (June 1965): 252–257; Heren, *No Hail, No Farewell*, 95; and Sherrill, *Accidental President*, 266–267.

64. U.S. Information Service, *Journey to the Pacific*, 64.

65. Johnson, *Vantage Point*, 363.

66. Ibid., 378–379; *Papers of Presidents: Lyndon Johnson, 1967*, 1178–1191, for the texts of President Johnson's addresses and joint statements. See also Hugh Sidey, "Around the World with Lyndon B. Magellan," *Life* (5 January 1968): 24c–24d, and Miller, *Lyndon: An Oral Biography*, 493–495.

67. For documentation on the president's Vatican visit, see Johnson, *Vantage Point*, 379–380; *Papers of Presidents: Lyndon Johnson, 1967*, 1189. This visit also is touched on in Bornet, *Presidency of Lyndon B. Johnson*, 267; Graff, *Tuesday Cabinet*, 148–149; Miller, *Lyndon: An Oral Biography*, 494–495; and Sidey, *A Very Personal Presidency*, 23–24.

68. For documentation on the president's visits to American troops at Cam Ranh Bay, see Johnson, *Vantage Point*, 363; *Papers of Presidents: Lyndon Johnson, 1966*, 1269–1270, 1303–1304, and *1967*, 1181–1187.

69. Quoted in Sherrill, *Accidental President*, 268.

70. Department of State, *American Foreign Policy: Current Documents, 1967*, 431.

71. Lyndon B. Johnson, *My Hope for America* (New York: Random House, 1964), 108; and Department of State, *American Foreign Policy: Current Documents, 1967*, 430.

72. Department of State, *American Foreign Policy: Current Documents, 1967*, 431. For commentary see Goldman, *Tragedy of Lyndon Johnson*, 406.

73. For additional discussion on this distinction, see Plischke, *Diplomat in Chief*, 218–224.

74. For additional comment, see ibid., 224–227.

75. Johnson, *Vantage Point*, 242–245, 259–260, 510–512; *Papers of Presidents: Lyndon Johnson, 1966*, 144–146, 148, 150–157 (with Declaration at 153–155); *1967*, 375–390; *1968*, 821–830. Also see Valenti, *A Very Human President*, 240–242.

76. *Papers of Presidents: Lyndon Johnson, 1968*, 511–518.

77. Johnson, *Vantage Point*, 248–249, 359–363, with text of Goals of Freedom at page 599; *Papers of Presidents: Lyndon Johnson, 1966*, 1256–1265, 1270–1273. Also see commentary in Sidey, *A Very Personal Presidency*, 132–155.

78. For preliminaries, see *Papers of Presidents: Lyndon Johnson, 1963–1964*, 65, 343, 363; *1965*, 133.

79. On the Glassboro Meeting, see Johnson, *Vantage Point*, 256–257, 481–485; *Papers of Presidents: Lyndon Johnson, 1967*, 643–652, 658–659, which includes President Johnson's remarks following each day's sessions; and Plischke, *Diplomat in Chief*, 334–

341. Also see Robert D. Bole, *Summit at Holly Bush* (Glassboro, N.J.: Glassboro State College Endowment Fund, 1969), and Hugh Sidney, "Eye to Eye at Holly Bush," *Life* (7 July 1967): 26b. It is interesting to note that few of Johnson's biographers wrote extensively on this summit meeting.

80. *Washington Post*, 26 June 1967.

81. Ibid.

82. *Washington Post*, 27 June 1967. For the Eisenhower statement to his cabinet in 1953, see Emmet John Hughes, *The Ordeal of Power* (New York: Atheneum, 1963), 151.

83. Johnson, *Vantage Point*, 585–588; Plischke, *Diplomat in Chief*, 530–533; Valenti, *A Very Human President*, 372–373; and Bornet, *Presidency of Lyndon B. Johnson*, 213. On transition relations of Presidents Johnson and Nixon regarding foreign affairs (without mentioning a possible Moscow summit meeting), see *Papers of Presidents: Lyndon Johnson, 1968–1969*, 1119–1120.

84. For general discussion of the presidential image, see Elmer Plischke, "The President's Image as Diplomat in Chief," *Review of Politics* 47 (October 1985): 544–549.

85. Some have also called him essentially a populist, inurbane, a sensual person in the sense that he sought to be an impressive physical presence, and that he was wont to engage in "tactile diplomacy"—poking a finger, gripping an arm, and the like. For comment on his sensual treatment, see Sherrill, *Accidental President*, 22–23.

86. See comparative table in Plischke, "The President's Image as Diplomat in Chief," 550, which was compiled from *The Gallup Poll Index*, October-November, 1980 and *The Gallup Report*. For additional comment on Johnson's polls and the media, see Bornet, *Presidency of Lyndon B. Johnson*, 157–159; Goldman, *Tragedy of Lyndon Johnson*, 415–416; Graff, *Tuesday Cabinet*, 154, 157–159, 162–163; and Sidey, *A Very Personal Presidency*, 194.

87. In addition, insofar as the Vietnam War was concerned, his rating rose eight points after the first bombing of Hanoi (1966) but fell seven points as a consequence of the Tet offensive (1968). It also declined after the *Maddox* incident and the enactment of the Gulf of Tonkin Resolution in 1964. His record reached its nadir in August 1968 as the people became disenchanted with the intensification of military involvement in Southeast Asia. Moreover, popular disapproval of his handling of the Vietnam War generally exceeded that of his overall performance in the presidency.

88. For a comparative table of presidential popular rating shifts related to major summit events, 1941–1981, see Plischke, "The President's Image as Diplomat in Chief," 557.

89. For a comparative table of eighteen surveys and individual assessments of presidents since 1940, see Elmer Plischke, "Rating Presidents and Diplomats in Chief," *Presidential Studies Quarterly* 15 (Fall 1985): Table 1, 730. President Johnson is not listed in the top eight to ten in four polls of experts, nor in the top ten listed by individuals, but he is listed as thirteenth among the strongest by Robert S. Hirschfield, *The Power of the Presidency: Concepts and Controversy* (Chicago: Aldine, 1973), 5–10. Nor is he regarded as among the "greats" in Thomas A. Bailey, *Presidential Greatness: The Image of the Man from George Washington to the Present* (New York: Appleton, Century, Crofts, 1966), which was published during the Johnson administration.

90. Gary M. Maranell, "The Evaluation of Presidents: An Extension of the Schlesinger Polls," *Journal of American History* 57 (June 1970): 104–113, which is summarized in Mary Klein, ed., *The Presidency: The Power and the Glory* (Minneapolis: Winston, 1973), 142–145. Also see Gary M. Maranell and Richard Dodder, "Political Orientation

and Evalution of Presidential Prestige: A Study of American Historians,'' *Social Science Quarterly* 51 (September 1970): 415–421.

91. Robert K. Murray and Tim H. Blessing, ''The Presidential Performance Study: A Progress Report,'' *Journal of American History* 70 (December 1983): 535–555; and *Chicago Tribune Magazine* (29 July 1982): 12–13, 40–41, 43. Comparative rankings are summarized in Murray and Blessing, Table 1, 540.

92. For an analysis of the Summit Hall of Fame, see Plischke, *Diplomat in Chief*, 483–485, and Plischke, ''Rating Presidents and Diplomats in Chief,'' 737–739.

93. For example, Eric Goldman reports that Lyndon Johnson's determination was that he ''was going to be a great president, a very great president, in all ways,'' and that he was driven ''to distinguish himself in international matters,'' *Tragedy of Lyndon Johnson*, 384.

94. Geyelin, *Lyndon B. Johnson and the World*, 232: also see Goldman, *Tragedy of Lyndon Johnson*, 384.

95. Johnson, *Vantage Point*, 565. He also declared that ''Doing what is right isn't the problem; it's knowing what is right;'' quoted in *New York Times*, 22 February 1975; also see commentary in Doris Kearns, *Lyndon Johnson and the American Dream* (New York: Harper & Row, 1976), 141–143, 215–216, 283–284; and Sidey, *A Very Personal Presidency*, 249–250, 262–264, 283. For Johnson's ''common law'' precepts for the functioning of the presidency—such as doing something for nothing is a violation of every law of practical politics, almost anybody or anything can be moved if you find the right levers, never slam doors even to the opposition, surprise is a fundamental weapon, and never lose or at least never be seen losing—see Geyelin, *Lyndon B. Johnson and the World*, 154–156. For discussion on Johnson and presidential greatness, see William V. Shannon, ''LBJ—Near Great,'' *Commonweal* (6 January 1967): 361–362; Harvey Cox, ''An Exchange of Views—LBJ Near Great,'' *Commonweal* (17 February 1967): 563–564; and William V. Shannon, ''Reply—LBJ Near Great,'' *Commonweal* (17 February 1967): 564–565.

V

VIETNAM

18

The Johnson Presidency and Foreign Policy: The Unresolved Conflict between National Interest and Collective Security

Kenneth W. Thompson

Historians and political observers, including some Johnson partisans, point to certain contradictions and tensions at the heart of his presidency. To some extent the tensions may be inherent in Lyndon Johnson himself. Shortly before he died, the late Justice Abe Fortas noted: "As you read the memoirs of people who were closely associated with Lyndon Johnson, you find many conflicting things. They probably all are true."[1] This may account for the fact that historians judging his presidency arrive at fundamentally opposing judgments. Robert Caro's biography paints Johnson as a leader tarnished by blemishes as man-sized as the president himself. Others find that few presidents have done more for the country, especially in education and civil rights. Yet for both sides in this historical controversy, the dark shadows of Vietnam hang over the Johnson presidency and confound every attempt at early objective evaluation.

Recognizing the controversies but sensing too the strengths of the Johnson presidency, the Miller Center from early 1984 through 1985 invited some of his close associates to visit us at the University of Virginia. We considered with them a broad range of issues concerning Lyndon Johnson: the man, his views on civil rights, relations with the press, the economy, foreign policy, and Vietnam. We invited assessments of his role as political leader and world statesman. In one way or the other, most of our discussions turned on the dilemmas of Johnson and Vietnam pointing up the tensions inherent in his thought and that of many Americans about politics, international politics, and collective security.

No problem in American foreign policy is more persistent than the discrepancies between the requirements of domestic and international politics. Lyndon Johnson was the master craftsman of congressional politics. No other postwar Senate leader quite matched his political skills. However, the failure of American political leaders from William Jennings Bryan through James F. Byrnes to Ronald

Reagan has been to translate know-how in domestic politics to international politics, and Lyndon Johnson was no exception.

Justice Fortas tried to explain one aspect of the problem as it related to Vietnam. He asked how was it that someone with such a clear understanding of power in American politics could misunderstand its role in Vietnam. Fortas wrote:

With the Vietnam situation, it was really sort of unbelievable to him that the application and demonstration of our nation's ever increasing and accelerating power would not cause the Communists to come to terms and to quit what they were doing and do what they ought to do instead of what they were doing.[2]

Through the skillful building of political coalitions, Johnson had organized power to achieve his ends in Congress. He had learned to use psychological pressures and the symbols of physical pressure in domestic politics. According to Fortas, Johnson in Vietnam "constantly felt that if a little more pressure were applied, the North Vietnamese and the communists would become convinced that they were not going to win, that they would come to terms."[3]

In summing up Johnson's predicament in the use of power, Fortas declared that "the real tragedy of President Johnson was the failure to realize that the usual results of the application of power, domestically in our own country, did not indicate that the application of an analogous force, internationally, would similarly result in changes being brought about."[4] The Johnson administration increased the American commitment to 550,000 men, but the circumstances of world politics and the conditions of revolutionary nationalism nullified the effort.

Another limitation that American politicians often bring to the conduct of foreign policy is the absence of a working theory of international relations. Running through the presentations at the Miller Center is a clear and unqualified statement that Johnson was not a conceptualizer but an operator. Some commentators consider his freedom from any fixed theoretical position a strength, for it gave him room to maneuver within changing political circumstances. He was not tied down by theoretical baggage. The majority leader of the Senate understood that "what the broad statement did . . . was to narrow the area for maneuver."[5] In Fortas' words, "He was a president who was much more comfortable with the use of a different kind of power than the power that resides in concepts and generalities."[6]

Yet even the most pragmatic leader is never wholly free of underlying assumptions, principles, and theories. In a lecture in the Rotunda, Harry McPherson reminded us that Lyndon Johnson came to the Congress in 1937, just a year before Munich. The prevailing wisdom in Washington for decades after Munich was that the West must avoid another Munich. "Stop the aggressor before the aggressor can climb all over you."[7] Columnists and political scientists described this philosophy as "the Munich syndrome," and in postwar American foreign policy it remained dominant until the reaction against policies in Vietnam. It is said when President Truman gathered a small group of advisers and decision makers in Blair House following the invasion of the South by North Korea, every man in the room was inspired by a single philosophy. Aggression must be turned back at its source if a larger and wider conflict comparable to World War II was to be prevented. The memory of Munich and its consequences was in everyone's mind the fateful night when American leaders decided to come to the aid of South Korea.

In seeking to understand the motivations for American foreign policy in Vietnam, several Miller Center speakers put forward another explanation. It was that the weight of the commitments of other presidents was such that no successor could disregard them. Justice Fortas believed that "Johnson pursued the Vietnam war because of Eisenhower's position and Kennedy's position."[8] That "inheritance affected his judgment." Fortas went on to say, "We are not talking about any sort of legal commitment or that he carried on because he was merely filling out President Kennedy's term. It was much more profound, much more subtle than that . . . [and] by the time he ran and was elected in his own right the die had been cast . . . and irreversible commitments had been made."[9] Once a superpower has entered a conflict and engaged its national prestige, all the forces that influence decision making push in the direction of staying the course.

American politics was of course another vital force that made retreat virtually impossible for the administration. As Harry McPherson saw it: "Given the nature of that war, and the nature of American politics, for Lyndon Johnson to have reversed John F. Kennedy's policy and pulled out of Vietnam early on was inconceivable. It would have been political suicide to let South Vietnam fall to either the NLF or to North Vietnam."[10] In Johnson's mind, turning back would have brought down not only his administration but unleashed critics to charge that "the Democrats had lost Vietnam."

In foreign policy, the primary question for those who resist aggression is "what is the threat?" "Who is the enemy?" There can be little doubt that the Johnson administration saw mainland China as the dominant threat. Harry McPherson asked himself essentially this question and responded:

He did not go in to save iron ore, oil, tin or a bunch of French Asian mandarins. He went in to try to prevent Asia from being rolled up by the Chinese Communists. That was what everybody thought was going to happen in 1963. We didn't realize that the Chinese and the Russians had already split badly, and that the Chinese and the North Vietnamese would later split so savagely.[11]

If the United States had not resisted "the yellow hoard," China would have overrun and captured all of Indochina.

When Lyndon Johnson became president, 16,500 troops were in Vietnam. Deterioration began to set in during the latter part of 1966. The Democrats lost some thirty-four seats in the congressional elections of that year. After that, everything was downhill. In Nicholas Katzenbach's phrase, "the great tragedy of Lyndon Johnson was Vietnam, which he didn't want. It wasn't within a field of . . . expertise that he felt he had."[12] He sought to buoy up his position by seeking a congressional resolution, but his associates told him that in the Tonkin Gulf resolution of the Congress he had all the authority he needed. Johnson thought "a great big vote . . . might discourage the North Vietnamese." Katzenbach considered this "a fairly naive judgment," but it illustrated once again the confusion of domestic and international politics.

Nicholas Katzenbach, when asked who applied specific pressures within the administration to escalate the war, replied, "the military primarily." It was not that they promised results for certain increases in troop strength. The restraints on them "drove them absolutely crazy." But Katzenbach's conclusion was that "it was mostly military pressure to increase" forces in Vietnam, and Johnson like Kennedy before him eventually responded to the pressure.

The focal point in the unresolved conflict in Johnson's foreign policy was the clash between collective security and U.S. interests in maintaining a balance of power and cooperating with the emerging nations in Asia. As majority leader in the Senate, Johnson delivered an address before the annual meeting of the American Political Science Association in which he pronounced that collective security must be the cornerstone of American foreign policy. The bedrock principle of collective security is that the nations must band together to oppose aggression wherever it occurs. One for all and all for one. The Southeast Asia Treaty created a regional collective security organization. Walt Rostow observed that "a failure to honor the treaty would weaken the credibility of U.S. commitments elsewhere; and the outcome of a U.S. withdrawal would not be peace but, sooner or later, a wider war."[13] Failure to come to the aid of any nation anywhere in the world would weaken security everywhere. Nineteen sixty-four had been a year of political instability "compounded by Indonesia's confrontation with Malaysia, its withdrawal from the United Nations, and alliance with the PRC."[14] In July 1965, regular units of the North Vietnam army entered Vietnam. President Johnson saw himself faced with the choice of accepting defeat in Southeast Asia or fighting. He chose to fight not only to protect South Vietnam but the other nations of Southeast Asia.

Walt Rostow offers reasons why Johnson's policy in Vietnam was burdened from the outset by nearly overwhelming obstacles to success. First, "Wilson and Franklin Roosevelt . . . confronted both urgent domestic problems and war, but the course of events permitted them to be dealt with in sequence; Johnson faced them together from his first day of responsibility."[15] Second, he believed he could carry the Congress with him on both of these fronts. As Thomas Corcoran observed, "He knows the players intimately. And he works at it day and night." But he underestimated the people's instincts, and therefore the Congress', for a prompt and decisive resolution of conflicts in which the United States was engaged. The people were not prepared to support a protracted and indecisive war with limited objectives and mounting casualties. Third, he was determined "to conduct the war in a way that minimized the chance that any U.S. action would lead to a large engagement with Chinese communist or Soviet

forces in a nuclear war.''[16] He failed, and perhaps was bound to fail, to communicate that objective to the American people. Both hawks and doves became
outspoken critics. Fourth, Rostow suggests a unique link between Johnson's
domestic policy and his policy in Asia. He concluded that Asians "wanted for
themselves and their children . . . what everyone else wanted: peace, higher living
standards, education, medical care. . . . A sense that he was standing in support
of an aspiring underdog of another race suffused Johnson's policy in Asia as
much as it did his civil rights and welfare policies at home."[17] As with Jimmy
Carter's equating universal human rights with American civil rights, Johnson
exaggerated the connections between American goals and those of Asian people.
Fifth, in Rostow's concluding observation:

There was yet another strand . . . which asserted itself throughout the advanced industrial
world: the reaction of a highly articulate margin of the middle class (inflated in numbers
by the post–1945 baby boom) not only against the war but also the material values of
the society . . . [and] viewing Johnson as the apotheosis of all they rejected.[18]

The drumbeat of these critics not only brought down Johnson but his would-be
successor, Hubert Humphrey.

American policy in Vietnam was of course influenced by concern over France.
Senator Fulbright explained, "We were afraid . . . after the war when Stalin was
still in power and the cold war was beginning that we had to support the French
or it would go Communist. . . . Vietnam was a side issue."[19] It was estimated
that the United States provided some $2 billion of money and arms to the French
to sustain them in Vietnam up to the time of their defeat in 1954 at Dien Bien
Phu. France was seen as part of the West's collective security system. During
this period, Ho Chi Minh, according to Senator Fulbright, wrote seven letters
to the U.S. government asking support on the grounds that Vietnam, like the
thirteen colonies, was a colony seeking national independence. Fulbright maintains that the letters were never answered. President Eisenhower was urged to
intervene with troops at Dien Bien Phu, but, because the British would not join
him, he did not go in, foreshadowing later arguments for the principles of
collective security.

Vietnam was also viewed by some as the scene of a clash of two collective
political movements and systems. From this standpoint, the Vietnam War was
"simply an expansion or extension of . . . the international Communist conspiracy
. . . inspired by the Russians using the Chinese as a puppet government. . . . If
we didn't stop it in Vietnam then we'd have to stop it at Los Angeles and San
Diego. . . . If Vietnam fell to communism, they would all fall."[20] In the clash
of two world-wide movements, the forms of resistance on both sides must be
collective and universal.

But collective security and resisting aggression everywhere in the world collide
with other powerful social and political forces. Senator Fulbright argued, "The

day of colonialism is over.'' Moreover, American policy around the world is more restricted that British policy in the nineteenth and twentieth centuries: ''They went in and took over the country and ran it.'' Even in Vietnam, the United States had no such plan or intention. We simply urged good government according to our views. Senator Fulbright concluded, ''That's much more difficult than taking it over and . . . running it yourself. We have a . . . time making our own government work, let alone do it in an alien culture that has little in common with ours.''[21]

It is always unfortunate in life and in politics when two competing goals or principles compete and conflict with one another without reconciliation. More unfortunate still is a situation in which the conflict remains permanently unresolved and is largely unrecognized by those who are involved. Beginning in the era of John Foster Dulles, some forty separate collective and bilateral security arrangements were fashioned by American foreign policy makers around the world. It was assumed that mobilizing the participants would be a relatively straightforward effort. Underestimated was the extent to which signatories would put their respective national interests first. While some half dozen nations carried most of the burden of fighting in Korea, South Vietnam and the United States were virtually alone in Vietnam.

Moreover, collective security was linked with the maintenance of the status quo. Movements for national independence, whether influenced or not by communist ideology, called for change in the status quo. The tides of history were dissolving the remnants of former colonial empires. If the United States were to align itself with history, it would be difficult to resist change wherever it occurred.

Thus, the national interest required the United States to identify its policies with the forces of change in Asia while collective security demanded pursuit of precisely the opposite goal. Historically, the one way of bringing the two objectives into harmony has been through persistent and skillful diplomacy directed to peaceful change. Either American foreign policy was found wanting in not organizing its priorities to place accommodation above strict preservation of the status quo or it sought peaceful change but failed because of the intractable position of its communist adversary. If the latter, the question that Harry McPherson and others addressed at the Miller Center arises once again. Who was the adversary and what was the threat? Apparently, policy makers in the Johnson administration saw China as the threat and Ho Chi Minh as a mere instrument of the Chinese. McPherson and others acknowledge the mistaken nature of this view and their judgment is confirmed by the subsequent struggle between China and Vietnam.

The question then that must be asked is whether this mistaken judgment was inspired by the unresolved conflict between collective security and the national interest in the minds of American leaders. Were the commitments made to collective security, that is, to resistance to change everywhere in the world, an obstacle to any clear-eyed evaluation of the national interest? Were considerations of the national interest brushed aside on grounds that conflicts or changes on the periphery of the world balance of power would move inescapably to the center unless they were opposed at the source? Was the "newfangled view" of foreign policy that placed international security above national interest an invitation to make minor wars or civil wars the direct interest of the superpowers and therefore a cause of war for them?

In the nineteenth century, before the dawn of the era of collective security, conflicts in Asia and Africa occurred in areas the great powers considered "empty spaces." The dominance of one power or the other, whether Germany, France, or Britain, was determined by negotiation and treaties. War when it broke out was localized and limited both in duration and number of participants. Conflicts broke out, the great powers drew a circle around the combatants and the exit from war was facilitated by sphere of influence arrangements based on assessments of national interest.

No such national interest assessments were made for Vietnam. No American policy maker declared unequivocally that Vietnam was a clear and unambiguous American national interest. The primacy of the collective security argument was assumed in all that was said about falling dominoes. In a brave new world with universal interests, nations were no longer seen as having to put national interest first.

What is tragic about Vietnam, then, is that the tensions and the conflicts between universal collective security and national interests remained unresolved. In fact, no one assumed such a resolution was required. Thus, the decision makers found themselves drawn ever more deeply into a conflict the rationale for which could not be explained or clarified for the American people. Collective security in the end became a unilateral American policy that was substituted for the national interest. Because nations continued to act on their national interests, broadly conceived, such a policy was doomed from the start. Neither the American public at home nor friends abroad were willing or able to do what universal collective security required.

The final aspect of the tragedy is that good and decent men with a vision of a better world were caught up in the conflict and eventually destroyed. They deserved better and so did the nation as a whole, which sought valiantly to build a security system that may have been ahead of its time.

NOTES

1. Abe Fortas, "The LBJ Presidency," a forum held at the White Burkett Miller Center of Public Affairs at the University of Virginia, 1 November 1981.

2. Ibid.

3. Ibid.

4. Ibid.

5. Ibid.

6. Ibid.

7. Harry McPherson, "The Johnson Presidency," a lecture held in the Dome Room of the Rotunda at the University of Virginia, 1 November 1985.

8. Fortas, "The LBJ Presidency."

9. Ibid.

10. McPherson, "The Johnson Presidency."

11. Ibid.

12. Nicholas Katzenbach, "Johnson and Foreign Policy," a Forum held at the White Burkett Miller Center of Public Affairs at the University of Virginia, 5 March 1984.

13. Walt Rostow, "Lyndon B. Johnson and Vietnam" (From a paper made available to the Miller Center).

14. Ibid.

15. Ibid.

16. Ibid.

17. Ibid.

18. Ibid.

19. Senator William J. Fulbright, "The Johnson Presidency and Vietnam," a Forum held at the White Burkett Miller Center of Public Affairs at the University of Virginia, 1 November 1984.

20. Ibid.

21. Ibid.

19

Tonkin Gulf Revisited: Vietnam, Military Mirage, and Political Reality in 1964

William F. Levantrosser

Those familiar with the U.S. naval incidents in the Gulf of Tonkin on 4 August 1964 and the subsequent controversy surrounding them are probably looking for some new evidence to clarify what has already been written and researched. Some may be hoping for greater confirmation that the attack on U.S. ships positively occurred while others may wish for a complete rebuttal of evidence that it did occur. Unfortunately, this chapter will disappoint both groups. This is not to say that it is impossible to provide additional perspectives on the incidents and the attendant circumstances. I hope this chapter contributes to that end.

The Southeast Asia resolution turned out to be a very significant step for enlarging U.S. participation in the Vietnam War. Although it is likely that the U.S. role would have eventually been expanded, the resolution gave President Johnson more secure political footing for deploying additional military forces in Southeast Asia and a better standing with the American electorate as he was campaigning for the presidency in his own right. However, since that time suspicions have been raised about the actual existence of a naval skirmish that triggered the final massive retaliatory air strike on North Vietnam by U.S. aircraft and the passage of a joint congressional resolution supporting whatever future action the president might think necessary and appropriate to meet the threats posed by North Vietnamese military actions. The alleged attack by North Vietnamese boats on American ships in the Gulf of Tonkin on 4 August 1964, has been a center of controversy since it affected the course of U.S. policy in Vietnam in such an important way and since it raised questions about the decision-making process for foreign policy at the highest levels of government.

This study will attempt to examine the evidence systematically and to provide a thorough explanation of the 4 August incident in the Gulf of Tonkin. While there have been previous attempts to assess this situation, my investigation seeks to determine whether more recent evidence on the matter will bring about a clearer and more complete understanding than has been possible heretofore.[1] Another objective of this research effort is to ascertain whether an understanding of the Tonkin Gulf episodes can provide guidelines for handling current and future conflict situations more effectively in terms of national interest. Presidential military decisions, political integrity, and the responsibility for providing information to the public in a democratic state are all vital ingredients of this analysis.

HOW THE UNITED STATES GOT INTO VIETNAM

As far back as the early 1900s, U.S. policy in the Far East included the objectives of maintaining access to trade in Asia and preventing any single power from dominating the region. Southeast Asia was a critical part of that region, so Japan's move into Indochina brought efforts by President Franklin Roosevelt to counter that push. Following World War II, President Truman made a commitment to support the French in their effort to reclaim control of Indochina. When the French effort failed, President Eisenhower pledged support for the establishment of a popular regime in Vietnam as determined by the outcome of a referendum authorized under the Geneva Accord of 1954. As it became apparent that the outcome of an election would be a communist government for all of Vietnam, the United States sought other alternatives. Gradually the United States increased its aid to South Vietnam in an effort to stabilize that government and strengthen its resistance to being taken over by the forces of Ho Chi Minh. By the time John F. Kennedy came into office, the United States was making advisers available to train and guide South Vietnamese Army units against guerrilla forces aided by North Vietnam.[2] Shortly before Kennedy's assassination a new government took over in the South in a coup resulting in the death of President Diem. During the early months of the Johnson administration the fortunes of the new government in South Vietnam began to decline as regular North Vietnamese units were introduced there.[3] In the first half of 1964 American officials discussed extensively a larger role for the United States in Vietnam.[4]

At that time, President Johnson also had to consider the dimensions of involvement in Vietnam as he developed his campaign strategy for the election of 1964.[5] Some observers feel that presidential election years in the United States are heavy on posturing but cautious on acting in foreign affairs and that this habitual stance might tempt adversaries of the United States to probe aggressively for gains on the assumption that the United States will not actually oppose military ventures of other countries at that time.[6] The Republicans played on this theme perhaps too strongly and the Democrats countered by attempting to portray Mr. Goldwater as trigger-happy, especially with nuclear weapons. President Johnson knew that a show of firmness in the Vietnamese setting through a prompt retaliatory strike would help allay any voter concerns on this issue.

THE CURTAIN GOES UP ON THE TONKIN GULF
INCIDENTS

Nineteen sixty-four was a year of transition in many ways for leaders dealing with policy in Vietnam. As President Johnson tightened his hold on the reins of power, three different governments in three months took the stage in South Vietnam. Since each South Vietnamese military commander also had control of the government in his area of operation, a change at the top in Saigon brought consequent changes in area commanders and in local governments as well. The resulting political turbulence undermined the people's confidence in their government while it abetted Vietcong guerrilla efforts.[7] On the U.S. side General Maxwell Taylor became ambassador to Vietnam, General William Westmoreland became head of the Military Assistance Command in Vietnam, Admiral U.S. Grant Sharp moved to the position of commander in chief Pacific, and Admiral Thomas Moorer took over as commander in chief of the Pacific Fleet under Admiral Sharp. If we include a newly installed president, we have an almost entirely new set of top leaders, including the government of South Vietnam in 1964.

Following his trip to Vietnam in March 1964, Secretary of Defense McNamara recommended reform in the South Vietnamese government, stepped-up aid, and a contingency program to initiate overt military pressure against North Vietnam.[8] Nguyen Khanh, the newest South Vietnamese leader, stressed the need for increased U.S. support, including direct action against North Vietnam to turn around the deteriorating situation.[9] Two tactical plans that eventually emerged are of particular concern for this analysis. The first was Operation Alpha–34, consisting of airdrops of propaganda leaflets and supplies for supporters in the North as well as raids by South Vietnamese patrol boats against the North Vietnamese coast. These fast patrol craft supplied by the United States and manned by Vietnamese crews concentrated on such critical targets as radar installations and communications facilities in addition to discouraging infiltration into South Vietnam by water.[10] Such a raid was conducted on the night of 30 July.[11] The second plan was an operation conducted entirely by the U.S. Navy, referred to as the DeSoto Patrol. Ostensibly, it was to operate in international waters to observe junk traffic and naval activity as well as to collect hydrographic data, but the patrols also collected intelligence concerning North Vietnamese electronic installations.[12] The destroyer USS Maddox entered the Gulf of Tonkin and was engaged in such a patrol on 2 August when it was attacked by three North Vietnamese PT boats firing torpedoes and machine guns.[13] Two PT boats ended up dead in the water and a third was damaged. The only damage sustained by the Maddox was a bullet hole in the after-gun director.

In view of the danger, the patrol commander, Captain John Herrick, requested a change in orders to suspend patrol activity.[14] The response from higher headquarters, however, not only reaffirmed the patrol's mission but directed patrol movements so as to arouse a greater response from North Vietnamese installations and register them for intelligence purposes.[15] In addition, the destroyer *Turner Joy* was directed to report to the *Maddox* for the continuation of the mission. During the next day personnel on the two destroyers were briefed on possible action and medical personnel on the *Maddox* distributed morphine styrettes to each crew member for use if wounded to ease the pain until medical attention was available. With many small Vietnamese junks in the vicinity of the patrol activity those on board the two destroyers were understandably edgy about being hit by a patrol boat bursting out of a group of junks.[16]

Finally, on the dark evening of 4 August the DeSoto Patrol began reporting action by two Swatows (boats without torpedoes) and a PT boat against the *Maddox* and the *Turner Joy*. For several hours the two ships weaved through the water in evasive tactics against reported torpedo wakes as they fired at suspected targets.[17] The air cover called to the scene also fired at suspected targets, but the planes were unable to confirm any torpedo sightings.[18] These reports, coming only two days after a confirmed attack on the *Maddox*, apparently convinced President Johnson that strong action had to be taken.[19] The entire machinery was then set in motion for planning a retaliatory strike and for the introduction of a resolution before Congress to support whatever additional action the president might deem necessary within the immediate time frame of the current combat actions.[20]

As these plans were being developed, Secretary of Defense McNamara was attempting to coordinate the initiation of the retaliatory strikes with a public announcement by President Johnson so as not to give any advance notice to North Vietnamese defenses and yet to make the first announcement of the retaliation. In the course of these efforts McNamara at the same time sought to confirm in phone conversations with Admiral Sharp that the attacks against the two American destroyers had in fact taken place.[21] The National Security Council met for the second time that day and congressional leaders were briefed on the situation by the president and his aides in the White House. As it turned out, the planes had not hit any targets before the president's announcement took place.[22] However, the retaliatory strikes were completed and the United States had entered another phase of the Vietnam War.

WHAT REALLY HAPPENED ON 4 AUGUST?

The credibility of early reports from the scene of action in the Gulf of Tonkin and the credibility of the interpretations of those reports at the highest level of government have been eroded to some degree by subsequent investigations and analyses. The atmosphere on board the two destroyers as well as the thinking at the highest military and civilian positions in the U.S. government prepared the participants to see and accept what they came to expect in the action at sea on a dark night. On both ships there were many cues anticipating an engagement. One destroyer had been attacked two days before and each individual received instructions on how to handle a similar situation the next time, which turned out to be the very next day. Continuation of the patrol mission would seem to place the destroyers in a very precarious position. Naval commanders at the headquarters of the Seventh Fleet, the Pacific Fleet, and the Pacific Command were strongly in favor of pressing the war to North Vietnam and certainly demonstrating their determination to maintain a navy presence in international waters adjoining an enemy of an ally.[23] To these ingredients one must add a very critical factor—the actual conditions at sea of limited visibility at night.[24] By American admission, the destroyers had challenged the electronic surveillance facilities of North Vietnam earlier in the day.[25] Each of these conditions cumulatively added up to a situation in which errors in perception and judgment could occur easily.[26]

Many of the immediate observations by naval personnel have been placed in doubt by the subsequent review of official communications connected to the episodes in the Gulf of Tonkin on 4 August. The task group commander, after acknowledging that there could not have been as many torpedoes fired as had been earlier reported, sent a message requesting evaluation before any further action was taken because the previous reports sent out by him were then thought to be in error.[27] Although there are still eyewitness accounts on record testifying to various sightings, these claims have not been subject to thorough public review and so they still stand.[28] The commander of aircraft flying cover over the area of action filed a negative report unable to confirm any of the action suggested by the early reports from the two destroyers.[29] It was acknowledged by senior naval officers that sonarmen may err on the side of being overly cautious in announcing torpedo noises when none may exist and are also actually misled by sounds reflected off the rudder from the propeller when the ship is involved in weaving action as the *Maddox* and the *Turner Joy* were in trying to evade what were perceived as hostile indications on the sonar.[30] Despite all the reported activity of over two hours duration, there was no damage to the destroyers, there were no casualties outside of several cases of heat exhaustion on the *Maddox*, and no debris was observed in the following days' aerial reconnaissance.[31]

The president's attitude at this point is also extremely important. From several close-at-hand observers we get a picture of a president ready for decisive, dramatic action.[32] Having shown restraint in response to the attack on the *Maddox* on 2 August and perhaps sensing potential disappointment among the public in addition to some criticism from the Republican candidate for president for failing to act, President Johnson saw a clear opportunity to accomplish several objectives with one decision.[33] In fact, aides sensed that the machinery was set in motion for a retaliatory strike almost as soon as the first reports reached the White House.[34] So the process became primarily one of determining the type of response and its orchestration rather than whether to respond. The targets were being considered long before the actual decision to strike back was made and this seemed to be more than mere contingency planning.[35]

One other crucial piece of evidence cited by Secretary of Defense McNamara was the series of radio intercepts of North Vietnamese communications purporting to show orders from North Vietnamese officers to attack the destroyers.[36]

These intercepts have never been made public, presumably because their reve-
lation would compromise the capability of U.S. intelligence operations. However, the cables have been examined by two former government officials and
were found to refer to some other engagement, probably to the one on 2 August,
but definitely *not* to the 4 August incident.[37] (Hereafter the 4 August incident
will be referred to as TG–2.) What we are left with then is a group of observations,
purporting to give proof of a naval battle that could not be examined entirely
by someone outside of government and the judgments of officials and military
officers based on these observations.[38] We are left with the threat of an ambush
blown into a two-hour naval engagement without any damage to ships or any
casualties. We cannot prove that there was not some threatening presence evoking
such extensive responses at the scene of activity but the evidence of the extent
of the engagement alleged to have occurred has been considerably weakened
over time.

The type of scenario likely to carry the most credence because it fits in with
the totality of evidence offered can then be only speculative. Since the DeSoto
Patrol continued to challenge the electronic installations of North Vietnam after
the 2 August engagement, at the very least, and since these actions probably
suggested other kinds of threats of action to them, the North Vietnamese continued to track the *Maddox* after the 2 August attack perhaps hoping to strike a
dramatic blow, but in any case to use the action for their own morale purposes.
These North Vietnamese craft approached the *Maddox* in the dark of night but
realized at the last moment they would be countered by not one but two U.S.
destroyers. They probably decided to retire and retreated just as the two destroyers
were working themselves into a frenzy weaving frantically trying to avoid suspected hostile action. Instead the U.S. ships were simply generating increased
sounds of suspected torpedo movements entirely by their own zig-zag
maneuvering.

WHAT CAN BE CRITICIZED IN U.S. ACTIONS?

Central to the American position on TG–2 was the claim that U.S. ships were
simply exercising their right to be on the high seas. (After all, the Soviets ply
the U.S. coastline continually keeping tabs on U.S. ships and installations.) The
accepted interpretation of international law in such cases would justify the American claim. However, within the context of TG–2 the issue of provocation
arises.[39] Now if one views the actions of the U.S. ships in this context, that
claim might not look the same to North Vietnam. Consider that the South
Vietnamese in the Alpha–34 maritime operations had recently attacked two off-
shore islands shortly before *Maddox* began its DeSoto Patrol mission.[40] Consider
that on 4 August the two destroyers had moved directly toward those islands on
their patrol mission.[41] Would it be reasonable for the North Vietnamese to make
some connection between the South Vietnamese boat attacks and the movement
of U.S. Navy destroyers, even with several days intervening? At the same time,

General Khanh was asking for aid to carry the war to the North. At the very least, the North Vietnamese had some cause for concern. The explanation by the United States for the DeSoto Patrol actions was not completely forthcoming in its insistence that by simply exercising its right of free passage on the high seas it was in no way being provocative.

What about the nature of the United States retaliatory strike and some kind of doctrine of proportionality? As the United States made plans for a retaliatory strike against North Vietnam, it should be repeated that as a result of TG–2 there were no American casualties and there was no damage to either destroyer or to covering aircraft. In the first engagement on 2 August only one bullet hit the *Maddox* and again there were no casualties or damage to U.S. aircraft.[42] Up to this point in the overall conflict American aircraft had not bombed North Vietnam. The American response in retaliation for what has to be assumed was the cumulative effect of two incidents on U.S. ships was to unleash fifty-nine bombing planes from two aircraft carriers. Estimates of the damage from the retaliatory strikes on 5 August also bear on the consideration of proportionality. Four patrol boat bases were hit and about twenty-five boats were damaged or destroyed, amounting to about half of the North Vietnamese high-speed patrol boats. In addition, the oil depot containing 10 percent of the petroleum capacity of North Vietnam was considered 90 percent destroyed.[43] Two U.S. planes were lost as one pilot died and the other was taken prisoner.[44]

The United States had significantly expanded the scope of the conflict and a new phase of the Vietnamese struggle had begun. If this strike is related strictly to the two incidents in the Gulf of Tonkin, it would seem the United States had exceeded what most observers would say was the doctrine of proportionality. Perhaps other objectives were satisfied but they were not mentioned by the United States.

Not only did TG–2 trigger off a massive retaliatory air strike against North Vietnam but it generated support for a congressional resolution authorizing President Johnson to take whatever action he deemed appropriate against threats to U.S. interests in Southeast Asia.[45] The first thing to mention in this regard is that the full story as known by the administration at that time was not given to Congress.[46] Constitutionally, the president already had authority as commander in chief to take the retaliatory action, so the congressional resolution was requested only to demonstrate national unity of purpose. It is not clear from the testimony in the debate how far and for how long presidential action was being endorsed.[47] It is true that some planning had taken place within the administration as early as June to develop the wording and substance of such a resolution if, and when, the United States contemplated an expansion of the conflict.[48] It is also fair to say that this contingency planning was not specifically designed to accompany a North Vietnamese reaction to some prearranged U.S. stimulus. Most observers would probably agree with Secretary of Defense McNamara and others on this point.[49] Since 1964 it has also become quite clear that one of the chief actors in gaining support for the resolution at the time was the chairman of the Senate Foreign Relations Committee and then a close friend of the president, Senator J. W. Fulbright. He had made it clear that at the very least he would have called for extended examination of the resolution had he been briefed on all the facts available to the administration at that time.[50] The chief opponent of the resolution at the time was Senator Wayne Morse, one of two in the entire Congress voting against the resolution, whose skepticism at the time turned out to have considerable merit in the light of later investigations.[51]

Perhaps Congress does have to shoulder some responsibility here because, even if the administration did not share all of its information, most members of Congress did not insist on asking the hard questions. It would have been possible to use more limiting terms in the resolution without clouding the matter of U.S. determination in foreign policy in a presidential election year. Democrats, probably eager to give the president a boost in the election campaign and knowing who the Republican opponent would be, were unusually reserved and even pliant considering later objections raised by some of them. Subsequent action by Congress undoubtedly took TG–2 into account as the nation moved into the 1970s with a new president. The War Powers Act of 1973 reflected this concern for similar circumstances in the future.[52] It probably has had some moderating effect on presidents in foreign policy endeavors although its constitutionality remains to be tested.

Here there are some judgments to be made about the nature of presidential leadership, political integrity, and the decision-making process insofar as the Johnson administration is concerned. From one point of view President Johnson could be credited with a masterful political stroke, as he orchestrated a response to domestic and foreign stimuli. He removed the Vietnam issue from the election while boosting his own political fortunes. In the short run, he gave a major lift to the troubled government of South Vietnam. He capitalized on events that presented golden opportunities with a superb sense of timing. In the longer run, however, matters of integrity and public trust in a democratic society arise. Even granting that the president acted in good faith, he failed to disclose completely the information needed by Congress. This later became part of the so-called credibility gap for the Johnson administration and it probably led to the high level of cynicism displayed by the public in its view of national political leadership.[53] Beyond this fault lies the public acknowledgment of error when it is discovered. This the Johnson administration refused to do when faced with evidence that revealed mistaken perceptions accepted as the basis for launching a retaliatory attack.[54] One lesson to be gained from this situation is that a democratic nation must be entirely clear about why it is taking military action if it is to succeed. As it turned out Vietnam became a tragedy not only for the Johnson administration but for the nation as a whole. The answer might have been for the president to take the matter of increasing the commitment to South Vietnam in 1965 to Congress and the country. In a way TG–2 started President Johnson on an easy road toward war without facing the problem of public debate.

The Tonkin Gulf incidents of early August 1964 gave President Johnson an opportunity to enlarge the Vietnam conflict, boost his presidential election campaign, and gain support from Congress for his actions in the future. Although President Johnson did not intend to stage developments as they finally unfolded, his decision did find the draft of a congressional resolution already drawn up, his action did benefit himself politically, his decision did aid the unsettled South Vietnamese government, and his action did push the United States in the direction he probably intended for it at a later date. President Johnson did fail to provide adequate information to Congress for considering the Southeast Asia resolution and he did fail to acknowledge errors when contrary evidence was unearthed. The Gulf of Tonkin decisions by the Johnson administration formed the beginning of a pattern of government disclosures leading to a credibility gap between the claims of the administration on Vietnam and reality. The United States did provoke the North Vietnamese government and did respond to its reaction in a disproportionately heavy retaliatory strike.

What are the consequences then of the heritage of the Tonkin Gulf incidents for future decisions in American foreign policy? One might hope that Congress and the American people will exercise a healthy degree of skepticism regarding presidential military decisions and that the process of making those decisions will be thorough and systematic. Events that might seem of little consequence at the time they happen can take on watershed significance in retrospect. For the most part military crisis decisions rarely turn out to require such quick action in developing a policy to meet them. The contest is not lost because a decision takes a week or two rather than an hour or two. If anything is gained from the Tonkin Gulf experience, it is that the president has to be careful in developing his perceptions of reality and that he has to acknowledge fully his biases so that the decision-making process merits public support. In this study the Johnson presidency was the historical example.

NOTES

1. The three most detailed accounts appear in Joseph C. Goulden, *Truth Is the First Casualty: The Gulf of Tonkin Affair—Illusion and Reality* (New York: Rand McNally, 1969); Anthony Austin, *The President's War* (New York: J. B. Lippincott, 1971); and Eugene G. Windchy, *Tonkin Gulf* (Garden City, N.Y.: Doubleday, 1971). Each comes close to, but not quite, claiming no attack occurred on 4 August. Gerald Kurland, *The Gulf of Tonkin Incidents* (Charlotteville, N.Y.: SamHar Press, 1975) is shorter but even closer to claiming no attack. The most recent journalistic analysis by Robert Scheer in the *Los Angeles Times* commemorating the tenth anniversary of the fall of Saigon focuses in part on the Gulf of Tonkin incidents and flatly denies the attack on 4 August ever occurred. See Robert Scheer, "Tonkin—Dubious Premise for a War," *Los Angeles Times*, 29 April 1985, 17. Samuel E. Halpern, *West Pac '64* (Boston: Branden Press, 1975) is the account of the medical officer on the *Maddox* on 4 August and he is not sure whether there was an attack on the *Maddox*. The most detailed recent account can be found in William Conrad Gibbons, *The U.S. Government and the Vietnam War: Executive and Legislative and Relationships, Part II, 1961–64* (December 1984), Chapter 5, prepared

for the U.S. Senate Committee on Foreign Relations, 98th Cong., 2d Sess., Prt. 98–185, Part 2 (Washington, D.C.: U.S. Government Printing Office, 1985).

2. "Legal Questions and Answers on the Gulf on Tonkin," Country File, Vietnam, National Security File 3A (1), Box 76 LBJ Library. Since 1961 the United States considered the South Vietnamese government justified in seeking military assistance at levels above the Geneva Accord of 1954. The Foreign Assistance Act of 1961 and the Mutual Defense Assistance Agreement with Vietnam are cited by the United States as the basis for giving aid.

3. Transcript, William P. Bundy Oral History, 29 May 1969, by Paige E. Mulhollan, 8–9, LBJ Library. Bundy claims regular North Vietnamese units came into South Vietnam as early as June 1964, although his predecessor, Roger Hilsman, contended they came in only after the U.S. bombing of North Vietnam following the Tonkin Gulf incidents.

4. Memo from Secretary of Defense 17 March 1964, vol. 1, Tab 5, "U.S. Policy Toward Vietnam," National Security File, National Security Council Meetings, Box 1, LBJ Library. Confirmed in William P. Bundy Oral History, 21–23. Also see Bill Berman, "Fulbright and Johnson: Before and After the Gulf of Tonkin Affair," Paper delivered to the Organization of American Historians in Detroit, 1981, 6, LBJ Library.

5. McGeorge Bundy, interview with author, New York, 17 October 1985.

6. Walt W. Rostow, interview with author, Austin, Texas, 5 July 1985.

7. Transcript, Admiral U.S. Grant Sharp Oral History, 13 December 1969, by Etta Belle Kitchen, 192, LBJ Library. Also reviewed in Memo to Rostow, 8 November 1968, from Marshall Wright and Sven F. Kraemer, "Presidential Decisions: The Gulf of Tonkin Attacks of August, 1964," National Security Council History, National Security File, Box 39, LBJ Library.

8. National Security Action Memorandum 288, approved 17 March 1964, and reviewed in Memo to Rostow, 8 November 1968; LBJ Library.

9. Memos to the President, McGeorge Bundy, June 1964 to February 1965, "Review of Secretary of State Rusk's Talk with General Khanh," Aides Files, National Security File, Box 15, LBJ Library.

10. Transcript, William P. Bundy Oral History Interview, 29 May 1969, 19. Bundy assigns less importance to the Alpha–34 raids. Gibbons describes the "303 Committee" organization responsible for U.S. covert operations and established by the NSAM of 2 June 1964, 283. This group, in turn, delegated the operational responsibility for Alpha–34 operations and the DeSoto patrols to the joint chiefs of staff. Secretary of Defense Robert McNamara refers to the connecting links in his testimony before the Senate Foreign Relations Committee on 20 February 1968, 72. Also mentioned in Admiral Sharp's Oral History, 13 December 1969, 207.

11. Central Intelligence Agency Memo to McGeorge Bundy, 6 August 1964, Country File, Southeast Asia, vol. 2, July-November 1964, National Security File, LBJ Library.

12. Transcript, Cyrus Vance Oral History, March 1970, by Paige E. Mulhollan, 2, LBJ Library.

13. "Chronology of Events Aug. 4–5," Country File, Vietnam, Gulf of Tonkin (Misc.) 1964, National Security File, Box 227, 1, LBJ Library.

14. Ibid., 2.

15. Transcript, Admiral Thomas H. Moorer Oral History, 8 August 1969, by Dorothy Pierce McSweeny, 10, LBJ Library.

16. Halpern, *West Pac*, 72–73.

17. "Chronology of Events Aug. 4–5," 3.

18. Memo, Bromley Smith to Walt Rostow, 27 January 1968, "Incidents in the Gulf of Tonkin August, 1964," Meeting Notes File, National Security File, Box 1, 2, LBJ Library.

19. Author's interview with McGeorge Bundy. Also Memo, Walter Jenkins, "Leadership Meeting," 4 August 1964, National Security Council Meeting File, National Security File, vol. 3, Tab 19, Box 38, LBJ Library, in which President Johnson is quoted as saying "We can tuck our tails and run, but if we do the countries will feel all they have to do is to scare us is to shoot the American flag. The question is how do we retaliate?" In addition, see transcript, General Earle Wheeler Oral History Interview, 21 August 1969, by Dorothy Pierce McSweeny, 22, LBJ Library.

20. Author's interview with McGeorge Bundy.

21. "Chronology of Events Aug. 4–5," 3.

22. Memo, Lt. Com. Ralph G. Spencer to Mr. Levinson, 25 August 1964, "Gulf of Tonkin," Chronologies, Archives Reference File, Gulf of Tonkin, LBJ Library.

23. Admiral Sharp Oral History, 12 December 1969, 106 and Admiral Moorer Oral History, 8 August 1969, 10.

24. Final Sitrep of DeSoto Patrol, 042158 Z, par. 5, Country File, Vietnam, Gulf of Tonkin (Misc.) 1964, National Security File, Box 228, LBJ Library.

25. Central Intelligence Agency Memo, 6 August 1964, 6.

26. Halpern, *West Pac*, 221.

27. Captain Herrick, Des. Div. on *Maddox* to CINCPACFLT, 01:27 EDT, Document #53, Cables and Messages, Gulf of Tonkin, Archives Reference File, LBJ Library.

28. Cable from CTG 72.1 to CINCPACFLT, 071051 Z and cable from CINCPACFLT and CINCPAC 071101 Z in Cables and Messages, Gulf of Tonkin, Archives Reference File, LBJ Library.

29. DeSoto Patrol Sitrep, Document #64, Gulf of Tonkin, Calls and Messages, Archives Reference Files. Also see Jim Sybil Stockdale, *In Love and War: The Story of a Family's Ordeal and Sacrifice During the Vietnam Years* (New York: Harper & Row, 1984), 22–23. Admiral Stockdale was the senior officer in the group of prisoners of war held by North Vietnam who organized the resistance against efforts to gain information from the prisoners through torture. He received the Congressional Medal of Honor for his heroism.

30. Final Sitrep of DeSoto Patrol, 042158 Z, par 4. Admiral Sharp, CINCPAC, tends to confirm the difficulties faced by sonarmen in his Oral History, 10 January 1970, 217. David Halberstam, *The Best and the Brightest* (New York: Random House, 1969), 414, quotes President Johnson as saying eight months after the 4 August incident, "For all I know, our Navy was hooting at whales out there."

31. Sitrep DeSoto Patrol, CTF 77 for August, 5,050514 Z, Country File, Vietnam, Operation Pierce Arrow, 5 August 1965, Box 228, LBJ Library. A search of the combat area showed no debris. Aerial reconnaissance came up with the same negative findings. This is confirmed in Memo for McGeorge Bundy, "Detailed Chronology of Events," Country File, Vietnam, 3A (3),Box 76, LBJ Library.

32. Author's interview with McGeorge Bundy. Mr. Bundy said he felt President Johnson knew what he wanted to do when he received the first reports of the 4 August incident. Also in Walter Jenkins' Memo "Leadership Meeting." Another close observer was the president's military aide, Major General Chester V. Clifton, who confirmed these perceptions in an interview with the author, Washington, D.C., 11 July 1985.

33. William P. Bundy Oral History, 29 May 1969, 28, LBJ Library. Also see Richard

A. Cherwitz, "The Need for Reconciliation: A Rhetorical Interpretation of the Gulf of Tonkin Crisis," Paper presented at the Central States Speech Association convention, St.Louis, Mo., 6 April 1970, LBJ Library.

34. Message from CINCPAC to JCS 041257 EDT, Cables and Messages, Document #52, Gulf of Tonkin, Archives Reference Files, LBJ Library. This was a request for authority to conduct punitive U.S. air strikes as soon as possible in stages of increasing severity for specific targets.

35. Even before suggestions from the field came in, the Pentagon was also researching targets. See "Chronologies," 041024 EDT.

36. Senate Committee on Foreign Relations, *The Gulf of Tonkin the 1964 Incidents*, 90th Cong., 2d Sess., hearing with Robert McNamara on 20 February 1968, 9, 17.

37. William Rust, "The 'Phantom Battle' That Led to War: Can It Happen Again?" *U.S. News and World Report*, 23 July 1984, 64. Louis Tondella, former deputy director of the National Security Agency, and Ray Cline, former deputy director of the Central Intelligence Agency, have concluded that the radio intercepts referred to by the Secretary of Defense McNamara could not have been connected with the 4 August incident. Mr. Cline later confirmed his view in an interview with the author, Washington, D.C., 11 July 1985.

38. The likelihood of being able to dispel the remaining evidence seems rather dim, particularly since public examination of the radio intercepts will probably never occur.

39. In Michael Charlton and Anthony Moncrief, *Many Reasons Why: The American Involvement in Vietnam* (New York: Hill and Wang, 1978), 108. George Ball, deputy secretary of state at the time, suggests that provocation was one goal of the DeSoto Patrol, "a tactical opportunity they were looking for." Senator Wayne Morse also introduced this element into congressional debate on the Southeast Asia Resolution on 5 August. See 5 August 1964, *Congressional Record*, 88th Cong., 2d Sess., 18135. For the other side of the argument see General Wheeler Oral History, Interview, 23. The administration position is also discussed in a memo to McGeorge Bundy from the State Department, 7 August 1964, National Security Council History File, Tab 19, National Security File, Box 38, LBJ Library.

40. Austin, *The President's War*, 67–68 and Goulden, *Truth Is the First Casualty*, 48. An unnamed source in the Pentagon had phoned Senator Morse to indicate the *Maddox* was an intelligence ship associated with the Alpha–34 raids carried out by South Vietnamese boats.

41. Admiral Sharp Oral History, 205. After the 2 August attack the commander of the DeSoto Patrol recommended discontinuation of the mission but instead he was directed to continue so as to stimulate North Vietnamese electronic signals to gain intelligence and to show the U.S. determination to maintain its freedom of movement in international waters.

42. Secretary of Defense McNamara held this bullet up for inspection when he appeared before the Senate Foreign Relations Committee on 20 February 1968, Hearing, 102.

43. CIA Memo 6 August 1964, has the most concise record of damage estimates.

44. The remains of the pilot who was the first to crash in North Vietnam twenty-one years ago on this retaliatory strike of 5 August have just recently been positively identified from among the twenty-six sets of remains returned to the United States by the North Vietnamese on 14 August 1985. The story from AP in Washington appeared in the *San Antonio Light*, "U.S., Laos Strike Accord on Searching for MIAs," 9 November 1985, A–1, A–24.

45. Public Law 88–408.

46. Among others, Senators Frank Church and Ernest Gruening subscribed to this point of view in their oral histories, the relevant transcripts for which may be found in Oral History Excerpts, Gulf of Tonkin, Archives Reference Files, LBJ Library.

47. U.S., Congress, House Report 88–1708. On the other hand, Clark Clifford, then a personal adviser to President Johnson, did not feel Congress had been misled on TG–2 while it was debating the resolution. See transcript, Clark Clifford Oral History, 7 July 1969, by Joe B. Frantz, 7, LBJ Library.

48. Memo of 10 June 1964 in "Presidential Decisions—Gulf of Tonkin Attacks," vol. II, Tab 23, National Security Council History File, National Security File, Box 39, LBJ Library. This document summarizes the debate then taking place within the administration on the advisability of proposing such a resolution.

49. Transcript, Wiliam P. Bundy Oral History Interview, 29 May 1969, p. 28, LBJ Library.

50. "Presidential Decisions—Gulf of Tonkin Attacks," vol. III, Tab 29, National Security Council History File, National Security File, Box 39, LBJ Library. Senator Fulbright states this point most directly in the Senate Foreign Relations Committee hearing on 20 February 1968 as he was questioning Secretary of Defense McNamara, p. 107. See also the transcript, Pat Mayo Oral History Interview, 10 November 1980 by Donald A. Ritchie for the Senate Historical Office, p. 179, National Archives. Mr. Holt was in charge of the Senate Foreign Relations Committee staff in 1964 while Carl M. Marcy was on leave.

51. 5 August 1964, *Congressional Record*, 88th Cong., 2d Sess., 18399–18471.

52. 87 Stat. 555, enacted in November 1973. As a congressman, Gerald Ford was aware of constituent concerns as he voted for the Southeast Asia Resolution and then later faced opposition when as president he had to consider the political consequences of not observing the provisions of this Act. Letter from Mrs. J. D. Eppinga to Representative Ford, 6 August 1964, and his response on 11 August 1964, Legislative File, Tab B, Box 12, Gerald R. Ford Library.

53. James Deakin, *Lyndon Johnson's Credibility Gap* (Washington, D.C.: Public Affairs Press, 1968), 9.

54. A feel for such situations can be obtained from the reports of officials not altogether happy with developments in Vietnam policy during the first year of the Johnson Administration. See transcript, David Nes Oral History Interviews, 10 November 1982 and 25 March 1983, by Ted Gittinger, LBJ Library.

20

President-Press Interaction: Media Influence on the Johns Hopkins Address

Kathleen J. Turner

Although the interaction between government officials and the press has commonly been described as adversarial, significant elements of the relationship may be lost if it is not also viewed as symbiotic. As Grossman and Rourke point out, "The adversary concept provides no mechanism for understanding the enormous amount of cooperation and even collaboration that takes place between press . . . and government."[1] Government officials, particularly the president with his national constituency, must have the cooperation of the press if they are to communicate effectively with their publics. The press, on the other hand, needs the government as a source of information.

In spite of their mutual dependency, however, the major goals of government officials and members of the media are not only different, but antithetical. Each side seeks to maximize its ability "to select the items of information that will be defined as news and disclosed to the public."[2]
Thus,

executive officials seek to confine the choice as much as possible to items that will be favorable to them. Reporters, on the other hand, try to broaden the choice so that all potential items of news—both favorable and unfavorable—are included in the pool from which the selection of items to be published will be made.[3]

Because of their conflicting needs, therefore, each side attempts to structure the government-press interaction in ways that will allow it to exploit the weaknesses of the other and enhance its own relative position. Members of the media seek interviews with officials and staff, emphasize their fair-minded support of the administration, and tender advice, both in print and in person, on proposed policies and statements. For their part, government officials are "willing to alter the content of their messages to make sure their messages will appear'' in the media, and "may be willing to alter them even more in order to have them appear with prominent display."[4]

In light of the foregoing considerations the purpose of this chapter is twofold. Its immediate goal is to provide a detailed account of the role played by the media in President Lyndon B. Johnson's first major policy speech on the U.S. involvement in Vietnam. In addition to the importance of the address itself, the evolution of the speech illustrates the ways in which Johnson's experiences with the media influenced his rhetorical decisions, especially concerning the Vietnam War, throughout his presidency. These decisions included whether to issue public statements, how to schedule public statements, and what the content, organization, and language of public statements would be. The address of April 1965 thus serves as an example of Lyndon Johnson's continued and calculated efforts both to adapt to and to influence the mass media.

In a large sense, however, the chapter is presented as an illumination of the nature of the more general relationship between presidents and the press. The chief executive's adaptation to and influence over members of the media are not limited to Lyndon Johnson's tenure in office, and the presidential-press relationship is one that, in the present age of mass communication dominance, appears to have become critically instrumental in shaping the public messages of all American chief executives.

BACKGROUND

By the time Lyndon Johnson succeeded to the presidency in 1963, the United States had been involved in the affairs of Southeast Asia for more than a decade. Johnson, however, had no intention of becoming a wartime president. He considered himself, both by training and by temperament, to be a man ideally suited to deal with the nation's domestic problems. As Johnson saw it, then, it was something akin to divine providence that had thrust him into the White House at that very moment in history when the nation was ready to move, through bold and innovative advances in education and civil rights, to establish a Great Society.

Despite his proclivity for domestic issues, Johnson found himself inextricably drawn, bit by bit, into increased military involvement in Vietnam. Unable to suppress the conflict through a quick show of force in the Gulf of Tonkin in August 1964, Johnson responded to an attack on the American officers' quarters at Pleiku by ordering retaliatory bombing raids on North Vietnam in February 1965. Lyndon Johnson did not formally address the American people after ordering these reprisals, for he preferred to minimize publicity about his actions. Yet his policies, by the spring of 1965, had resulted in both the intensification and the polarization of public opinion concerning U.S. involvement in Southeast Asia. It was during this period, historian Eric Goldman points out, that the terms *hawk* and *dove* gained currency. Although, as Goldman observes, "they did as much to confuse as to classify," the growing popularity of the terms did capture the spirit of two strong strains of public opinion on the issue.[5]

The news media reflected these conflicting positions as well. The *New York Times'* editorials grew more and more critical of the American bombing policy, as they urged Johnson to reduce our involvement before it was too late.[6] In contrast, columnist Joseph Alsop rejected neturalization as "selling out," and he encouraged Johnson to adopt a course of continued air strikes to demonstrate that "the president now means business at last" rather than simply employing "another fruitless one-shot stunt" like the Gulf of Tonkin reprisals.[7] Meanwhile, columnist James Reston admitted that he might lack sufficient information on the war to second guess Johnson's decisions, but he argued that "the least the president can do is to go before the country and explain his objectives," to still the "babble of influential voices in Washington" muttering along without guidance from their leader.[8]

One commentator of special interest to the Johnson administration was columnist Walter Lippmann. Early in Johnson's presidency, veteran Democratic political adviser James Rowe had warned Johnson that the Washington press corps is

worse than a wolf pack when it comes to attacking public officials. But they are like a bunch of sheep in their own profession and they will always follow the bellwether sheep. . . . The only two newspapermen practically all of them admire are Walter Lippmann and Scotty Reston. As long as those two are for Lyndon Johnson he will, on the whole, get a good press from the rest of them. You certainly have Lippmann and Reston in your pocket now. I hope you do not lose them.[9]

Johnson doubted, as he said both at the time and in his memoirs, that a southern president could ever receive fair treatment from what he called "the metropolitan press of the eastern seaboard."[10] Yet he knew the "bellwether" columnists could be useful to him—particularly Lippmann, who in one poll of the Washington press corps had garnered an exceptional 42 percent of the vote as the fairest and most reliable columnist on the political scene.[11] Lippmann had been enthusiastically supportive of Johnson in the first year of his presidency and praised his healing influence during a time of trial. Johnson had reciprocated by awarding him the Presidential Medal of Freedom, the nation's highest civilian honor, in September 1964. Vietnam, however, brought an increasing sense of disillusionment to the columnist. The key to American foreign policy lay in Europe, Lippmann argued, not Asia. Moreover, in the wake of Johnson's reprisal policy, the columnist complained that even

apart from the question of morality and the gigantic risks of escalating war, there is not sufficient reason to think that the Northern communists can be bombed into submission. . . . For this country to involve itself [further] in such a war in Asia would be an act of supreme folly. . . . There is no tolerable alternative except a negotiated truce.[12]

As the bombings of North Vietnam continued through the spring of 1965 and no truce appeared, Lippmann's disenchantment deepened.

Against this background of conflicting pressures and criticism, Lyndon Johnson called for a speech on Vietnam.[13] For two months following the Pleiku attacks, public messages on Vietnam had been limited to White House statements and remarks at press conferences; in addition, Johnson had spoken with individuals and small groups about American goals there.[14] On those occasions when staff members had outlined foreign policy speeches for the president, Johnson had rejected them.[15] In late March 1965, however, he decided that it was time for a full-fledged public statement on American policy regarding Southeast Asia.

RESPONSE TO THE PRESS: PREPARING THE MESSAGE

McGeorge Bundy, national security adviser to Johnson, outlined the original draft of the speech, which focused on the history of American commitments to the region and our continuing refusal "to accept aggression as the price of lowered tension." The United States wanted no wider war, Bundy insisted, but any settlement of the conflict demanded that "the aggression against the people and Government of South Vietnam" must stop. Such a settlement would allow the United States "to cooperate in Southeast Asia in regional development." Bundy concluded with recommendations to include references to the South Vietnamese government throughout the speech, "so that this is not just a U.S. policy and a U.S. program," and to end the address "on the note of steadfastness for peace—with a reprise on our hope to do those things—and only those things—which are necessary to repel aggression and which give promise of a brighter future of all concerned."[16]

The potential importance of this address, which as yet had no firm date or setting for delivery, soon became apparent to Johnson's aides. In a memorandum to Johnson that was attached to a second draft of the statement, Bundy suggested that "this may well be the most important foreign policy speech you have yet planned."[17] Bundy, along with Secretary of State Dean Rusk and Secretary of Defense Robert McNamara, recommended an emphasis on the history of American involvement in Vietnam, complete with quotations from John Kennedy to, as Bundy explained, "give us protection and encouragement with some of the 'liberals' who are falsely telling each other that our policy is different from his."

From Bundy the draft went to Richard Goodwin, the brash but bright aide whose eloquence as a ghostwriter for Kennedy had attracted Johnson to him. It was Goodwin who had captured Johnson's domestic vision in the phrase, "the Great Society." Working with Valenti, Goodwin produced a two-pronged plan after Johnson's own heart: a proposal to create a team of experts to design a food program for South Vietnam, paired with a plan to develop the Mekong River region, the latter to be seeded with a billion dollar contribution from the United States.[18]

Johnson responded enthusiastically. Here was an approach he could endorse.

After his trip to Vietnam as vice president, Johnson's report to Kennedy had warned that the greatest danger that the country faced was not the communist threat, which he felt was considerable, but "hunger, ignorance, poverty, and disease."[19] Now he could envision expanding his war on poverty from the home front to the Third World region and thus battle those enemies common to all of humanity.

Over the next week—the end of March and the beginning of April—Bundy, Goodwin, Valenti, and others pored over drafts of the speech and made changes that ranged from minute to massive. In one instance they inserted a carefully worded passage on "energetically" moving toward a peaceful settlement, to respond to an appeal from seventeen nonaligned nations to begin immediate negotiations. In justifying the phrasing of the insertion, the writers' notation referred not to the dangers of international misunderstanding, but to the fear that "without these paragraphs the speech might not strike the sophisticated correspondents as saying anything important."[20]

In further revisions, the American response to the peace appeal was then moved, for greater emphasis, from the middle of the speech to the introduction. It was replaced by a passage of special significance: "We will never be second in the search for such a peaceful settlement in Vietnam. . . . We have stated this position over and over again, fifty times and more, to friend and foe alike. And we remain ready, with this purpose, for unconditional discussions."[21]

In the media and in and out of Congress, members of the peace bloc had been pressuring Johnson to proclaim his openness to negotiations, and the plea from the seventeen nations increased that pressure. Johnson had resisted such recommendations earlier; he protested that he had been publicly open to negotiations, but that Hanoi had responded only with further aggressive acts. Thus, it was consistent with Johnson's perception of the situation for this "new" offer to be cast as one made "fifty times and more" which "we remain" ready to make again. In addition, the offer was for unconditional discussions, not negotiations; the former promised only to talk, not necessarily to reach a settlement.

At this stage, four days before the scheduled delivery, preparations for the speech intensified. Valenti showed the address to Philip Potter, bureau chief of the *Baltimore Sun*, and Jack Horner of the *Washington Star*.[22] Horner cautioned that Reedy should background the press to clarify Johnson's usage of "unconditional talks" (for example, whether that included a ceasefire); other than that, he felt the speech was "fine." Potter, a friend and supporter of Johnson, composed two paragraphs that were used almost verbatim. The first contradicted "those who say" that China is destined to dominate Southeast Asia, by contending that "there is no end to that argument until all of the nations of Asia are swallowed up"—a version of the domino theory that implicitly extended to the United States as well. The second paragraph, paralleling American responsibility in Asia to that in Europe, noted that World War II was fought on both continents. "When it ended," Potter's passage maintained, "we found ourselves with continued responsibility for the defense of freedom."[23] The two paragraphs constituted a refutation of arguments, like Lippmann's, that the United States had no vital stakes in Southeast Asia.

In addition, the president himself joined the round of previews, as he read a draft to the *New York Times'* Charles Mohr, AP correspondent Doug Cornell, and two other reporters on the day before the speech.[24] Of greater significance, however, was Johnson's off-the-record meeting that day with columnist Walter Lippmann.[25] In a memorandum to Johnson before the conference, McGeorge Bundy suggested that it would be

perfectly proper to show the current draft of your speech to Walter Lippmann and get his opinion. *A part of our purpose, after all, is to plug his guns*, and he can tell us better than anyone to what degree we have done so. The only risk I see in this is that we want to be awfully careful that the language we finally use is not harder than what he sees, and for that reason it may be better to read to him from the speech and to slide gently past the words "unconditional discussions." While I recommend these words myself and believe that they put us in a strong, balanced position, there is no doubt that some commentators will think they are not so much a clarification as a softening of the position. [emphasis added][26]

Bundy clearly articulated an important rhetorical purpose for the Johns Hopkins speech: to "plug the guns" of Walter Lippmann on Vietnam. In addition, the adviser's concern for press perception of the "hardness" or "softness" of the administration's stand indicates his cognizance of the fine line they were walking: to be "hard" enough to reassure "hawks" that the United States would not shirk its responsibilities and yet to be "soft" enough that "doves" knew of America's openness to and hope for a peaceful settlement. As Goldman indicated, the labels may confuse as well as classify; Lippmann, like substantial portions of the public at this stage, did not want to withdraw at any cost. At the same time, the commentator did not want further American personnel and financial aid committed to Vietnam; to Lippmann, a negotiated truce was the only tolerable solution.[27]

Recognizing the complexity of the columnist's stand, Bundy recommended that Johnson further explore Lippmann's views. In particular, the aide advised inquiries as to "why he is pushing so hard for the notion of a single Vietnam," for "if he is going to advise negotiations, it seems to me he ought to be telling us what he expects to get" from North Vietnam.[28] Otherwise, the president might inquire whether negotiations are "his idea of a quiet way of giving it to the communists." Moreover, Bundy continued:

You may also want to make it clear to Lippmann that when we say we are ready to talk, we do not mean that we are ready for a ceasefire. . . . Walter needs to understand this, and if he gets it straight from you, he is likely to be less objectionable about it. Under pressure he will admit that the Secretary of Defense is excellent, but he will still think him wrong. He had a useful tendency to think the President himself is right.[29]

While there is no way of knowing the extent to which Johnson slid "gently past the words 'unconditional discussion,' " Lippmann's colleagues reported him to be well satisfied with the speech after his preview.[30] Although presidential Press Secretary George Reedy attributes perceptions of the columnist's satisfaction to the fact that Johnson had not given the man a chance to speak, Steele reconciles the two views. He contends that it was a session with Bundy following the lengthy conference with Johnson that gave Lippmann his optimism, for he came from it with the hope that the president would announce not only unconditional discussions but also an unconditional ceasefire—contrary to Bundy's memorandum.[31]

On the afternoon of the speech, the text was distributed to the White House press corps. In addition, McGeorge Bundy, Secretary of Defense Robert McNamara, and Undersecretary of State George Ball filmed capsule background statements on Vietnam to be televised as previews for the president's message. Several correspondents who found this to be a peculiar device for a presidential statement christened these spots "the singing commercials."[32] In final preparation for this major address, Johnson informed Ball that the White House, not the State Department, would release the reply to the seventeen nonaligned nations' appeal on Vietnam.[33]

RESPONSE BY THE PRESS: REACTIONS TO THE JOHNS HOPKINS ADDRESS

On that Wednesday night—7 April 1965—Lyndon Johnson faced more than a thousand faculty and students in Johns Hopkins University's Shriver Auditorium, as well as an estimated sixty million television viewers throughout the country and an international audience. He delivered, as several contemporary descriptions characterized it, a "carrot-and-stick" speech, in which America's determination to defend liberty against aggression joined with America's proposals for peace and economic development in Southeast Asia.[34]

Initial reports of reactions at home and abroad appeared to fulfill Bundy's early prediction that the Johns Hopkins address would be Johnson's "most important foreign policy speech" to date. *Newsweek*'s account observed that "few U.S. foreign-policy declarations of recent years met with such an immediate and overwhelmingly favorable response. At home, the editorial reaction was little short of lyrical. . . . Abroad, the response to the speech was even more striking."[35]

The *New York Times*' previous editorial criticism turned into praise for "an American policy . . . in which the country can take pride," while the *Washington Post* admired Johnson's skillful twin brandishment of the sword and the olive branch.[36] Columnist Joseph Alsop, who had felt that "overlong waiting" to explain his policy on Vietnam "had left the president in a position of weakness," called the Johns Hopkins address "a great speech" that acquitted its speaker well.[37]

Amidst these enthusiastic responses, however, the seeds of future dissent, to
be nurtured by subsequent events, were apparent. The day before the Johns
Hopkins speech, the *New York Times* editorialized that ''a major task for President
Johnson'' in his address

is to explain to the American people and to the world the basic American contention that
Vietnam is crucial to American security, to the freedom of all Southeast Asia, to small
nations everywhere, and to the hopes of containing Communism in Asia and the Far
East. It is important that he explain that the methods the United States is employing to
defend South Vietnam are the wisest and most effective.[38]

Yet the explanations of America's presence in Vietnam that Johnson provided
were to receive scant attention in the *New York Times'* front page account of
the speech. Perhaps such justifications were considered ''old hat,'' and thus not
as newsworthy as Johnson's offer for unconditional discussions; perhaps they
lacked the conflict basic to ''news.'' Even the Southeast Asian development
plan, newsworthy enough to gain part of the headline, received only a third of
the column space devoted to the offer of unconditional discussions and the refusal
to quit fighting. As a result, although the title of Johnson's address was ''Peace
without Conquest,'' the *New York Times'* stress on the conflict between nations
and the intrigue of possible discussions greatly muted the peaceful images. The
Times' main account, written by one of the four correspondents backgrounded
by Johnson on the day of the speech, emphasized military concerns far more
than did the speech itself, and the sidebars echoed this tone.[39]

In addition to the *Times'* orientation toward ''the stick,'' articles in both the
New York Times and the *Washington Post* noted a disparity between recent
administration declarations and the Johns Hopkins speech. Citing Johnson's offer
of unconditional discussions, with his insistence that it was one made many
times before, the *Times'* story reported: ''Government sources maintained, as
did the president, that the offer to talk unconditionally was not a marked change
in policy. However, the emphasis had been on the futility of negotiations and
there had been nothing like tonight's clear offer.''[40]

The *Washington Post* devoted part of its front page to a news analysis head-
lined, ''President's Use of 'Unconditional' in Speech Viewed as Significant.''[41]
While not calling Johnson and his staff liars, the articles nonetheless clearly cast
doubt upon the strict reliability of the administration's versions of past and present
policy. The skepticism conveyed by this aspect of the *Times'* and the *Post's*
coverage was perhaps among those events that led to the first use of the term
''credibility gap'' in print within two months after the Johns Hopkins speech.[42]

Other elements of dissatisfaction with Johnson's address among members of
the media were more obvious. In his column on the speech, Walter Lippmann,
whose approval Johnson had courted and coveted so much, wrote that while the
address did ''in some measure correct some of the defects of the public relations
of the administration,'' it was nonetheless ''certainly too little, perhaps because

it was too late, to change the course of the war.''[43] The opening paragraph of the column reflected his conference with Johnson as presaged in the memorandum from Bundy; for example, Lippmann cautioned that "there was no illusion that the Viet Cong and Hanoi would be willing to cease and desist, and it was no less evident that the president's offer of 'unconditional discussions' was not meant to bring about a ceasefire.''[44] The failure to announce a ceasefire helps explain why Lippmann's reported support of the speech after his preview failed to appear in his column. The man who before Johns Hopkins had been puzzled as to "why the Administration persists in keeping its war aims uncertain" afterward wondered why the administration bothered to articulate them now that it was to late. Within a month, Lippmann was warning that "the president is in grave trouble" on his Vietnam policy, and the sizable opposition was a fact that "the Administration should put . . . in its pipe and smoke.''[45] Later, Lippmann would say more bluntly of Johnson, "He misled me.''[46]

For his part, Johnson felt misled and betrayed by what he viewed as Lippmann's quicksand support. "I thought my speech in Baltimore would satisfy Lippmann," he said after the Johns Hopkins address. "I went over it with him, but I find out now about Mr. Lippmann and Martin Luther King and some others—old slow me just catches up with them, then they are gone ahead of me.''[47] Bundy and other administration officials continued to encourage the columnist to accept the president's arguments, but Johnson's disillusionment with Lippmann soon turned to bitterness.[48] Within a year staff members were preparing lengthy reports outlining the inconsistencies of Lippmann's views during his long career.''[49]

At the moment, however, all of this bad news lay in the future. Lippmann's column was only a small annoyance amidst the general joy of stemming the tide of criticism and outlining constructive action for Southeast Asia. Lyndon Johnson was exultant over Vietnam that April night in 1965 when he made the Johns Hopkins speech. As Lady Bird recorded in her memoirs:

I had the thrilling feeling that we have taken the initiative. We are beginning to really explain to the world about Vietnam, about what we can do, about the promise of this epoch in history—that we are on the move against the negation of war and communism. It was exciting. I felt as if the stalemate had had a firecracker put under it.[50]

Three years and many speeches after delivering his Johns Hopkins address, Lyndon Johnson would again face the camera to "speak . . . of peace in Vietnam and Southeast Asia''—but this time he would also announce his decision not to seek reelection.[51] The role of Lyndon Johnson's relationship with the press in that decision was foreshadowed during the evolution of the speech of 7 April 1965.

CONCLUSION

The foregoing description of the evolution of the Johns Hopkins speech yields observations about Lyndon Johnson's relationship with the press on two levels. First, it provides an account of the press's role in the preparation and evaluation of Johnson's first major policy statement on Vietnam, a critical speech on an issue of major importance. From his initial reticence to speak about the retaliatory raids to the careful casting of phrases that would impress "the sophisticated correspondents," Johnson's processes of invention, disposition, style, and delivery depended to a significant extent upon the anticipation of media responses. That the Johns Hopkins address should be so motivated by and modeled to press reaction points to a source of influence deserving scrutiny. The process of creating contemporary presidential messages necessarily includes attention to the media as both audience and gatekeeper.

In addition to the accounting of this particular speech, the evolution of the Johns Hopkins address is indicative of Lyndon Johnson's relationship with the media throughout his term in office. As president he continually sought to gain the understanding and support of the media, which he recognized as a prerequisite to reaching the American public as he wished. Valenti's lobbying efforts with Horner and Potter, Bundy's caution concerning the thin line that they trod with commentators, and Johnson's own sessions with journalists demonstrated both the administration's desire to gain favorable coverage for the message, and the journalists' desire to gain as much information about the message as possible. With the Johns Hopkins address as with other messages, the efforts to "slide gently past" points of contention during the briefings led to media dissatisfaction, a natural outcome of the perpetual tug between cooperation and competition in the government-press relationship. Johnson's sense of betrayal at Lippmann's column and Mohr's article was typical, for he believed that his efforts to communicate with the American public were neither understood nor appreciated by members of the press. Lyndon Johnson thus in large part blamed his inability to quiet the opposition to his policies in Vietnam on the ability of the media

to create a climate of dissent and opposition in Washington and New York and the academic community that was a tremendous distortion of the way the country felt. But this had its effect. . . . The overall effect, I think, was to weaken the effectiveness of America's action [and] to diminish the chances for a successful negotiation of a peace settlement.[52]

Understanding Johnson's efforts to marshal the media as well as the country on behalf of America's efforts in Vietnam, as indicated by the evolution of the Johns Hopkins address, thus provides a significant perspective on the rhetorical climate of the country in the mid–1960s.

This examination of Johnson's Johns Hopkins speech also may be viewed as a case study that provides insight into the complex interweavings of the presidential-press relationship. By exploring such dimensions as the influence of the administration's perceptions of the media in the message's development, the differences in the roles played by "friendly" journalists like Potter and important but wavering journalists like Lippmann, and the connections among briefings, speech texts, and media accounts, we better understand that blend of the symbiotic and the adversarial that constitutes government-press interaction. Moreover, such investigations further our understanding of the relationships among interpersonal, public, and mediated communication, with implications that extend well beyond the evolution of the Johns Hopkins speech.

This chapter thus points to questions for further investigation of that competitive yet cooperative relationship between government officials and members of the media. Particularly intriguing are the possibilities involved in a systematic study of the strategies employed by the presidents to gain media access in ways that will produce favorable publicity. Equally promising are investigations into the numerous rhetorical decisions that either must or may be made by the press, and how these are influenced by particular media. Intensive investigations of such questions may lead to the development of generalizations about the rhetorical interaction between presidents and the press and its effect on public communication.

NOTES

1. Michael Baruch Grossman and Francis E. Rourke, "The Media and the Presidency: An Exchange Analysis," *Political Science Quarterly* 91 (1976): 455. Following the practice of the White House Press Corps and the White House Press Office, the term *press* in this chapter refers to both print and broadcast media.

2. Ibid., 456–457.

3. Ibid.

4. Delmer D. Dunn, *Public Officials and the Press* (Reading, Mass.: Addison-Wesley Publishing Co., 1969), 169.

5. Eric Goldman, *The Tragedy of Lyndon Johnson* (New York: Knopf, 1969), 402–403.

6. See, for example, "Black Day in Vietnam," editorial, *New York Times*, 11 February 1965, 38.

7. Joseph Alsop, " 'We Can' or 'We Can't,' " *Washington Post*, 8 February 1965, sec. A, 17.

8. James B. Reston, "What Are Our Aims in Vietnam?" *New York Times*, 12 February 1965, 28.

9. Letter, James Rowe to Johnson, 9 April 1964, Ex PR 18, Box 356, LBJ Library. This letter and other materials similarly cited are from the holdings of the Lyndon B. Johnson Library in Austin, Texas.

10. Rowe's letter had been stimulated by a conversation with Reston after the columnist met with Johnson; Reston was concerned about this attitude of the president. Yet Johnson held it strongly enough to repeat it in his memoirs. See Lyndon B. Johnson, *The Vantage Point: Perspectives of the Presidency, 1963–1969* (New York: Holt, Rinehart and Winston, 1971), 95.

11. William L. Rivers, *The Opinionmakers: The Washington Press Corps* (Boston: Beacon Press, 1970), 55.

12. Walter Lippmann, "The Viet Nam Debate," *Washington Post*, 18 February 1965, sec. A, 21.

13. According to "Mr. Valenti's notes on the Johns Hopkins speech" (Statements, Box 126, 7 April 1965 Remarks), the "President gave orders to prepare such a speech two weeks before" it was delivered on 7 April 1965, which would have been around March 24. McGeorge Bundy's first outline is dated March 26, verifying the recollections of Jack Valenti, the president's special assistant and right-hand man. See the memorandum, Bundy to Dean Rusk, 26 March 1965, National Security Files: Vietnam, Box 12, #164 (these files are hereafter designated NSF:VN). The two pages of notes by Valenti, undated and typed up in very rough form, follow the evolution of the speech from Johnson's original call for a draft to shortly before its delivery.

14. See the 1965 news conferences of 13 March, 20 March, and 1 April, in *Public Papers of the Presidents of the United States: Lyndon B. Johnson* (Washington, D.C.: Office of the *Federal Register*, National Archives and Records Service, 1965), 278–279, 300–302, 305–307, and 367–369. The Johnson administration attended to press coverage of Vietnam during this period, thanked editors for supportive pieces (e.g., letter, Johnson to E. Palmer Hoyt, 4 March 1965, NSF:VN, Box 23, #200b), and refuted columns alleging McNamara's opposition to retaliatory strikes, e.g., letter, George W. Ball to Drew Pearson, 26 February 1965, NSF:VN, Box 12, #149; and letter, Pearson to Ball, 6 March 1965, in Bill Moyers' files, Box 72, File Drew Pearson. Referring to one piece in the *Minneapolis Tribune*, Carl T. Rowan of the USIA mused to Johnson: "What a help it would be if we could get more of the columnists and editorial writers in the country to replace the emotional axe-grinding with this kind of constructive comment," Memorandum, 26 February 1965, NSF:VN, Box 12, #148, regarding a 21 February article by John Cowles, Jr.

15. See, for example, Goldman, *Tragedy*, 275–280.

16. Memorandum, Bundy to Rusk, 26 March 1965, NSF:VN, Box 12, #164.

17. Memorandum, Bundy to Johnson, 28 March 1965, NSF:VN, Box 12, #160.

18. Valenti's notes.

19. Memorandum, Johnson to Kennedy, 23 May 1964, "Mission to Southeast Asia, India, and Pakistan," in Vice Presidential Security File, Vice Presidential Travel, Vice President's Visit to Southeast Asia, 9–24 May 1961 (I).

20. Draft, 5 April 1965, Statements, Box 126, Baltimore.

21. Unindicated draft, Statements, Box 126, Baltimore.

22. Valenti's notes.

23. Potter's paragraphs are attached to a memorandum, Nell Yates to Dorothy Territo, 8 April 1965, Statements, Box 126, Baltimore; they closely parallel the passage as it appears in the Address at Johns Hopkins University: "Peace without Conquest," 7 April 1965, *Public Papers of the Presidents: Lyndon Johnson, 1965*, 395. Valenti's notes comment on the politics of ghostwriting: "Goodwin took out Potter's revisions, but we [Valenti and Potter] put them back in."

24. Ibid.

25. Unindicated memorandum, Diary Back-up, 6 April 1965.

26. Memorandum, Bundy to Johnson, 6 April 1965, Diary Back-up, 6 April 1965.

27. Walter Lippmann, "The Viet-Nam Debate," *Washington Post*, 18 February 1965, sec. A, 21.

28. Memorandum, Bundy to Johnson, 6 April 1965, Diary Back-up, 6 April 1965.

29. Ibid.

30. See, for example, Hugh Sidey, *A Very Personal Presidency: Lyndon Johnson in the White House* (New York: Atheneum, 1968), 85–86; and Rowland Evans and Robert Novak, *Lyndon B. Johnson: The Exercise of Power* (New York: New American Library, 1966), 567. Valenti's notes unfortunately do not refer to Lippmann's conference with the president at all.

31. Reedy, interview with the author, Milwaukee, 19 May 1978; and Ronald Steel, *Walter Lippmann and the American Century* (Boston: Little, Brown, 1980), 562–564.

32. Sidey, *Very Personal Presidency*, 129.

33. In a memorandum to Johnson, 7 April 1965, CF SP 3, Box 80, George Ball told him that he would receive the ambassadors of Yugoslavia, Ghana, Afghanistan, and Ethiopia at the State Department the next day "as a follow up of your speech," with Ball giving them the American response to the plea for peace negotiations. Johnson's handwritten note at the bottom of the memorandum reads: "Jack—we want to release at WH."

34. The text of the Johns Hopkins address is contained in Johnson's *Public Papers* for 1965, 394–399. For the "carrot and stick" characterization, see, for example, Joseph Alsop, "Matter of Fact: A Great Speech," *Washington Post*, 9 April 1965, sec. A, 25; and Walter Lippmann, "The Baltimore Address and After," *Washington Post*, 9 April 1965, sec. A, 13.

35. "A Path for Reasonable Men," *Newsweek*, 19 April 1965, 25. The Ex ND 19/CO files, Box 215 contain a number of letters from Johnson to editors thanking them for their support following the speech.

36. "The President Opens the Door," editorial, *New York Times*, 8 April 1965, 38; "Sword and Olive Branch," editorial, *Washington Post*, 9 April 1965, sec. A, 24.

37. Joseph Alsop, "Matter of Fact: A Great Speech," *Washington Post*, 9 April 1965, sec. A, 25.

38. Editorial, "Vietnam's 'Wider War,' " *New York Times*, 6 April 1965, sec. A, 38. The title refuted the administration's continual insistence that "we seek no wider war."

39. See Charles Mohr, "President Makes Offer to Start Vietnam Talks Unconditionally: Proposes $1 Billion Aid for Asia," *New York Times*, 8 April 1965, sec. A, as well as other front-page stories of that day. The news coverage of the *Washington Post* on 8 April 1965 also follows this trend.

40. Mohr, "President Makes Offer."

41. Murray Marder, "President's Use of 'Unconditional' in Speech Viewed as Significant," *Washington Post*, 8 April 1965, 1.

42. According to Goldman, *Tragedy*, 409, the phrase was used among White House correspondents and other journalists for some time before it first made the newspapers as a headline over David Wise's article in the New York *Herald-Tribune* of 23 May 1965.

43. Walter Lippmann, "The Baltimore Address and After," *Washington Post*, 13 April 1965, sec. A, 13.

44. Ibid. Compare with memorandum, Bundy to Johnson, 6 April 1965, Diary Back-up, April 6, 1965.

45. Walter Lippmann, "Is Uncertainty Necessary?" *Washington Post*, 6 April 1965, sec. A, 17; Lippmann, "The Falling Dominoes," *Washington Post*, 23 April 1965, sec.

A, 21. By August 1966, Lippmann endorsed a peace candidate for senator from Massachusetts as a man who "not only tells the truth, but . . . tells it without weasling and hedging and fudging" (see the *New York Times* advertisement in Marvin Watson's files, Vietnam I, 18 August 1966).

46. Cited in Steel, *Walter Lippmann*, 572.

47. Sidey, *Very Personal Presidency*, 85–86.

48. See, for example, letter, Bundy to Lippmann, 20 April 1965; letter, Lippmann to Bundy, 23 April 1965; and letter, Bundy to Lippmann, 28 April 1965 (all in Ex ND 19/DO 312, Box 214). The last letter rebuked Lippmann for the tone of his 23 April column on "the things [about Vietnam] which the president's advisers should stick in their pipes and smoke."

49. See memorandum, Panzer to Moyers, 17 March 1966, an eleven-page memorandum with thirty-four footnotes on Lippmann's inconsistencies (filed with 31 March 1967 memorandum to Johnson on the credibility gap, Ex FG 1, Box 14); and memorandum, Robert Kinner to Johnson, 13 August 1966, on a book on Lippmann's views over the years (Ex PR 18, Box 358). In addition, a memorandum from Walt W. Rostow to Johnson, 9 May 1966, outlining Lippmann's positions over the preceding twenty years has been withdrawn from CF PR 18, Box 83, because of security classifications.

50. Lady Bird Johnson, *A White House Diary* (New York: Holt, Rinehart and Winston, 1970), 256.

51. The President's Address to the Nation Announcing Steps to Limit the War in Vietnam and Reporting His Decision Not to Seek Reelection, 31 March 1968, *Public Papers of the Presidents: Lyndon Johnson, 1968–1969*, 469–475.

52. Lyndon B. Johnson Oral History, by Elspeth Rostow, transcript #2, 28 September 1970, 1, LBJ Library.

21

"In What Direction Are We Going in Vietnam?" The U.S. Senate, Lyndon Johnson, and the Vietnam War, 1964–1965

Philip J. Avillo, Jr.

In June 1965 Senator Mike Mansfield, the Democratic majority leader from Montana, sent a series of confidential memoranda to President Lyndon B. Johnson. "You know it is a view which I have long held," Mansfield wrote in one, that "there are no significant American interests which dictate an essentially massive, unilateral American military effort to control the events in Vietnam or even on the Southeast Asian mainland as a whole." Several days later he asked Johnson, "In what direction are we going in Vietnam?" The absence of a clear answer to that question, he continued, "seems to me to be the crux of the difficulty which has confronted us all along."[1]

Mansfield's concern was well placed. During the first six months of 1965, the American military effort in Vietnam had escalated gradually, but steadily. That escalation continued throughout the remainder of the year, and, as 1965 drew to a close, the number of American troops in that country had grown from 23,000 at the year's beginning to over 180,000. The number of Americans killed in Vietnam had increased apace as well, numbering over 1,600 at year's end.[2]

Few political observers would have predicted this turn of events as the year began. President Johnson had just been elected and envisioned at his January 1965 inaugural a future characterized by domestic progress and world peace.[3] Indeed, throughout the presidential election campaign of 1964, Johnson reminded the electorate that he was a man of peace. Unlike his opponent, Barry Goldwater, Johnson pledged to keep the United States from becoming embroiled in a war in Southeast Asia.[4] Even when alleged attacks in August 1964 by North Vietnamese patrol boats against U.S. naval ships patrolling the waters just off the coast of North Vietnam prompted Johnson to order retaliatory air strikes against North Vietnam, he couched the strikes in terms of peace, emphasizing that they were limited in scope and restrained both quantitatively and geographically. His only purpose was to prevent aggression in Vietnam and to preserve the peace in Southeast Asia. To this end, Johnson in August persuaded the Congress to endorse the Tonkin Gulf Resolution, which authorized him to use whatever means necessary, including the use of force, to ensure that peace.[5]

Only two senators, Democrats Wayne Morse of Oregon and Ernest Gruening of Alaska, voted against the Tonkin Gulf Resolution. Both of them had argued since well before the Gulf of Tonkin incident that events in Vietnam had little to do with American interests. As early as October 1963, Gruening articulated his concern on the floor of the Senate. So-called technicians in Vietnam, he insisted, were in reality "troops," and already the war had taken the "lives of 100 young [American] men."[6] Wayne Morse, too, had voiced similar objections for a number of years.[7]

When the Senate considered Johnson's Gulf of Tonkin Resolution, Morse and Gruening used the opportunity to challenge the president's claim that such a measure was necessary to ensure peace in Southeast Asia. President Johnson, Morse said, was "dead wrong on this issue." The resolution bypassed Congress' constitutional authority to declare war and provided the president with a "pre-dated declaration of war." Passage of the resolution, he warned, will plant "seeds not of peace, but of war," and "Senators who vote for it will live to regret it."[8] Gruening argued that "American security is not involved" in Vietnam. "I do not consider this our war," Gruening insisted, urging his country "to disengage" itself from Vietnam immediately. "We have lost too many American lives already," and should this resolution be enacted, he predicted, "their number will steadily increase."[9]

Eventually a number of other senators joined them in their protest, including Senator J. William Fulbright of Arkansas, the chairman of the Senate Foreign Relations Committee, who had maneuvered the Tonkin Gulf Resolution through the Senate floor. Fulbright's shift typified that which many senators experienced. During the debate over the Tonkin Gulf Resolution, Fulbright had reassured his colleagues that Johnson proposed only to prevent future attacks by the North Vietnamese similar to those that had occurred only a few days earlier. The resolution had limited objectives, Fulbright commented in the Senate, "calculated to prevent the spread of war." Echoing classic military wisdom, Fulbright emphasized that "the last thing we want to do is become involved in a land war in Asia." Fulbright had supported Johnson earlier in 1964 as well, suggesting both publicly and privately that the president was dealing with a difficult situation and that he was convinced the president would "not do anything rash that would cause many thousands of deaths."[10] As Fulbright confided to one correspondent after passage of the Tonkin Resolution, the American involvement in Vietnam may have been unwise but "it is difficult to know how to disengage without disastrous consequences, especially immediately prior to an election."[11]

Fulbright's doubts surfaced in 1965.[12] Initially, he questioned the policy privately, either in the confines of the Senate Foreign Relations Committee's closed hearings or to the president himself. Fulbright himself marks the break with

President Johnson in September 1965, when he spoke publicly against U.S. policy, but as early as 8 February 1965, political analysts had noted strains in the relations between these long-time friends and former Senate colleagues. On that particular day, Fulbright was absent from a White House briefing given by McGeorge Bundy. He missed two White House briefings for congressional leaders given the previous two days. His exclusion from these meetings, coupled with the fact that Johnson had not consulted privately with the senator for some time, indicated that Fulbright had begun already to fall from presidential favor.[13]

The rift between Fulbright and Johnson over his Vietnam policy widened later that spring. Fulbright challenged Secretary of State Dean Rusk's arguments against a bombing pause in North Vietnam, suggesting that a cessation of the bombing might lead more readily to negotiations. In May Fulbright urged that a settlement be devised based on the 1954 Geneva accords, which in effect placed him at odds with Johnson's decision to increase American forces in Vietnam.[14] The following month in a major speech to the Senate, Fulbright distanced himself even further from Johnson's policy. The United States should pursue a "resolute but restrained" path, sufficiently strong, he reasoned, to bring the communists to the negotiating table. Emphasizing his opposition either to unconditional withdrawal or to continued American escalation of the war, Fulbright insisted nevertheless that the effort necessary to win a protracted military action in Vietnam far exceeded American interests there. Later, he urged President Johnson to cease bombing North Vietnam in an effort to initiate negotiations with the North Vietnamese.[15]

Perhaps no senator tried more in private to alter the president's path in South Vietnam than did Mike Mansfield. He sent memorandum after memorandum in staccatolike fashion to Johnson, frequently in flurries of two or three within only a few days of each other, and in particular when the American involvement in Vietnam appeared so fluid during the early period of escalation in 1965. In February he wrote pessimistically, "I have grave doubts about the ability of General Khanh's government. I have no doubt but that the great majority of the population of South Vietnam are tired of the war and will give us no significant assistance." Two days later he reiterated this theme, commenting that the American weakness in Vietnam is on the ground, "where isolated pockets of Americans are surrounded by, at best, an indifferent population and, more likely, by an increasingly hostile population."[16] By June, Mansfield was suggesting to the president that in order "to get this business to the conference table as quickly as possible, I think we should throw out some clear signs and signals of our own instead of waiting for the other side."[17]

Mansfield warned Johnson, too, that the congressional support for his policy had limits. Many senators had voted for his resolutions, but had voted "with grave doubts and much trepidation." They had acted "largely on faith, out of loyalty to you and on the premise that the president should have their legislative support in a time of crisis."[18] Several weeks later, Mansfield sent an even more ominous memorandum to the president in which he described a meeting he had with five other Senate leaders. They articulated a number of points for the president to consider, including: Vietnam is a no-win situation; the bombing of North Vietnam was a mistake; the people are "concerned," "confused," and support the president "primarily because he is the president." In addition, Secretary of Defense McNamara came under attack for his role, as did the South Vietnamese military forces who were of "dubious quality" when compared to the "highly skilled and formidable" enemy soldiers. Mansfield's concluding comment offered the president little consolation. While unanimity did not emerge on all of these issues, a certain consensus did. "As far as Vietnam is concerned," Mansfield informed the president, the senators agree that "we are deeply enmeshed in a place where we ought not to be; . . . the situation is rapidly going out of control; and . . . every effort should be made to extricate ourselves."[19]

A number of other senators concurred with this appraisal. Senator Allen J. Ellender (D-La.) recommended in early 1965 immediate American withdrawal from Vietnam, "without any ifs or ands." Senators Frank Church of Idaho and Olin D. Johnston of South Carolina, both Democrats, sought a solution through UN intervention. "I suggest the United Nations handle it, set up a buffer zone between North and South Vietnam and police it," Johnston told the Associated Press, while Church insisted that only an internationally enforced guarantee of South Vietnam's independence and neutrality would resolve the crisis in that country.[20] When the United States increased its military aid to South Vietnam and increased its bombing sorties into North Vietnam, Senator George McGovern (D-S.D.) expressed his concern that the United States was embarked on a fruitless exercise. A military victory in South Vietnam was unlikely if not impossible, he commented. Moreover, the United States was not experiencing gains in South Vietnam and was supporting a government in South Vietnam "that is incapable either of winning a military struggle or governing its people." An expanded American military effort, he argued, would be "an act of folly designed in the end to create a larger, more inglorious debacle."[21]

If Johnson heard voices from the Senate raised in protest of his Vietnam policy, he heard a chorus as well supporting the measures he had taken to date. Most senators early in 1965 considered the Vietnam issue a frustrating one, one that offered the United States few alternatives to its current course. The United States should continue its efforts to bring about a negotiated settlement in Vietnam, they suggested, but the negotiations should be conducted from a position of strength. Senator William Proxmire (D-Wisc.) underlined that premise, insisting that "it's a mistake to negotiate when losing."[22]

Indeed, a number of senators emphasized the need for an expanded American presence in Vietnam. Strom Thurmond (R-S.C.) suggested that the South Vietnamese should bring the war to North Vietnam, but "if necessary, bomb [North Vietnam] with United States troops, planes and ammunition." Republicans John Tower of Texas and Jack Miller of Iowa agreed at least about the need for South Vietnam to interdict the infiltration of men and supplies from the North. "Continuation of the present policy means continuation of a policy that is losing the war," Tower informed the Associated Press, while Miller believed that "under this present policy, the situation has deteriorated."[23] Several others indicated that the achievement of American objectives in South Vietnam might necessitate eventually the deployment of American combat troops on a limited and clearly defined scale.[24]

Political considerations tempered Senate criticism of the growing U.S. involvement in Vietnam, perhaps reinforcing the president in his policy as well. Few senators, even those most critical of that policy, proved anxious to strain relations with President Johnson. When J. W. Fulbright disagreed in May 1965 with Secretary of State Dean Rusk over the merits of a bombing pause, he did so reluctantly.[25] Senators Church and McGovern responded quickly to the president's speech at Johns Hopkins in April 1965 in which he had expressed a willingness to discuss unconditionally the Vietnam situation. They praised it for its moderation, cancelled prepared Senate speeches critical of Johnson's Vietnam policy, and deflected in the process potentially strained relations with the White House.[26] In August 1965 Senator Gruening, one of the most outspoken of the early critics of the war, refrained from introducing in the Senate legislation barring the deployment of draftees to Vietnam in response to an "earnest request" from the president.[27]

Domestic politics had a similar impact. Throughout 1964 and most of 1965, the American people generally supported President Johnson's policies in Vietnam. Senators, although partially removed from immediate public pressure due to the electoral cushion afforded by their six-year terms, moved cautiously in an area where the public response reinforced Johnson's escalation of the war. In October 1965, for instance, Senator Edward M. Kennedy (D-Mass.) acknowledged in a news conference that the "overwhelming majority" of Americans supported the president's Vietnam policy. While he used that opportunity to caution the Vietnamese communists not to be misled by what appeared to be substantial opposition to the Johnson administration, he disclosed simultaneously the Senate's perception of the public pulse.[28]

An opportunity for the senators to demonstrate clearly their position toward Johnson's program of escalation came in May 1965 when the president submitted to the legislature a $700 million supplemental military appropriation bill. In his accompanying message, Johnson informed the Congress that everyone "who supports this request is also voting to persist in our effort to halt communist aggression in South Vietnam."[29] Most of the senators recognized that these monies were unnecessary, that they were available elsewhere in the current budget, and many attempted to disassociate themselves from Johnson's maneuver to obtain a vote of confidence. Senator Robert F. Kennedy (D-N.Y.), fuming over the tactic, echoed the sentiments of many of his colleagues when he denied in the Senate that any vote in support of the measure constituted a "blank check."[30] Notwithstanding such qualifications, the Senate voted overwhelmingly in favor of the measure. No doubt most of its members were as conscious as Robert Kennedy that their constituents would consider the appropriation crucial for the safety of the men fighting in Vietnam.[31]

Johnson had his vote and, as already noted, the pattern of escalation continued throughout the remaining months of 1965. Nevertheless, within the Senate strong misgivings persisted, and Senator Mansfield continued to press Johnson for a hard, close review of the American policy. Mansfield's efforts prevailed. In November 1965, the president authorized him and several other senators to travel throughout Europe and Asia for the purpose of discussing the Vietnam issue with foreign leaders.[32]

Mansfield's report, compiled after over a month of travel, meetings, and discussions, offered the president little consolation. Few other nations, he informed the president, expressed a willingness to assist the United States either in its bid for a negotiated settlement or with military assistance. Moreover, the Vietnamese communists remained steadfast and showed "no signs of acquiescing." "If the objectives of our policy remain the same," Mansfield insisted, "the war in Vietnam is just beginning for the United States." Worse, he concluded, "all the choices open to us are bad choices." Pointing out that the United States stood to lose in Vietnam even should it follow a path of restraint, Mansfield also emphasized that this country "stood to lose far more at home and throughout the world by the more extensive military pursuit of an elusive objective in Vietnam."[33]

Mansfield acknowledged that his views did not necessarily reflect those of the entire Senate, but because he was the majority leader, Johnson was acutely aware that Mansfield spoke for many of his Senate colleagues.[34] By the end of 1965, these senators knew the direction of American policy in Vietnam and they encouraged Johnson to reverse it. Johnson chose continued escalation, and Mansfield's report proved to be for the president and the nation an ominous prophecy.

NOTES

1. Mike Mansfield to Lyndon Johnson, 5, 9, 14 June 1965, attached to McGeorge Bundy to Mike Mansfield, 29 June 1965, Name File, National Security File, Box 5, LBJ Library.

2. The figures appear in Peter Braestrup, ed., "Appendices," *Vietnam as History: Ten Years after the Paris Peace Accords* (Washington, D.C.: University Press of America, 1984). The best short account of that escalation and the American involvement in Vietnam is George C. Herring, *America's Longest War: The United States and Vietnam, 1970–1975* (New York: John Wiley and Sons, 1979).

3. *New York Times*, 17 January 1965.

4. For details of the election of 1964, see Allen J. Matusow, *The Unraveling of America: A History of Liberalism in the 1960s* (New York: Harper & Row, Publishers, 1984), 131–152.

5. Accounts of the Tonkin Gulf incident appear in Joseph C. Goulden, *Truth Is the First Casualty: The Gulf of Tonkin Affair, Illusion and Reality* (Chicago: Rand McNally,

1969); John Galloway, *The Gulf of Tonkin Resolution* (Rutherford, N.J.: Fairleigh Dickinson University Press, 1970); and Eugene C. Windchy, *Tonkin Gulf* (Garden City, N.Y.: Doubleday and Co., 1971).

6. U.S. Congress, 88th Cong., 1st Sess., 7 October 1963, *Congressional Record*, 18814; Ernest Gruening, *Many Battles: The Autobiography of Ernest Gruening* (New York: Liveright, 1973), 467.

7. *Congressional Record*, 88th Cong., 2d Sess., 10 March 1964, 4832.

8. *Congressional Record*, 88th Cong., 2d Sess., 7 August 1964, 18425, 18447–18449.

9. Ibid., 6 August 1964, 18413.

10. Fulbright to W. C. Holland, 5 June 1964, cited in William Berman, "Fulbright and Johnson: Before and After the Gulf of Tonkin Affair," unpublished manuscript, LBJ Library, 5–6.

11. Fulbright to Fred W. Neal, 25 September 1964, quoted in ibid., 18.

12. See, for example, Fulbright's comments reported in the *New York Times*, 3, 19 April, 6 May, 16 June, 20 July, and 25 October 1965.

13. *New York Times*, 6 January, 9 February, 1965; J. William Fulbright interview, Former Members of Congress Collection, Box #4, 21, Manuscripts Division, Library of Congress, Washington, D.C.

14. *New York Times*, 19 April, 6 May 1965.

15. *Record*, 89th Cong., 1st Sess., 15 June 1965; *New York Times*, 25 October 1965.

16. Mansfield to LBJ, 8, 10 February 1965, Johnson Papers, National Security File, Name File, National Security File, Box 5, LBJ Library.

17. Mansfield to LBJ, 14 June 1965, Name File, National Security File, Box 5, LBJ Library.

18. Mansfield to LBJ, 9 June 1965, ibid.

19. Mansfield to LBJ, 27 July 1965, Johnson Papers, National Security File, National Security Council Histories: Deployment of Major U.S. Forces to Vietnam, July 1965, Box 40.

20. *New York Times*, 7 January 1965.

21. Ibid., 16 January 1965.

22. Ibid., 7 January 1965.

23. Ibid.

24. See, for example, the comments of Wallace F. Bennett (R-Utah), and Harrison A. Williams (D-N.J.) made in response to an Associated Press survey. Ibid.

25. Ibid., 19 May 1965.

26. Lyndon Baines Johnson, *The Vantage Point: Perspectives of the Presidency, 1963–1969* (New York: Holt, Rinehart and Winston, 1971), 132–134; *New York Times*, 8 April 1965; Kathleen J. Turner, *Lyndon Johnson's Dual War* (Chicago: University of Chicago Press, 1985), 130.

27. Ernest Gruening to LBJ, 20 August 1965, and LBJ to Gruening, 21 August 1965, Confidential File, Country File, Vietnam, Box 71, LBJ Library. Gruening did eventually introduce the amendment in 1966. *New York Times*, 26 January 1966.

28. John Mueller, "Reflections on the Vietnam Antiwar Movement and on the Curious Calm at the War's End," 151, and, "A Summary of Public Opinion and the Vietnam War," both in Peter Braestrup, ed., "Appendices," *Vietnam as History*; *New York Times*, 24 October 1965.

29. Johnson's statement appears in Ernest Gruening and Herbert W. Beaser, *Vietnam Folly* (Washington: National Press, 1968), 21.

30. *Congressional Record*, 89th Cong., 1st Sess., 6 May 1965, 9760–9763; Arthur M. Schlesinger, Jr., *Robert Kennedy and His Times* (Boston: Houghton Mifflin Company, 1978), 729–730. Others expressing similar sentiments were George Aiken (R-Vt.), Albert Gore (D-Tenn.), and Jacob Javits (R-N.Y.). *New York Times*, 6 May 1965.

31. Schlesinger, *Robert Kennedy*, 729. The appropriation bill passed in the Senate, eighty-seven to three. The three dissenters were Wayne Morse (D-Ore.), Ernest Gruening (D-Alaska), and Gaylord Nelson (D-Wisc.). *Congressional Record*, 89th Cong., 1st Sess., 6 May 1965, 9367. The bill received a similar endorsement in the House, 408–407. Ibid., 5 May 1965.

32. The group was bipartisan and included besides Mansfield, George Aiken (R-Vt.), Edmund Muskie (D-Me.), Daniel Inouye (D-Hawaii), and Hale Boggs (D-La.). Jack Valenti to Johnson, 10 November 1965, Confidential File, FG 431 F, WHCF, Box 34, and Mansfield to Johnson, 17 December 1965, Int. Mtg. & Travel, National Security File, Box 30, LBJ Library.

33. Mansfield to Johnson, 18 December 1965, ibid.

34. Mansfield to Johnson, 17 December 1965, ibid.

22

The Vietnam War in Perspective: A Panel Discussion

Editors' Note: The Vietnam War was Lyndon Johnson's tragedy, and ultimately his undoing. While there were many other triumphs and failures associated with the Johnson administration, no other played an equivalent role in affecting the president's political fortunes. The war helped to end Johnson's mastery over Congress, dramatically altered his standing in public opinion, provoked the challenge from within his own party that would eventually lead to his withdrawal from the 1968 elections, and robbed him of the status in history that his accomplishments might otherwise have earned him. In the following panel discussion, former administration officials, an anti-war activist, and a leading scholar explore the reasons underlying Johnson's approach to the war and examine the consequences for him and the nation. Among the former officials are National Security Adviser W. W. Rostow, Assistant Secretary of State William P. Bundy, Ambassador William H. Sullivan, and Undersecretary of the Air Force Townsend Hoopes, perhaps better known for his critical study of the administration's Vietnam policy, *The Limits of Intervention*. Anti-war activist Tom Hayden reviews his own role, and political scientist Larry Berman, author of *Planning a Tragedy*, discusses his current research. Historian Herbert Parmet moderates.

MODERATOR: HERBERT PARMET

Greetings to everybody here. We are, thirteen years since the last American troops were removed from Vietnam, in danger of having [the lessons of] that experience [govern our approach to today's world]—just as the Cold War response was largely determined by what had happened before World War II and, in fact, the so-called lessons of World War I had colored our reactions in the 1930s. We have, in other words, at this point, been moving from the World

War II maxims, it seems to me, to the Vietnam maxims, and there are a number of [such maxims] which may to some extent constitute a consensus. One is stated very cogently in a most recent book by a respected American historian who has written that "Vietnam cut short the rush to the Great Society, smashed Johnson's consensus and made him one of the most hated chief executives in a hundred years." The other side of that indicates that because of our inability to pursue the objective and because of the congressional undermining of the war, Southeast Asia—at this point certainly what had been Indochina—is now entirely communist, whereas it need not have been. These and many other ideas are going to be discussed in the following two hours. I would now like to present Mr. Walt Rostow.

W. W. ROSTOW

In the short time properly made available to me, I evidently cannot present an analysis of all the factors that determined President Johnson's position on Southeast Asia and Vietnam. When a president makes the kind of solemn decision President Johnson did in July of 1965, it is almost always because a number of quite different factors converge, and I think that was so in July of 1965. But I shall confine myself to one proposition and a brief comment on it. The proposition I have in mind is this: President Johnson's perspective on Vietnam and Southeast Asia was strongly affected by his judgment of the greatly increased importance to the United States of Asia as a whole.

But there was a second related strand that surprised me when I first ran across it, and it may surprise you; and I find it may even surprise my distinguished younger colleague in history, Professor Berman. Johnson's vision of a future where Asians and Americans would live and work in increasing intimacy converged in the late 1950s with his assumption—in the Senate on the issue of civil rights—of leadership leading to the legislation of 1957, the first civil rights legislation since Reconstruction.

This convergence of his views on Asia and civil rights accounts for the reversal of his position on statehood for Hawaii. The mixture of races in Hawaii became in his eyes not as it had been to those who opposed statehood—a dangerous example and precedent—but a dual asset, an asset in our relations with Asia and an asset as we struggled to build a peaceful, multiracial society of equal opportunity at home.

I would underline that Johnson's position on civil rights was, of course, not wholly determined by his view of the future importance of Asia; but his views of Asia reinforced his position on civil rights, and he understood that a segregationist America could not be a valid and effective partner with the Asia beginning to demonstrate its dynamism in the second half of the 1950s.

My first insight into this linkage occurred on October 17, 1966, en route from Washington to Hawaii on the first leg of the president's three weeks' tour through Asia. Johnson had worked hard with several of us—including, if my memory is correct, Bill Bundy and Bill Moyers—on his major speech in Honolulu which was to be delivered at the East-West Center. On Air Force One, however, after reading over the draft in which he had been actively participating, he decided to add something. He dictated a passage which included the following:

My forebears came from Britain and Germany. People in my section of the country regarded Asia as totally alien in spirit as well as nationality. We therefore looked away from the Pacific, away from its hopes as well as from its great crisis. Even the wars that many of us fought here were often with leftovers of preparedness, and they did not heal our blindness. One consequence of that blindness was that Hawaii was denied its rightful part in our union of states for many years. Frankly, for two decades, I opposed its admission as a state until at last the undeniable evidence of history, as well as the irresistible persuasiveness of Jack Burns removed the scales from my eyes. Then I began to work and fight for Hawaiian statehood, and I hold that to be one of my proudest achievements of my twenty-five years in the Congress.

Later in the speech he referred to Hawaii as a model of how men and women of different races and different cultures can come and live and work together, to respect each other in freedom and in hope. There is no doubt that John Burns had a considerable impact on Johnson in this matter. Burns was the Hawaiian delegate without voting rights in Congress in the late 1950s and, later, governor of the state. Johnson also referred, in his Honolulu speech, to the East-West Center as "this very special place to me," and indeed it was that. That was not a statement of courtesy for the occasion. It was Johnson who initiated the legislation creating the center, nurtured it in the Senate and was active as vice president in assuring its funding. It remained to him a living part of his vision of future relations in the Pacific Basin.

The theme of President Johnson's 1966 tour through Asia was not Vietnam. It was the future of Asia—the need for Asia to organize regionally to shape its own destiny. His hope and faith: "Sooner or later, the pragmatic and compassionate spirit of the Chinese people will prevail and the policies of mainland China will offer and permit reconciliation, and the future role of the United States as a neighbor among equals, a partner in the great adventure of bringing peace, order, and progress to a part of the world where more than half of the entire human race lives."

President Johnson saw the frustration of aggression in Southeast Asia—with the assistance of New Zealand and Australia, South Korea, the Philippines, and Thailand—as a condition for this positive vision to come to life; and I can attest that this was a major part of the framework within which he viewed our task in Southeast Asia from April 1, 1966, when I went over from the State Department to the White House, to January 20, 1969.

In Asia and the Pacific, Johnson's view was fully understood. Indeed, leadership in building Asian regionalism was in the hands of a remarkable group of statesmen in the whole arc from Wellington and Canberra through Djakarta and Singapore and Bangkok to Tokyo and Seoul. Without the leadership of these

Asian statesmen of the 1960s who continued creative work in the 1970s and down to the present, American advocacy would have been fruitless. But neither at the time, nor in retrospect, was it widely appreciated in the west that Johnson's approach to the problem of Vietnam was deeply rooted in his vision of the inevitable [and] increasing importance of Asia and the need for the fragmented states of Asia to organize on a regional and subregional basis. Among western journals, only the *London Economist* and *Fortune*, for example, discussed seriously the significance of these themes in reporting his 1966 tour through the region. I would guess that most analysts would accept the central thesis of Leslie Gelb and Richard Betts in their serious study *The Irony of Vietnam*, and I quote: "United States leaders," they write, "considered it vital not to lose Vietnam by force to communism. They believed Vietnam to be vital not for itself, but for what they thought its loss would mean internationally and domestically." I have no doubt that there were some officials in the executive branch in the 1960s who took precisely the view Gelb and Betts asserted. But Lyndon Johnson— and I would add John Kennedy—was not among them.

But in mid–1965, when Johnson made his critical decision on Vietnam, the meaning of Asia and its future was not a long-term abstract, mystical, historical question. It was real and urgent. [President] Sukarno [of Indonesia] had taken Indonesia out of the United Nations late in 1964. He had entered an explicit alliance with North Korea, China, North Vietnam, and Cambodia. Together they mounted what Sukarno called a nutcracker movement of which one arm was the Malaysian confrontation, the other, the movement of North Vietnamese regular forces to South Vietnam via Laos. At the New Year's Day diplomatic reception in January in Peking in 1965, the Chinese foreign minister announced that "Thailand was next." The governments of the whole region were authentically alarmed, including those of New Zealand, Australia, Singapore, Malaysia, Thailand, and Laos. The wobbly dominos were not a theory in the summer of 1965, as any historian can easily establish from documents now available. And one vivid source, incidentally, is the memoir of the Australian diplomat, the late Sir Howard Beale. It was only after Johnson's July decision on Vietnam and the later failure of the coup backed by Sukarno that noncommunist Asia began to breathe a bit easier.

But to return to the thesis of Gelb and Betts, Johnson did indeed consider the impact of the failure to honor successfully the Southeast Asia treaty on other American alliances and on American society and on our politics. But that treaty unambiguously spread the mantle of U.S. protection and commitment over South Vietnam, and he believed that treaty reflected an abiding American interest in Asia. He did not require a super computer, even an abacus, to understand that Asia would soon be at least as important to the United States as Europe if not more important. Incidentally, he would have chuckled with satisfaction at learning that 25 percent of the undergraduate students at the University of California at Berkeley are now Asian or of Asian extraction.

I have presented this theme today not to argue that President Johnson was correct. None of us knows whether any of us—including presidents with whom we worked and supported—was correct. I happen to believe he was; but that's not the point. I chose this theme as a historian in the hope that after our discussion today this dimension of Johnson's perspective on Vietnam will be understood and simply taken into account in future analyses of the 1960s.

Johnson's perspective may be worth considering for another reason. Southeast Asia as of 1986 is both a hopeful and precarious place. President [Jimmy] Carter and President [Ronald] Reagan have reaffirmed the continued applicability of the Southeast Asian Treaty to Thailand, including the 1962 supplementary U.S. commitment, to act in support of the treaty, whether or not other signatories respond. It's by no means certain that we shall again confront military crisis in that region. The Asian countries used well the time painfully bought between 1965 and 1975. They are much stronger and more confident now than twenty years ago. Hanoi has had great difficulty trying to consolidate its empire in Indochina as well as expanding and modernizing the Vietnamese economy. President [Gerald] Ford and his two successors did not accept the actions of the Congress in the mid–1970s as determining long-run U.S. policy towards Southeast Asia or Asia as a whole. Our relations with China and the region, as elsewhere, have changed for the better.

On the other hand, large Vietnamese forces are on the long and highly vulnerable Thai border. Substantial Soviet naval and air forces operate every day out of the bases we built at Camranh Bay and around Da Nang just across from Subic Bay and Clark Field in the Philippines. The sea routes of the South China Sea through the straits to the Indian Ocean, so literally vital to Japan and China and indeed to all the other countries of the Pacific Basin, are not as secure as they were. Not many Americans recall that Franklin Roosevelt cut off from Japan the flow of scrap iron and oil and sequestered their assets when they threatened these routes by moving their forces from northern to southern Indochina in 1941. I would say, incidentally, as a historian, that is where the *Pentagon Papers* should have begun, but didn't. And Franklin Roosevelt's eight successors, without exception, have all asserted our security interest in the area. The nine presidents who have taken successively a consistent position in the past forty-five years may have been wrong, but I suggest that it would be useful in this period of relative calm and hope for the Pacific Basin that we as a nation look far back and far forward and come to a stable consensus on our policy toward the region.

TOM HAYDEN

I am pleased to journey so far to be here. So far not only into the past but from the area that I now reside in, Santa Monica, California, which is an area which has an unusually large number of a subgroup of a subgroup of the Yuppies called the Frumpies, the formerly radical upwardly mobile young professionals, which may explain why I am now in office.

I recently, for the first time, visited the Lyndon Baines Johnson Library in Austin. I had other business there. I knew I was coming here to speak. I dropped by to see Professor Rostow. I have never been to the LBJ Library and I don't know if you have, but I for the first time felt an urge or an ability to reconnect and try to see what I could learn and what it had to communicate as an institution that housed a particular memory. There is a lovely grassy hill there with a fountain where one can reflect on the past and the 1960s before one goes into what is rather a larger windowless building, something like a tomb. Inside on the first floor I toured the foreign policy exhibit, where the visitor learns the LBJ years were "crowded with events, dramatic, tragic, hopeful, which related to foreign affairs," and the exhibit presents three of those events each [about] which it says "for a while commanded the world's attention"—Glassboro, the Six Day War, and Vietnam. Glassboro, a forgotten summit, the Six Day War, an area of Israeli conflict, are equated with Vietnam, which for a while commanded the world's attention, as if each were equal in our measurement of the Lyndon Baines Johnson years and the impact on our lives.

Going further, the Vietnam exhibit in the library told me that first Lyndon Baines Johnson continued the policies of Eisenhower and Kennedy to preserve the independence of South Vietnam; that the war began, or in the words of the exhibit, "was triggered by North Vietnamese attack in the Gulf of Tonkin"; that "LBJ chose the middle course between a pullout and an all-out war"; that "our forces were able generally to stabilize the situation by 1968, but the communists achieved a marked psychological advantage as frustrations over the war grew." There is reference to the bombing of military targets and improving the lives of the people of South Vietnam, although the exhibit notes that this was not widely noted or reported in the press. Before leaving office, the exhibit concludes, "Lyndon Baines Johnson persuaded the communists to begin peace talks" and when he left office 35,541 Americans, in the words of the exhibit, "had given their lives."

As best I can tell, twenty years later, none of this is true. President Johnson radically departed from the past policies by escalating a war and eventually sending 500,000 troops. The Gulf of Tonkin incident was more a pretext than a cause. It was hardly a middle course that we pursued. The tonnage of bombs dropped, the number of lives lost far exceeded anything in recent memory. Nineteen hundred sixty-eight was, far from being a year of stability, the year of greatest upheaval for this generation. And as for military targets, while there were many military targets bombed, I can say from personal experience that there were plenty of nonmilitary targets as well.

If this were simply a personal epitaph, I would not raise it. In ordinary life such things are allowed in order to allow the deceased and their kin to rest more easily, but this is a perpetuation of deceit beyond death. It's an epitaph of evasion which lays the foundation for the current surge of what I could call [the] politics of denial of what happened in Vietnam—the politics of illusion, which is easily perpetuated apparently in a country that is easily comforted by myth and nostalgia, a country which is still to an unfortunate degree capable of confusing Custer and John Wayne, Rambo and Ronald Reagan. Despite these efforts to rewrite history which is all about us, I believe that for most Americans, Vietnam was not a "noble cause," as President Reagan refers to it. Vietnam was not a "noble cause," but was an American tragedy. It was, for those of us who look coldly at it, the end of innocence and the beginning of a new American experience, an experience of frustration of not being able to win. This is not an attitude that has been accepted by all Americans, and it is currently fashionable, as I said, to rewrite the history of the time. Those who say that we should not have been there and could not have prevailed are considered by some to be weak and the attitude of no regrets still prevails in official circles too much in this country.

I believe that at least my generation wants not to put the war behind us—that can never happen—but wants to reconcile, wants to heal the divisions that were imposed upon my generation by the experience of the war, but not at the expense of the truth. There are several things that can help us overcome the divisions that were imposed on the Vietnam generation. For one, the fact that we were *all* deceived. We served in Vietnam or served in the protest movement. Second, a common sense that many of us paid our dues—whether we were in Vietnam or whether we were here. We sacrificed, we felt persecution; in some cases we were cut off from our society. Many who served in Vietnam felt that for years and years and years they could not communicate with their brothers and sisters of their own age group who had protested. In my case, which is not an unusual one, I could not speak to my father for twelve years because of my protest of the war.

So I believe that a certain strength, if you will, can come from having second thoughts and that strength can be the basis of reconciliation. None who participated in those times ought to feel or does feel utterly righteous in their role. I have my particular regrets as do others. Mine include the regret that I was infected with a hostility that alienated me from this country for years. I regret now than Hanoi has an imperial design on impoverished Cambodia and has largely done away with pluralism in the southern part of Vietnam. I regret that I was not more critical of the cynical motives of the Soviet Union and, most of all, I regret that I inadvertently compounded the pain of many Americans who lost sons or loved ones in Vietnam. I think though that regrets can be a basis of strengths rather than weaknesses.

In looking at the lessons of Vietnam nothing could be worse than to remain frozen in the premises and perspectives that we had a generation ago. None of us should be prisoners of that experience, as if it contains clear lessons that are permanent guideposts to the future. In fact, I think that often the lessons of the past become the pitfalls of the future. I think it is true that we cannot be the policemen of the world, but it is also true that we cannot withdraw from it or naively believe that all conflicts can simply be peacefully negotiated. It is true, in my opinion, that a Vietnam-style war in Central America would be dishonorable and tragic, but it's also true that Third World revolutions bring new forms of repression. It is true, I think, that we must confront the root causes of unrest, but it is also true that we need a strong military defense against terror. It is true that we are strengthened by democratic controversy about foreign policy and that we are weakened by an imperial presidency, but it is also true that we do need a post-Vietnam foreign policy consensus, and we lack one. These are among the issues that face today's generation, and I don't believe the answers to these questions can be found in Vietnam.

The Vietnam experience cannot provide answers, but it can provide humility—a humility, that I think, we need to be strong enough to hear each other and to arrive at meaningful consensus. The attitude I have in mind can be found in visiting a very different sort of monument to Vietnam—that is the Vietnam Memorial in Washington, D.C. Far different from the LBJ Library in Austin, in Washington, for those of you who have not been there, you come to a city of monuments, pillars, majestic sorts of monuments, that hearken to times of previous glory in this nation's history, and you almost stumble as we did into Vietnam. You almost stumble into the Vietnam memorial, which is a black scar on the green earth of Washington, and as you descend into it you feel that you are enveloped in a mirror in which you see other monuments to past moments of glory. You see the names of the dead, and you see yourself reflected over and behind the names of those dead. There is no attempt in that memorial to hide the truth. No attempt to repeat the deceit, no euphemistic declaration about men giving their lives. Only the fact that those men lost died for nothing, unless we can turn their tragedy into a better future.

WILLIAM H. SULLIVAN

To me the supreme irony of Vietnam is this: The United States, its allies, and its friends did not win the war in Indochina. Indeed, we lost the war. But the irony is that in strategic terms the current situation is far more satisfactory to the U.S., its allies, and its friends than it would have been had we won the war. Now let me make clear what I am saying. I am not talking about the enormous losses of life. I'm not talking about the enormous expenditure of the treasury. I am not talking about the disruption, turmoil in American society, that resulted from Vietnam. In cold strategic terms, I am just saying that the United States, its allies, and its friends are now better off than they would have been had they won the war. Let me explain that.

If we had won the war, we would doubtless continue to have American troops in South Vietnam. If we had American troops doubtless in South Vietnam, China would doubtless feel obligated to sublimate its distaste to North Vietnam and to continue to supply logistics to them. In order to do that, China would have had to continue to have some sort of policy of association with the Soviet Union, which it has since ruptured. Now, as Walt Rostow explained, the intervention President Johnson and three other American presidents undertook militarily in

Indochina was not solely due to the actions of the Vietnamese pushing against South Vietnam and Laos. It was also due to their perceptions of what he called the nutcracker movement—Chinese subversion in Thailand, the Philippines, and, above all, Indonesia. We don't know entirely what turned the Chinese leadership around, but it is very clear that by the end of the 1960s to the beginning of the 1970s, the Chinese leadership's view of the world and the Soviet Union, and of the United States, had changed enormously. The Chinese leadership was probably affected by the failure of the coup in Indonesia in 1965, something historians have not given adequate attention to. It was probably also affected by the extremism and by the radicalism of the Cultural Revolution and the Gang of Four. It was probably also affected by the fact that American presidents did put American troops into Indochina and were not paper tigers. They [American presidents] might have been frustrated to the point where they might have used a nuclear weapon [and] that certainly acted to deter the great zeal that the Chinese never felt toward North Vietnam. Whatever the reasons were, the Chinese shift at the end of the Vietnam time was made possible because the United States no longer had troops there, and when they made that shift, I don't think that I can express the cosmic proportions of the change in [the] strategic balance in Asia, because the Soviet Union and the Chinese were allied from 1950 down 'till that change.

The United States used to think in contingency terms of fighting two and a half wars. Now we have to think only in terms of fighting one and a half wars. Our whole so-called SIOP—our Single Integrated Operational Plan of deploying forces in the Western Pacific—has been changed. The attitude of the Chinese toward the Soviets is not an ephemeral one. The conditions they've made for improving relations are fundamental, and therefore we can consider the change fundamental. The change has produced an equilibrium in Asia that has brought about a better prospect for peace and prosperity since any time since the sixteenth century in the Pacific region.

This was all an inadvertent consequence of American intervention in Vietnam, but it proves, it seems to me, that even when we get into circumstances when we don't win that sometimes there can be consequences that we have not contemplated. I don't know what lesson to draw from that. I'm not suggesting that we should have a policy of entering wars for the purpose of losing them, but I would like to say that when we put the whole perspective of Vietnam in perspective, in strategic terms, I think ironic conclusions of historians will be rather remarkable.

TOWNSEND HOOPES

If viewed in the long perspective of the whole period from 1945–1975, the Vietnam War looks very much today like a series of false assumptions, miscalculations, repeated mistakes, and missed opportunities, all adding up to failure writ large. The Johnson administration certainly did not have a monopoly of these shortcomings, but it did fail to learn from the earlier mistakes of others and it was no doubt the victim of conditions created by those earlier errors of perception and judgment. George Kennan once said that if you trace back along the chain of cause and effect treating each cause as the effect of an earlier cause and so on until you arrive at the first cause, then you are forced to make a philosophical judgment of either cosmic forgiveness or cosmic unforgiveness, and, viewed in perspective, I think the Vietnam War seems rather like that. We failed out of understandable ignorance and the accident of President [Franklin] Roosevelt's death to prevent the return of the French to Indochina in 1945. This led to a nasty colonial war in which we [lost] a real opportunity to recognize Ho Chi Minh as a legitimate Vietnamese nationalist, and we ended up supporting and bankrolling the French war because they demanded it as a price for their support for NATO, and NATO was central to our strategic concerns. Especially after the Korean War, we became obsessed by the domino theory and acted on the assumption that Ho Chi Minh was merely an agent of international communism, ignoring the deep historic enmity between China and Vietnam.

After the French defeat, we refused to underwrite the Geneva Accords because that involved legitimizing [a] communist conquest of Vietnam, and this was anathema in our domestic politics, but this drove away all of the other potential great power guarantors of that settlement. We did manage to abide by the accords, but we said that we would view any renewal of aggression with grave concern. For two years we supported President [Ngo Dinh] Diem's refusal to hold the Vietnam elections promised in 1956 by those Geneva Accords, and when this refusal, not surprisingly, led Ho Chi Minh to reopen the civil war we found ourselves the only willing guarantor of South Vietnam. We then construed an essential civil war as a conclusive global test of Khrushchev's newly proclaimed wars of national liberation doctrine. We then jumped to the conclusion that this was of vital interest to the U.S., and we committed our support to a government and a series of governments that intrinsically lacked both competency and legitimacy. To assure success and to protect our own prestige, we took over the conduct of the war, and as we assumed a heavier and heavier share of the burden, the South Vietnamese governments were less and less motivated to stand on their own feet. Our effort was first conceived as a counterinsurgency when it turned out the only war we were prepared for was a war of mass firepower and mobility, and this was the only kind of war for which we had trained the 175,000-man South Vietnamese Army.

This kind of massively destructive campaign was inconsistent with our stated political aim to win the hearts and minds of the peasantry. The [General William] Westmoreland campaign destroyed millions of crops, drove millions of peasants into swallowed refugee camps, and uprooted the whole economic structure of South Vietnam. The Westmoreland strategy of attrition was that the U.S. could accept greater casualties and over a longer period of time than the North Vietnamese and the Vietcong. The bombing strategy assumed that we could cripple the North Vietnamese productivity and morale, but it strengthened the national morale and cohesion just as had happened as a result of Hitler bombing London, since North Vietnam was basically a conduit for supplies from Russia and China and needed only five tons per day to carry on the war in the south.

To save the cherished Great Society program, President Johnson proclaimed a goal of limited objectives in South Vietnam but refused in fact to countenance any solution involving Vietcong participation in South Vietnamese government. This meant, in fact, that the only acceptable solution to us was total victory and that implied a war effort without any definable limits. The war effort indeed became impaled on this fundamental contradiction.

In another consequential maneuver to save the Great Society program by disguising the cost of the war, President Johnson declined to ask for [higher] taxes until about two and a half years after we were well into it, in mid–1967, but the total cost of the war outran even new taxes and thus began the dizzying inflationary spiral that brought us to the 20 percent interest rates in the 1970s.

In all of this it appears that we were propelled by our sense of great power responsibility to our conception of world order by the dynamics of internal politics and by our sense of omnipotence. As the war went on, we were concerned chiefly increasingly to save our own national prestige. Our options were limited by our cumulative costs of blood and treasure expended and the fear of right wing retribution in the event of a negotiated solution that fell short of clear victory. And so the enterprise ended in serious, perhaps total, failure and tore the remaining shreds of our postwar foreign policy consensus.

WILLIAM BUNDY

I want to talk in the vein that Tom Hayden tried to steer us into and very movingly. I feel very humble about Vietnam. I have deep regrets about it. I never go to Washington without going to the memorial, practically. I also had a very different interpretation of the exhibits in the LBJ Library, which I also visited, as it happens, within the last month. I don't think the exhibits on Vietnam are open entirely to the interpretations that Tom Hayden has drawn. And I most certainly do not think that the existence of exhibits on Glassboro and the Six Day War [lend themselves to the same interpretation]. [There] could equally be at any given time an exhibit on the Nuclear Nonproliferation Treaty or on how Lyndon Baines Johnson pressed India to learn to grow its own food with fantastic results for the benefit of the Indian people over the next generation.

But in any case, it is a basic truth that the Vietnam War was not solely a matter of the Johnson administration—that point has now been made by others—and that the Johnson administration's foreign policy was by no means confined to Vietnam. That's one point. I found my points incidentally being taken by the other speakers so I'm speaking almost extemporaneously. I, of course, agree with Tom Hayden that the war was deeply tragic.

I do think that we have on this panel only two of the three basic points of view toward the war that exist in this country, and that is perhaps unfortunate, but I think we could come quite close to an agreement on the tragic interpretation between those who are here who are backers, often with regret, and those who became critics. The one we lack, the third element we lack, are what I would call hawk-critics of the war who think the tragedy was that we didn't go all out and win. We would have a balanced panel if we had a contemporary representative of that view of which there were many—and many who voted for Gene McCarthy in the New Hampshire primary in March 1968, where, as you know, later studies show that the majority of those who voted for him wanted to do more rather than less. It would be represented perhaps contemporaneously by one who came only laterally to that view like Norman Podhoretz, the editor of *Commentary*. We are talking among backers, backers with regrets, and I would call, just shorthand, dove-critics among this panel, and that must be borne in mind. We are not responding to the views of our contemporary president on the war, and we must again bear that in mind.

One point I thought I could still make, although Tim Hoopes just mentioned it, came to me particularly forcefully yesterday listening to the Great Society panel and reaching the conclusion that it was the war that prevented the Great Society from a fair test in many ways. I think Frank Keppel [Johnson's commissioner of education] mentioned it. We were only allowed to go three innings, and that is emphatically true. There is no question about it, and to me the greatest depth of the tragedy is that Lyndon Johnson tried in his presidency to do two terribly hard things. He tried to conduct a policy in Vietnam that would see it through and carry on what he saw as the tradition and the view that he accepted of its importance in Asia. Vietnam was a *duty*. The Great Society was a *passion* with Lyndon Johnson, and that is basic. And I would think that it was time, perhaps for historians, and I am looking at my colleagues on the panel Mr. Parmet and Mr. Berman, to try to put along side each other the chronology of the Great Society and the chronology of the Vietnam War. You cannot examine in my view key decisions by Johnson concerning at least the presentation of the war to the people and to the Congress unless you understand that in the background was his passion for going ahead with the Great Society for the benefit of the American people, and as was noted in an earlier panel today, taking advantage of that third window of opportunity in this century where the Congress could be persuaded to adopt a needed program of sweeping reform and where that need had become in his view burning and palpable.

I, with respect to many episodes that contributed to the credibility gap, think that contributed to what he said in the 1964 campaign because he wanted a big enough majority and mandate to start and initiate the Great Society. It contributed to the way he was less than totally candid about the initiation of the bombing and the introduction of the marines and so on and the other events in the early part of 1965, where he was trying to keep the way clear for the legislative first steps to the Great Society. It affects particularly what I regard as the single most clear error in the presentation of the war to the people and in the making of it a war in which we at least understood what we were doing—namely, the failure to have a great debate in August of 1965, because that would have entailed a filibuster by [Senator] Wayne Morse that would have delayed or possibly prevented the passage of 30 or 40 percent of the initial authorizing bills of the Great Society. And then in the early part of 1966 where the true foreseen costs of the war were not fairly presented to the Congress, because of the president's desire to keep the decks clear for the authorizing legislation and because of his view that he would lose crucial votes in the center and on the conservative side if he was totally blunt about what the war was going to cost. In other words, the Great Society was a planetary influence on the way he presented the war. I do not suggest that he changed his basic policy on Vietnam or the basic decisions, but I think it made a great deal of difference to the way the war was understood, to the honesty with which it was debated, an honesty that was not perfect on either side, I think it is fair to say. Definitely not fair on many of the opponents' side who never were able to admit that what they were really after was total withdrawal and that any idea of a negotiated answer, with all respect [to] Tim Hoopes, was nonsense, and [had no] serious chance of maintaining an independent South Vietnam.

Now, it's that that I hope we can look at a little more. It's an interesting point for historians. It's a terribly important point in judging Lyndon Johnson. He was attacked at the time as devious, manipulative, many of those things, and he was not free of qualities of that sort, but in the case of Vietnam, I deeply believe that nine-tenths of what he did—that was not simply honest misjudgment, easily mistaken for deception but of course entirely different—but nine-tenths of what he did in this regard that was designed not to present Vietnam totally candidly was because he cared so passionately about the Great Society, and the depth of the tragedy for him and for the country was that in the end, of course he got the worst of both worlds.

LARRY BERMAN

Herb Parmet pointed out that we are involved in a reexamination of Vietnam. I think that is a crucial word—*reexamination*. As a scholar I have been involved in the reexamination of the war in the past four years in my writing and in my speaking. In that regard I want to say a word about the Johnson Library, and I want to take the elevator up from the exhibits to the eighth floor of the library where the ongoing vital nerve or center where Vietnam research is being conducted. I might point out that Harry Middleton, the director of the library, and the Johnson Foundation have done everything possible to expedite the research by scholars into the area of Vietnam by making declassifications available, and I think both the archivists in the library and the staff, from the researcher's perspective up on the eighth floor, have expedited the nature of the Vietnam inquiry. I wanted to make that point because most people do in fact stop on that first floor or second floor, and I think the reassessment of Vietnam is occurring in the research room where we are aptly served by the Johnson Library. As a scholar of the war, I have always used John Roche, his wonderful requirement that he would be waiting at heaven's gate demanding footnotes of those who wrote on Vietnam and sought to bring malice towards Johnson and that if we came with documents, we would get through. And I have accepted that as a primary requirement for my own research, because I really do feel that Vietnam was a very important part of my life and the research and documentation become essential to it.

I have always wondered, as John Roche said, why Lyndon Johnson played a middle hand in a game of high-low poker and why he did it from 1965 to 1968. And ultimately some of the issues just addressed by Bill Bundy about the Great Society and his passion to see the Great Society reach fulfillment would give you a good answer [as] to why this man of tremendous political talents and instincts—there was no man who came to the presidency with a better vita for the presidency than LBJ, having done his internships in the House and the Senate, the master of political consensus—seemed to fail in the real critical test of trying to build a national consensus to lead us either into war or out of war.

The puzzle of Lyndon Johnson becomes one I think for political scientists and historians: the fact that we really only had three innings for the Great Society. I'm also always aware of the admonition that those who write history have the gift of revision and those who make it get only one chance, and in that sense it is easy to see with more sympathy than I once did while protesting the war the tremendous pressure that came to bear on Lyndon Johnson in July of 1965, where on the one hand George Ball recommended something tantamount to negotiated surrender and Johnson would be the first president to lose a war.

And put yourself in a time capsule back in 1965. There would have been no Great Society had he walked away, and I think Johnson understood that because the backlash would have been so great. And there would have been no Great Society had he taken the recommendation of the joint chiefs and bombed to smithereens North Vietnam or mined the harbors. I think it was real that he thought that the Soviets or the Chinese [could intervene], when would [come] the accident that would lead us to a World War III. The tremendous pressure of a president sitting in a situation room or in the White House trying to make the right decision. In hindsight, I don't believe he made the right decision, but in that time capsule, it's necessary to go back and to view these things, never forgetting there is a whole context of history.

My own Berman corollary to all this is that those who participated in these decisions—as one reads the depositions in the Westmoreland-CBS trial or one reads oral histories—those who participated often have recollections of amnesia victims in the sense of exactly what did and what did not occur in July of 1965 or of 1966. The release of new documents bearing on decisions of President Johnson in Vietnam some twenty years ago really does cast history as a dynamic process. What we see often seems schizophrenic. Private debates between advisers stand in stark contrast to the lights at the end of the tunnel that we heard so much about in 1967.

My task as a researcher is complicated even more by the trauma of Vietnam, its effect upon America today. The war divided a nation, destroyed the president, left an indelible image of defeat. America simply did not make good on its promise to save Vietnam from communist control. Political leadership failed to motivate overwhelming public support or mold a governing consensus necessary for the means to achieve the goal of building a free and independent South Vietnam.

America's failure in Vietnam is a difficult digestive chore for a national ethos unfamiliar with seeing such public disgrace as helicopters carrying American embassy personnel from rooftops of a Saigon Embassy in April of 1975. It took ten years for us to awaken from our collective amnesia that Vietnam had occurred and that there were some lessons to be drawn. The battle on Vietnam frequently shifts from understanding Vietnam to justifying it, so therefore this bumper sticker mentality of 1986. I am now supposed to somehow understand what "No More Vietnam" in Central America means, as if somehow the lesson is really clear. Or what is a noble cause? One is struck by the difficulty my own students have in deciphering those lessons.

Military sources now argue we won the battle, every battle when we combated North Vietnamese forces, but we lost a war in Washington, D.C., where protestors were turning America against the war, and here I would side with Tom Hayden that the protestors did not make contradictions in policy. They merely pointed up those contradictions. Someone had to take it upon themselves to point out contradictions in policy. I believe that anti-war movement sought to do that.

During a moment of confidentiality prior to his death, Johnson told General Westmoreland, these releases are now in the new Tuesday minutes, that had he to fight the war over again, he would have liked to impose press censorship, as if the press had been responsible for pointing out these inconsistencies or they themselves aided the credibility gap.

Let me just say in a closing minute that, in my own book, *Planning a Tragedy*, I focused on a single decision—the way Lyndon Johnson maneuvered and sought to legitimize America's taking over of a ground war in Southeast Asia in July of 1965. It's true, Eisenhower, Truman, and Kennedy had simply with increments of money been able to pass off the real question. Johnson faced in July of 1965 the fundamental fact that he was about to lose South Vietnam under his shift, so to speak. I view Johnson as a historically tragic figure, boxed in by the way his own advisers had defined situations for him—George Ball on one side, the joint chiefs on the other, and I think the most acceptable middle ground proposal by Bill Bundy which wasn't accepted, unfortunately. Limited in options, Johnson took his case to the country at the lowest possible denominator. He sought to achieve a political consensus so he could get the Great Society through. And he did it. In July, Johnson had that legislative mandate that he knew he would lose in two years, so he soft-sold the war, despite on his desk the fact from his military advisers that within six months he would need another 100–150,000 troops in Vietnam to stave off defeat.

By 1967, and I think this is where I want to close, the inconsistencies in policies were obvious and in my new study I focus on the role of Robert McNamara, secretary of defense, the man who merged from mechanical optimist to mechanical pessimist as he realized by 1967 that optimistic calculations and scenarios that Johnson had presented to the public were not bearing out.

For John Roche and those who demand documents or proof, I happen to have, not knowing I was going to speak today, but never knowing when an idea would occur to me on a plane, I brought some of my notes so I could keep writing my new book. I'll just read four dates to you in closing: December 18, 1965, Johnson says, at a meeting of his military advisers, ''Then no matter what we do militarily, there is no sure victory.'' McNamara tells Johnson, ''That's right, we have been too optimistic.'' McNamara on January 13, 1966, in a memo to the President, ''Prognosis is bad the war can be brought to a satisfactory conclusion within the next two years.'' McGeorge Bundy, writing to the president regarding Ambassador [Henry Cabot] Lodge's weekly memo, ''He is as optimistic as McNamara is pessimistic about the timing and likelihood of straight military successes against pacification.'' Juxtaposed to McNamara's negative views, and I know Walt Rostow will want to enter a fray, on March 18, 1967, Walt writes to President Johnson, ''If victory is not in sight, it is on the way.'' On November 1, it was McNamara who wrote to the president arguing that there was no military victory in sight, and within a month McNamara was in the World Bank.

The questions of contradictions in policy, solid progress versus internal debate, that is the historian's obligation, and I come to you here today not as a participant but as a scholar of that historical period. And the documents speak for themselves. With the documents along with interviews, we can start reconstructing the events of Vietnam and in that respect I think the frontier of scholarship is just beginning, particularly on these crucial decisions of 1965–1967.

Epilogue: Second Thoughts

Bill D. Moyers

The angel Gabriel, we are told, once informed an Englishman, a Frenchman, and an American that they had only six months to live, but were also being granted one final wish. They could have anything they wanted. The Frenchman asked for vintage wine and a villa on the Riviera with Brigitte Bardot. The Englishman wanted tea with the Queen. And the American wanted a second opinion. If President Johnson were alive and had been invited he would have come. If he had not been invited, he would have come anyway. He would have wanted to hear all the second opinions and second thoughts and to embrace or rebut them.

Reinhold Niebuhr wrote a book in his old age to revise his previously held opinions. LBJ would never have written down his thoughts. It would have taken too long for a man who believed that action was the measure of the day. He would have been here in the front row—listening, kibitzing, occasionally interrupting to seize the podium—to revise his opinions and ours face to face. I think he would have been the first to agree that any estimate of his role in history will require a continuing round of second opinions. There is no last judgment on a president, only a series of interim reports.

This is mine. It is subjective. It is biased. And it is circumscribed by the reality that while Lyndon Johnson was in Washington thirty-one years, I worked for him fewer than four of those years. There are many people in this room who served him longer and more wisely than I. Their portrait of him would be fuller, their judgments sounder, their memories richer. I was present for only three of his campaigns and just over three of the five White House years. But my experiences with him were exhilarating and excruciating.

He was thirteen of the most interesting and difficult men I ever met—at times proud, sensitive, impulsive, flamboyant, sentimental, bold, magnanimous, and graceful (the best dancer in the White House since George Washington); at times, temperamental, paranoid, ill of spirit, strangely and darkly uneasy with himself. He owned and operated a ferocious ego, and he had an animal sense of weakness in other men. He could inflict on them a thousand cuts before flying in at his own expense the best doctor to heal them; or if that failed, a notable for the last rites.

I came to love him as the recruit loves the shrewd, tough, and vulgar CO who swaggers and profanes too much in order to hide fears more threatening than the private's. He had that passion for fame which is the force of all great ambitions, but he suffered violent dissent in the ranks of his own personality. He is, in death as in life, damned to everlasting scrutiny.

If character is destiny, choice is history. Long after the last witness to those days is dead and buried, the consequences of Lyndon Johnson's decisions will be studied, sifted, and weighed for the manner in which they turned, to large or trivial directions, the tributaries of the American experience.

I have for a long time been reluctant to speak about the Johnson years for fear of unwittingly revising a history I did not understand even as I lived it. Perhaps Freud was right when he said that we all experience our presence naively. I certainly experienced it frenetically, possessed of far more energy than wisdom. Even now I am tentative about how all the pieces fit together. Only as I listen to others who shared the time and scholars who are examining it do I understand why I still believe and doubt.

On the plane back from Dallas that dark Friday afternoon, he was as he had always been—a man of infinite practicality unencumbered with theory. He once told me that every experience creates a new reality and a good politician takes his mandate from opportunity. He reveled in the vocation of politics, and—in the Senate especially—his mastery of it, yielding here, standing firm there, then delaying again before acting to resolve the conflicting forces and interests. Huey Long of Louisiana used to talk about the differences between a "scrooch" owl and a "hoot owl." "A 'hoot owl,' " said Huey, "bangs into the roost and knocks the hen clean off and catches her, but a 'scrooch' owl slips into the roost, 'scrooches' up to the hen and talks softly to her, and the hen just falls in love, and the next thing you know there ain't no hen." Lyndon Johnson was both a "scrooch" owl and a "hoot owl." The ancient Greeks employed two words for time. One was chronos, from which comes our word chronology. It means time as a measurable quantity, the regular march of seconds into minutes and hours. If you ask me for the time of the evening, I'll give you chronos. The second word was kyros, a critical and decisive point which taken boldly becomes fateful. Euripides described this kind of time as the moment when "he who sees the helm of fate, forces fortune." The scribes in the New Testament used this term to suggest the fullness of time. Lyndon Johnson on that plane that afternoon believed he had come to power in just such a time.

Grasping though he had been in life, no amount of wily exertion would have brought him the office now delivered by a cruel and capricious fate. Only days before he had said to friends that his future was behind him. Now suddenly he sought to consummate it in a swift and decisive series of events that would give his country and the world their first impression of him. With a materially decisive sense of the fateful, acting from the accumulated experiences of a lifetime in public office, and with antennae that swept the political landscape of Washington like the strong beam of a searchlight, he reckoned in those first few days to complete the agenda in waiting—and to shape his own. "This is the time to act," he said as he dressed that first fall day in office. "This is the time to act." Sure enough, by nightfall of that same day he had instructed his chief economic adviser to proceed full steam ahead on planning the anti-poverty program. Within days, he met with the leaders of every major civil rights organization in the country, he called in the powers of Congress, he talked to old friends and new advisers. On the map of his mind there was already appearing in bold relief the routes he would ask the country to follow. No detour yet marked the exit of Vietnam. That would come later.

This was, thought LBJ, *the fullness of time economically*. Our resources were growing at the rate of 5 percent a year, and his economic advisers assured him (in the words of Walter Heller) that "in our time, the engine of our economy would be the mightiest engine of human progress the world has ever seen." Just by shifting a small portion of the additional resources created by growth, it was thought, we could abolish poverty without raising taxes. The Council of Economic Advisers had only been created in 1946. The measurement of our GNP as the chief indicator of economic performance and growth was only established as an official government task twenty years before LBJ became president. Already the economists had been enshrined as the great reckoners of cost—a science dubbed dismal because the first and foremost principle concerned itself with scarcity. One of the greatest principles of economics, said the economist Kenneth Boulding, had been enunciated by the dutchess in *Alice in Wonderland*, "The more there is of yours, the less there is of mine." But now the economists were changing their tune and inviting all of us to sing with them, "More for everybody and more for me too." Lyndon Johnson came to believe we could all join in that delightful, positive-sum game of getting richer together. This, said one observer, was a time "when the number of chickens comfortably exceeded the number of pots."

He thought this *the fullness of time politically, as well*. Twenty-five years ago scholars and political observers had been debating the deadlock of democracy, the impasse of a system choked on huge indigestible issues. Now a country shocked by the murder of John F. Kennedy yearned for proof the system could work again. It had in Lyndon Johnson a virtuoso of Washington politics. For him happiness was something for everybody. The British journalist, Godfrey Hodgson, would write that Johnson's ambition to build a great society was not the vulgar megalomania it was pictured to be. "Here instead," said Hodgson, "was one of those rare moments when a government had real freedom to compose a national agenda, with some assurance that it would be able to do most of the things it chose to do, because they were economically and politically affordable.''

This was also for Lyndon Johnson *the fullness of time personally*. As a young congressman from the hill country of Texas, he had been what Theodore White calls "a country liberal." He supported rural electrification, social security, soil conservation, farm price support, and federal aid to build power. Ambition turned him to the right. Running for the Senate he probed for the core of a state-wide constituency more conservative than those central Texas voters who first sent him to the House to do Franklin Roosevelt's bidding. To win the support of powerful business interests, he supported the Taft-Hartley Act to curb labor. In his successful race for the Senate in 1948, he denounced as socialized medicine what sixteen years later as president he would hail as salvation for the elderly. In that same race he condemned the civil rights portion of Harry Truman's Fair Deal as "a farce and a sham"—an effort, he said, to set up a police state in the guise of history.

But while he was a man of time and place, he felt the bitter paradox of both. I was a young man on his staff in 1960 when he gave me a vivid account of that southern schizophrenia he understood and feared. We were in Tennessee. During the motorcade he spotted some ugly racial epithets scrawled on signs by a few plain—he called them homely—white women on the edge of a crowd on a street corner. Late that night in the hotel when the local dignitaries had finished the last bottles of bourbon and branch water and departed, he started talking about those signs. And long past midnight with an audience of one, he was still going on about how poor whites and poor blacks had been kept apart so they could be separately fleeced. "I'll tell you what's at the bottom of it," he said. "If you can convince the lowest white man he's better than the best colored man he won't notice you're picking his pocket. Hell, give him somebody to look down on, and he'll empty his pockets for you. But even the best politician," he said, "even those on the little man's side, drew the line at color. They might read Shakespeare and quote Shelley, but out there in the crowds they shouted, 'Nigger, Nigger, Nigger!' ''

He said if he could talk to just one man who had passed through the Senate before him, it wouldn't be Daniel Webster or Henry Clay or any of the other great figures other men might summon. The senator with whom he would have conversed was Pitchfork Ben Tillman—Benjamin Ryan Tillman of South Carolina. "Here," said LBJ, "was a fella who stood up for the farmers and sent the bankers and the lawyers packing. Here was a fella who took on the railroads, started colleges, and invited women to get a first class education and persuaded the legislature to jack up money for schools. And yet," said Lyndon Johnson that night, "here was a fella who wanted to repeal the fifteenth amendment, who took the vote away from the colored folks, who got so passionate about these things that he almost got kicked out of the United States Senate." Except for the poison of race, Lyndon Johnson said of Pitchfork Ben Tillman, "he might have been president of the United States. I'd like to sit with him and ask how it was to throw it away for the sake of hating.''

Some years later when his old friend Richard Russell of Georgia had left the White House after a visit, the president said, ''God damn it. Jim Crow put a collar on more smart men as sure as if they were sentenced to a chain gang in Georgia. If Dick Russell hadn't had to wear Jim Crow's collar, Dick Russell would be sitting here now instead of me.'' So for Lyndon Johnson who could once look right through blacks, the presidency offered a reprieve from the past.

There was a press conference in the East Room. A reporter unexpectedly asked the president how he could explain his sudden passion for civil rights when he had never had much enthusiasm for the cause. The question hung in the air. I could see those huge nostrils as the president stared directly at the reporter. I could almost hear the cue cards flipping through his mind and his silent cursing of a press secretary who had not anticipated this one. But then he relaxed, and from an instinct no assistant could brief—one seasoned in the double life from which he was now delivered and hoped to deliver others—he said in effect: Most of us don't have a second chance to correct the mistakes of our youth. I do and I am. That evening, sitting in the White House, discussing the question with friends and staff, he looked around the room, gestured broadly about the mansion where he was living, and said, ''Eisenhower used to tell me that this place was a prison. I never felt freer.''

Roy Wilkins of the NAACP came to the White House soon after the president, in that historic speech long to be remembered, declared to the Congress and the nation, ''We shall overcome.'' Wilkins said he wept as the president moved toward the climactic moment when he put the whole armor of the White House behind the conscience of the nation. Now, waiting for the president to finish a phone call, Wilkins recalled how as Senate majority leader LBJ had perfected ''the three-two trot of racial progress: Three steps forward and two steps back.'' But ''ever since he got in there,'' Wilkins said, pointing toward the Oval Office, ''it's been rock-around-the-clock.'' And so it had. For weeks in 1964 the president carried in his pocket the summary of a census bureau report showing that the lifetime earnings of an average black college graduate were actually lower than that of a white man with an eighth-grade education. And when the *New York Times* in November 1964 reported racial segregation actually to be increasing instead of disappearing, he took his felt tip pen and scribbled across it ''Shame, shame, shame,'' and sent it to Everett Dirksen, the Republican leader in the Senate.

I have a hard time explaining to our two sons and daughter—now in their twenties—that when they were little America was still deeply segregated. The White House press corps, housed in Austin when the president was on vacation in Texas, would often go to the faculty club at the University of Texas, which was still off limits to blacks, still segregated in 1964. I remember the night it changed. There was a New Year's party for one of the president's favorite assistants, Horace Busby. About half way into the evening, there was a stir and everyone looked up. The president of the United States was entering with one of his secretaries on his arm—a beautiful black woman. A professor of law at the University of Texas, Ernest Goldstein, had come to the club that evening out of friendship for Busby, although he resented and had opposed its segregationist policies. Now, joyously but increduously, he slipped up to me and asked, "Does the president know what he's doing?" "He knows," I said. But I wasn't sure. The next day Goldstein called the club to announce he intended to bring back some black associates to a meeting there. "No problem at all," said the woman on the phone. "Are we really integrated?" Goldstein asked. "Yes sir," she answered, "the president of the United States integrated us last night."

In those days our faith was in integration. The separatist cries would come later, as white flight and black power ended the illusion that an atmosphere of genuine acceptance and respect across color lines would overcome in our time the pernicious effects of a racism so deeply imbedded in American life. But Lyndon Johnson championed that faith. He genuinely believed that money spent on integrated education would produce a greater equality in scholastic achievement and a greater equality in society as well. He thought the opposite of integration was not just segregation but disintegration—a nation unraveling.

America *was* a segregated country when LBJ came to power. It *wasn't* when he left. But I am certain he would be appalled to discover today how many American blacks are still caught in that undertow of discrimination—that circle of segregated slum housing—leading to inferior schooling, subemployment, broken homes, and low incomes, which lead inevitably back to segregated slums. He knew instinctively, I think, the peril of this disastrous converging of class and color. Whatever his motives—whether from a moral imagination now freed from expediency or from expediency now free to seize a higher ground—he swore in those very first hours in office that he would move to combat on a broad front.

But he also knew not an inch would be won cheaply. The Civil Rights Act of 1964 is to many of us a watershed in American history and one of the most exhilarating triumphs of the Johnson years. With it, blacks gained access to public accommodations across the country. When he signed the act he was euphoric, but late that very night I found him in a melancholy mood as he lay in bed reading the bulldog edition of the *Washington Post* with headlines celebrating the day. I asked him what was troubling him. "I think we just delivered the south to the Republican party for a long time to come," he said.

Throughout that heady year, even as his own popularity soared the president saw the gathering storm of a backlash. George Wallace took 34 percent of the presidential vote in liberal Wisconsin, 30 percent in Indiana, and 43 percent in Maryland. Watching the newscasts one night, the president said, "George Wallace makes these working folks think whatever is happening to them is all the Negro's fault. He runs around throwing gasoline on coals that ought to be dying out; he'd burn down the whole goddamn house just to save his separate drinking water.'' Once Whitney Young came to visit and the president sent me searching for a copy of Wallace's defiant proclamation for the preservation of segregation. Over and over he read it aloud, ''Segregation now, segregation tomorrow, segregation forever! Segregation now, segregation tomorrow, segregation forever!'' Then he handed it to Whitney Young and said, ''Remember that when you think we are about to cross the Jordan.''

He wanted to cross the Jordan, all right, and take everybody with him. In those days he longed to integrate us all. He called in business, he called in labor, he called in the clergy, he even went skinny dipping in the White House pool with Billy Graham before dressing in black tie for dinner with Cardinal Spellman. He called in ethnic groups, trade associations, school children, and graduate students. Liz Carpenter reminded us last night of the time the president appointed fifty-three women to office—with a single announcement. I remembered the time someone sent him a copy of Thomas Jefferson's statement that ''The appointment of a woman to office is an innovation for which the public is not prepared, nor am I.'' ''Well,'' said LBJ, ''I'm damn sure ready!'' And he handed the quote to an aide with orders to find a qualified woman to name as an ambassador before the week was over. Which was done.

Critics attacked his notion of consensus, but the president kept insisting to some of us that in politics you cast your stakes wide and haul up a big tent with room for everybody who wants in. The only time I can remember any kind of discussion with him about his political philosophy, he said he was ''a little bit left, a little bit right, and a lot of center.'' Peter Drucker wrote at the time that President Johnson's Great Society ''represents a first response to some of the new issues, both at home and abroad. But it approaches those largely within the old alignments. It appeals primarily to the old values and it employs mostly the traditional rhetoric. The voice is Jacob's but the hands are the hands of Esau.''

There were more recent analogies that could have been used because in the fullness of time, thought LBJ, his was the glory to finish what Roosevelt, Truman, and Kennedy started. Like them, he sought to stimulate the private sector into generating growth and jobs. So—the budgetary deficit, the growth rate of the money supply and, in the beginning, the ratio of social to defense spending were all moderately increased to promote growth.

I am one of those who think it worked. I agree with those scholars like Jonathan Schwartz, who believe those policies in 1964 and 1965 had a positive impact. Largely because of the baby boom and the huge increase in the number of women wanting jobs, 55 million Americans poured into the work force from 1965 to 1980. As Schwartz points out, no other major western nation experienced soaring birthrates spanning the two decades following World War II. The number in America caused our work force to increase by an extraordinary 40 percent. Unemployment could not help but rise, and it did—by 2.5 percent between 1965 and 1980. Yet the number of jobs almost doubled, in no small part of the result of economic and social policies begun in the Johnson years and intended mostly to propel the growth of the private economy. It seems to me we can fairly ask, what might have happened if the crowded baby boom generation had arrived in the work force without those jobs?

On poverty LBJ was often of two minds simultaneously. One was traditional, the other flirted with the radical. Poverty could be ended, he believed, if the economy grew and the poor were better managed and trained for better jobs. Help them to a better doctor, move them into a better house. He remembered those Mexican children who couldn't read or write and he told me a dozen times at least that he would have missed it all if he hadn't stayed in school. "I didn't learn a whole lot in classes in college but I made a lot of contacts and sure learned how to get ahead," he said. That was education to LBJ: get up and get out. So with school, training, and equal opportunity poor people would make the system work for them. "Give them skills and rewards and they will become taxpayers instead of tax eaters," he said. When he signed into law the anti-poverty program he said, "You tell Sargent Shriver no doles, we don't want any doles."

But as Franklin Roosevelt did, he thought the government should be adventuresome. He was willing to experiment. He thought there would be time to find out what worked and what didn't. He turned around the direction of one meeting on the defense budget by saying, "You know, you can't take a tank from the blueprint to the battlefield, you test it over and over. That's true of the social programs as well. You can't take a poor kid and turn him around just by getting Congress to pass a bill and the president to sign it and one of those agencies in Washington to run it. You have to experiment and keep at it until you find what it takes." So if he shared the liberal faith that by enlarging the size of the economic pie of total income everyone would gain, he instinctively sensed it wasn't enough. As he said once, "Sometimes when that tide raises all those boats, some of those boats got leaks in the bottom." And he said if income grew without any change in relative shares, there would be no increase in equality. He certainly wasn't a flat equality man, but he believed equality was the moving horizon that America had been chasing for all of its history.

Moreover, LBJ believed, income was not the only measure of well-being. Here he was getting a little daring. What about such goods of the public household as schools and police protection? Quality schools, quality protection. Those were assets the poor would never be able to afford for want of personal income. "We wouldn't leave poor people undefended just because they couldn't buy a piece of the Air Force or the Navy," he told me: Why leave them uneducated and unhoused for the same reason? What about status, self-respect, opportunities for upward mobility, and political power? Could these be left only to those who could afford them? "Not on your life," he said. I'm pretty sure LBJ never read John Stuart Mill, but in his bones, planted there from the experience of childhood and youth, he believed that in the absence of its natural defenders the interests of the excluded are always in danger of being overlooked.

So with no popular mandate—we took no poll—except the conviction that what the best and wisest parents want for their child, the community should want for all its children, he okayed an anti-poverty program that would try an end run around deeply ingrained institutional obstacles to social justice. It was a token, a start, but in the words of one observer, it also represented "a real social invention which may have large consequences for the future and the whole idea that the poor should organize themselves." In his more expansive moments LBJ talked of going all the way—of rebuilding the cities, restoring the country-side, redeeming public education. "It isn't enough just to round out the New Deal," he said one day to a congressman. "There has to be a better deal." He talked of "the Great Society," but the slogan was no more precise than others in currency in those days. Remember them? Nelson Rockefeller's "Just Soci-ety," Ronald Reagan's "Creative Society," Barry Goldwater's "Free Society." Sometimes LBJ despised the term: It just didn't fit his way of talking. In simplest terms he was trying to raise our sights beyond sheer size and the grandeur of wealth. A full stomach yes, but a fuller life too.

One day he made a request. He asked for a genealogy of the phrase. And we searched. And there in the family tree of its forebears was this passage from Adam Smith's *The Wealth of Nations*:

According to the system of natural liberty, the sovereign has only three duties to attend to. Three duties of great importance indeed, but plain and intelligible to common un-derstandings: First, the duty of protecting the society from the violence and invasion of other independent societies. Secondly, the duty of protecting as far as possible, every member of the society from the injustice or oppression of every other member of it, or the duty of establishing an exact administration of justice; and thirdly, the duty of erecting and maintaining certain public works and certain public institutions which can never be for the interest of any individual or small number of individuals to erect and maintain because the profit could never repay the expense to any individual or small number of individuals, though it may frequently do much more than repay it to a great society.

"That's it," LBJ said, "That's it. I'm an Adam Smith man."

He could talk privately as he talked publicly. "Let's conquer the vastness of space, create schools and jobs for everyone. Let's care for the elderly, let's build schools and libraries, let's increase the affluence of the middle class. Let's improve the productivity of business, let's do more for civil rights in one Congress than the last one hundred combined, and let's get started in all of these by summer"—with no increase in spending.

He really did believe he might have it all ways. "We can continue the Great Society while we fight in Vietnam," he told the country. Friend or foe, scholar or laity, champion or critic, if you would understand him you must see that both to him were the unfinished business of his generation. With his domestic programs he would consummate a long tradition of social and economic reform. They were linked in his mind to Theodore Roosevelt's crusades against monopolies, FDR's regulatory intervention in the economy, Harry Truman's assumption of responsibility for full employment, and John Kennedy's emerging commitment to the abolition of poverty. Hans Morgenthau was a critic of the president's foreign policy, but of LBJ's Great Society vision in 1965 he said, "It is oriented toward an intelligible and generally accepted set of values. It seeks the enhancement and ultimate consummation of the individual's dignity and self-sufficiency."

So—to the president—was Vietnam a piece of America's Cold War tradition of opposing communism where not to do so might affect adversely the nation's interests. If he could do it without troops as Truman did in Greece, he would. But if he could do it with only the implied threat of force as Kennedy had done in the Cuban missile crisis, he would do so. But, he said, if it took force as Truman had to use force in Korea, he would do that too. What was new was the president's decision to put those intentions into effect simultaneously. It proved an improvident and costly combination. The result in Vietnam was a loss out of proportion to the ends sought. The increasing cruelty and futility of it sapped his morale and vigor, robbed him of that tolerance and tranquility he always had difficulty negotiating from the warring factions of his own nature. They whipped him into fits of depression and delusion—those unconscious impulses that sometimes stormed his ego, which not even Lady Bird could quiet.

At home, his cherished consensus eroded into strenuous and violent political conflict. This was almost certain to happen if there had been no Vietnam War. We had the first hint of it in those racial riots in Rochester, New York, in 1964—the prelude of things to come. But there was also no way the more ambitious policies could have failed in time to provoke the ire of many of those interests on which consensus relied. This, too, was signaled early.

Sometime in the spring of 1965 I read and sent to the president an essay by Herbert Marcuse applauding LBJ's objectives—but doubting the government's ability to stay the course. "Rebuilding the cities, restoring the countryside, redeeming the poor, and reforming education," said Marcuse, "could produce nondestructive full employment. This requires, nothing more, nothing less than the actual reconstruction outlined in the president's program. But the very program requires the transformation of power structures standing in the way of its fulfillment."

I underlined that part of the article that dealt with the highway beautification program so dear to Lady Bird. It was a modest program, but Marcuse had seized upon it as a shining example of how he thought the president's ambitions irreconcilable with capitalist interests. The rigidly enforced elimination of all billboards, neon signs, and other commercial blights on nature meant the abrogation of some of the most powerful lobbies in the country. Marcuse felt the president wouldn't go this far. "Who is this fella Marcuse?" the president demanded on the phone. I explained that he was a philosopher who fled Germany when Hitler came to power, that he was teaching at Brandeis University where some students thrilled to his ideas about revolution and radical politics, and that his book *One Dimensional Man* was being widely read on other campuses too. "What are you doing reading him?" the president asked. "Well, I'm trying to keep up," I answered. "I even read Barry Goldwater's *Conscience of a Conservative* last year and sent it over to you, remember?'' ''Well,'' he said, ''don't send this fella's book, but call him and tell him Lady Bird's the revolutionary on this bill. Not me!''

Actually, both the president and Mrs. Johnson initially fought and lobbied hard for the Highway Beautification Act, but in the end we compromised almost to the point of capitulation. The legislation passed, but it since has been so weakened by loopholes and tax enforcement that recently the *Wall Street Journal* said, ''It protects billboards more than it causes their removal.''

Then there was the call I got from Richard Daley (as so many others did too). Almost before I could say hello he asked, ''What in the hell are you people doing? Does the president know he's putting money in the hands of subversives?'' Now, Richard Daley's definition of subversion was the intervention of anyone outside his political machine. Suddenly the president was pouring money—''M-O-N-E-Y,'' Mr. Daley spelled it on the phone to me—''money to people that aren't a part of our organization.'' Didn't the president know they'd take that money to bring him down?

I don't think I'll ever know whether LBJ knew in advance that the community action program was going to generate so much political controversy. He did say to [Sargent] Shriver and others that we couldn't fight poverty from some of the traditional agencies of government. Especially the older ones—full of mediocrities, protected by civil service. He knew from twenty-five years in Washington that bureaucracies are inert. He said, ''You'll have to run some guerrilla raids.'' That was his term, ''guerrilla raids,''—like J.E.B. Stuart to run around the traditional agencies, covering up and outflanking them—getting that help right to poor people themselves. This meant inevitably in some places challenging the political status quo. And in places like Chicago, Richard Daley was Mayor Status Quo. When I told the president about Daley's call, he immediately called the mayor with a message the contents of which were never divulged to me because I had been by then disinvited from the scene. I found out only yesterday, from Wilbur Cohen, that the community action director eventually hired for Chicago was one of Richard Daley's own men. The operative saying goes, ''He might be a subversive, but he's our subversive.'' So Chicago was made safe for poverty and democracy.

I repeat, such conflicts would have been serious enough without the Vietnam War, but an unpopular war created defection on the part of people who might otherwise have supported the changes envisioned by new policies. I barely noticed at the time that in 1964 student rebels in Berkeley were uttering their first expletives deleted—obscenities in the cause of free speech. Thoreau had urged nineteenth-century dissidents to ''let your life be a counter friction to stop the machine.'' Now Mario Savio was calling for students to put their bodies on the machine and stop it.

When the Berkeley uprising was followed by the escalation of the war in Vietnam and the draft began, the call to the young to stop the machine took on an urgent and personal meaning. Pickets showed up across from the White House wearing huge IBM cards that read "I am a student. Do not fold, spindle, or mutilate." Burners of draft cards and advocates of Viet Cong victory were joined by young people who felt, for many other reasons, deeply alienated from American society.

Opponents of the war and critics of the Great Society were soon finding one another's company against a government that was their common foe. Lyndon Johnson belonged to the generation that saluted when the commander-in-chief said, "Do your duty." Now he had begun to confuse patriotism for blind loyalty. Dissent began as the mischief of "nervous nellies" and then became the work of traitors. The more he sought to drive them to the fringe of the public square, the more the square blazed with the fires of his own effigies. By 1967, neither the president nor the country talked anymore of a grand vision.

I had left early that year, my morale hemorrhaging from self-inflicted wounds and from those unintended blows two proud and sensitive people suffer in the turbulent close quarters of a relationship so personal it cannot be mediated and so painful it cannot be continued. When I told him I was leaving he had me come to the ranch and for several hours the two of us rode around the pastures as he talked almost without interruption. Once he said, "If I had to do it over again, I'd come to the White House as a presidential assistant, not as president." "Why?" I asked. "Because you can quit and I can't."

He had talked at times to Mrs. Johnson and others of not wanting to run again, but then he would talk of what remained to be done once he brought the boys home from Vietnam. Now, out there on the rim of a hill overlooking the pasture, he leaned against the steering wheel and said, "We'll just be getting to the end of the runway with that first term and we'll be taking off on the second. You ought to be around for the take off." But he didn't sound as if he himself relished the trip or believed that it would really happen. He seemed to know the fullness of time had come and passed.

What worked? Well, in 1967, 75 percent of all Americans over sixty-five had no medical insurance and a third of the elderly lived in poverty. More than 90 percent of all black adults in the south were not registered to vote and across the nation there were only about 200 elected public officials who were black. There was no Head Start for kids. Today, Medicare, food stamps, and more generous Social Security benefits have helped reduce the poverty rate for the elderly by half, and they are no poorer than Americans as a whole. Nearly 6,000 blacks hold elected office, including the office once held by Richard Daley. A majority of small children attend preschool programs. The bedrock of the Great Society—Medicare, Medicaid, federal aid to education, the right of blacks to citizenship—are permanent features of the American system. So much so that in the first debate between Ronald Reagan and Walter Mondale, Reagan presented himself as the man who saved your safety net.

What went wrong? Some things that went wrong were unjustly blamed on the Great Society. As my former colleague Ben Wattenberg has pointed out, there was no "soft-on-crime act" of 1966. There was no "permissive curriculum act" of 1967. There was no "get vindictive with business act" of 1968. But plenty of things went wrong. Progress fell victim to pork-barrel politics. The idea of giving the poor resources for leadership never got the support it deserved. Employment training projects suffered from high drop out rates. There were often no jobs when the training ended. And the cost exceeded the estimate.

We had jumped too fast, spread out too far and too thinly over too vast a terrain, and then went to war on a distant front—against an enemy that would not bargain, compromise, or reason together. The enemy wanted only to win. For once in his career, Lyndon Johnson sat down at the table, divided up the chips, cut the cards—and no one showed up to deal.

A slogan is a dangerous thing. Those who create it can lose control of its meaning. Others read into it what was not there. Friends put their own spin on it. It can mean everything or nothing. But slogans aside, at the root the Great Society was only an idea and not a new one. It was the idea that free men and women can work with their goverment to make things better. Lyndon Johnson's generation had been traumatized by the Great Crash—by the sight of lean hungry men wandering the countryside in search of food and work—by the collapse of the economic system they had trusted. His generation came to maturity at a time when state governments were failing or verged on bankruptcy. Only the national government could move to help. And many of the local governments were as morally bankrupt in matters of race as they were financially woeful, masquerading in the high-falutin' rhetoric of states' rights. They held themselves up as the arbitrary judges of their own conduct no matter how unjust or dangerous to the social fabric.

Furthermore, by the time Lyndon Johnson reached the White House, the United States was in the throes of one of the most perplexing and painful transitions in its history. We were becoming a national society with an intricately intertwined economy; a metropolitan society with many people living in a small number of densely populated areas; a pluralistic society with huge organizations with multitudes of activities that must mesh to make the system work.

Government did not grow bigger and become more centralized on whim or caprice. Big government was the response to two worlds, the Cold War, the Great Depression, urbanization, an unjust social system, and market forces that did not stay around to help losers. Big government is symptomatic of the fact that modern society depends on a far-reaching and complex organizational network that extends across the nation and the world. The welfare and health of each member of this society is dependent on the health and welfare of the whole enterprise.

In the old mythology of Hollywood westerns, the rugged individual rides alone toward the sunset without the thought of Holiday Inns at the next exit ramp or whether the food has been inspected. But there is no escape for us today to some simpler place like the good old days. Bigness is here to stay. His own rhetoric notwithstanding, Ronald Reagan has not presided over a diminishing government. Rather, he has shifted resources from social services to the defense establishment. The result is not a reduction in federal spending but a doubling of the national debt in five years with a higher percentage of the gross national product going to government than when he entered office.

The problem of big government is real. Finding ways to make this complex system work, of making it responsive and responsible with a due regard for the integrity of the individual and well-being of the country, was the challenge we set out to wrestle twenty years ago. It will be so far into the future.

"The Great Society," said Lyndon Johnson, "is a challenge constantly renewed." Back in 1964, Syracuse University convened a scholarly seminar on the Great Society and President Johnson proposed the scholars consider five questions. The scholars turned them into two. First, just what is it and what should become the content of the Great Society? Second, how can we best measure desired and actual change in any society? The first has to do with the most complex and controversial aspects of human values, national purposes, and political leadership. The second goes to the heart of our ability to understand the complexity of social reality. If Lyndon Johnson were around today, he would have shown up this week at Hofstra to badger, poke, and parry—above all, to listen, eager to hear your answers to those questions.

Hofstra University gratefully acknowledges the significant support of the National Endowment for the Humanities (NEH) in funding programs of the Hofstra Cultural Center through a challenge grant. Under the terms of the challenge, the funds raised through the Conference will generate an additional contribution by the federal government of one-third of the total raised. Since 1983, this generous NEH funding has enabled Hofstra to increase humanities activities on campus for the benefit of the community, students, and faculty.

IN COOPERATION WITH THE LYNDON BAINES JOHNSON LIBRARY, AUSTIN, TEXAS

FIFTH ANNUAL PRESIDENTIAL CONFERENCE

LYNDON BAINES JOHNSON

A TEXAN IN WASHINGTON

APRIL 10-12, 1986

HOFSTRA
HEMPSTEAD, NEW YORK 11550
UNIVERSITY

HOFSTRA CULTURAL CENTER

Founding Director
JOSEPH G. ASTMAN
1916-1985

Acting Co-Directors
NATALIE DATLOF
ALEXEJ UGRINSY

Special Assistant to the Director
BARBARA LEKATSAS

Development Coordinator
DONNA TESTA

Conference Coordinators
JO-ANN G. MAHONEY
KARIN BARNABY

Secretaries
MARILYN SEIDMAN
ATHELENE A. COLLINS

Conference Assistants
MUSA G. BADAT
KAREN CASTRO
REMELINE C. DAMASCO
WILLIAM KRUEGER
MOHAMMED OMAR
DIANE PATERSON
JOSEPH PIZZIMENTI
TARA STAHMAN

GALLERIES

David Filderman Gallery
MARGUERITE M. REGAN
Activities Coordinator
NANCY E. HERB
ANNE RUBINO
Gallery Staff

Emily Lowe Gallery
GAIL GELBURD
Director
ELEANOR RAIT
Curator of Collections
MARY WAKEFORD
Executive Secretary

MUSICAL ORGANIZATIONS

American Chamber Ensemble
BLANCHE ABRAM
NAOMI DRUCKER
Directors

Hofstra String Quartet
SEYMOUR BENSTOCK
Artistic Director

Cover Photo: Frank Wolfe

FIFTH ANNUAL PRESIDENTIAL CONFERENCE

On the Occasion of the 50th Anniversary of Hofstra University

A CONFERENCE

LYNDON BAINES JOHNSON:
A TEXAN IN WASHINGTON

April 10 -12, 1986

JAMES M. SHUART	*President*
ROBERT C. VOGT	*Conference Co-Director* *Dean, Hofstra College of Liberal Arts and Sciences*
BERNARD J. FIRESTONE	*Conference Co-Director* *Associate Professor of Political Science*
NATALIE DATLOF ALEXEJ UGRINSKY	*Acting Co-Directors, Hofstra Cultural Center* *Conference Coordinators*

Hofstra University Lyndon Baines Johnson Conference Committee: Faculty Members

BRUCE ADKINSON
Political Science
RICHARD T. BENNETT
Government Relations
SHERI DAVID
History
MICHAEL D'INNOCENZO
History
ROBERT L. DOUGLAS
Law

ANDREW J. GRANT
Grant Development
PAUL F. HARPER
Political Science
LOUIS KERN
History
HAROLD A. KLEIN
University Relations
HARVEY J. LEVIN
Economics

MARK L. LANDIS
Political Science
WILLIAM F. LEVANTROSSER
Political Science
JOHN L. RAWLINSON
History
HERBERT D. ROSENBAUM
Political Science
SONDRA RUBENSTEIN
Communication Arts

ERIC J. SCHMERTZ
Law
RONALD H. SILVERMAN
Law
LINTON S. THORN
History
LYNN TURGEON
Economics
JOHN E. ULLMANN
Management & Marketing

Hofstra University Lyndon Baines Johnson Conference Committee: Student Members

SUSAN ACKERMAN, *Student Government Association*
PRISCILLA ALMODOVAR, *Student Government Association*
JEAN NICOLA BOURA, *President, Organization of International Students*
MARIJN BRAADBAART, *Organization of International Students*
MARY CASSARA, *Vice President, Organization of International Students*
CRAIG COHEN, *Political Affairs Club*
ANDRE CROPPENSTEDT, *Organization of International Students*
MICHELLE CYR, *Student Government Association*
JIM DAGUANNO, *President, Student Government Association*
CONRAD DAVIES, *Political Science*
HEATHER FELLMAN, *New College*

WALKER FLANARY, *Political Science*
ANN MARIE GOLDWAIT, *Vice President, Student Government Association*
RON GORDON, *Student Government Association*
ARLENE GUTMAN, *Student Government Association*
PRABHAT GUPTA, *Organization of International Students*
ANTHONY IADEVAIA, *Treasurer, Political Affairs Club*
KAREN JOHNSTON, *President, Hofstra University Young Democrats*
JOAN KENYON, *Student Government Association*
SCOTT KESSLER, *Political Science*
KEN LANDEN, *Vice President, Hofstra University Young Democrats*
LISA ANN LANE, *Student Government Association*

STEVEN LESTER, *Secretary, Political Affairs Club*
SLOAN MAHONE, *Drama*
HELEN PANAGIOTOPOULOS, *Student Government Association*
JOANN PICCIONNONO, *Political Science*
DARREN PORT, *Political Science*
WILLIAM F. RABCHUK, *Political Science*
STEVE RACHLIN, *Student Government Association*
GINA RICCIO, *Student Government Association*
LYNNE ROWAN, *Student Government Association*
KAREN SATINOFF, *Organization of International Students*
HARRY SHLYONSKY, *Political Science*
ALYCE STONE, *President, Political Affairs Club*
SONDRA TANDJUNG, *Secretary, Organization of International Students*

LYNDON BAINES JOHNSON
INTERNATIONAL HONORARY COMMITTEE

Honorary Committee Co-Chairpersons:
Mrs. Lynda Johnson Robb
Hon. Charles S. Robb
Mrs. Luci Johnson Turpin

Hon. Gardner Ackley
Hon. Joseph P. Addabbo
Hon. Carl Albert
Hon. Clifford L. Alexander, Jr.
Hon. Robert B. Anderson
Hon. George W. Ball
Hon. Robert M. Ball
Hon. Joseph W. Barr
Hon. Lindy Boggs
Hon. Richard Bolling
Hon. Julian Bond
Hon. Bernard L. Boutin
Hon. John Brademas
Hon. Willy Brandt
Hon. Daniel Brewster
Hon. Edward W. Brooke
Hon. Edmund G. "Pat" Brown
Hon. Harold Brown
Hon. McGeorge Bundy
Hon. William P. Bundy
Prof. James MacGregor Burns
Hon. Robert C. Byrd
Hon. Joseph A. Califano, Jr.
Hon. Hugh L. Carey
Hon. Elizabeth S. Carpenter
Hon. Jimmy Carter
Hon. Douglass Cater
Hon. Anthony J. Celebrezze
Hon. John Chancellor
Mr. Cesar E. Chavez
Hon. George Christian
Hon. Ramsey Clark
Hon. Clark M. Clifford
Hon. Wilbur J. Cohen
Hon. John B. Connally
Hon. John Conyers, Jr.
Hon. Maurice Couve de Murville
Hon. Archibald Cox
Hon. Mario M. Cuomo
Hon. Alfonse M. D'Amato
Hon. Hedley Donovan
Hon. Thomas J. Downey
Amb. Abba Eban
Hon. Alain Enthoven
Hon. James Farmer
Hon. Gerald R. Ford
Hon. Henry H. Fowler
Prof. John Hope Franklin
Hon. Orville L. Freeman
Hon. J. William Fulbright
Amb. John Kenneth Galbraith

Hon. John W. Gardner
Hon. John H. Glenn, Jr.
Amb. Arthur J. Goldberg
Prof. Eric F. Goldman
Hon. Barry Goldwater
Hon. Lincoln Gordon
Hon. John A. Gronouski
Hon. Robert L. Hardesty
Amb. W. Averell Harriman
Prof. Fred R. Harris
Hon. Walter W. Heller
Hon. Richard Helms
Rev. Theodore M. Hesburgh, C.S.C.
Prof. Charles J. Hitch
Hon. Townsend Hoopes
Prof. Donald F. Hornig
Dr. R. Gordon Hoxie
Hon. Ralph K. Huitt
Rev. Jesse L. Jackson
Hon. Jacob K. Javits
Hon. U. Alexis Johnson
Hon. Barbara Jordan
Vernon E. Jordan, Jr., Esq.
Hon. Nicholas deB. Katzenbach
Ms. Rossie D. Kelly
Hon. Francis Keppel
Hon. Paul G. Kirk, Jr.
Mr. Lane Kirkland
Hon. Robert W. Komer
Mr. Arthur B. Krim
Mrs. Albert D. Lasker
Hon. Norman F. Lent
Amb. Sol M. Linowitz
Hon. Russell B. Long
Hon. Warren G. Magnuson
Amb. Mike Mansfield
Hon. Leonard H. Marks
Hon. Burke Marshall
Hon. Ray Marshall
Hon. Louis E. Martin
Hon. William McChesney Martin
Hon. Gale W. McGee
Hon. Raymond J. McGrath
Hon. Robert S. McNamara
Hon. Harry McPherson
Hon. Martin Mellman
Hon. Harry J. Middleton
Hon. Wilbur D. Mills
Juanita Jackson Mitchell, Esq.
Hon. Walter F. Mondale
Hon. Joseph N. Mondello
Adm. Thomas H. Moorer, USN (Ret.)

Hon. Bill D. Moyers
Hon. Daniel Patrick Moynihan
Hon. Robert J. Mrazek
Hon. Edmund S. Muskie
Hon. Paul H. Nitze
Hon. Richard Nixon
Hon. John O. Pastore
Hon. Basil A. Paterson
Amb. Robert L. Payton
Hon. Esther Peterson
Hon. J. J. Pickle
Hon. Francis T. Purcell
Hon. Charles B. Rangel
Hon. George E. Reedy
Hon. Edwin O. Reischauer
Hon. Stanley R. Resor
Hon. Abraham Ribicoff
Ms. Nan Robertson
Hon. John P. Roche
Hon. Franklin D. Roosevelt, Jr.
Prof. Elspeth Rostow
Hon. Eugene V. Rostow
Hon. W. W. Rostow
Hon. Dean Rusk
Mr. Bayard Rustin
Hon. Barefoot Sanders
Mr. Richard M. Scammon
Prof. Glenn T. Seaborg
Hon. Sargent Shriver
Hon. Otis A. Singletary
Hon. Joseph J. Sisco
Hon. John C. Stennis
Hon. Roger L. Stevens
Hon. Robert S. Strauss
Hon. William H. Sullivan
Col. Harry G. Summers, Jr., USA (Ret.)
Hon. Herman E. Talmadge
Hon. Jack Valenti
Hon. Cyrus Vance
Hon. Paul C. Warnke
Hon. W. Marvin Watson
Hon. Ben J. Wattenberg
Hon. Robert C. Weaver
Hon. James E. Webb
Gen. William C. Westmoreland, USA (Ret.)
Hon. Lee C. White
Rt. Hon. Lord Wilson of Rievaulx
Hon. Willard Wirtz
Hon. Robert Wood
Hon. Ralph W. Yarborough
Prof. Adam Yarmolinsky
Hon. Andrew Young

Co-Sponsor: Lufthansa German Airlines

2

DIRECTORS' MESSAGE

It is difficult to identify a post-World War II American presidency of more enduring historical importance than the presidency of Lyndon Baines Johnson. The Johnson legacy can be found today in government programs that feed the poor, educate the middle class and provide medical care for the elderly. It resonates in the voting power and civil equality of Black Americans. It achieves contemporary relevance in the political debate over the wisdom and utility of the "Great Society."

The images of the Johnson era—with their sharply contrasting evocations—live equally in our memories. Etched in our minds are the tragedy of Dallas and the triumph of the 1964 campaign, the legislative brilliance and the anguish of Vietnam, the soaring eloquence of the president's "We Shall Overcome" speech and the bitter turbulence of the riots in the streets, the great personal popularity of the early presidential years and the fall from public grace culminating in the unexpected withdrawal from the 1968 presidential race.

Lyndon Johnson, a man of enormous energy and political skill, was a product of his times. Raised to political maturity under the ideological umbrella of New Deal liberalism, Johnson came to believe, as did an entire generation of Americans, that government could offer its citizens the promise of a better life. Abroad, he embraced the standard Cold War faith in the superiority of democratic values and the dangers of appeasement. Probably never as heroic as his unquestioning admirers claimed him to be, nor as venal and devoid of vision as his detractors would have had us believe, Lyndon Johnson was, above all, a master politician. His administration faltered when the foreign policy assumptions he had grown to accept as articles of faith came under sustained attack, but he will nonetheless be long remembered for succeeding in translating the liberal vision of a just society into legislative reality.

Hofstra University's Lyndon Baines Johnson Presidential Conference, the fifth in a series that began in 1982 with a retrospective on the presidency of Franklin D. Roosevelt, assembles a rich assortment of former government officials and notables from the Johnson era to supplement the contributions of the outstanding scholars who are scheduled to present papers during the three days of the conference. Panels have been organized to assess the president's efforts in the fields of civil rights and social welfare policy and to explore his relations with the press. A distinguished forum on the Vietnam War brings together former members of the Johnson administration and opponents of the war to survey the issues which so convulsed the nation twenty years ago. An extraordinary panel of foreign dignitaries, including Maurice Couve de Murville, Joseph M.A.H. Luns, B.K. Nehru, Gerhard Schröder and Lord Harold Wilson meets under the direction of former National Security Advisor W.W. Rostow to examine President Johnson's foreign policy record.

A number of invitational addresses are also scheduled. The opening ceremony features *The New York Times* columnist, Tom Wicker, who will initiate the proceedings, and former Congresswoman Barbara Jordan, who will address the topic, "LBJ: An Atypical Texan in Washington." Friday afternoon, President Johnson's two daughters, Mrs.

Lynda Johnson Robb and Mrs. Luci Johnson Turpin, reminisce about life in the White House. Former Presidential Assistant and Press Secretary Bill D. Moyers highlights Friday evening's banquet with a major address, and President Johnson's son-in-law, the former Governor of Virginia, Charles S. Robb, speaks Saturday morning on the future of the Democratic Party. Saturday afternoon, Pulitzer prize-winning biographer, Robert A. Caro, who has published the first volume of a planned three-volume study of the life of Lyndon Johnson, addresses the topic "Lyndon Johnson: Dark and Bright."

We urge you to visit the Lyndon Baines Johnson Exhibit in the David Filderman Gallery on the 9th floor of the Hofstra Library. The exhibit will include interesting memorabilia on loan from the Lyndon Baines Johnson Library in Austin, Texas and a large selection of books on President Johnson. The exhibit has been arranged by the Hofstra Library's Special Collections staff.

A program of this magnitude does not materialize without substantial assistance, and many thanks are due to those who have helped make this conference possible. A special thanks goes to the scholars who submitted papers and to the notables who agreed to participate in the various conference forums. Thanks also to the Hofstra faculty committee who read the papers and helped to choose from among them for inclusion in the conference proceedings.

The willing assistance and cooperation of Harry J. Middleton, Director of the Lyndon Baines Johnson Presidential Library, is greatly appreciated.

We are especially grateful to Bill D. Moyers. His good sense, graciousness and enthusiastic support were invaluable in making this project a reality.

Finally, our sincere thanks are extended to members of the Hofstra community with whom we have worked so closely over the last several months: Harold A. Klein, Jim Merritt, Marge Regan, Donna Testa and the Cultural Center student assistants, a group of extraordinarily talented, resourceful and hard-working young men and women, all students here at Hofstra University. They include: Musa G. Badat, Karen Castro, Remeline C. Damasco, William Krueger, Mohamed Omar, Diane Paterson, Joe Pizzimenti and Tara Stahman. A special word of thanks is extended to the Cultural Center's staff, Athelene A. Collins, Jo-Ann G. Mahoney and Marilyn Seidman, whose dedication to the daily tasks contributed to the overall success of the conference. The Cultural Center's acting co-directors, Natalie Datlof and Alexej Ugrinsky, have worked tirelessly to build on the legacy of the late Professor Joseph G. Astman, who founded the Center ten years ago, and this conference is a tribute to their efforts, as well as to those of the staff that serves them and the University so well.

We welcome our guests and we hope our three days together will be enjoyable, intellectually rewarding and historically significant.

Robert C. Vogt
Dean, Hofstra College of
Liberal Arts & Sciences
Conference Co-Director

Bernard J. Firestone
Associate Professor of
Political Science
Conference Co-Director

Thursday, April 10, 1986   Student Center Theater
                                                           North Campus

---

| 8:30 a.m. | Registration |

9:30 a.m.   Opening Ceremonies

Greetings   *James M. Shuart,* President
                       Hofstra University

                       Robert C. Vogt, Dean
                       Hofstra College of Liberal Arts and Sciences
                       Co-Director, Lyndon B. Johnson Conference

                       Bernard J. Firestone
                       Associate Professor of Political Science
                       Co-Director, Lyndon B. Johnson Conference

Opening Address   *Tom Wicker*
                       Chief, Washington Bureau of *The New York Times,* 1964-1966
                       Author, *JFK and LBJ: The Influence of Personality Upon Politics* (1968)
                       Political Columnist, "In the Nation,"
                       The New York Times
                       New York, NY

                       "LBJ: 'The Strength of a Giant'"

Greetings and   *Harry J. Middleton*
Introduction of   Staff Assistant to President Lyndon B. Johnson, 1967-1969
Keynote Speaker   Director, Lyndon Baines Johnson Library, 1970–
                       Austin, TX

Keynote Address   *Barbara Jordan*
                       Texas State Legislature, 1966-72
                       U.S. House of Representatives, 1972-1978
                       Holder of the Lyndon Baines Johnson Centennial Chair in National Policy
                       Lyndon B. Johnson School of Public Affairs
                       University of Texas at Austin
                       Austin, TX

                       "LBJ: An Atypical Texan in Washington"

Refer to page 35 for photo credits and captions.

LBJ Exhibits schedule on page 30.

5

Thursday, April 10, 1986

11:00 a.m.-1:00 p.m.   Student Center Theater, North Campus

Panel I a   BUILDING THE GREAT SOCIETY

Moderator/Commentator:
Herbert D. Rosenbaum
Professor of Political Science
Hofstra University

Michael L. Reopel
Lance W. Bardsley
Department of Political Science
United States Military Academy
"Strategies for Governance: Domestic Policymaking
in the Johnson Administration"

Michael J. Rockler
Graduate School of Education
Rutgers University/Camden
"Lyndon Baines Johnson and Education"

Sheri David
Department of History
Hofstra University
"Medicare: Hallmark of the Great Society"

Phillip M. Simpson
Department of Political Science
Cameron University
"Lyndon B. Johnson and the 1964-68 Revenue Acts:
Congressional Politics and 'Fiscal Chickens Coming
Home to Roost'"

11:00 a.m.-12:30 p.m.   Dining Rooms ABC, North Campus

Panel I b   GUNS AND BUTTER

Moderator/Commentator:
Helen Hill Updike
Associate Dean, Hofstra College of Liberal Arts and Sciences
Associate Professor of Economics

Donald K. Pickens
Department of History
North Texas State University
"LBJ, The Council of Economic Advisers, and the
Burden of New Deal Liberalism"

Thomas Riddell
Department of Economics
Smith College
"The Vietnam War and Inflation Revisited"

John E. Ullmann
Department of Business Computer Information
Systems/Quantitative Methods
Hofstra University
"Lyndon Johnson and the Limits of American Resources"

Thursday, April 10, 1986   Dining Rooms ABC
                                                                North Campus

12:30-1:30 p.m.   Lunch: Student Center, North Campus

1:30-3:00 p.m.   Dining Rooms ABC, North Campus

Panel II a   FOREIGN POLICY

                                       Moderator/Commentator:
                                       Paul F. Harper
                                       Chair and Professor of Political Science
                                       Hofstra University

                                       Thomas M. Gaskin
                                       Department of History
                                       Everett Community College
                                       "Senate Majority Leader Lyndon B. Johnson:
                                       The Formosa and Middle East Resolutions"

                                       Elmer Plischke
                                       Professor Emeritus, University of Maryland
                                       American Enterprise Institute
                                       Gettysburg College
                                       "Lyndon Johnson as Diplomat-in-Chief"

                                       Morris Honick
                                       Historian
                                       Supreme Headquarters Allied Powers Europe, (SHAPE)
                                       Brussels, Belgium
                                       "The French Initiatives of 1966"

1:30-3:00 p.m.   Hofstra Cultural Center Lecture Hall
                                       Library, 1st Floor, South Campus

Panel II b   MINORITIES AND THE GREAT SOCIETY

                                       Moderator/Commentator:
                                       Ronald H. Silverman
                                       Professor of Law
                                       Hofstra University School of Law

                                       Robert D. Loevy
                                       Department of Political Science
                                       The Colorado College
                                       "'To Write It in the Books of Law': President Lyndon B. Johnson
                                       and the Civil Rights Act of 1964"

                                       James Findlay
                                       Department of History
                                       University of Rhode Island
                                       "Religion and Politics in the Sixties: The Churches
                                       and the Civil Rights Act of 1964"

                                       Julie Leininger Pycior
                                       Department of History
                                       Fordham University
                                       "Lyndon, *La Raza* and the Paradox of Texas History"

7

8

Thursday, April 10, 1986   Hofstra Cultural Center Lecture Hall
                                             Library, 1st Floor, South Campus

3:00-4:30 p.m.   Hofstra Cultural Center Lecture Hall
                                 Library, 1st Floor, South Campus

Law Forum   LYNDON BAINES JOHNSON AND THE COURTS

                                 Moderator/Commentator:
                                 Burton C. Agata
                                 Max Schmertz Distinguished Professor of Law
                                 Special Counsel to the New York State Senate Minority
                                 Member, State Antitrust Law Committee on the ABA
                                     Section on Antitrust Law
                                 Former Consultant to the United States State Department

                                 David M. O'Brien
                                 Woodrow Wilson Department of Government &
                                 Foreign Affairs
                                 University of Virginia
                                 "LBJ and Supreme Court Politics in the Light of History"

                                 Bruce Murphy
                                 Department of Political Science
                                 Pennsylvania State University
                                 "Abe Fortas: The Justice and The Friend"

                                 Bernard E. Jacob
                                 Hofstra University School of Law
                                 Clerk to Justice William O. Douglas, 1960-1961
                                 "Supreme Court Justices: Presidential Advising and Other Non-judicial Roles"

                                 Sponsored by the Hofstra University School of Law

4:30-6:00 p.m.   Student Center Theater
                                 North Campus

Forum   THE GREAT SOCIETY—THEN AND NOW

                                 Moderator/Commentator:
                                 Sargent Shriver
                                 Director, Peace Corps, 1961-1966
                                 Director, Office of Economic Opportunity, 1964-1968
                                 Special Assistant to the President, 1965-1968
                                 U.S. Ambassador to France, 1968-1970
                                 Partner—Fried, Frank, Harris, Shriver & Jacobson
                                 Washington, DC

                                 Wilbur J. Cohen
                                 Assistant Secretary, 1961-1965; Under
                                     Secretary, 1965-1968;   Secretary, 1968-1969;
                                     Department of Health, Education and Welfare
                                 Chairman, President's Committee on Mental Retardation, 1968
                                 Chairman, President's Committee on Population
                                     and Family Planning, 1968
                                 Sid W. Richardson Professor of Public Affairs
                                 Lyndon B. Johnson School of Public Affairs
                                 University of Texas at Austin

Thursday, April 10, 1986

Student Center Theater
North Campus

Francis Keppel
U.S. Commissioner of Education, 1962-1965
Assistant Secretary of Education, HEW, 1965-1966
Senior Fellow, Aspen Institute for Humanistic Studies
Senior Lecturer, Harvard University
Cambridge, MA

Adam Yarmolinsky
Special Assistant to the Secretary of Defense, 1961-1964
Deputy Director, President's Anti-Poverty Task Force, 1964
Chief, U.S. Emergency Relief Mission to the
    Dominican Republic, 1965
Principal Deputy Assistant to the Secretary of
    Defense for International Security Affairs, 1965-1966
Policy Science Graduate Program
University of Maryland, Baltimore County
Catonsville, MD

Robert C. Weaver
Administrator, Housing and Home Finance Agency, 1961-1966
Secretary of HUD, 1966-1968
New York City Municipal Assistance Corporation, 1975–
Distinguished Professor of Urban Affairs Emeritus
Hunter College/CUNY
New York, NY

6:00-7:30 p.m.   Dinner: Student Center, North Campus

Thursday, April 10, 1986

7:30-9:30 p.m.

Forum   STAFF RECOLLECTIONS

Moderator/Commentator:
Harry McPherson
Special Assistant and Counsel to President
   Lyndon B. Johnson, 1965-1966
Special Counsel to the President, 1966-1969
Partner—Verner, Liipfert, Bernhard, McPherson & Hand
Washington, DC

Bess Abell
White House Social Secretary
President, Bess Abell Enterprises
Washington, DC

Liz Carpenter
Executive Assistant to Vice President
   Lyndon B. Johnson, 1961-1963
Presidential Secretary and Staff Director to
   Mrs. Lyndon B. Johnson, 1963-1969
Austin, TX

Harry J. Middleton
Staff Assistant to President Lyndon B. Johnson, 1967-1969
Director, Lyndon Baines Johnson Library, 1970–
Austin, TX

John P. Roche
White House Special Consultant, 1966-1968
Dean *ad interim*
Tufts University
The Fletcher School of Law and Diplomacy
Medford, MA

Lee C. White
Associate Counsel to President Lyndon B. Johnson, 1963-1965
Special Counsel to the President, 1965-1966
Chairman, Federal Power Commission, 1966-1969
Partner—White, Fine & Verville
Washington, DC

Reception

11

Friday, April 11, 1986   Hofstra Cultural Center Lecture Hall
                                                Library, 1st Floor, South Campus

---

8:00 a.m.   Registration
                                       Student Center Theater Lobby, North Campus

---

8:30-10:00 a.m.   Hofstra Cultural Center
                                       Library, First Floor, South Campus

Panel III   THE GREAT SOCIETY RE-EVALUATED

                                       Moderator/Commentator:
                                       Robert C. Wood
                                       Henry R. Luce Professor of Democratic Institutions
                                            and the Social Order
                                       Wesleyan University
                                       Middletown, CT

                                       Attiat F. Ott
                                       Institute for Economic Studies
                                       Clark University
                                       and
                                       Paul Hughes-Cromwick
                                       Department of Health and Human Resources
                                       Washington, DC

                                       "The War on Poverty: Two Decades Later"

                                       Marlan Blissett
                                       Lyndon B. Johnson School of Public Affairs
                                       University of Texas at Austin

                                       "Untangling the Mess"

                                       Michael P. Riccards
                                       Department of Political Science
                                       Hunter College/CUNY

                                       "Failure of Nerve: How the Liberals Killed Liberalism"

14

Friday, April 11, 1986

John Cranford Adams Playhouse, South Campus

10:15 a.m.-12:30 p.m.
Forum   THE VIETNAM WAR IN PERSPECTIVE

Sponsored by the Political Affairs Club of Hofstra University
Introductions: *Alyce Stone*,
                        President, Political Affairs Club
                        Bernard J. Firestone, Conference Co-Director

Moderator/Commentator:
Herbert S. Parmet
Distinguised Professor of History
Queensborough Community College/CUNY
The Graduate Center/CUNY
New York, NY

William P. Bundy
Assistant Secretary of Defense for International Security, 1963-1964
Assistant Secretary of State
    for East Asian and Pacific Affairs, 1964-1969
Editor, *Foreign Affairs,* 1972-1984
Princeton, NJ

Daniel Ellsberg
Member of *McNamara Task Force on History of U.S.*
    Decision-making in Vietnam, 1945-1968
Special Assistant to Assistant Secretary of Defense for
    International Security Affairs, 1964-1965
Lecturer and writer
Kensington, CA

Tom Hayden
Co-founder, 1961; President, 1962-1963;
    Students for a Democratic Society (SDS)
Leader, Indochina Peace Campaign
Founder and Chairman, Campaign for Economic Democracy
California State Assembly
Santa Monica, CA

Townsend Hoopes
Principal Deputy Assistant Secretary of Defense for
    International Affairs, 1965-1967
Under Secretary of the Air Force, 1967-1969
President, Association of American Publishers
Washington, D.C.

W.W. Rostow
Special Assistant to the President for National Security Affairs, 1966-1969
Rex G. Baker, Jr. Professor of Political Economy
University of Texas at Austin
Austin, TX

William H. Sullivan
UN Advisor, Bureau of Far Eastern Affairs, 1960-1963
Ambassador to Laos, 1964-1969
President, The American Assembly
Columbia University, 1979–
New York, NY

Friday, April 11, 1986

12:30 p.m.   Lunch: Student Center, North Campus

1:15-2:00 p.m.
Roundtable   WHITE HOUSE RECOLLECTIONS

Lynda Johnson Robb
McLean, VA

Luci Johnson Turpin
Toronto, Canada

Introductions and Remarks:
Harry J. Middleton
Director, Lyndon B. Johnson Library
Austin, TX

17

Friday, April 11, 1986

Student Center Theater
North Campus

2:00-4:00 p.m.

International Forum

LYNDON B. JOHNSON AND THE WORLD

Co-sponsored by The International Students Office and
The Organization of International Students of
Hofstra University

Introduction: *Bernard J. Firestone,* Associate Professor of Political Science

Moderator/Commentator:
W.W. Rostow
Special Assistant to the President for National Security Affairs, 1966-1969
Rex G. Baker, Jr. Professor of Political Economy
University of Texas at Austin
Austin, TX

The Honorable Maurice Couve de Murville
Minister for Foreign Affairs, 1958-1968
Prime Minister of France, 1968-1969
Deputy, National Assembly, 1981—
Paris, France

The Honorable Joseph M. A. H. Luns
Minister of Foreign Affairs, The Netherlands, 1956-1971
Secretary-General, NATO, 1971-1983
Brussels, Belgium

The Honorable B. K. Nehru
Ambassador to the United States, 1961-1968
Governor of Gujarat, 1984—
Gujarat, India

The Honorable Gerhard Schröder
Member of the Bundestag, 1949-1980
Minister of Foreign Affairs, 1961-1966
Minister of Defense, 1966-1969
Bonn, Federal Republic of Germany

The Right Honorable Lord Wilson of Rievaulx
Member, House of Lords
Member, House of Commons, 1945-1983
Prime Minister of Great Britain, 1964-1970; 1974-1977
Chairman, The Great Britain-USSR Society
London, England

Friday, April 11, 1986   Student Center Theater
                                                North Campus

4:00-5:45 p.m.   CIVIL RIGHTS

Forum   Moderator/Commentator:
                                Louis E. Martin
                                Deputy Chairman,
                                Democratic National Committee, 1961-1969
                                Assistant Vice President for Communications
                                Howard University
                                Washington, DC

                                Ramsey Clark
                                Assistant Attorney General, 1961-1965;
                                Deputy Attorney General, 1965-1967;
                                Attorney General, 1967-1969;
                                U.S. Department of Justice
                                Ramsey Clark Law Office
                                New York, NY

                                James Farmer
                                Founder; National Director, 1961-1966;
                                Congress of Racial Equality (CORE)
                                Assistant Secretary for Administration, HEW, 1969-1970
                                Author and civil rights activist
                                Washington, DC

                                Nicholas deB. Katzenbach
                                Deputy Attorney General, 1962-1964;
                                Acting Attorney General, 1964;
                                Attorney General, 1965-1966;
                                U.S. Department of Justice
                                Under Secretary of State, 1966-1969
                                IBM Corporation
                                Armonk, New York

                                Floyd B. McKissick, Sr.
                                National Chairman, 1963-1966;
                                National Director, 1966-1968;
                                Congress of Racial Equality, (CORE)
                                President, Soul City Company, 1974—
                                Oxford, NC

                                Joseph L. Rauh, Jr.
                                National Chairman,
                                Americans for Democratic Action (ADA), 1955-1957
                                General Counsel of Leadership Conference on Civil Rights, 1964—
                                Chairman, D.C. Democratic Committee, 1964-1967
                                National Board of Directors, NAACP
                                Partner—Rauh & Silard, 1961—
                                Washington, DC

20

21

Friday, April 11, 1986   EVENING PROGRAM

7:00 p.m. **Exhibits**	Hofstra University Library, South Campus *Lyndon Baines Johnson* Book, Manuscript, Photo and Memorabilia Exhibition David Filderman Gallery, Ninth Floor
	Images of America Hofstra Cultural Center, Tenth Floor
	Reception and Opening
8:00 P.M.	LYNDON B. JOHNSON PRESIDENTIAL CONFERENCE BANQUET
	Dining Room, Student Center, North Campus
Presiding	*James M. Shuart* President Hofstra University
Introduction	*Paul F. Harper* Chairman, Department of Political Science Director, John F. Kennedy Conference
Greetings and **Introductions**	*Robert C. Vogt* Dean, Hofstra College of Liberal Arts and Sciences Co-Director, Lyndon Baines Johnson Conference
	Bernard J. Firestone Associate Professor of Political Science Co-Director, Lyndon Baines Johnson Conference
Greetings from **the Johnson Family**	*Charles S. Robb* Former Governor of Virginia, 1982-1986 Partner–Hunton & Williams Fairfax, VA
Introduction of **Banquet Speaker**	*George G. Dempster* Chairman Emeritus Board of Trustees Hofstra University

Banquet Address	*Bill D. Moyers*
	White House Special Assistant
	    to President Lyndon B. Johnson, 1963-1965
	White House Press Secretary, 1965-1966
	Publisher, *Newsday,* 1967-1970
	Editor-in-Chief,
	    Bill Moyers Journal, 1971-1976; 1978-1981
	Editor and Chief Correspondent, CBS Reports
	Senior News Analyst, CBS News
	New York, NY

	"Second Thoughts"
Presentation	*James M. Shuart* President
	Emil V. Cianciulli Chairman Board of Trustees Hofstra University

Saturday, April 12, 1986

Student Center Theater
North Campus

8:00 a.m.

Registration
Complimentary Continental Breakfast
Student Center Theater Lobby, North Campus

8:45-10:45 a.m.

Student Center Theater, North Campus

Panel IV

VIETNAM

Moderator/Commentator:
Larry Berman
Department of Political Science
University of California/Davis
Davis, CA

William F. Levantrosser
Department of Political Science
Hofstra University
"Tonkin Gulf Revisited: Vietnam, Military Mirage, and
Political Reality in 1964"

Kathleen J. Turner
Department of Communication
University of Tulsa
"Presidential-Press Interaction: Media Influence
on the Johns Hopkins Address"

Kenneth W. Thompson
Director, White Burkett Miller Center
of Public Affairs
University of Virginia
"The Johnson Presidency and Foreign Policy: The Unresolved Conflict
Between National Interest and Collective Security"

Philip J. Avillo, Jr.
Department of History & Political Science
York College of Pennsylvania
"'In What Direction Are We Going In Vietnam?' The U.S. Senate,
Lyndon Johnson and the Vietnam War, 1964-1965"

Saturday, April 12, 1986   Student Center Theater
                                                                    North Campus

11:00 a.m.- 12:00 noon   **Introduction:** *Robert C. Vogt*
                                            Dean, Hofstra College of Liberal Arts and Sciences
                                            Conference Co-Director

Invitational Address   *Charles S. Robb*
                                    Former Governor of Virginia, 1982-1986
                                    Partner—Hunton & Williams
                                    Fairfax, VA

                                    "Democratic Legacy: Whither the Future"

12:00 noon   Lunch: Student Center, North Campus

12:45-2:00 p.m.   Dining Rooms ABC, North Campus
Panel V   SCIENCE, TECHNOLOGY AND SPACE

                                    Moderator/Commentator:
                                    Sanford Hammer
                                    Provost & Dean of Faculties
                                    Hofstra University

                                    Henry Lambright
                                    Department of Political Science
                                    Syracuse University
                                    "Lyndon Johnson and National Science Policy: The Continuing Issues"

                                    Nancy Brendlinger
                                    Department of Political Science
                                    Kent State University
                                    "Lyndon Johnson's Involvement in the American Space Program"

2:00-3:15 p.m.   Student Center Threater

                                    Introduction: *Robert C. Vogt*

Invitational Address   *Robert A. Caro*
                                    New York, NY

                                    Author
                                    The Years of Lyndon Johnson: The Path to Power (1982)
                                    The Power Broker: Robert Moses and the Fall of New York (1974)
                                    Pulitzer Prize in Biography
                                    National Book Critics Circle Award
                                    Francis Parkman Prize of the Society of American Historians
                                    Carr P. Collins Award of the Texas Institute of Letters
                                    H.L. Mencken Award

                                    "Lyndon Johnson: Dark and Bright"

Saturday, April 12, 1986   Student Center Theater
                                                                         North Campus

3:30-5:30 p.m.
Forum   THE PRESS CORPS

                                             Moderator/Commentator:
                                             James Lynn
                                             Senior Editor for Editorials
                                             Newsday
                                             Melville, NY

                                             Douglass Cater
                                             Special Assistant to President Lyndon B. Johnson, 1964-1968
                                             President, Washington College
                                             Chestertown, MD

                                             Frank Cormier
                                             Chief White House Correspondent, Associated Press, 1962-1980
                                             Fairfax, VA

                                             Sid Davis
                                             White House Correspondent,
                                             Westinghouse Broadcasting Company, 1959-1968
                                             Chief, Washington News Bureau, 1968-1977
                                             Senior Correspondent, NBC News
                                             Washington, D.C.

                                             Sarah McClendon
                                             White House Correspondent since the Roosevelt Administration
                                             Publisher, *Sarah McClendon's Report*
                                             Columnist, "Sarah McClendon's Washington"
                                             Washington, D.C.

                                             George E. Reedy
                                             Special Assistant
                                                 to Vice President Lyndon B. Johnson, 1961-1963
                                             Press Secretary
                                                 to President Lyndon B. Johnson, 1964-1965
                                             Dean and Nieman Professor, 1972-1977;
                                             Nieman Professor of Journalism, 1977;
                                             College of Journalism
                                             Marquette University
                                             Milwaukee, WI

                                             Ray Scherer
                                             White House Correspondent, NBC News, 1951-1968
                                             Vice President, Washington RCA Corporation, 1975-
                                             Washington D.C.

                                             George Tames
                                             Chief Photographer, Washington Bureau, 1945-
                                             The New York Times
                                             Washington, D.C.

5:30 p.m.   Reception

"Pressing the Flesh"

Lyndon Baines Johnson and Senator Theodore F. Green (D, R.I.)
Photo by George Tames/The New York Times

Conference Exhibits Schedule

ART:
Images of America

Hofstra Cultural Center—Library, 10th Floor (South Campus)
April 10-12, 1986

Images of America is a selection of 19th and 20th century works of art from the permanent collection of Hofstra University. This view of American life by American artists ranges from historical prints, Currier & Ives lithographs to modern and contemporary masters such as Thomas Hart Benton, John Stewart Curry, Louis Lozowick, Ben Shahn, Berenice Abbott, Red Grooms and Robert Rauschenberg.

Gallery Hours: Thursday, April 10: 10:00 a.m.-7:30 p.m.
Friday, April 11: 10:00 a.m.-5:00 p.m.
Saturday, April 12: 10:00 a.m.-6:00 p.m.

For Information: (516) 560-5672

BOOK, MANUSCRIPT AND POLITICAL MEMORABILIA:
Lyndon Baines Johnson

David Filderman Gallery, Library 9th Floor (South Campus)
April 10-June 10, 1986

Gallery Hours: Thursday, April 10: 10:00 a.m.-7:30 p.m.
Friday, April 11: 10:00 a.m.-5:00 p.m.
Saturday, April 12: 10:00 a.m.-6:00 p.m.
From April 14-June 10: Monday-Friday, 9:00 a.m.-5:00 p.m.

For Information: (516) 560-5974

Hofstra University at the Golden Milestone

The depth of the depression was hardly an ideal time to found an institution of higher learning, but the visionaries who established Hofstra University in 1935 were planners with foresight and courage. Undaunted by the problems of the day, they sought to utilize the opportunities that were available, and now, half a century later, it is apparent they succeeded far beyond their initial expectations.

They established the college on the 15-acre estate of William S. and Kate Mason Hofstra on the outskirts of the Village of Hempstead, and affiliated it with New York University. The first class of 150 students was taught by a faculty of 13. The institution, which they named Nassau College-Hofstra Memorial, was housed in a single building that was the former Hofstra estate house, now known as Hofstra Hall.

In 1939 the New York State Board of Regents granted a charter to Hofstra College as an independent institution. After achieving university status in 1963, Hofstra went on to become one of the foremost institutions of higher education in the country.

This fledgling liberal arts college of 50 years ago is now a nationally and internationally recognized university with an enrollment of more than 11,500 students and a distinguished faculty of more than 700. Eighty percent of the full-time faculty have terminal degrees in their various fields.

The original Hofstra Hall is now just one of 78 buildings on a campus of 238 acres which in today's market has a value in excess of $150 million. The budget in 1939 was $150,000; today it exceeds $75 million.

A significant measure of a university's stature is its library. In the beginning the Hofstra library holdings fit adequately in one room and served the small student body well. Fifty years later, the Libraries house more than a million volumes. Only five percent of the colleges and universities in the nation have collections of this magnitude.

For the first three decades, all Hofstra students commuted to campus. Today, approximately half of Hofstra University's full-time undergraduates live in university residences on campus. Enrollment includes students from 25 states and 60 foreign countries.

From its inception, Hofstra has stressed high educational standards. Hofstra is the only private institution of higher learning on Long Island with a Phi Beta Kappa chapter, and is nationally accredited by 11 educational and professional associations.

The University has the only School of Business on Long Island accredited by the American Assembly of Collegiate School of Business and the only School of Education on the Island accredited by the National Council for Accreditation of Teacher Education. Its School of Law is rated 28 out of 174 law schools in the nation. Hofstra is listed in Barron's 227 *Most Prestigious Colleges* and in Barron's 350 *Best, Most Popular, and Most Exciting Colleges*.

There is a vitality on the Hofstra campus not usually found in higher education today. While many other colleges and universities have been retrenching—particularly in the private sector—Hofstra in the past five years has completed 28 new buildings to meet growing academic, recreational, and residential needs.

Fifty years is a comparatively brief span in the life of a university, but it is a significant milestone in the establishement of a truly remarkable record of growth and achievement. The great accomplishments of Hofstra's past and present are harbingers of even greater progress in the years to come.

Credit for the success of the Conference goes to more people than can be named herein, but those below deserve special commendation:

HOFSTRA UNIVERSITY OFFICERS
James M. Shuart, *President*
Emil V. Cianciulli, *Chairperson, Board of Trustees*
Sanford Hammer, *Provost and Dean of Faculties*
J. Richard Block, *Assistant to the President
for Information Systems*
Anthony T. Procelli, *Vice President
for Finance and Treasurer*
James Fellman, *Vice President for Operational Services*
Rochelle Lowenfeld, *Vice President for Development*
Robert C. Vogt, *Dean, Hofstra College of Liberal Arts
and Sciences*
Eric J. Schmertz, *Dean, School of Law*

HOFSTRA ASSOCIATES
Howard L. Weingrow

OFFICE OF THE PRESIDENT
Richard T. Bennett, *Assistant to the President
for Governmental Relations*
Roland H. Davis, *Coordinator for Community
Development*
Laura Scher, *Administrative Assistant and Office Manager*
Ruth Collins, *Adminstrative Assistant*

DEPARTMENT OF DRAMA
James Van Wart, *Chairperson*
Richard Mason

DEPARTMENT OF POLITICAL SCIENCE
Paul F. Harper, *Chairperson*
Marilyn Shepherd, *Senior Executive Secretary*

DEVELOPMENT OFFICE
Rochelle Lowenfeld, *Assistant to the President*
Donna Testa, *Coordinator*
Martin Malinofsky, *Coordinator*
Alice Castle, *Administrative Assistant*
Joan Tiedge, *Senior Executive Secretary*
Eileen Meserole, *Senior Clerk*
Margaret Scheihing, *Senior Clerk*

HCLAS, Office of the Dean
Robert C. Vogt, *Dean*
Linton S. Thorn, *Associate Dean*
Helen Hill Updike, *Associate Dean*
Jerome H. Delamater, *Teaching Dean*
Sylvia P. Osswald, *Administrative Assistant to the Dean*
Peggy M. Bossett, *Senior Executive Secretary*
Emilie Cantante, *Senior Executive Secretary*
Sophie I. Fronckwicz, *Senior Secretary*

HOFSTRA UNIVERSITY LIBRARY
Charles R. Andrews, *Dean*
Wayne Bell, *Associate Dean*

HOFSTRA USA
Albert Passuelo, *Manager*

MAIL SERVICES
Dolores Pallingayan, *Administrator*
Bob Henry, *Supervisor*
Mail Room Staff

MEDIA SERVICES
Elizabeth Weston, *Director*
Laura Campbell, *Coordinator*
William Gray, *Audio-visual Technician*
Robert Certo, *Audio-visual Technician*
John Nixon, *Audio-visual Technician*

OFFICE OF INTERNATIONAL STUDENTS
Graydon Vanderbilt, *Dean*
Helen Boland, *Senior Clerk*
Rachel Reyes, *Director, Ambassador Program*

OPERATIONAL SERVICES
James Fellman, *Vice President*

Public Safety and Technical Services
Robert L. Crowley, *Director*
Edward N. Bracht, *Deputy Director of Public Safety*
Robert J. Kleinhans, *Director of Technical Services*

Physical Plant
Richard J. Drury, *Director*
Charles J. Rubel, *Associate Director*
David G. Blanchard, *Associate Director*

Facilities Management
Charles L. Churchill, *Manager*
Margaret A. Shields, *Hospitality Services Manager*
Dorothy Fetherston, *Director of Scheduling*
Anthony Internicola, *Director of Dining Services*
Dawn Smith, *Assistant Director of Dining Services &
Catering Manager*

Theatre Facilities
Donald H. Swinney, *Director of the
John Cranford Adams Playhouse*
Jean Morris, *Playhouse Manager*

PUBLICATIONS OFFICE
Jack Ruegamer, Director, Printing & Publications
Vicki Anderson
Lisa San Sonette
Margaret Mirabella
Veronica Fitzwilliam
Catherine Healy
Doris Brown, *Administrative Supervisor Printing Department*
Printing Department Staff

SPECIAL SECRETARIAL SERVICES
Stella Sinicki, *Supervisor*
Secretarial Staff

UNIVERSITY RELATIONS
Harold A. Klein, *Director*
James Merritt, *Assistant Director*
M. F. Klerk, *Editor/Writer*
Frances B. Jacobsen, *Administrative Assistant*

Hofstra University Student Sponsoring Groups

POLITICAL AFFAIRS CLUB
ORGANIZATION OF INTERNATIONAL STUDENTS
STUDENT GOVERNMENT ASSOCIATION
HOFSTRA UNIVERSITY YOUNG DEMOCRATS
SOCIETY FOR COLLEGIATE JOURNALISTS

We gratefully acknowledge the
cooperation of

ABRAHAM & STRAUS
Hempstead, NY

ROBERT BERKS
Orient, NY

INTERNTIONAL RESEARCH AND
EXCHANGES BOARD (IREX)
New York, NY

NASSAU LIBRARY SYSTEM
Uniondale, NY

THE NATIONAL ARCHIVES
Washington, D.C.

NEW YORK PUBLIC LIBRARY
New York, NY

STEPHEN V. RUSSELL
Belle Vernon, PA

SUFFOLK COOPERATIVE LIBRARY SYSTEM
Bellport, NY

UNITED STATES DEPARTMENT OF STATE
OFFICE OF PROTOCOL
Washington, D.C.

USSR ACADEMY OF SCIENCES
INSTITUTE FOR THE UNITED STATES AND
CANADA
Moscow, USSR

WALDEN THEATRE CONSERVATORY
New York, NY

Special Acknowledgements Should
Be Given To

B & B
Compliments of B & B Liquors

COUNTRY ARTS AND FLOWERS
West Hempstead, NY

GARDEN CITY HOTEL
Garden City, NY

HEMPSTEAD LIMOUSINE SERVICE
CORPORATION
Hempstead, NY

THE ISLAND INN
Westbury, NY

L.F. O'CONNELL ASSOCIATES
Garden City, NY

THE NEW YORK TIMES
New York, NY

SEMPE ARMAGNAC
Compliments of Regal Brands, Inc.

34

Photo Credits

Page 4. LBJ waves through auto window to Australian well-wishers.
　　　　Photo by Okamoto

Page 8. President Johnson pauses for applause during a 1966 address to a Joint Session of the Congress.
　　　　Photo by Wolfe

Page 10. President Johnson in his early days in the White House meets in the Oval Office with Pierre Salinger, Bill Moyers, Theodore Sorensen, and Jack Valenti.
　　　　Photo by Okamoto

Page 12. LBJ "presses the flesh" after a rally during the 1964 Presidential campaign.
　　　　Photo by Stoughton

Page 14. Top military and civilian advisors at a 1964 meeting with LBJ at his Texas ranch.
　　　　Photo by Okamoto

Page 16. Johnson family portrait during the Presidency at the White House.

Page 17. Lady Bird Johnson holds an umbrella over the President as he delivers greetings to a crowd in 1966.
　　　　Photo by Wolfe

Page 19. LBJ listens intently to Soviet Premier Kosygin at their 1967 summit conference at Glassboro State College in New Jersey.
　　　　Photo by Okamoto

Page 21. President Lyndon B. Johnson signs the historic Civil Rights Act in 1964 at the White House (Martin Luther King is seen behind the President).
　　　　Photo by Stoughton

Page 22. President Johnson stands at the podium at a White House Press Conference in July, 1965.

Page 26. LBJ holds an informal press conference in the White House Oval Office.
　　　　Photo by Okamoto

Page 29. LBJ looks at Chicago Tribune headline announcing that he will not be a candidate for re-election in 1968.
　　　　Photo by Okamoto

Page 30. Bronze portrait bust of President Lyndon Baines Johnson
　　　　by Robert Berks

Page 34. On his last day as President (January 20, 1969), LBJ confers with his successor, Richard Nixon at the White House.
　　　　Photo by Wolfe

HOFSTRA CULTURAL CENTER

Conference Schedule and Publications Listing

•George Sand Centennial—November 1976
•Heinrich von Kleist Bicentennial—November 1977
+ The Chinese Woman—December 1977
•George Sand: Her Life, Her Works, Her Influence—April 1978
•William Cullen Bryant and His America—October 1978
 The Trotsky-Stalin Conflict in the 1920's—March 1979
 Albert Einstein Centennial—November 1979
 Renaissance Venice Symposium—March 1980
+ Sean O'Casey—March 1980
•Walt Whitman—April 1980
 Nineteenth-Century Women Writers—November 1980
 Fedor Dostoevski—April 1981
 Gotthold Ephraim Lessing—November 1981
 Franklin Delano Roosevelt: The Man, the Myth, the Era—March 1982
 Johann Wolfgang von Goethe—April 1982
 James Joyce—October 1982
 Twentieth-Century Women Writers—November 1982
 Harry S. Truman: The Man from Independence—April 1983
••John Maynard Keynes—September 1983
 Romanticism in the Old and the New World—Washington Irving, Stendhal, and Zhukovskii—October 1983
 Espectador Universal: Jose Ortega y Gasset—November 1983
 Dwight D. Eisenhower: Soldier, President, Statesman—March 1984
+ Victorian Studies—April 1984
 Symposium on Eighteenth-Century Venice—April 1984
 George Orwell—October 11-13, 1984
 Friedrich von Schiller—November 8-10, 1984
 John F. Kennedy: The Promise Revisited—March 28-30, 1985
 Higher Education: Today and Tomorrow—April 18-19, 1985
 Heritage: A Reappraisal of the Harlem Renaissance—May 2-4, 1985
 Fourth Annual Edward F. Carlough Labor Law Conference—May 23-24, 1985
 New York State History Conference—June 7-8, 1985
 Eighteenth-Century Women and the Arts—October 10-12, 1985
 Johann Sebastian Bach—October 24-26, 1985
 Law School Conference: Sixteen Years of the Burger Court, 1969-1985—November 7-8, 1985
 Avant-Garde Art and Literature—November 14-16, 1985
 Television 1985-1986: Issues for the Industry and the Audience—November 19-21, 1985
 Artificial Intelligence—February 27-March 1, 1986
 Evolution of Business Education—March 13-14, 1986
 Lyndon B. Johnson: A Texan in Washington—April 10-12, 1986
 Long Island Studies—May 2-3, 1986
 Attitudes Toward Persons with Disabilities—June 4-6, 1986
 Fifth Annual Edward F. Carlough Labor Law Conference—September 23, 1986
 The World of George Sand—October 16-18, 1986
 Miguel de Unamuno/Ramon Valle-Inclán/Frederico García-Lorca—November 6-8, 1986
 C. G. Jung and the Humanities—November 20-22, 1986
 Bicentennial of the United States Constitution—April 24-26, 1987

•Volumes available from AMS Press, Inc., 56 East 13th Street, New York, NY 10003
••Volume available from M.E. Sharpe, Inc., 80 Business Park Drive, Armonk, NY 10504
+ No publication
*Volume available from Greenwood Press,
 88 Post Road West, Westport, CT 06881

All other volumes forthcoming from Greenwood Press

For further information and "Calls for Papers":
Hofstra Cultural Center
Hofstra University
Hempstead, NY 11550
(516) 560-5669/5670

Index

About the Contributors

PHILIP J. AVILLO, JR., is associate professor of history at York College of Pennsylvania. He has written several articles examining the role of southern Republicans who served in Congress during Reconstruction. He is currently preparing a study of the U.S. Senate and the Vietnam War.

LANCE W. BARDSLEY is a major in the U.S. Army and is presently attending the Command and General Staff College. He was assigned as an assistant professor of political science within the Department of Social Sciences at the U.S. Military Academy, West Point. His primary research interest is presidential-congressional relationships with particular emphasis on domestic politics.

MARLAN BLISSETT is professor of public affairs at the Lyndon B. Johnson School of Public Affairs, University of Texas at Austin. He is the author of *Politics in Science* and numerous articles on energy and environmental policy. His most recent book—co-authored with Emmette S. Redford—is *Organizing the Executive Branch: The Johnson Presidency*.

SHERI I. DAVID is assistant professor of history at Hofstra University. She specializes in twentieth-century American history and social policy. Her most recent work is *With Dignity: The Search for Medicare and Medicaid*.

BERNARD J. FIRESTONE is associate professor of political science at Hofstra University. He is the author of *The Quest for Nuclear Stability* and is currently writing a book on U Thant.

THOMAS M. GASKIN is an instructor of history at Everett Community College, Everett, Washington. He is completing his doctoral dissertation on Senator Lyndon B. Johnson and U.S. foreign policy at the University of Washington. Grants from the Lyndon B. Johnson Foundation and an Albert J. Beveridge Grant from the American Historical Association helped fund the research for this article.

PAUL HUGHES-CROMWICK is a research analyst currently working on long-term care insurance for the elderly and assessing housing needs to the year 2000 for the Office of Policy and Management, State of Connecticut Government. In addition, he is a visiting lecturer in public policy studies at Trinity College. Prior to this, he served as an economist in the office of the assistant secretary for planning and evaluation, U.S. Department of Health and Human Services, where he was involved principally with designing and monitoring policy research spanning the areas of retirement and elderly studies and poverty and long-term welfare dependency.

WILLIAM F. LEVANTROSSER is professor of political science and director of the Colloquium on the American Presidency at Hofstra University. His principal research interests involve U.S. defense policy, the Pacific area, and the modern American presidency. He is the author of *Congress and the Citizen-Soldier* and the editor of *Harry S. Truman: The Man from Independence* (Greenwood Press, 1986).

ROBERT D. LOEVY is professor of political science at The Colorado College. An expert on public opinion and elections, he is the author of numerous articles appearing in scholarly publications and newspapers.

BILL D. MOYERS was special assistant and press secretary to President Lyndon Baines Johnson. An award-winning journalist, Moyers has been publisher of *Newsday*, editor-in-chief of *Bill Moyers Journal*, editor and chief correspondent for CBS Reports, and news analyst for CBS News. He is currently affiliated with Public Affairs Television, Inc.

BRUCE MURPHY, associate professor of political science at Pennsylvania State University, is the author of *The Brandeis/Frankfurter Connection: The Secret Political Activities of Two Supreme Court Justices* and has recently written *Fortas: The Rise and Ruin of a Supreme Court Justice*.

DAVID M. O'BRIEN is an associate professor of government at the University of Virginia. He is author of eight books, including *Storm Center: The Supreme Court in American Politics*. He has been a Visiting Postdoctoral Fellow at the Russell Sage Foundation, a Judicial Fellow at the Supreme Court of the United

States, and in 1987–1988 a Fulbright Scholar and Visiting Fellow in Constitutional Studies at Nuffield College, Oxford.

ATTIAT F. OTT is professor of economics and director of the Institute for Economic Studies at Clark University in Worcester, Massachusetts. She is the author of numerous articles and books including *Macroeconomic Theory*. Her primary fields of research are tax policy and public economics.

DONALD K. PICKENS is professor of history at the University of North Texas, Denton, Texas. Among his several publications is "Truman's Council of Economic Advisers and the Legacy of New Deal Liberalism," *Harry S. Truman: The Man from Independence*, ed. William F. Levantrosser. In addition to his research into the ideologies of feminism and republicanism, he is working on a biography of Leon H. Keyserling.

ELMER PLISCHKE, former professor and head, Department of Government and Politics, is now professor emeritus, University of Maryland and adjunct scholar, American Enterprise Institute. He has written extensively for professional journals and authored more than twenty-five books and monographs, including *Conduct of American Diplomacy*, *Foreign Relations Decisionmaking*, *United States Diplomats and Their Missions*, *Microstates in World Affairs*, *Modern Diplomacy: The Art and the Artisans*, and *Diplomat in Chief: The President at the Summit*.

JULIE LEININGER PYCIOR is a research associate of the Institute for Research in History, New York City and adjunct assistant professor of history at Fordham University. She has written extensively on Chicano history, as well as on immigration and on Latin America. She is the author of *Chicanos in South Bend: Some Historical Narratives* and of articles such as "Assimilation and Pluralism in Recent Studies of American Immigration History," which recently appeared in *Ethnic and Immigration Groups*, edited by William Zeisel.

MICHAEL R. REOPEL is a management consultant with McKinsey and Company, Inc., and a former assistant professor of social sciences at the U.S. Military Academy, West Point. He is a lecturer in executive politics and management. As a former White House Fellow, he was a contributor to domestic policymaking within the Reagan administration while serving in the Office of Policy Development.

MICHAEL P. RICCARDS is president of St. John's College, Santa Fe, New Mexico. He has previously been provost and professor of political science at Hunter College (CUNY) and dean of arts and sciences at the University of Massachusetts at Boston. He holds a Ph.D. from Rutgers University, has been a Fulbright Fellow to Japan, a National Endowment for the Humanities Fellow at Princeton University, and a Henry Huntington Fellow. He is the author of

The Making of the American Citizenry: An Introduction to Political Socialization and co-editor of *Reflections in American Political Thought: From Past to Present*.

TOM RIDDELL is associate professor of economics at Smith College where he also teaches in the American Studies program. He has previously taught at the University of Massachusetts at Amherst, Bucknell University, and the American University. His research focuses on the economic dimensions of military spending. He is co-author of *Economics: A Tool for Understanding Society*, a widely used introductory text, and is staff director of the Center for Popular Economics.

PHILLIP M. SIMPSON is professor and chair in the department of political science, Cameron University, Lawton, Oklahoma. He has a companion publication, also with Greenwood Press, which treats extensively the tax and fiscal policies of the Kennedy administration. In addition to the American presidency, his other areas of interest include the legislative process, economic policy, the judicial process, state politics, criminal justice policy, and American political theory.

KENNETH W. THOMPSON is director of the White Burkett Miller Center of Public Affairs at the University of Virginia. He is the author of numerous books and articles including *The Moral Issue in Statecraft*, *Masters of International Thought*, and *Understanding World Politics*. He recently revised Hans J. Morgenthau's *Politics Among Nations*.

KATHLEEN J. TURNER is associate professor in the Department of Communication at Tulane University. She is the author of numerous publications, including *Lyndon Johnson's Dual War: Vietnam and the Press*.

JOHN E. ULLMANN is professor of management and quantitative methods at Hofstra University. An industrial engineer, he has written extensively on industrial development, with special reference to the technical, economic, and political aspects of the arms race. His recent books include *The Anatomy of Industrial Decline* (Quorum, 1988) and *The Prospects of American Industrial Recovery* (Quorum, 1985). He was a member of the Executive Committee of the National Committee for a Sane Nuclear Policy (SANE) from 1961 to 1983.

ROBERT C. VOGT is dean of the Hofstra College of Liberal Arts and Sciences and associate professor of political science. He received his Ph.D. from the State University of New York.

TOM WICKER is a political columnist and former Washington bureau chief for the *New York Times*. A graduate of the University of North Carolina (1948) and a Nieman Fellow at Harvard (1957–1958), he is the author of seven novels and four books of nonfiction. His most recent novel was *Unto This Hour* (1984).

Hofstra University's
Cultural and Intercultural Studies
Coordinating Editor, Alexej Ugrinsky

Harry S. Truman: The Man from Independence
(Editor: William F. Levantrosser)

Nineteenth-Century Women Writers of the English-Speaking World
(Editor: Rhoda B. Nathan)

Lessing and the Enlightenment
(Editor: Alexej Ugrinsky)

Dostoevski and the Human Condition After a Century
(Editors: Alexej Ugrinsky, Frank S. Lambasa, and Valija K. Ozolins)

The Old and New World Romanticism of Washington Irving
(Editor: Stanley Brodwin)

Woman as Mediatrix
(Editor: Avriel Goldberger)

Einstein and the Humanities
(Editor: Dennis P. Ryan)

Dwight D. Eisenhower: Soldier, President, Statesman
(Editor: Joann P. Krieg)

Goethe in the Twentieth Century
(Editor: Alexej Urginsky)

Franklin D. Roosevelt: The Man, the Myth, the Era, 1882–1945
(Editors: Herbert D. Rosenbaum and Elizabeth Bartelme)

The Stendhal Bicentennial Papers
(Editor: Avriel Goldberger)

Faith of a (Woman) Writer
(Editors: Alice Kessler-Harris and William McBrien)

Jośe Ortega y Gasset: Proceedings of the *Espectador universal* International
Interdisciplinary Conference
(Editor: Nora de Marval-McNair)

George Orwell
(Editors: Courtney T. Wemyss and Alexej Ugrinsky)

John F. Kennedy: The Promise Revisited
(Editors: Paul Harper and Joann P. Krieg)